AutoCAD
and its applications
Advanced

by

Terence M. Shumaker
Manager
Autodesk Premier Training Center
Clackamas Community College, Oregon City, OR

David A. Madsen
Chairperson
Drafting Technology
Autodesk Premier Training Center
Clackamas Community College, Oregon City, OR
Former Board of Director
American Design Drafting Association

Autodesk
Registered Author/Publisher

Publisher
The Goodheart-Willcox Company, Inc.
Tinley Park, Illinois

Library of Congress Catalog Number 97-20231
International Standard Book Number 1-56637-414-6 (Softcover)
International Standard Book Number 1-56637-422-7 (Loose-leaf drilled)

1 2 3 4 5 6 7 8 9 10 98 01 00 99 98 97

Library of Congress Cataloging-in-Publication Data
Shumaker, Terence M.
  AutoCAD and its applications: advanced: release 14 /
by Terence M. Shumaker, David A. Madsen.

  p. cm.
Includes index.
ISBN 1-56637-414-6

  1. Computer graphics. 2. AutoCAD for Windows
I. Madsen, David A. II. Title.
T385.S46132 1998
620'.0042'02855369—dc21   97-20231
                                     CIP

Introduction

AutoCAD and its Applications—Advanced, Release 14 is a write-in text that provides complete instruction in mastering the AutoCAD® Release 14 3D modeling commands, Internet access, and various customizing techniques. These topics are covered in an easy-to-understand sequence, and progress in a way that allows you to become comfortable with the commands as your knowledge builds from one chapter to the next. In addition, *AutoCAD and its Applications—Advanced, Release 14* offers the following features:

- Step-by-step use of AutoCAD commands.
- In-depth explanations of how and why commands function as they do.
- Extensive use of font changes to specify certain meanings. This is fully explained in the next section, *Fonts used in this text*.
- Examples and discussions of industrial practices and standards.
- Actual screen captures of AutoCAD and Windows features and functions.
- Professional tips explaining how to use AutoCAD effectively and efficiently.
- Over 75 exercises to reinforce the chapter topics. These exercises also build on previously learned material.
- Chapter tests for review of commands and key AutoCAD concepts.
- A large selection of modeling and customizing problems supplement each chapter. Problems are presented as 3D illustrations, actual plotted drawings, and engineering sketches.

With *AutoCAD and its Applications—Advanced, Release 14*, you not only learn AutoCAD commands, but you also become acquainted with:

- Constructing models using different 3D coordinate systems.
- 3D object construction and layout techniques.
- User coordinate systems.
- Model space viewports.
- 3D editing and display techniques.
- 3D text and dimensioning.
- Surface modeling and rendering.
- Solid model construction, editing, and display.
- AutoCAD's structured query language (SQL) functions.
- Internet access from AutoCAD.
- Customizing the AutoCAD environment.
- Customizing toolbars, pull-down menus, and image tiles.
- Customizing screen, button, and tablet menus.
- The basics of AutoLISP and dialog box (DCL) programming.
- Advanced AutoCAD features such as OLE.

Fonts used in this text

Different typefaces are used throughout each chapter to define terms and identify AutoCAD commands. Important terms always appear in *bold-italic face, serif* type. AutoCAD menus, commands, variables, dialog box names, and tool button names are printed in **bold-face, sans serif** type. File names, directory names, paths, and keyboard-entry items appear in the body of the text in Roman, sans serif type. Keyboard keys are shown inside of square brackets [ ] and appear in Roman, sans serif type. For example, [Enter] means to press the enter (return) key. In addition, commands, menus, and dialog boxes related to Microsoft Windows appear in Roman, sans serif type.

Prompt sequences are set apart from the body text with space above and below, and appear in Roman, sans serif type. Keyboard entry items in prompts appear in **bold-face, sans serif** type. In prompts, the [Enter] key is represented by the ↵ symbol.

Checking the AutoCAD reference manuals

No other reference should be needed when using this text. However, the authors have referenced relevant topic areas to the *AutoCAD User's Guide* and the *AutoCAD Customization Guide*. An icon in the margin identifies the specific chapter within the reference where additional information can be found. For example, the icon next to this paragraph tells you that you can find more information in Chapter 5 of the *AutoCAD User's Guide*.

The *AutoCAD User's Guide* and *AutoCAD Customization Guide* are part of the help file installed with AutoCAD. To reference these materials, select **AutoCAD Help Topics** from the **Help** pull-down menu.

The AutoCAD help file also includes the *AutoCAD Command Reference*. Commands and variables are presented in alphabetical order in this manual. Refer to it for additional information on specific commands and system variables.

Other text references

This text focuses on advanced AutoCAD applications. Basic AutoCAD applications are covered in *AutoCAD and its Applications—Basics, Release 14*, which is also available from Goodheart-Willcox. *AutoCAD and its Applications* texts are also available for AutoCAD Releases 10, 11, 12, and 13.

For your convenience, other Goodheart-Willcox textbooks are referenced. Textbooks that are referenced include *AutoLISP Programming—Principles and Techniques*, and *AutoCAD AME—Solid Modeling for Mechanical Design*. All of these textbooks can be ordered directly from Goodheart-Willcox.

Introducing the AutoCAD commands

There are several ways to select AutoCAD drawing and editing commands. Selecting commands from a toolbar or pull-down menu is slightly different than entering them from the keyboard. All AutoCAD commands and related options are presented in this text using a variety of command entry methods.

Unless otherwise specified, command entries are shown as if typed at the keyboard. This allows the text to present the full command name and the prompts that appear on-screen. Commands, options, and values you must enter are given in **bold** text, as shown in the following example. Pressing the [Enter] (return) key is indicated with the ↵ symbol. (Also, refer to the earlier section *Fonts used in this text*.)

```
Command: 3DFACE↵
First point: 2,2↵
Second point: 4,2↵
Third point: 4,6↵
Fourth point: 2,6↵
```

General input, such as picking a point or selecting an object, is presented in *italic, serif font*, as shown below.

Command: **3DFACE**↵
First point: *(pick a point)*
Second point: *(pick another point)*
Third point: *(pick a third point)*
Fourth point: *(pick the last point)*

The command line, toolbar button, and pull-down menu entry methods are presented throughout the text. When a command is introduced, these methods are illustrated in the margin next to the text reference. The toolbar in which the button is located is also identified. The example in the margin next to this paragraph illustrates the various methods of initiating the **HIDE** command.

Features new for Release 14

Autodesk has introduced many new features in Release 14 of AutoCAD. When a new or updated feature is presented in this text, the AutoCAD R14 icon appears in the margin next to the material. This serves as an aid to users upgrading to Release 14 from earlier releases.

Flexibility in design

Flexibility is the key word when using *AutoCAD and its Applications—Advanced, Release 14*. This text is an excellent training aid for both individual and classroom instruction. *AutoCAD and its Applications—Advanced, Release 14* teaches you how to apply AutoCAD to common modeling and customizing tasks. It is also an invaluable resource for any professional using AutoCAD.

When working through the text, you will see a variety of notices. These notices include Professional Tips, Notes, and Cautions that help you develop your AutoCAD skills.

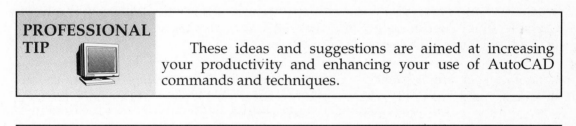

PROFESSIONAL TIP These ideas and suggestions are aimed at increasing your productivity and enhancing your use of AutoCAD commands and techniques.

NOTE A note alerts you to important aspects of a command function, menu, or activity that is being discussed. These aspects should be kept in mind while you are working through the text.

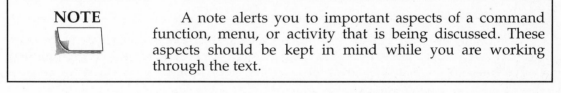

CAUTION A caution alerts you to potential problems if instructions or commands are used incorrectly, or if an action can corrupt or alter files, folders, or disks. If you are in doubt after reading a caution, always consult your instructor or supervisor.

AutoCAD and its Applications—Advanced, Release 14 provides several ways for you to evaluate your performance. Included are:

- **Exercises.** Each chapter contains in-text Exercises. These Exercises allow you to perform tasks that reinforce the material just presented. You can work through the Exercises at your own pace.

- **Chapter Tests.** Each chapter includes a written test at the end of the chapter. Questions require you to give the proper definition, command, option, or response to perform a certain task.
- **Drawing Problems.** There are a variety of drawing, design, and customizing problems at the end of each chapter. These are presented as real-world CAD drawings, 3D illustrations, and engineering sketches. The problems are designed to make you think, solve problems, use design techniques, research and use proper drawing standards, and correct errors in the drawings or engineering sketches.

Each drawing problem deals with one of six technical disciplines. Although doing all of the problems will enhance your AutoCAD skills, you may be focusing on a particular discipline. The discipline that a problem addresses is indicated by a graphic in the margin next to the problem number. Each graphic and its description is as follows:

 These problems address mechanical drafting and design applications, such as manufactured part designs.

 These problems address architectural and structural drafting and design applications, such as floor plans, furniture, and presentation drawings.

 These problems address civil drafting and design application, such as plot plans, plats, and landscape drawings.

 These problems address graphic design applications, such as text creation, title blocks, and page layout.

 These problems address piping drafting and design applications, such as piping flow diagrams, tank drawings, and pipe layout.

 These problems address a variety of general drafting, design, and customization applications. These problems should be attempted by everyone learning advanced AutoCAD techniques for the first time.

NOTE

Some problems presented in this text are given as engineering sketches. These sketches are intended to represent the kind of materials a drafter is expected to work from in a real-world situation. As such, engineering sketches often contain errors or slight inaccuracies, and are most often not drawn according to proper drafting conventions and applicable standards. Errors in these problems are *intentional* to encourage the user to apply appropriate techniques and standards in order to solve the problem. As in real-world applications, sketches should be considered preliminary layouts. Always question inaccuracies in sketches and designs, and consult the applicable standards or other resources.

Disk Supplements

To help you develop your AutoCAD skills, Goodheart-Willcox offers a disk supplement package to use with *AutoCAD and its Applications—Advanced, Release 14*. The Autodesk software AutoCAD Release 14 is required for Goodheart-Willcox software to operate properly.

The *Student Work Disk* contains additional AutoCAD pull-down menus with a variety of activities. These activities are intended to be used as a supplement to the exercises and activities found in the text. The *Work Disk* activities correspond to Chapter 1–Chapter 14 of the text. These activities allow you to progress at your own pace.

About the Authors

Terence M. Shumaker is Manager of the Autodesk Premier Training Center, and a Drafting Technology instructor at Clackamas Community College. Terence has been teaching at the community college level since 1977. He has commercial experience in surveying, civil drafting, industrial piping, and technical illustration. He is the author of Goodheart-Willcox's *Process Pipe Drafting*, and is coauthor of the *AutoCAD and its Applications Release 14* series, *AutoCAD and its Applications* (Release 10, 11, 12, and 13 editions), and *AutoCAD Essentials*.

David A. Madsen is the Chairperson of Drafting Technology and the Autodesk Premier Training Center at Clackamas Community College. David has been an instructor/department chair at Clackamas Community College since 1972. In addition to community college experience, David was a Drafting Technology instructor at Centennial High School in Gresham, Oregon. David also has extensive experience in mechanical drafting, architectural design and drafting, and construction practices. He is the author or coauthor of several Goodheart-Willcox drafting and design textbooks, including *Geometric Dimensioning and Tolerancing*, the *AutoCAD and its Applications Release 14* series, *AutoCAD and its Applications* (Release 10, 11, 12, and 13 editions), and *AutoCAD Essentials*.

Acknowledgments

The authors and publisher would like to thank the following individuals and companies for their assistance and contributions.

Contributing authors

The authors are indebted to Rod Rawls for his professional expertise in providing in-depth research and testing, technical assistance, reviews, and development of new materials for Chapter 15–Chapter 24. Rod is an AutoCAD consultant and principal instructor at the AutoCAD Premier Training Center, Clackamas Community College. He is also the coauthor of *AutoLISP Programming Principles and Techniques* published by Goodheart-Willcox.

Technical assistance and contribution of materials

Rachel Cederdahl, student at Clackamas Community College
Margo Bilson of Willamette Industries, Inc.
Fitzgerald, Hagan, & Hackathorn
Dr. Stuart Soman of Briarcliffe College
Gil Hoellerich of Springdale, AR

Contribution of materials

Cynthia B. Clark of the American Society of Mechanical Engineers
Marty McConnell of Houston Instrument, A Summagraphics Company
Grace Gallego of Autodesk, Inc.
Dave Hall of the Harris Group, Inc.

Contribution of photographs or other technical information

Amdek Corporation
Applications Development, Inc.
Arthur Baker
Autodesk, Inc.
CADalyst magazine
CADENCE magazine
CalComp
Chris Lindner
Computer-Aided Design, Inc.
Digital Equipment Corp.
EPCM Services Ltd.
Far Mountain Corporation
FLIR Systems Inc.
Gateway 2000
GTCO Corporation
Harris Group, Inc.
Hewlett-Packard
Houston Instrument, A Summagraphics Company
International Source for Ergonomics

IOLINE Corporation
JDL, Inc.
Jerome Hart
Jim Armstrong
Jim Webster
Kunz Associates
Mark Stennfeld
Matt Slay
Microsoft Corporation
Mitsubishi Electronics America, Inc.
Mouse Systems Corporation
Myonetics Inc.
NEC Technologies, Inc.
Norwest Engineering
Schuchart & Associates, Inc.
The American Society of Mechanical Engineers
The Xerox Engineering Systems Weiser, Inc.
Willamette Industries, Inc.

Trademarks

Autodesk, AutoCAD, and AutoLISP are registered in the U.S. Patent Trademark Office by Autodesk, Inc.

Autodesk Animator Studio, Autodesk 3D Studio, and DXF are trademarks of Autodesk, Inc.

dBase is a registered trademark of Ashton Tate

IBM is a registered trademark of International Business Machines

MS-DOS, Windows, Windows NT, Windows 95, and Microsoft Word are trademarks of Microsoft Corporation

Pizazz Plus is a registered trademark of Applications Software Corporation

Contents

Three-Dimensional Construction and Display

Solid Modeling with ACIS

Presentation Graphics and Rendering

Advanced AutoCAD Applications

Customizing AutoCAD

Introduction to Three-Dimensional Drawing

Learning Objectives

After completing this chapter, you will be able to:
- O Describe the nature and function of rectangular 3D coordinate systems.
- O Describe the "right-hand rule" of 3D visualization.
- O Construct extruded and wireframe 3D objects.
- O Display 3D objects from any viewpoint.

The use of three-dimensional (3D) drawing and design as a tool is becoming more prevalent throughout industry. Companies are discovering the benefits of 3D modeling in design, visualization, testing, analysis, manufacturing, assembly, and marketing. Three-dimensional models also form the basis of computer animations and *virtual worlds* used with virtual reality systems. Persons who can design objects, buildings, and "worlds" in 3D are in demand for a wide variety of positions, both inside and outside of the traditional drafting and design disciplines.

The first twelve chapters of this book provide you with a variety of skills and techniques for drawing and designing 3D wireframes, surfaces, and solids. These skills provide you with the ability to construct any object in 3D, and prepare you for entry into an exciting aspect of graphic communication.

To be effective creating and using 3D objects, you must first have good 3D visualization skills, including the ability to see an object in three dimensions and to visualize it rotating in space. These skills can be obtained by using 3D techniques to construct objects, and by trying to see two-dimensional sketches and drawings as 3D models. This chapter provides an introduction to several aspects of 3D drawing and visualization. Subsequent chapters expand on these aspects and provide a detailed examination of 3D drawing, editing, visualization, and display.

Rectangular 3D Coordinates

AutoCAD User's Guide **13**

In two-dimensional drawing, you see one plane defined by two dimensions. These dimensions are usually located on the X and Y axes. However, in 3D drawing, another plane and coordinate axis is added. The additional plane is defined with a third dimension located along the Z axis. If you are looking at a standard AutoCAD screen, the positive Z axis comes directly out of the screen toward your face. AutoCAD can only draw lines in 3D if it knows the X, Y, and Z coordinate values of each point on the object. For 2D drawing, only two of the three coordinates are needed.

Compare the 2D coordinate system and the 3D coordinate system shown in Figure 1-1. Notice that the positive values of Z in the 3D system come up from the XY plane of a 2D drawing. Consider the surface of your screen as the XY plane. Anything behind the screen is negative Z and anything in front of the screen is positive Z. The object in Figure 1-2A is a 2D drawing showing the top view of an object. The XY coordinate values of the origin and each point are shown. Think of the object as being drawn directly on the surface of your screen.

Figure 1-1.
A comparison of 2D and 3D coordinate systems.

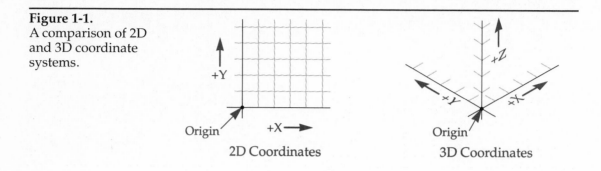

2D Coordinates   3D Coordinates

To convert this object to its three-dimensional form, Z values are given to each corner. Figure 1-2B shows the object pictorially with the XYZ values of each point listed. Positive Z coordinates are used. Therefore, the object comes out of your screen. The object can also be drawn using negative Z coordinates. In this case, the object extends behind, or into, the screen.

Study the nature of the 3D coordinate system. Be sure you understand Z values before you begin constructing 3D objects. It is especially important that you carefully visualize and plan your design when working with 3D constructions.

Three-dimensional objects can be drawn in AutoCAD using two additional coordinate systems—spherical and cylindrical. These two systems allow you to work with point locations using distances and angles. A complete discussion of spherical and cylindrical coordinate systems is provided in Chapter 2.

PROFESSIONAL TIP Although the sign of the Z value (positive or negative) makes no difference to AutoCAD, it can be time-consuming to use negative values.

Figure 1-2.
A—The corners of a 2D object need only two coordinates. B—Each corner of a 3D object must have an X, Y, and Z value.

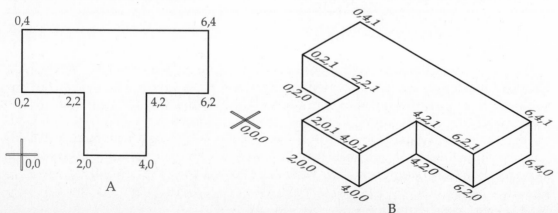

A   B

❏ Study the multiview sketch below.
❏ Freehand sketch the object pictorially on the 3D coordinate axes. Each tick mark
is one unit. Use correct dimensions as given in the multiview sketch.
❏ When you complete the freehand sketch, draw the object in AutoCAD with the
LINE command by entering XYZ coordinates for each point.
❏ Save the drawing as EX1-1 and quit.

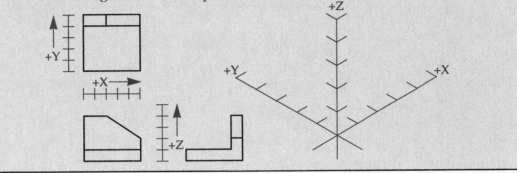

Creating Extruded 3D Shapes

Most shapes drawn with AutoCAD are extruded shapes. *Extruded* means that a
2D shape is given a base elevation and a thickness. The object then rises up, or
"extrudes" to its given thickness. The **ELEV** command is used to extrude an object.
ELEV does not draw, it merely sets the base elevation and thickness for the next object
drawn. To use this command, type ELEV at the Command: prompt.

> **NOTE**
>
> Keep in mind that the current elevation established by the
> value set using the **ELEV** command is the level at which the next
> object is drawn. Therefore, if you set the elevation at 1.0, then
> draw the bottom of a machine part, the bottom of that part is
> now sitting at an elevation of 1.0 units above the zero elevation.
>
> On the other hand, the setting of the *thickness* is the value
> that determines the height of the next object you draw.
> Therefore, if you want to draw a part one unit high with the
> bottom of the part resting on the zero elevation plane, set ele-
> vation to 0.0 and thickness to 1.0.

To draw the "T"-shaped object shown in Figure 1-3A with sides that are one unit
high, first use the **ELEV** command as follows:

    Command: **ELEV**↵
    New current elevation ⟨0.0000⟩: ↵
    New current thickness ⟨0.0000⟩: **1**↵

After you have entered this command sequence, nothing happens on-screen.
However, an elevation of 0 and thickness of 1 are now the current settings. Next, use
the **LINE** command to draw the outline. Although it appears that you are drawing
lines, you are actually drawing X and Y planes. Each plane has a height (thickness) of
one unit that you cannot see in this view.

Now, use the following instructions to add two hexagons and a circle, as shown
in Figure 1-3B. The hexagons should sit on top of the "T" and extend .25 units above.
The circle should appear to be a hole through the leg of the "T." Since the circle has
the same elevation and thickness as the "T," draw it first. This way you will only need
to use the **ELEV** command when drawing the hexagons.

Chapter 1   Introduction to Three-Dimensional Drawing   **15**

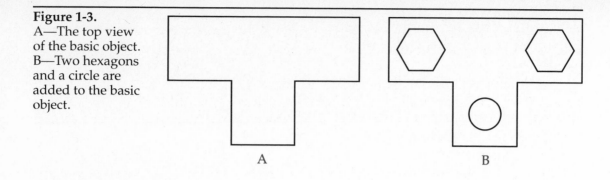

Figure 1-3.
A—The top view of the basic object.
B—Two hexagons and a circle are added to the basic object.

A   B

To draw the hexagons, set the base elevation and thickness (height) using the **ELEV** command as follows. The base elevation is set to the top surface of the "T."

> Command: **ELEV**↵
> New current elevation ⟨0.0000⟩: **1**↵
> New current thickness ⟨1.0000⟩: **.25**↵

The value of 1 is entered for the elevation because the hexagons sit on top of the "T," which is 1 unit thick. The value of .25 is the thickness, or height, of the hexagons above the base elevation. Now, draw the hexagons. With all of the elements drawn, the object is ready to be viewed in 3D.

Displaying quick 3D views

AutoCAD has several ways to quickly display a 3D drawing. You can select a preset view by picking **3D Viewpoint** in the **View** pull-down menu, picking the appropriate button in the **Viewpoint** toolbar, or selecting a view from the **Viewpoint** flyout on the **Standard** toolbar, Figure 1-4.

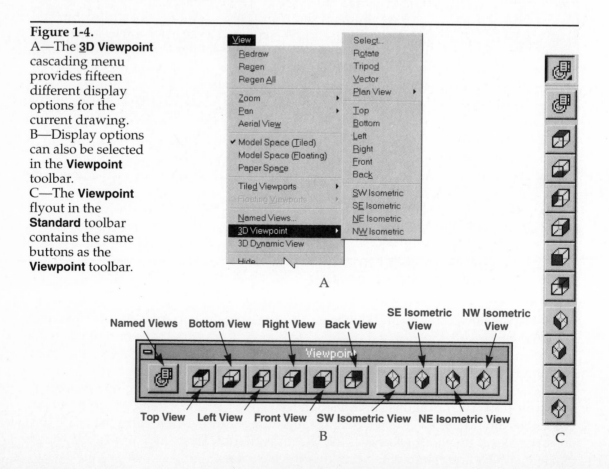

Figure 1-4.
A—The **3D Viewpoint** cascading menu provides fifteen different display options for the current drawing.
B—Display options can also be selected in the **Viewpoint** toolbar.
C—The **Viewpoint** flyout in the **Standard** toolbar contains the same buttons as the **Viewpoint** toolbar.

AutoCAD and its Applications—Advanced

Picking **Plan View** from the **3D Viewpoint** cascading menu displays the current drawing in a plan view of the current user coordinate system. This option is not available in the **Viewpoint** toolbar. User coordinate systems are discussed in detail in Chapter 3.

Using either the pull-down menu or the toolbar, pick the **SW Isometric View** button. The display should look like the one shown in Figure 1-5. If you want to return to the previous 2D display, just pick **Plan View**, and then pick **Current UCS** in the **3D Viewpoint** cascading menu.

Figure 1-5.
The object shown in Figure 1-3B is viewed here as a wireframe by looking at it from the southwest.

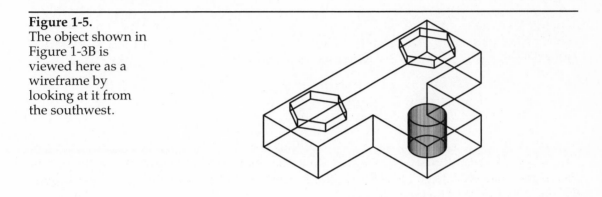

Removing hidden lines in 3D displays

In a wireframe display, every edge can be seen. This view can be confusing, especially if there are several circular features in your drawing. The best way to mask all lines that would normally be hidden is to use the **HIDE** command. Activate the **HIDE** command by entering HI or HIDE at the Command: prompt, picking **Hide** from the **View** pull-down menu, or picking the **Hide** button on the **Render** toolbar.

```
Command: HI or HIDE↵
Regenerating drawing
```

Use **HIDE** only after you have selected a 3D viewpoint. The complexity of the drawing and the speed of your computer determine how long you must wait for the lines to be hidden. The object in Figure 1-5 is shown in Figure 1-6 with hidden lines removed.

The view in Figure 1-6 may not look quite right. You probably expected the "T" to appear solid with a circle in the top representing a hole. Think back to the initial construction of the object. When drawn in the plan view, it consisted of lines, or planes. It was not drawn with a top or bottom, just sides. Then, you placed hexagons on top of the "box" and a cylinder inside. However, the object still is made up of only sides. That is why the "hidden line removed" display appears as it does.

Figure 1-6.
The hidden lines of this object were removed using the **HIDE** command.

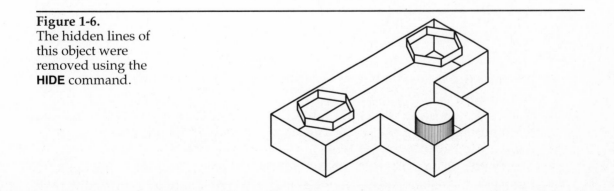

The individual features that compose the object in Figure 1-5 are shown in Figure 1-7. Both wireframe and hidden-line views are given. To redisplay the wireframe view, just select another viewpoint or enter REGEN and press [Enter]. A regeneration displays all lines of the objects.

Figure 1-7.
The individual features of the object in Figure 1-6 are shown here as a wireframe (A) and with hidden lines removed (B).

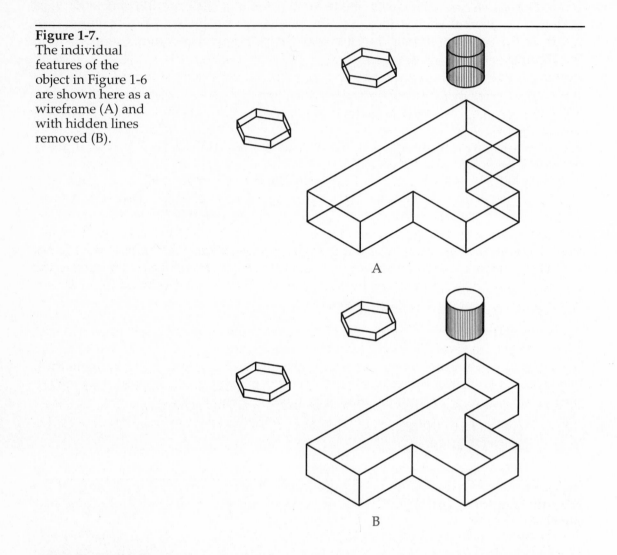

A

B

PROFESSIONAL TIP

Keep in mind that a "hole" drawn using **ELEV** and **CIRCLE** is not really a hole to AutoCAD. It is a cylinder with solid ends. This becomes clear when you display the objects in a 3D view with hidden lines removed, as shown in Figure 1-6.

Some 3D drawing hints

- Erasing a line drawn with the thickness set to a value other than zero erases an entire plane.
- Shapes drawn using the **LINE** and **ELEV** commands are open at the top and bottom. Shapes drawn with the **CIRCLE** and **ELEV** commands are closed at the ends.
- The **PLINE**, **POLYGON**, **RECTANG**, and **TRACE** commands give thickness to lines and make them appear as walls in the 3D view, similar to using the **LINE** command.

The Right-Hand Rule of 3D

In order to gain a more thorough understanding of how AutoCAD displays 3D objects, it is important for you to become familiar with the method used to present them. The following method is simple and helps you visualize the 3D coordinate system.

The *right-hand rule* is a graphic representation of positive coordinate values in the three axis directions of a coordinate system. AutoCAD's **UCS** (User Coordinate System) is based on this concept of visualization. To use the right-hand rule, position the thumb, index finger, and middle finger of your right hand as shown in Figure 1-8. Although this may seem a bit unusual to use (especially if you are sitting in a school library or computer lab), it can do wonders for your understanding of the nature of the three axes. It can also help in understanding how the UCS can be rotated about each of the axis lines (fingers).

Imagine that your thumb is the X axis, your index finger the Y axis, and your middle finger the Z axis. Hold your hand directly in front of you so that your middle finger is pointing directly at you, as shown in Figure 1-8. This is the plan view. The positive X axis is pointing to the right and the positive Y axis is pointing up. The positive Z axis comes toward you, and the origin of this system is the palm of your hand.

This concept can be visualized even better if you are sitting at a computer and the AutoCAD graphics screen is displayed. If the UCS icon is not displayed in the lower-left corner of the screen, turn it on as follows:

Command: **UCSICON**↵
ON/OFF/All/Noorigin/ORigin ⟨*current*⟩: **ON**↵

Now orient your right hand as shown in Figure 1-8 and position it next to the UCS icon on the screen. Your index finger and thumb should point in the same directions as Y and X, respectively, on the UCS icon. Your middle finger will be pointing out of the screen directly at you. This technique can also be used to eliminate confusion when the UCS is rotated to odd angles.

Figure 1-8.
Try positioning your hand like this to understand the relationship of the X, Y, and Z axes.

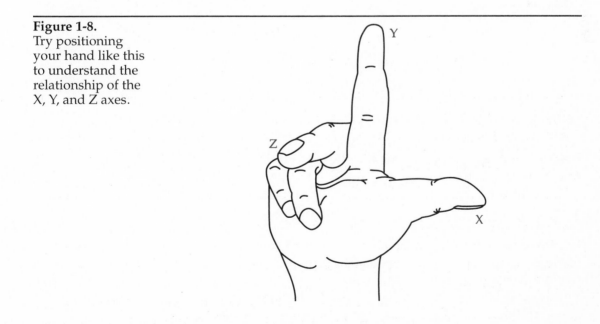

When you use the **VPOINT** command (discussed later in this chapter), a tripod appears on the screen. It is composed of three axis lines—X, Y, and Z. When you see the tripod, you should be able to make the comparison with the right-hand rule. See Figure 1-9.

The UCS can be rotated to any position desired. The coordinate system rotates on one of the three axis lines, just like a wheel rotates on an axle. Therefore, if you want to rotate the X plane, keep your thumb stationary, and turn your hand. If you wish to rotate the Y plane, keep your index finger stationary and turn your hand to the left or right. When rotating the Z plane, you must keep your middle finger stationary and rotate your entire arm to the right or left.

If your 3D visualization skills are weak or you are having trouble with the UCS method, don't be afraid to use the right-hand rule. It is a useful technique for improving your 3D visualization skills. The ability to rotate the UCS around one or more of the three axes can become confusing if proper techniques are not used to visualize the rotation angles. A complete discussion of these techniques is provided in Chapter 3.

Figure 1-9.
Compare the use of three fingers on the right hand and the tripod used by AutoCAD for 3D viewing.

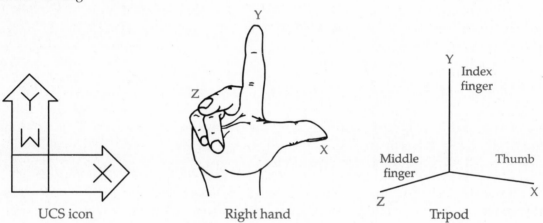

UCS icon   Right hand   Tripod

Displaying 3D Drawings

AutoCAD User's Guide 13

There are two ways to generate a 3D display in AutoCAD. The easiest to understand is the **VPOINT** command. This is discussed next. The second method is the **DVIEW** command. It is considerably more complex than the **VPOINT** command. It is discussed in detail in Chapter 7.

The **VPOINT** command allows you to display the current drawing at any angle. It may be easier to understand the function of this command as establishing your position relative to the object.

Imagine that you can position yourself at a coordinate location in 3D space in relation to the object. The **VPOINT** command provides AutoCAD with the XYZ coordinates of your eyes, so the object can be positioned properly. To use the **VPOINT** command, enter -VP or VPOINT at the Command: prompt or select **Tripod** from the **3D Viewpoint** cascading menu in the **View** pull-down menu.

VPOINT
-VP

View
 ↳ 3D Viewpoint
   ↳ Tripod

Command: **-VP** *or* **VPOINT**↵
Rotate/⟨View point⟩ ⟨0.0000,0.0000,1.0000⟩:

The three numbers in the prompt reflect the XYZ coordinates of the current viewpoint. Change these coordinates to select a different viewpoint. The values shown in the command sequence represent the coordinates for the plan view. This means that you see the XY plane.

It is difficult to visualize a viewpoint as a number. You can also display a graphic representation of the XYZ axes and pick the desired viewpoint with your pointing device. Press [Enter] at the Rotate: prompt or select the **Axes** option from the screen menu. The screen display changes to one similar to Figure 1-10A.

As you move the pointing device, notice what happens on-screen. The XYZ coordinate tripod and the small crosshairs near the concentric circles move. When the small crosshairs are inside the small circle, you are viewing the object from above. When the crosshairs are located between the two circles, you are viewing the object from below.

The concentric circles are divided into quarters to represent a compass. Figure 1-10B shows what the circles look like with the directions of a compass added. Notice that the small crosshairs are located in the southwest quadrant. Therefore, this display appears similar to one achieved by picking the **SW Isometric View** option. However, it is hard to create an exact isometric viewpoint using the tripod.

Figure 1-10.
A—The **VPOINT** axes display allows you to position yourself in relation to the object. B—Compass directions added to the concentric circles of the **VPOINT** axes display.

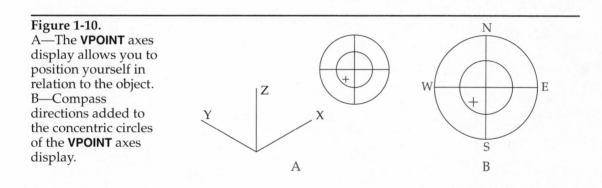

The easiest way to locate the viewpoint is to move the cursor while observing the XYZ axes tripod movement. Pick the location where you are satisfied with the appearance of the axes. It may take some practice. Remember that in the top, or plan, view, the X axis is horizontal, Y axis is vertical, and Z axis comes out of the screen. As you move the tripod, keep track of where the crosshairs are located inside the compass. Compare their position to that of the tripod. Move the tripod until it is positioned like the one given in Figure 1-11. This is similar to picking the **SW Isometric View** button in the **Viewpoint** toolbar.

Figure 1-11.
The three axes and a 3D view from the southwest quadrant.

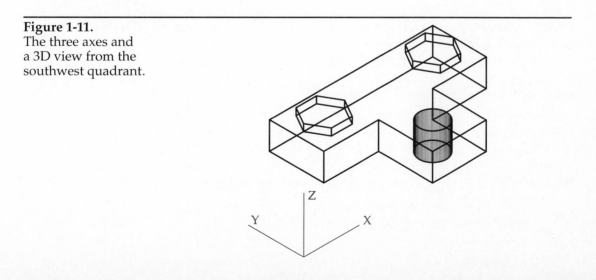

The number of viewpoints you can select is endless. To get an idea of how the axes tripod and compass relate to the viewpoint, see the examples in Figure 1-12.

It can be hard to distinguish top from bottom in wireframe views. Therefore, the viewpoints shown in Figure 1-12 are all from above the object and the **HIDE** command has been used to clarify the views. Use the **VPOINT** command to try each of these 3D positions on your computer.

When you are ready to return to the plan view, type PLAN at the Command: prompt and select the default option (**Current UCS**), or type the XYZ coordinates for the plan view using the **VPOINT** command:

> Command: **-VP** or **VPOINT**↵
> Rotate/⟨View point⟩ ⟨*current*⟩: **0,0,1**↵

This returns your original top view, which fills the screen. You can use the **All** option of the **ZOOM** command to display the drawing limits.

Figure 1-12.
Examples of viewpoint locations and their related axes positions.

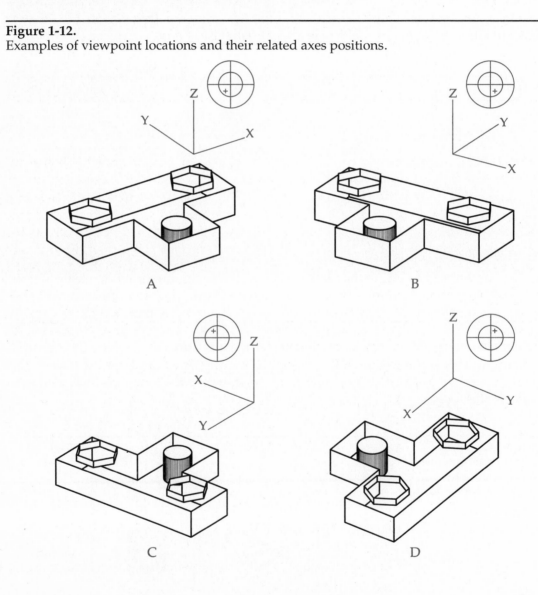

❏ Set the grid spacing to .5 and snap spacing to .25.
❏ Use the **LINE** command to draw the figure in A below to the dimensions given. Do not dimension the drawing.
❏ Use the **CIRCLE** command to draw the figure in B below to the dimensions given. Do not dimension the drawing.
❏ Use the **VPOINT** command to display the 3D view of your drawing. Display it from three viewpoints using the axes tripod.
❏ Save the drawing as EX1-2.

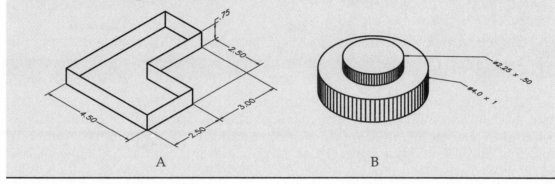

A   B

Creating extruded 3D text

Text added on the plan view is displayed in 3D when you use the **VPOINT** command. However, the displayed text does not have thickness, and it always rests on the zero elevation plane. You can give text thickness with the **DDCHPROP** command or by picking the **Properties** button in the **Object Properties** toolbar. After selecting the text, the **Modify Text** dialog box appears. See Figure 1-13. Enter a new value in the **Thickness** text box and pick **OK**. The selected text now has a thickness. Figure 1-14 shows examples of 3D text with thickness added, before and after using the **HIDE** command.

Figure 1-13.
Thickness of text can be changed using the **Modify Text** dialog box.

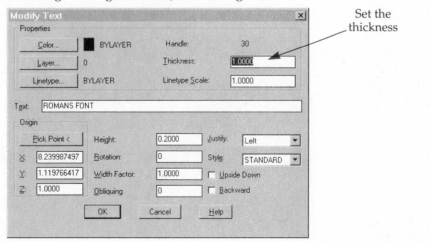

Set the thickness

Figure 1-14.
Thickness is applied to 3D text with, and without, the **HIDE** option.

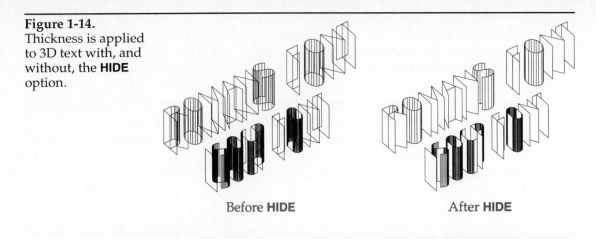

Before **HIDE**   After **HIDE**

3D Construction Techniques

Three-dimensional objects can be drawn in three basic forms—wireframe, surface models, and solid models. The following section discusses the construction of wireframes and the use of 3D faces to apply a surface to the wireframe. Additional information on wireframe construction is provided in Chapter 2, Chapter 3, and Chapter 4. A complete discussion of surface modeling is found in Chapter 5. Solid model construction and editing is covered in Chapter 10, Chapter 11, and Chapter 12.

A *wireframe construction* is an object that looks like it is made of wire. You can see through it. There are not a lot of practical applications for wireframe models unless you are an artist designing a new object using coat hangers. Wireframe models can be hard to visualize because it is difficult to determine the angle of view and the nature of the surfaces. Compare the two objects in Figure 1-15.

Surface modeling, on the other hand, is much easier to visualize. A surface model looks more like a real object. Surface models can be used to imitate solid models. Most importantly, color, surface textures, lights, and shadows can be applied for realistic presentations. These "shaded and rendered" models can then be used in any number of presentation formats including slide shows, black and white or color prints, walk-around or walk-through animations, and animations that are recorded to videotape. A surface model can also be exported from AutoCAD for use in animation and rendering software, such as Autodesk's 3D Studio.

Figure 1-15.
A wireframe object may be harder to visualize than a surface model. (Autodesk, Inc.)

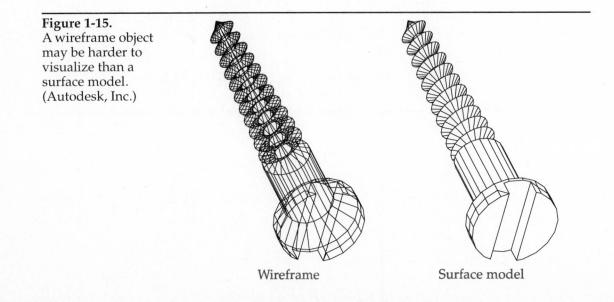

Wireframe   Surface model

Surface models are the basis for the construction of composite 3D models, often called *virtual worlds*, which are used in the field of virtual reality. These 3D rendered worlds can then be used with virtual reality software such as the Autodesk Cyberspace Developers Kit (CDK). The possibilities are endless. However, remember that the usefulness of surface models is defined by the word "presentation." This means *seeing* what the model looks like while viewing it from different angles, with different lighting, shading, and surface textures.

On the other hand, *solid modeling* more closely represents designing an object using the materials it is to be made from. This type of 3D design involves using primitive solid shapes such as boxes, cylinders, spheres, and cones to construct an object. These shapes are added and subtracted to create a finished product. The solid model can then be shaded and rendered. More importantly, solid models can be analyzed and tested for mass, volume, moments of inertia, and centroids. Some third-party programs allow you to perform finite element analysis on solid models.

Before constructing a 3D model, you should determine the purpose of your design. What will the model be used for—presentation, analysis, or manufacturing? This helps you determine which tools you should use to construct the model. The discussions and examples in this chapter provide an introduction to the uses of wireframe, 3D faces, and basic surfaced objects in order to create 3D constructions.

Constructing Wireframes and 3D Faces

Wireframes can be constructed using the **LINE**, **PLINE**, **SPLINE**, and **3DPOLY** commands. There are a number of different ways to use these commands to construct wireframes, but one particularly useful method is called filters. A *filter* is an existing point or vector in your drawing file. When using a filter, you instruct AutoCAD to find the coordinate values of a selected point, then you supply the missing value—X, Y, Z, or a combination. Filters can be used when working in two-dimensional space or when using a pictorial projection resulting from the **VPOINT** command.

Using filters to create 3D wireframe objects

When using **LINE**, you must know the XYZ coordinate values of each corner on the object. To draw an object, first decide the easiest and quickest method using the **LINE** command. One technique is to draw the bottom surface. Then, make a copy at the height of the object. Finally, connect the corners with lines. The filters can be used with the **COPY** command, or by using grips to copy.

For example, first draw the 2D object shown in Figure 1-2A using the **LINE** command. Next, copy the shape up to the height of one unit.

```
Command: CO or COPY↵
Select objects: (select the shape using a window or crossing box)
Select objects: ↵
⟨Base point or displacement⟩/Multiple: (pick a corner of the shape)
Second point of displacement: .XY↵
of (pick the same corner)
(need Z): 1↵
```

The new object is directly above the original object, so there still appears to be a single object on the screen. The top surface has the same XY values as the bottom surface. That is why .XY was entered as the second point of displacement. This filter picks up the XY values of the point specified and applies them to the location of the new copy. Now, all AutoCAD needs is the Z value, which it requests. Check your progress by looking at the object using the **VPOINT** command. Enter the coordinates given below. Your display should look like that in Figure 1-16.

> Command: **-VP** *or* **VPOINT**↵
> Rotate/〈View point〉 〈*current*〉: **1,-1,0.75**↵

Return the drawing to the plan view and finish the object using **LINE** command and point filters. The eight remaining lines are vertical and one unit long. You can draw these lines using the **Intersection** object snap or by using filters as follows:

> Command: **L** *or* **LINE**↵
> From point: *(pick the lower-left corner)*
> To point: **.XY**↵
> of *(pick the lower-left corner again)*
> (need Z): **1**↵
> To point: ↵

In this example, you are instructing the computer to draw a line from the lower-left corner of the object to the same XY position one unit above. The new line connects the top and bottom planes of the object. The same process can be used to draw the other vertical lines. If you forget to enter the XY filter at the To point: prompt, AutoCAD will not ask for the Z distance. If this happens, cancel the command and start again. Your drawing should look like Figure 1-17.

Figure 1-16.
A partially constructed 3D shape using **LINE** and XYZ filters.

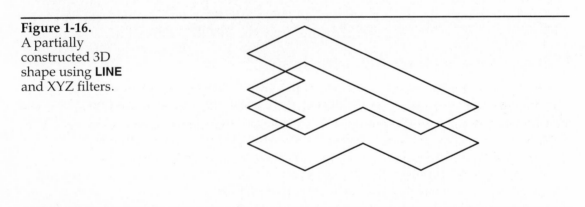

Figure 1-17.
A 3D wireframe object created with the **LINE** command.

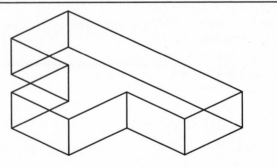

EXERCISE 1-3

❏ Set the grid spacing at .5, snap spacing at .25, and elevation at 0.
❏ Draw the 3D object below to the dimensions indicated. Use the **LINE** and **COPY** commands to construct the object. Construct the top and bottom planes in the plan view. Connect the vertical lines in a 3D view.
❏ Save the drawing as EX1-3.

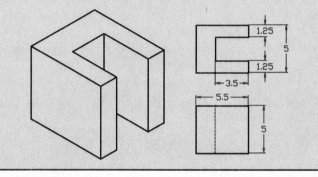

Constructing 3D faces

Surfaces that appear solid (not wireframe) are called *3D faces*. They can be made with the **3DFACE** command. Its prompt structure is similar to that of the **SOLID** command, but you can specify points in a clockwise or counterclockwise manner. The **3DFACE** command is accessed by picking the **3D Face** button in the **Surfaces** toolbar, selecting **3D Face** from the **Surfaces** cascading menu in the **Draw** pull-down menu, or entering 3F or 3DFACE at the Command: prompt.

A 3D face must have at least three corners, but cannot have any more than four corners. Therefore, to draw the top surface of the "T"-shaped box in Figure 1-17, two 3D faces are required. The resulting shape will look somewhat different than the one drawn as a wireframe. Use the following steps to draw the "T" object with 3D faces:

1. Set the elevation to zero.
2. Draw the bottom faces.
3. Copy the bottom faces up a positive Z value (the thickness) to create the top faces.
4. Draw 3D faces on all sides.

3DFACE
3F

Draw
➡ Surfaces
➡ 3D Face

Surfaces
toolbar

3D Face

Draw the first 3D face. Then the second, adjoining 3D face can be drawn using the following command sequence. Refer to Figure 1-18 as you work.

Command: **3F** *or* **3DFACE**↵
First point: **FROM**↵
Base point: **END**↵
of *(pick point A)*
⟨Offset⟩: **@2,0**↵
Second point: *(pick point 2)*
Third point: *(pick point 3)*
Fourth point: *(pick point 4)*
Third point: ↵

The 3D faces can be copied using the same steps taken to copy the wireframe line surface.

Finally, draw the vertical sides of the shape. First, set a viewpoint and then connect corners of each 3D face using the **Endpoint** or **Intersection** running object snap mode.

Command: **-VP** *or* **VPOINT**↵
Rotate/⟨View point⟩ ⟨*current*⟩: **1,-1,.75**↵

The drawing should look like that shown in Figure 1-19. Zoom in if the view is too small.

To complete the object in Figure 1-19, first set the **Intersect** running object snap mode, then pick points 1 through 4 on the right side. You can construct a series of connected faces without exiting the **3DFACE** command. After picking the fourth point, the Third point: prompt reappears. Continue picking points 3 and 4 around the object until you pick the last points 3 and 4 that coincide with the original points 1 and 2. Press [Enter] to exit the command.

Command: **3F** *or* **3DFACE**↵
First point: *(pick point 1)*
Second point: *(pick point 2)*
Third point: *(pick point 3)*
Fourth point: *(pick point 4)*
Third point: *(pick point 3)*
Fourth point: *(pick point 4)*
Third point: *(continue picking points 3 and 4 to complete the object)*

Figure 1-18. The bottom of the object is composed of two 3D faces.

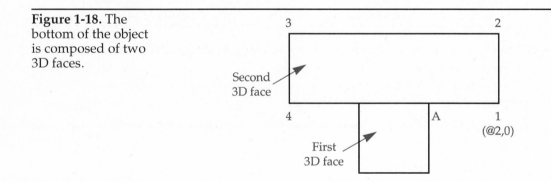

Figure 1-19.
After the top and bottom are created, the sides must be added. The numbers indicate the points to pick when using the **3DFACE** command.

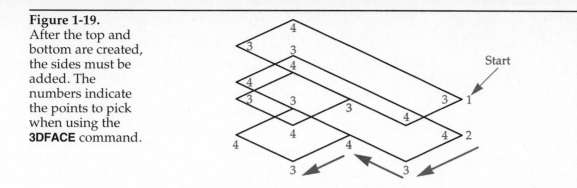

The finished box should appear similar to that in Figure 1-20.

Notice in Figure 1-20B that an intersection line is visible between the two faces on the top surface. This surface, and similar arrangements of attached 3D faces, can be drawn so that all intersecting edges are invisible. The procedure requires some planning and is discussed in Chapter 2.

How does a 3D face object differ from ones drawn using the **ELEV** and **LINE** commands? For comparison, Figure 1-21 shows boxes drawn using the **ELEV**, **LINE**, and **3DFACE** commands with hidden lines removed by **HIDE**.

Figure 1-20.
A—The completed object appears to be a wireframe construction before using **HIDE**.
B—The object after using **HIDE**.

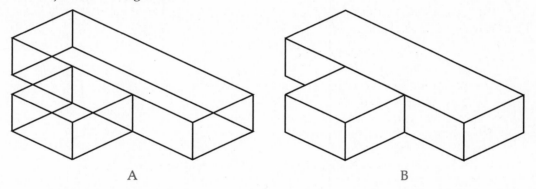

A

B

Figure 1-21.
A comparison of boxes drawn with **ELEV**, **LINE**, and **3DFACE**, all after the **HIDE** command.

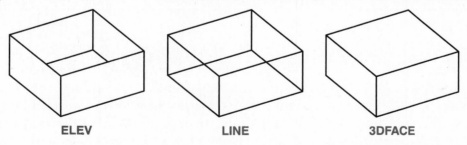

ELEV

LINE

3DFACE

When moving or copying objects in 3D space, it can simplify matters to use the displacement option to specify positioning data. This allows you to specify the X, Y, and Z movement simultaneously. For example, to copy a 3D face to a position three units above the original on the Z axis, use the following command sequence:

Command: **CO** *or* **COPY**↵
Select objects: *(pick the 3D face)*
Select objects: ↵
⟨Base point or displacement⟩/Multiple: **0,0,1**↵
⟨Second point of displacement⟩: ↵

Because [Enter] was pressed at the ⟨Second point of displacement⟩: prompt, the X,Y,Z values entered are used as a relative displacement instead of a base point.

EXERCISE 1-4

❑ Set the grid spacing at .5, snap spacing at .25, and elevation at 0.
❑ Use the **3DFACE** command to construct the object shown below to the dimensions given. The front surface should be drawn with two faces, shown below as A and B.
❑ Use the **HIDE** command when you complete the object.
❑ Save the drawing as EX1-4.

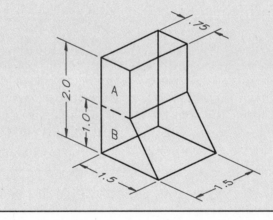

Constructing 3D Surface-Modeled Objects

Several predrawn 3D objects can be quickly drawn by providing AutoCAD with a location and basic dimensions of the object. These objects can be selected by picking the appropriate button in the **Surfaces** toolbar or from the **3D Objects** dialog box, Figure 1-22. To access this dialog box, you can pick **3D Surfaces...** from the **Surfaces** cascading menu in the **Draw** pull-down menu.

In the **3D Objects** dialog box, notice the list box to the left. These are the names of all the objects shown. An object can be selected by picking either the name or the image. When an image or its name is selected, the image is highlighted with a box, and the name in the list box is also highlighted. Pick **OK** to draw the highlighted object.

Figure 1-22.
A—The **3D Objects** dialog box displays a group of 3D surface-modeled objects that can be quickly drawn by supplying a few basic dimensions. B—The same objects can be selected from the **Surfaces** toolbar.

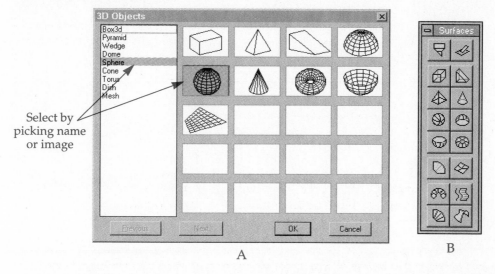

Select by picking name or image

A

B

The first prompt requests a location point for the object. The remaining prompts request the length, width, height, diameter, radius, or number of longitudinal and latitudinal segments, depending on the object selected. For example, select **Dome** in the **3D Objects** dialog box. The following prompts appear:

Center of dome: *(pick a point)*
Diameter/⟨radius⟩: *(enter a radius or pick on the screen)*
Number of longitudinal segments ⟨16⟩: ↵
Number of latitudinal segments ⟨8⟩: ↵

The object is drawn in the plan view, as shown in Figure 1-23A. Use the **VPOINT** command to produce a 3D view of the object, and use **HIDE** to remove hidden lines.

Figure 1-23B illustrates longitudinal and latitudinal segments. Longitudinal refers to an east-west measurement, and latitudinal refers to north-south measurement.

Remember that if you draw 3D objects in the plan view, you must use the **VPOINT** command in order to see a 3D view. The illustrations in Figure 1-24 show all of the dimensions required to construct the predrawn 3D objects provided by AutoCAD.

Figure 1-23.
A—The plan view of a dome.
B—Longitudinal segments are measured east-west, and latitudinal segments are measured north-south.

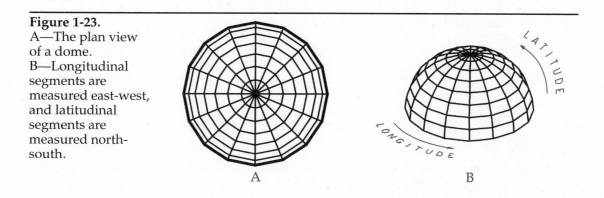

A

B

Figure 1-24.
These dimensions are required to draw AutoCAD's various 3D surface objects.

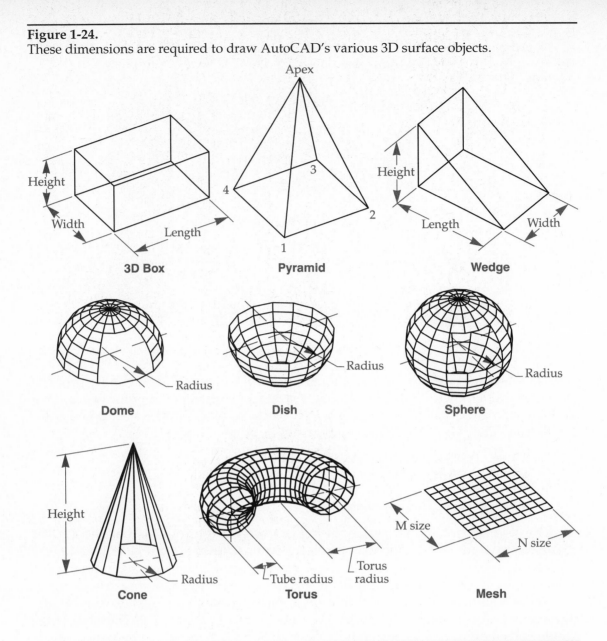

Chapter Test

Write your answers in the spaces provided.

1. When looking at the screen in plan view, in which direction does the Z coordinate project?_____

   _____

   _____

2. Which command allows you to give objects thickness?_____

   _____

3. If you draw a line after setting a thickness, what have you actually drawn?_____

   _____

   _____

4. What is the purpose of the right-hand rule? _____
_____
_____
_____

5. According to the right-hand rule, name the coordinate axes represented by the following fingers:
Thumb— _____
Middle finger— _____
Index finger—_____

6. What is the purpose of the **VPOINT** command?_____
_____
_____
_____

7. How are you viewing an object when the little crosshairs are inside the small circle in the **VPOINT** command display? _____
_____
_____

8. How are you viewing an object when the little crosshairs are between the small circle and the large circle in the **VPOINT** command display?_____
_____

9. How do you create 3D extruded text? _____
_____
_____

10. What is the function of the **HIDE** command? _____
_____
_____

11. Define "point filters." _____
_____
_____
_____
_____

12. Compare the **3DFACE** and **SOLID** commands. _____
_____
_____
_____
_____

13. How do you select one of AutoCAD's predrawn 3D shapes? _____
_____

Drawing Problems

*Problems 1–12. Draw the following objects as extruded 3D objects using the **ELEV** command. Where possible, draw additional 3D faces to enclose the object. Do not dimension the objects. Display the problems in two different 3D views. Use the **HIDE** command in one view. Do not dimension the drawings. Use your own dimensions for objects shown without dimensions. Save the drawings as **P1-1, P1-2,** etc.*

1.

2.

3.

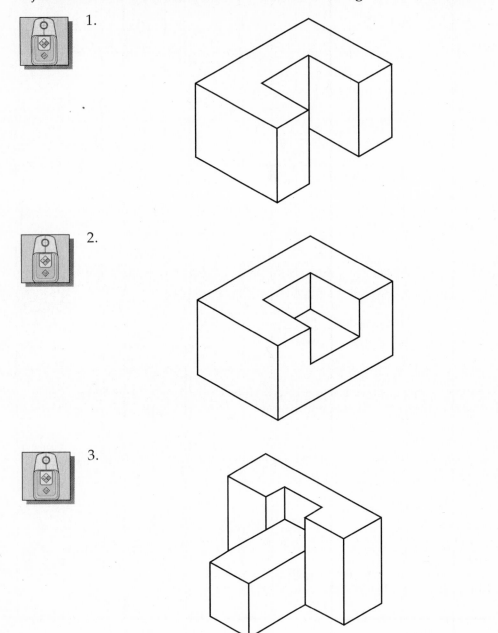

4.

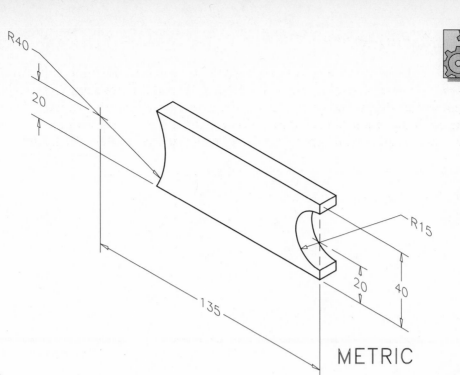

R40

20

R15

135

20

40

METRIC

5.

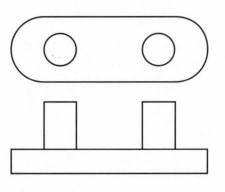

6.

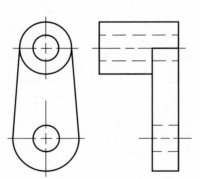

7.

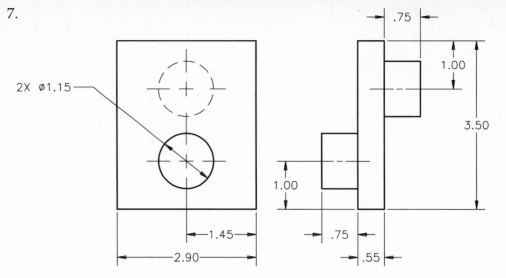

8.

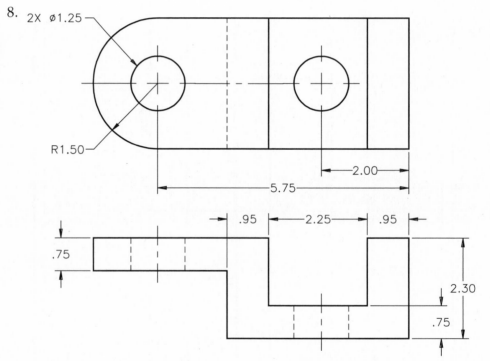

9.

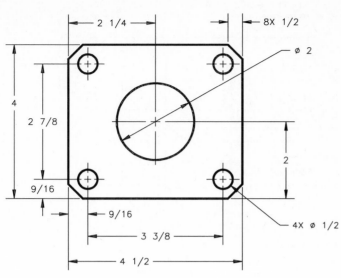

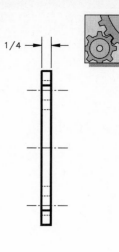

10.

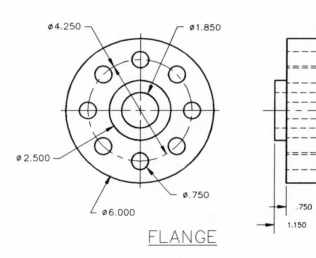

FLANGE

11.

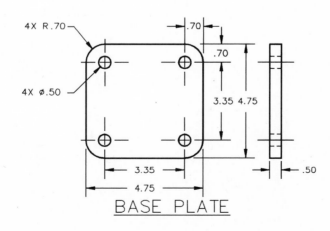

BASE PLATE

12.

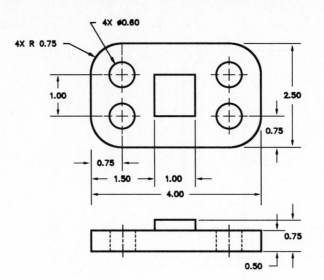

Problems 13–16. *Draw the following objects in 3D form. Use the **LINE** and **3DFACE** commands with the dimensions given to create the drawings. Display the drawings from three different viewpoints. Select the **HIDE** command for one of the views. Save the drawings as **P1-13, P1-14**, etc.*

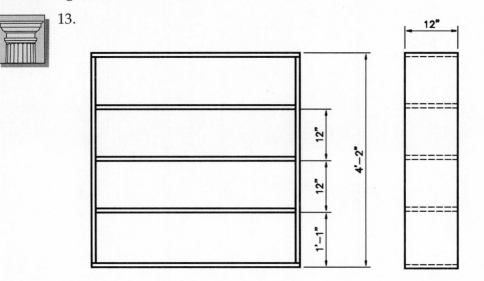 13.

14.

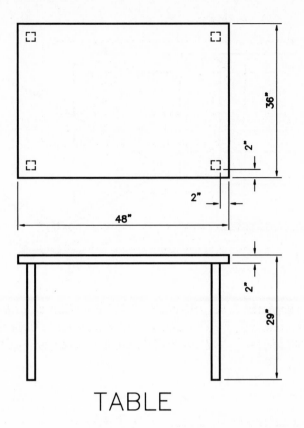

36"

2"

2"

48"

2"

2"

29"

TABLE

15.

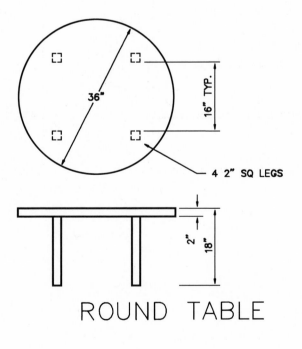

16" TYP.

36"

4 2" SQ LEGS

2"

18"

ROUND TABLE

16.

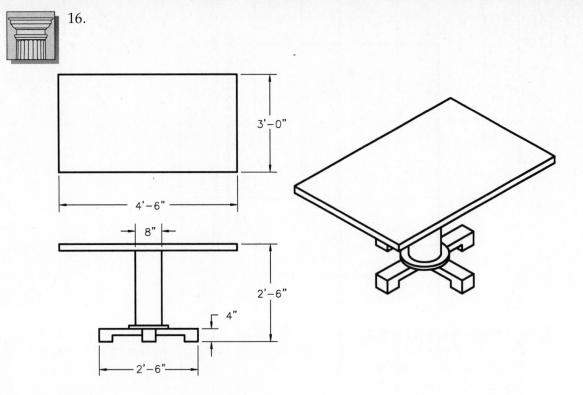

3'-0"

4'-6"

8"

2'-6"

4"

2'-6"

Three-Dimensional Coordinates and Constructions

Learning Objectives

After completing this chapter, you will be able to:
- O Describe rectangular, spherical, and cylindrical 3D coordinate systems.
- O Create 3D surface-modeled objects.
- O Use 3D construction tools.

With AutoCAD, you can display 3D models at any angle. This gives you unlimited possibilities. However, the display and presentation of your models should always be accurate and realistic. Therefore, it is important to be familiar with a variety of coordinate entry methods that can be used with different geometric shapes. This chapter covers the three principal forms of coordinate entry. Drawing and display examples are also given for each type.

3D Coordinate Systems

AutoCAD User's Guide **13**

You can enter 3D coordinates in three different formats. Rectangular coordinates are the most commonly used form of 3D coordinate entry. Refer to Chapter 1 for a discussion on rectangular coordinates. Two other common coordinate systems are spherical coordinates and cylindrical coordinates. These two systems are similar.

Spherical coordinates

Spherical coordinates are similar to locating a point on the earth using longitude, latitude, and the center of the earth as an origin. The origin value can be the default WCS (World Coordinate System) or the current UCS (User Coordinate System). Lines of longitude connect the north and south poles. This gives an east-west measurement on the earth's surface. The longitude measurement is the angle *in* the XY plane. The latitude measurement is the angle *from* the XY plane. Refer to Figure 2-1A. This is a measurement from the equator toward either the north pole or the south pole on the earth's surface. Spherical coordinates are entered like polar coordinates. However, there is an additional angle value, as shown below and in Figure 2-1B:

7.5<35<55

Figure 2-1.
A—Latitudinal segments run from north to south. Longitudinal segments run from east to west. B—Spherical coordinates require a distance, an angle *in* the XY plane, and an angle *from* the XY plane.

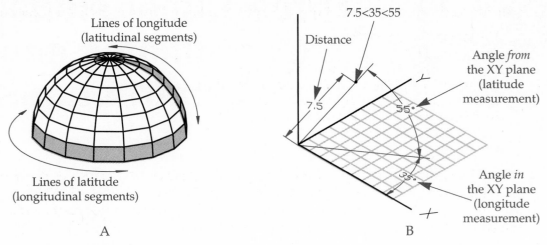

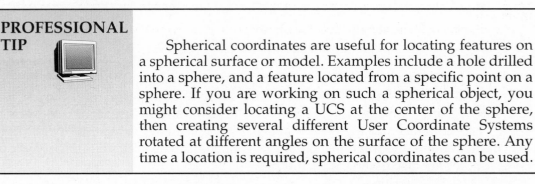

Lines of longitude (latitudinal segments)

Lines of latitude (longitudinal segments)

A

7.5<35<55

Distance

7.5

55°

35°

Angle *from* the XY plane (latitude measurement)

Angle *in* the XY plane (longitude measurement)

B

PROFESSIONAL TIP

Spherical coordinates are useful for locating features on a spherical surface or model. Examples include a hole drilled into a sphere, and a feature located from a specific point on a sphere. If you are working on such a spherical object, you might consider locating a UCS at the center of the sphere, then creating several different User Coordinate Systems rotated at different angles on the surface of the sphere. Any time a location is required, spherical coordinates can be used.

Using spherical coordinates

Spherical coordinates are well-suited for locating points on the surface of a sphere. The first value that is entered is the radius of the sphere. The following example shows how to locate a new object on the surface of a sphere.

First, a sphere is drawn in the plan view. Then, a preset 3D viewpoint is selected. To draw a second sphere on the surface of the first, locate a node at the center of the sphere using the **POINT** command. Be sure to set an appropriate **PDMODE** value. Next, pick **Surfaces** from the **Draw** pull-down menu, and then pick **3D Surfaces**. Pick the sphere image, or select **Sphere** from the list, then pick **OK**. Continue as follows:

> Command: (*pick* **Sphere** *from the* **3D Objects** *dialog box or the* **Surfaces** *toolbar*)
> Center of sphere: **7,5.**↲
> Diameter/⟨radius⟩: **1.5.**↲
> Number of longitudinal segments ⟨16⟩: ↲
> Number of latitudinal segments ⟨16⟩: ↲
> Command:

NOTE

Create a separate layer for construction aids. For example, create a layer named Construct and give it the color blue. Be sure this is the current layer before drawing any construction objects, such as the point used in this example.

AutoCAD and its Applications—Advanced

Use the **POINT** command to draw a point at the center of the sphere. Next, pick **SE Isometric** from the **3D Viewpoint** cascading menu in the **View** pull-down menu. You can also pick the **SE Isometric View** button in the **Viewpoint** toolbar. This displays the object in 3D. Center the object on the screen. Your drawing should look like Figure 2-2A. Pick **Sphere** again. Continue as follows. Use object snaps to assist in accurate location:

```
Center of sphere: FROM↵
Base point: NODE↵
of (pick the point at the center of the sphere)
⟨Offset⟩ @1.5<30<60↵ (1.5 is the radius of the first sphere)
Diameter/⟨radius⟩: .4↵
Number of longitudinal segments ⟨16⟩: ↵
Number of latitudinal segments ⟨16⟩: ↵
Command:
```

The objects should now appear as shown in Figure 2-2B. The center of the new sphere is located on the surface of the original sphere. This is clear after the **HIDE** command is used. See Figure 2-2C. If you want the surfaces to be tangent, add the radius of each sphere (1.5 + .4) and enter that value as the offset (@1.9<30<60).

Figure 2-2.
A 3-unit diameter sphere shown from the SE isometric viewpoint. B—A .8-unit diameter sphere with its center located on the surface of the original object. C—The objects after using the **HIDE** command.

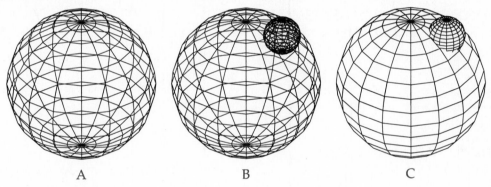

| A | B | C |

Notice in Figure 2-2C that the polar axis lines of both spheres are parallel. This is because both objects were drawn with the same User Coordinate System (UCS). This can be misleading unless you are aware of how objects are constructed based on the current UCS. Test this by locating a cone on the surface of the large sphere, just below the small sphere. Pick **Cone** from the **3D Objects** dialog box or the **Surfaces** toolbar. Continue with the process as follows. Use object snaps to assist in accurate location. The result of this construction is shown in Figure 2-3.

```
Base center point: FROM↵
Base point: NODE↵
of (pick the point at the center of the sphere)
⟨Offset⟩: @1.5<30<30↵
Diameter/⟨radius⟩ of base: .25↵
Diameter/⟨radius⟩ of top ⟨0⟩: ↵
Height: 1↵
Number of segments ⟨16⟩: ↵
Command:
```

Figure 2-3.
The axis lines of objects drawn in the same coordinate system are parallel. Notice that the cone does not project from the center of the large sphere.

Changing the UCS

The axis of the cone is a line from the center of the base to the tip of the cone. In Figure 2-3, the axis is tangent to the sphere, not pointing to the center. This is because the Z plane of the large sphere and the cone are both the World Coordinate System (WCS). This is the default coordinate system of AutoCAD. In order for the axis of the cone to project from the sphere's center point, the UCS must be changed. This is discussed in Chapter 3. However, here is a quick overview.

Study Figure 2-4 and the steps listed below. This describes how the UCS can be rotated in order to draw a cone that projects from the center of the sphere. First, move the UCS icon to the center of the sphere:

> Command: **UCS**↵
> Origin/ZAxis/3point/OBject/View/X/Y/Z/Prev/Restore/Save/Del/?/⟨World⟩: **O**↵
> Origin point ⟨0,0,0⟩: **NODE**↵
> of *(pick the point at the center of the sphere and press* [Enter]*)*

Figure 2-4.
A—The World Coordinate System must be rotated to create a new UCS.
B—The new UCS is rotated 30° in the XY plane.
C—A line rotated up 30° from the XY plane is the axis of the new object.
D—The UCS is rotated 60° about the Y axis. The centerline of the cone coincides with the Z axis.

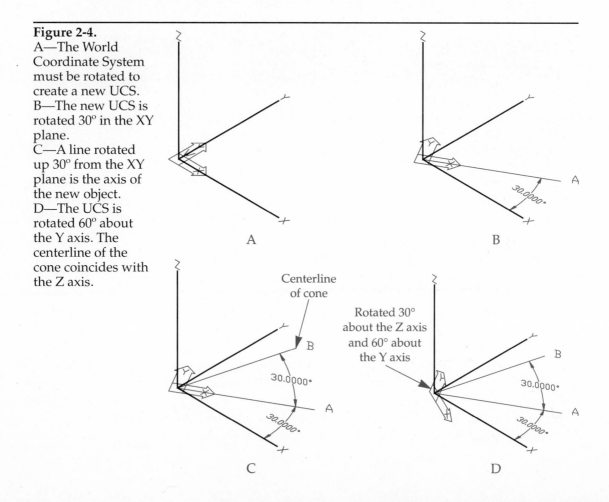

Now, continue as follows. Keep in mind that the point you are locating is 30° from the X axis and 30° from the XY plane.

```
Command: UCS↵
Origin/ZAxis/3point/OBject/View/X/Y/Z/Prev/Restore/Save/Del/?/⟨World⟩: Z↵
Rotation angle about Z axis ⟨0⟩: 30↵
Command: UCS↵
Origin/ZAxis/3point/OBject/View/X/Y/Z/Prev/Restore/Save/Del/?/⟨World⟩: Y↵
Rotation angle about Y axis ⟨0⟩: 60↵
```

Save the new coordinate system with the **Save** option of the **UCS** command.

This new UCS can be used to construct a cone with its axis projecting from the center of the sphere. Figure 2-5A shows the new UCS located at the center of the sphere. Pick **Cone** from the **3D Objects** dialog box or the **Surfaces** toolbar. With the UCS rotated, rectangular coordinates can be used to locate the cone.

```
Base center point: 0,0,1.5↵
Diameter/⟨radius⟩ of base: .25↵
Diameter/⟨radius⟩ of top ⟨0⟩: ↵
Height: 1↵
Number of segments ⟨16⟩: ↵
Command:
```

The completed cone is shown in Figure 2-5B. You can see that the axis projects from the center of the sphere. Figure 2-5C shows the objects after using **HIDE**.

Figure 2-5.
A—A new UCS is created with the Z axis projecting from the center of the sphere.
B—A cone is drawn using the new UCS. C—The objects after using **HIDE**.
The cone projects from the center of the sphere.

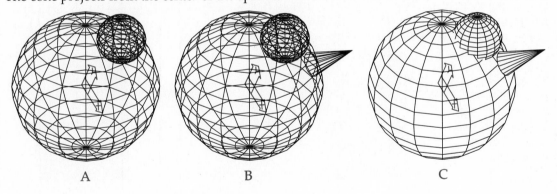

A   B   C

Constructing accurate intersections

When an object is located on a curved surface, there may be a small space between the curved surface and the object. See Figure 2-6A. In order for the model to display properly when rendered or animated, you need to make up for this space.

For example, refer to the cone and sphere in Figure 2-5. First, lay out an orthographic view of the radius of the sphere. Then, draw a radial centerline for the intersecting cone. Draw a line tangent to the curve with a length equal to the diameter of the cone's base. See Figure 2-6A. Project a new line perpendicular from one end of the tangent through the curve. Then, move the baseline of the cone to the intersection of the projection and the curve. This is the new base. See Figure 2-6B. Next, measure the distance from the center of the sphere perpendicular to the new base. See Figure 2-6C. Use this distance when locating the cone. See Figure 2-6D.

Figure 2-7 shows the cone from Figure 2-5 and Figure 2-6 after using the **HIDE** and **SHADE** commands. Notice in Figure 2-7A and Figure 2-7B that the edge of the base can be seen as a line. This is because the cone is sitting above the surface of the sphere. In Figure 2-7C and Figure 2-7D, the edge of the base cannot be seen because it is *inside* the sphere. Therefore, the objects appear correct when rendered.

Figure 2-6.
A—A gap is created when the base of the cone is located tangent to the sphere's surface.
B—Lay out the base of the cone so that its edge intersects the surface of the sphere.
C—Measure the distance from the center of the sphere to the base of the cone.
D—The cone intersects the surface of the sphere with no gap.

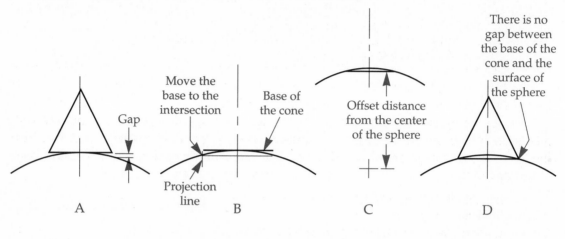

Figure 2-7.
A—A cone with the center of its base located on the surface of the sphere. B—When rendered, the edge of the base is visible. C—A cone with the edge of its base intersecting the surface of the sphere. D—When rendered, the edge of the base is not visible.

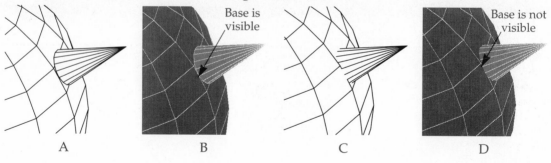

NOTE

You may have expected a line to define the intersection of the cone and the sphere in Figure 2-7C and Figure 2-7D. This is not the case when objects created with surface modeling techniques intersect. AutoCAD retains the definitions of two separate objects and does not automatically create a line at intersections. If you want a defining line to be placed at the intersection of two shapes, it may be necessary to draw them as solids and then join them in a union. Solid model construction and editing is covered in Chapter 10, Chapter 11, and Chapter 12.

❏ Open AutoCAD and begin a new drawing named EX2-1.

❏ Set **PDMODE** to 3. Set the color to blue and draw a point at 6,4.

❏ Set the color to white and draw a 4" diameter sphere centered on the point.

❏ Set the color to red and draw two .75" diameter spheres. Center both on the surface of the 4" diameter sphere. For the first sphere, use angular coordinates of 15° *in* the XY plane and 50° *from* the XY plane. For the second, use angular coordinates of –15° *in* the XY plane and 50° *from* the XY plane.

❏ Set the color to green and draw a cone with a .5" diameter base. Center the cone on the surface of the 4" diameter sphere using angular coordinates of 0° *in* the XY plane and 30° *from* the XY plane. Create a UCS and construct a cone with a centerline projecting from the center of the sphere.

❏ Display the objects using **SE Isometric View**. Use the **HIDE** command.

❏ Save the drawing as EX2-1.

Displaying drawings using spherical coordinates

When using spherical coordinates to change the viewpoint, AutoCAD only needs the two angle values. This is because the viewpoint does not set a distance from the "center." Enter spherical coordinates using the **Rotate** option of the **VPOINT** command as follows:

```
Command: -VP or VPOINT↵
Rotate/⟨View point⟩ ⟨current⟩: R↵
Enter angle in XY plane from X axis ⟨current⟩: 45↵
Enter angle from XY plane ⟨current⟩: 45↵
Regenerating drawing.
Command:
```

In Figure 2-8, the viewpoint is counterclockwise 45° from the X axis and 45° from the XY plane. Notice in the command sequence above that no "distance" value is entered.

Figure 2-8.
This view was created using the **Rotate** option of the **VPOINT** command. The rotation angles used are 45° *in* the XY plane and 45° *from* the XY plane.

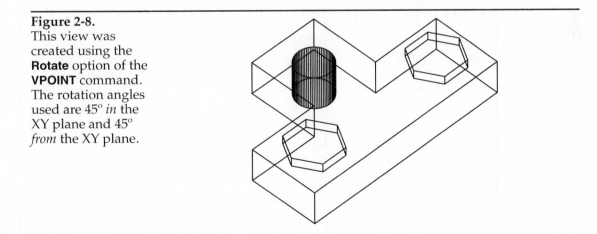

Cylindrical coordinates

Cylindrical coordinates provide coordinate locations for a cylindrical shape. The first value is the horizontal distance from the origin. The second value is the angle in the XY plane. The third value is a vertical, or Z, dimension. A cylindrical coordinate is entered as follows. See Figure 2-9.

7.5<35,6

Figure 2-9.
Cylindrical
coordinates require
a horizontal
distance from the
origin, an angle in
the XY plane, and
a Z dimension.

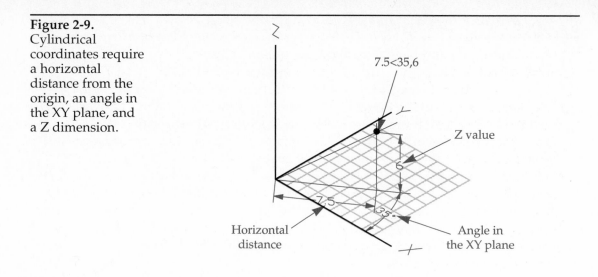

Figure 2-10.
A—A plan view of a tank shows the angle of the pipe attachment. B—A 3D view from the SE quadrant shows the pipe attachment point located with cylindrical coordinates. The point was located with **PDMODE** set to 3. C—The pipe is located on the tank using a new UCS.

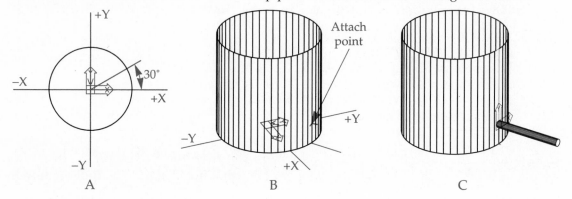

A   B   C

Using cylindrical coordinates

Cylindrical coordinates work well for attaching new objects to a cylindrical shape. An example is a pipe that must be attached to another pipe, a tank, or a vessel. In Figure 2-10, a pipe must be attached to a 12′ diameter tank at a 30° angle from horizontal and 2′-6″ above the floor.

An attachment point can easily be created to begin the pipe run. First, move the UCS origin to the center of the tank. Then, set an appropriate **PDMODE**. Next, locate the attachment point with cylindrical coordinates as follows:

> Command: **UCS**↵
> Origin/ZAxis/3point/OBject/View/X/Y/Z/Prev/Restore/Save/Del/?/⟨World⟩: **O**↵
> Origin point ⟨0,0,0⟩: *(pick the center point of the tank)*

Placing the UCS origin at the center of the tank makes it easier to enter the exact coordinates of the pipe attachment location.

> Command: **POINT**↵
> Point: **6′<30,2′6**↵
> Point: ↵
> Command:

Look at Figure 2-10B. Notice that the point drawn with **PDMODE** set to 3 appears as two legs of an X sticking out of the tank. It is drawn in the same plane as the current UCS, which is parallel to the bottom of the tank. A new UCS can be established and the pipe attached at its origin. See Figure 2-10C.

❑ Open AutoCAD and begin a new drawing named EX2-2.
❑ Set the current elevation to 0 and the thickness to 3.
❑ Draw a 1.5″ diameter circle.
❑ Use the **SW Isometric View** button.
❑ Set **PDMODE** to the shape of your choice. Locate the following points on the surface of the extruded circle.
  ❑ Point 1 = <25,1.5
  ❑ Point 2 = <295,1.5
❑ Draw separate lines from points 1 and 2 that project from the center of the circle, and extend 2″ from the surface of the extruded circle.
❑ Project new lines from each of the previous lines at 90° angles so that they intersect, as shown in the plan view below.
❑ Save the drawing as EX2-2.

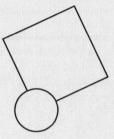

3D Surface Models

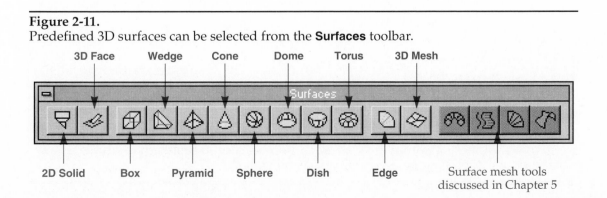

A group of predefined 3D objects is supplied in AutoCAD. These 3D objects are box, wedge, pyramid, cone, dish, dome, sphere, torus, and mesh. You only need to enter basic dimensions and a location to draw these objects. The result is a surfaced 3D object. The **HIDE** command makes the object appear solid. Therefore, the design can be used in presentation and animation programs, such as 3D Studio. The next sections discuss these predefined 3D objects.

The 3D objects can be accessed using the **Surfaces** toolbar or the **3D Objects** dialog box. The **Surfaces** toolbar displays buttons for all of the 3D objects, Figure 2-11. Picking **3D Surfaces...** from the **Surfaces** cascading menu in the **Draw** pull-down menu displays the **3D Objects** dialog box, Figure 2-12.

These objects are created as a 3D mesh, so each is a single entity. If you wish to edit any part of the object, first use the **EXPLODE** command. After exploding, each object is made up of 3D faces.

AutoCAD User's Guide **13**

Figure 2-11.
Predefined 3D surfaces can be selected from the **Surfaces** toolbar.

3D Face   Wedge   Cone   Dome   Torus   3D Mesh

2D Solid   Box   Pyramid   Sphere   Dish   Edge   Surface mesh tools discussed in Chapter 5

Figure 2-12.
Predefined 3D
surfaces can be
selected from the **3D
Objects** dialog box.

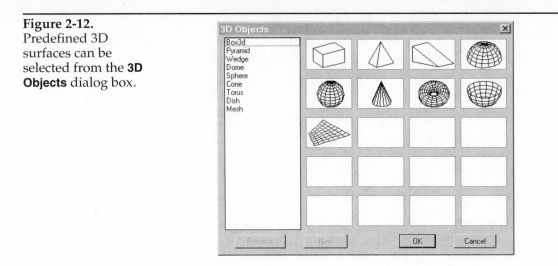

If you prefer to work from the Command: prompt, you
can use the **3D** command to select any of the 3D objects available in the **Surfaces** toolbar and **3D Objects** dialog box.

NOTE

AutoCAD creates two types of 3D shapes—solid primitives and surfaced wireframes. They are:

Solid Primitives	Surface Wireframes
Box	Box
Cone	Cone
Cylinder	Dome
Sphere	Dish
Torus	Mesh
Wedge	Pyramid
	Sphere
	Torus
	Wedge

If you type the name of one of the solid primitives listed
above at the Command: prompt, the solid model version of
that shape is created. If you want to use the surfaced wireframe version, use the **Surfaces** toolbar, **3D Objects** dialog
box, or type 3D at the Command: prompt. You can also enter
the following:

Command: **AI_CONE**↵

The "AI" refers to an "Autodesk Incorporated"
AutoLISP command definition that is found in the 3d.lsp file.
When you select an object from either the dialog box or the
toolbar, you will notice this entry on the command line. The
underscore character (_) is used in the acad.mnu file to allow
commands to be automatically translated in foreign language versions of AutoCAD.

Box

You can construct a surface-modeled box by selecting the **Box** button from the **Surfaces** toolbar or the **Box** image in the **3D Objects** dialog box. You can also enter AI_BOX at the Command: prompt. You must provide the location of one corner, the box dimensions, and the rotation angle about the Z axis (with the first corner as the base). Enter the values using the keyboard or pick them with your pointing device.

AI_BOX

Surfaces toolbar

Box

> Command: **AI_BOX**↵
> Corner of box: **3,3**↵
> Length: **1**↵
> Cube/⟨Width⟩: **C**↵
> Rotation angle about Z axis: **0**↵

If you select the **Cube** option, AutoCAD applies the value entered at the Length: prompt to the width and height. If you accept the default and enter a number for the width, you are prompted for the height. See Figure 2-13.

NOTE	The **BOX** command draws a solid 3D model of a box. This is different than the surface-modeled box discussed in this chapter. Solid models are discussed in Chapter 10.

Figure 2-13.
A surface-modeled box requires a location, length, width, height, and rotation angle.

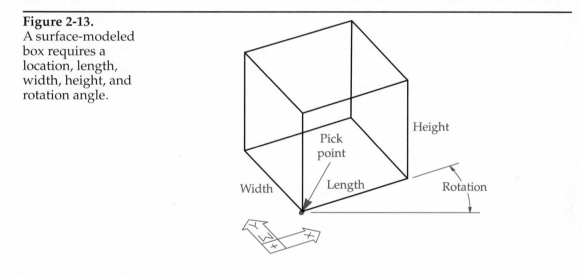

Wedge

You can quickly create a right-angle surface-modeled wedge by picking the **Wedge** button from the **Surfaces** toolbar, selecting the **Wedge** image from the **3D Objects** dialog box, or entering AI_WEDGE at the Command: prompt. You are prompted to locate a corner of the wedge, then enter the length, width, height, and rotation angle. A wedge and its values are shown in Figure 2-14.

AI_WEDGE

Surfaces toolbar

Wedge

Figure 2-14.
The surface-modeled wedge requires a location, length, width, height, and rotation angle.

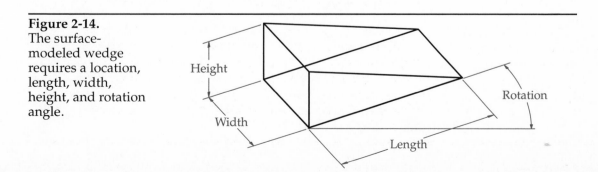

```
Command: AI_WEDGE↵
Corner of wedge: 6,3↵
Length: 3↵
Width: 2↵
Height: 2↵
Rotation angle about Z axis: 15↵
Command:
```

> **NOTE** The **WEDGE** command draws a solid 3D model of a wedge. This is different than the surface-modeled wedge discussed in this chapter. Solid models are discussed in Chapter 10.

Pyramid

Five varieties of surface-modeled pyramids are available in AutoCAD. You can draw three types of four-sided pyramids, Figure 2-15. You can also draw two types of three-sided pyramids called *tetrahedrons.*

Draw a pyramid by picking the **Pyramid** button from the **Surfaces** toolbar, selecting the **Pyramid** image from the **3D Objects** dialog box, or entering AI_PYRAMID at the Command: prompt.

To draw a pyramid, first draw the base. When you have located the third point, you can draw a tetrahedron or the fourth point of the base. If you draw the fourth point on the base, the options **Ridge**, **Top**, and **Apex** appear. The default is **Apex**. When drawing the apex, use XYZ filters or enter an XYZ coordinate. The following example shows how to draw a four-sided pyramid with an apex:

```
Command: AI_PYRAMID↵
First base point: 2,6↵
Second base point: @2,0↵
Third base point: @0,2↵
Tetrahedron/⟨Fourth base point⟩: @-2,0↵
Ridge/Top/⟨Apex point⟩: .XY↵
of 3,7↵
(need Z): 3↵
Command:
```

Figure 2-15.
Three options are available for pyramids with four-sided bases.

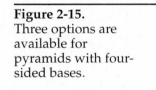
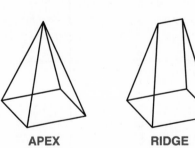

APEX   RIDGE   TOP

The **Ridge** option requires two points to define the ridge. After you draw the fourth point on the base, select **Ridge**. The last line drawn on the base is highlighted. This indicates that the first point of the ridge will begin perpendicular to the highlighted line. However, the first point does not have to touch the highlighted line.

Ridge/Top/⟨Apex point⟩: **R**↵
First ridge point: **.XY**↵
of *(pick a point inside the highlighted line)*
(need Z): **3**↵
Second ridge point: **.XY**↵
of *(pick a point inside the second highlighted line)*
(need Z): **3**↵

The **Top** option creates a *truncated* (flattened) top. This option works similar to **Ridge**. However, a rubber band line is attached from the first corner of the pyramid to the crosshairs. Then, the First top point: prompt appears. Use filters or XYZ coordinates to locate the top points. After the first top point is located, the rubber band line is attached to the second base point, and so on. When the fourth top point is located, the pyramid is complete.

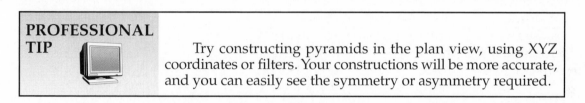

PROFESSIONAL TIP

Try constructing pyramids in the plan view, using XYZ coordinates or filters. Your constructions will be more accurate, and you can easily see the symmetry or asymmetry required.

A tetrahedron has a three-sided base with an apex or flattened top. The following example illustrates how to construct a tetrahedron. Refer to Figure 2-16.

Command: **AI_PYRAMID**↵
First base point: **2,2**↵
Second base point: **@3,0**↵
Third base point: **@0,3**↵
Tetrahedron/⟨Fourth base point⟩: **T**↵
Top/⟨Apex point⟩: **.XY**↵
of *(pick P1 in the middle of the triangle)*
(need Z): **3**↵

A truncated (flattened) top can be given to a tetrahedron by selecting the **Top** option. Refer to Figure 2-16B.

Tetrahedron/⟨Fourth base point⟩: **T**↵
Top/⟨Apex point⟩: **T**↵
First top point: *(use filters to pick the first top point)*
Second top point: *(use filters to pick the second top point)*
Third top point: *(use filters to pick the third top point)*
Command:

Figure 2-16.
A—A tetrahedron is a pyramid with a three-sided base.
B—A truncated tetrahedron requires three pick points for the top surface.

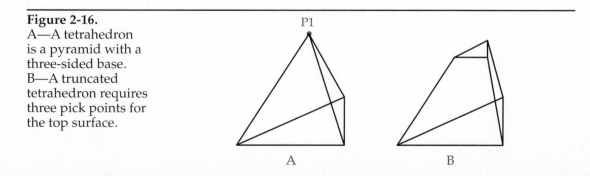

A

B

Cone

Pointed and truncated cones can be easily created in AutoCAD. Three dimensions are required for a cone—the base diameter, the top diameter, and the height. A pointed cone has a zero top diameter. A truncated cone has a top diameter other than zero.

To draw a surface-modeled cone, pick the **Cone** button from the **Surfaces** toolbar, select the **Cone** image from the **3D Objects** dialog box, or type AI_CONE at the Command: prompt:

AI_CONE

Surfaces
toolbar

Cone

> Command: **AI_CONE**↵
> Base center point: **3,3**↵
> Diameter/⟨radius⟩ of base: **1**↵
> Diameter/⟨radius⟩ of top ⟨0⟩: **.15**↵
> Height: **2**↵
> Number of segments ⟨16⟩: ↵
> Command:

If you want a pointed cone, simply press [Enter] at the Diameter/⟨radius⟩ of top: prompt. The two types of cones are shown in Figure 2-17.

Figure 2-17.
Surface-modeled cones can be truncated or pointed.

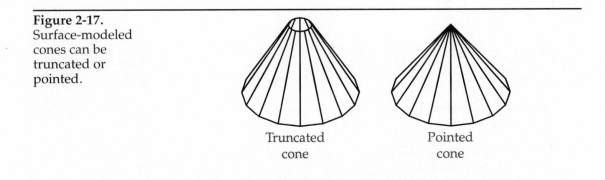

Truncated
cone

Pointed
cone

NOTE   The **CONE** command draws a solid 3D model of a cone. This is different than the surface-modeled cone discussed in this chapter. Solid models are discussed in Chapter 10.

Dome and dish

AI_DOME

Surfaces
toolbar

Dome

AI_DISH

Surfaces
toolbar

Dish

Think of a dome or a dish as a hemisphere, or half of a sphere. If a dome is placed on top of a dish, a sphere is formed. The top of the dome is the north pole. The bottom of the dish is the south pole. Longitudinal segments run east and west around the circumference. Latitudinal segments run north and south. See Figure 2-1A.

To draw a dome or dish, pick the **Dome** or **Dish** button in the **Surfaces** toolbar or the **Dome** or **Dish** image in the **3D Objects** dialog box. You can also type the following:

> Command: **AI_DOME**↵ (or **AI_DISH** to draw a dish)
> Center of dome: (pick a point)
> Diameter/⟨radius⟩: **2**↵
> Number of longitudinal segments ⟨16⟩: (enter a value or press [Enter])
> Number of latitudinal segments ⟨8⟩: (enter a value or press [Enter])
> Command:

> **NOTE**
> The more segments you use, the smoother the curved surface, but the longer drawing regeneration takes. Use as few segments as possible.

Sphere

A sphere requires the same information as a dish or dome. Since the sphere is a complete globe, the default values for latitudinal and longitudinal segments are the same.

To draw a surface-modeled sphere, pick the **Sphere** button from the **Surfaces** toolbar or the **Sphere** image from the **3D Objects** dialog box, or enter AI_SPHERE at the Command: prompt:

    Command: **AI_SPHERE.**↵
    Center of sphere: *(pick a center point)*
    Diameter/⟨radius⟩: *(pick or type a radius, or type D to provide a diameter)*
    Number of longitudinal segments ⟨16⟩: *(type number of segments and press [Enter])*
    Number of latitudinal segments ⟨16⟩: *(type number of segments and press [Enter])*
    Command:

Figure 2-18 shows three spheres composed of 8, 16, and 32 segments.

Figure 2-18.
The more segments in a sphere the smoother it appears, but the longer it takes to regenerate.

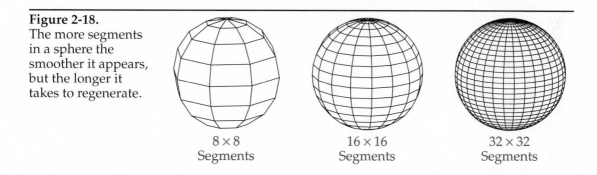

8×8
Segments

16×16
Segments

32×32
Segments

Torus

A *torus* looks like an inflated inner tube. See Figure 2-19. To draw a torus, you need to enter the diameter (or radius) of the torus and the tube. You also need to enter the number of segments around the torus circumference and around the tube circumference. To draw a torus, pick the **Torus** button from the **Surfaces** toolbar, select the **Torus** image from the **3D Objects** dialog box, or enter AI_TORUS at the Command: prompt:

    Command: **AI_TORUS.**↵
    Center of torus: *(pick the center point)*
    Diameter/⟨radius⟩ of torus: **2**↵
    Diameter/⟨radius⟩ of tube: **.5**↵
    Segments around tube circumference ⟨16⟩: ↵
    Segments around torus circumference ⟨16⟩: ↵
    Command:

Figure 2-19.
To draw a torus, you must specify the radius (or diameter) of the torus and of the tube. You must also specify the number of segments around each.

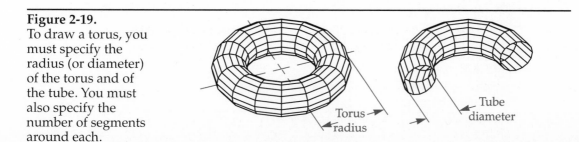

Torus radius

Tube diameter

There are several different 3D constructions. These include 3D arrays, 3D poly-lines, and 3D faces. These constructions are covered in the next sections.

Arraying 3D objects

3DARRAY
3A

Modify
➥ **3D Operation**
 ➥ **3D Array**

The **3DARRAY** command lets you array an object in 3D space. This works in much the same way as the **ARRAY** command, but with a third dimension. You need to enter the number of rows and columns, as with the **ARRAY** command. However, *levels* give the third (Z) dimension. There are two types of 3D arrays—rectangular and polar. The command sequence is the same as the 2D array command, with two added prompts.

To create a 3D array, select **3D Array** from the **3D Operation** cascading menu in the **Modify** pull-down menu or type 3A or 3DARRAY at the Command: prompt. The following example creates a rectangular array of a pyramid. See Figure 2-20.

 Command: **3A** *or* **3DARRAY**↵
 Select objects: *(pick the pyramid)*
 Select objects: ↵
 Rectangular or Polar array (R/P): **R**↵
 Number of rows (---) ⟨1⟩: **2**↵
 Number of columns (┊┊┊) ⟨1⟩: **3**↵
 Number of levels (...) ⟨1⟩: **3**↵
 Distance between rows (---): **1.5**↵
 Distance between columns (┊┊┊): **1.5**↵
 Distance between levels (...): **1.5**↵
 Command:

Figure 2-20.
A rectangular 3D array is made up of rows, columns, and levels.

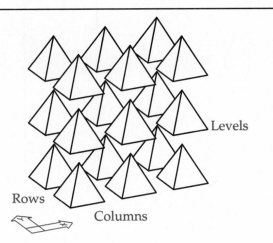

When creating a 3D polar array you need to enter an axis of rotation. The axis does not need to be a line in the XY plane. Any line can be used. A polar array of pyramids is created in Figure 2-21 using the following command sequence:

 Command: **3A** *or* **3DARRAY**↵
 Select objects: *(pick the pyramid)*
 Select objects: ↵
 Rectangular or Polar array (R/P): **P**↵
 Number of items: **5**↵
 Angle to fill ⟨360⟩: **-180**↵
 Rotate objects as they are copied? ⟨Y⟩: **N**↵
 Center point of array: *(pick P1)*
 Second point on axis of rotation: *(pick point P2 in the XY plane)*
 Command:

Figure 2-21.
The axis of rotation
of a 3D polar array
can be any line.

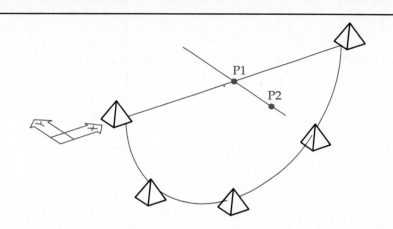

In Figure 2-21, the 3D array is tilted 90° to the current UCS. This is because the axis of rotation defined for the 3D array is parallel to the XY plane of the current UCS.

PROFESSIONAL TIP

3D Rectangular Array and **3D Polar Array** buttons can be used in a custom toolbar or added to an existing toolbar. Refer to Chapter 18 for information on customizing toolbars.

EXERCISE 2-3

❑ Begin a drawing named EX2-3.
❑ Set the limits to 34,22, the grid to 1, and snap to .5.
❑ Draw the following 3D objects using the sizes indicated. Space them evenly in your drawing.

    ❑ Box   2 × 3 × 1.5h
    ❑ Wedge   3 × 1 × 1.25h
    ❑ Pyramid (apex)   2 × 2 × 2.5h
    ❑ Pyramid (ridge)   2 × 2 × 2.5h
    ❑ Pyramid (top)   2 × 2 × 2.25h
    ❑ Tetrahedron (apex)   2 × 2 × 1.5h
    ❑ Tetrahedron (top)   2 × 2 × 1.5h
    ❑ Cone (apex)   Ø2 × 1.5h
    ❑ Cone (truncated)   Ø2 × 1.5h
    ❑ Dome   Ø2
    ❑ Dish   Ø2
    ❑ Sphere   Ø2.5
    ❑ Torus   Ø3 torus, Ø.5 tube

❑ Display the completed objects in three different 3D viewpoints. Use the **HIDE** command in each.
❑ Save the drawing as EX2-3.

3D polyline

3DPOLY
3P

Draw
➥ 3D Polyline

A *3D polyline* is drawn using the **3DPOLY** command. To access this command, pick **3D Polyline** in the **Draw** pull-down menu or type 3P or 3DPOLY at the Command: prompt. A 3D polyline is the same as a regular polyline with an added third (Z) dimension. Any form of coordinate entry is valid for drawing 3D polylines.

```
Command: 3P or 3DPOLY↵
From point: 4,3,6↵
Close/Undo/⟨Endpoint of line⟩: @2,0,1↵
Close/Undo/⟨Endpoint of line⟩: @0,2,1↵
Command:
```

The **Close** option is used to draw the final segment and create a closed shape. The **Undo** option removes the last segment without canceling the command.

The **PEDIT** command can be used to edit 3D polylines. The **Spline** option of **PEDIT** is used to fit a B-spline curve to the 3D polyline. Figure 2-22 shows a regular 3D polyline and the same polyline fit with a B-spline curve. The **SPLFRAME** system variable controls the display of the original polyline frame, and is either on (1) or off (0).

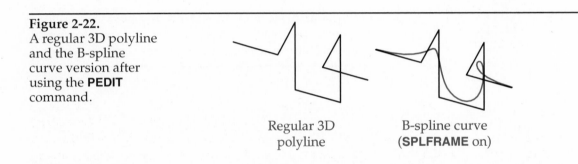

Figure 2-22.
A regular 3D polyline and the B-spline curve version after using the **PEDIT** command.

Regular 3D
polyline

B-spline curve
(**SPLFRAME** on)

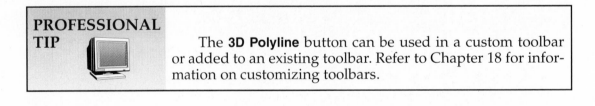

PROFESSIONAL TIP The **3D Polyline** button can be used in a custom toolbar or added to an existing toolbar. Refer to Chapter 18 for information on customizing toolbars.

3D faces

Surfaces that appear solid and not as wireframes are called 3D faces. These are created using the **3DFACE** command. This command was introduced in Chapter 1.

You may recall that a 3D face can only have three or four straight edges. In Chapter 1, you created a "T"-shaped box using 3D faces. When the **HIDE** command was used, the edge between the faces was visible. This line can be made invisible. The next section briefly describes the procedure.

Invisible 3DFACE edges

The **3DFACE** command allows you to remove, or hide, edges that should not appear as lines on a surface. This is done with the **Invisible** option. Before picking the first point of the invisible edge, enter I for the **Invisible** option. The following example shows how to do this. See Figure 2-23.

Figure 2-23.
The **Invisible** option of the **3DFACE** command hides edges that are normally visible.

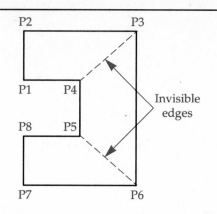

```
Command: 3DFACE↵
First point: (pick P1)
Second point: (pick P2)
Third point: I↵ (pick P3)
Fourth point: (pick P4)
Third point: I↵ (pick P5)
Fourth point: (pick P6)
Third point: (pick P7)
Fourth point: (pick P8)
Third point: ↵
Command:
```

If the **SPLFRAME** system variable is set to its default value of 0, invisible edges are *not* shown. If **SPLFRAME** is set to 1, invisible edges *are* shown. When screen menus are configured to display, **SPLFRAME** can be set using the **ShowEdge** and **HideEdge** options that appear in the **3Dface:** menu, Figure 2-24. Their functions are as follows:

- **ShowEdge. SPLFRAME** is set to 1 and hidden edges are shown. This option displays the following message:

     Invisible edges will be shown after next Regeneration.

- **HideEdge. SPLFRAME** is set to 0 and edges drawn with the **Invisible** option are *not* shown. This option displays the following message:

     Invisible edges will be HIDDEN after next Regeneration.

Figure 2-24.
When AutoCAD is configured to display screen menus, the **ShowEdge** and **HideEdge** options can be used to control the visibility of invisible edges.

```
AutoCAD
****
3Dface:

Invisibl

ShowEdge
HideEdge

Edge:
Ddmodif:
```
Controls
visibility of
invisible
edges

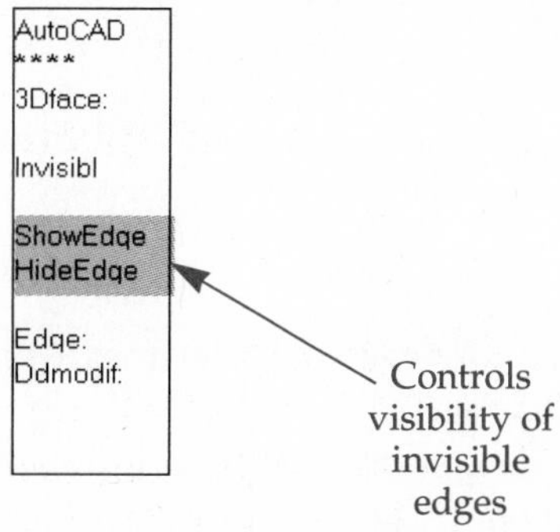

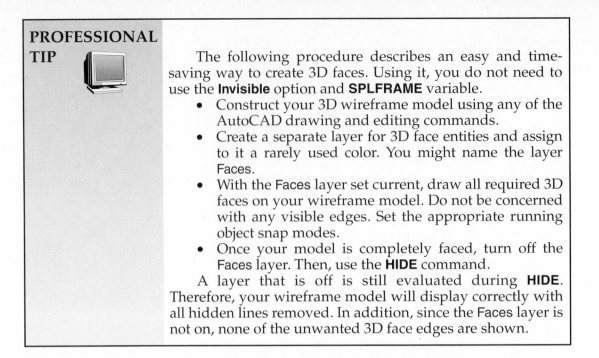

PROFESSIONAL TIP

The following procedure describes an easy and time-saving way to create 3D faces. Using it, you do not need to use the **Invisible** option and **SPLFRAME** variable.

- Construct your 3D wireframe model using any of the AutoCAD drawing and editing commands.
- Create a separate layer for 3D face entities and assign to it a rarely used color. You might name the layer Faces.
- With the Faces layer set current, draw all required 3D faces on your wireframe model. Do not be concerned with any visible edges. Set the appropriate running object snap modes.
- Once your model is completely faced, turn off the Faces layer. Then, use the **HIDE** command.

A layer that is off is still evaluated during **HIDE**. Therefore, your wireframe model will display correctly with all hidden lines removed. In addition, since the Faces layer is not on, none of the unwanted 3D face edges are shown.

Things to Consider When Working with 3D

Working in 3D, like working with 2D drawings, requires careful planning to get the desired results efficiently. Use the following suggestions when working in 3D.

Planning

✓ Determine the type of final drawing you need. Then, choose the method of 3D construction that best suits your needs.

✓ Isometric is quickest and most versatile for objects needing only one pictorial view. Ellipses and arcs are easy to work with in isometric drawings.

✓ Objects and layouts that need to be viewed from different angles for design purposes are best constructed using the 3D commands.

✓ Construct only the details needed for the function of the drawing. This saves space and time, and makes visualization much easier.

✓ Use the object snap modes **Midpoint**, **Endpoint**, and **Intersection** with the **LINE** and **3DFACE** commands.

✓ Keep in mind that the grid appears at the current elevation and viewpoint angle.

✓ Create layers having different colors for different entities. Turn them on and off as needed, or freeze those not being used.

Editing

✓ Use the **CHPROP** command to change color, layer, linetype, or thickness of 3D objects.

✓ Use the **STRETCH** command or grips in the 3D view to change only one dimension of the object (see Chapter 6). Use the **SCALE** command in the 3D view to change the size of the entire object proportionally.

✓ Do as much editing as possible from a 3D viewpoint. It is quicker and the results are seen immediately.

Displaying

✓ The **HIDE** command can help you visualize complex drawings.

✓ To change views quickly, use the preset views in the **Viewpoint** toolbar or in the **3D Viewpoint** cascading menu in the **View** pull-down menu.

✓ Use the **VIEW** command to create and save 3D views for quicker pictorial displays. This avoids having to use the **VPOINT** or **DVIEW** commands.

✓ Freeze unwanted layers before displaying objects in 3D, and especially before using **HIDE**. Also, remember that AutoCAD still regenerates layers that are off.

✓ Before using **HIDE**, zoom in on the part of a drawing to display. This saves time in regenerating the view because only the entities that are visible are regenerated.

✓ Objects that touch or intersect may have to be moved slightly if the display removes a line you need to see or plot.

Chapter Test

Write your answers in the spaces provided.

1. Explain the differences between spherical and cylindrical coordinates. _____

   _____

   _____

   _____

2. A new point is to be located 4.5″ from the last point. It is to be at a 63° angle *in* the XY plane, and at a 35° angle *from* the XY plane. Write the proper spherical coordinate notation. _____

   _____

3. Write the proper cylindrical coordinate notation for a point located 4.5″ in the horizontal direction, 3.6″ along the Z axis, and at a 63° angle in the XY plane.

   _____

4. How do you select one of AutoCAD's predrawn 3D shapes? _____

   _____

   _____

   _____

5. When using the **3DFACE** command, how do you indicate that an edge is invisible?

   _____

   _____

6. What predrawn 3D shapes are available? _____

   _____

7. How many different types of pyramids can you draw with the **PYRAMID** command (*not* including the tetrahedrons)? _____

8. How does **SPLFRAME** affect the **3DFACE** command? _____

   _____

   _____

9. Define "longitudinal segments" in reference to a dome or dish. _____

_____

10. What command can you enter at the keyboard to draw a surface-modeled cone?

_____

11. Which 3D shape is used to draw a tetrahedron? _____

12. What two measurements are required to draw a torus? _____

_____

13. Name the system variable and value that is used to control the following functions of **3DFACE** display.

ShowEdge _____

HideEdge _____

14. Name the five different shapes that can be constructed with the **PYRAMID** command.

_____

_____

Drawing Problems

*Problems 1–4. Draw each of these objects as wireframes. Then, use the **3DFACE** command to place surfaces on all sides of the objects. Measure the objects directly to obtain dimensions. Use A-size limits. Plot the drawings at a 3:1 scale with hidden lines removed. Save the drawings as **P2-1**, **P2-2**, etc.*

1.
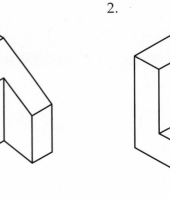

2.
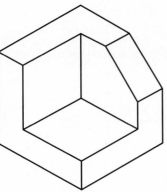

3.
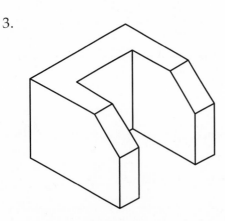

4.
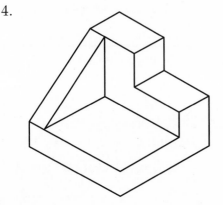

AutoCAD and its Applications—Advanced

*Problems 5–9. Draw each of these objects using the dimensions given. Use 3D objects to create the models. Use grips and editing commands to aid in construction. Do not dimension the objects. Save the drawings as **P2-5, P2-6**, etc.*

5.

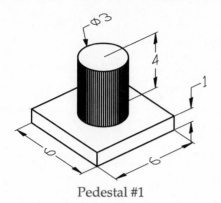

Pedestal #1

6.

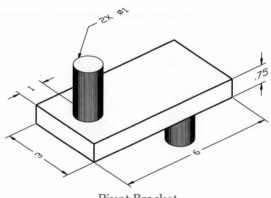

Pivot Bracket

7.

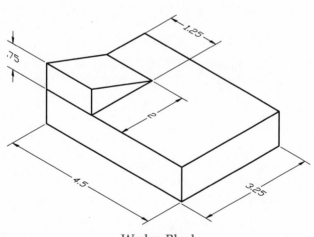

Wedge Block

8.

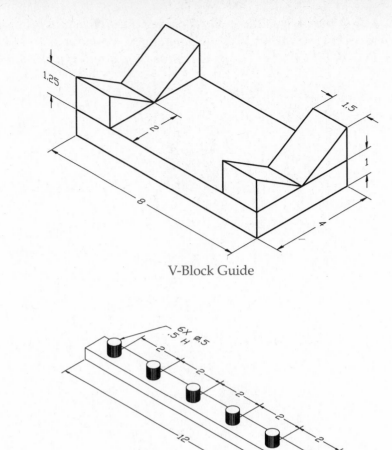

V-Block Guide

9.

Pin Bar

10. Draw the Ø8" pedestal .5" thick. Four Ø.75" feet are centered on a 7"
diameter circle and are .5" high. Use elevation and thickness to assist in
creating this model. Save the drawing as P2-10.

Pedestal #2

11. Four wedges, each 3" long, 1" wide, and 1" high, support this Ø10"
globe. Each wedge sits .8" away from the center of the Ø12" circular
base. The base is .5" thick. Save the drawing as P2-11.

Globe

*Problems 12–17. Construct 3D models of each of the objects shown. Use only 3D objects found in the **Surfaces** toolbar. Construct each object using the specific instructions given. Save the drawings as **P2-12**, **P2-13**, etc.*

12. Table legs (A) are 2″ square and 17″ tall. Table top (B) is 24″ × 36″ × 1″.

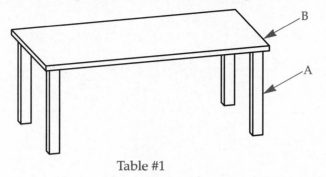

Table #1

13. Table legs (A) are Ø2″ and 17″ tall. Table top (B) is 24″ × 36″ × 1″. Table legs (C) are Ø2″ and 11″ tall. Table top (D) is 24″ × 14″ × 1″.

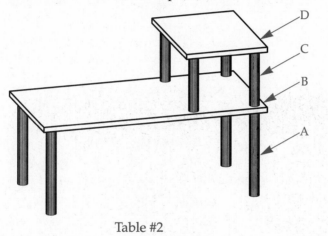

Table #2

14. Object A is Ø6″. Object B is 6″ long and Ø1.5″.

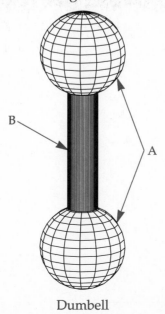

Dumbell

15. Object A is ∅8″ at the base, ∅7″ at the top, and is 1″ tall. Object B is ∅5″ and 7″ tall. Object C is ∅2″ and 6″ tall. Item D is .5″ × 8″ × .125″, and there are four pieces. Object E is ∅18″ at the base, ∅6″ at the top, and is 12″ tall.

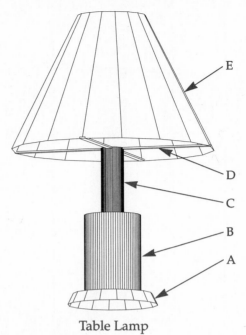

Table Lamp

16. Objects A and B are 5′ high brick walls. The walls are two courses of brick thick. Research the dimensions of standard brick and draw accordingly. Wall B is 7′ long and wall A is 5′ long. Lamps are placed at each end of the walls. Object C is ∅2″ and 8″ tall. Object D is ∅10″.

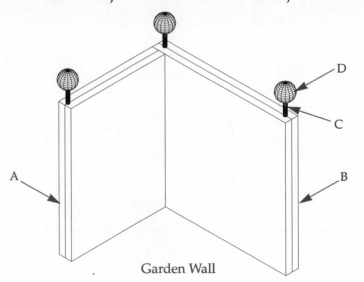

Garden Wall

17. Object A is ∅18″ and 1″ tall. Object B is ∅1.5″ and 6′ tall. Object C is ∅6″ and .5″ tall. Object D is a ∅10″ sphere. Object E (four items) is an L-shaped bracket to support the shade to object C. Draw these an appropriate size. Object F has a base of ∅22″ and is 12″ tall.

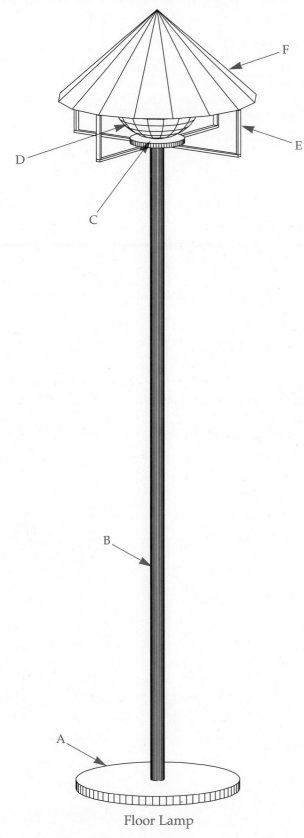

Floor Lamp

Changing the User Coordinate System makes 3D construction easier.
Five different systems are used in creating this basic object.

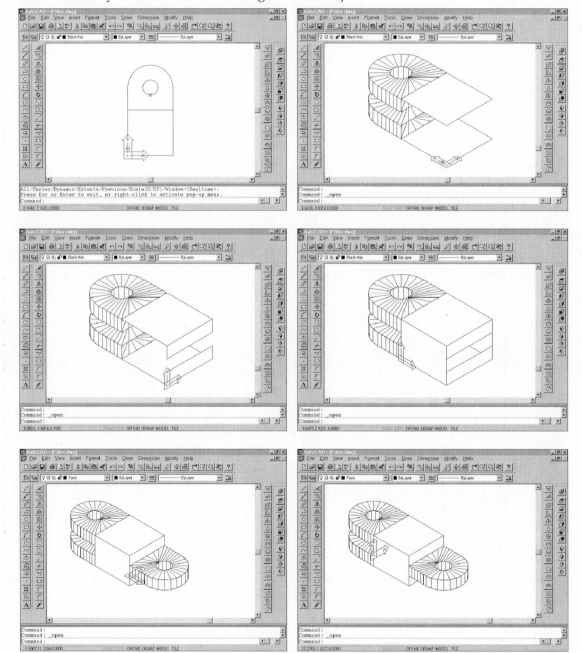

AutoCAD and its Applications—Advanced

Chapter 3

Understanding User Coordinate Systems

Learning Objectives

After completing this chapter, you will be able to:
- ○ Describe the function of the world and user coordinate systems.
- ○ Move the coordinate system to any surface.
- ○ Rotate the coordinate system to any angle.
- ○ Change the coordinate system to match the plane of a geometric object.
- ○ Save named user coordinate systems.
- ○ Restore and use named user coordinate systems.

Part of the flexibility of 3D construction with AutoCAD is the ability to create and use different 3D coordinate systems. All drawing and editing commands can be used in any coordinate system you create. Objects that are drawn will always be parallel to the plane, or coordinate system, you are working in. Therefore, you must be able to change your point of view so it is perpendicular to the plane you want to draw on. Your view is then said to be "plan" to that plane. This chapter provides you with detailed instructions in constructing and working with coordinate systems. This will allow you to draw any type of 3D shape that you need.

Introduction to User Coordinate Systems

All points in a drawing or on an object are defined with XYZ coordinate values measured from the 0,0,0 origin. Since this system of coordinates is fixed and universal, AutoCAD refers to it as the *World Coordinate System (WCS)*. The *User Coordinate System (UCS)*, on the other hand, can be defined at any orientation desired. The **UCS** command is used to change the origin, position, and rotation of the coordinate system to match the surfaces and features of an object under construction.

Changes in the UCS are reflected in the orientation and placement of the UCS icon symbol at the lower-left corner of the graphics window. The available options for creating and managing a UCS, as well as the UCS icon symbol, are found under **UCS** cascading menu in the **Tools** pull-down menu, Figure 3-1A. In addition, UCS options can be selected from the **UCS** flyout in the **Standard** toolbar, and from the **UCS** toolbar. See Figure 3-1B.

Figure 3-1.
UCS options can be accessed in several ways. A—The **UCS** cascading menu in the **Tools**
pull-down menu. B—The **UCS** toolbar. All of these buttons are also contained in the
UCS flyout in the **Standard** toolbar.

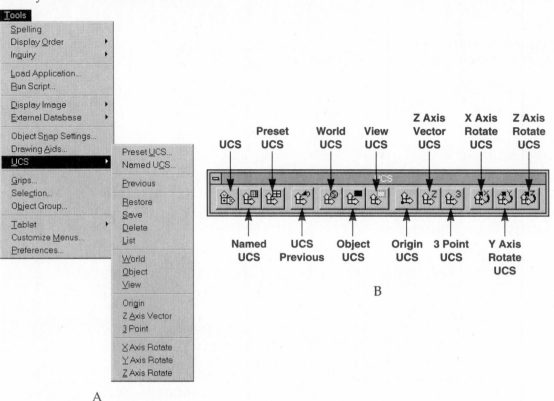

A

B

Displaying the UCS icon

The symbol that identifies the orientation of the coordinate system is called the
UCS icon. It is located in the lower-left corner of the viewport. The display of this
symbol is controlled by the **UCSICON** command. If your drawing does not require
viewports and altered coordinate systems, you may want to turn the icon off.

Command: **UCSICON**↵
ON/OFF/All/Noorigin/ORigin ⟨*current*⟩: **OFF**↵
Command:

The icon disappears until you turn it on again using the **UCSICON** command. You can
also turn the icon on or off and change the icon origin using the options under **UCS**
Icon in the **Display** cascading menu in the **View** pull-down menu.

Changing the coordinate system

To construct a three-dimensional object, you must visualize shapes at many
angles. Different planes are needed to draw features on angled surfaces. It is easy to
rotate the UCS icon to match any surface on an object. The following example illustrates this process.

The object in Figure 3-2 has a cylinder on the angled surface. The base of the object
is five units long and four units wide. The height is five units, and the cut horizontal
and vertical surfaces are each two units long. The cylinder is 1.5 units in diameter
with a height of .35 units.

The first step in creating this model is to draw the base in the plan view. See
Figure 3-3A. Now, display the object in the SE isometric view.

With the base of the object constructed, draw the vertical lines. You can draw the
vertical lines using XYZ filters. However, it is easier to rotate the UCS so you can

Figure 3-2.
This object can be constructed by changing the orientation of the coordinate system. You will construct this object in this chapter.

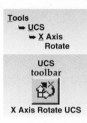

draw the vertical lines as if you are drawing a front view. Rotate the UCS so that the Y axis is pointing up from the bottom surface of the object and the X axis is pointing to the right side. When this happens, the Z axis is pointing out of the screen to the left.

Tools
→ UCS
→ X Axis Rotate

UCS toolbar

X Axis Rotate UCS

Rotate the UCS on the X axis by picking the **X Axis Rotate UCS** button from the **UCS** toolbar, selecting **X Axis Rotate** from the **UCS** cascading menu in the **Tools** pull-down menu, or using the **X** option of the **UCS** command as follows:

        Command: **UCS**↵
        Origin/ZAxis/3point/OBject/View/X/Y/Z/Prev/Restore/Save/Del/?/⟨World⟩: **X**↵
        Rotation angle about X axis ⟨0⟩: **90**↵
        Command:

The UCS icon changes to reflect the new UCS. See Figure 3-3B.

Figure 3-3.
A—The base of the object is constructed on the plan view of the WCS.
B—The UCS icon is rotated 90° around the X axis to draw the sides. Notice how the UCS icon has changed.

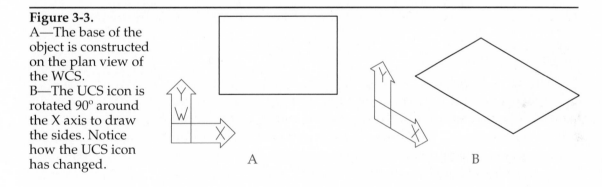

A   B

NOTE	The UCS icon can be rotated about the Y axis and Z axis using the **Y** and **Z** options of the UCS command, the **Y Axis Rotate UCS** and **Z Axis Rotate UCS** buttons, or the **Y Axis Rotate** and **Z Axis Rotate** pull-down selections. The process is the same as rotating around the X axis.

The next step is to draw the front face of the object, Figure 3-4A. Use the **LINE** command and your choice of tools and methods (snap and grid, direct distance entry, coordinate entry, object snaps) to complete the side.

The lines just drawn represent the front face of the object. First, copy them to the back edge. Since the back edge is not in the drawing plane, you must use object snap or coordinate entry to specify the location where the lines are copied. Lines connecting the two surfaces can then be drawn. You may want to draw one line and then copy it to the other locations. See Figure 3-4B and Figure 3-4C.

Figure 3-4.
A—The front surface of the wedge is added using the **LINE** command. B—The front surface is copied on the Z axis to create the back surface. C—The object is completed by connecting the front and back surfaces with lines.

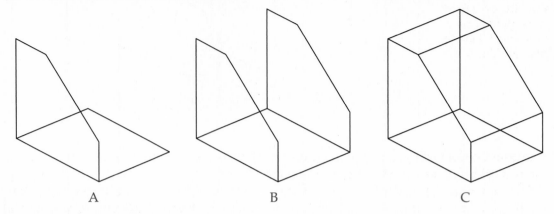

A   B   C

Saving a named UCS

Once you have created a new UCS that can be used to construct a model it is best to save it for future use. You can save a UCS by picking **Save** from the **UCS** cascading menu in the **Tools** pull-down menu or by using the **Save** option of **UCS** command:

> Command: **UCS.↵**
> Origin/ZAxis/3point/OBject/View/X/Y/Z/Prev/Restore/Save/Del/?/⟨World⟩: **S.↵**
> ?/Desired UCS name: *(enter a name for the UCS, such as* FRONT*)*
> Command:

Now the coordinate system is saved and can be easily recalled for future use.

Aligning the UCS and UCS icon with an angled surface

The cylinder in Figure 3-2 needs to be drawn on the angled surface. In 2D drafting, an angled surface is seen in its true shape and size only when projected to an auxiliary view. An auxiliary view places your line of sight perpendicular to the angled surface. This means that you see the angled surface as a "plan" view.

AutoCAD draws objects aligned with the plan view of the current UCS. For the construction in Figure 3-4, the plan view of the UCS looks like Figure 3-5. A plan view is always perpendicular to your line of sight.

Notice that the UCS icon has exactly the same orientation as the vertical and horizontal lines of the object. The UCS and the front surface are parallel, and your line of sight is perpendicular to those planes. Therefore, if you draw the cylinder with this UCS, it will be perpendicular to this view. You must align the UCS with the angled surface of the object.

The **3point** option of the **UCS** command can be used to change the UCS to any angled surface. This option requires that you locate a new origin, a point on the positive X axis, and a point on the positive Y axis. Refer to Figure 3-6 for pick points as

Figure 3-5.
Planes
perpendicular to the
XY plane appear as
lines in the plan view.

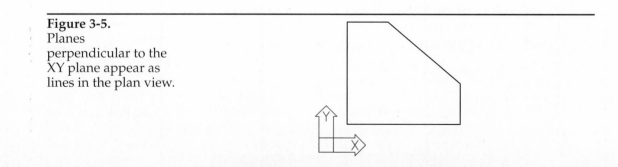

Figure 3-6.
A new UCS can be established by picking three points. P1 is the origin, P2 is the positive X axis, and P3 is the positive Y axis.

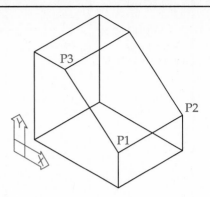

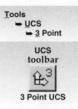

Tools
→ UCS
→ 3 Point

UCS toolbar

3 Point UCS

you use the following command sequence. Use the **Endpoint** or **Intersection** object snap to select points that are not in the XY plane.

To use this option, pick the **3 Point UCS** button in the **UCS** toolbar, select **3 Point** from the **UCS** cascading menu, or use the **3point** option of the **UCS** command as follows:

> Command: **UCS**↵
> Origin/ZAxis/3point/OBject/View/X/Y/Z/Prev/Restore/Save/Del/?/⟨World⟩: **3.**↵
> Origin point: ⟨0,0,0⟩: *(pick P1)*
> Point on positive portion of the X-axis ⟨10.0000,0.0000,−2.0000⟩: *(pick P2)*
> Point on positive-Y portion of the UCS XY plane ⟨9.0000,1.0000,−2.0000⟩: *(pick P3)*
> Command:

After you pick P3, the UCS icon changes its orientation to align with the angled surface of the wedge. However, it is still located at the lower-left corner of the view. To help you visualize the drawing, move the icon to the origin of the new UCS. Use the **Origin** option of the **UCSICON** command or pick **Origin** after **UCS Icon** in the **Display** cascading menu of the **View** pull-down menu.

The icon is now located on the origin of the User Coordinate System. Any coordinate locations you enter will be relative to the new origin.

The cylinder can be drawn in 3D view or "plan" to the current UCS. For this example, the current 3D view is used. First set the thickness. Then, draw the cylinder using the **CIRCLE** command. In this example, tracking is used to locate the center of the face.

> Command: **ELEV**↵
> New current elevation ⟨0.0000⟩: ↵
> New current thickness ⟨0.0000⟩: **.35.**↵
> Command: **C** *or* **CIRCLE**↵
> 3P/2P/TTR/⟨Center point⟩: **TRA.**↵
> First tracking point: **MID.**↵
> of *(pick near the midpoint of a line on the side of the face)*
> Next point (Press ENTER to end tracking): **MID.**↵
> of *(pick near midpoint of line at bottom of face)*
> Next point (Press ENTER to end tracking): ↵
> Diameter/⟨Radius⟩: **.75.**↵
> Command: ↵

The circle appears in its correct orientation on the angled surface. All edges and features can be seen, Figure 3-7A. The cylinder appears solid when **HIDE** is used, Figure 3-7B.

Figure 3-7.
A—The completed wireframe wedge shows the properly placed cylinder. B—When **HIDE** is used, the cylinder is solid while the rest of the object is a wireframe.

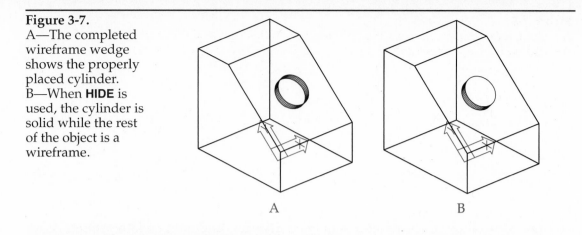

A   B

EXERCISE 3-1

❑ Begin a new drawing named EX3-1.
❑ Construct the 3D object shown using the techniques discussed in this section. Do not include dimensions. Rotate the UCS as needed.
❑ Save the drawing as EX3-1.

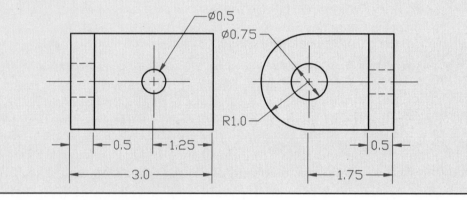

Drawing wireframe "holes"

Wireframe holes can be created by drawing a circle and copying it to new location. To add a hole to the lower surface of the object in Figure 3-7, first move the UCS. Use the **3point** option of the **UCS** command. Place it on the lower-right vertical surface of the object using the pick points shown in Figure 3-8A.

Set the elevation and thickness to zero before you draw any objects. Then, draw the first circle as follows:

```
Command: CIRCLE↵
3P/2P/TTR/⟨Center point⟩: TRA↵
First tracking point: MID↵
of (pick near the midpoint of a line on the side of the face)
Next point (Press ENTER to end tracking): MID↵
of (pick near midpoint of line at bottom of face)
Next point (Press ENTER to end tracking): ↵
Diameter/⟨Radius⟩: .5↵
Command:
```

Figure 3-8B shows the new circle. Since the UCS is aligned with the lower-right vertical surface, the circle can be copied using a negative Z value. This produces the appearance of a wireframe "hole." You can copy the circle using the **COPY** command with coordinate entry or filters or by using grips. To use grips, first pick the circle to display the grips. Select one of the grips to make it hot, then copy the circle as follows:

Figure 3-8.
A—Use the **3point** option to set the UCS parallel to the lower-right vertical surface.
B—The first circle representing the hole is drawn. C—The completed wireframe hole.

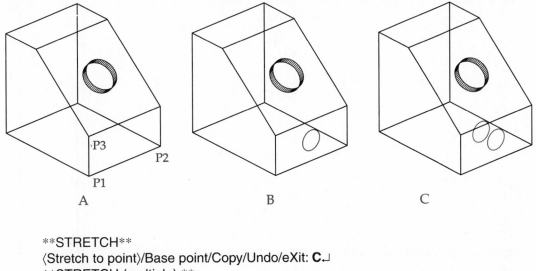

A   B   C

```
**STRETCH**
⟨Stretch to point⟩/Base point/Copy/Undo/eXit: C↵
**STRETCH (multiple) **
⟨Stretch to point⟩/Base point/Copy/Undo/eXit: @0,0,-1↵
**STRETCH (multiple) **
⟨Stretch to point⟩/Base point/Copy/Undo/eXit: ↵
Command:
```

The wireframe hole is shown in Figure 3-8C.

Additional Ways to Change the UCS

There are other ways to change the UCS. These options include selecting a new Z axis, picking a new origin for the UCS, rotating the Y and Z axes, and setting the UCS to an existing entity.

Selecting a new Z axis

The **ZAxis** option of the **UCS** command allows you to select the origin point and a point on the positive Z axis. Once the new Z axis is defined, AutoCAD sets the new X and Y axes. Figure 3-9A shows the current UCS on the model from Figure 3-8. The command sequence is as follows. You must use an object snap mode to select points P1 and P2 because they are not in the XY plane.

```
Command: UCS↵
Origin/ZAxis/3point/OBject/View/X/Y/Z/Prev/Restore/Save/Del/?/⟨World⟩: ZA↵
Origin point ⟨0,0,0⟩: (use an object snap mode to pick P1)
Point on positive portion of Z-axis ⟨current⟩: (use an object snap mode to pick P2)
Command:
```

The UCS icon now appears as shown in Figure 3-9B.

The same option can be used to quickly move the UCS to the front plane of the wedge, Figure 3-9C. Select point P2 as the origin and press [Enter] to accept the default coordinates of the second prompt.

```
Command: UCS↵
Origin/ZAxis/3point/OBject/View/X/Y/Z/Prev/Restore/Save/Del/?/⟨World⟩: ZA↵
Origin point ⟨0,0,0⟩: (use an object snap mode to pick P2)
Point on positive portion of Z-axis ⟨current⟩: ↵
Command:
```

Figure 3-9.
A—The **ZAxis** option of the **UCS** command requires that you select the new origin and a point on the positive Z axis. B—The UCS icon is located at the new origin. C—The same process can be used to set the front plane as the UCS.

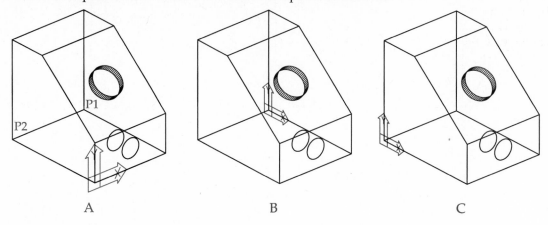

A   B   C

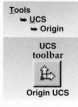

Selecting a new origin

The **Origin** option of the **UCS** command sets a new origin point. This option can also be accessed by picking the **Origin UCS** button from the **UCS** toolbar or by selecting **Origin** from the **UCS** cascading menu.

The UCS icon moves to the specified point and remains parallel to the current UCS. Figure 3-10 shows the UCS icon moved to three different origin points using the **Origin** option. Notice how all of the new locations remain parallel to the current UCS. All coordinate measurements begin at the new UCS origin.

Figure 3-10.
The UCS icon remains parallel to the current UCS when you move the origin using the **Origin** option.

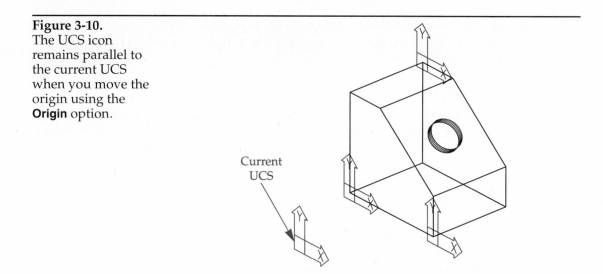

Current
UCS

Rotating the X, Y, and Z axes

Earlier, you rotated the current UCS about the X axis. This same technique is used to rotate the Y or Z axis. Rotating a single axis is useful when you need to rotate the UCS to match the angle of a surface on a part. Figure 3-11 shows the direction of rotation around each axis when a 90° angle is specified. You can also enter negative angles. The following sequence rotates the Z axis 90°.

Figure 3-11.
The UCS icon can be rotated around the X, Y, and Z axes by entering an angle. The angle can be positive or negative, as appropriate.

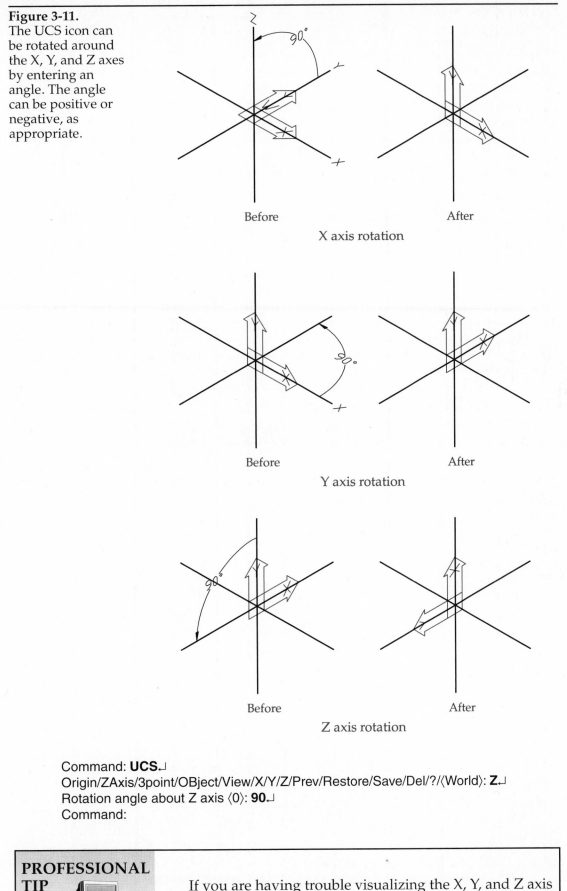

Before   After
X axis rotation

Before   After
Y axis rotation

Before   After
Z axis rotation

Command: **UCS**↵
Origin/ZAxis/3point/OBject/View/X/Y/Z/Prev/Restore/Save/Del/?/⟨World⟩: **Z**↵
Rotation angle about Z axis ⟨0⟩: **90**↵
Command:

PROFESSIONAL TIP

If you are having trouble visualizing the X, Y, and Z axis rotations, try using the right-hand rule. The right-hand rule is covered in Chapter 1.

Setting the UCS to an existing object

Tools
→ UCS
→ Object

UCS
toolbar

Object UCS

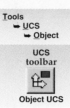

The **Object** option of the **UCS** command can be used to define a new UCS on any object, except a 3D polyline or polygon mesh. This option can also be accessed by picking the **Object UCS** button on the **UCS** toolbar or by selecting **Object** in the **UCS** cascading menu.

There are certain rules that control the orientation of the UCS icon. For example, if you select a circle, the center point becomes the origin of the new UCS. The pick point on the circle determines the direction of the X axis. The Y axis is relative to X, and the UCS Z axis is the same as the Z axis of the entity selected. In the following example, the cylinder in Figure 3-10 is selected for the new UCS:

> Command: **UCS.**↵
> Origin/ZAxis/3point/OBject/View/X/Y/Z/Prev/Restore/Save/Del/?/⟨World⟩: **OB.**↵
> Select object to align UCS: *(pick the top edge of the cylinder)*
> Command:

The UCS icon probably looks like the one shown in Figure 3-12A. This may not be what you expected. The X axis is determined by the pick point on the circle. In this case, the pick point was in the lower-left quadrant of the cylinder. To rotate the UCS in the current plane so the X and Y axes are parallel with the sides of the object, use the **ZAxis** option. Refer to Figure 3-12B.

> Command: **UCS.**↵
> Origin/ZAxis/3point/OBject/View/X/Y/Z/Prev/Restore/Save/Del/?/⟨World⟩: **ZA.**↵
> Origin point ⟨0,0,0⟩: **CEN.**↵
> of *(pick the cylinder)*
> Point on positive portion of Z-axis ⟨0.0000,0.0000,1.0000⟩: ↵
> Command:

Figure 3-12.
A—The X axis of the UCS icon placed at the pick point of the circle. B—The UCS rotated parallel to the object with the **ZAxis** option.

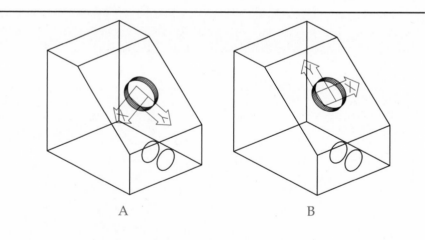

A   B

Setting the UCS perpendicular to current view

Tools
→ UCS
→ View

UCS
toolbar

View UCS

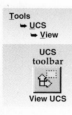

You may need to add notes or labels that appear horizontal in the current view to a 3D drawing, Figure 3-13. This is easy to do using the **View** option of the **UCS** command. This option can also be accessed by picking the **View UCS** button in the **UCS** toolbar or selecting **View** in the **UCS** cascading menu.

When using the **View** option, the UCS icon rotates to a position perpendicular to the current view.

> Command: **UCS.**↵
> Origin/ZAxis/3point/OBject/View/X/Y/Z/Prev/Restore/Save/Del/?/⟨World⟩: **V.**↵
> Command:

Now, anything added to the drawing appears horizontal in the current view.

Figure 3-13.
The **View** option allows you to place text horizontally in the current view.

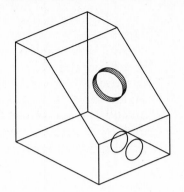

WIREFRAME OBJECT

Preset UCS orientations

AutoCAD has six preset orientations that can be selected from the **UCS Orientation** dialog box. To use one of these, select **Preset UCS...** from the **UCS** cascading menu in the **Tools** pull-down menu, pick the **Preset UCS** button from the **UCS** toolbar, or enter UCP or DDUCSP at the Command: prompt. See Figure 3-14.

Six icons in the dialog box allow you to select a preset UCS. The icon at the upper-left corner returns to the World Coordinate System. If you wish to restore the previous UCS you were working with, pick **Previous** in the lower-right corner. The **Current View** icon creates a UCS that is perpendicular to the current view. The two option buttons in the dialog box allow you to create a new UCS relative to the current UCS or absolute to the WCS.

If you have a UCS set, keep in mind that a plan view of any coordinate system can also be considered a top view. Therefore, if you select the **FRONT** icon to set a new UCS relative to the current one, you are basically rotating the UCS icon 90° around the X axis. This can be an easy way to create a new UCS. Then, move the UCS icon to a new origin using the **Origin** option of the **UCS** command.

DDUCSP
UCP

Tools
→ UCS
↳ Present
UCS...

UCS
toolbar

Preset UCS

Figure 3-14.
The **UCS Orientation** dialog box has six preset UCS configurations.

WCS

Same as **View** option of **UCS** command

Return to previous UCS

Select coordinate system

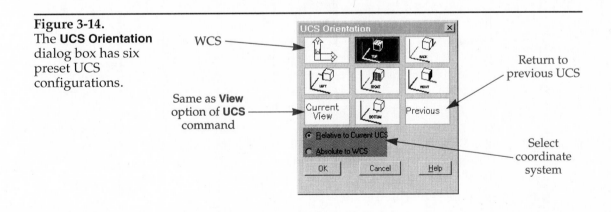

When you select a preset UCS from the dialog box, the **Absolute to WCS** option button is on by default if the WCS is current. Therefore, any UCS icon you pick sets a new UCS based on the World Coordinate System. However, if any coordinate system other than the WCS is current when the dialog box appears, the **Relative to Current UCS** option button is the default. In this case, the icon you pick rotates the new coordinate system 90° relative to the current one.

UCS dialog boxes

DDUCS
UC

Tools
→ UCS
  → Named UCS

UCS
toolbar

Named UCS

User Coordinate Systems can be created, selected, and modified using dialog boxes. The **DDUCS** (dynamic dialog UCS) command activates the **UCS Control** dialog box, Figure 3-15. This dialog box is accessed by picking **Named UCS...** from the **UCS** cascading menu in the **Tools** pull-down menu, picking the **Named UCS** button in the **UCS** toolbar, or entering UC or DDUCS at the Command: prompt.

Figure 3-15.
The **UCS Control** dialog box allows you to rename, list, delete, and set current an existing UCS.

Saved coordinate systems

Pick to set highlighted UCS current

Pick to list origin and axis points for the selected UCS

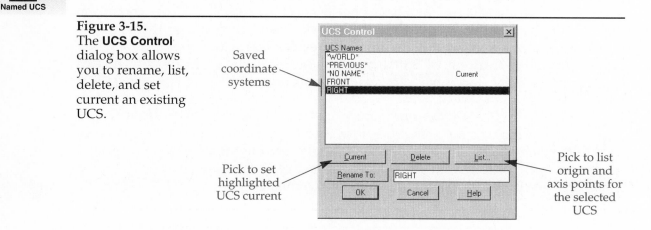

The **UCS Names** area of the dialog box contains names of all saved coordinate systems, plus *WORLD*. If other coordinate systems have been used, the word *PREVIOUS* appears in the list. The entry *NO NAME* appears if the current coordinate system has not been named. Make any of the listed coordinate systems active by highlighting the name and picking the **Current** button.

A list of coordinate and axis values of the current UCS can be displayed by picking the **List...** button. This displays the **UCS** dialog box shown in Figure 3-16.

Use the following steps to define and name a new User Coordinate System:
1. Open the **UCS Orientation** dialog box to display the preset icons.
2. Select the orientation you need and pick the **OK** button.
3. Select the **UCS** command and use the **Save** option to enter a name for the new UCS.

Figure 3-16.
The **UCS** dialog box displays the coordinate values of the current UCS.

	Name: *WORLD*			
Origin	X Axis	Y Axis	Z Axis
X= -1.5937	X= 0.3713	X= 0.8510	X= -0.3713
Y= 0.6784	Y= -0.6018	Y= 0.5252	Y= 0.6018
Z= -3.8891	Z= 0.7071	Z= 0.0000	Z= 0.7071

OK

❑ Begin a new drawing named EX3-2.
❑ Construct the 3D object shown below. Do not include dimensions or labels.
❑ Rotate and relocate the UCS as needed.
❑ Create and save named User Coordinate Systems as follows:

Label	UCS name
A	Front
B	Right

❑ Save the drawing as EX3-2.⏎

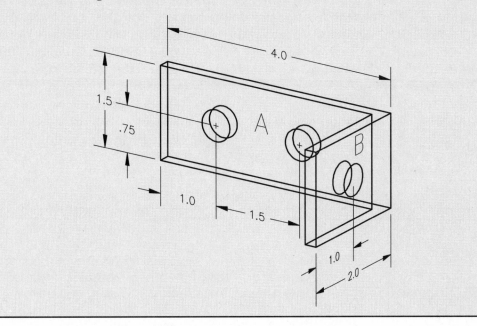

Setting an automatic plan display

Earlier, you learned how to display a plan view to the current UCS using the **PLAN** command. After changing the UCS, a plan view is often needed to give you a better feel for the XYZ directions. The plan view also allows you to visualize the object in a pictorial view. This makes it easier to decide the best viewpoint orientation to pick.

If the **UCSFOLLOW** system variable is set to 1, AutoCAD automatically generates a plan view in the current viewport when the UCS is changed. Viewports are discussed in Chapter 4. The default setting of **UCSFOLLOW** is 0 (off). The **UCSFOLLOW** variable can be set for each viewport individually. The following example sets **UCSFOLLOW** to 1 for the current viewport only.

Command: **UCSFOLLOW**⏎
New value for UCSFOLLOW ⟨0⟩: **1**⏎
Command:

Working with more than one UCS

You can create as many User Coordinate Systems as needed to construct your model or drawing. AutoCAD allows you to name coordinate systems for future use. Several options of the **UCS** command allow you to work with multiple coordinate systems. These are explained below.

- **?.** Switches the graphics window to the text window and displays all of the named coordinate systems. The display includes the coordinate values of the XYZ axes of each UCS relative to the current UCS. The name of the current UCS is given first. If the current UCS does not have a name and is different than the WCS, *NO NAME* appears.
- **Previous (P).** Allows you to display previously used coordinate systems. AutoCAD remembers ten previous systems in both model space and paper space, for a total of twenty. You can step back through them in the same way that **ZOOM Previous** displays previous zooms.
- **Restore (R).** Requires the name of the UCS you wish restored. If you forget the names, enter a question mark (?) to list saved coordinate systems. Only the orientation of the UCS icon will change. The views remain the same.
- **Save (S).** Save a UCS by entering a name having 31 characters or less. Numbers, letters, dollar signs ($), hyphens (–), and underscores (_) are valid.
- **Delete (D).** Enter the name of the UCS to be deleted. You can use wild card characters and a question mark (?), or delete a list by separating the names with commas.
- **World (W).** Resets the World Coordinate System (WCS) as the current UCS.

PROFESSIONAL TIP

Most drawings can be created using a single named UCS. This UCS is rotated and placed on any plane that you are working on. If the drawing is complex with several planes containing a large amount of detail, you may wish to establish a named UCS for each detailed face. Then, to work on a different plane, just restore the proper UCS. For example, when working with architectural drawings, you may wish to establish a different UCS for each floor plan and elevation view, and for roofs that require detail work.

UCS variables

As mentioned earlier in this chapter, the **UCSFOLLOW** system variable allows you to change how an object is displayed in relation to the UCS. There are also variables that display a variety of information about the current UCS. These variables include the following:

- **UCSFOLLOW.** Has an integer value of 0 or 1. When set to 1 it displays a plan view when the UCS is changed. This feature is discussed in Chapter 4.
- **UCSNAME.** (Read only) Displays the name of the current UCS.
- **UCSORG.** (Read only) Displays the XYZ origin value of the current UCS.
- **UCSXDIR.** (Read only) Displays the XYZ value of the X axis direction of the current UCS.
- **UCSYDIR.** (Read only) Displays the XYZ value of the Y axis direction of the current UCS.

Chapter Test

Write your answers in the spaces provided.

1. Define the meaning of WCS. _____

   _____

2. What is a User Coordinate System (UCS)?_____

   _____

   _____

   _____

3. What command controls the display of the User Coordinate System icon? _____

   _____

4. What is the function of the **3point** option of the **UCS** command?_____

   _____

   _____

   _____

5. How do you create a display perpendicular to the current UCS? _____

   _____

   _____

6. How is the UCS icon moved to the origin of the current coordinate system? ____

   _____

   _____

7. When you use the **Object** option of the **UCS** command, how does AutoCAD determine the X axis if you pick a circle for the new UCS? _____

   _____

   _____

8. How do you move the UCS along the current Z axis? _____

   _____

9. What is the function of the **Object** option of the **UCS** command?_____

   _____

10. When is the **View** option of the **UCS** command used? _____

    _____

    _____

11. How can you make sure that a view will always be plan to the current UCS? ___

    _____

    _____

12. How do you access the **UCS Orientation** dialog box? _____

    _____

13. What command displays the **UCS Control** dialog box? _____

    _____

14. What appears in the **UCS Control** dialog box if the current UCS has not been named?

    _____

Drawing Problems

Problems 1–3. These problems are engineering design sketches. They are the types of sketches a drafter is expected to work from in a real-world situation. Therefore, they may contain dimensioning errors and some information may be incomplete. It is up to you to supply appropriate information as needed.

 1. This is a concept sketch of a desk organizer. Create a 3D drawing, either wireframe or surfaced, using the dimensions given. Create new User Coordinate Systems as needed. Length dimensions of the compartments are up to you. Plot your drawing to scale on a B-size sheet of paper. Save the drawing as P3-1.

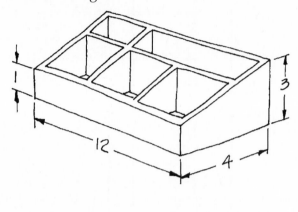

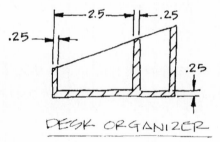

DESK ORGANIZER

 2. This is a concept sketch of a desk pencil holder. Create a 3D wireframe drawing using the dimensions given. Create new User Coordinate Systems as needed. Plot your drawing to scale on a B-size sheet of paper. Save the drawing as P3-2.

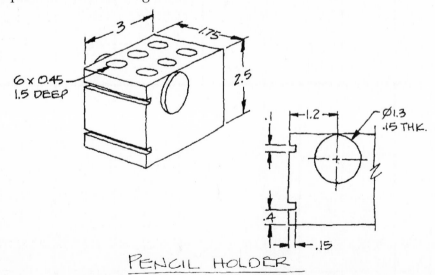

PENCIL HOLDER

3. This is an engineering sketch of a window blind mounting bracket. Create a 3D drawing using the dimensions given. Create new User Coordinate Systems as needed. Plot two views of your drawing to scale on a C-size sheet of paper. Save the drawing as P3-3.

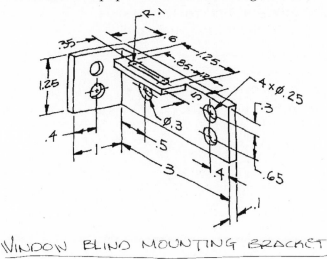

WINDOW BLIND MOUNTING BRACKET

4. This is a two-view orthographic drawing of a window valance mounting bracket. Convert it to a 3D wireframe drawing. Use the dimensions given. Similar holes have the same offset dimensions. Create new User Coordinate Systems as needed. Plot two views of your drawing to scale on a C-size sheet of paper. Save the drawing as P3-4.

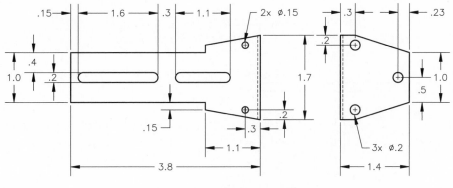

MATERIAL THICKNESS = .125"

5. This is an orthographic drawing of a light fixture bracket. Convert it to a 3D wireframe drawing. Use the dimensions given. Similar holes have the same offset dimensions. Create new User Coordinate Systems as needed. Plot two views of your drawing to scale on a C-size sheet of paper. Save the drawing as P3-5.

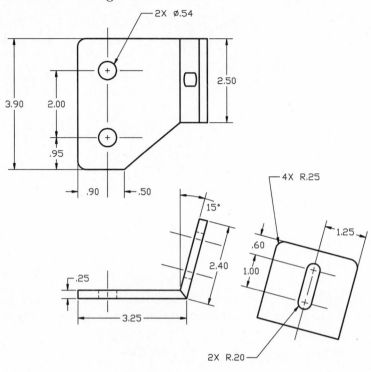

Problems 6–8. These problems are mechanical parts. Create a 3D wireframe drawing of each part. Do not dimension the model. Plot the finished drawings on B-size paper.

6.

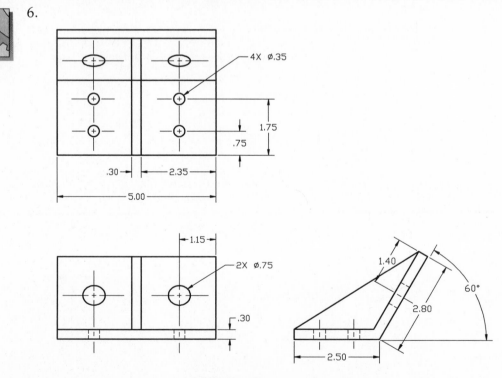

Angle Bracket

7.

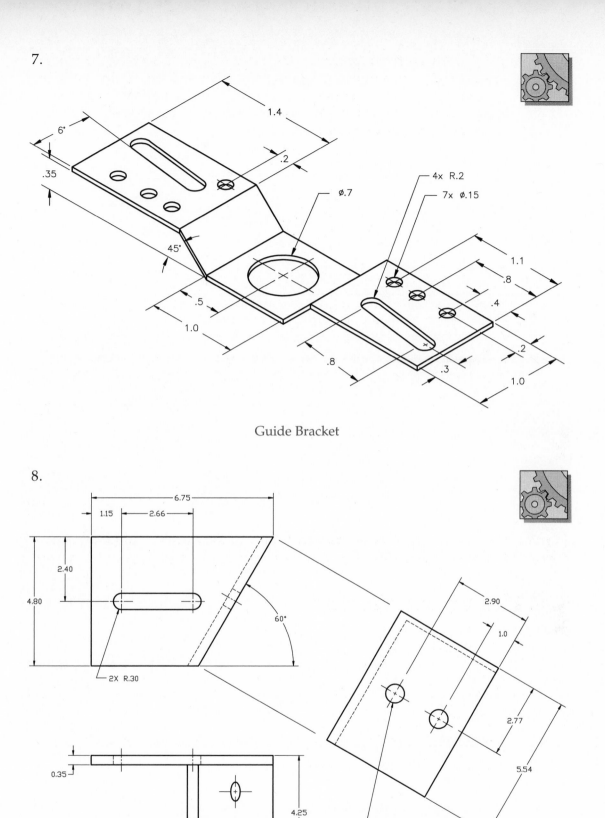

Guide Bracket

8.

Angle Mount

When working with 3D construction, you do not need to construct each orthographic view separately. Simply select the appropriate viewpoint for each viewport.

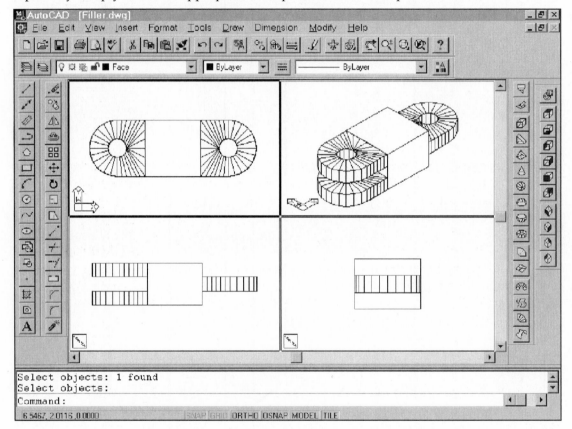

Using Model Space Viewports

Learning Objectives

After completing this chapter, you will be able to:
- ○ Describe the function of model space viewports.
- ○ Divide the screen into multiple viewports.
- ○ Create and save a variety of viewport configurations.
- ○ Alter the current viewport configuration.
- ○ Construct a drawing using multiple viewports.

A variety of views can be displayed at one time using model space viewports. This is useful when constructing 3D models. Using the **VPORTS** command, the screen can be divided into two or more smaller screens. These smaller screens are called *viewports.* Each viewport can be configured to display a different 2D or 3D view of the model.

The *active viewport* is the viewport where the model is constructed. Any viewport can be made active, but only one can be active at a time. As objects are added or edited, the results are shown in all viewports. A variety of viewport configurations can be saved and recalled as needed. This chapter discusses the use of viewports and shows how they can be used for 3D constructions.

Understanding Viewports

The AutoCAD graphics window can be divided into a maximum of 48 viewports. However, this is impractical due to the small size of each viewport. Four viewports is the maximum number practical to display at one time. The number of viewports you need depends on the model you are drawing. Each viewport can show a different view of an object. This makes it easier to construct 3D objects.

A variety of **VPORTS** command options can be found by selecting **Tiled Viewports** in the **View** pull-down menu. See Figure 4-1. Tiled viewports are created in model space, while floating model space is the area inside a paper space viewport.

Model space viewports are created with the **VPORTS** command. In order to use **VPORTS**, model space must be active. Model space is active by default when you enter AutoCAD. The **TILEMODE** system variable must also be set to the default of 1. Model space viewports cannot be plotted because they are not entities. Viewports are simply for display purposes.

Paper space viewports are used to lay out the views of a drawing before plotting. Detailed discussions of paper space viewports are found in Chapter 10 and Chapter 24 of *AutoCAD and its Applications—Basics, Release 14*. The **MVIEW** command is

AutoCAD User's Guide **6**

Figure 4-1.
The **VPORTS**
command options
can be selected from
the **Tiled Viewports**
cascading menu.

```
View
  Redraw
  Regen
  Regen All
  Zoom          ▶
  Pan           ▶
  Aerial View
✓ Model Space (Tiled)
  Model Space (Floating)
  Paper Space
  Tiled Viewports   ▶    Layout...
  Floating Viewports ▶
                         1 Viewport
  Named Views...         2 Viewports
  3D Viewpoint      ▶    3 Viewports
  3D Dynamic View        4 Viewports
  Hide                   Restore
  Shade             ▶    Delete
  Render            ▶    Join
  Display           ▶    Save
  Toolbars...
```

used to create paper space viewports. These viewports are like "windows" cut into a sheet of paper. Paper space viewports are entities and can be edited. You can then insert, or "reference" different scaled drawings (views) into these windows. For example, architectural details or sections and details of complex mechanical parts may be referenced. These viewports can be used at the end of a project when preparing the layout for plotting. Hence the name "paper space." The **TILEMODE** variable must be set to 0 to create viewports with the **MVIEW** command.

NOTE

The **MAXACTVP** (maximum active viewports) variable sets the number of paper space viewports that can be active at one time. Type MAXACTVP at the Command: prompt to set this value. This number depends on the operating system of your computer.

Creating Viewports

Creating model space viewports is similar to working with a multiview layout in manual drafting. In a manual multiview layout, several views are on the same sheet. You can switch from one view to another simply by moving your pencil. With model space viewports, pick with your pointing device in the viewport you wish to work in. The picked viewport becomes active. Using viewports is a good way to construct 3D models because all views are updated as you draw. However, viewports are also good for creating 2D drawings.

The project you are working on determines the number of viewports needed. Keep in mind that the more viewports on your screen, the smaller they get. Small viewports may not be useful to you. Figure 4-2 shows four different viewport configurations. As you can see, when 16 viewports are displayed, the viewports become very small. Two to four viewports are normally used. The command sequence appears as follows:

```
Command: VPORTS↵
Save/Restore/Delete/Join/SIngle/?/2/⟨3⟩/4: ↵
```

Figure 4-2.
A—Two vertical viewports. B—Two horizontal viewports. C—The default arrangement of
three viewports. D—Sixteen viewports.

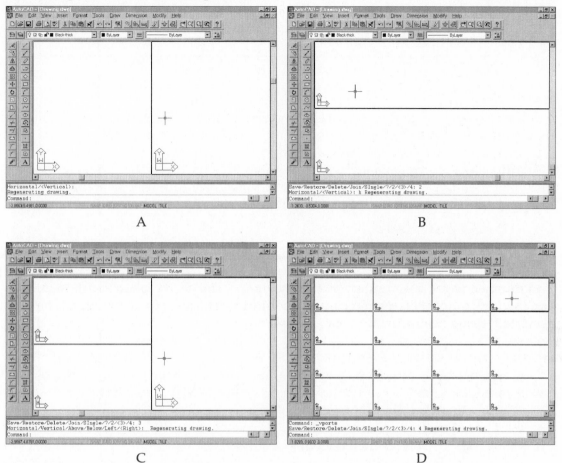

A

B

C

D

Notice that 3 is the default value. After entering a value or accepting the default, you
need to enter the configuration. For the default of three viewports, the prompt is:

Horizontal/Vertical/Above/Below/Left/⟨Right⟩: ↵

The **Right** option places two viewports on the left side of the screen and a large viewport on the right. Viewports can be arranged in several ways. Selecting three viewports has the greatest number of possibilities. The options for a three-viewport layout
are shown in Figure 4-3.

Figure 4-3.
Three viewports can
be arranged in six
different ways.

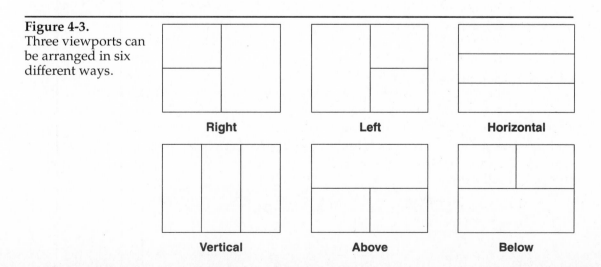

Right   Left   Horizontal

Vertical   Above   Below

Making a viewport active

Only one viewport can be active at one time. The cursor appears as crosshairs in the active viewport. A thick line also surrounds the active viewport. When moved into an inactive viewport, the cursor becomes an arrow.

Any viewport can be made active. Simply move the arrow to that viewport and pick, or press [Ctrl]+[R] to switch viewports. Viewports can also be made active by using the **CVPORT** (current viewport) command.

Command: **CVPORT**⏎
New value for CVPORT ⟨*current*⟩: **3**⏎
Command:

The number is the ID number of the viewport. The ID number is automatically assigned by AutoCAD. It is discussed later in this chapter. This command is also a good way to determine the ID number of viewports.

Setting viewports with a dialog box

A layout of one to four viewports can be quickly created using a dialog box. Select **Tiled Viewports** from the **View** pull-down menu. Then, pick the **Layout...** option. This displays the **Tiled Viewport Layout** dialog box, Figure 4-4. There are twelve viewport configurations from which to choose. You can pick the image tile or the name in the list. Pick **OK** when you are finished.

Notice that there are eight empty spaces in this dialog box. These are for additional viewport image tiles. You can create your own viewport arrangements and place new images in this menu. If you create more than eight image tiles, the **Previous** and **Next** buttons allow you to see other "pages." Chapter 20 details customizing image tiles.

Figure 4-4.
The **Tiled Viewport Layout** dialog box. Custom configurations can be added to the blank tiles.

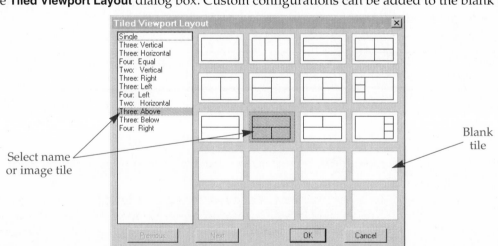

Select name or image tile

Blank tile

Saving, restoring, and deleting viewports

Viewport configurations are not permanent. Once you change the configuration, only the previous one can be recalled. Although viewports are easy to create, it still saves time if you save individual configurations to use later. The **Save** option of the **VPORTS** command allows you to do this. Pick **Save** from the **Tiled Viewports** cascading menu of the **View** pull-down menu, or use the Command: prompt as follows:

```
Command: VPORTS↵
Save/Restore/Delete/Join/SIngle/?/2/⟨3⟩/4: S↵
?/Name for new viewport configuration: FIRST↵
```

This command sequence saves the current viewport configuration with the name FIRST. This configuration can be recalled (restored) at any time. To list the configuration names, enter a question mark after selecting the **Restore** option as follows:

```
Command: VPORTS↵
Save/Restore/Delete/Join/SIngle/?/2/⟨3⟩/4: R↵
?/Name of viewport configuration to restore: ?↵
Viewport configuration(s) to list ⟨*⟩: ↵
Current configuration:
id# 2
   corners: 0.0000,0.5000 0.5000,1.0000
id# 3
   corners: 0.5000,0.0000 1.0000,1.0000
id# 4
   corners: 0.0000,0.0000 0.5000,0.5000
Configuration FIRST:
   0.0000,0.0000 0.5000,0.5000
   0.0000,0.5000 0.5000,1.0000
   0.5000,0.0000 1.0000,1.0000
?/Name of viewport configuration to restore: FIRST↵
Regenerating drawing.
Command:
```

The order in which the above coordinates appear may vary, but the values will be the same. All viewports are automatically given an ID number by AutoCAD. This number is independent of any name you might give the viewport configuration. Each viewport is also given a coordinate location with 0.0000,0.0000 as the lower-left corner of the graphics area and 1.0000,1.0000 as the upper-right corner. Look at the coordinate locations above. Can you determine the layout of the viewports by reading the coordinate values? Figure 4-5 shows the coordinate values of the viewport configuration saved as FIRST.

Unwanted viewport configurations can be removed. Select the **VPORTS** command and then enter the **Delete** option as follows:

```
Command: VPORTS↵
Save/Restore/Delete/Join/SIngle/?/2/⟨3⟩/4: D↵
?/Name of viewport configuration to delete: FIRST↵ (enter ? to list the names)
Command:
```

PROFESSIONAL TIP   Each viewport can have its own viewpoint, zoom scale, limits, grid spacing, and snap setting. Specify the drawing aids in all viewports before saving the configuration. When a viewport is restored, all settings are restored as well.

Figure 4-5.
The viewport coordinate values of the configuration named FIRST. The ID numbers are also identified.

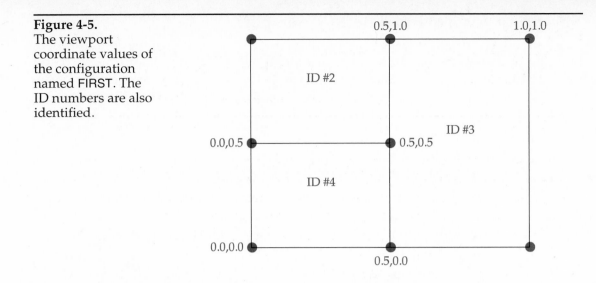

Altering the current viewport configuration

You can join two adjacent viewports to form a single one. This process is quicker than trying to create an entirely new configuration. However, the two viewports must form a rectangle when joined, Figure 4-6. The **Join** option of the **VPORTS** command is used to join viewports.

When you enter the **Join** option, AutoCAD first prompts you for the *dominant viewport*. All aspects of the dominant viewport are used in the new viewport. These aspects include limits, grid, and snap settings. Pick **Tiled Viewports** from the **View** pull-down menu, then pick **Join** to join two viewports or use the following command sequence:

    Command: **VPORTS**↵
    Save/Restore/Delete/Join/SIngle/?/2/⟨3⟩/4: **J**↵
    Select dominant viewport ⟨current⟩: *(select the viewport or press* [Enter]*)*
    Select viewport to join: *(select the other viewport)*
    Regenerating drawing.
    Command:

The two viewports selected are eliminated and joined into a single viewport. If you select two viewports that do not form a rectangle, AutoCAD returns this message:

    The selected viewports do not form a rectangle.
    Select dominant viewport ⟨current⟩:

The screen can also be restored to a single viewport. To do so, select the **Single** option of the **VPORTS** command as follows:

    Command: **VPORTS**↵
    Save/Restore/Delete/Join/SIngle/?/2/⟨3⟩/4: **SI**↵
    Command:

Figure 4-6.
Two viewports can be joined if they will form a rectangle. If the two viewports will *not* form a rectangle, they cannot be joined.

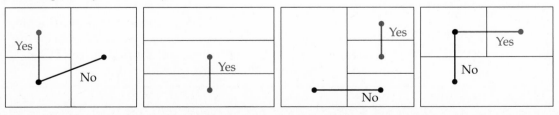

EXERCISE 4-1

❏ Start a new drawing. Select the **VPORTS** command, create the following viewports, and save them with the viewport name indicated:

Number of Viewports	Configuration	Name
1		ONE
2	Vertical	TWO
3	Above	THREE-A
3	Left	THREE-L
3	Right	THREE-R
4		FOUR

❏ List the viewports to be sure all were saved.
❏ Restore each named configuration.
❏ Restore configuration THREE-A and join the two small viewports. Save the new configuration under the name TWO. Answer YES when asked if you want to replace the existing configuration named TWO.
❏ Restore configuration TWO. It should have two horizontal viewports.
❏ Delete configuration THREE-A.
❏ Restore configuration THREE-L. Set the grid and snap spacing in each viewport to different values. Save the configuration as THREE-L.
❏ Select the **Single** option in the **VPORTS** command.
❏ Restore configuration THREE-L. Check the drawing aids in each viewport to be sure they have the same values previously set.
❏ Save your work as EX4-1.

Drawing in Multiple Viewports

For 2D drawings, viewports allow you to display a view of the entire drawing plus views showing portions of the drawing. This is similar to the **VIEW** command, except you can have several views on-screen at once. Adjust the zoom scale to a different area of the drawing in each viewport. Save the viewport configuration if you plan to continue working with it during other drawing sessions. You can create an unlimited number of viewport configurations.

Viewports are also a powerful aid when constructing 3D models. You can specify different viewpoints in each port and see the model take shape as you draw. A model can be quickly constructed because you can switch from one viewport to another while drawing and editing the object.

The following example gives the steps to construct a simple 3D part using two viewports. Refer to Figure 4-7 as you go through the following command sequence:

Command: **VPORTS**↵
Save/Restore/Delete/Join/SIngle/?/2/⟨3⟩/4: **2**↵
Horizontal/⟨Vertical⟩: ↵
Regenerating drawing.
Command: *(make sure the right viewport is active)* **L** *or* **LINE**↵
From point: **3,2**↵
To point: **@7,0**↵
To point: **@0,5**↵
To point: **@-7,0**↵
To point: **C**↵
Command: **C** *or* **CIRCLE**↵
3P/2P/TTR/⟨Center point⟩: **@3.5,-2.5**↵
Diameter/⟨Radius⟩: **1**↵
Command: **-VP** *or* **VPOINT**↵
Rotate/⟨View point⟩ ⟨0.0000,0.0000,1.0000⟩: **-1,-1,1**↵
Regenerating drawing.

Use **PAN** and **ZOOM** to center and enlarge the object in the left viewport.

The screen now displays two viewports. The left viewport contains a top view of the part and the right viewport displays the part in a 3D viewpoint, Figure 4-7.

The next step is to copy the shape in the left viewport up 2 units along the Z axis. This can be done using the **COPY** command and XY filters, or with grips. For this example, grips are used. Select the entire object in the left viewport so that all grips on the rectangle and circle are displayed. Pick any one of the grips to make it hot.

** STRETCH **
⟨Stretch to point⟩/Base point/Copy/Undo/eXit: ↵
** MOVE **
⟨Move to point⟩/Base point/Copy/Undo/eXit: **C**↵
** MOVE (multiple) **
⟨Move to point⟩/Base point/Copy/Undo/eXit: **@0,0,2**↵
** MOVE (multiple) **
⟨Move to point⟩/Base point/Copy/Undo/eXit:↵
Command:

Figure 4-7.
The screen is divided into two viewports. The top view appears in the left viewport and a 3D view appears in the right viewport.

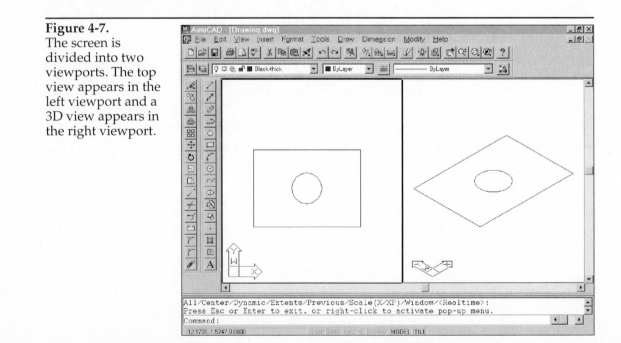

The screen now appears as shown in Figure 4-8. The right viewport shows the result of the copy.

The final step is to connect the corners of the object with vertical lines. Draw the lines in the right viewport. Set the **Endpoint** running object snap and use the **LINE** command. You can draw one line and copy it to the other locations, or use the **MULTIPLE LINE** command as follows:

> Command: **MULTIPLE.**⏎
> Multiple command: **LINE.**⏎
> From point: *(pick the corner on upper shape)*
> To point: *(pick the adjacent corner on the lower shape)*
> To point: ⏎
> LINE From point: *(continue joining the corners)*

Press [Esc] to cancel the command when all corners have been joined. The completed object appears in Figure 4-9.

PROFESSIONAL TIP

Displaying saved viewport configurations can be automated by using custom menus. Custom menus are easy to create. If a standard naming convention is used, these named viewports can be saved with template drawings. This creates a consistent platform all students or employees can use.

Figure 4-8.
The copied shapes appear automatically in the 3D (right) viewport.

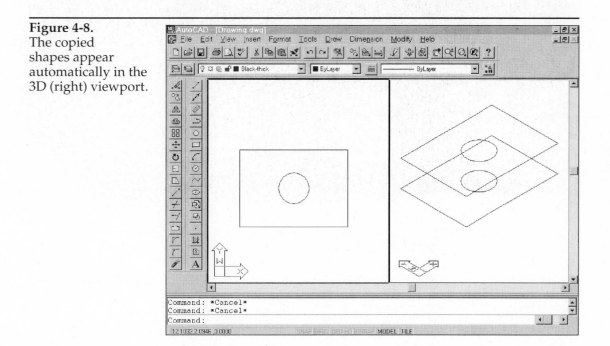

Figure 4-9.
The corners of the
upper and lower
planes are
connected with lines
in the right
viewport to create
the wireframe.

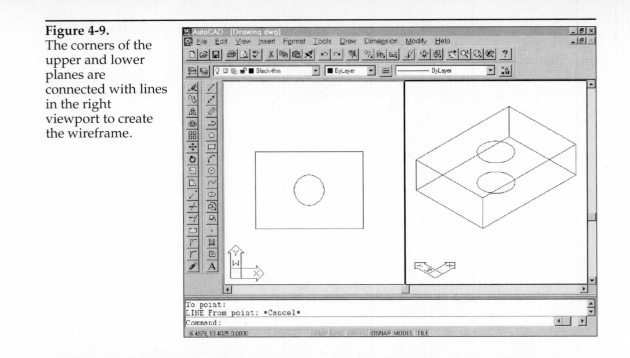

❑ Start a new drawing named EX4-2.
❑ Create a viewport configuration with two viewports arranged horizontally. Save it as TWO.
❑ Construct the object shown below. Draw a top view in the upper viewport. Display a 3D viewpoint in the lower viewport. Connect the corners in the lower viewport.
❑ Save the drawing as EX4-2.

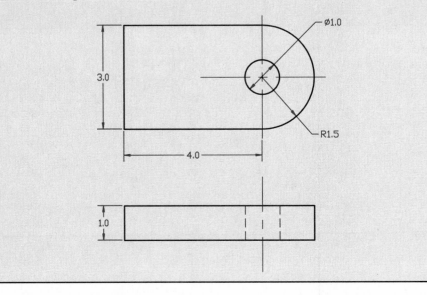

Working with the UCS in viewports

When an object is displayed in a multiple viewport configuration, the UCS is the same in all viewports. The viewpoints can vary, but the origin and orientation of the UCS must be the same. For example, notice in Figure 4-10 that the UCS icon is the same in all views. You cannot have a variety of User Coordinate Systems set in different viewports.

Figure 4-10.
Only one UCS can be set at a time, and it applies to all viewports.

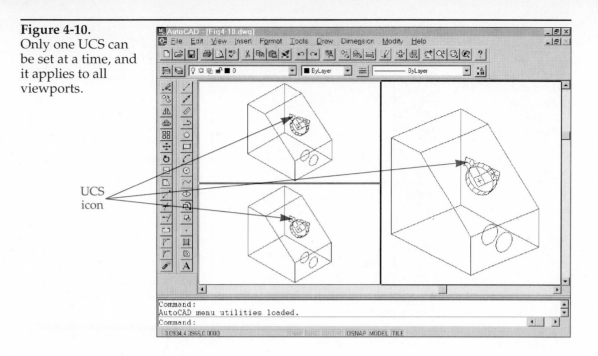

UCS icon

When working on a surface, it may help if the viewpoint is plan to the surface. Simply use the **PLAN** command in the appropriate viewport to do this. Figure 4-11 shows the upper-left viewport plan to the current UCS. If you change the UCS, the viewport with the plan view has a *broken pencil* icon in the lower-left corner. See Figure 4-12. The broken pencil icon indicates that the view is perpendicular (or nearly so) to the current UCS. If you draw objects in a viewport with a broken pencil, unexpected results may occur.

You can set up one viewport so that it is always plan to the current UCS. If you change the UCS, the viewport automatically changes to the plan view of the new coordinate system. To do this, set the **UCSFOLLOW** variable to 1 in the viewport:

```
Command: UCSFOLLOW↵
New value for UCSFOLLOW ⟨0⟩: 1↵
Command:
```

Figure 4-11.
The **PLAN** command is used in the upper-left viewport.

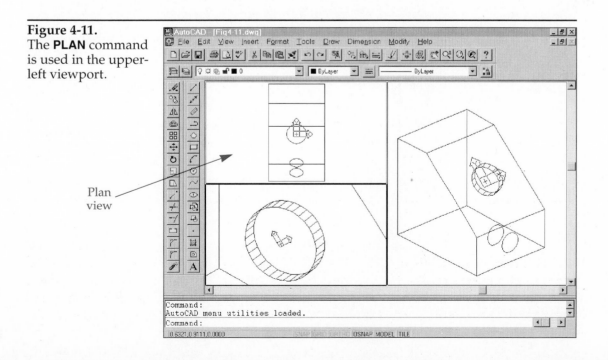

Plan view

Figure 4-12.
The broken pencil icon means that the view is perpendicular to the current UCS.

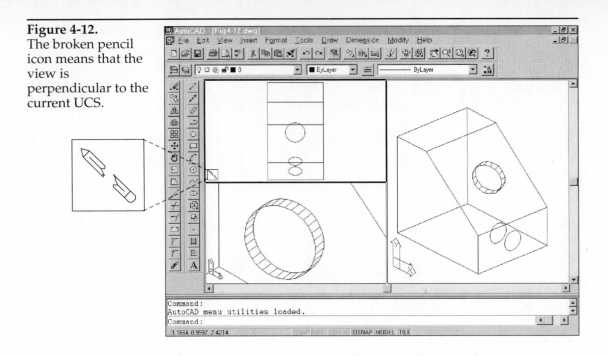

Figure 4-13 shows the upper-left viewport with **UCSFOLLOW** set to 1 after the current UCS was changed. Keep in mind that if you change the **UCSFOLLOW** variable in a viewport, the display will not change to a plan view until the UCS is changed.

PROFESSIONAL TIP

The **UCSFOLLOW** variable can be a very useful tool. This feature can be even more useful if the origin of the UCS is the lower-left corner (or some other meaningful reference point) of the plan surface.

Figure 4-13.
When the **UCSFOLLOW** variable is activated in a viewport, that viewport displays a view plan to the current UCS.

Viewport automatically shows plan view when UCS is charged

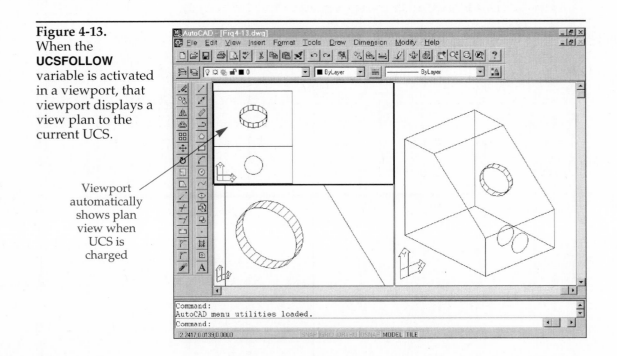

AutoCAD and its Applications—Advanced

Redrawing and regenerating viewports

The **REDRAW** and **REGEN** commands affect the current viewport only. To redraw or regenerate all viewports at the same time, use the **REDRAWALL** and **REGENALL** commands. These commands can be selected from the **View** pull-down menu or typed at the Command: prompt. The **Redraw All** button can also be selected from the **Standard** toolbar.

The **QTEXT** display feature is controlled by the **REGEN** command. Therefore, if you are working with text in viewports, be sure to use the **REGENALL** command in order for **QTEXT** to affect all viewports.

Chapter Test

Write your answers in the spaces provided.

1. Identify the purpose of the **VPORTS** command. _____
   _____
   _____

2. How do you name a configuration of viewports? _____
   _____

3. What is the purpose of naming a configuration of viewports?_____
   _____

4. Name the system variable that retains the number of viewports that can be active
   at one time. _____

5. What is the total number of viewports allowed with the **VPORTS** command?
   How many viewports are practical? _____
   _____

6. How can a named viewport be redisplayed on the screen? _____
   _____
   _____

7. How can a list of the named viewports be displayed on the screen?_____
   _____
   _____

8. What relationship must two viewports have before they can be joined? _____
   _____
   _____

9. What is the significance of the dominant viewport when two viewports are
   joined? _____
   _____
   _____

10. List three ways to change the active viewport.
    _____
    _____
    _____

Drawing Problems

1. Construct seven template drawings, each with a preset viewport configuration. Use the following configurations and names:

Configuration	Name
Two viewports horizontal	TWO-H
Two viewports vertical	TWO-V
Three viewports—large on right	THREE-LR
Three viewports—large on left	THREE-LL
Three viewports—large above	THREE-LA
Three viewports—large below	THREE-LB
Three viewports vertical	THREE-V

2. Construct one of the problems from Chapter 3 using viewports. Use one of your template drawings from Problem 1. Save the drawing as P4-2.

Chapter 5

Three-Dimensional Surface Modeling Techniques

Learning Objectives

After completing this chapter, you will be able to:
- ○ Construct a 3D surface mesh.
- ○ Create a variety of surface-modeled objects using the **EDGESURF**, **TABSURF**, **RULESURF**, and **REVSURF** commands.
- ○ Construct a detailed surface model using multiple viewports.

There are several ways to construct surface models using AutoCAD. The method you use will depend on the object you are creating. A surface mesh, or "patch," can be created using the **3DMESH** or **PFACE** command. The **EDGESURF** command creates a surface mesh using four edges joined at the endpoints. The **RULESURF** command creates a mesh of ruled surfaces between two curves. The **TABSURF** command creates a tabulated-surface mesh using a curve and a specified direction to extend the surface. The **REVSURF** command creates a surface of revolution. A surface of revolution is a profile rotated around an axis.

3D Mesh Techniques

AutoCAD User's Guide 13

Three-dimensional face meshes are used to create surface models that cannot be constructed using surfacing commands. There are four types of 3D face meshes: planar mesh, 3D mesh, pface mesh, and surface patch.

A *planar mesh* is made up of four sides. The corners can have different Z values. However, the mesh lies in a single plane. In other words, a mesh is "flat." A planar mesh is created with the **Mesh** option of the **3D** command.

A *3D mesh* is a polygon mesh composed of 3D faces. This type of mesh is not restricted to a single plane. The **3DMESH** command is used to create a 3D mesh.

A *pface mesh*, or *polyface mesh*, is a general polygon mesh of 3D faces. Each face can have an infinite number of vertices and can occupy a different plane. The **PFACE** command is used to create a polyface mesh.

The fourth type of mesh is a *surface patch*. This is created with the **EDGESURF** command. The **EDGESURF** command is discussed later in this chapter.

Constructing a 3D mesh

The **3DMESH** command creates a 3D mesh. The mesh is defined in rows and columns. The *N value* defines the number of rows. An N value of three produces two rows. The *M value* defines the number of columns. An M value of four produces three columns. See Figure 5-1.

Figure 5-1.
A 3D polygon mesh
is similar to a grid
of XY coordinates.
M values define
columns and N
values define rows.
This example has an
M value of 4 and an
N value of 3.

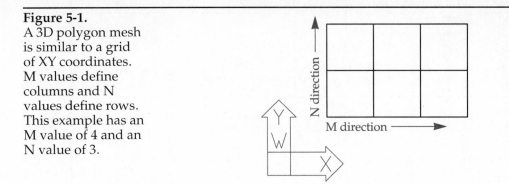

When using the **3DMESH** command, each vertex in the mesh must be given an XYZ coordinate location. The vertices of the mesh are its definition points. A mesh must have between 2 and 256 vertices in both directions.

When prompting for coordinates, the M and N location of the current vertex is indicated. See the command sequence below. The values for each vertex of the first M column must be entered. Then, values for the second, third, and remaining M columns must be entered.

3D MESH

Draw
→ Surfaces
→ 3D **M**esh

Surfaces
toolbar

3D Mesh

To draw a 3D mesh, select **3D Mesh** from the **Surfaces** cascading menu in the **Draw** pull-down menu, pick the **3D Mesh** button from the **Surfaces** toolbar, or type 3DMESH at the Command: prompt. Use the following command sequence to get the feel for the **3DMESH** command. When complete, use **VPOINT** to view the mesh from different angles. The mesh should look like the one shown in Figure 5-2 after using **VPOINT**.

```
Command: 3DMESH↵
Mesh M size: 4↵
Mesh N size: 3↵
Vertex (0,0): 3,2,1↵
Vertex (0,1): 3,3,1.5↵
Vertex (0,2): 3,4,1↵
Vertex (1,0): 4,2,.5↵
Vertex (1,1): 4,3,1↵
Vertex (1,2): 4,4,.5↵
Vertex (2,0): 5,2,1.5↵
Vertex (2,1): 5,3,1↵
Vertex (2,2): 5,4,1.5↵
Vertex (3,0): 6,2,2.5↵
Vertex (3,1): 6,3,2↵
Vertex (3,2): 6,4,2.5↵
Command:
```

Figure 5-2.
A 3D polygon mesh.
The M value is 4
and the N value is 3.

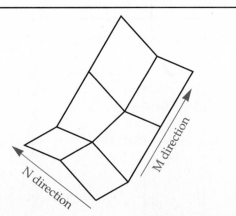

Constructing a single-plane mesh

A *planar mesh* is a 3D mesh that lies in a single plane. It has between 2 and 256 vertices in both M and N directions. To draw a planar mesh, pick **3D Surfaces...** from the **Surfaces** cascading menu in the **Draw** pull-down menu. This displays the **3D Objects** dialog box. Pick **Mesh** from the list or pick the **Mesh** icon. You can also select the **Mesh** option of the **3D** command or enter AI_MESH at the Command: prompt:

    Command: **AI_MESH**↵

or

    Command: **3D**↵
    Box/Cone/DIsh/DOme/Mesh/Pyramid/Sphere/Torus/Wedge: **M**↵

You are then asked for the four corners of the mesh and the number of vertices.

    First corner: **4,3**↵
    Second corner: **9,3**↵
    Third corner: **9,8**↵
    Fourth corner: **4,8**↵
    Mesh M size: **10**↵
    Mesh N size: **8**↵
    Command:

The resulting mesh is shown in Figure 5-3.

Figure 5-3.
A planar mesh has between 2 and 256 vertices in both directions.

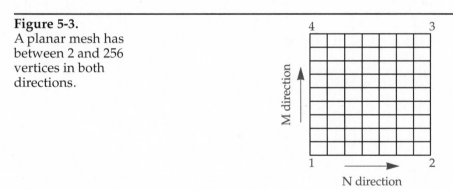

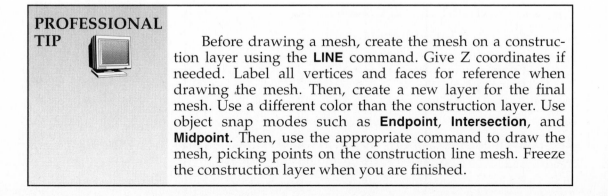

Constructing a 3D polyface mesh

A general polygon mesh can be constructed using the **PFACE** command. This creates a mesh similar to the **3DFACE** command. However, you do not need to pick vertices that join another face twice. You can also create faces that have an infinite number of vertices, rather than the maximum of four specified by the **3DFACE** command. You can use the **PFACE** command to construct surfaces that cannot be "faced" using any of the standard surfacing commands. However, using this command is time-consuming, and is best suited for AutoLISP or ADS (Autodesk Development System) applications.

To create a pface mesh, first define all of the vertices for the mesh. Then, assign those vertices to a face. The face is then given a number and is composed of the vertices you assign to that face. While creating a pface, you can change the color, layer, or linetype by entering the **COLOR**, **LAYER**, or **LINETYPE** commands at the Face *n*, vertex *n*: prompt. The following example creates a pface mesh consisting of two faces. See Figure 5-4A. The first portion of the command defines all the vertices of the two faces.

```
Command: PFACE↵
Vertex 1: 3,3↵
Vertex 2: 7,3↵
Vertex 3: 7,6↵
Vertex 4: 3,6↵
Vertex 5: 2,7,3↵
Vertex 6: 2,2,3↵
Vertex 7: 3,3↵
Vertex 8: ↵
```

The next sequence assigns vertices to face number 1.

```
Face 1, vertex 1: 1↵
Face 1, vertex 2: 2↵
Face 1, vertex 3: 3↵
Face 1, vertex 4: 4↵
Face 1, vertex 5: ↵
```

Now you can change the color of the second face without exiting the command.

```
Face 2, vertex 1: COLOR↵
New color ⟨BYLAYER⟩: GREEN↵
```

The last sequence assigns vertices to face number 2.

```
Face 2, vertex 1: 4↵
Face 2, vertex 2: 5↵
Face 2, vertex 3: 6↵
Face 2, vertex 4: 1↵
Face 2, vertex 5: ↵
Face 3, vertex 1: ↵
```

Now use the **VPOINT** and **HIDE** commands to view the faces.

```
Command: -VP or VPOINT↵
Rotate/⟨View point⟩ ⟨current⟩: -1,-1,.75↵
Regenerating drawing.
Command: HIDE↵
Regenerating drawing.
Command:
```

The pface mesh first appears as a wireframe. However, after using the **HIDE** command, the 3D faces can be clearly seen. See Figure 5-4B.

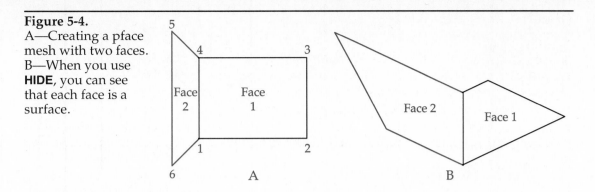

Figure 5-4.
A—Creating a pface mesh with two faces.
B—When you use **HIDE**, you can see that each face is a surface.

Polygon mesh variations

A polygon mesh created with **3DMESH** can be smoothed using the **PEDIT** command. The smoothness of the surface depends on the value set in the **SURFTYPE** system variable:

SURFTYPE setting	Surface type
5	Quadratic B-spline
6	Cubic B-spline
8	Bezier surface

Before smoothing a polygon mesh, set the **SURFU** (M direction) and **SURFV** (N direction) system variables larger than the M and N values. If you do not change these values, the resulting surface may have less 3D faces than the original. Figure 5-5 illustrates the different types of surfaces that can be created using **SURFTYPE** and **PEDIT** smoothing.

Figure 5-5.
A—The **SPLFRAME** variable set to 1. B—A quadratic B-spline (**SURFTYPE** = 5).
C—A cubic B-spline (**SURFTYPE** = 6). D—A Bezier surface (**SURFTYPE** = 8).

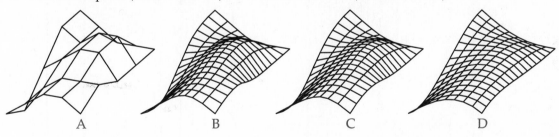

Constructing enclosed surfaces with EDGESURF

The **EDGESURF** command allows you to construct a 3D mesh between four edges. The edges can be lines, polylines, splines, or arcs. The endpoints of the objects must meet precisely. However, a closed polyline *cannot* be used. The four objects can be selected in any order. The resulting surface is a smooth mesh, similar to a planar mesh. The *AutoCAD User's Guide* calls this type of surface mesh a *Coons patch*.

The number of faces are determined by the variables **SURFTAB1** (M direction) and **SURFTAB2** (N direction). To draw an edge surface, pick **Edge Surface** from the **Surfaces** cascading menu in the **Draw** pull-down menu, pick the **Edge Surface** button in the **Surfaces** toolbar, or enter EDGESURF at the Command: prompt:

```
Command: EDGESURF↵
Select edge 1: (pick edge 1)
Select edge 2: (pick edge 2)
Select edge 3: (pick edge 3)
Select edge 4: (pick edge 4)
```

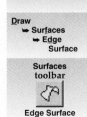

EDGESURF

Draw
➥ Surfaces
  ➥ Edge
    Surface

Surfaces
toolbar

Edge Surface

Figure 5-6.
A completed surface
patch with both
SURFTAB variables
set to 12.

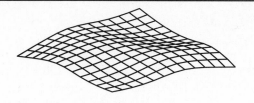

A completed surface patch with the **SURFTAB** variables set to 12 is shown in Figure 5-6.

Creating a surface mesh with RULESURF

A surface mesh can be constructed between two objects using the **RULESURF** command. This mesh is called a *ruled surface*. The two objects can be lines, arcs, circles, polylines, splines, enclosed objects, or a single plane. The two objects must both be either open or closed. A variety of constructions are shown in Figure 5-7. A point can be used with any object to create constructions such as those shown in Figure 5-8. A ruled surface is useful for surfacing holes in parts, exterior fillets (rounds), interior fillets, or flat surfaces of various shapes.

Figure 5-7.
Many different
objects can be used
to create a ruled
surface.

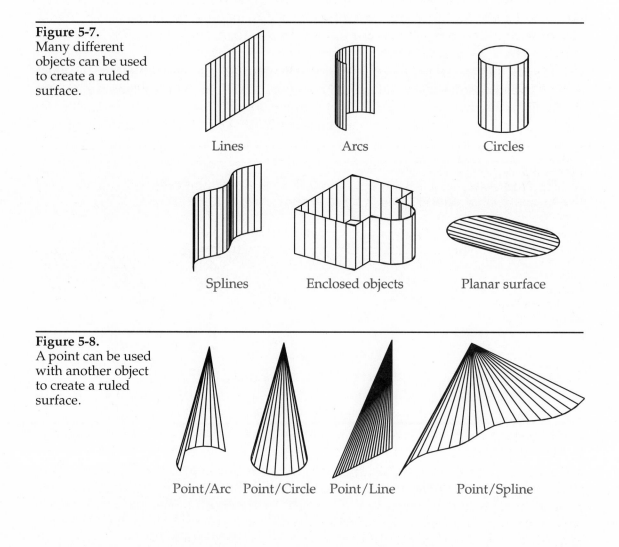

Lines   Arcs   Circles

Splines   Enclosed objects   Planar surface

Figure 5-8.
A point can be used
with another object
to create a ruled
surface.

Point/Arc   Point/Circle   Point/Line   Point/Spline

PROFESSIONAL TIP

When constructing holes in surface-modeled objects, always draw the original circles on a separate construction layer. After the hole has been surfaced with the **RULESURF** command, turn off or freeze the construction layer. If you do not turn off the construction layer, the inside of the hole will not be displayed when **HIDE** is used or the object is rendered.

RULESURF

Draw
➡ **Surfaces**
➡ **Ruled Surface**

Surfaces toolbar

Ruled Surface

Select the **RULESURF** command by picking **Ruled Surface** from the **Surfaces** cascading menu in the **Draw** pull-down menu, picking the **Ruled Surface** button in the **Surfaces** toolbar, or entering RULESURF at the Command: prompt:

Command: **RULESURF**↵
Select first defining curve: *(pick first object)*
Select second defining curve: *(pick second object)*
Command:

When using **RULESURF** to create a surface between two objects such as those shown in Figure 5-9A, it is important to select both objects near the same end. If you pick near opposite ends of each object, the resulting figure may not be what you want, Figure 5-9B. The correctly surfaced object is shown in Figure 5-9C.

The number of elements that compose the ruled surface is determined by the **SURFTAB1** system variable. The greater the number of elements, the smoother the surface appears.

Figure 5-9. When creating a ruled surface, be sure to select the objects near the same end. A—The original objects. B—If you pick incorrectly, the surface is "twisted." C—The surface using the correct pick points.

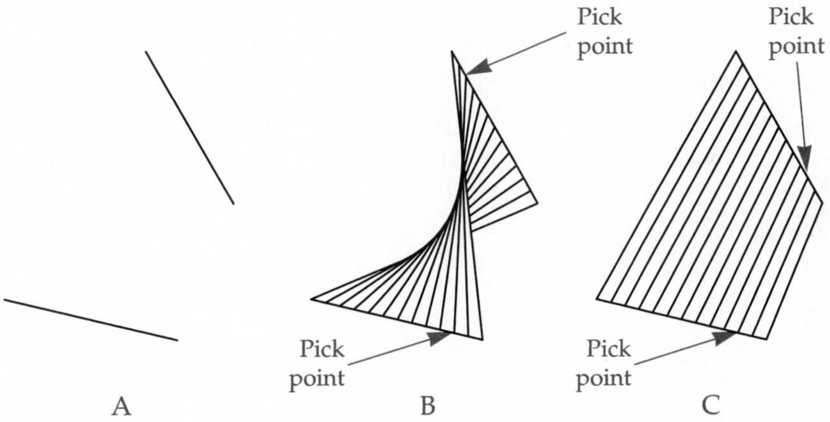

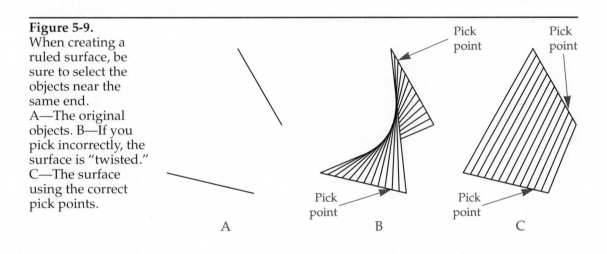

Constructing tabulated surfaces with TABSURF

A ***tabulated surface*** is similar to a ruled surface. However, only one entity is needed. This entity is called the ***path curve***. Lines, arcs, circles, 2D polylines, and 3D polylines can all be used. A line called the ***direction vector*** is also required. This line indicates the direction and length of the tabulated surface. AutoCAD finds the endpoint of the direction vector closest to your pick point. It sets the direction toward the opposite end of the vector line. The tabulated surface follows the direction and length of the direction vector. The **SURFTAB1** system variable controls the number of "steps" that are constructed. Figure 5-10 shows the difference the pick point makes when assigning the direction.

Figure 5-10.
The point you pick
on the direction
vector determines in
which direction the
tabulated surface is
extruded.

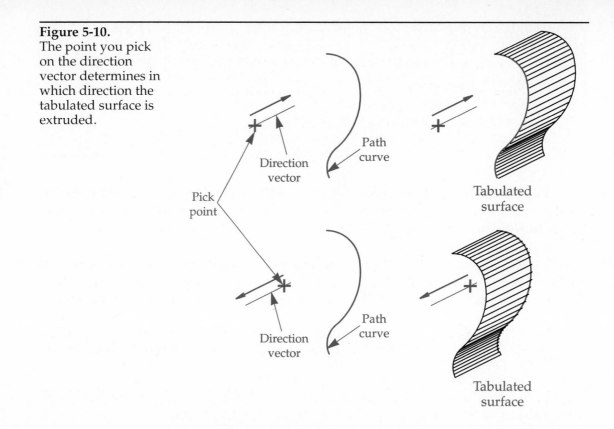

To create a tabulated surface, select **Tabulated Surface** from the **Surfaces** cascading menu of the **Draw** pull-down menu, pick the **Tabulated Surface** button in the **Surfaces** toolbar, or enter TABSURF at the Command: prompt:

> Command: **TABSURF**↵
> Select path curve: *(pick the curve)*
> Select direction vector: *(pick correct end of vector)*
> Command:

Constructing revolved surfaces with REVSURF

With the **REVSURF** command, you can draw a profile and then rotate that profile around an axis to create a symmetrical object. This is a powerful tool and will greatly assist anyone who needs to draw a symmetrical three-dimensional shape. The profile, or *path curve*, can be drawn using lines, arcs, circles, 2D polylines, and 3D polylines. The rotation axis can be a line or an open polyline. Notice the initial layout of the revolved surface in Figure 5-11.

Figure 5-11.
A path curve
(profile) and an axis
are needed to create
a revolved surface.

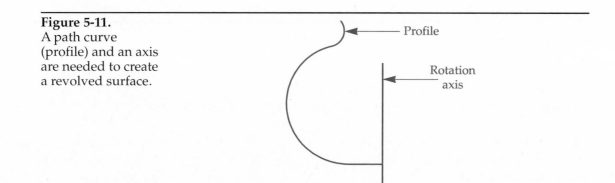

Begin the command by selecting **Revolved Surface** from the **Surfaces** cascading menu of the **Draw** pull-down menu, picking the **Revolved Surface** button in the **Surfaces** toolbar, or typing REVSURF at the Command: prompt:

> Command: **REVSURF**↵
> Select path curve: *(pick the profile)*
> Select axis of revolution: *(pick an axis line)*
> Start angle ⟨0⟩: ↵
> Included angle (+ = ccw, − = cw) ⟨Full circle⟩: ↵
> Command:

The Start angle: prompt allows you to specify an offset angle at which to start the surface revolution. The Included angle: prompt lets you draw the object through 360° of rotation or just a portion of that. Figure 5-12 shows the rotated Figure 5-11 profile displayed with hidden lines removed.

The **SURFTAB1** and **SURFTAB2** system variables control the mesh of a revolved surface. The **SURFTAB1** value determines the number of segments in the direction of rotation around the axis. The **SURFTAB2** value divides the path curve into segments of equal size.

The **REVSURF** command is powerful because it can create a symmetrical surface using any profile. Figure 5-13 illustrates additional examples of **REVSURF** constructions.

Figure 5-12.
The revolved surface created with the profile and axis in Figure 5-11.

Figure 5-13.
Revolved surfaces created with a variety of profiles.

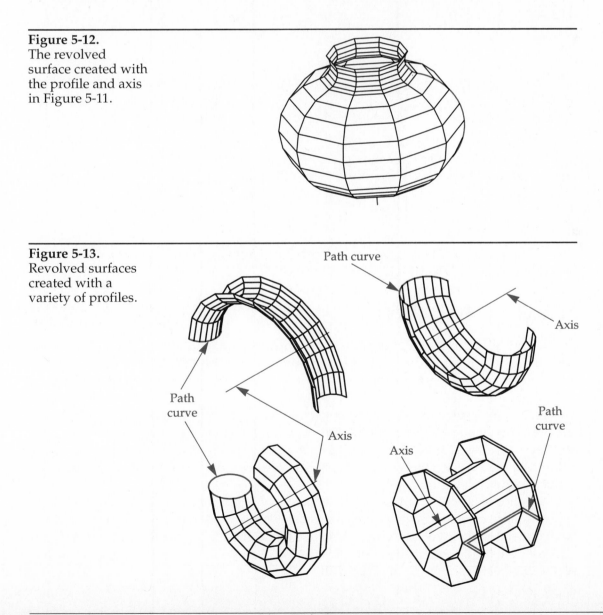

Path curve

Axis

Path curve

Axis

Axis

Path curve

❏ Begin a new drawing and name it EX5-1.
❏ Draw the objects shown below and display them in a 3D viewport.
❏ Set the **SURFTAB1** and **SURFTAB2** variables to values of your choice.
❏ Create the surface model constructions as indicated.
❏ Save your drawing as EX5-1.

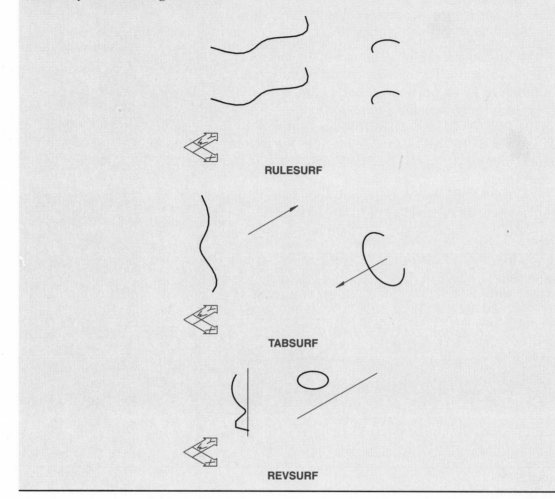

RULESURF

TABSURF

REVSURF

Surfacing around Holes

AutoCAD cannot automatically create surfacing around a hole. A series of steps is required to do this. A common method is to use the **RULESURF** and **3DFACE** commands to create the required surfaces.

For example, the object in Figure 5-14A must be surfaced. This object has a hole through it. To surface the hole, first construct two 180° arcs where the hole is. Use a construction layer. Next, use **RULESURF** to create the surface connecting the large arc and the hole. Use **RULESURF** again to create the surface connecting the arc and the left end of the object. The two remaining surfaces can be created using **3DFACE**. The result is shown in Figure 5-14B.

Another example is surfacing the space between two holes, as shown in Figure 5-15A. Again, create arcs where the circles are. Then, use **RULESURF** to create the surface connecting the two inside arcs. Also use **RULESURF** to create the surface between the outer arcs and the outside edges. Use **3DFACE** to surface the remaining faces. The surfaced object is shown in Figure 5-15B.

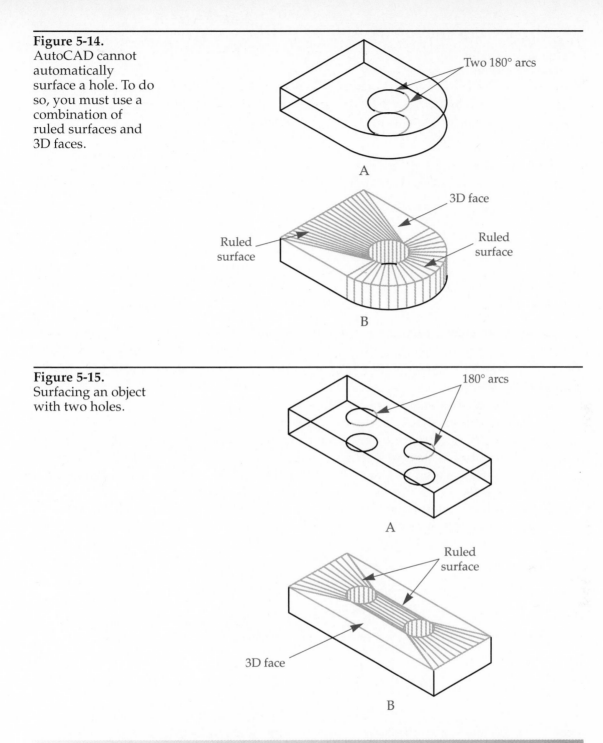

Figure 5-14.
AutoCAD cannot automatically surface a hole. To do so, you must use a combination of ruled surfaces and 3D faces.

Two 180° arcs

A

3D face

Ruled surface

Ruled surface

B

Figure 5-15.
Surfacing an object with two holes.

180° arcs

A

Ruled surface

3D face

B

Constructing a Surface Model

The following tutorial shows how surface modeling can be used to create an object composed of several different shapes. A twelve-button digitizer puck will be constructed. See Figure 5-16. If possible, enter the commands on your workstation as you go through this example. It is not necessary to complete this tutorial in one drawing session. Complete what you can, save your work, and return when you have available time.

> **NOTE** Follow the instructions in this tutorial exactly. Once you are experienced with these commands, experiment on your own with different ways of using them.

Figure 5-16.
A 3D surface model of a twelve-button puck.

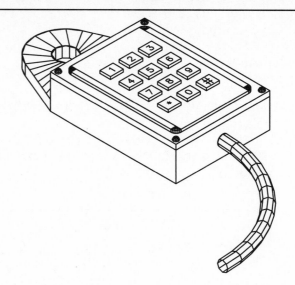

Drawing setup

You should plan your work carefully before beginning any 3D drawing. Draw the least amount of elements that can be used to complete the project. Also, use the following guidelines:

✓ Let the computer do as much work as possible.
✓ Use predrawn shapes and create blocks when possible.
✓ Save display configurations, such as views and viewports.
✓ As an optional step, make slides of each step of your work for later reference. Slides are covered in Chapter 28 of *AutoCAD and its Applications—Basics, Release 14.*

Begin your drawing by setting units as decimal and limits to 18,12. Set the grid spacing to .5 and snap spacing to .25. Then, create the following layers with the color indicated:

Layer name	Color
Body	red
Body-cap	white
Buttons	magenta
Button1	magenta
Button2	blue
Cable	green
Constr	blue
Edgesurf	green
Eyepiece	yellow
Eyesurf	yellow
Face1	green
Face2	cyan
Numbers	cyan
Screws	red

Using 3D shapes

The individual parts of the digitizer puck are shown in Figure 5-17. The first step is to create a one-unit cube as a basic 3D building block. This block can then be used for at least three of the parts on the puck. Rather than drawing the box as a wireframe and adding 3D faces to it, you can use the 3D surface-modeled box from the **3D Objects** dialog box or the **Box** button in the **Surfaces** toolbar.

```
Command: AI_BOX↵
Corner of box: 0,0↵
Length: 1↵
Cube/⟨Width⟩: C↵
Rotation angle about Z axis: 0↵
```

The box appears to be a wireframe, but it is actually a single entity composed of 3D faces.

Next, use the **BLOCK** command to make a block of the cube. Name it BOX. You can do this in the 3D display. Pick one of the corners as an insertion point using the **Endpoint** object snap, Figure 5-18.

Figure 5-17.
The components needed to make the puck.

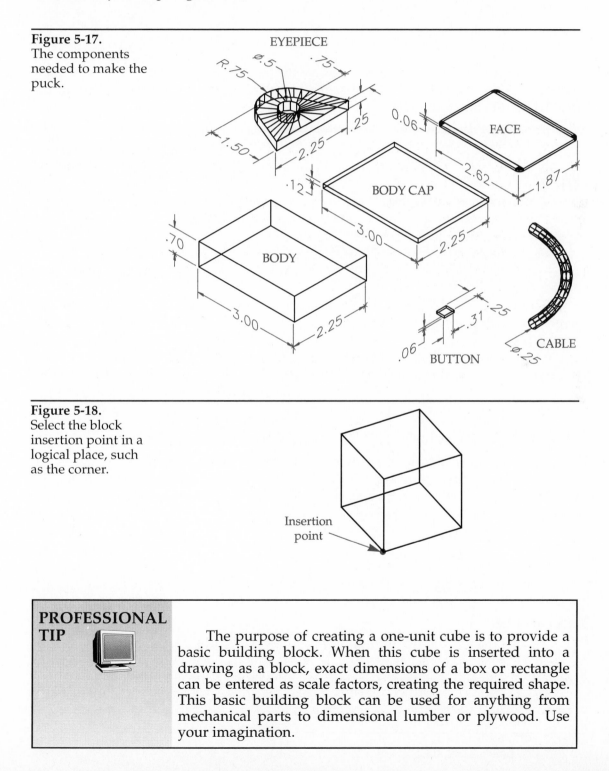

Figure 5-18.
Select the block insertion point in a logical place, such as the corner.

Insertion point

PROFESSIONAL TIP

The purpose of creating a one-unit cube is to provide a basic building block. When this cube is inserted into a drawing as a block, exact dimensions of a box or rectangle can be entered as scale factors, creating the required shape. This basic building block can be used for anything from mechanical parts to dimensional lumber or plywood. Use your imagination.

Inserting a 3D block

The block can now be inserted into the drawing to create the body of the puck. Change the current layer to Body. Return the display to the plan view. Use the **DDINSERT** or **INSERT** command to insert the BOX block. Use the following scale factors:

```
Command: I or DDINSERT↵
(Select the BOX block from the Insert dialog box and pick OK)
Insertion point: 0,0,0↵
X scale factor ⟨1⟩ / Corner / XYZ: X↵
    X scale factor ⟨1⟩ / Corner: 2.25↵
    Y scale factor (default=X): 3↵
    Z scale factor (default=X): .7↵
    Rotation angle ⟨0⟩: ↵
Command:
```

The body of the puck is now in place with the required dimensions. As an alternative, you can visually place and size a 3D block using the **Corner** option of the **INSERT** command. You might try it again for practice to see what the dynamic sizing of the **Corner** option provides.

Select the SW isometric viewpoint. Make layer 0 current and insert a copy of the BOX block. This time the cube is used to create a block for the puck's buttons. Insert the block as follows:

```
Command: I or DDINSERT↵
(Select the BOX block from the Insert dialog box and pick OK)
Insertion point: (pick a point)↵
X scale factor ⟨1⟩ / Corner / XYZ: X↵
    X scale factor ⟨1⟩ / Corner: .31↵
    Y scale factor (default=X): .25↵
    Z scale factor (default=X): .06↵
    Rotation angle ⟨0⟩: ↵
Command:
```

Now, make a block of the box you just inserted. Name it BUTTON and give it the same insertion point as shown in Figure 5-18. This block is used later to create an array of buttons. The next section shows how to construct a more detailed button having a curved surface.

Constructing a wireframe curved button (optional step)

The following example shows one way to create a wireframe model that you can place surface patches on using the **EDGESURF** command. A *surface patch* is a 3D mesh that creates a surface for a specified area. Begin construction of the button using the **LINE** command.

```
Command: LINE↵
From point: (pick a point)
To point: @.31,0↵
To point: @0,.25↵
To point: @-.31,0↵
To point: C↵
```

This creates the base of the button. Zoom in on the object so that it nearly fills the screen. This makes it easier to draw the vertical lines of the corners. Figure 5-19A shows these lines, which can be drawn using the **LINE** command as follows:

```
Command: LINE↵
From point: END↵
of (pick point P1)
To point: @0,0,.03↵
```

```
To point: ↵
Command: ↵
LINE From point: END↵
of (pick point P2)
To point: @0,0,.06↵
To point: ↵
```

The next step is to construct an arc connecting the tops of the two vertical lines. This arc represents the curved shape of the button surface. However, the UCS must be changed so that the X axis is the same direction as the line between P1 and P2. This places the new UCS in the same plane where the arc will be drawn. See Figure 5-19B.

```
Command: UCS↵
Origin/ZAxis/3point/OBject/View/X/Y/Z/Prev/Restore/Save/Del/?/⟨World⟩: ZA↵
Origin point ⟨0,0,0⟩: END↵
of (pick point P2)
Point on positive portion of Z-axis ⟨defaults⟩: @-1,0,0↵
```

If the UCS icon does not move to the new origin, use the **Origin** option of the **UCSICON** command to move the icon.

```
Command: UCSICON↵
ON/OFF/All/Noorigin/ORigin/⟨ON⟩: OR↵
```

The icon moves to the new origin. The UCS icon is a good reminder of the location of the origin of the current UCS.

Now the arc can be drawn. Refer to Figure 5-19C for the pick points of the arc. Use the **ARC** command as follows:

```
Command: ARC↵
Center/⟨Start point⟩: END↵
of (pick point P3)
Center/End/⟨Second point⟩: E↵
End point: END↵
of (pick point P4)
Angle/Direction/Radius/⟨Center point⟩: A↵
Included angle: 20↵
```

Figure 5-19.
Creating a wireframe of a curved button.

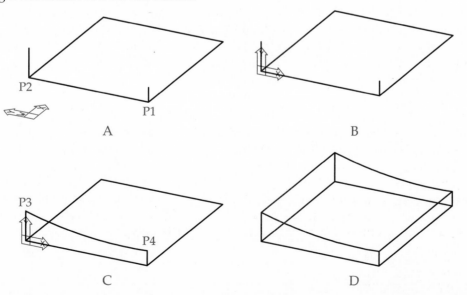

The final steps are to copy the two vertical lines and the arc to the opposite end of the button, and to connect the top edges of the button with straight lines. The completed drawing should look like Figure 5-19D.

Creating edge defined surfaces

Curved surfaces having four sides can be created using the **EDGESURF** command. This command was discussed earlier in this chapter. An *edge surface* is actually a matrix of 3D faces. The number of rows and columns of faces is controlled by the **SURFTAB1** and **SURFTAB2** system variables. Keep in mind that the greater the number of faces you have, the longer the regeneration time is, and the longer it takes to remove hidden lines using the **HIDE** command. Keep the **SURFTAB** values low for small objects.

PROFESSIONAL TIP   When working with 3D surfaces, determine the purpose of your drawing. How will you be viewing it? What other programs will you use to shade, render, or animate the object? If you will not be looking at certain sides of an object, do not apply surfacing to those sides. Also, avoid using large values for the **SURFTAB** variables.

First, set the **SURFTAB** variables. Then, set the current layer to Button1 and create the first surface patch. Refer to Figure 5-20A.

    Command: **SURFTAB1**↵
    New value for SURFTAB1 ⟨current⟩: **6**↵
    Command: **SURFTAB2**↵
    New value for SURFTAB2 ⟨current⟩: **2**↵
    Command: **EDGESURF**↵
    Select edge 1: (pick edge 1)
    Select edge 2: (pick edge 2)
    Select edge 3: (pick edge 3)
    Select edge 4: (pick edge 4)

The first line you pick is divided into six segments (**SURFTAB1**). The second edge is divided into two segments (**SURFTAB2**). See Figure 5-20B.

Next, copy the surface patch to the opposite end of the button. Your object should look like Figure 5-20C. Now, turn off layer Button1 and make layer Button2 current. This allows you to select the edges without the surface patch getting in the way. If you select the surface patch while defining a new surface patch, the message Object not usable to define surface patch appears on the command line.

Now, use **EDGESURF** to create the curved top surface of the button. Pick one of the ends that is already surfaced as the first edge. When the curved surface is completed, turn on layer Button1. Finally, use the **3DFACE** command on the two remaining sides. There is no need to use the **3DFACE** command on the bottom because it will sit on another surface. After using the **HIDE** command, the button looks like Figure 5-20D.

This shape can now be saved as a block or wblocked as a file. It is also a good idea to save your drawing at this point. You will use the blocks you have created to complete the digitizer puck later.

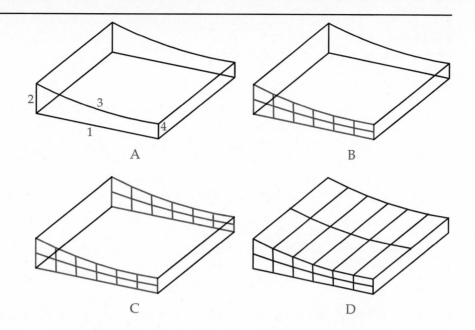

Figure 5-20.
Surfacing the curved button.

A

B

C

D

Using viewports to help create the puck

Viewports can be a great help in drawing 3D objects. Viewports will be used to help create the puck. To set the viewports, first zoom out so that the entire body shape is displayed. Then, use the **UCS** command to return to the World Coordinate System.

Use the **VPORTS** command and the default options to display three views of the part, Figure 5-21. Create a pictorial view in the right and lower-left viewports. First, pick in the right viewport to make it active. Select the SW isometric view. Make the lower-left viewport active and select the NW isometric viewpoint. Use the **ZOOM** command to magnify these views. Use **PAN** if necessary to center the objects in the viewports.

Next, pick the upper-left viewport to make it active and use the **PLAN** command to create a plan view. Use **ZOOM** and **PAN** to adjust all of the views as needed. The final arrangement of the viewports should be similar to Figure 5-22.

After you have adjusted all three viewports, study the orientation of the views in relation to the UCS icon. The ability to visualize the XYZ axes as they relate to the object is imperative to understanding 3D construction and multiple view layouts.

Figure 5-21.
Create a three-viewport display to help you draw the puck. The viewpoint for this display is -1,2,1.

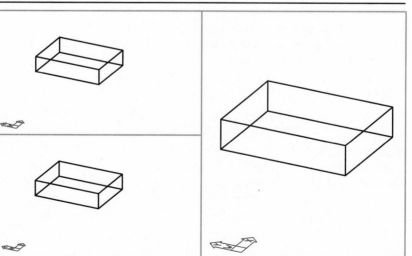

Figure 5-22.
Change the views so that each viewport shows a different aspect of the puck.

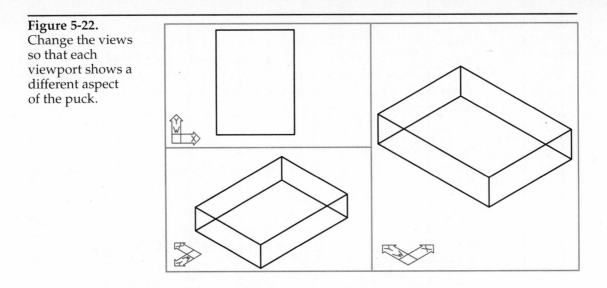

An important tool when working with viewports is the ability to store a configuration. If you need the configuration again, it can simply be recalled instead of created over again. Use the **Save** option of the **VPORTS** command to store a configuration. Save your current viewport configuration as follows:

    Command: VPORTS↵
    Save/Restore/Delete/Join/SIngle/?/2/⟨3⟩/4: S↵
    ?/Name for new viewport configuration: THREE↵

This viewport arrangement is now a named entity and can be recalled at any time. For example, use the **VPORTS** command and the **Single** option to return to one viewport. Then, use **VPORTS** again and the **Restore** option. Enter the name THREE for viewport configuration to restore. The configuration you just saved is restored.

Next, you need to add a "cap" to the puck body. First, set the current layer to Body-cap. Then, make the large viewport active. Insert the BOX block and attach it to the body at the insertion point shown in Figure 5-23A. Remember, the box is a one unit cube so you can enter the dimensions of the cap as scale factors.

    Command: I or DDINSERT↵
    (Select the BOX block from the Insert dialog box and pick OK)
    Insertion point: (pick the insertion point shown in Figure 5-23A)
    X scale factor ⟨1⟩ / Corner / XYZ: X↵
        X scale factor ⟨1⟩ / Corner: 2.25↵
        Y scale factor (default=X): 3↵
        Z scale factor (default=X): .12↵
        Rotation angle ⟨0⟩: ↵
    Command:

The inserted body cap is shown in Figure 5-23B.

Figure 5-23.
Inserting the BOX block to create the cap.

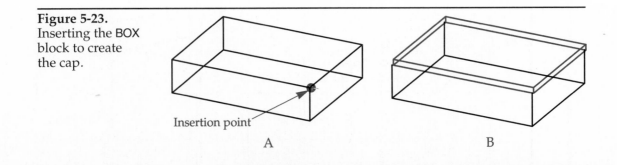

Insertion point

A

B

Using polylines in 3D

Next, you need to construct the face of the puck. Notice in Figure 5-17 that the face has filleted corners. You must construct it using a combination of polylines, ruled surfaces, and 3D faces. Since the face is placed on top of the body cap, create a UCS on that surface. Also, save the UCS for future use. Be sure the large viewport is active and use the following command sequence:

```
Command: UCS↵
Origin/ZAxis/3point/OBject/View/X/Y/Z/Prev/Restore/Save/Del/?/⟨World⟩: O↵
Origin point ⟨0,0,0⟩: (pick the top corner of the body cap above the insertion point)
Command: UCSICON↵
ON/OFF/All/Noorigin/ORigin ⟨ON⟩: A↵ (this applies the next option to all viewports)
ON/OFF/Noorigin/ORigin ⟨ON⟩: OR↵
Command: UCS↵
Origin/ZAxis/3point/OBject/View/X/Y/Z/Prev/Restore/Save/Del/?/⟨World⟩: S↵
?/Desired UCS name: FACE↵
```

Notice that the UCS icon is at the new origin in all three viewports. See Figure 5-24. With the UCS saved, it can be recalled at any time with the **Restore** option of the **UCS** command.

Begin drawing the puck face by making the upper-left viewport active. Change to the layer Face1. If you return to a single viewport, the object will be larger. This may make it easier to work on. Since you have saved the three-viewport configuration, you can always go back to it later. Next, turn off any running object snaps. Then, use the **PLINE** command to draw the face. Be sure to use the **Close** option to complete the shape.

```
Command: PLINE↵
From point: .19,.19↵
Arc/Close/Halfwidth/Length/Undo/Width/⟨Endpoint of line⟩: @1.87,0↵
Arc/Close/Halfwidth/Length/Undo/Width/⟨Endpoint of line⟩: @0,2.62↵
Arc/Close/Halfwidth/Length/Undo/Width/⟨Endpoint of line⟩: @1.87<180↵
Arc/Close/Halfwidth/Length/Undo/Width/⟨Endpoint of line⟩: C↵
```

If you returned to a single viewport, restore the three-viewport configuration. Your drawing should now look like Figure 5-25.

Figure 5-24.
Placing the UCS icon at the origin helps you visualize coordinates better.

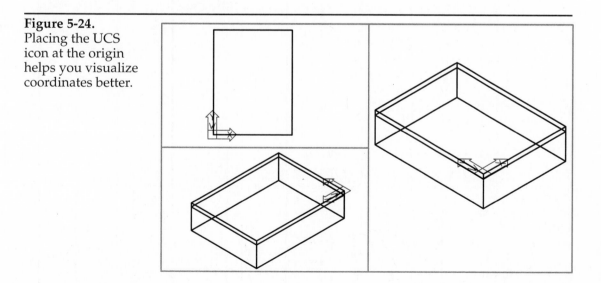

Figure 5-25.
Creating a wireframe of the face starts with drawing a closed polyline "on top" of the cap.

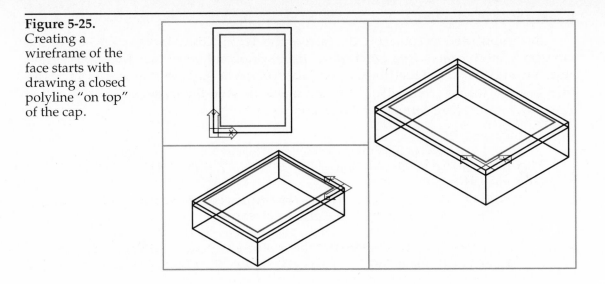

Next, place a .125 radius fillet on the corners of the polyline. Then, copy the filleted polyline on the Z axis using the following command sequence. Use the viewport that will allow you to draw most efficiently.

> Command: **CO** or **COPY**↵
> Select objects: *(select polyline)*
> 1 found
> Select objects: ↵
> ⟨Base point or displacement⟩/Multiple: **@**↵
> Second point of displacement: **@0,0,.06**↵

The result is shown in Figure 5-26.

Figure 5-26.
The face wireframe is completed by filleting the polyline and copying it on the Z axis.

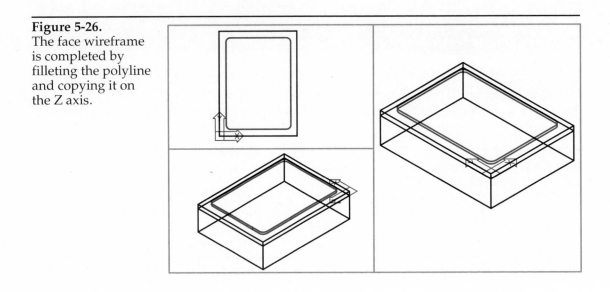

Using RULESURF to surface fillets

The **RULESURF** command is used to surface the round corners of the face and the top surface of the face at the corners. To do this efficiently, make a single view of the large viewport. Save this viewport configuration as ONE. Next, zoom in so that the object fills the screen. Use the **VIEW** command to save the current display as ALL. Now, zoom in on the front corner (insertion point) of the face and body cap. Save this display with the name CORNER.

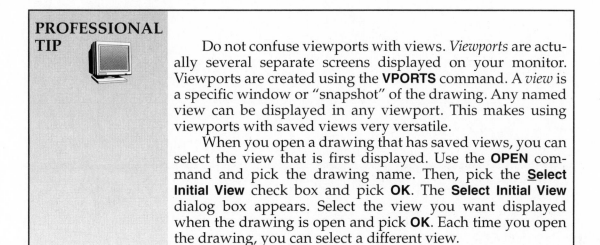

PROFESSIONAL TIP

Do not confuse viewports with views. *Viewports* are actually several separate screens displayed on your monitor. Viewports are created using the **VPORTS** command. A *view* is a specific window or "snapshot" of the drawing. Any named view can be displayed in any viewport. This makes using viewports with saved views very versatile.

When you open a drawing that has saved views, you can select the view that is first displayed. Use the **OPEN** command and pick the drawing name. Then, pick the **Select Initial View** check box and pick **OK**. The **Select Initial View** dialog box appears. Select the view you want displayed when the drawing is open and pick **OK**. Each time you open the drawing, you can select a different view.

Next, you need to place a point at the center of a fillet radius on the top of the face. This point is needed to construct the ruled surface. Change to the Constr layer, set an appropriate value for **PDMODE**, and set **PDSIZE** to .04. In this example, a **PDMODE** value of 3 is used so that the point appears as an "X." Then, use the **POINT** command to place a point at the center of the arc, Figure 5-27A. The **Center** object snap can be quickly accessed from the right-button cursor menu to locate the center of the arc.

Use the **EXPLODE** command to break apart the two polylines that represent the face. This lets you select the corner arcs with the **RULESURF** command, Figure 5-27B. Change to the Face2 layer, set **SURFTAB1** to 6, and select the **RULESURF** command.

> Command: **RULESURF**↵
> Select first defining curve: (*pick curve 1 in Figure 5-27B*)
> Select second defining curve: (*pick curve 2 in Figure 5-27B*)

The corner is now surfaced with six segments. See Figure 5-27C. If you want more or fewer segments, erase the ruled surface and redraw it with a different **SURFTAB1** setting.

Next, a ruled surface must be applied to the top of the face. This will connect the corner arc to the point at the center of the arc. You must pick the arc as the first defining curve, not the ruled surface. If you pick the ruled surface, the message Object not usable to define ruled surface appears on the command line. To avoid picking the ruled surface, zoom in on the arc and the point, Figure 5-27D. Notice that the ruled surface on the corner is composed of straight segments and the corner arc is smooth. Use the **RULESURF** command to pick the top curve and the center point. After the top is surfaced, you can either erase the point or turn off the Constr layer. The corner should look like Figure 5-27E. Save your work before continuing.

Figure 5-27.
Surfacing the corners of the face. A—Place a point at the center of the fillet.
B—Create a ruled surface using the corner arcs. C—The ruled surface on the edge of the corner.
D—Zoom in to make sure you pick the arc, not the first ruled surface, to create an edge
surface on the top of the corner. E—The surfaced corner.

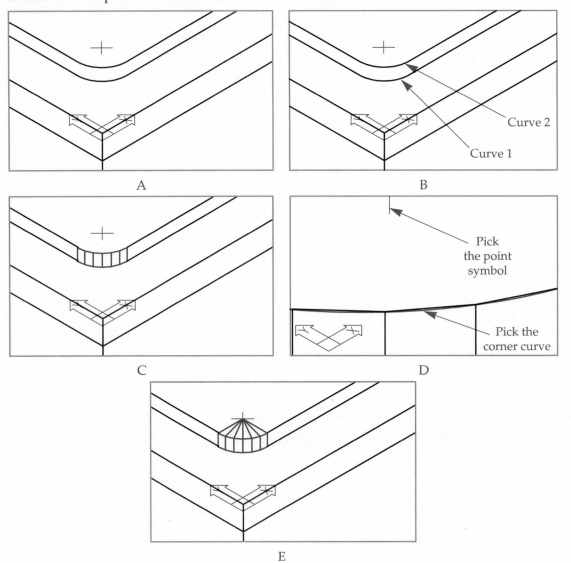

❑ Begin a new drawing and name it EX5-2.
❑ Draw a circle 2″ (50mm) in diameter.
❑ Copy the circle up four units on the Z axis.
❑ Use the **VPOINT** command to get an isometric view (-1,-1,1) of the circles.
❑ Make two copies of the circles so that your drawing looks like the one shown on the following page.
❑ Set the **SURFTAB1** variable to 4 and use the **RULESURF** command on the first set of circles.
❑ Set the **SURFTAB1** variable to 8 and use the **RULESURF** command on the second set of circles.

❑ Set the **SURFTAB1** variable to 16 and use the **RULESURF** command on the third set of circles.
❑ Save your drawing as EX5-2.

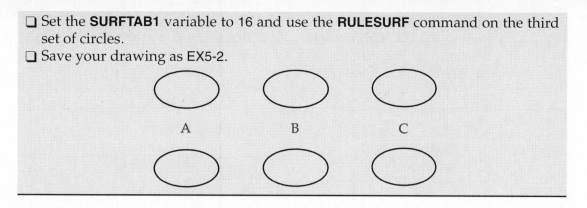

Using **MIRROR** and **3DFACE** on 3D objects

You can repeat the above procedure for each of the three remaining corners. However, it is much faster to let AutoCAD do this for you with the **MIRROR** command. Be sure you have a single viewport and restore the ALL view. For this example, turn ortho on and reflect the surfaces along the X axis. Then reflect *both* corners along the Y axis. Use the **Midpoint** object snap to pick the mirror line. Do not delete the old objects.

Now, there are two 3D faces that must be constructed. Use the **VIEW** command to create a view of the upper-left corner. Name this view CORNER2. Next, use the **VPORTS** command to create a two-viewport vertical configuration. Save it as TWO. Restore the CORNER2 view in the left viewport and the CORNER view in the right viewport. You may also want to remake the CORNER view so that it more closely matches CORNER2. To do this, use the following command sequence:

```
Command: VIEW↵
?/Delete/Restore/Save/Window: R↵
   View name to restore: CORNER.↵
Command: ↵
?/Delete/Restore/Save/Window: W↵
   View name to save: CORNER.↵
First corner: (pick first window corner)
Other corner: (pick second window corner)
```

Your screen should look like Figure 5-28.

Now, you can apply 3D faces to the vertical side of the puck face and the top surface between the rule-surfaced corners. Make sure the Face2 layer is current. Set the **Endpoint** running object snap.

Figure 5-28.
To draw a 3D face on the edge of the puck face, create two viewports. Then, display a different corner in each.

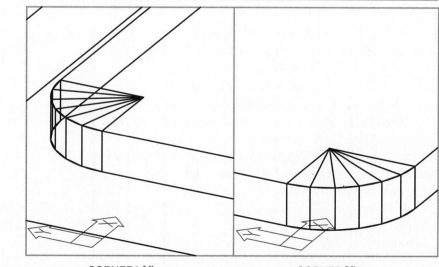

CORNER2 View   CORNER View

Draw the vertical 3D face using the pick points shown in Figure 5-29A. Then, press [Enter] to end the **3DFACE** command. Remember, to activate a viewport, simply move the cursor to the viewport and pick. Next, draw the top face between the centers of the arcs and the edge of the previous face, Figure 5-29B.

Figure 5-29.
A—Creating a 3D face on the edge of the puck face. B—Creating a 3D face on the top of the puck face. C—The finished 3D faces.

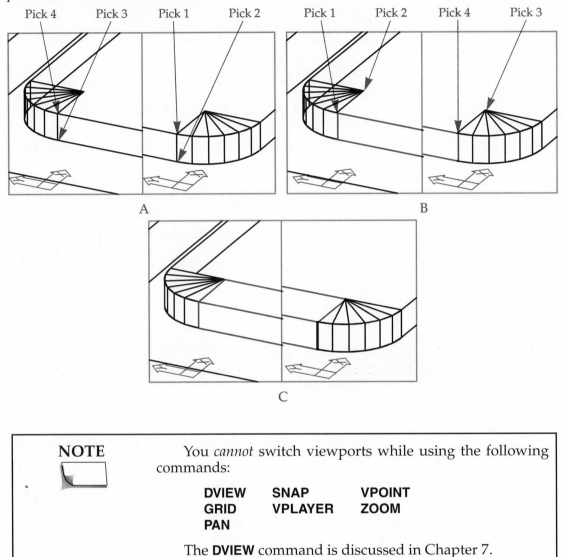

A

B

C

NOTE	You *cannot* switch viewports while using the following commands:

DVIEW	SNAP	VPOINT
GRID	VPLAYER	ZOOM
PAN		

The **DVIEW** command is discussed in Chapter 7.

Restore the ONE viewport and the ALL view. Use the **MIRROR** command to copy the 3D faces and ruled surfaces to the opposite side of the face. See Figure 5-30.

Next, you need to add 3D faces to the narrow vertical ends of the puck face. Then, add one large 3D face to the top of the puck face. It may be easier to change the viewpoint, or even return to a plan view, to draw the 3D face on the top. Use the **3DFACE** command and pick the four corners indicated in Figure 5-31. Use the **Endpoint** object snap to help.

The completed face is shown in Figure 5-32 after using the **HIDE** command. Your screen display may have a line or two missing where the face rests on the body cap. This is because those two surfaces are at the same elevation and AutoCAD "thinks" some lines on the face may be hidden.

AutoCAD and its Applications—Advanced

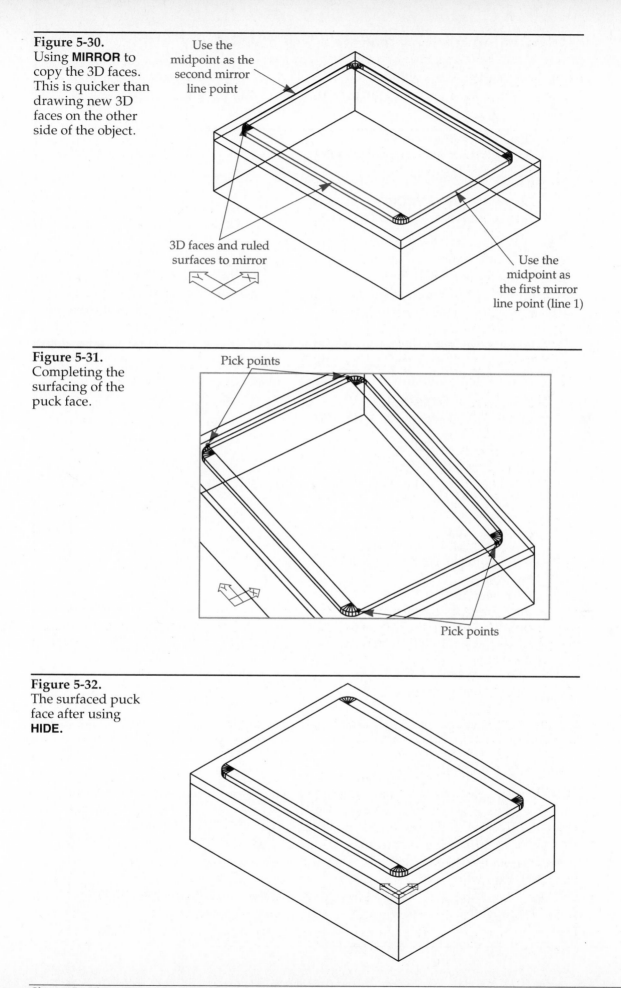

Figure 5-30.
Using **MIRROR** to copy the 3D faces. This is quicker than drawing new 3D faces on the other side of the object.

Use the midpoint as the second mirror line point

3D faces and ruled surfaces to mirror

Use the midpoint as the first mirror line point (line 1)

Figure 5-31.
Completing the surfacing of the puck face.

Pick points

Pick points

Figure 5-32.
The surfaced puck face after using **HIDE.**

Constructing the eyepiece with RULESURF

To draw the eyepiece, first set the Eyepiece layer current and restore the viewport configuration THREE. Make the upper-left viewport active and display a plan view showing the upper half of the object. Then, make the large viewport active and use **VPOINT** as follows:

    Command: **-VP** *or* **VPOINT**↵
    Rotate/⟨View point⟩ ⟨*current*⟩: **-2,1.5,1**↵

Next, pick the lower-left viewport, and continue as follows:

    Command: **-VP** *or* **VPOINT**↵
    Rotate/⟨View point⟩ ⟨*current*⟩**: -1,-1,1**↵

Your display should now look like Figure 5-33A.

Now, create a new UCS by moving the origin to where the eyepiece attaches to the body. See Figure 5-33B. Save the new UCS as EYEPIECE. Move the UCS icon to the new origin in all viewports. Save this viewport configuration as THREE. Replace the existing viewport. This new UCS allows you to enter the dimensions of the eyepiece from the origin.

To begin drawing the eyepiece, make the upper-left viewport active and return to a single viewport. Use the **CIRCLE** and **LINE** commands to draw the outline as follows. Then, use the **TRIM** command to cut away the unused portion of the circle.

    Command: **C** *or* **CIRCLE**↵
    3P/2P/TTR/⟨Center point⟩: **1.125,.75**↵
    Diameter/⟨Radius⟩: **D**↵
    Diameter: **.5**↵
    Command: ↵
    CIRCLE 3P/2P/TTR/⟨Center point⟩: **@**↵
    Diameter/⟨Radius⟩: **.75**↵
    Command: **L** *or* **LINE**↵
    From point: **0,0**↵
    To point: **TAN**↵
    to (*pick the left side of the large circle*)
    To point: ↵
    Command: ↵
    LINE From point: **2.25,0**↵
    To point: **TAN**↵
    to (*pick the right side of the large circle*)
    To point:↵
    Command: **TR** *or* **TRIM**↵
    Select cutting edge(s)...

Figure 5-33.
A—Change the views to help you draw the eyepiece. B—Place a new UCS at the bottom corner of the puck body to help you locate coordinates better.

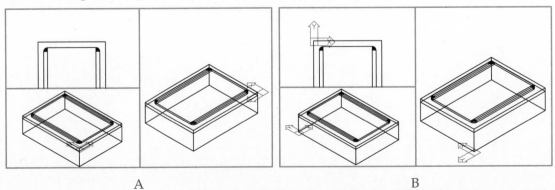

A   B

Select objects: (*pick the two tangent lines*)
Select objects: ↵
⟨Select object to trim⟩/Project/Edge/Undo: (*pick the inside portion of the large circle*)
⟨Select object to trim⟩/Project/Edge/Undo: ↵

Restore the viewport configuration named THREE. Use the **VIEW** command to window a view called EYEPIECE2 in the right viewport. Window in closely on the eyepiece. Restore this view. Your drawing should look similar to Figure 5-34A.

Activate the right viewport and copy the eyepiece outline .25″ on the Z axis. Draw a line connecting the two ends of the top surface of the eyepiece. The 3D wireframe of the eyepiece is complete, Figure 5-34B.

However, before you begin surfacing, it is important to determine how to surface the top plane of the eyepiece. Remember that **RULESURF** requires two separate entities, and closed objects, such as circles, cannot be used with an open object. Therefore, you must redraw the circle as arcs on the Constr layer before surfacing.

First, set the Constr layer current. Then, change the UCS origin to the top surface of the eyepiece directly above the current origin. Zoom in on the top circle of the eyepiece. Use the **ARC** command's **Center, Start, End** option to draw three arcs. Use the **Center**, **Quadrant**, and **Endpoint** object snaps, as indicated in Figure 5-35A. Then, draw a point at the quadrant between arcs two and three. Be sure **PDMODE** is set to 3 and **PDSIZE** is set to .08.

Figure 5-34.
A—First, draw the bottom of the eyepiece. B—Then, copy the objects on the Z axis to create the top.

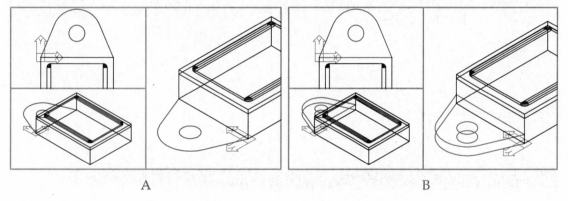

Figure 5-35.
A—Draw three arcs and a point to help you surface the top of the eyepiece.
B—The pick points to use when surfacing the eyepiece.

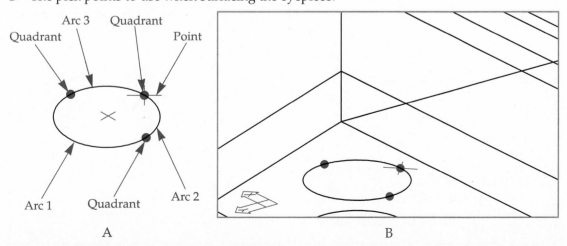

You can now use the **RULESURF** command to surface the entire eyepiece. Change the current layer to Eyesurf. Then, create the following four ruled surfaces:
- The first ruled surface uses the point on the circle and the adjacent line, Figure 5-36A.
- The second ruled surface uses arc 2 and the adjacent angled line, Figure 5-36B.
- The third ruled surface uses arc 1 and the large outside arc, Figure 5-36C.
- The fourth ruled surface uses arc 3 and the adjacent angled line, Figure 5-36D.

Figure 5-36.
Use **RULESURF** four times to completely surface the top of the eyepiece.

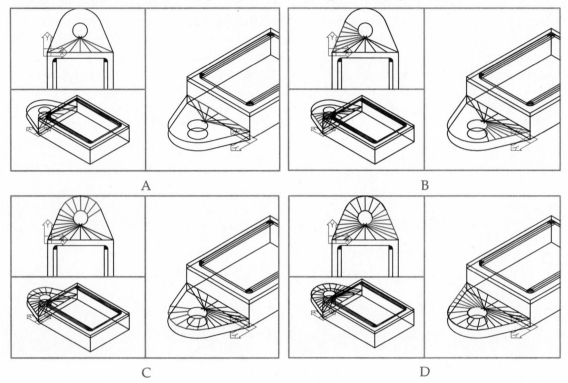

A   B

C   D

NOTE

Be sure to pick near the same end of both entities when using the **RULESURF** command. If you pick near opposite ends of the two entities, the surfacing segment lines cross over each other. For example, notice in A below that the first pick is located near the far end of the line. Pick number 2 is at the near end of the arc, diagonal to pick 1. This results in crossed segments. In B below, pick points 1 and 2 are near the same ends of the line and arc, or adjacent to each other. This creates a properly ruled surface.

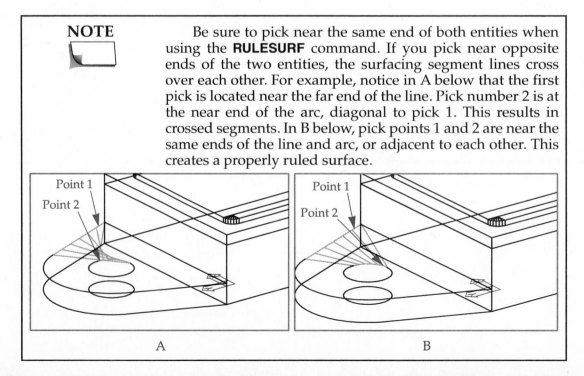

A   B

The hole and the round end of the eyepiece must also be surfaced. These two surfaces are created just like the filleted corners on the puck face. Use zoom so you can pick the original circle and not the ruled surface. Since you cannot mix open and closed paths, remove the arcs from the drawing by turning off the Constr layer. This ensures you will not select an arc and a circle. Use a tight zoom and pick the circles, Figure 5-37. Also, use the **RULESURF** command to surface the curved end of the eyepiece.

Be sure to change **SURFTAB1** if you want more than six segments for the surface of the hole. A **SURFTAB1** setting of **8** is used for the illustration in Figure 5-38. The larger the value, the smoother the circle.

The final step in constructing the eyepiece is to create a 3D face on each vertical side. You can either draw two separate faces, or draw one face and mirror it. When you are finished, use the **HIDE** command to be sure that you have created all of the needed surfaces. See Figure 5-38.

Figure 5-37.
Use zoom to make sure you pick the circles, and not the ruled surface.

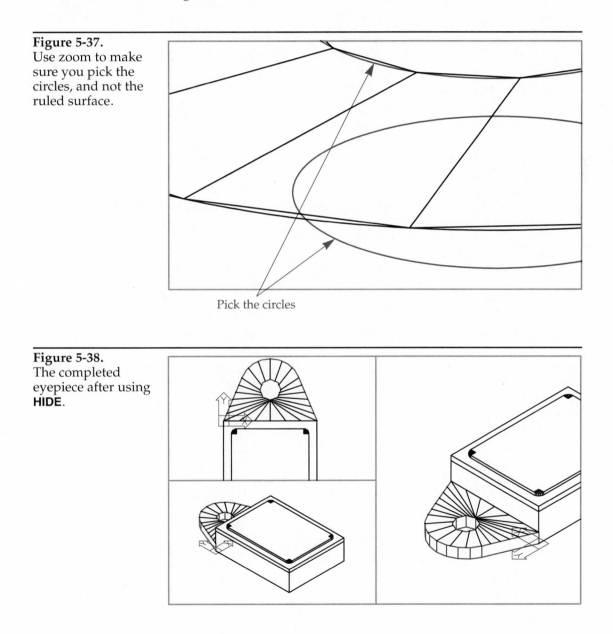

Pick the circles

Figure 5-38.
The completed eyepiece after using **HIDE**.

Constructing a cable with REVSURF

The **REVSURF** (revolved surface) command draws a symmetrical shape revolved around a central axis. To draw a revolved surface, you need a profile and an axis (line). The profile is the shape to be revolved. AutoCAD calls this profile the *path curve*. The *axis* is a line that the shape is revolved around. For the puck cable, the path curve is a circle. A revolved surface can be drawn to fill any angle. A 360° angle creates a full circle. For the puck cable, the circle is revolved 90°.

The **SURFTAB1** variable controls the number of segments on the surface around the axis. The **SURFTAB2** variable controls the number of segments on the path curve. Before using the **REVSURF** command, determine the number of segments needed and set the **SURFTAB** variables. For the puck cable, set **SURFTAB1** to 12 and **SURFTAB2** to 8. This creates eight segments around the circumference of the circle and twelve segments around the axis.

To draw the cable, first make the Cable layer current. Then, use the **VPORTS**, **VPOINT**, **PAN**, and **ZOOM** commands to adjust the viewports so they look like Figure 5-39. For the lower-left viewport, you need to change the UCS. Use the **UCS** command as follows:

```
Command: UCS↵
Origin/ZAxis/3point/OBject/View/X/Y/Z/Prev/Restore/Save/Del/?/⟨World⟩: X↵
Rotation angle about X axis ⟨0⟩: 90↵
Command: ↵
Origin/ZAxis/3point/OBject/View/X/Y/Z/Prev/Restore/Save/Del/?/⟨World⟩: Y↵
Rotation angle about Y axis ⟨0⟩: -90↵
Command: ↵
Origin/ZAxis/3point/OBject/View/X/Y/Z/Prev/Restore/Save/Del/?/⟨World⟩: O↵
Origin point ⟨0,0,0⟩: END↵
of (pick the corner shown in the large viewport of Figure 5-39)
```

Then, make the lower-left viewport active. Use the **PLAN** command to make the viewport plan to the current UCS. Once your display looks like Figure 5-39, save the viewport configuration as CABLE.

Now, create a new UCS on the end of the puck. Name this UCS CABLE. Use the **3point** and **Save** options of the **UCS** command as follows. Refer to Figure 5-40.

Figure 5-39.
Create a new viewport configuration to help draw the cable.

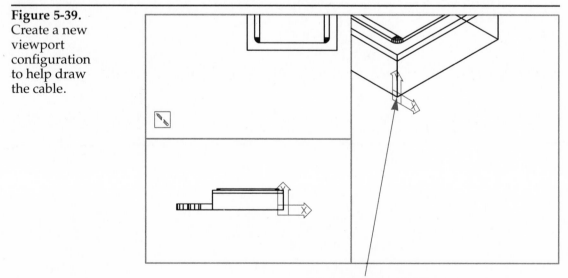

Origin of the new UCS

Figure 5-40.
Create a new UCS
on the end of the
puck body. Pick the
origin, X axis, and Y
axis as shown here.

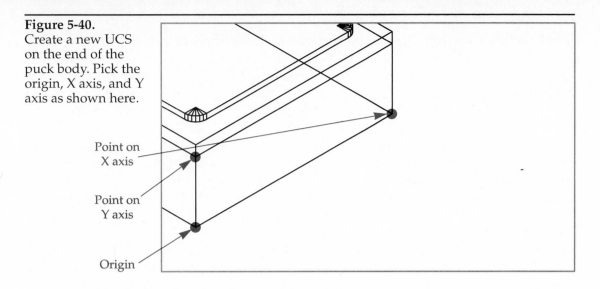

Point on
X axis

Point on
Y axis

Origin

```
Command: UCS↵
Origin/ZAxis/3point/OBject/View/X/Y/Z/Prev/Restore/Save/Del/?/⟨World⟩: 3↵
Origin point ⟨0,0,0⟩: END↵
of (pick the origin)
Point on positive portion of the X-axis ⟨current⟩: END↵
of (pick a point on the new X axis)
Point on positive-Y portion of the UCS XY plane ⟨0.00,1.00,0.00⟩: END↵
of (pick a point on the new Y axis)
Command: UCS↵
Origin/ZAxis/3point/OBject/View/X/Y/Z/Prev/Restore/Save/Del/?/⟨World⟩: S↵
?/Desired UCS name: CABLE↵
```

Make the large viewport active. You can now create the profile and the axis. Use the **CIRCLE** and **LINE** commands as follows:

```
Command: CIRCLE↵
3P/2P/TTR/⟨Center point⟩: 1.125,.35,0↵
Diameter/⟨Radius⟩: D↵
Diameter: .25↵
Command: LINE↵
From point: -1.5,1,0↵
To point: -1.5,-1,0↵
To point: ↵
```

Set the two **SURFTAB** variables and then use the **REVSURF** command to complete the cable as follows:

```
Command: SURFTAB1↵
New value for SURFTAB1 ⟨current⟩: 12↵
Command: SURFTAB2↵
New value for SURFTAB2 ⟨current⟩: 8↵
Command: REVSURF↵
Select path curve: (pick the path curve circle as shown in Figure 5-41A)
Select axis of revolution: (pick the axis as shown in Figure 5-41A)
Start angle ⟨0⟩: ↵
Included angle (+ = ccw, − = cw) ⟨Full circle⟩: -90↵
Command:
```

You can now erase the axis line. The completed cable is shown in Figure 5-41B after using the **HIDE** command. Save your work before continuing.

Figure 5-41.
A—The path curve on the end of the puck and the axis of revolution. B—The completed cable.

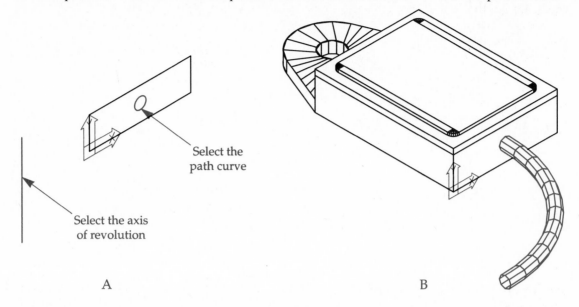

Select the
path curve

Select the axis
of revolution

A

B

Creating screw heads with the DOME command

The **3D Objects** dialog box and the **Surfaces** toolbar both contain three different spherical shapes. These are dome, dish, and sphere. The dome and the dish are simply one half of a sphere. For the puck, domes are used to represent screw heads on the face.

To draw the screw heads, first set the Screws layer current. Then, restore the FACE UCS. It may be easiest to switch to a single viewport and zoom in on the origin corner of the puck. Next, draw the screw heads as follows:

> Command: *(pick **Dome** from the **3D Objects** dialog box or **Surfaces** toolbar)*
> Center of dome: **.095,.095.**↵
> Diameter/⟨radius⟩: **D**↵
> Diameter: **.125**↵
> Number of longitudinal segments ⟨16⟩: **8**↵
> Number of latitudinal segments ⟨8⟩: **4**↵

This places one screw head on the face, Figure 5-42A. Now, use the **ARRAY** command to create the other three screw heads as follows:

> Command: **AR** *or* **ARRAY**↵
> Select objects: **L**↵
> Select objects: ↵
> Rectangular or Polar array (⟨R⟩/P): ↵
> Number of rows (---) ⟨1⟩: **2**↵
> Number of columns (⫿⫿⫿) ⟨1⟩: **2**↵
> Unit cell distance between rows (---): **2.81**↵
> Distance between columns (⫿⫿⫿): **2.06**↵
> Command:

Figure 5-42B shows the array of four domes on the digitizer puck after using **HIDE**.

Figure 5-42.
Use domes to represent screw heads on the face of the puck. A—Draw one dome in the lower-left corner. B—Use **ARRAY** to copy the dome to the other three locations.

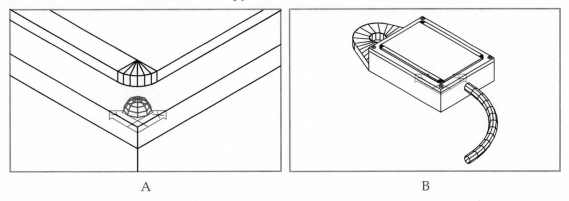

A   B

Inserting the button 3D block

The last thing to do is add the buttons. This digitizer has twelve buttons. Earlier, you created a block called BUTTON. You must insert this block on the face of the puck. First, set the Buttons layer current. Then, create and save a new UCS as follows:

    Command: **UCS**↵
    Origin/ZAxis/3point/OBject/View/X/Y/Z/Prev/Restore/Save/Del/?/⟨World⟩: **O**↵
    Origin point ⟨0,0,0⟩: **.19,.19,.06**↵
    Command: ↵
    Origin/ZAxis/3point/OBject/View/X/Y/Z/Prev/Restore/Save/Del/?/⟨World⟩: **S**↵
    ?/Desired UCS name: **BUTTON**↵
    Command:

For the insert operation, you need only a single view of the object on the screen. If you did not switch to a single view for the screw heads, switch to one now. Then, insert the buttons as follows:

    Command: **MINSERT**↵
    Block name: (or ?): **BUTTON**↵
      Insertion point: **.3125,.5**↵
    X scale factor ⟨1⟩ / Corner / Corner / XYZ: ↵
      Y scale factor ⟨1⟩ (default=X): ↵
      Rotation angle ⟨0⟩: ↵
    Number of rows (---) ⟨1⟩: **4**↵
    Number of columns (⁞⁞⁞) ⟨1⟩: **3**↵
    Unit cell or distance between rows (---): **.457**↵
    Distance between columns (⁞⁞⁞): **.457**↵

The completed puck is shown in Figure 5-43.

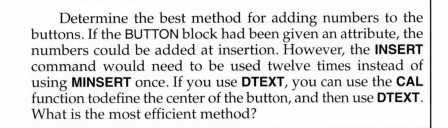

NOTE   Determine the best method for adding numbers to the buttons. If the BUTTON block had been given an attribute, the numbers could be added at insertion. However, the **INSERT** command would need to be used twelve times instead of using **MINSERT** once. If you use **DTEXT**, you can use the **CAL** function todefine the center of the button, and then use **DTEXT**. What is the most efficient method?

Figure 5-43.
The completed puck
with buttons.

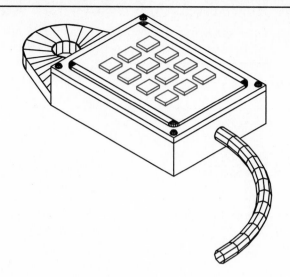

Chapter Test

Write your answers in the spaces provided.

1. Name three commands that allow you to create different types of meshes._____

   _____

2. What command creates a surface mesh between four edges?_____
3. How must the four edges be related when using the command in Question 2?

   _____

   _____

4. What values does AutoCAD need to know for a 3D mesh? _____

   _____

5. AutoCAD's surface meshing commands create what type of entities? _____

   _____

6. Which surface mesh command allows you to rotate a profile about an axis to
   create a symmetrical object? _____

7. What object does **TABSURF** create? _____

   _____

   _____

8. What do the **SURFTAB1** and **SURFTAB2** variables control?_____

   _____

   _____

9. Name three entities that can be connected with the **RULESURF** command._____

   _____

10. When using **RULESURF**, what happens if the two objects are selected near oppo-
    site ends? _____

    _____

    _____

11. Why should you avoid using large numbers for the **SURFTAB** settings? _____

_____

_____

12. What objects can be used to create a ruled surface with **RULESURF**? _____

_____

Drawing Problems

Construct 3D surface models of the following problems. For objects without dimensions, measure directly from the text. Problems 1–8 are objects that were drawn as problems in Chapter 1, problems 9–13 are problems from Chapter 3. Save the models as **P5-1**, **P5-2**, *etc.*

1.

2.

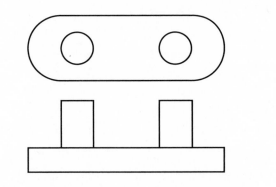

3.

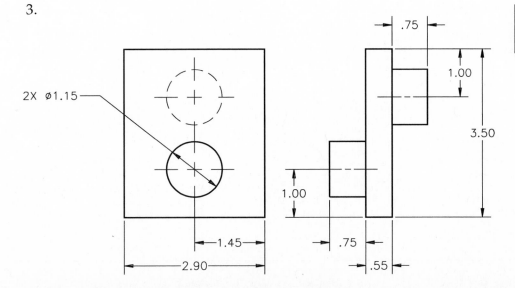

2X ⌀1.15

.75

1.00

3.50

1.00

1.45

2.90

.75

.55

4.

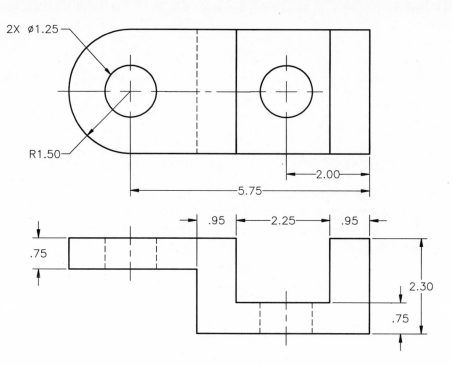

5.

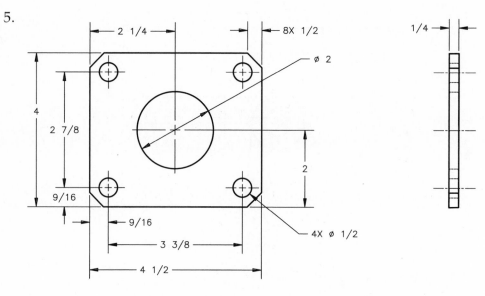

6.

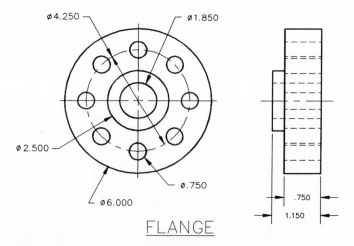

FLANGE

7.

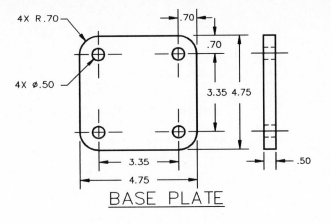

4X R.70

.70

.70

4X Ø.50

3.35 4.75

3.35

4.75

.50

BASE PLATE

8.

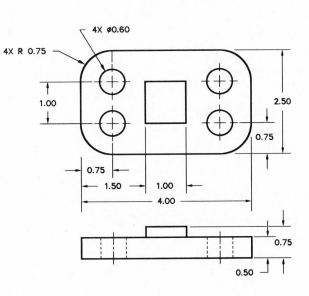

4X Ø0.60

4X R 0.75

1.00

2.50

0.75

0.75

1.50   1.00

4.00

0.75

0.50

9.

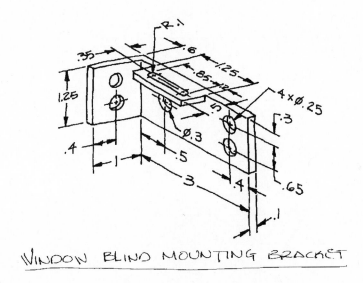

R.1

.35

.6

1.25

.85

1.25

.3

4XØ.25

Ø.3

.5

.4

.5

3

.4

.65

.1

WINDOW BLIND MOUNTING BRACKET

10.

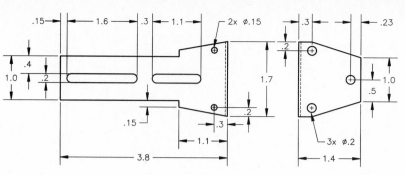

MATERIAL THICKNESS = .125"

11.

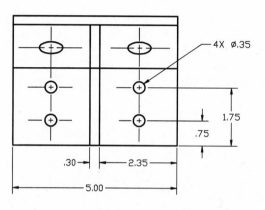

4X Ø.35

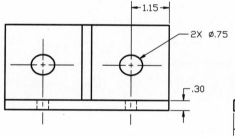

2X Ø.75

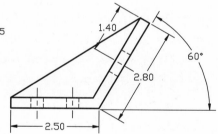

12.

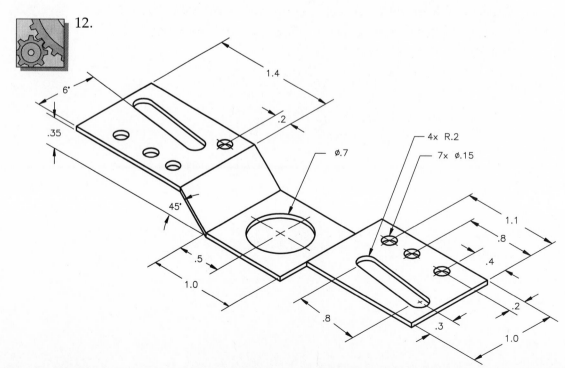

13.

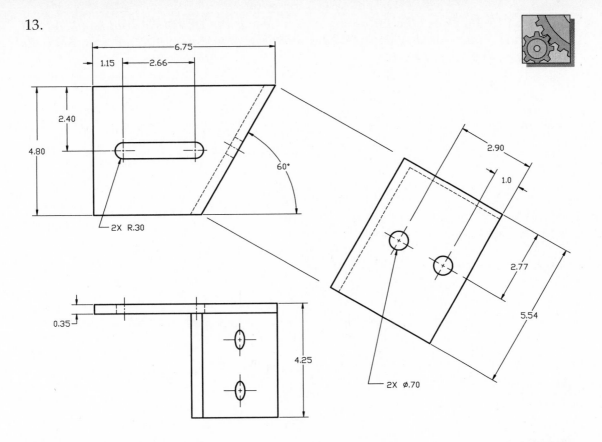

14. Create a surface model of a glass using the profile shown.

A. Use the **REVSURF** command to construct the glass.

B. Use the dimensions given for height and radii.

C. Set the **SURFTAB1** variable to 16.

D. Set the **SURFTAB2** variable to 8.

E. Use **HIDE** to remove hidden lines.

F. Construct the glass a second time using different **SURFTAB** settings.

G. Plot the drawing on B-size bond both as a wireframe and with hidden lines removed.

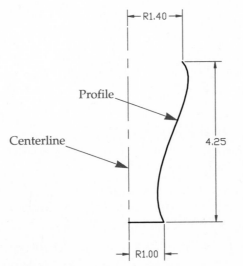

*Problems 15–16. Draw the following objects using the **REVSURF** command. Accept the default values for segments. Display the objects and use **HIDE** on each. Save the drawings as P5-15 and P5-16.*

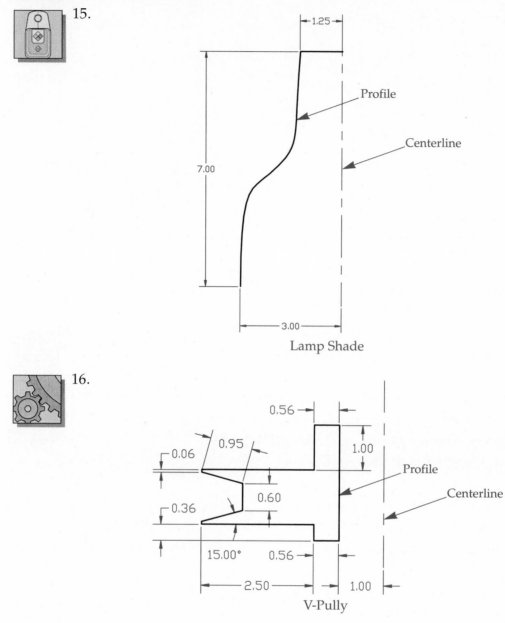

15.

Lamp Shade

16.

V-Pully

Problems 17–19. Problems 17 through 19 are plans of two houses and a cabin. Create a 3D model of the house(s) assigned by your instructor. Use all modeling techniques covered in this chapter.

A. Establish multiple viewports.

B. Create named User Coordinate Systems for the floor plan and the various wall elevations.

C. Create named viewport configurations (using one viewport) of single floors or walls so you can display the working areas as large as possible on the screen.

D. Use the dimensions given or alter the room sizes and arrangements to suit your own design. Use your own dimensions for anything not specified.

E. Plot the model on B-size or C-size sheet with hidden lines removed.

17.

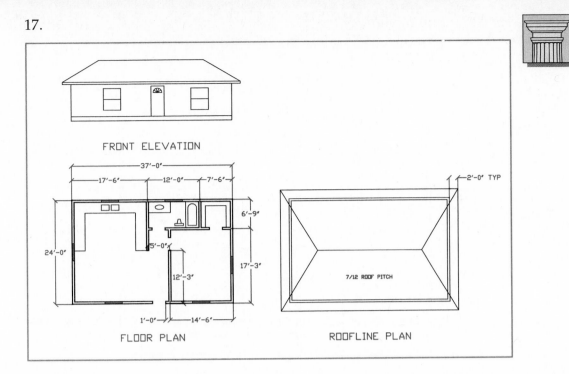

FRONT ELEVATION

FLOOR PLAN

ROOFLINE PLAN

18.

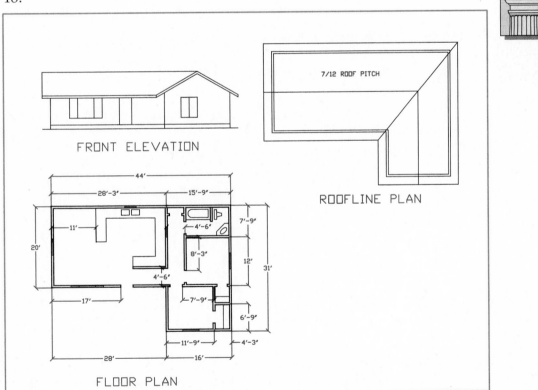

FRONT ELEVATION

ROOFLINE PLAN

FLOOR PLAN

19.

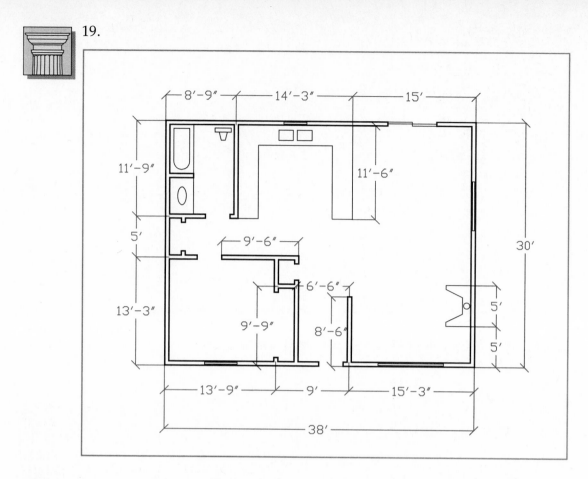

20. Complete the digitizer puck that was demonstrated in the tutorial.

  A. Add numbers to the buttons.

  B. Redraw as many 3D faces as possible using the **Invisible** option of the **3DFACE** command.

  C. Delete the square buttons and insert the curved buttons.

  D. Generate laser prints or pen plots on A-size or B-size paper showing the view in each of the four compass quadrants.

Editing Three-Dimensional Objects

Learning Objectives

After completing this chapter, you will be able to:
- ○ Use grips to edit 3D objects.
- ○ Align, rotate, and mirror 3D objects.
- ○ Trim and extend 3D objects.
- ○ Create fillets and rounds.
- ○ Edit polygon meshes.

It is always important to use proper editing techniques and commands. This is especially true when using a variety of User Coordinate Systems and 3D objects. This chapter covers the correct procedures for editing 3D objects.

Changing Properties

The **CHANGE** command is often used to change the properties of 2D objects. However, it has some limitations when an object is not perpendicular to the Z axis of the current UCS. If you use the **CHANGE** command on this type of object, AutoCAD displays this message:

> n found
> n was not parallel with UCS.

Instead of the **CHANGE** command, use the **DDCHPROP** or **CHPROP** command. These commands can change an entity even if it is not parallel to the current UCS. The **DDCHPROP** command allows you to change properties in the **Change Properties** dialog box. If you use the **CHPROP** command, you must specify the information on the command line.

To change all aspects of the object, including the location, use the **DDMODIFY** command. This can be accessed by picking the **Properties** button in the **Object Properties** toolbar. This opens the **Modify** dialog box. In this dialog box, you can change the properties, size, and coordinate location of the object.

Using Grips to Edit 3D Objects

Using grips is an efficient way to edit 3D objects. For an in-depth discussion on using grips, refer to Chapter 12 of *AutoCAD and its Applications, Basics—Release 14*. Editing should be done in a 3D view where you can see the change dynamically. For example, to change the height of a cone using grips, first change to a 3D view, such as the SW isometric view. Next, pick anywhere on the cone and the grips appear, Figure 6-1A. Then, pick the grip at the apex of the cone so it becomes hot, Figure 6-1B. A hot grip is a red square that is filled solid. The **STRETCH** operation can be completed as follows:

```
**STRETCH**
⟨Stretch to point⟩/Base point/Copy/Undo/eXit: .XY↵
of (pick the grip at the cone apex again)
(need Z): 5↵
Command:
```

You can move a hot grip around the screen with your pointing device. It appears that the grip is moving in all three (XYZ) directions. However, this is misleading. You are actually moving the grip in the XY plane. If you pick a point, the Z value of the grip is changed to 0. In other words, you have placed the grip on the current XY plane. Therefore, use XYZ filters or enter relative coordinates to edit 3D objects.

AutoCAD User's Guide **13**

ALIGN
AL

Modify
↦ 3D Operation
↦ Align

Aligning 3D Object

The **ALIGN** command enables you to correct errors of 3D construction and quickly manipulate 3D shapes. **ALIGN** requires existing points (source), and the new location of those existing points (destination). The **ALIGN** command can be issued by selecting **Align** from the **3D Operation** cascading menu of the **Modify** pull-down menu, or entering AL or ALIGN at the Command: prompt.

For an example, refer to Figure 6-2. The wedge in Figure 6-2A is aligned in its new position as follows. Set the **Intersection** running object snap to make point selection easier. Refer to the figure for the pick points.

Figure 6-1.
Using grips to edit a 3D object. A—First, pick on the object to make the grips warm. Then, pick the grip to edit so that it becomes hot. B—Next, enter coordinates at the keyboard for the new location of the grip. C—The edited object.

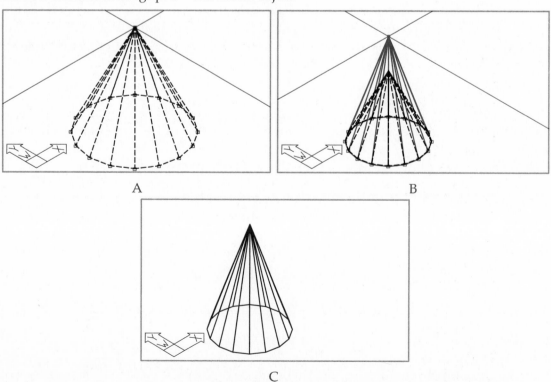

AutoCAD and its Applications—Advanced

Command: **AL** *or* **ALIGN**↵
Select objects: *(pick the wedge)*
Select objects: ↵
Specify 1st source point: *(pick P1)*
Specify 1st destination point: *(pick P2)*
Specify 2nd source point: *(pick P3)*
Specify 2nd destination point: *(pick P4)*
Specify 3rd source point: *(pick P5)*
Specify 3rd destination point: *(pick P1 again)*
Command:

The aligned object should look like Figure 6-2B.

Figure 6-2.
The **ALIGN** command can be used to properly orient 3D objects.

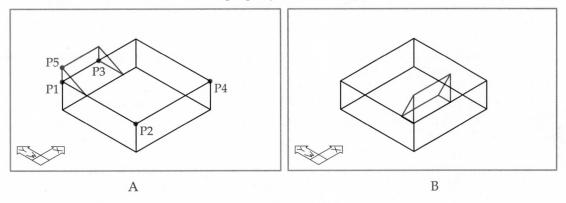

A   B

PROFESSIONAL TIP

The **Align** button can be used in a custom toolbar or added to an existing toolbar. Refer to Chapter 18 for information on customizing toolbars.

EXERCISE 6-1

❑ Begin a new drawing.
❑ Draw a box and a wedge arranged like those shown in Figure 6-2A.
❑ Use the **ALIGN** command to create the arrangement shown below.
❑ Save the drawing as EX6-1.

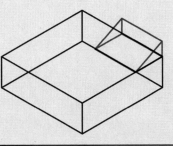

PROFESSIONAL TIP

Before using 3D editing commands, set running object snap modes to enhance your accuracy and speed.

The **ROTATE3D** command can rotate objects on any axis, regardless of the current UCS. This is an extremely powerful editing and design feature. When using the default option, you must pick two points to define an axis of rotation and specify a rotation angle. The rotation angle is defined by looking down the axis from the second pick point and specifying an angle. A positive angle rotates the object counterclockwise.

ROTATE3D

Modify
➥ **3D Operation**
  ➥ **Rotate 3D**

To use the **ROTATE3D** command, select **Rotate 3D** from the **3D Operation** cascading menu in the **Modify** pull-down menu, or enter ROTATE3D at the Command: prompt. The following example rotates the wedge in Figure 6-2 –90° on a selected axis. See Figure 6-3A for the pick points.

Command: **ROTATE3D**↵
Select objects: *(pick the wedge)*
Select objects: ↵
Axis by Object/Last/View/Xaxis/Yaxis/Zaxis/⟨2points⟩: *(pick P1)*
2nd point on axis: *(pick P2)*
⟨Rotation angle⟩/Reference: **-90**↵
Command:

The rotated object is shown in Figure 6-3B.

There are several different ways to define an axis of rotation with the **ROTATE3D** command. These are explained as follows:

- **Axis by Object (O).** Objects such as lines, arcs, circles, and polylines can define the axis. A line becomes the axis. The axis of a circle or arc passes through its center, perpendicular to the plane of the circle. For a polyline, the selected segment (line or arc) is used to determine the axis.
- **Last (L).** Uses the last axis of rotation defined.
- **View (V).** The viewing direction of the current viewport is aligned with a selected point to define the axis.
- **Xaxis/Yaxis/Zaxis (X, Y, or Z).** Aligns the axis of rotation with the X, Y, or Z axis and a selected point.

Figure 6-3.
The **ROTATE3D** command is used to rotate objects in 3D space.

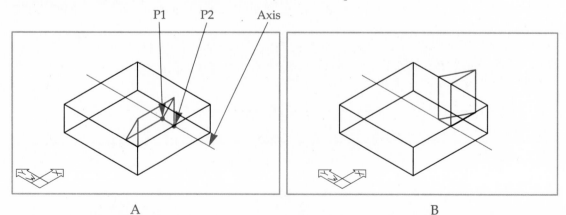

PROFESSIONAL TIP   The **3D Rotate** button can be used in a custom toolbar or added to an existing toolbar. Refer to Chapter 18 for information on customizing toolbars.

❑ Open the drawing created in the last exercise (EX6-1).
❑ Use the **ROTATE3D** command to rotate the wedge to the position shown below.
❑ Save the drawing as EX6-2.

3D Mirroring

AutoCAD User's Guide **13**

The **MIRROR3D** command allows you to mirror objects about any plane, regardless of the current UCS. The default option is to define a mirror plane by picking three points on that plane, Figure 6-4A. Object snap modes should be used to accurately define the mirror plane.

To use the **MIRROR3D** command, select **Mirror 3D** from the **3D Operation** cascading menu in the **Modify** pull-down menu, or enter MIRROR3D at the Command: prompt. To mirror the wedge in Figure 6-3, set the **Midpoint** running object snap and use the following command sequence:

MIRROR3D

Modify
➥ 3D Operation
   ➥ Mirror 3D

    Command: **MIRROR3D**↵
    Select objects: *(pick the wedge)*
    Select objects: ↵
    Plane by Object/Last/Zaxis/View/XY/YZ/XZ/⟨3points⟩: *(pick P1)*
    2nd point on plane: *(pick P2)*
    3rd point on plane: *(pick P3)*
    Delete old objects? ⟨N⟩ ↵
    Command:

The drawing should now look like Figure 6-4B.

There are several different ways to define a mirror plane with the **MIRROR3D** command. These are explained as follows:

- **Plane by Object (O).** The plane that a circle, arc, or 2D polyline segment is in can be used as the mirror plane.
- **Last (L).** Uses the last mirror plane defined.

Figure 6-4.
The **MIRROR3D** command allows you to mirror objects on any 3D axis, regardless of the current UCS.

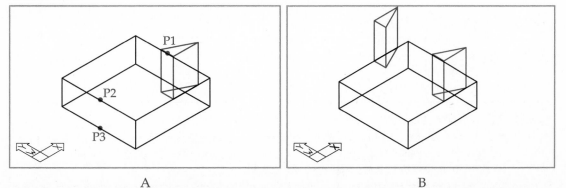

    A   B

- **Zaxis (Z).** Defines the plane with a pick point on the plane and a point on the Z axis of the mirror plane.
- **View (V).** The viewing direction of the current viewpoint is aligned with a selected point to define the axis.
- **XY/YZ/XZ.** The mirror plane is placed in one of the three basic planes, and passes through a selected point.

PROFESSIONAL TIP The **3D Mirror** button can be used in a custom toolbar or added to an existing toolbar. Refer to Chapter 18 for information on customizing toolbars.

EXERCISE 6-3

❏ Open the drawing created in the last exercise (EX6-2).
❏ Use the **MIRROR3D** command to mirror the wedge to the position drawn below.
❏ Save the drawing as EX6-3.

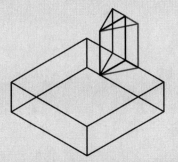

Creating 3D Arrays

Creating an array of 3D objects in 3D space is discussed and illustrated in Chapter 2. However, this type of construction is sometimes considered editing. Therefore, a brief discussion also appears here.

Rectangular 3D arrays

3DARRAY
3A

Modify
↳ **3D Operation**
  ↳ **3D Array**

An example of a rectangular 3D array is the layout of structural steel columns on multiple floors of a commercial building. To use the **3DARRAY** command, select **3D Array** from the **3D Operation** cascading menu in the **Modify** pull-down menu, or enter 3A or 3DARRAY at the Command: prompt.

In Figure 6-5A, you can see two concrete floor slabs of a building and a single steel column. It is now a simple matter of arraying the steel column in rows, columns, and levels. Use the following procedure:

```
Command: 3A or 3DARRAY↵
Select objects: (pick the object)
n found
Select objects: ↵
Rectangular or Polar array (R/P): R↵
Number of rows (---) ⟨1⟩: 3↵
Number of columns (¦¦¦) ⟨1⟩: 5↵
Number of levels (...) ⟨1⟩: 2↵
Distance between rows (---): 10'↵
Distance between columns (¦¦¦): 10'↵
Distance between levels (...): 12'8↵
```

Figure 6-5.
A—Two floors and one steel column are drawn. B—A rectangular 3D array is used to place steel columns on both floors.

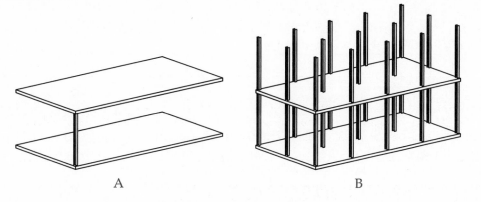

A   B

The result is shown in Figure 6-5B. Constructions like this can be quickly assembled for multiple levels using the **3DARRAY** command only once.

Polar 3D arrays

A polar 3D array is similar to a polar 2D array. However, you must also select a centerline axis of rotation. You can array an object in a UCS different from the current one. Unlike a rectangular 3D array, a polar 3D array does not allow you to create levels of the object. The object is arrayed in a plane defined by the object and the selected centerline (Z) axis.

To use the **3DARRAY** command, select <u>**3D Array**</u> from the <u>**3D Operation**</u> cascading menu in then <u>**Modify**</u> pull-down menu, or enter 3A or 3DARRAY at the Command: prompt.

For example, the tank nozzle in Figure 6-6A must be placed at the four quadrant points around the tank at the same elevation. Before using **3DARRAY**, an axis line must be drawn through the center of the tank. Then, continue as follows:

> Command: **3A** *or* **3DARRAY**↵
> Select objects: *(select the object)*
> *n* found
> Select objects: ↵
> Rectangular or Polar array (R/P): **P**↵
> Number of items: **4**↵
> Angle to fill 〈360〉: ↵
> Rotate objects as they are copied? 〈Y〉: ↵
> Center point of array: *(pick center of tank base)*
> Second point on axis of rotation: *(pick top end of axis line)*
> Command:

The completed 3D polar array is shown in Figure 6-6B. If additional levels of a polar array are needed they can be copied.

3DARRAY
3A

Modify
➟ 3D Operation
➟ 3D Array

Figure 6-6.
A—The tank and one inlet are drawn. B—A polar 3D array is used to create the three other inlets.

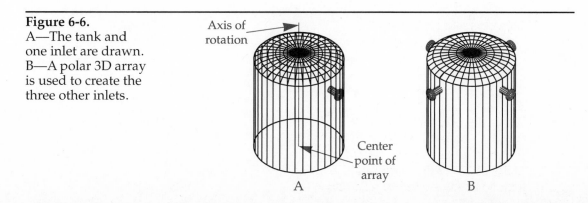

Axis of rotation

Center point of array

A   B

AutoCAD
User's
Guide **13**

Trimming and Extending 3D Objects

Correct use of the **TRIM** and **EXTEND** commands on 3D objects may be confusing at first. However, both of these commands can be powerful tools when working in 3D. This section covers using these commands on 3D objects.

Figure 6-7 shows three wireframe objects. The left viewport is a plan view of the objects. The right viewport is a 3D view. The circle is three inches directly above the ellipse on the Z axis. The bottom edge of the rectangle sits on the same plane as the ellipse. The rectangle passes through the circle at an angle. The right edge of the rectangle in the left viewport is used as the cutting edge in the following example. Use **TRIM** as follows:

```
Command: TRIM↵
Select cutting edges: (Projmode = None, Edgemode = Extend)
Select objects: (pick the bottom-right edge of the rectangle) 1 found
Select objects: ↵
⟨Select object to trim⟩/Project/Edge/Undo: P↵
None/Ucs/View ⟨Ucs⟩: N↵
⟨Select object to trim⟩/Project/Edge/Undo: (pick the right side of the ellipse)
⟨Select object to trim⟩/Project/Edge/Undo: ↵
Command:
```

Figure 6-8 shows the results.

Figure 6-7.
Three wireframe objects in 3D space that will be trimmed.

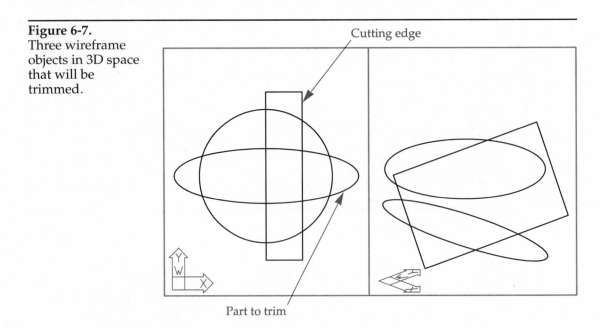

Cutting edge

Part to trim

Figure 6-8.
With the **None** suboption of the **TRIM** command **Project** option, the ellipse is trimmed where it actually intersects the rectangle.

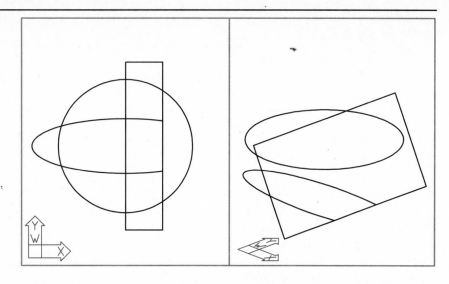

The **TRIM** command has two options—**Project** and **Edge**. The **Project** option establishes the projection method for objects to be trimmed in 3D space. This option is also controlled by the **PROJMODE** system variable. The **Project** option displays the following suboptions:

None/Ucs/View ⟨Ucs⟩:

- **None. (PROJMODE = 0)** No projection method is used. Objects to be trimmed in 3D space must form an actual intersection with the cutting edge. In Figure 6-8, you can see that the edge of the rectangle and the ellipse actually intersect.
- **Ucs. (PROJMODE = 1)** Cutting edges and edges to be trimmed are all projected onto the XY plane of the current UCS. Objects are trimmed even if they do not intersect in 3D space. See Figure 6-9.
- **View. (PROJMODE = 2)** Objects are projected along the current view direction and onto the current viewing plane. Objects are trimmed even if they do not intersect in 3D space. See Figure 6-10.

Figure 6-9.
With the **Ucs** suboption of the **TRIM** command **Project** option, the circle is trimmed where it intersects the cutting edge as the edge is projected to the current UCS.

Cutting edge   Trimmed object

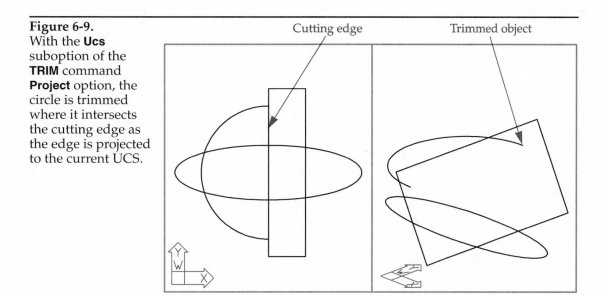

Figure 6-10.
With the **View** suboption of the **TRIM** command **Project** option, the rectangle is trimmed where it intersects the cutting edge and the edge is projected along the current viewing angle to the XY plane. If the objects were selected in the right viewport, more of the rectangle would have been trimmed.

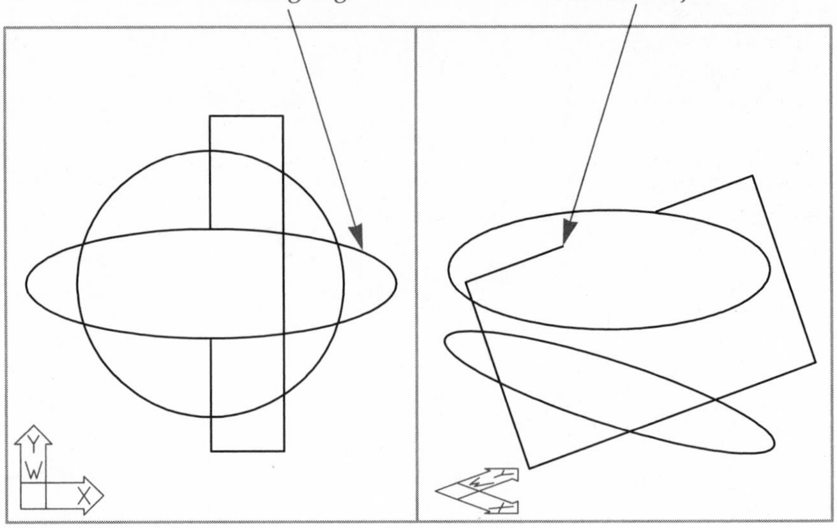

Cutting edge   Trimmed object

The **Edge** option of the **TRIM** command determines if an object is to be trimmed at an implied edge or at the actual intersection of an object in 3D space. This option applies specifically to the projection of an edge and *not* a plane. The **Edge** option is selected as follows:

⟨Select object to trim⟩/Project/Edge/Undo: **E**↵
Extend/No extend ⟨No extend⟩:

- **Extend.** The cutting edge is extended into 3D space to intersect objects to be trimmed. The objects must intersect exactly when the cutting edge is extended.
- **No extend.** The cutting edge is not extended, and the object to be trimmed must intersect the cutting edge in 3D space.

Creating Fillets and Rounds

Fillets are rounded inside corners. Rounds are rounded outside corners. Both of these are easily created with the surfacing commands **RULESURF** and **TABSURF**. Choose the one you prefer. Notice in Figure 6-11A that arcs have been drawn on the inside and outside corners of a wireframe object in order to create a fillet and round. The arcs are copied to the opposite side and lines are drawn connecting the tangent points of the arcs.

If you use **TABSURF**, you then only need to give direction vectors. If **RULESURF** is used, the lines connecting the arcs are not needed. Select one arc as the first defining curve and the opposite arc as the second defining curve. The result of either process is shown in Figure 6-11B.

The face of the arcs on both sides of the object must be surfaced with **RULESURF**. First, put points at the center of the arc on the round and at the intersection of the two inside edges of the part. See Figure 6-11C. Then, pick the point and the arc as the two defining curves. Now, the **3DFACE** command can be used to construct faces on the object. Three 3D faces must be drawn on the left side of the object. The completed object is shown in Figure 6-11D.

Hiding 3D face edges with the EDGE command

Notice in Figure 6-11D that the 3D face edges are visible on the left side of the object. These edges can be created as hidden edges by using the **Invisible** option of the **3DFACE** command while drawing them. However, you can quickly hide an existing edge with the **EDGE** command.

Figure 6-11.
A—To construct fillets and rounds, arcs are drawn first. The direction vectors are needed if **TABSURF** is used, but not for **RULESURF**.
B—The "edges" of the fillet and round. Now, the "faces" must be drawn.
C—Use construction points and **RULESURF** to surface the "faces" of the fillet and round.
D—Use the **3DFACE** command to complete the surfacing of the entire side of the object.

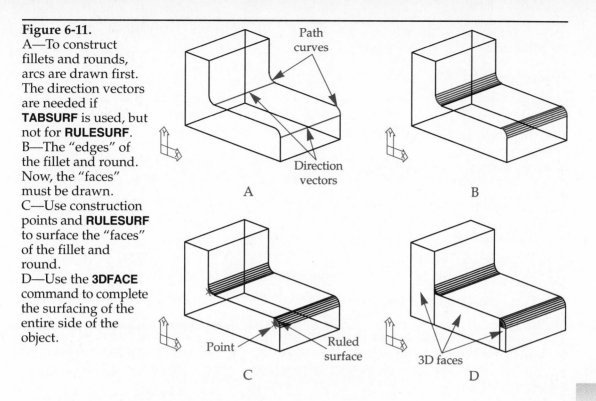

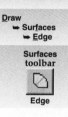

To use this command, pick **Edge** from the **Surfaces** cascading menu in the **Draw** pull-down menu, pick the **Edge** button in the **Surfaces** toolbar, or enter EDGE at the Command: prompt:

Command: **EDGE**↵
Display/〈Select edge〉: *(pick the edge to hide)*
Display/〈Select edge〉: ↵
Command:

The edge is hidden and the object appears as shown in Figure 6-12. Invisible edges can be made visible using the **Display** option of the **EDGE** command as follows:

Command: **EDGE**↵
Display/〈Select edge〉: **D**↵
Select/〈All〉: **S**↵
Select objects: *(pick an edge of the 3D face)* 1 found
Select objects: ↵
** Regenerating 3DFACE objects…done.
Display/〈Select edge〉: *(pick the highlighted invisible edge)*
Display/〈Select edge〉: ↵
Command: ↵

Figure 6-12.
In Figure 6-11D, the edges of the 3D faces can be seen in the middle of the object. The **EDGE** command can be used to make these edges invisible, as shown here.

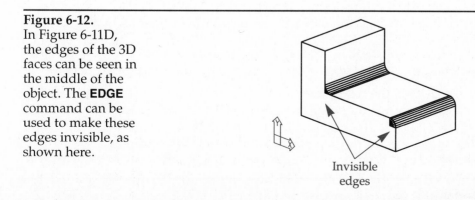

The edge is now visible. Notice that the two suboptions of the **Display** option are to **Select** a single edge or to select **All** edges.

Using **SPLFRAME** to control visibility

The **SPLFRAME** system variable can also be used to control the visibility of 3D face edges. To set this variable, type SPLFRAME at the Command: prompt. A value of 0 does not display invisible 3D face edges. A value of 1 displays invisible 3D face edges.

Editing Polygon Meshes

The **PEDIT** command is used to edit polygon meshes. The entire mesh can be smoothed, individual vertices can be moved, or the mesh can be closed. The following options are displayed when a polygon mesh is selected:

Command: **PEDIT**⏎
Edit vertex/Smooth surface/Desmooth/Mclose/Nclose/Undo/eXit ⟨X⟩:

The **Edit vertex** option is used to alter individual vertices. This option is explained in detail later. The following options are also available:

- **Smooth surface.** Applies a smooth surface to the mesh based on the value of the **SURFTYPE** variable. These types of surfaces are also discussed in Chapter 5.

SURFTYPE setting	Surface type
5	Quadratic B-spline
6	Cubic B-spline
8	Bezier surface

- **Desmooth.** Removes smoothing and returns the mesh to its original vertices.
- **Mclose.** The polylines in the M direction are closed if the M direction mesh is open.
- **Mopen.** Opens the polylines in the M direction if they are closed.
- **Nclose.** The polylines in the N direction are closed if the N direction mesh is open.
- **Nopen.** Opens the polylines in the N direction if they are closed.

Figure 6-13A shows a polygon mesh. Figure 6-13B shows the results of using the **Nclose** option on the mesh.

The **Edit vertex** option of the **PEDIT** command allows you to move individual vertices of the polygon mesh. When you select the **Edit vertex** option, you get several suboptions:

Edit vertex/Smooth surface/Desmooth/Mclose/Nclose/Undo/eXit ⟨X⟩: **E**⏎
Vertex (0,0). Next/Previous/Left/Right/Up/Down/Move/REgen/eXit ⟨N⟩:

Notice in Figure 6-14A that an X marker appears at the first vertex. This X can be moved to the vertex you want to edit. The **Edit vertex** suboptions are explained as follows:

- **Next.** The X moves to the next vertex in the order drawn. When the end of a line is reached, the X jumps to the start of the next line.
- **Previous.** The X moves to the previous vertex in the order drawn.
- **Left.** The X moves to the previous vertex in the N direction. When the end of a line is reached, the X jumps to the start of the next line.
- **Right.** The X moves to the next vertex in the N direction. See Figure 6-14B.
- **Up.** The X moves to the next vertex in the M direction. When the end of a line is reached, the X jumps to the start of the next line. See Figure 6-14B.
- **Down.** The X moves to the previous vertex in the M direction.
- **Move.** The vertex where the X is can be moved to a new location.

You may notice in Figure 6-14B that the **Right** option is actually moving the vertex to the left of the screen. This is because the right/left and up/down directions are determined by the order in which the vertices were drawn.

AutoCAD and its Applications—Advanced

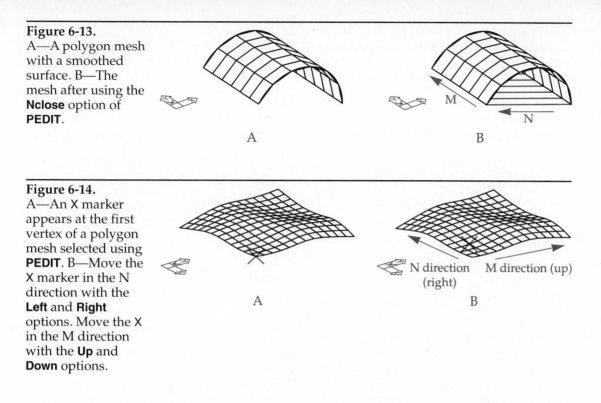

Figure 6-13.
A—A polygon mesh with a smoothed surface. B—The mesh after using the **Nclose** option of **PEDIT**.

A

B

Figure 6-14.
A—An X marker appears at the first vertex of a polygon mesh selected using **PEDIT**. B—Move the X marker in the N direction with the **Left** and **Right** options. Move the X in the M direction with the **Up** and **Down** options.

A

N direction (right)   M direction (up)

B

When the **Move** option is selected, the crosshairs are attached to the vertex with a rubber band line and the following prompt appears.

　　Enter new location:

If a new point is picked, the mesh appears to be altered properly, Figure 6-15A. However, when the viewpoint is changed, as in Figure 6-15B, it is clear that the new point does not have the intended Z value. This is because the Z value will always be zero on the current XY plane. Therefore, do not pick a new polygon mesh location with the pointing device. Instead, enter the coordinates or use XYZ filters.

　　Enter new location: **@0,0,.6**↵

The new location in Figure 6-16A appears similar to Figure 6-15A. However, when viewed from another direction, it is clear that entering coordinates produced the correct results, Figure 6-16B.

Figure 6-15.
A—A new point picked with the cursor appears correct. B—When the viewpoint is changed, the pointing device may produce inaccurate results.

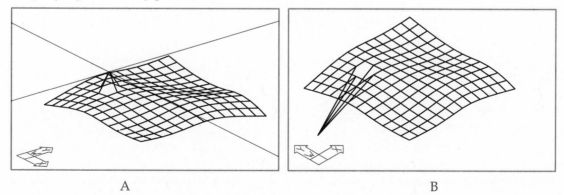

A

B

Figure 6-16.
A—When coordinates are entered at the keyboard, the results at first appear the same as when using the pointing device. B—When the viewpoint is changed, you can see that entering coordinates produces correct results.

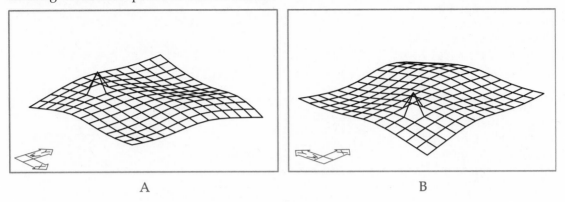

A   B

Editing polygon meshes with grips

When a polygon mesh is selected, all of its grips are displayed. See Figure 6-17A. Individual vertices can be edited by picking the grip you wish to move and entering the new coordinates at the keyboard, Figure 6-17B.

If **EXPLODE** is used on a polygon mesh, the mesh is broken into individual 3D faces. Pick any edge on the mesh and four grips that define the corners of the 3D face appear. See Figure 6-18A. The vertices of each face can be edited using grips. See Figure 6-18B. If you edit a vertex of a 3D face created by exploding a polygon mesh, the vertex will no longer be attached to the original mesh. See Figure 6-18C.

Figure 6-17.
A—When a polygon mesh is selected, the grips become warm. B—Select a single grip to make it hot. This grip can then be moved.

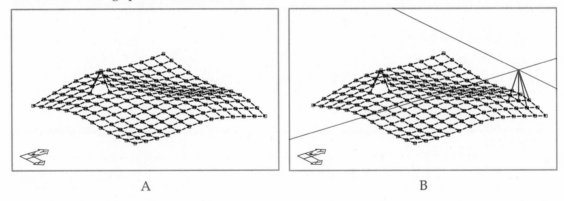

A   B

PROFESSIONAL TIP

With careful planning, you can minimize the number of faces you construct. Draw only the number needed and use editing commands to create the rest. As shown in Figure 6-18, a 3D face is easily edited using grips. Use all of the grip editing functions—move, rotate, scale, and mirror—to quickly manipulate 3D faces.

Figure 6-18.
A—When you select an edge of an exploded polygon mesh, you can see that it is made up of 3D faces. B—A single vertex on a 3D face can be edited using grips. C—The edited 3D face vertex is detached from the original mesh.

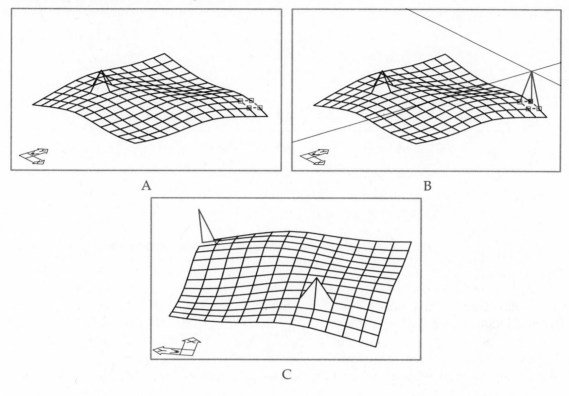

A

B

C

Chapter Test

Write your answers in the spaces provided.

1. What command allows you to both move and rotate a 3D object? _____
   _____

2. What feature do you define when using the **ROTATE3D** command? _____
   _____

3. What option of the **ROTATE3D** command allows you to use the center axis of a circle as the feature about which to rotate? _____

4. What is the default method of picking a **MIRROR3D** mirror plane? _____
   _____
   _____

5. What are the three dimensions of a 3D array?_____
   _____

6. Indicate the **PROJMODE** values, give the name, and define the function of the three suboptions of the **Project** option of the **TRIM** command.

   PROJMODE = _____

   PROJMODE = _____

   PROJMODE = _____

7. What is the function of the **Edge** option of the **TRIM** command? _____

_____

_____

8. Which surfacing commands are good for creating fillets and rounds? _____

_____

9. What is the function of the **EDGE** command? _____

_____

10. How can invisible 3D face edges be displayed? _____

_____

11. How can the angular faces of a polygon mesh be rounded?_____

_____

12. Name the three types of smooth curves that can be applied to a polygon mesh, and give their **SURFTYPE** values.

    SURFTYPE = _____

    SURFTYPE = _____

    SURFTYPE = _____

13. What command, option, and suboption are used to edit a single vertex of a polygon mesh? _____

_____

14. What is the most accurate way to move a polygon mesh vertex when using the grip method?_____

_____

15. When a polygon mesh is exploded, what type of objects are created? _____

Drawing Problems

1. Open Problem 2 from Chapter 1. If you have not done this problem, draw it as a 3D wireframe using your own measurements. Then, do the following:

   A. Construct a box the exact width and depth of the slot in the object, but twice as high as the opening in the object. Draw the box sitting outside the object.

   B. Use the **ALIGN** command to place the box inside the slot.

   C. Edit the object so that the slot is moved half the distance to the left edge of the object. Move the box along with the slot.

   D. Save the drawing as P6-1.

2. Open Problem 1 from Chapter 1. If you have not done this problem, draw it in 3D wireframe using your own measurements. Then, do the following:

A. Use **ROTATE3D** to rotate the object 90°.

B. Use **MIRROR3D** to place a second copy at a 180° rotation using the **YZ** option.

C. Use the **XZ** option of **MIRROR3D** to create a copy of the last operation. The final drawing should look like the one shown below.

D. Save the drawing as P6-2.

3. Open Problem 3 from Chapter 1. If you have not done this problem, draw it in 3D wireframe using your own measurements. Then, do the following:

A. Use **ALIGN** to rotate the block that is inserted into the slot of the main body. The block should be rotated 90° so its tall side is aligned with the tall dimension of the body.

B. Mirror and copy the body 180° so that the copy and the original fully enclose the block.

C. Save the drawing as P6-3.

4. Draw Problem 5 from Chapter 1 as a 3D surface model using the measurements given. Use the following guidelines:

A. Construct fillets where the two cylinders join the base.

B. Construct chamfers at the top of each cylinder.

C. Apply a fillet around the top edge of the base.

D. Save the drawing as P6-4.

5. Draw Problem 8 from Chapter 1 as a 3D surface model using the dimensions given. Use the following guidelines:

A. Construct a .25 radius fillet on all three inside corners.

B. Construct a .125″ × 45° chamfer at the top of each hole.

C. Save the drawing as P6-5.

6. Draw Problem 9 from Chapter 1 as a 3D surface model using the dimensions given. Use the following guidelines:

A. Create a .125″ × 45° chamfer on the top edge of the large hole.

B. Construct the small holes using **RULESURF**.

C. Use **3DARRAY** to create a polar array of the four small holes.

D. Save the drawing as P6-6.

7. Draw Problem 11 from Chapter 1 as a 3D surface model using the dimensions given. Use the following guidelines:

   A. Create a .25″ radius fillet around the top edge of the base plate.

   B. Construct the small holes using **RULESURF**.

   C. Use **ARRAY** to create a rectangular array of the four small holes.

   D. Save the drawing as P6-7.

8. Draw Problem 9 from Chapter 2 as a 3D surface model using the dimensions given. Use the following guidelines:

   A. Draw a bar of the same dimensions to fit over the pin bar in Problem 2-9. Construct it alongside the pin bar.

   B. Use **RULESURF** to construct the holes in the new bar, and be sure to erase the original circles used to construct the holes.

   C. Use **ALIGN** to place the new bar over the pin bar.

   D. Rotate the entire assembly 90°.

   E. Save the drawing as P6-8.

9. Draw Problem 11 from Chapter 2 as a 3D surface model. Use the following guidelines:

   A. Explode the sphere mesh. Remove 20 3D faces—12 above the equator and 8 below.

   B. Draw a new sphere in the exact center of the existing one, and 1/2 its diameter.

   C. Draw a small diameter tube protruding at a 45° angle from the center of the new sphere into the northern hemisphere. It should extend out through the large sphere.

   D. Create a 3D polar array of six tubes.

   E. Save the drawing as P6-9.

10. Draw Problem 1 from Chapter 3 as a 3D surface model. Use the following guidelines:

    A. Place a .25″ radius fillet on all inside vertical corners.

    B. Place a .125″ radius round on all outside vertical corners.

    C. Save the drawing as P6-10.

11. Draw Problem 3 from Chapter 3 as a 3D surface model using the dimensions given. Use the following guidelines:

    A. Give the object a .25″ radius bend at the "L".

    B. Save the drawing as P6-11.

12. Draw Problem 8 from Chapter 3 as a 3D surface model using the dimensions given. Use the following guidelines:

    A. Draw the 4.80 side at a 15° angle from vertical.

    B. Give the object a .25″ inside radius at the bend.

    C. Save the drawing as P6-12.

Viewing and Displaying Three-Dimensional Models

Learning Objectives

After completing this chapter, you will be able to:
○ Use all options of the **VPOINT** command to display 3D models.
○ Describe how to hide lines in a variety of situations.
○ Use the **DVIEW** command to view 3D models.
○ Create a standard engineering layout using **MVSETUP**.
○ Apply shading to objects using the **SHADE** command.
○ Use the **SHADEDGE** and **SHADEDIF** system variables to create shading variations.
○ Use the **RENDER** command to produce quick renderings.

There are two different ways to select a viewpoint for 3D models. These are the **VPOINT** command and the **DVIEW** command. The **VPOINT** command, which was discussed in Chapter 1, is a "static" method. The viewpoint is established first, then the object is displayed. The **DVIEW** command is a "dynamic" viewing method. You can select a viewpoint while the model is being moved. Once a viewpoint has been selected, you can enhance the display in several ways. You can pan and zoom in "real time." This means that you can see the object move as it is panned or zoomed.

The **MVSETUP** command enables you to create a standard engineering layout of any 3D model. The layout contains three orthogonal views—top, front, and right side—and a 3D view. The views are placed inside four floating model space viewports in a paper space layout.

You can use the **HIDE** command to temporarily remove hidden lines. This command has been used in previous chapters. You can also use the **SHADE** command to create a simple rendering. A more advanced rendering is created with the **RENDER** command. This command creates the most realistic display of the model. The **RENDER** command is introduced in this chapter, but is discussed in detail in Chapter 9 and Chapter 14.

Using the VPOINT Command

The **VPOINT** command can be accessed in three different ways. It can be selected from the **View** pull-down menu by picking **3D Viewpoint** and then **Tripod**. This is covered in Chapter 1. Viewpoint angles can also be established using the **Viewpoint Presets** dialog box, the **Viewpoint** flyout, or the **Viewpoint** toolbar. For an overview of the **VPOINT** command and the "right-hand rule," refer to Chapter 1.

Using the Rotate option

Using the **Rotate** option of the **VPOINT** command, you can enter two angles to set the viewpoint. The angles are similar to spherical coordinates, but do not include a distance from the center point. Spherical coordinates can locate any point on, inside, or outside a sphere.

Figure 7-1 shows an example of a point located with spherical coordinates. Notice that the 90° angle is the angle *in* the XY plane from the X axis. The 45° angle is the angle *from* the XY plane. These are the two angles used with the **Rotate** option of the **VPOINT** command.

Figure 7-1.
Spherical coordinates are made up of three values. These three values define a point in space.

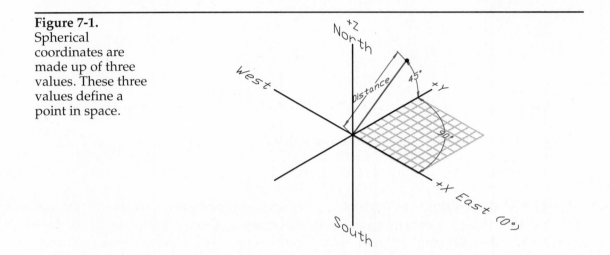

The **Rotate** option can be selected by picking **Rotate** from the **3D Viewpoint** cascading menu in the **View** pull-down menu, or it can be entered at the Command: prompt as follows:

    Command: **-VP** *or* **VPOINT↵**
    Rotate/⟨View point⟩ ⟨*current*⟩: **R↵**
    Enter angle in XY plane from X axis ⟨*current*⟩: **45↵**
    Enter angle from XY plane ⟨*current*⟩: **45↵**
    Regenerating drawing.
    Command:

In Figure 7-2, the viewpoint in the right-hand viewport is moved counterclockwise 45° in the XY plane and 45° from the XY plane.

Figure 7-2.
The viewpoint in the right viewport was created using the **Rotate** option of the **VPOINT** command. Both rotation angles are 45°.

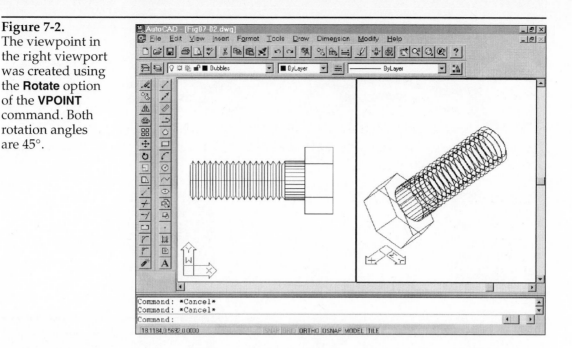

3D display options using a pull-down menu

The **View** pull-down menu provides additional options of viewpoint selection. Pick the **View** pull-down menu, then select **3D Viewpoint**. A cascading menu displays viewpoint options. See Figure 7-3. This selection of preset views allows you to display six orthographic and four isometric views of the current drawing. Figure 7-4 shows how these different selections affect the drawing display. The appropriate **Viewpoint** toolbar button also appears next to each view.

Figure 7-3.
The **3D Viewpoint** cascading menu has several options for creating a 3D viewing angle.

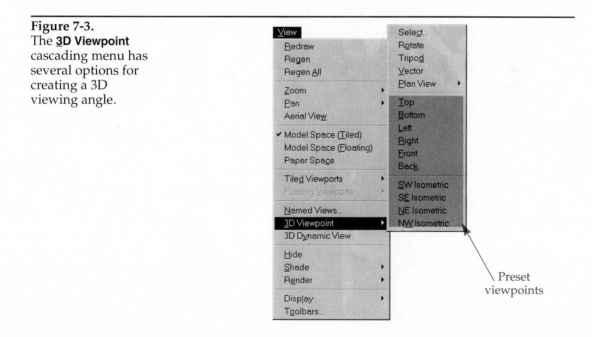

Preset viewpoints

Figure 7-4.
Each of the 3D viewpoint presets applied to a link rod model.

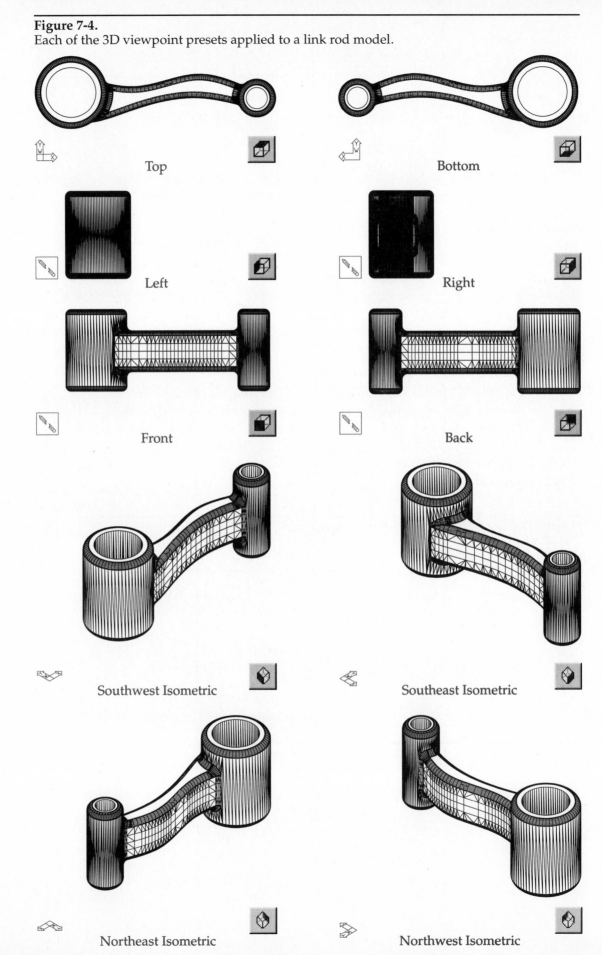

Top

Bottom

Left

Right

Front

Back

Southwest Isometric

Southeast Isometric

Northeast Isometric

Northwest Isometric

Specifying the camera angle

If the initial **DVIEW** display is a plan view, it is best to use the **Camera** option first. This option lets you locate your eye position in two directions relative to object. A vertical movement is the angle *from* the XY plane. A horizontal movement is *in* the XY plane from the X axis.

After selecting the **Camera** option, you can move the pointing device to pick the best display. Placing the cursor at the center of the screen represents an angle of 0° *in* the XY plane and 0° *from* the XY plane. Move the cursor horizontally and the house rotates 180° to the left or right in the XY plane. This allows the camera to be positioned at any angle in the XY plane. Move the cursor vertically and the house "tips" forward or backward 90°. Experiment moving the cursor first horizontally and then vertically while observing how the view changes. Separating the cursor movement into its two components makes the relationship between the cursor location and the resulting view clear.

Picking a point with the cursor actually selects two angles—the angle *in* the XY plane and the angle *from* the XY plane. These angles can also be entered directly from the keyboard. There is a prompt for each angle.

> CAmera/TArget/Distance/POints/PAn/Zoom/TWist/CLip/Hide/Off/Undo/⟨eXit⟩: **CA**↲
> Toggle angle in/Enter angle from XY plane ⟨*current*⟩: **15**↲
> Toggle angle from/Enter angle in XY plane from X axis ⟨*current*⟩: **-60**↲

The second prompt requests the angle of the camera in the XY plane. A 0° value results in a view looking straight down the X axis. This is looking into the window of DVIEWBLOCK. A positive value moves the camera to the right, or counterclockwise, around the house. A negative rotation angle moves the camera left, or clockwise.

The result of the settings is shown in Figure 7-8A. The effect of these camera settings on the link rod model is shown in Figure 7-8B.

While the **Camera** option prompts are on the screen, you can toggle between the horizontal and vertical angle input by using the **Toggle** option. If the prompt reads Toggle angle in, you can switch to this option to input the angle *in* the XY plane by typing T and pressing [Enter]. The prompt changes to Toggle angle from. This allows you to try several angles while still in the **Camera** option.

You can limit the movement of the camera to one direction by specifying an angle and pressing [Enter]. For example, if you enter 20 for the angle from the XY plane as follows, the object remains stationary at that angle and only moves clockwise or counterclockwise on the X axis.

> Toggle angle in/Enter angle from XY plane ⟨*current*⟩: **20**↲

Figure 7-8.
A—This view was created with values of 15° *from* the XY plane and –60° *in* the XY plane.
B—The settings in A applied to the link rod model.

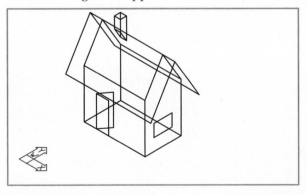

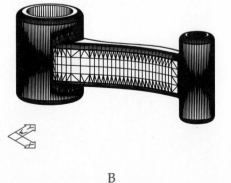

A   B

This allows you to view the object at one vertical angle from any horizontal angle in the XY plane. You can also enter an angle in the XY plane from the X axis to limit the horizontal movement of the camera.

Toggle angle in/Enter angle from XY plane ⟨*current*⟩: **T**↵
Toggle angle from/Enter angle in XY plane from X axis ⟨*current*⟩: **30**↵

A plan view is 90° from the XY plane. This places your line of sight perpendicular to the XY plane of the current UCS. With the DVIEWBLOCK drawing displayed, a 90° camera angle places your line of sight looking down onto the roof. A 0° camera angle places the line of sight looking into the door.

Select the target angles

Another way to change your view is with the **Target** option. The *target* is the point where the camera looks. The target can be rotated around the camera to any angle. A 90° vertical rotation angle creates a view of the opposite side of the object, Figure 7-9.

The following angle settings for the **Target** option create a view from below the floor of the house, Figure 7-10A. These are the same values used above for the **Camera** option. The effect of this **DVIEW** target setting on the link rod model is shown in Figure 7-10B.

Figure 7-9.
The vertical rotation angle for the target is opposite that of the camera.

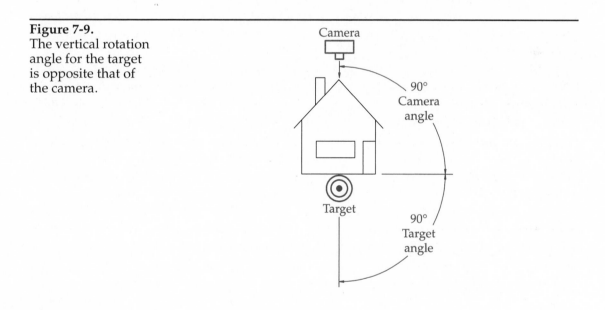

Figure 7-10.
A—When the target is moved using the values entered for the camera in Figure 7-8, the view is from under the house. B—The settings in A applied to the link rod model.

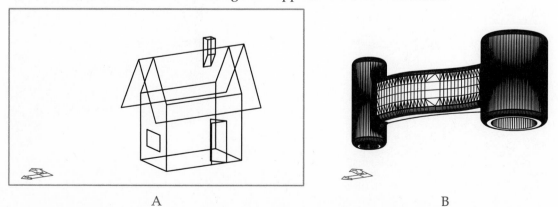

A   B

```
Command: DVIEW↵
Select objects: ↵
CAmera/TArget/Distance/POints/PAn/Zoom/TWist/CLip/Hide/Off/Undo/⟨eXit⟩: TA↵
Toggle angle in/Enter angle from XY plane ⟨current⟩: 15↵
Toggle angle from/Enter angle in XY plane from X axis ⟨current⟩: -60↵
```

Setting a distance between camera and target (perspective)

To this point, you have created views that are parallel projections. A perspective is not a parallel projection. The **Distance** option creates a perspective by moving the camera closer to or farther from the target. This is how your eye actually sees the object. Lines in a perspective view project to vanishing points. Therefore, lines farther from the camera appear to meet. AutoCAD indicates the perspective mode by placing a perspective icon in the lower-left corner of the screen.

```
CAmera/TArget/Distance/POints/PAn/Zoom/TWist/CLip/Hide/Off/Undo/⟨eXit⟩: D↵
New camera/target distance ⟨current⟩: 15↵
```

The new view should look like Figure 7-11A. Press [Enter] to return to the Command: prompt. The effect of this **DVIEW Distance** setting on the link rod model is shown in Figure 7-11B.

A slider bar appears when you select the **Distance** option. See Figure 7-12. When you move the slider bar to the right, the camera moves away from the object. You can pick a distance with the slider bar or enter a distance at the keyboard. You may need to enter a distance greater than the width of your drawing to see all of the objects.

The perspective view achieved with the **Distance** option is great for display and plotting purposes, but not practical for working. The **PAN** and **ZOOM** commands do not function in a perspective view, nor can you select points for drawing. Therefore, turn the **Distance** option off as follows before continuing to work on the drawing:

```
CAmera/TArget/Distance/POints/PAn/Zoom/TWist/CLip/Hide/Off/Undo/⟨eXit⟩: O↵
CAmera/TArget/Distance/POints/PAn/Zoom/TWist/CLip/Hide/Off/Undo/⟨eXit⟩: ↵
Regenerating drawing.
Command:
```

Figure 7-11.
A—The DVIEWBLOCK drawing with distance values applied. Notice the perspective icon in the lower-left corner. B—The setting in A applied to the link rod model.

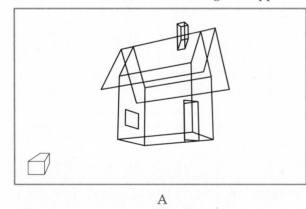

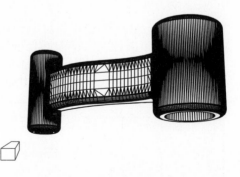

A

B

Figure 7-12.
A slider bar appears for many of the **DVIEW** command options.

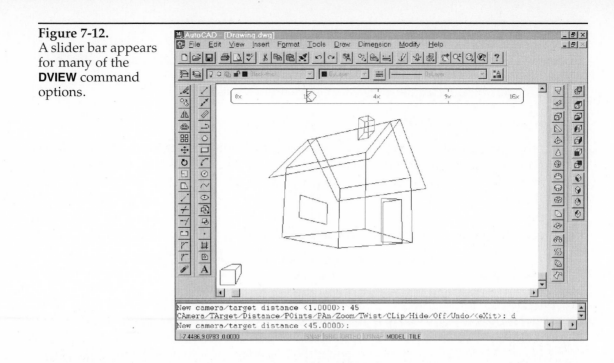

Picking points for the target and camera

The **Points** option allows you to pick the target and camera locations using XYZ coordinates, filters, or object snap modes. When entering XYZ coordinates, keep in mind that the coordinates are based on the current UCS. The **Points** option is best used when you have already created a display other than the initial plan view. As you select the pick points, a rubber band connects the camera and target to help you see the new line of sight.

Figure 7-13 shows target (P1) and camera (P2) pick points and the resulting view. The command sequence for Figure 7-13 follows:

    Command: **DVIEW**↵
    Select objects: *(select the objects on the screen)*
    CAmera/TArget/Distance/POints/PAn/Zoom/TWist/CLip/Hide/Off/Undo/⟨eXit⟩: **PO**↵
    Enter target point ⟨*default*⟩: **MID**↵
    of *(pick P1)*
    Enter camera point ⟨*default*⟩: **END**↵
    of *(pick P2)*

Notice in Figure 7-13B that the target and camera points are aligned. The camera point at the top of the tripod touches the target point. These two points are the line of sight. A perspective display changes to a parallel projection to help you select camera and target points. The display then returns to perspective.

PROFESSIONAL TIP

Several **DVIEW** options display a horizontal slider bar. Use this bar to visually set your display or read approximate values. The diamond in the bar indicates position. Rubber band lines are anchored to a short line in the slider bar. This short line indicates the present position of the drawing. When the diamond is centered on the short line, the current dynamic position is the same as the present drawing position. The value of the current slider setting appears in the coordinate display window.

Figure 7-13.
A—The target (P1) and camera (P2) are located using the **Points** option of the **DVIEW** command. B—The resulting pictorial view.

A   B

EXERCISE 7-2

❑ Open one of the 3D models you created in an earlier chapter.
❑ Set **TILEMODE** to 0.
❑ Use the **DVIEW Distance** option to move your viewpoint farther away from the object.
❑ Use the **DVIEW Off** option to turn off the perspective display.
❑ Set the **DVIEW Camera** and **Target** options to both positive and negative angle values. Check each view using the **Hide** option.
❑ Set the **DVIEW Points** option to view the object from two different viewpoints.
❑ Close the drawing without saving.

Change the position of the drawing

The **Pan** option of the **DVIEW** command is similar to the **PAN** command. It allows you to move the entire drawing in relation to the graphics display area. Use the **Pan** option as follows:

        CAmera/TArget/Distance/POints/PAn/Zoom/TWist/CLip/Hide/Off/Undo/⟨eXit⟩: **PA.**↵
        Displacement base point: (*pick a point to move from*)
        Second point: (*pick a point to move to*)

Using a zoom lens

You can change the lens on the **DVIEW** camera just as you can a real camera. Lens lengths are measured in millimeters. A zoom, or telephoto, lens is greater than 50mm. It allows you to get a close-up view while not changing the camera and target positions. A wide angle lens is less than 50mm. It takes in a wider field of vision as the lens length gets smaller. You can change lenses with the **Zoom** option.

        CAmera/TArget/Distance/POints/PAn/Zoom/TWist/CLip/Hide/Off/Undo/⟨eXit⟩: **Z.**↵
        Adjust lens length ⟨50.000mm⟩: **28.**↵

If your display is not in perspective, **Zoom** requests a scale factor. If the display is in perspective, **Zoom** allows you to adjust the lens length.

A 28mm lens is commonly known as a "fish-eye." This lens creates a wide field of vision. However, a fish-eye lens can distort the sides of your drawing and make the model appear farther away, depending on the current distance setting. Two views of the DVIEWBLOCK drawing are shown in Figure 7-14 using a distance of 40 feet.

Figure 7-14.
A—A 28mm lens at a distance of 40 feet. B—A 100mm lens at a distance of 40 feet.

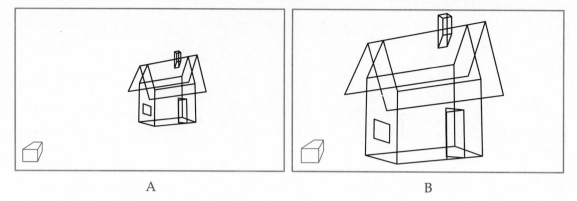

A   B

Rotating the drawing around a point

The **Twist** option allows you to rotate the drawing around the center point of the screen. When the twist, or *tilt angle*, is set with the pointing device, the angle appears in the coordinate display window. A rubber band line connects the center point to the crosshairs. An exact positive or negative angle can be entered at the keyboard.

Clipping portions of the drawing

Portions of a drawing can be eliminated from the display by using *clipping planes*. Think of a clipping plane as a wall that hides everything behind it. A clipping plane can also hide everything in front of it. The plane is always perpendicular to your line of sight. Lines behind the back clipping plane or in front of the front clipping plane are removed.

The **Clip** option of the **DVIEW** command is used to dynamically place a clipping plane, or enter its distance from the target. The front and back planes are turned on by entering a distance, or turned off by selecting the **Off** option. The camera is the default position of the front plane. The front clipping plane can be returned to the camera position with the **Eye** option.

> CAmera/TArget/Distance/POints/PAn/Zoom/TWist/CLip/Hide/Off/Undo/⟨eXit⟩: **CL**↵
> Back/Front/⟨Off⟩: **B**↵
> ON/OFF/ ⟨Distance from target⟩ ⟨*current*⟩: (*enter a distance or use the slider bar to pick*)
> CAmera/TArget/Distance/POints/PAn/Zoom/TWist/CLip/Hide/Off/Undo/⟨eXit⟩: **CL**↵
> Back/Front/⟨Off⟩: **F**↵
> Eye/ON/OFF/⟨Distance from target⟩ ⟨*default*⟩: **E**↵

When perspective is on, the front clipping plane is automatically on. The **On** and **Off** suboptions of the **Front** option are available only if perspective is off. Figure 7-15 shows a drawing with front and back clipping planes.

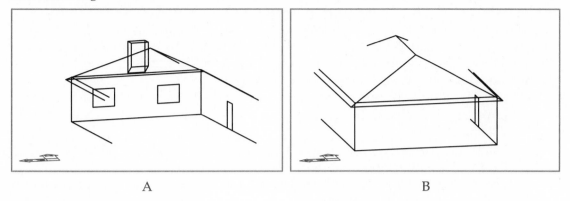

A   B

Other DVIEW options

The two remaining options of the **DVIEW** command are **Undo** and **Exit**. These are explained below.

- **Undo (U).** Undoes the previous **DVIEW** option. Like the **UNDO** command, this option lets you step back through previous **DVIEW** functions.
- **Exit (X).** Exits the **DVIEW** command and regenerates the drawing using the last view established.

EXERCISE 7-3

❑ Begin a new drawing. Draw a 3D house similar to the DVIEWBLOCK drawing in Figure 7-7.
❑ Select the **DVIEW** command to select a camera angle. Select the **Zoom** option to see the entire house.
❑ Draw a small box in the center of the house.
❑ Draw another object of your choice outside the house.
❑ Use the **Points** option of the **DVIEW** command to place the camera on the object outside the house. Place the target on a corner of the box inside the house.
❑ Select the **Distance** option to move farther away. Then, move closer to the target.
❑ Zoom to a point on or near the box inside the house.
❑ Select the **Target** option. Pick an angle from the XY plane near zero. Move the pointer to several positions when picking the horizontal rotation. Notice how the house moves around you. Pick a view that allows you to see the object outside the house.
❑ Use the **Clip** option to place a back clipping plane that hides the object outside the house.
❑ Save the drawing as EX7-3.

Creating a Standard Engineering Layout

The **MVSETUP** command can be used to create a paper space layout of four floating model space viewports of any 3D model. Many of the functions of **MVSETUP** have been replaced with the new setup wizards and template files in Release 14, but some features are still useful. One such feature is the standard engineering layout option. This powerful function automatically converts a 3D model into a layout of the top, front, and right side orthogonal views and a 3D (isometric) view.

MVSETUP is actually an AutoLISP routine. The command provides you with a variety of options useful in constructing a paper space layout on a border and title block template drawing. The use of **MVSETUP** with 2D drawing layout was discussed in Chapter 10 of *AutoCAD and its Applications—Basics, Release 14*.

When **MVSETUP** is used to create a standard engineering layout from a 3D model, a step-by-step procedure must be followed in order to achieve properly aligned views. The following list is a general outline of these steps. It is assumed that the 3D model has already been constructed in model space.

- Use **MVSETUP** options, or wizards and template files, to establish drawing limits and layers. Create a paper space border and title block layout using the **Title block** option.
- Establish paper space viewports with the **Create** option of **MVSETUP**, using the **Standard Engineering** option.
- The **Scale** and **Align** options must be used to adjust the size and placement of each view within its viewport.
- Complete the views by adding dimensions and notes, and revise any solid lines that should appear as hidden lines.

NOTE

The process of adding dimensions and notes to views created with **MVSETUP** is time-consuming. Care must be taken to create specific layers for each viewport. Use the **VPLAYER** command to handle viewport visibility of layers, or use the options contained in the **Layer and Linetype Properties** dialog box.

Creating hidden lines for each viewport is also tedious, but can be accomplished by changing linetypes in each viewport and assigning hidden lines to new layers specific to each viewport. Another method for creating multiview layouts suitable for dimensioning is provided with the **SOLVIEW** command. See Chapter 12 for a detailed discussion of this process.

Prior to starting the layout process, be sure the following items have been completed:

- Open the 3D model.
- Create a layer for the title block.
- Create a layer for viewports.
- Set the Viewports layer as current before using **MVSETUP**.

The following step-by-step procedure can be used to create a standard engineering layout using a 3D model. This example illustrates a title block and border inserted using **MVSETUP**. The 3D model is displayed on the screen as shown in Figure 7-16.

Figure 7-16.
The 3D model displayed in model space.

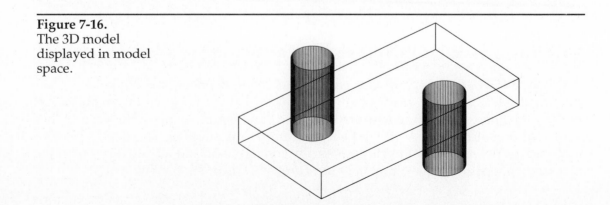

1. With the 3D model displayed on the screen, execute **MVSETUP**. Use **Options** to set a title block layer and establish paper space limits.

> Command: **MVSETUP**↲
> Enable paper space? (No/⟨Yes⟩): ↲
> Entering Paper space. Use MVIEW to insert Model space viewports.
> Regenerating paperspace.
> Align/Create/Scale viewports/Options/Title block/Undo: **O**↲
> Choose option to set — Layer/LImits/Units/Xref: **L**↲
> Layer name for title block or . for current layer: **TITLE_BLOCK**↲
> Choose option to set — Layer/LImits/Units/Xref: **LI**↲
> Set drawing limits? ⟨N⟩: **Y**↲
> Choose option to set — Layer/LImits/Units/Xref: ↲
> Align/Create/Scale viewports/Options/Title block/Undo:

2. Insert a title block using the **Title block** option.

> Align/Create/Scale viewports/Options/Title block/Undo: **T**↲
> Delete objects/Origin/Undo/⟨Insert title block⟩: ↲
> Available title block options:
>
> | | |
> |---|---|
> | 0: | None |
> | 1: | ISO A4 Size (mm) |
> | 2: | ISO A3 Size (mm) |
> | 3: | ISO A2 Size (mm) |
> | 4: | ISO A1 Size (mm) |
> | 5: | ISO A0 Size (mm) |
> | 6: | ANSI-V Size (in) |
> | 7: | ANSI-A Size (in) |
> | 8: | ANSI-B Size (in) |
> | 9: | ANSI-C Size (in) |
> | 10: | ANSI-D Size (in) |
> | 11: | ANSI-E Size (in) |
> | 12: | Arch/Engineering (24 x 36in) |
> | 13: | Generic D size Sheet (24 x 36in) |
>
> Add/Delete/Redisplay/⟨Number of entry to load⟩: **8**↲
> Align/Create/Scale viewports/Options/Title block/Undo:

The title block and border are now inserted in paper space over the model space drawing. See Figure 7-17.

3. Use the **Create** option of **MVSETUP** to place an arrangement of four viewports on the paper. Select number 2, the Standard Engineering layout.

> Align/Create/Scale viewports/Options/Title block/Undo: **C**↲
> Delete objects/Undo/⟨Create viewports⟩: ↲
> Available Mview viewport layout options:
>
> | | |
> |---|---|
> | 0: | None |
> | 1: | Single |
> | 2: | Std. Engineering |
> | 3: | Array of Viewports |
>
> Redisplay/⟨Number of entry to load⟩: **2**↲
> Bounding area for viewport(s). First point: *(pick first viewport corner)*
> Other point: *(pick second viewport corner)*
> Distance between viewports in X. ⟨0.0⟩: **.25**↲
> Distance between viewports in Y. ⟨0.25⟩: ↲
> Align/Create/Scale viewports/Options/Title block/Undo:

Figure 7-18 shows the resulting viewport arrangement.

Figure 7-17.
The **Title block** option of **MVSETUP** is used to insert a border and title block in paper space.

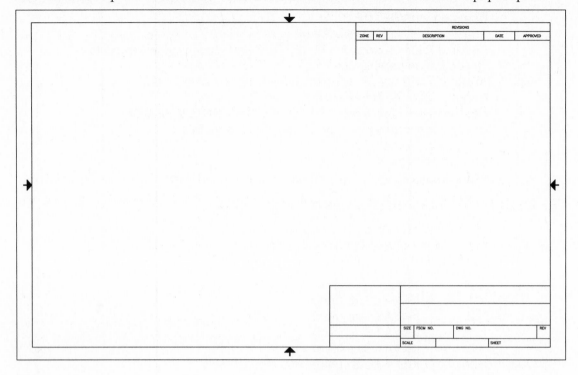

Figure 7-18.
A standard engineering layout is generated using the **Create** option of the **MVSETUP** command.

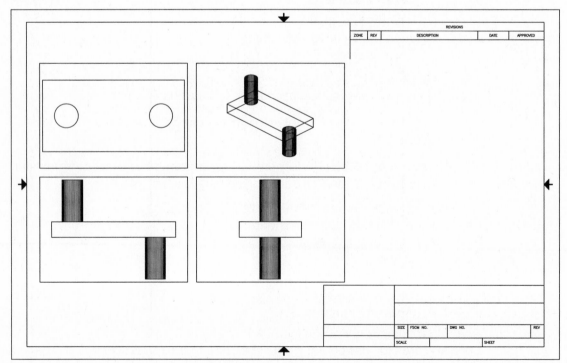

4. Next use the **Scale** option to set a scale in the orthogonal viewports.

> Align/Create/Scale viewports/Options/Title block/Undo: **S**↵
> Select the viewports to scale…
> Select objects: *(pick the three orthogonal viewport outlines)*
> Select objects: ↵
> Set zoom scale factors for viewports. Interactively/⟨Uniform⟩: ↵
> Number of paper space units. ⟨1.0⟩: ↵
> Number of model space units. ⟨1.0⟩: **2**↵
> Align/Create/Scale viewports/Options/Title block/Undo:

The scaled arrangement is shown in Figure 7-19. The 3D viewport can be scaled in the same manner using a different scale if desired.

5. The objects in the three orthogonal viewports are automatically aligned when the layout is first created. If the objects become misaligned for any reason, they can be quickly adjusted using the **Align** option as follows:

> Align/Create/Scale viewports/Options/Title block/Undo: **A**↵
> Angled/Horizontal/Vertical alignment/Rotate view/Undo: **V**↵
> Basepoint: **END**↵
> of *(pick inside the front viewport, then pick an endpoint)*
> Other point: **END**↵
> of *(pick inside the top viewport, then pick a corresponding endpoint)*
> Angled/Horizontal/Vertical alignment/Rotate view/Undo: **H**↵

Proceed in the same manner to align horizontal viewports.

The standard engineering layout is now complete. Remember, this procedure is sufficient for objects that have few hidden features in the views. If hidden features do exist, additional layers must be created and they must be frozen in all viewports except the one in which they are visible. See Chapter 24 of *AutoCAD and its Applications—Basics, Release 14* for a detailed discussion of the **VPLAYER** command.

Figure 7-19.
Objects in all viewports can be resized using the **Scale** option of the **MVSETUP** command.

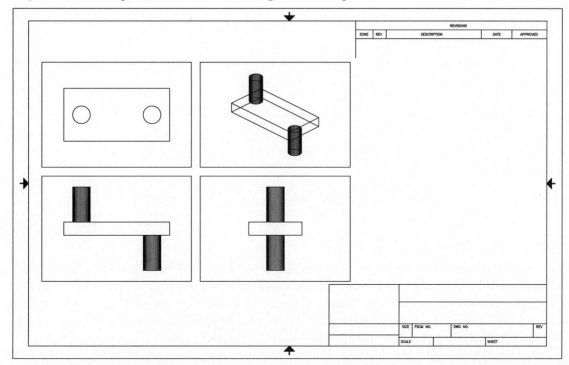

AutoCAD User's Guide **14**

Displaying a 3D Model

The *display* of a 3D model is how the model is presented. This does not refer to the viewing angle. The simplest display technique is to remove hidden lines using the **HIDE** command. A simple rendered model can be created with the **SHADE** command. An advanced rendered model can be created with the **RENDER** command. This is the most realistic presentation.

Using the HIDE command

HIDE
HI

View
↳ Hide

Render
toolbar

Hide

The **HIDE** command removes hidden lines from the display. The command regenerates the drawing and removes all lines that are behind other objects. Invisible edges of 3D faces are also removed. To use this command, select **Hide** from the **View** pull-down menu, pick the **Hide** button from the **Render** toolbar, or type HI or HIDE at the Command: prompt.

Hiding lines on a plotted drawing can be done in one of two ways. These are described below:

- **Plotting.** Hidden lines are removed in a plot only if the **Hide-Lines** check box is selected in the **Plot Configuration** dialog box.
- **Paper space plotting.** Hidden lines are not automatically removed in floating model space viewports when a drawing is plotted in paper space. To hide these lines, turn on the **Hideplot** option of the **MVIEW** command. Then, select the viewport to hide as follows:

  Command: **MVIEW**↵
  ON/OFF/Hideplot/Fit/2/3/4/Restore/⟨First Point⟩: **H**↵
  ON/OFF: **ON**↵
  Select objects: *(pick the viewport to hide lines when plotting)*
  1 found
  Select objects: ↵
  Command:

When you pick the viewport, pick the border of the viewport. Do not pick the objects in the viewport.

CAUTION

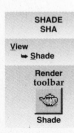

Layers that are turned off are still regenerated. Frozen layers are not regenerated. Therefore, objects on layers that are turned off may block your view of objects on visible layers. On the other hand, objects on layers that are frozen will not obscure objects on visible layers.

Using the SHADE command

SHADE
SHA

View
↳ Shade

Render
toolbar

Shade

The **SHADE** command can be accessed by selecting **Shade** from the **View** pull-down menu, picking the **Shade** button in the **Render** toolbar, or typing SHA or SHADE at the Command: prompt. If the **Shade** button or Command: prompt is used, the objects are shaded using the current **SHADEDGE** value. The default value is 3. If you select the command from the **View** pull-down menu, a cascading submenu appears, Figure 7-20. The options in this submenu temporarily change the **SHADEDGE** variable and then shade the object. The different **SHADEDGE** settings are explained below.

Figure 7-20.
Selecting an option from the **Shade** cascading menu in the **View** pull-down menu temporarily changes the **SHADEDGE** variable.

View
- Redraw
- Regen
- Regen All

- Zoom ▶
- Pan ▶
- Aerial View

✓ Model Space (Tiled)
- Model Space (Floating)
- Paper Space

- Tiled Viewports ▶
- Floating Viewports ▶

- Named Views...
- 3D Viewpoint ▶
- 3D Dynamic View

- Hide
- Shade ▶
  - 256 Color ────────── **SHADEDGE=0**
  - 256 Color Edge Highlight ── **SHADEDGE=1**
  - 16 Color Hidden Line ──── **SHADEDGE=2**
  - 16 Color Filled ──────── **SHADEDGE=3**
- Render ▶

- Display ▶
- Toolbars...

SHADEDGE value	Pull-down menu option	Explanation
0	**256 Color**	Faces are shaded and edges are not highlighted.
1	**256 Color Edge Highlight**	Faces are shaded and edges are drawn in the background color.
2	**16 Color Hidden Line**	Faces are not shaded and edges are drawn in the object color.
3	**16 Color Filled**	Faces are shaded in the object color and edges are drawn in the background color.

Figure 7-21 shows the effects of the four different **SHADEDGE** settings.

Diffuse light is light reflected off the surface of an object. The amount of diffuse light from an object is controlled by the **SHADEDIF** (shade diffuse) system variable. This value is the percent of light from the source behind your eyes that is diffused from the surface. The default value is 70, or 70%. The remaining 30% of light you see in a shaded drawing is ambient light. *Ambient light* is the natural light that surrounds you. The **SHADEDIF** value can be set at the Command: prompt:

Command: **SHADEDIF**↵
New value for SHADEDIF ⟨*current*⟩: **100**↵

Figure 7-21.
The **SHADEDGE** values produce different display effects.
A—**SHADEDGE** = 0.
B—**SHADEDGE** = 1.
C—**SHADEDGE** = 2.
D—**SHADEDGE** = 3.

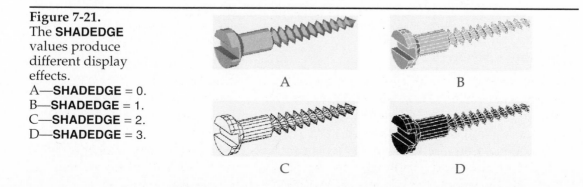

A

B

C

D

Since the **SHADEDIF** value is a percentage, the setting can be from 0 to 100.

The effects of several **SHADEDIF** settings are shown in Figure 7-22. All of the images in Figure 7-22 were produced with a **SHADEDGE** value of 0. This setting does not create edge highlighting.

Figure 7-22.
SHADEDIF can be set to values from 0 to 100.
A—**SHADEDIF** = 10.
B—**SHADEDIF** = 40.
C—**SHADEDIF** = 70.
D—**SHADEDIF** = 100.

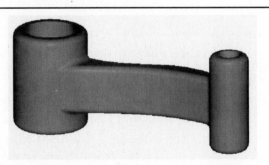

A   B

C   D

Producing a quick rendering

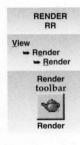
Rendering is covered in detail in Chapter 9 and Chapter 14. The **Render** dialog box is used to specify rendering variables. To access this dialog box, select **Render** from the **Render** cascading menu in the **View** pull-down menu, pick the **Render** button from the **Render** toolbar, or enter RR or RENDER at the Command: prompt.

Open a model from an earlier chapter and select a 3D viewpoint. Use the defaults shown in the **Render** dialog box and pick the **Render** button (or press [Enter]). A shaded and rendered image is then created, Figure 7-23.

Figure 7-23.
A rendering of the link rod model.

EXERCISE 7-4

❑ Open one of your 3D models from an earlier chapter.
❑ Pick each of the four shading options in the **Shade** submenu. Notice the difference in the displays.
❑ Change the **SHADEDIF** setting and select one of the shading options. Do this for three different **SHADEDIF** settings.
❑ Use the **RENDER** command to produce a shaded rendering of the object.
❑ Do not save the drawing.

Chapter Test

Write your answers in the spaces provided.

1. What kind of coordinates can you use with the **Rotate** option of the **VPOINT** command? _____

2. What two angles are needed when using the **Rotate** option of the **VPOINT** command?

    _____

    _____

3. What command produces a view that is perpendicular to the current UCS?_____

    _____

4. What does the image on the left side of the **Viewpoint Presets** dialog box represent?

    _____

5. What is the function of the DVIEWBLOCK? _____

    _____

6. How do you specify a camera angle using the **DVIEW** command?_____

    _____

7. What two values must be set to complete the **DVIEW** option in Question 6? _____

    _____

8. What point does the camera look at in the **DVIEW** command? What option is used to set it? _____

9. Which option of the **DVIEW** command allows you to create a perspective view?

    _____

10. After a perspective view is created and you are at the Command: prompt, which commands and activities are *not* allowed?_____

    _____

11. How is a lens length selected in the **DVIEW** command? _____

    _____

12. What portions of an object are removed when **DVIEW** clipping planes are set?

    _____

    _____

13. What is the function of the **Hideplot** option of the **MVIEW** command?_____

    _____

14. What system variable controls the appearance of surfaces and edges when the **SHADE** command is used? _____

15. Which value of the variable in Question 14 produces faces that are shaded in the object color and edges that are drawn in the background color? _____

16. What is the function of the **SHADEDIF** system variable? _____

    _____

    _____

    _____

17. What is the range of values that **SHADEDIF** can be set to?_____

18. What command produces the most realistic shaded image?_____

Drawing Problems

1. Open one of your 3D drawings from a previous chapter and do the following:

   A. Use **VPOINT** to produce a display with a 30° rotation in the XY plane and a 40° rotation from the XY plane.

   B. Shade the object so that faces are shown in object colors and edges are highlighted.

   C. Produce a slide of the image. Refer to Chapter 28 of *AutoCAD and its Applications—Basics, Release 14* for information on creating slides.

2. Open one of your 3D drawings from a previous chapter and do the following:

   A. Create an arrangement of three floating model space viewports in a paper space layout.

   B. Display the drawing from a different viewpoint in each viewport.

   C. Set the **SHADEDGE** variable to a different value in each viewport. Create a shaded image using **SHADE** in each viewport.

3. Open one of your 3D drawings from a previous chapter and perform the following:

   A. Create an arrangement of three floating model space viewports in a paper space layout.

   B. Display the drawing in a different viewpoint in each viewport.

   C. Set the **SHADEDGE** variable to a different value in two viewports. Set **SHADEDIF** to different values in those two viewports as well.

   D. Shade the objects in the two viewports, and use **RENDER** in the third viewport.

4. Open one of your 3D drawings from a previous chapter and perform the following:

   A. Create a standard engineering layout on a sheet of paper that requires a scale other than full.

   B. Display the 3D viewport drawing in a scale different than the other viewports.

   C. Create dimensioning layers for each of the three orthogonal viewports and apply some basic dimensions to each view.

   D. Use the **Hideplot** option of the **MVIEW** command to hide the hidden lines in the 3D viewport.

   D. Plot the drawing in paper space using a scale of 1:1.

Three-Dimensional Text and Dimensioning

Learning Objectives

After completing this chapter, you will be able to:
- ○ Create text with a thickness.
- ○ Apply horizontal text and titles to 3D views.
- ○ Rotate 3D text to a different plane.
- ○ Describe how 3D objects can hide text.
- ○ Create 3D dimensioning.
- ○ Apply leaders to different UCS planes.

Creating 3D Text with Thickness

Text does not have a thickness when created. This is true even if thickness is set with the **ELEV** command before drawing text. Text must be given thickness after it is created using the **CHANGE**, **DDMODIFY**, or **DDCHPROP** command. Once a thickness is applied, the hidden lines can be removed by using **HIDE**. Figure 8-1 shows six different fonts as they appear after being given a thickness with hidden lines removed.

Figure 8-1.
Six different fonts with thickness after hidden lines are removed.

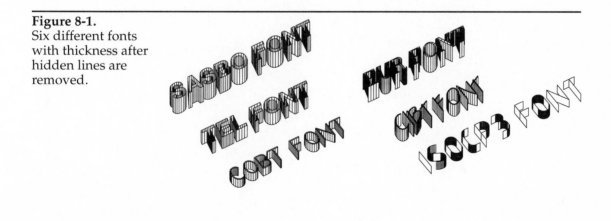

AutoCAD comes with a variety of TrueType fonts, which are listed with a .ttf file extension. These fonts *cannot* be given thickness. Standard AutoCAD fonts have an .shx extension. This is a compiled version of the corresponding .shp, or *shape*, file. Although none are shipped with Release 14, PostScript fonts have a .pfb file extension, which is not useable until it is compiled into a .pfm file. To compile a .shp or .pfb font into a file type that can be used in AutoCAD, type COMPILE at the Command: prompt. The **Select Shape or Font File** dialog box shown below appears. If AutoCAD was installed using default values, the directory that contains the fonts is \AutoCAD R14\Fonts. Pick either .shp or .pfb in the **Files of type:** list box. Next, select the font you wish to compile and pick **OK**. The font can now be used in AutoCAD, and the .shx or .pfm font can be given thickness.

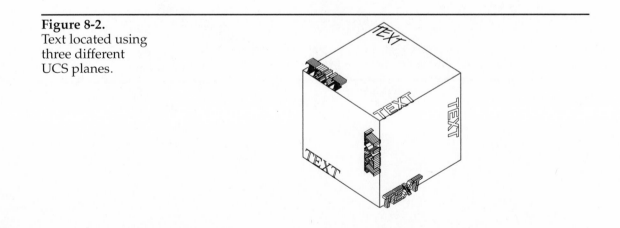

Text and the UCS

Text is parallel to the UCS in which it is drawn. Therefore, if you wish to show text appearing on a specific plane, make that plane the current UCS before placing the text. Figure 8-2 shows several examples of text on different UCS planes.

Figure 8-2.
Text located using three different UCS planes.

Changing the UCS of a text object

If text is placed improperly or on the wrong UCS, it can be edited using grips or 3D editing commands. For example, if the text at the upper-left corner of Figure 8-2 should be "lying" on the top surface, it can be edited as follows:

Command: **ROTATE3D**↵
Select objects: (*pick the text object*)
Select objects: ↵
Axis by Object/Last/View/Xaxis/Yaxis/Zaxis/⟨2points⟩: **X**↵
Point on X axis ⟨0,0,0⟩: **END**↵
of (*pick line along the bottom of the text*)
⟨Rotation angle⟩/Reference: **-90**↵
Command:

This command sequence is based on the UCS in which the text was drawn. The axis of rotation may be different if another UCS is current.

After hidden lines are removed, the object appears as shown in Figure 8-3A. Since this text has a thickness, it appears to be recessed into the surface of the box with its "feet" showing through the side. To place the text on the top surface, use grips to move it the thickness of the text along the appropriate axis. The edited object is shown in Figure 8-3B.

Figure 8-3.
A—Text that
appears recessed
in the box.
B—After being
moved using grips.

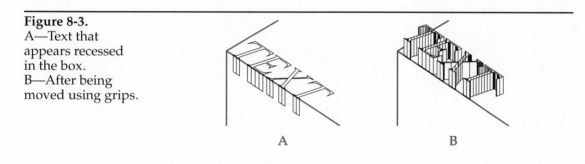

A   B

Using the **UCS** View option to create a title

Text does not always need to be placed in a 3D plane. It can be drawn perpendicular and horizontal to your point of view regardless of the 3D viewpoint displayed. This application is used to insert the title of a 3D view. This is done with the **View** option of the **UCS** command:

Command: **UCS**↵
Origin/ZAxis/3point/OBject/View/X/Y/Z/Prev/Restore/Save/Del/?/⟨World⟩: **V**↵

A new UCS is created perpendicular to your viewpoint. However, the view remains a 3D view. Name and save the UCS if you will use it again. Since inserted text is placed parallel to the new UCS, it will be horizontal (or vertical) in the current view. See Figure 8-4.

Figure 8-4.
Titles can be placed correctly using the **View** option of the **UCS** command.

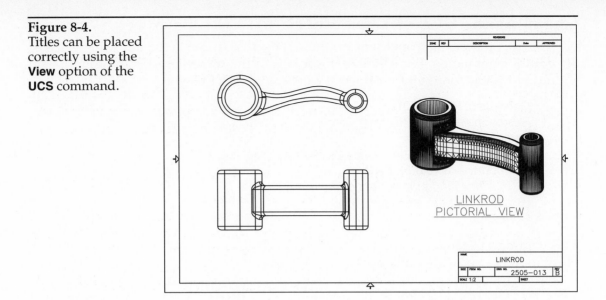

The limitations of hiding text

Text that is drawn without a thickness will not be properly hidden by the **HIDE** command, even if it is placed behind a 3D object. In order for text behind a 3D object to be hidden, it must be given a thickness. Text that has a thickness will appear correctly when placed inside, outside, or protruding through a 3D object. If you want text to be hidden but not appear to have a thickness, give it a thickness of .001.

Figure 8-5A shows a variety of text placements in and around a 3D box. The two text objects at the upper left are sitting outside the box. Figure 8-5B shows the display after **HIDE** is used.

Figure 8-5.
A—Text objects placed in and around a 3D box.
B—The display after **HIDE** is used.

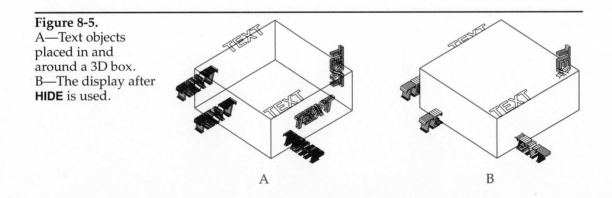

A   B

3D Dimensioning

Dimensioned 3D objects are seldom used for manufacturing, but may be used for assembly. Most often dimensioned 3D drawings are used for some sort of presentation, such as displays, illustrations, parts manuals, or training manuals. Therefore, dimensions shown in 3D must be clear and easy to read. The most important aspect of applying dimensions to a 3D object is planning. That means following a few basic guidelines.

Create a 3D dimensioning template drawing

If you often create dimensioned 3D drawings, make a template drawing containing a few 3D display settings. These are outlined below:

- Create named dimension styles with appropriate text heights. See Chapters 18–21 of *AutoCAD and its Applications—Basics, Release 14* for detailed information on dimensioning and dimension styles.
- Establish several named User Coordinate Systems that match the planes where dimensions will be placed. See Figure 8-6 for examples of standard named systems.
- Establish several 3D viewpoints that can be used for different objects. These viewpoints will allow you to select the display best for reading dimensions. Name and save these views.

Figure 8-6.
Three named User Coordinate Systems that can be used for dimensioning.

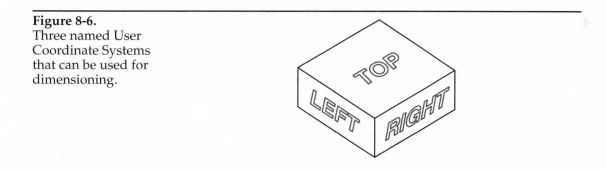

Placing dimensions in the proper plane

To create dimensions that display properly, it may be necessary to create more than one UCS for a single plane. Notice in Figure 8-7A that the left dimension is inverted. Note the orientation of the UCS. A second UCS is created and the dimension is redrawn correctly in Figure 8-7B.

Figure 8-7.
More than one UCS for a given plane may be needed to properly create dimensions. A—The left-hand dimension is inverted. B—The left-hand dimension drawn correctly using a different UCS.

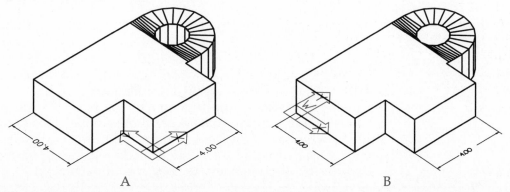

A   B

The location and plane where dimensions are placed is often a matter of choice. For example, Figure 8-8 shows several options for placing a thickness dimension on the object. All of these are correct. However, several of the options can be eliminated when other dimensions are added. This illustrates the importance of planning.

The key to good 3D dimensioning is to avoid overlapping dimension and extension lines in different planes. A freehand sketch can help you plan this. As you lay out the 3D sketch, try to group information items together. Dimensions, notes, and item tags should be grouped so that they are easy to read and understand. This technique is called *information grouping*.

Figure 8-9A shows the object from Figure 8-8 fully dimensioned using the aligned technique. Notice that the location dimension for the hole is placed on the top surface. This avoids dimensioning to hidden points. Figure 8-9B shows the same object dimensioned using the unilateral technique.

Figure 8-8.
The thickness dimension can be located in many different places. All of the locations shown here are correct.

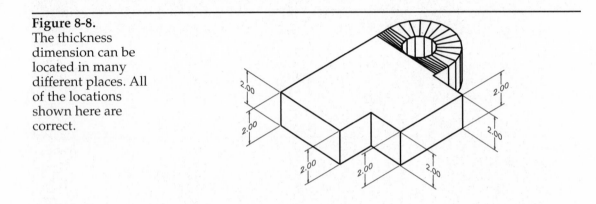

Figure 8-9.
A—An example of a 3D object dimensioned using the aligned technique. B—The object dimensioned with unilateral dimensions.

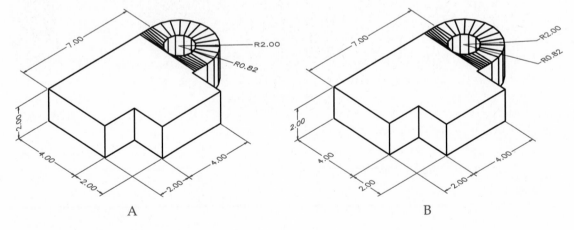

A   B

PROFESSIONAL TIP

Prior to placing dimensions on a 3D drawing, you should determine the purpose of the drawing. What will it be used for? Just as dimensioning a drawing for manufacturing purposes is based on the function of the part, 3D dimensioning is based on the function of the drawing. This determines whether you use chain, datum, arrowless, architectural, or some other style of dimensioning. It also determines how completely the object is dimensioned.

Placing leaders and radial dimensions in 3D

Although standards such as ASME Y14.5M-1994 should be followed, the nature of 3D drawing and the requirements of the project may determine how dimensions and leaders are placed. Remember, the most important aspect of dimensioning a 3D drawing is its presentation. Is it easy to read and interpret?

Leaders and radial dimensions can be placed in, or perpendicular to, the plane of the feature. Figure 8-10A shows the placement of leaders in the plane of the top surface. Figure 8-10B illustrates the placement of leaders and radial dimensions in a UCS that is perpendicular to the top surface of the object.

In Figure 8-10B, notice the arrowhead on the R2.00 dimension. The bottom half is missing. That is because it is below the top surface of the object and will not be visible when **HIDE** is used. Keep this in mind when choosing a plane for 3D dimensions.

Remember that text, dimensions, and leaders are always placed in the XY plane of the current UCS. Therefore, to create the layout in Figure 8-10B, you must use more than one UCS. Figure 8-11A and Figure 8-11B show the UCS icon orientations for the two radial dimensions.

Figure 8-10.
A—Leaders placed in the plane of the top surface. B—Leaders placed in a UCS perpendicular to the top surface. Notice the arrowhead on the radius dimension is half hidden.

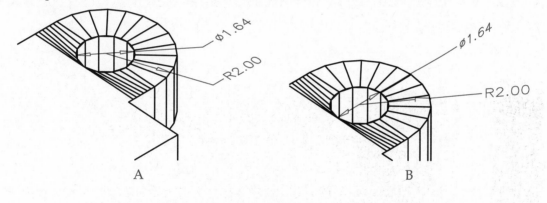

Figure 8-11.
A—The UCS used to draw the diameter dimension. B—The UCS used to draw the radius dimension.

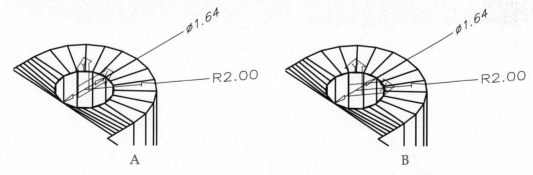

NOTE	When you are dimensioning 3D objects, AutoCAD does not fill in the arrowheads of dimensions and leaders.

Chapter 8 Three-Dimensional Text and Dimensioning

❏ Begin a new drawing and name it EX8-2.
❏ Draw the object shown in Figure 8-9 using the dimensions given. Create as many different User Coordinate Systems needed to draw and dimension the object.
❏ Place dimensions and leaders to achieve the best presentation.
❏ Save the drawing as EX8-2.

Chapter Test

Write your answers in the spaces provided.

1. How does the **ELEV** command affect the thickness of text? _____

   _____

   _____

2. What commands are used to alter text thickness? _____

   _____

3. What file extension is used for PostScript font shape files? _____

4. How can PostScript fonts be used for 3D text with thickness? _____

   _____

5. If text is placed using the wrong UCS, how can it be edited to appear on the correct one? _____

   _____

6. How can text be placed horizontally in your viewpoint if the object is displayed in 3D? _____

   _____

   _____

   _____

7. How can text be made to appear hidden when it is behind a 3D object and **HIDE** is used?_____

   _____

   _____

8. What is the most common use of dimensioned 3D drawings?_____

   _____

9. Give three items that should be a part of a 3D dimensioning template drawing.

   _____

   _____

10. What is information grouping? _____

   _____

   _____

Drawing Problems

1. Construct a 4" cube. Create a named UCS for each of the six sides. Name them FRONT, BACK, RIGHT, LEFT, TOP, and BOTTOM. Place a text label with a .75" thickness centered on each face of the cube. Use TrueType fonts for at least two faces. Save the drawing as P8-1.

*Problems 2–10. Create a fully dimensioned 3D drawing of the following problems. Save the drawings as **P8-2**, **P8-3**, etc.*

2. Chapter 2, Problem 1.

3. Chapter 2, Problem 2.

4. Chapter 2, Problem 3.

5. Chapter 2, Problem 4.

6. Chapter 2, Problem 6.

7. Chapter 2, Problem 7.

8. Chapter 2, Problem 8.

9. Chapter 2, Problem 9.

10. Chapter 2, Problem 12.

*Problems 11–18. Create a fully dimensioned 3D drawing of the following problems. Place a text label below each drawing. The text should be horizontal in the current viewpoint. Use a label such as **3D VIEW**, or the name of the object, such as **GUIDE BRACKET**. Save the drawings as **P8-11**, **P8-12**, etc.*

11. Chapter 3, Problem 1.

12. Chapter 3, Problem 2.

 13. Chapter 3, Problem 3.

 14. Chapter 3, Problem 4.

 15. Chapter 3, Problem 5.

 16. Chapter 3, Problem 6.

 17. Chapter 3, Problem 7.

 18. Chapter 3, Problem 8.

Chapter 9

Introduction to Shading and Rendering

Learning Objectives

After completing this chapter, you will be able to:
- ○ Shade a 3D model.
- ○ Display a model using the **SHADEDGE** system variable.
- ○ Display a model using the **SHADEDIF** system variable.
- ○ Render a 3D model.
- ○ Render windowed areas in a 3D model.

In previous chapters, you used the **HIDE** command to make it easier to visualize a 3D model. The **SHADE** command displays the model more realistically than the **HIDE** command. The **SHADEDGE** and **SHADEDIF** system variables control how the shaded object appears. The **RENDER** command produces the most realistic image with highlights and shading. An example of a 3D model after using **HIDE**, **SHADE**, and **RENDER** is shown in Figure 9-1. This chapter discusses the **SHADE** command and the default settings of **RENDER**.

Shading a Model

The **SHADE** command is used to shade an object. The color of the shaded image is controlled by the color of the model. A single light source located behind the viewer points at the object. The **SHADEDGE** variable controls how the object's edges are displayed. The **SHADEDIF** variable controls the intensity of the light.

An object can be shaded from any viewpoint. A shaded model *cannot* be selected for editing until the screen is regenerated. You cannot plot a shaded image. However, you can copy a shaded image to the Windows Clipboard. The image can then be "pasted" into Windows Paintbrush or other software. The image can then be edited, printed, and saved in different file formats. See Chapter 13 and Chapter 24 for more detailed information on working with images using the Clipboard.

Figure 9-1.
A—Hidden lines removed. B—Shaded. C—Rendered. (J.P. Pond, Unified Technical
Education Center, Grand Junction, CO)

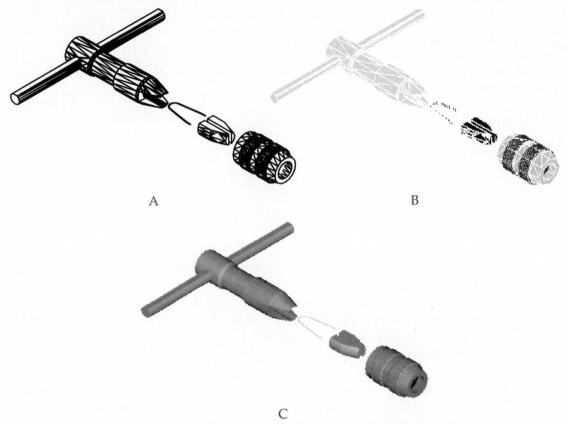

A

B

C

EXERCISE 9-1

❏ The 3D model created in this exercise is used in the remainder of the chapter.
You can use this model or substitute one of your own surfaced or solid models.
❏ Begin a new drawing.
❏ Set units to decimal and limits to 12, 9. **ZOOM All**.
❏ Create the following layers and colors:

Layer name	Color
Box	red
Cone	yellow
Cylinder	magenta
Torus	blue
Surfaces	white

❏ Make the Surfaces layer current. Use the **3DFACE** command to draw a square
floor surface with the coordinates (0,0), (8,0), (8,8), and (0,8). Draw a backdrop
surface with the coordinates (0,8), (8,8), (8,8,8), and (0,8,8).
❏ Set a viewpoint of (–3,–2,2).
❏ Use solid primitives to draw the following objects:
  ❏ Make the Box layer current. Draw a 3D primitive box (**BOX** command) with
  the corner at (5.5,6,2). Select the **Cube** option with a length of 2.
  ❏ Make the Cone layer current. Draw a 3D primitive cone (**CONE** command)
  with the center at (4,4), a diameter of 3 and a height of 6.
  ❏ Make the Torus layer current. Draw a 3D primitive torus (**TORUS** command)
  with the center at (7,1,2), a diameter of 3 and a tube radius of 1.

❏ Make the Cylinder layer current. Draw a 3D primitive cylinder (**CYLINDER** command) with the center at (1,7), a diameter of 1.5 and a height of 6.

❏ Save the drawing as EX9-1. Leave AutoCAD open. Your drawing should look like the one shown below.

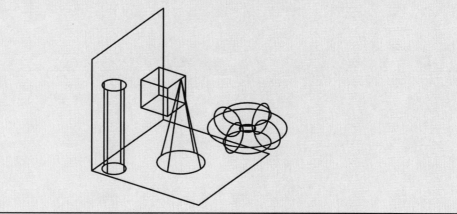

Performing a quick shade

SHADE
SHA

View
⮡ Shade

RENDER
toolbar

Shade

The quickest way to display a shaded image is to select the **Shade** button in the **Render** toolbar. See Figure 9-2. You also can select <u>**Shade**</u> from the <u>**View**</u> pull-down menu or type SHA or SHADE at the Command: prompt.

Using the **SHADE** command on the objects created in Exercise 9-1 produces the image shown in Figure 9-3A. Notice the difference between the **HIDE** image in Figure 9-3B and the shaded version. The model is shaded using the colors of the objects. The default settings of **SHADEDGE** = 3 and **SHADEDIF** = 70 were used in Figure 9-3. These variables are discussed in the next section.

Figure 9-2.
The **Shade** and **Render** buttons are found in the **Render** toolbar.

Shade   Render

Figure 9-3.
A—The **SHADE** command used on the objects created in Exercise 9-1. B—Hidden lines removed from the objects.

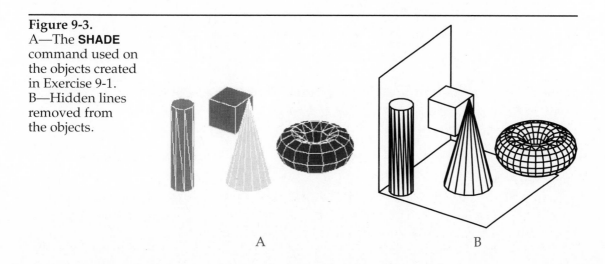

A   B

The SHADEDGE system variable

The **SHADEDGE** system variable controls how edges are displayed and how the faces are shaded. The four **SHADEDGE** options can be set at the Command: prompt. The options also can be selected from the **Shade** cascading menu in the **View** pull-down menu, Figure 9-4. If you set the variables using the Command: prompt, the settings stay until they are changed.

Figure 9-4.
The **SHADE** command can be selected from the **View** pull-down menu.

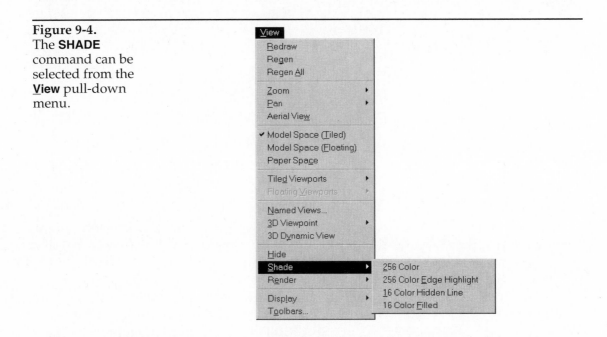

The **SHADEDGE** options are explained below. The corresponding pick in the **Shade** cascading menu is also given. You need a display with at least 256 colors using the standard AutoCAD 256 color map to see the full effect of values 0 and 1.

SHADEDGE setting	Description
0	Faces are shaded and edges are not highlighted. Pick **256 Color**.
1	Faces are shaded and edges are drawn in the background color. Pick **256 Color Edge Highlight**.
2	Faces are not shaded but are displayed in the background color, and edges are drawn in the object color. Pick **16 Color Hidden Line**.
3	Faces are shaded in the object color with no lighting effect, and edges are drawn in the background color. Pick **16 Color Filled**.

Figure 9-5 shows the effects of the four different SHADEDGE settings.

Figure 9-5.
Different **SHADEDGE** values produce different display effects. A—**SHADEDGE** = 0.
B—**SHADEDGE** = 1. C—**SHADEDGE** = 2. D—**SHADEDGE** = 3.

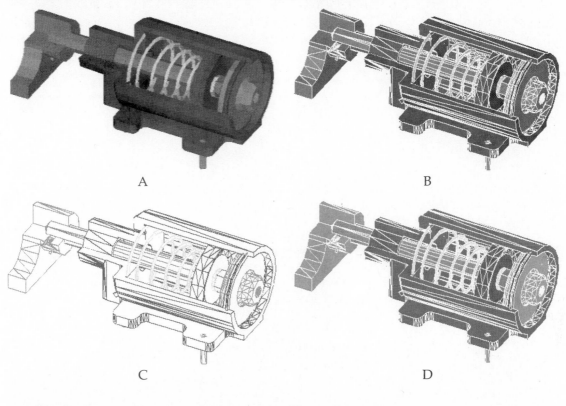

A   B

C   D

EXERCISE 9-2

❑ Open the drawing named EX9-1 if it is not displayed on your screen.
❑ Type SHADEDGE and enter the value 0. Use the **SHADE** command to shade the model.
❑ Set **SHADEDGE** to 1. Shade the model.
❑ Set **SHADEDGE** to 2. Shade the model.
❑ Set **SHADEDGE** to 3. Shade the model.
❑ How did each display differ?
❑ Do not save the drawing.

Using **SHADEDIF** to control lighting

The amount of diffuse light reflection from the surfaces of the object is controlled by the **SHADEDIF** (shade diffuse) system variable. The **SHADEDIF** value is the percent of light from the source behind your eyes that is reflected, or diffused, from the surface of the object. The higher the diffused value, the higher the contrast between surfaces in the image. The default value of SHADEDIF is 70. This means that 70% of the light striking the object is reflected. The remaining 30% is ambient light. Ambient light is the light that surrounds you, such as from a lamp or the sun. All surfaces receive the same amount of ambient light. Ambient light cannot create highlights.

The **SHADEDIF** value must be entered at the Command: prompt:

    Command: **SHADEDIF**↵
    New value for SHADEDIF ⟨70⟩: **100**↵

The effects of several **SHADEDIF** settings are shown in Figure 9-6. All of the images in Figure 9-6 have a **SHADEDGE** value of 0. This creates no edge highlighting.

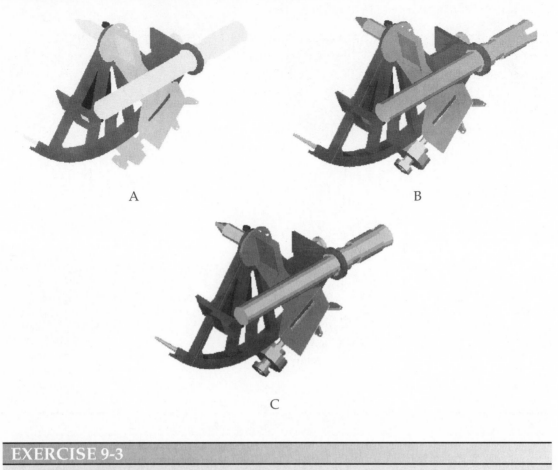

A

B

C

❏ Open the drawing named EX9-1 if it is not displayed on your screen.
❏ Set the **SHADEDGE** variable to 0 and the **SHADEDIF** variable to 0. Shade the model. Observe the results.
❏ Change **SHADEDGE** to 1 and shade the model again.
❏ Set **SHADEDIF** to values of 30, 70, and 100 and shade the model after each setting.
❏ Experiment with combinations of **SHADEDGE** and **SHADEDIF**.
❏ Do not save the drawing.

AutoCAD
User's **14**
Guide

Rendering a Model

The **RENDER** command creates a realistic image of a model. However, **RENDER** takes longer than **SHADE**. There are a variety of settings that you can change with the **RENDER** command to allow you to fine-tune renderings. These include scenes, lights, materials, backgrounds, fog, and preferences. These can all be changed in dialog boxes. The **RENDER** settings are discussed in detail in Chapter 14. This chapter covers the default settings of **RENDER**.

The **RENDER** command default settings display an image that is rendered in only the current viewport using a single light source located behind the viewer. The light intensity is set to 1 and the material is steel. All of these options are discussed in Chapter 14.

To render a model, select **Render** from the **Render** cascading menu in the **View** pull-down menu. You can also pick the **Render** button in the **Render** toolbar or type RR or RENDER at the Command: prompt. The **Render** dialog box appears, Figure 9-7. Pick the **Render** button to render the model.

RENDER
RR

View
➥ Render
  ➥ Render

Render
toolbar

Render

EXERCISE 9-4

❑ Open the drawing named EX9-1 if it is not displayed on your screen.
❑ Change the viewpoint to the SW isometric.
❑ Render the drawing.
❑ The image should look like the one shown below.

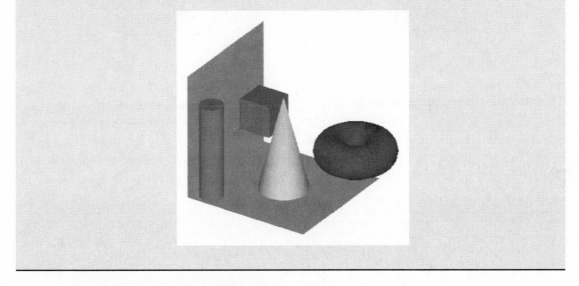

A smooth shaded rendering

Notice in Figure 9-7 that the **Smooth Shade** check box is active. This produces a rendering where individual polygon faces are smoothed to create a more realistic image. However, this is a more complicated process and takes longer to display. Figure 9-8 shows the effect of smooth shading.

Figure 9-7.
Basic rendering options are set in the **Render** dialog box.

Figure 9-8.
A—A rendering without smooth shading. B—A rendering with smooth shading applied.

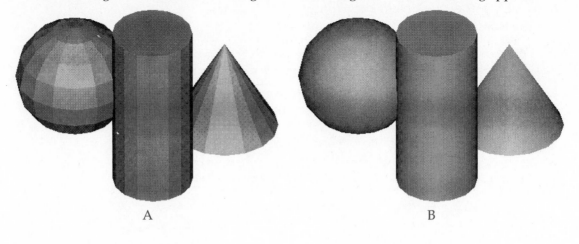

A   B

Rendering specific areas

A time-saving option in the **Render** dialog box is the **Crop Window** check box in the **Rendering Procedure** area. This feature allows you to render a windowed area in the model. Only the objects inside the specified window are rendered. A small area of the model from Exercise 9-1 is rendered in Figure 9-9.

Figure 9-9.
Cropping a window to be rendered. The portion of the screen outside the window is black.

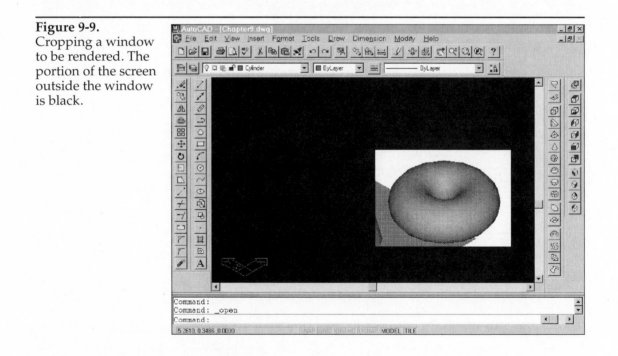

Chapter Test

Write your answers in the spaces provided.

1. What is the difference between the **HIDE** and **SHADE** commands? _____

   _____

   _____

2. What affects the color of the objects to be shaded? _____

   _____

   _____

3. What is the purpose of the **SHADEDGE** system variable? _____

   _____

4. What does a **SHADEDGE** value of 2 do? _____

   _____

   _____

5. What hardware do you need for the **SHADEDGE** values of 0 and 1 to be effective?

   _____

   _____

6. What system variable controls the lighting effects in the **SHADE** command? ____

   _____

7. What is ambient light? _____

   _____

   _____

   _____

8. What is diffused light? _____

   _____

   _____

   _____

9. The default setting for **SHADEDIF** is 70. What does this mean? _____

   _____

   _____

10. What is the function of the **RENDER** command? _____

    _____

    _____

    _____

11. When rendering, what are the benefits of the **Crop Window** option? _____

    _____

    _____

    _____

Drawing Problems

1. Open one of your 3D drawings from a previous chapter. Set the **SHADEDIF** to 30. Shade the drawing. Set **SHADEDIF** to 70 and **SHADEDGE** to 1. Shade the drawing.

2. Open one of your 3D drawings from a previous chapter.

   A. Create a four-viewport configuration.

   B. Set **SHADEDGE** to 3. Shade the objects in the upper-left viewport.

   C. Set **SHADEDGE** to 2. Shade the objects in the upper-right viewport.

   D. Change **SHADEDGE** variable to 1 and shade the lower-left viewport. If you do not have a 256 color display, skip this step.

   E. Shade the objects in the lower-right viewport after changing **SHADEDGE** to 0. If you do not have a 256 color display, you do not need to do this step.

3. Using a 3D drawing from the last chapter, **RENDER** the current scene. Use the same drawing to render two different windowed areas.

4. Begin a new drawing named P9-4.

   A. Make a Box layer and set the color to yellow. Make a Cone layer and set the color to blue. Make a Torus layer and set the color to green. Make the Torus layer current.

   B. Create a torus with a center point at (3,3,3), a diameter of 5, and a tube diameter of 1.

   C. Make the Cone layer current. Create a 3D solid cone. Place the center of the cone at (7,9,1) with a diameter of 2 and height of 7.

   D. Make the Box layer current. Create a solid box. Place the first corner at (1,6,8) and make the box a 2 unit cube.

   E. Make 2 vertical viewports. In the left viewport, set your viewpoint to the SW isometric. In the right viewport, set the viewpoint to the SE isometric.

   F. Shade the right viewport. Render the left viewport.

   G. Experiment with different **SHADEDGE** and **SHADEDIF** settings.

Chapter 10

Introduction to Solid Modeling

Learning Objectives

After completing this chapter, you will be able to:
- ○ Create regions that can be analyzed.
- ○ Construct 3D solid primitives.
- ○ Create complex solids using the **UNION** command.
- ○ Remove portions of a solid using the **SUBTRACT** command.
- ○ Create a new solid from the common intersection of two or more solids.
- ○ Verify for interference between two solids and create a new solid from the interference volume.

Working with Regions

A *region* is a closed two-dimensional solid. It can be extruded into a 3D solid object. A region can also be analyzed for its mass properties. Therefore, regions are useful for 2D applications where area and boundary calculations must be quickly obtained from a drawing. In addition, a 2D section view can be converted to a region, then extruded into a 3D solid model.

Constructing a 2D region model

The **REGION** command allows you to convert closed two-dimensional entities into regions. A region has all the 3D solid model properties except for thickness (Z value). When regions are added to, subtracted from, or intersected with other regions, a *composite region* is created. A composite region is also called a *region model*. A region can be given a thickness, or *extruded*, quickly and easily. This means that you can convert a 2D shape into a 3D solid model in just a few steps.

The example on the following page creates a base for a support bracket. First, set your limits to 18,12 and perform a **Zoom all**. Next, use the **RECTANG**, **CIRCLE**, and **ARRAY** commands to create the profile geometry. Then, convert the profile into a 2D composite region model.

```
Command: REC or RECTANG↵
Chamfer/Elevation/Fillet/Thickness/Width/⟨First corner⟩: 3,3↵
Other corner: 11,11↵
Command: C or CIRCLE↵
3P/2P/TTR/⟨Center point⟩: 4,4↵
Diameter/⟨Radius⟩: D↵
Diameter: .75↵
Command: AR or ARRAY↵
Select objects: L↵
1 found
Select objects: ↵
Rectangular or Polar array (⟨R⟩/P): ↵
Number of rows (---) ⟨1⟩: 2↵
Number of columns (|||): 2↵
Unit cell or distance between rows (---): 6↵
Distance between columns (|||): 6↵
Command:
```

REGION
REG

Draw
➥ Region

Draw
toolbar

Region

This creates AutoCAD entities that can now be converted into regions. See Figure 10-1. Convert the rectangle and circles to regions using the **REGION** command. You can select this command by picking the **Region** button in the **Draw** toolbar, selecting **Region** in the **Draw** pull-down menu, or typing REG or REGION at the Command: prompt:

```
Command: REG or REGION↵
Select objects: (pick the rectangle and circles)
Select objects: ↵
5 loops extracted.
5 Regions created.
Command:
```

The rectangle is now a region and each circle is a region. In order to create the surface of the rectangle, the circles must be subtracted from it. Use the **SUBTRACT** command by picking the **Subtract** button in the **Modify II** toolbar, selecting **Subtract** from the **Boolean** cascading menu in the **Modify** pull-down menu, or entering SU or SUBTRACT at the Command: prompt:

SUBTRACT
SU

Modify
➥ Boolean
➥ Subtract

Modify II
toolbar

Subtract

```
Command: SU or SUBTRACT↵
Select solids and regions to subtract from...
Select objects: (pick the rectangle)
Select objects: ↵
Select solids and regions to subtract...
Select objects: (pick the four circles)
Select objects: ↵
Command:
```

Now if you select the rectangle or any of the circles, you can see that all five objects have been changed into one region.

Figure 10-1.
These 2D objects can be made into a region. The region can then be made into a 3D solid.

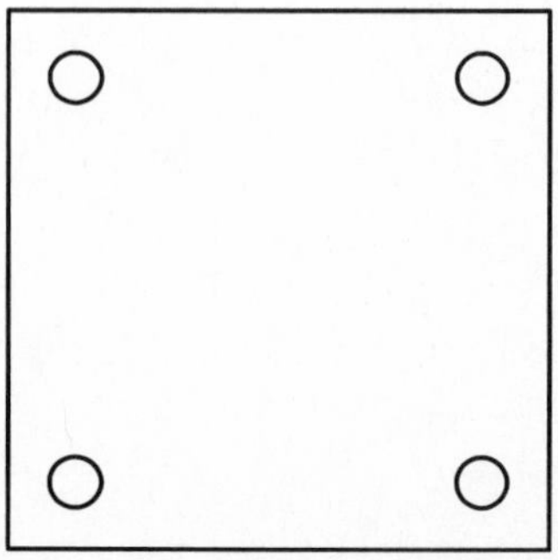

AutoCAD and its Applications—Advanced

Using the BOUNDARY command to create a region

The **BOUNDARY** command is often used to create a polyline for hatching or an inquiry. In addition, this command can be used to create a region. To do so, pick **Boundary** from the **Draw** pull-down menu or type BO or BOUNDARY at the Command: prompt. The **Boundary Creation** dialog box is displayed. See Figure 10-2.

To create a region, pick the **Object Type:** drop-down menu, then pick **Region**. Next, select the **Pick Points** button. You are returned to the graphics display and prompted to select an internal point. Pick a point inside the object you wish to convert to a region. Press [Enter] when you are finished and the region is created. You can always check to see if an object is a polyline or region by using the **LIST** command.

BOUNDARY
BO

Draw
➥ Boundary

Figure 10-2.
Regions can be created using the **Boundary Creation** dialog box.

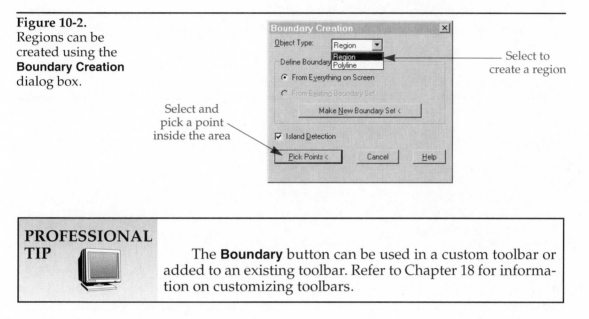

Select to create a region

Select and pick a point inside the area

PROFESSIONAL TIP

The **Boundary** button can be used in a custom toolbar or added to an existing toolbar. Refer to Chapter 18 for information on customizing toolbars.

Extruding a 2D region into a 3D solid

The final step in creating a 3D solid model from a 2D region is to apply a thickness to the region. The **EXTRUDE** command is used for this. A 2D region can be extruded in either a positive or negative Z direction. To use this command, pick the **Extrude** button in the **Solids** toolbar, select **Extrude** from the **Solids** cascading menu in the **Draw** pull-down menu, or enter EXT or EXTRUDE at the Command: prompt:

EXTRUDE
EXT

Draw
➥ Solids
➥ Extrude

Solids
toolbar

Extrude

Command: **EXT** or **EXTRUDE**↵
Select objects: *(pick anywhere on the region)*
Select objects: ↵
Path/⟨Height of Extrusion⟩: **1**↵

At the next prompt, you can enter an angle value. A positive angle tapers the extruded solid. Press [Enter] to accept the default of 0 for no taper.

Extrusion taper angle ⟨0⟩: ↵

The base is now a 3D solid object. A 3D solid object is called a *primitive.*

Use the **VPOINT** or **DVIEW** command to see a 3D view of the extruded solid. Notice that the holes are shown with four lines connecting the circles. See Figure 10-3. These lines are used to represent the wireframe outline of the objects. This feature is discussed in Chapter 12.

Figure 10-3.
The extruded 3D
solid. Notice the
wireframe display
of the holes.

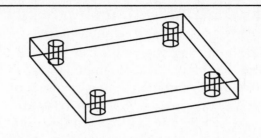

EXERCISE 10-1

❑ Start a new drawing named EX10-1.
❑ Using the **RECTANG** and **CIRCLE** commands, draw a two-dimensional top view of the object shown below. Use the dimensions given, but do not dimension the object.
❑ Using the appropriate commands, create a 2D composite region.
❑ Extrude the region model into a 3D solid with the given thickness.
❑ Save the model as EX10-1.

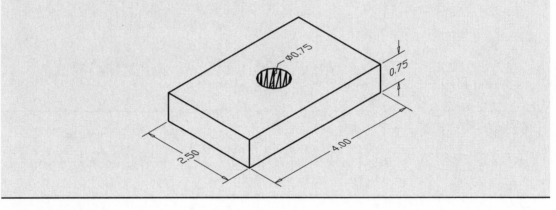

Calculating the area of a region

A region is not a polyline. It is an enclosed area called a *loop*. Certain values of the region, such as area, are stored as a value of the region primitive. The **AREA** command can be used to determine the length of all sides and the area of the loop. This can be a useful advantage of using a region.

For example, suppose a parking lot is being repaved. You need to calculate the surface area of a parking lot to determine the amount of material needed. This total surface area excludes the space taken up by planting dividers, sidewalks, and light posts, because you will not be paving under these items. If the parking lot and all objects inside it are drawn as a region, the **AREA** command can give you this figure in one step. If a polyline is used to draw the parking lot, all internal features must be subtracted each time the **AREA** command is used.

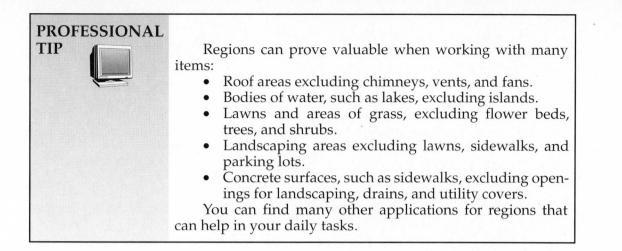
Regions can prove valuable when working with many items:

- Roof areas excluding chimneys, vents, and fans.
- Bodies of water, such as lakes, excluding islands.
- Lawns and areas of grass, excluding flower beds, trees, and shrubs.
- Landscaping areas excluding lawns, sidewalks, and parking lots.
- Concrete surfaces, such as sidewalks, excluding openings for landscaping, drains, and utility covers.

You can find many other applications for regions that can help in your daily tasks.

Constructing Solid Primitives

AutoCAD User's Guide | 13

Solid primitives are basic 3D geometric shapes such as boxes, spheres, cylinders, cones, wedges, and tori. Unlike 3D surfaced objects, they have the mass properties of a solid. Solid primitives can also be used as building blocks for complex solid models. To create a solid primitive, pick the appropriate button in the **Solids** toolbar, select the object from the **Solids** cascading menu in the **Draw** pull-down menu, or type the primitive name at the Command: prompt. The pull-down menu and toolbar are shown in Figure 10-4.

Figure 10-4.
A—The **Solids** cascading menu. B—The **Solids** toolbar.

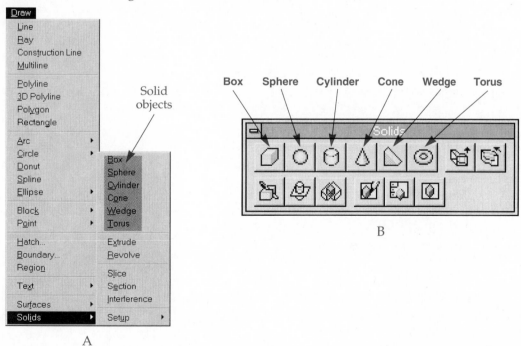

All the solid primitives discussed in this chapter can be created by typing their name at the Command: prompt. To construct a *surfaced* 3D object, type AI_ followed by the name of the object (AI_BOX, for example). You can also select the object from the **Surfaces** toolbar or **3D Objects** dialog box. There is not a command to create a surface-modeled cylinder directly. Chapter 5 discusses surface modeling.

Box

BOX

Draw
➥ Solids
➥ Box

Solids
toolbar

Box

A box can be constructed from an initial corner or the center. These options are available by picking the **Box** button from the **Solids** toolbar, selecting **Box** from the **Solids** cascading menu in the **Draw** pull-down menu, or entering BOX at the Command: prompt. Refer to Figure 10-5 as you read the following command sequence:

Command: **BOX**⏎
Center/⟨Corner of box⟩ ⟨0,0,0⟩: *(pick a corner or type C for the* **Center** *option)*
Cube/Length/⟨other corner⟩: *(pick the diagonal corner of the base, or type L and press* [Enter] *to provide a length)*
Height: **2**⏎

If the **Cube** option is selected, the length value is applied to all dimensions.

Figure 10-5.
A—A box created using the **Cube** option.
B—A box created by selecting the center point.

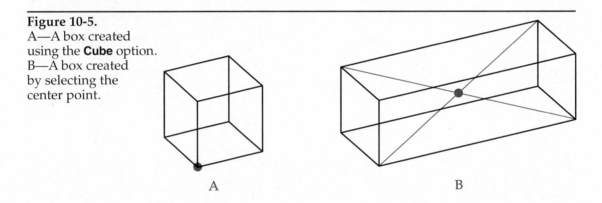

A   B

Sphere

SPHERE

Draw
➥ Solids
➥ Sphere

Solids
toolbar

Sphere

A sphere is drawn by first picking its center point, then entering a radius or diameter. To draw a sphere, pick the **Sphere** button in the **Solids** toolbar, select **Sphere** from the **Solids** cascading menu in the **Draw** pull-down menu, or enter the following at the Command: prompt:

Command: **SPHERE**⏎
Center of sphere ⟨0,0,0⟩: *(pick a point or enter coordinates)*
Diameter/⟨Radius⟩ of sphere: *(pick a point or enter a value)*
Command:

Notice in Figure 10-6A that the display is a wireframe with few lines defining the shape. The lines that form the wireframe of a solid are called *isolines*. Isolines are controlled by the **ISOLINES** system variable, which is discussed in Chapter 12.

Also, notice in Figure 10-6A that there is no outline or silhouette. The **DISPSILH** system variable controls the display of wireframe silhouettes. This variable is set to 0 by default. When **DISPSILH** is set to 1, the silhouette shown in Figure 10-6B is displayed. When hidden lines are removed, only the silhouette appears, Figure 10-6C. The sphere is shown with hidden lines removed and **DISPSILH** set to a value of 0 in Figure 10-6D. System variables that affect display are discussed in detail in Chapter 12.

Figure 10-6.
A—The basic wireframe display of spheres. B—The **DISPSILH** variable is set to 1.
C—The **DISPSILH** variable is set to 1 and the **HIDE** command used. D—Spheres displayed after using **HIDE** with **DISPSILH** is set to 0.

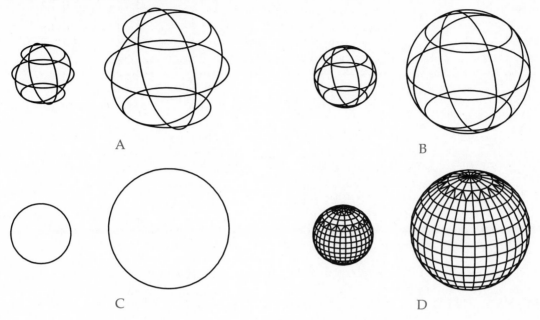

A   B

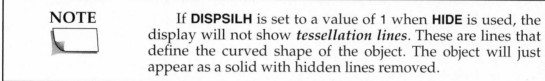

C   D

> **NOTE**
>
> If **DISPSILH** is set to a value of 1 when **HIDE** is used, the display will not show *tessellation lines*. These are lines that define the curved shape of the object. The object will just appear as a solid with hidden lines removed.

Cylinder

A cylinder can be drawn circular or elliptical. To draw a solid cylinder, pick the **Cylinder** button in the **Solids** toolbar, select **Cylinder** from the **Solids** cascading menu in the **Draw** pull-down menu, or enter CYLINDER at the Command: prompt:

CYLINDER

Draw
→ Solids
 → Cylinder

Solids
toolbar

Cylinder

Command: **CYLINDER.**↵
Elliptical/⟨center point⟩⟨0,0,0⟩: *(pick a center point)*
Diameter/⟨Radius⟩: **1**↵
Center of other end/⟨Height⟩: **3**↵

The cylinder shown in Figure 10-7A is displayed.

You can draw an elliptical cylinder two different ways. The default method prompts you to specify the two endpoints of the first axis and the second axis distance. This prompt sequence is as follows:

Elliptical/⟨center point⟩⟨0,0,0⟩: **E**↵
Center/⟨Axis endpoint⟩: *(pick the first axis endpoint)*
Axis endpoint 2: *(pick the second axis endpoint)*
Other axis distance: *(pick the other axis distance)*
Center of other end/⟨Height⟩: **3**↵

The cylinder in Figure 10-7B is created. The second option allows you to select the center point.

Figure 10-7.
A—A circular
cylinder.
B—An elliptical
cylinder.

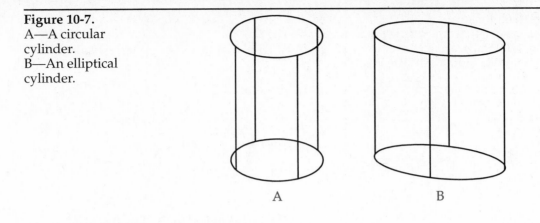

A B

Elliptical/⟨center point⟩⟨0,0,0⟩: **E**↵
Center/⟨Axis endpoint⟩: **C**↵
Center of ellipse ⟨0,0,0⟩: *(pick the center of the ellipse)*
Axis endpoint: *(pick the axis endpoint)*
Other axis distance: *(pick the other axis distance)*
Center of other end/⟨Height⟩: **3**↵

To set the height, pick two points with the cursor or enter a value at the keyboard. When setting the height, you have the option of picking the center point of the opposite end of the cylinder. This is useful if you are placing a cylinder inside another object to create a hole. The cylinder can then be subtracted from the other object to create a hole. Refer to Figure 10-8 as you go through the following sequence:

Center of other end/⟨Height⟩: **C**↵
Center of other end: **CEN**↵
of *(pick the top end of the cylinder)*
Command:

Figure 10-8.
A—A cylinder is
drawn inside
another cylinder
using the **Center of
other end** option.
B—The large
cylinder appears to
have a hole after
SUBTRACT is used.

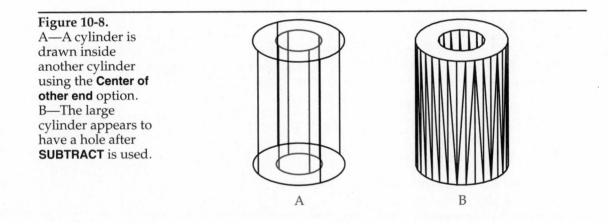

A B

CONE

Draw
↪ Solids
  ↪ Cone

Solids
toolbar

Cone

Cone

The cone can also be drawn circular or elliptical. To draw a cone, pick the **Cone** button in the **Solids** toolbar, select **Cone** from the **Solids** cascading menu in the **Draw** pull-down menu, or enter CONE at the Command: prompt:

Command: **CONE**↵
Elliptical/⟨center point⟩⟨0,0,0⟩: *(pick the center point)*
Diameter/⟨Radius⟩: **1**↵
Apex/⟨Height⟩: **3**↵

The cone in Figure 10-9A is displayed. An elliptical cone can be created as follows:

Elliptical/⟨center point⟩⟨0,0,0⟩: **E**↵
Center/⟨Axis endpoint⟩: *(pick the axis endpoint)*
Axis endpoint 2: *(pick the other axis endpoint)*
Other axis distance: *(pick the other axis distance)*
Apex/⟨Height⟩: **3**↵
Command:

The cone shown in Figure 10-9B is displayed. Just as with a cylinder, you can select the center of the cone at the following prompt:

Center/⟨Axis endpoint⟩:

The **Apex** option is similar to the **Center of other end** option for drawing a cylinder. This option allows you to orient the cone at any angle, regardless of the current UCS. For example, to place a tapered cutout in the end of a block, locate the cone base and give a coordinate location of the apex. Refer to Figure 10-10. Use tracking and the **Midpoint** running object snap to locate the center of the cone's base as follows:

Command: **CONE**↵
Elliptical/⟨center point⟩⟨0,0,0⟩: **TRA**↵
First tracking point: *(pick P1)*
Next point (Press ENTER to end tracking): *(pick P2)*
Next point (Press ENTER to end tracking): ↵
Diameter/⟨Radius⟩: **1**↵
Apex/⟨Height⟩: **A**↵
Apex: **@2,0,0**↵

Figure 10-10 illustrates the construction of the cone and its appearance after being subtracted from the box.

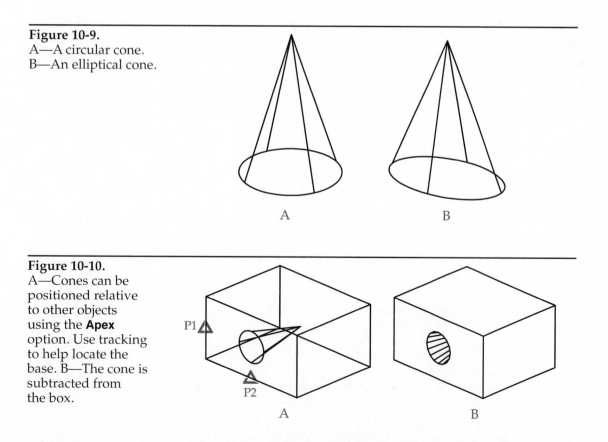

Figure 10-9.
A—A circular cone.
B—An elliptical cone.

A   B

Figure 10-10.
A—Cones can be positioned relative to other objects using the **Apex** option. Use tracking to help locate the base. B—The cone is subtracted from the box.

P1

P2

A   B

Wedge

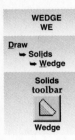

WEDGE
WE

Draw
➥ Solids
➥ Wedge

Solids
toolbar

Wedge

A wedge can be constructed by picking corners or by picking the center point. The center point of a wedge is the middle of the angled surface. To draw a wedge, pick the **Wedge** button from the **Solids** toolbar, select <u>Wedge</u> from the **Solids** cascading menu in the **<u>D</u>raw** pull-down menu, or enter WE or WEDGE at the Command: prompt:

> Command: **WE** *or* **WEDGE**↵
> Center/⟨Corner of wedge⟩⟨0,0,0⟩: *(pick a corner location)*
> Cube/Length/⟨other corner⟩: *(pick the diagonal corner location)*
> Height: **2.**↵

See Figure 10-11A. You can also specify the length, width, and height instead of picking the diagonal corner.

> Cube/Length/⟨other corner⟩: **L**↵
> Length: **3.**↵
> Width: **2.**↵
> Height: **2.**↵

The **Center** option is used as follows. Refer to Figure 10-11B.

> Center/⟨Corner of wedge⟩⟨0,0,0⟩: **C**↵
> Center of wedge ⟨0,0,0⟩: *(pick the center point)*
> Cube/Length/⟨corner of wedge⟩:

You can pick a corner of the wedge or use the **Length** option to specify length, width, and height. The **Cube** option uses the length value for all three sides.

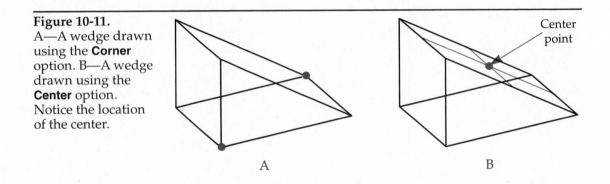

Figure 10-11.
A—A wedge drawn using the **Corner** option. B—A wedge drawn using the **Center** option. Notice the location of the center.

A

B

Center point

Torus

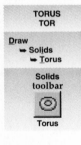

TORUS
TOR

Draw
➥ Solids
➥ <u>T</u>orus

Solids
toolbar

Torus

A torus can be drawn in three different ways. Refer to Figure 10-12. To draw a torus, pick the **Torus** button in the **Solids** toolbar, select **<u>T</u>orus** from the **Solids** cascading menu in the **<u>D</u>raw** pull-down menu, or enter TOR or TORUS at the Command: prompt:

> Command: **TOR** *or* **TORUS**↵
> Center of torus ⟨0,0,0⟩: *(pick the center point)*
> Diameter/⟨Radius⟩ of torus: **1.**↵
> Diameter/⟨Radius⟩ of tube: **.4.**↵

The basic torus shown in Figure 10-12A is drawn. Notice that you can enter either a diameter or a radius.

A torus with a tube diameter that touches itself has no center hole. This type of torus is called *self-intersecting*. See Figure 10-12B. To create a self-intersecting torus, the tube radius must be greater than the torus radius.

The third type of torus looks like a football. It is drawn by entering a negative torus radius and a positive tube diameter of greater value. See Figure 10-12C.

Figure 10-12.
The three types of tori are shown as wireframes and with hidden lines removed.

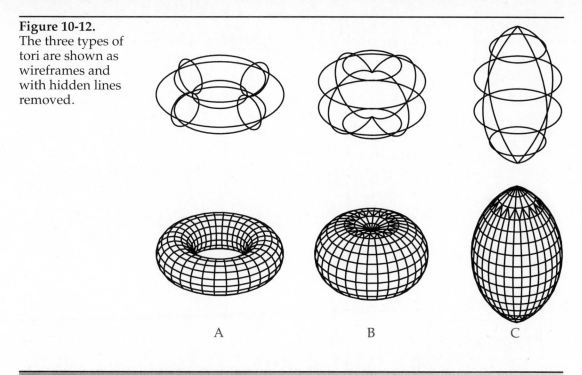

A   B   C

EXERCISE 10-2

❏ Begin a new drawing named EX10-2.
❏ Construct the following solid primitives:
  ❏ A sphere 1.5″ in diameter.
  ❏ A box 3″ × 2″ × 1″.
  ❏ A cone 2.5″ high with a base diameter of 1.5″.
  ❏ An elliptical cone 3″ high with a major base diameter of 2″ and a minor diameter of 1″.
  ❏ A wedge 4″ long, 3″ wide, and 2″ high.
  ❏ A cylinder 1.5″ in diameter and 2.5″ high.
  ❏ An elliptical cylinder with a major axis of 2″, a minor axis of 1″, and 3″ high.
  ❏ A basic torus with a radius of 2″ and a tube diameter of .75″.
  ❏ A self-intersecting torus.
  ❏ A football-shaped torus.
❏ Save your drawing as EX10-2.

PROFESSIONAL TIP

When you are working with surface-modeled boxes, wedges, pyramids, and cones, you can select corners using the **Intersection** object snap. However, when working with solid models, you must use the **Endpoint** object snap to select corners.

Creating Composite Solids

AutoCAD User's Guide **13**

A *composite solid* is a solid model constructed of two or more solid primitives. Primitives can be subtracted from each other, joined to form a new solid, or overlapped to create an intersection or interference. When primitives are joined, it is called a *union*. The commands used to create composite solids are found in the **Boolean** cascading menu in the **Modify** pull-down menu, and within the **Modify II** toolbar . See Figure 10-13.

Figure 10-13.
Boolean commands can be selected from the pull-down menu or the **Modify II** toolbar.

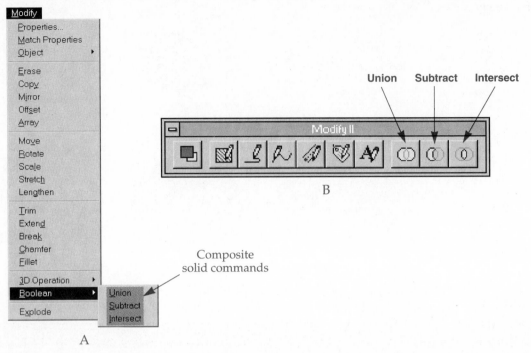

A

B

These commands perform *Boolean operations*. George Boole (1815–1864) was an English mathematician who developed a system of mathematical logic where all variables have the value of either one or zero. Boole's two-value logic, or *binary algebra*, is the basis for the mathematical calculations used by computers, and specifically for those required in the construction of composite solids.

Subtracting solids

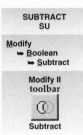

SUBTRACT
SU

Modify
➥ Boolean
  ➥ Subtract

Modify II
toolbar

Subtract

The **SUBTRACT** command allows you to remove the volume of one or more solids from another solid. The first object selected is the object to be subtracted *from*. The next object is the object to be subtracted from the first. You can subtract solids by picking the **Subtract** button in the **Modify II** toolbar, selecting **Subtract** from the **Boolean** cascading menu in the **Modify** pull-down menu, or entering SU or SUBTRACT at the Command: prompt:

Command: **SU** *or* **SUBTRACT**↵
Select solids and regions to subtract from...
Select objects: *(pick the object)*
Select objects: ↵
Select solids and regions to subtract...
Select objects: *(pick the objects to subtract)*
Select objects: ↵
Command:

Several examples are shown in Figure 10-14.

Figure 10-14.
A—Solid primitives shown here have areas of intersection and overlap. B—Composite solids after using the **SUBTRACT** command.

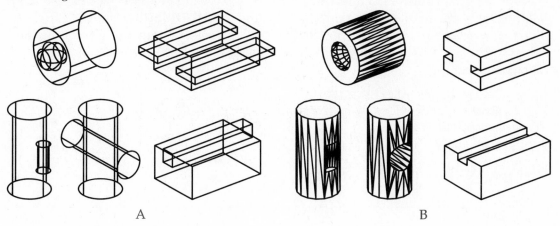

A   B

Joining two or more objects

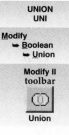

Composite solids can be created using the **UNION** command. The primitives do not need to touch or intersect to form a union. Therefore, locate the primitives accurately when drawing them. To create a union, pick the **Union** button in the **Modify II** toolbar, select **Union** from the **Boolean** cascading menu in the **Modify** pull-down menu, or enter UNI or UNION at the Command: prompt:

Command: **UNI** *or* **UNION**.↵
Select objects: (*select all primitives to be joined*)
Select objects: ↵
Command: ↵

In the examples shown in Figure 10-15B, notice that lines, or edges, are shown at the new intersection points of the joined objects.

Figure 10-15.
A—Solid primitives shown here have areas of intersection and overlap.
B—Composite solids after using the **UNION** command.

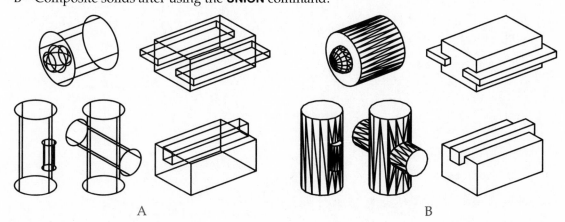

A   B

Creating solids from the intersection of primitives

INTERSECT
IN

Modify
➡ Boolean
  ➡ Intersect

Modify II
toolbar

⟨0⟩

Intersect

When solid primitives intersect, they form a common volume. This is an area in space that both primitives share. This shared space is called an *intersection*. An intersection can be made into a composite solid using the **INTERSECT** command. To do so, pick the **Intersection** button in the **Modify II** toolbar, select **Intersect** from the **Boolean** cascading menu in the **Modify** pull-down menu, or enter IN or INTERSECT at the Command: prompt:

Command: **IN** *or* **INTERSECT**↵
Select objects: *(select the objects that form the intersection)*
Select objects: ↵
Command:

Figure 10-16 shows several examples.

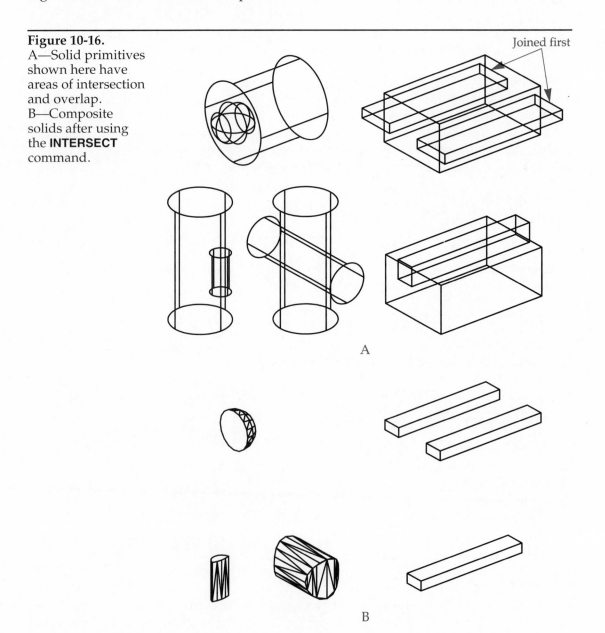

Figure 10-16.
A—Solid primitives shown here have areas of intersection and overlap.
B—Composite solids after using the **INTERSECT** command.

Joined first

A

B

EXERCISE 10-3

❑ Begin a new drawing named EX10-3.
❑ Construct objects similar to those shown in Figure 10-14A using your own dimensions. Be sure the objects intersect and overlap. Make two copies of all objects.
❑ Perform subtractions on all of the objects and observe the results.
❑ Perform unions on the copy of the objects and observe the results.
❑ Use the **INTERSECT** command on all of the objects and observe the results.
❑ Save your drawing as EX10-3.

Creating new solids using the INTERFERE command

When you use the **SUBTRACT**, **UNION**, and **INTERSECT** commands, the original solid primitives are deleted. They are replaced by the new composite solid. The **INTERFERE** command does not do this. A new solid is created from the interference, but the original objects remain.

To use the **INTERFERE** command, pick the **Interfere** button in the **Solids** toolbar, select **Interference** from the **Solids** cascading menu in the **Draw** pull-down menu, or enter INF or INTERFERE at the Command: prompt:

Command: **INF** or **INTERFERE.**↵
Select the first set of solids:
Select objects: *(select the first solid)*
Select objects: ↵
Select the second set of solids: *(select the second solid)*
Select objects: ↵
Comparing 1 solid against 1 solid.
Interfering solids (first set): 1
   (second set):   1
Interfering pairs: 1
Create interference solids? ⟨N⟩: **Y**↵

The result is shown in Figure 10-17B. Notice that the original solids are intact, but new lines indicate the new solid.

The new solid is a separate object. It can be moved, copied, and manipulated just like any other object. Figure 10-17C shows the new object after it has been moved and lines have been hidden.

AutoCAD compares the first set of solids with the second set. Any solids that are selected for both the first and second sets are automatically included as part of the first selection set, and are eliminated from the second. If you do not select a second set of objects, AutoCAD calculates the interference between the objects in the first selection set. You can do this by pressing [Enter] instead of picking the second set.

Figure 10-17.
A—Two solids form an area of intersection.
B—After using **INTERFERE**, a new solid is defined and the original solids remain.
C—The new solid can be moved or copied.

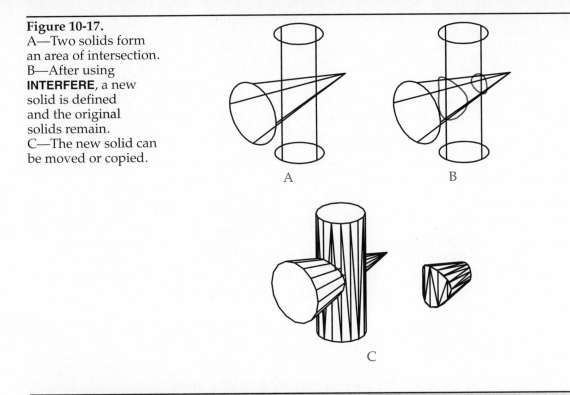

A

B

C

EXERCISE 10-4

❑ Begin a new drawing named EX10-4.
❑ Construct objects similar to those shown in Figure 10-17A using your own dimensions. Be sure the objects intersect and overlap.
❑ Use the **INTERFERE** command on the objects and observe the results. Be sure to make a solid of the interference. Use the **HIDE** command.
❑ Make a copy of the new solid and move it to a new location.
❑ Save your drawing as EX10-4.

Chapter Test

Write your answers in the spaces provided.

1. What is a region? _____

_____

2. How can a 2D section view be converted to a 3D solid model? _____

_____

3. What is created when regions are added to or subtracted from one another? ____

_____

4. What command allows you to remove the area of one region from another region?

_____

5. What are two types of objects that can be created with the **BOUNDARY** command?

_____

_____

6. Why is it useful to create a region instead of a polyline if an object's area must be calculated? _____

_____

_____

7. What is a solid primitive? _____

_____

_____

8. How is a solid cube created? _____

_____

_____

9. Name two system variables that control the display of lines in the wireframe view of a solid. _____

_____

10. How is an elliptical cylinder created? _____

_____

_____

11. What is the function of the **Apex** option of the **CONE** command? _____

_____

_____

_____

12. Where is the center of a wedge located? _____

_____

13. A torus can be drawn in how many different shapes? _____

_____

14. What is a composite solid? _____

_____

_____

15. What type of mathematical calculations are used in the construction of solid models? _____

_____

_____

16. How are two or more solids combined to make a composite solid? _____

_____

_____

17. What is the function of the **INTERSECT** command? _____

_____

_____

18. How does the **INTERFERE** command differ from **INTERSECT** and **UNION**? _____

_____

_____

_____

Drawing Problems

1. Construct a solid model of the object in Problem 1 of Chapter 1. Save the drawing as P10-1.

2. Construct a solid model of the object in Problem 2 of Chapter 1. Save the drawing as P10-2.

3. Construct a solid model of the object in Problem 3 of Chapter 1. Save the drawing as P10-3.

4. Construct a solid model of the object in Problem 4 of Chapter 1. Save the drawing as P10-4.

5. Construct a solid model of the object in Problem 5 of Chapter 1. Save the drawing as P10-5.

6. Construct a solid model of the object in Problem 6 of Chapter 1. Save the drawing as P10-6.

7. Construct a solid model of the object in Problem 7 of Chapter 1. Save the drawing as P10-7.

8. Construct a solid model of the object in Problem 8 of Chapter 1. Save the drawing as P10-8.

9. Construct a solid model of the object in Problem 1 of Chapter 3. Save the drawing as P10-9.

10. Construct a solid model of the object in Problem 2 of Chapter 3. Save the drawing as P10-10.

11. Construct a solid model of the object in Problem 3 of Chapter 3. Save the drawing as P10-11.

12. Construct a solid model of the object in Problem 4 of Chapter 3. Save the drawing as P10-12.

13. Construct a solid model of the object in Problem 5 of Chapter 3. Save the drawing as P10-13.

14. Construct a solid model of the object in Problem 6 of Chapter 3. Save the drawing as P10-14.

AutoCAD and its Applications—Advanced

Solid Model Construction and Features

Learning Objectives

After completing this chapter, you will be able to:
- ○ Create solid objects by extruding closed 2D profiles.
- ○ Revolve closed 2D profiles to create symmetrical 3D solids.
- ○ Apply fillets to solid objects.
- ○ Apply chamfers to solid objects.
- ○ Construct a variety of detailed solid shapes and features.

Complex shapes can be created by applying a thickness to a two-dimensional profile. This is called *extruding* the shape. Two or more profiles can be extruded to intersect. The resulting union can form a new shape. Objects having symmetry can be created by revolving a 2D profile about an axis to create a new solid. Rounded and angular corners can be constructed using the **FILLET** and **CHAMFER** commands.

Creating Solid Extrusions

An *extrusion* is a closed two-dimensional shape that has been given thickness. The **EXTRUDE** command allows you to create extruded solids using closed objects such as polylines, polygons, splines, regions, circles, ellipses, and donuts. Objects in a block cannot be extruded. Extrusions can be created along a straight line or along a path curve. A taper angle can also be applied as you extrude an object.

Create an extruded solid by picking the **Extrude** button in the **Solids** toolbar, selecting **Extrude** from the **Solids** cascading menu in the **Draw** pull-down menu, or typing EXT or EXTRUDE at the Command: prompt:

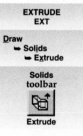

```
Command: EXT or EXTRUDE↵
Select objects: (pick object to extrude)
Select objects: ↵
Path/⟨Height of Extrusion⟩: .35↵
Extrusion taper angle ⟨0⟩: ↵
Command:
```

Figure 11-1 illustrates a polygon that is extruded into a solid.

The taper angle can be any value between +90° and −90°. A positive angle tapers to the inside of the object from the base. A negative angle tapers to the outside of the object from the base. See Figure 11-2.

Figure 11-1.
The **EXTRUDE**
command creates a
solid by adding
thickness to a closed
2D profile. A—The
initial 2D profile.
B—The extruded
solid object shown
with hidden lines
removed.

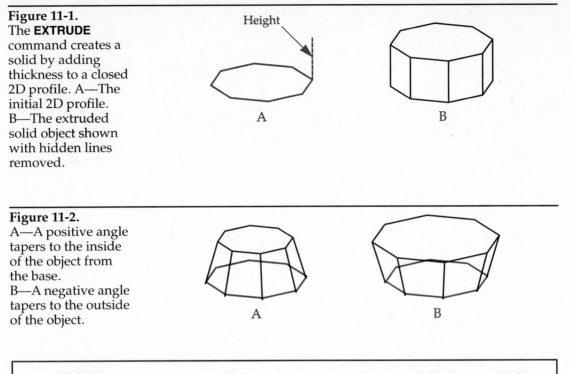

A

B

Figure 11-2.
A—A positive angle
tapers to the inside
of the object from
the base.
B—A negative angle
tapers to the outside
of the object.

A

B

NOTE   The height of extrusion is always applied in the Z direction. A positive value extrudes above the XY plane. A negative height value extrudes below the XY plane.

Extrusions along a path

A closed 2D shape can be extruded along a path to create a 3D solid. The path can be a line, circle, arc, ellipse, polyline, or spline. Line segments and other objects can be joined to form a polyline path. The corners of angled segments are mitered, while curved segments are smooth. See Figure 11-3.

Objects can also be extruded along a line at an angle to the base object, Figure 11-4. Notice that the plane at the end of the extruded object is perpendicular to the path. Also notice that the length of the extrusion is the same as that of the path.

```
Command: EXT or EXTRUDE.↵
Select objects: (pick object to extrude)
Select objects: ↵
Path/⟨Height of Extrusion⟩: P↵
Select path: (pick the path)
```

Figure 11-3.
A—Angled
segments are
mitered when
extruded.
B—Curves are
smoothed when
extruded.

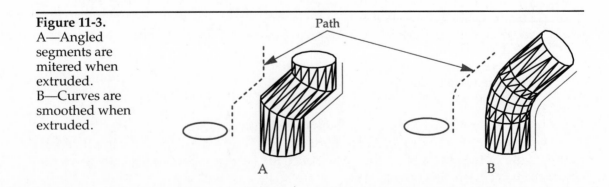

Path

A

B

AutoCAD and its Applications—Advanced

Figure 11-4.
A—An object extruded along a path.
B—The end of an object extruded along an angled path is perpendicular to the path.

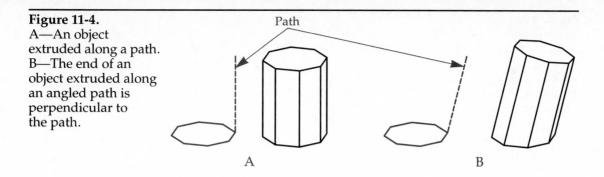

The path does not need to be perpendicular to the object. However, the new solid is created so its base is perpendicular to the path. Also, one of the endpoints of the path should be on the plane of the object to be extruded. If it is not, the path is temporarily moved to the center of the profile. The following prompts may appear after the path is selected:

Select path: *(pick the path)*
Path was moved to the center of the profile.
Profile was oriented to be perpendicular to the path.
Command: ↵

An example is shown in Figure 11-5.

Figure 11-5.
When the path is not perpendicular to the 2D profile (both shown here in color), the base profile is rotated to be perpendicular to the path.

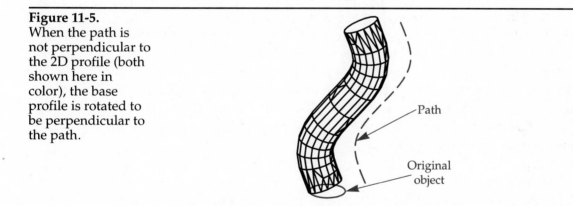

Creating features with EXTRUDE

You can create a wide variety of features with the **EXTRUDE** command. With some planning, you can use regions and **SUBTRACT** to construct solids. Study the shapes shown in Figure 11-6. These detailed solid objects were created by drawing a profile and then using the **EXTRUDE** command. The objects in Figure 11-6C and Figure 11-6D must first be constructed as regions before they are extruded. For example, the five holes in Figure 11-6D must be removed from the base object using the **SUBTRACT** command.

Figure 11-6.
Detailed solids can be created by extruding the profile of an object. The profiles are shown here in color.

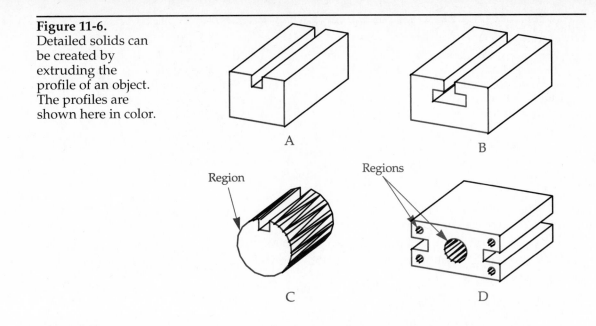

A

B

Region

Regions

C

D

AutoCAD User's Guide **13**

REVOLVE
REV

Draw
➥ Solids
  ➥ Revolve

Solids
toolbar

Revolve

Creating Revolved Solids

The **REVOLVE** command allows you to create solids by revolving closed shapes such as circles, ellipses, polylines, closed splines, regions, and donuts. The selected object can be revolved at any angle up to 360°. To create a solid by revolving, pick the **Revolve** button in the **Solids** toolbar, select **Revolve** from the **Solids** cascading menu in the **Draw** pull-down menu, or enter REV or REVOLVE at the Command: prompt. The default option is to pick the two endpoints of an axis of revolution. This is shown in Figure 11-7.

Command: **REV** *or* **REVOLVE**↵
Select objects: *(pick the objects to revolve)*
Select objects: ↵
Axis of revolution - Object/X/Y/⟨Start point of axis⟩: *(pick P1)*
⟨End point of axis⟩: *(pick P2)*
Angle of revolution ⟨full circle⟩: ↵
Command:

Figure 11-7.
Points P1 and P2 are
selected as the axis
of revolution.

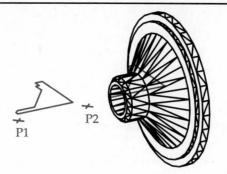

Revolving about an axis line object

You can select an object, such as a line, as the axis of revolution. Figure 11-8 shows a solid created using the **Object** option of the **REVOLVE** command. Both a full circle (360°) revolution and a 270° revolution are shown.

```
Axis of revolution - Object/X/Y/〈Start point of axis〉: O↵
Select an object: (pick the axis line)
Angle of revolution 〈full circle〉: ↵
```

Figure 11-8.
An axis of
revolution can be
selected using the
Object option of the
REVOLVE command.
Here, the line is
selected as the axis.

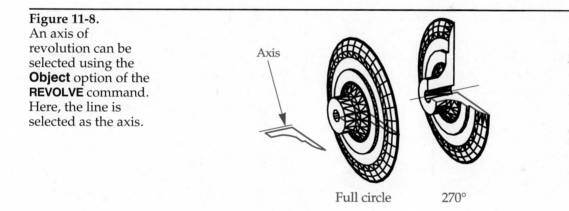

Axis

Full circle   270°

Revolving about the X axis

The X axis of the current UCS can be used as the axis of revolution by selecting the **X** option of the **REVOLVE** command. The origin of the current UCS is used as one end of the X axis line. Notice in Figure 11-9 that two different shapes can be created by changing the UCS origin point of the same 2D profile. No hole appears in the object in Figure 11-9B because the profile was revolved about an edge that coincides with the X axis.

```
Axis of revolution - Object/X/Y/〈Start point of axis〉: X↵
Angle of revolution 〈full circle〉: ↵
```

Figure 11-9.
A—A solid is
created using the
X axis as the axis
of revolution.
B—A different
object is created by
changing the UCS
origin.

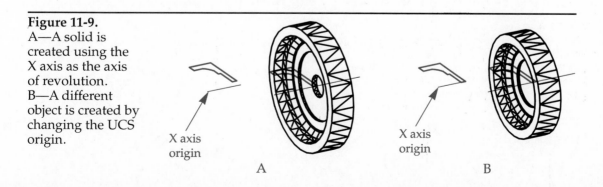

X axis
origin

X axis
origin

A   B

Revolving about the Y axis

The Y axis of the current UCS can be used as the axis of revolution by selecting the **Y** option of the **REVOLVE** command. The UCS origin determines the shape of the final object. See Figure 11-10. Notice the different shapes created by revolving the same profile with different UCS origins.

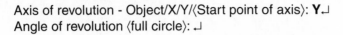

Axis of revolution - Object/X/Y/〈Start point of axis〉: **Y**↵
Angle of revolution 〈full circle〉: ↵

Figure 11-10.
A—A solid is created using the Y axis as the axis of revolution. B—A different object is created by changing the UCS origin.

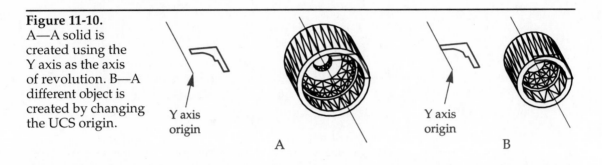

Y axis origin

A

Y axis origin

B

EXERCISE 11-2

❑ Begin a new drawing.
❑ Examine the objects shown below. Determine the shape of the closed profiles revolved to create the solids. The dimensions of the objects are not important.
❑ Draw the profiles and revolve them to create a solid.
❑ Use the **RENDER** command to see if your objects match those shown.
❑ Save the drawing as EX11-2.

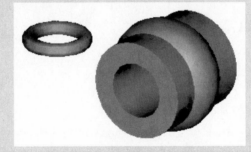

Filleting Solid Objects

A fillet rounds the edges of an object. Before a fillet is created, solid objects that intersect need to be joined using the **UNION** command. Then, use the **FILLET** command. See Figure 11-11. Since the object being filleted is actually a single solid and not

Figure 11-11.
A—Pick the edge where two unioned solids intersect to create a fillet. B—The fillet after using **HIDE**.

Pick the edge

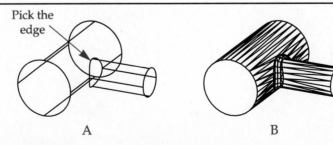

A

B

two objects, only one edge is selected. In the following sequence, first the fillet radius is set at .25, then the fillet is created:

> Command: **F** *or* **FILLET**↵
> (TRIM mode) Current fillet radius = *current*
> Polyline/Radius/Trim/⟨Select first object⟩: **R**↵
> Enter fillet radius ⟨*current*⟩: **.25**↵
> Command: ↵
> FILLET
> (TRIM mode) Current fillet radius = 0.2500
> Polyline/Radius/Trim/⟨Select first object⟩: *(pick edge to be filleted)*
> Enter radius ⟨.025⟩: ↵
> Chain/Radius/⟨Select edge⟩: ↵ *(this fillets the selected edge, but you can also select other edges at this point)*
> 1 edges selected for fillet.
> Command:

Examples of fillets and rounds are shown in Figure 11-12.

Figure 11-12.
Examples of fillets and rounds.

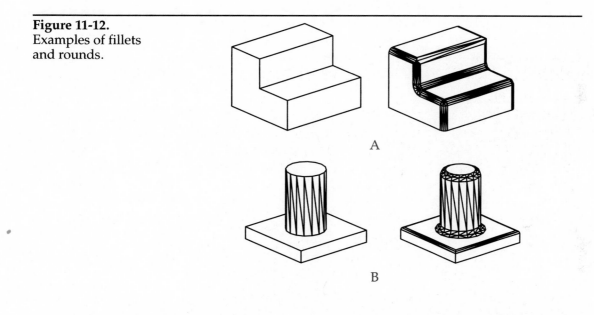

A

B

Chamfering Solid Objects

To create a chamfer on a 3D solid, use the **CHAMFER** command. Just as when chamfering a 2D line, there are two chamfer distances. Therefore, you must specify which surfaces correspond to the first and second distances. If you are chamfering a hole, the two objects must first be subtracted. If you are chamfering an intersection, the two objects must first be unioned.

After you enter the command, you must pick the edge you want to chamfer. The edge is actually the intersection of two surfaces. One of the two surfaces is highlighted when you select the edge. The highlighted surface is associated with the first chamfer distance. This surface is called the *base surface*. If the highlighted surface is not the one you want as the base surface, enter N at the Next/⟨OK⟩: prompt and press [Enter]. This highlights the next surface. When the proper base surface is highlighted, press [Enter] for **OK**. Chamfering a hole is shown in Figure 11-13A.

```
Command: CHA or CHAMFER↵
(TRIM mode) Current chamfer Dist1 = 0.5000, Dist2 = 0.5000
Polyline/Distance/Angle/Trim/Method/〈Select first line〉: (pick edge 1)
Select base surface:
Next/〈OK〉: N↵
Next/〈OK〉: ↵
Enter base surface distance 〈0.5000〉: .125↵
Enter other surface distance 〈0.5000〉: .125↵
Loop/〈Select edge〉: (pick edge 2, the edge of the hole)
Loop/〈Select edge〉: ↵
Command:
```

The end of the cylinder in Figure 11-13B is chamfered by first picking one of the vertical isolines, then picking the top edge.

Figure 11-13.
A—A hole is chamfered by picking the top surface, then the edge of the hole. B—The end of a cylinder is chamfered by first picking the side, then the end. Both ends can be chamfered at the same time, as shown here.

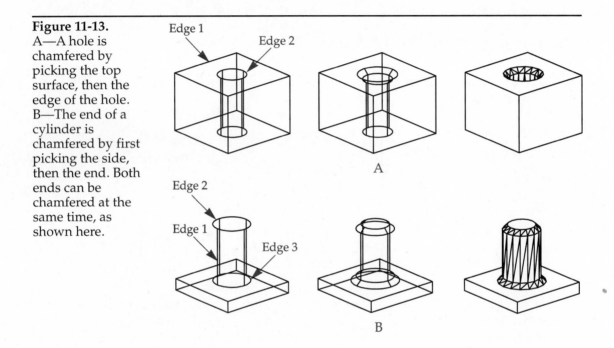

A

B

❑ Begin a new drawing.
❑ Draw the locking pin shown below using the appropriate solid modeling and editing commands.
❑ The pin is 3″ long and .5″ diameter.
❑ The two cotter pin holes are .2″ diameter and .35″ from each end.
❑ The chamfer on each end is .1″ and the fillet on each hole has a .02″ radius.
❑ When you complete the object, use **HIDE** and then **RENDER**.
❑ Save the drawing as EX11-3.

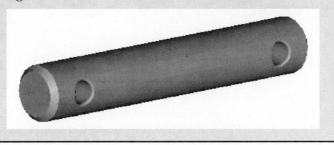

Constructing Solid Details and Features

A variety of machining, structural, and architectural details can be created using some basic solid modeling techniques. The features discussed in the next sections are just a few of the possibilities.

Counterbore and spotface

A *counterbore* is a recess machined into a part, centered on a hole, that allows the head of a fastener to rest below the surface. Create a counterbore as follows:

1. Draw a cylinder representing the diameter of the hole, Figure 11-14A.
2. Draw a second cylinder the diameter of the counterbore and center it at the top of the first cylinder. Move the second cylinder so it extends below the surface of the object, Figure 11-14B.
3. Subtract the two cylinders from the base object, Figure 11-14C.

A *spotface* is similar to a counterbore, but is not as deep. It provides a flat surface for full contact of a washer or underside of a bolt head. Construct it in the same way as a counterbore. See Figure 11-15.

Figure 11-14.
Constructing a counterbore. A—Draw a cylinder to represent a hole. B—Draw a second cylinder to represent the counterbore. C—Subtract the two cylinders from the base object. The object is shown here with hidden lines removed.

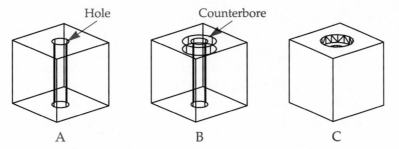

Figure 11-15.
Constructing a spotface. A—The bottom of the second cylinder should be located at the exact depth of the spotface. However, the height may extend above the surface of the cube. Then, subtract the two cylinders from the base. B—The spotface is much shallower than a counterbore.

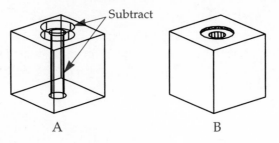

Countersink

A *countersink* is like a counterbore with angled sides. The sides allow a flat head machine screw or wood screw to sit below the surface of an object. A countersink can be drawn in one of two ways. You can draw an inverted cone centered on a hole, or you can chamfer the top edge of a hole. The chamfering technique is the quickest.

1. Draw a cylinder representing the diameter of the hole, Figure 11-16A.
2. Subtract the cylinder from the base object.
3. Select the **CHAMFER** command and enter the chamfer distance(s).
4. Select **CHAMFER** again and pick the top edge of the base object, then pick the top edge of the hole.

Figure 11-16.
Constructing a countersink. A—Subtract the cylinder from the base. B—Chamfer the top of the hole to create a countersink. The object is shown here with hidden lines removed.

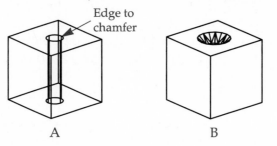

Boss

A *boss* does the same thing as a spotface, but has an area raised above the surface of an object. Draw a boss as follows:

1. Draw a cylinder representing the diameter of the hole. Extend it above the base object higher than the boss is to be, Figure 11-17A.
2. Draw a second cylinder the diameter of the boss. Place the base of the cylinder above the top surface a distance equal to the height of the boss. Give the cylinder a negative height value so that it extends inside the base object, Figure 11-17B.
3. Union the base object and the second cylinder. Subtract the hole from the new unioned object, Figure 11-17C.
4. Fillet the intersection of the boss with the base object, Figure 11-17D.

Figure 11-17.
Constructing a boss. A—Draw a cylinder for the hole extending above the surface of the object.
B—Draw a cylinder the height of the boss on the top surface of the object. C—Union the
large cylinder to the base. Then, subtract the small cylinder (hole) from the unioned objects.
D—Fillet the edge to form the boss. The final object is shown here with hidden lines removed.

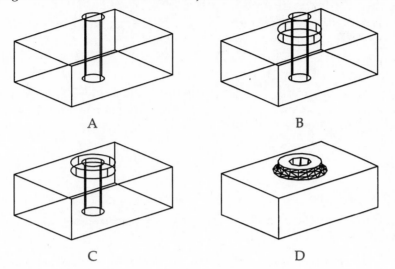

A   B

C   D

O-ring groove

An *o-ring* is a circular seal that resembles a torus. It sits inside a groove so that at
least half of the o-ring is above the surface. The groove can be constructed by placing
the center of a circle on the outside surface of a cylinder. Then, revolve the circle
around the cylinder. Finally, subtract the extrusion from the cylinder.

1. Construct the cylinder to the required dimensions, Figure 11-18A.
2. Rotate the UCS on the X axis.
3. Draw a circle with a center point on the surface of the cylinder, Figure 11-18B.
4. Revolve the circle 360°, Figure 11-18C.
5. Subtract the revolved object from the cylinder, Figure 11-18D.

The object is shown after using **HIDE** and **RENDER** in Figure 11-18E.

Figure 11-18.
Constructing an o-ring groove. A—Construct a cylinder. B—Draw a circle centered on the
surface of the cylinder. C—Revolve the circle 360°. D—Subtract the revolved object from the
cylinder. E—The completed o-ring groove.

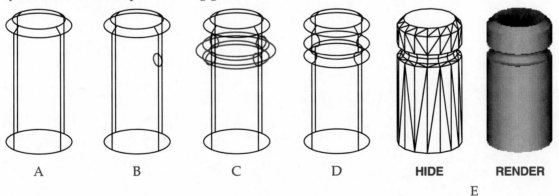

A   B   C   D   **HIDE**   **RENDER**

E

Architectural molding

Architectural details that contain molding can be quickly constructed using extrusions. The procedure is as follows:

1. Construct the profile of the molding as a closed shape, Figure 11-19A.
2. Extrude the profile the desired length, Figure 11-19B.

Molding intersections at corners can be quickly created by extruding the same shape in two different directions, then joining the two objects.

1. Copy and rotate the molding profile to orient the Z axis in the direction desired for the second extrusion, Figure 11-20A.
2. Extrude the copied profile the desired length, Figure 11-20B.
3. Union the two extrusions to create the new mitered corner molding, Figure 11-20C. A quick rendering of this corner molding clearly displays the features, Figure 11-20D.

Figure 11-19.
A—The molding profile. B—The profile extruded to the desired length.

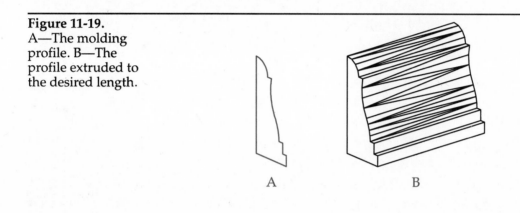

A   B

Figure 11-20.
Constructing corner molding. A—Copy and rotate the molding profile. B—Extrude the copied profile to the desired length. C—Union the two extrusions to create the mitered corner. D—A rendered view of the molding.

Copy and rotate
the profile

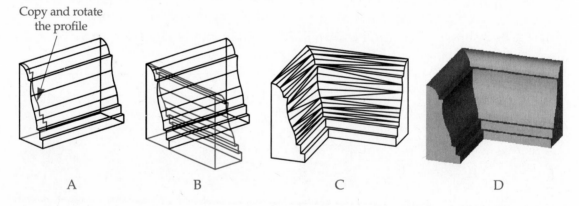

A   B   C   D

Multiple intersecting extrusions

Many solid objects have complex curves and profiles. These can often be constructed using two or more extrusions joined by intersection. The resulting solid is a combination of only the intersecting volume of the extrusions. The following example shows the construction of a coat hook.

1. Construct the first profile, Figure 11-21A.
2. Construct the second profile located on a common point with the first, Figure 11-21B.
3. Construct the third profile located on a common point with the first two, Figure 11-21C.

4. Extrude each profile the required dimension into the same area. Be careful to specify positive or negative heights for each extrusion, Figure 11-21D and Figure 11-21E.
5. Use **INTERSECT** to join the extrusions into a composite solid, Figure 11-21F.

Figure 11-21.
Constructing a coat hook. A—Draw the first profile. B—Draw the second profile. C—Draw the third profile. All three profiles should have a common origin. D—Extrude each profile so that the extruded objects intersect. E—The extruded objects with hidden lines removed. F—Use **INTERSECT** to create the composite solid. The final solid is shown here with hidden lines removed.

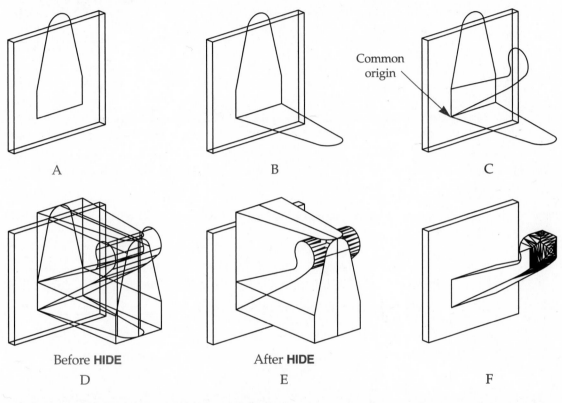

A

B

Common origin

C

Before **HIDE**
D

After **HIDE**
E

F

Chapter Test

Write your answers in the spaces provided.

1. What is an extrusion? _____

2. How can an extrusion be constructed to extend below the current UCS? _____
_____

3. What is the range in which a taper angle can vary? _____

4. How can a curved extrusion be constructed? _____

5. If an extrusion is created as indicated in Question 4, how is the base of the extruded object oriented? _____
_____

6. What are the four different options for selecting the axis of revolution for a revolved solid? _____
_____
_____

7. How can a profile be revolved twice (or more) about the same axis and create different shaped solids? _____

8. Why must only one edge of a solid be selected when using the **FILLET** command?
_____
_____

9. When you are chamfering a solid, how can you select the proper surface if the wrong surface is highlighted when you select an edge? _____
_____

10. What can be edited on a solid? _____

Drawing Problems

1. Construct an 8″ diameter tee pipe fitting using the dimensions shown below.

   A. Use **EXTRUDE** to create two sections of pipe at 90° to each other, then **UNION** the two pieces together.

   B. Use **FILLET** and **CHAMFER** to finish the object. The chamfer distance is .25″.

   C. The outside diameter of all three openings is 8.63″ and the pipe wall thickness is .322″.

   D. Save the drawing as P11-1.

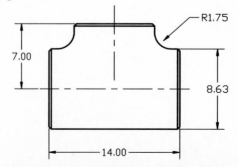

2. Construct an 8″ diameter 90° elbow pipe fitting using the dimensions shown below.

   A. Use **EXTRUDE** to create the elbow.

   B. Use **CHAMFER** to finish the object. The chamfer distance is .25″.

   C. The outside diameter is 8.63″ and the pipe wall thickness is .322″.

   D. Save the drawing as P11-2.

12.00

3. Construct a 12′ long section of wide flange structural steel with the cross section shown below. Use the dimensions given. Save the drawing as P11-3.

.288   8.00   .433   8.00

*Problems 4–13. These problems require you to use a variety of solid modeling functions to construct the objects. Use **EXTRUDE, REVOLVE, FILLET,** and **CHAMFER** to assist in construction.*

4.

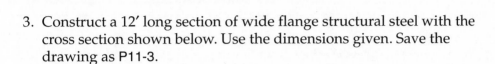

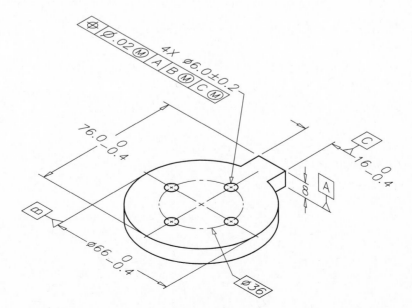

Spring clip

5.

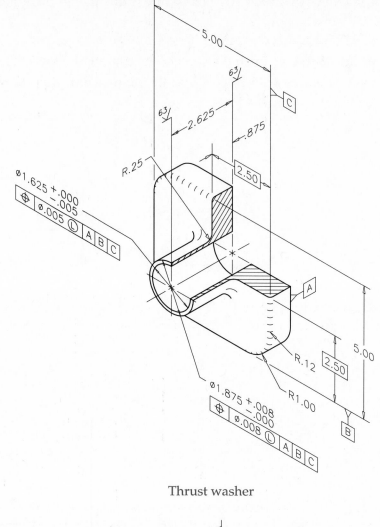

Thrust washer

6.

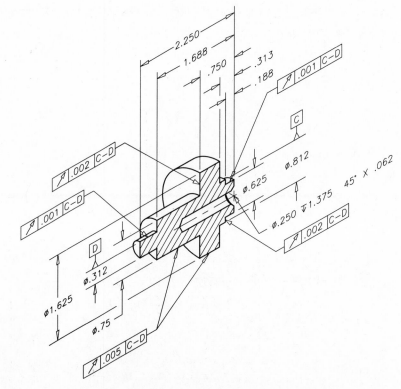

Valve pin

7.

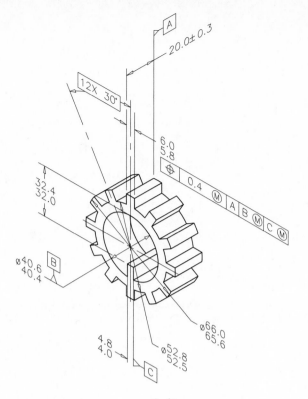

A

20.0± 0.3

12X 30°

6.0
5.8

⌖ 0.4 Ⓜ A B Ⓜ C Ⓜ

32.4
32.0

⌀40.6
40.4 B

ø66.0
65.6

4.8
4.0

⌀52.8
52.5

C

Spline

8.

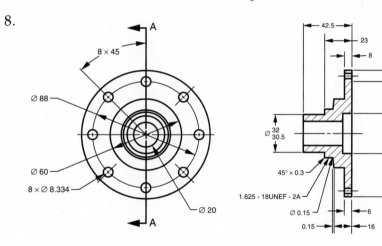

A

8 × 45

Ø 88

Ø 60

8 × Ø 8.334

Ø 20

A

42.5

23

8

Ø 32
30.5

Ø 36
34

Ø 110

45° × 0.3

1.625 - 18UNEF - 2A

Ø 0.15

0.15

6

16

Flange

9.

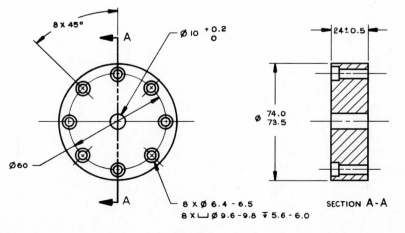

8 X 45°

A

Ø 10 + 0.2
        0

Ø60

A

8 X Ø 6.4 - 6.5
8 X ⌴ Ø 9.6 - 9.8 ▼ 5.6 - 6.0

24± 0.5

Ø 74.0
73.5

SECTION A-A

Collar

10.

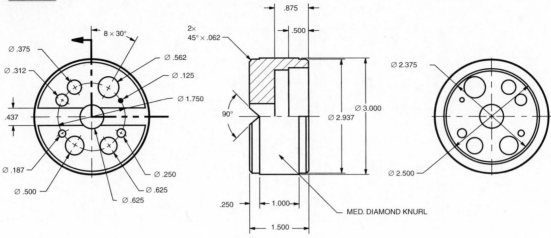

Diffuser

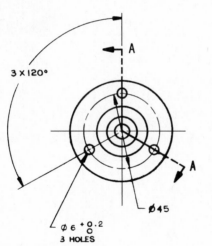

11.

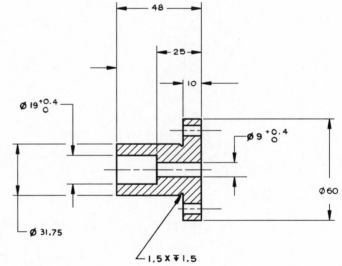

SECTION A-A

Bushing

12.

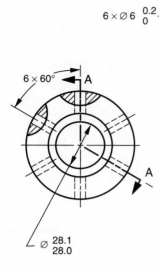

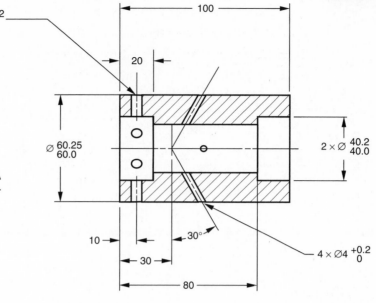

6 × Ø6 $^{0.2}_{0}$

6 × 60°

A

A

Ø 28.1
28.0

100

20

Ø 60.25
60.0

2 × Ø $^{40.2}_{40.0}$

10

30°

30

4 × Ø4 $^{+0.2}_{0}$

80

SECTION A-A

Nozzle

13.

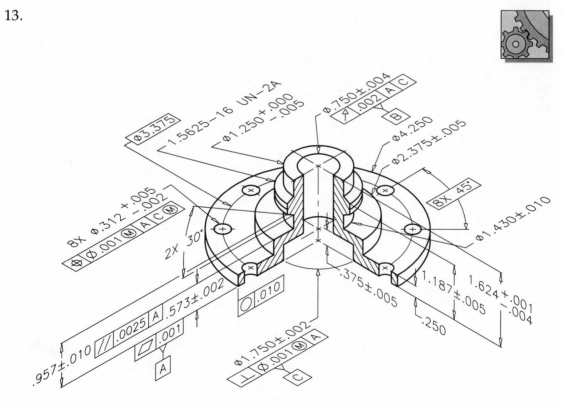

Ø3.375

1.5625–16 UN–2A

Ø1.250 $^{+.000}_{-.005}$

Ø.750±.004

☐ .002 A C

B

Ø4.250

Ø2.375±.005

8X 45°

Ø1.430±.010

8X Ø.312 $^{+.005}_{-.002}$

⊕ Ø.001 Ⓜ A C Ⓜ

2X 30°

◯ .010

.375±.005

1.187 ±.005

1.624 $^{+.001}_{-.004}$

.250

.957±.010

∥ .0025 A

.573±.002

⬦ .001

A

Ø1.750±.002

⊥ Ø.001 Ⓜ A

C

Hub

14. Construct picture frame moldings using the profiles shown below.

   A. Draw each of the closed profiles shown. Use your own dimensions for the details of the moldings.

   B. The length and width of A and B should be no larger than 1.5″ × 1″.

   C. The length and width of C and D should be no larger than 3″ × 1.5″.

   D. Construct 8″ × 12″ picture frames using moldings A and B.

   E. Construct 12″ × 24″ picture frames using moldings C and D.

   F. Save the drawing as P11-14.

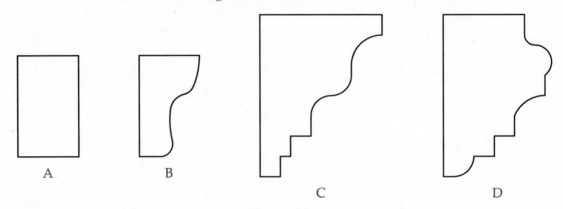

A   B   C   D

15. Construct a solid model of the faucet handle shown below.

   A. Create three User Coordinate Systems. Use a common origin for each UCS.

   B. Draw each profile using the dimensions given.

   C. Extrude each profile into a common space. Be sure to use the proper Z value when extruding.

   D. Create an intersection of the three profiles to produce the final solid.

   E. Save the drawing as P11-15.

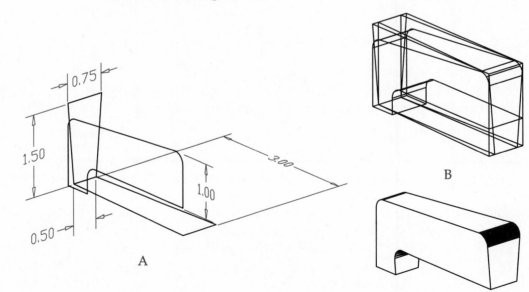

A   B   C

Chapter 12

Solid Model Display and Analysis

Learning Objectives

After completing this chapter, you will be able to:
- ○ Control the appearance of solid model displays.
- ○ Construct a 2D section through a solid model.
- ○ Construct a 3D section of a solid model.
- ○ Create a multiview layout of a solid model using **SOLVIEW** and **SOLDRAW**.
- ○ Construct a profile of a solid using **SOLPROF**.
- ○ Perform an analysis of a solid model.
- ○ Export and import solid model files and data.

The appearance of a solid model is controlled by the **ISOLINES, DISPSILH**, and **FACETRES** system variables. Internal features of the model can be shown using the **SLICE** and **SECTION** commands. This chapter looks at how these sections can be combined with 2D projections created with **SOLVIEW** and **SOLDRAW** to create a drawing layout for plotting. This chapter also covers how a profile of a solid can be created using the **SOLPROF** command.

Controlling Solid Model Display

AutoCAD solid models can be displayed as a wireframe, with hidden lines removed, shaded, or rendered. A wireframe is the default display and is the quickest to create. The hidden, shaded, and rendered displays require a longer regeneration time.

> AutoCAD User's Guide **14**

Isolines

The appearance of a solid model in wireframe form is controlled by the **ISOLINES** system variable. An *isoline* is a line that connects points of equal value. In other words, all points on a horizontal isoline have the same Z value. All points on a vertical isoline have the same X or Y values.

The default value for the **ISOLINES** system variable is 4. It can have a value from 0 to 2047. All solid objects in the drawing are affected by changes in the **ISOLINES** value. Change the **ISOLINES** setting as follows:

> Command: **ISOLINES**↵
> New value for ISOLINES ⟨*current*⟩: **12**↵

Figure 12-1 illustrates the difference between **ISOLINES** set to 4 and 12.

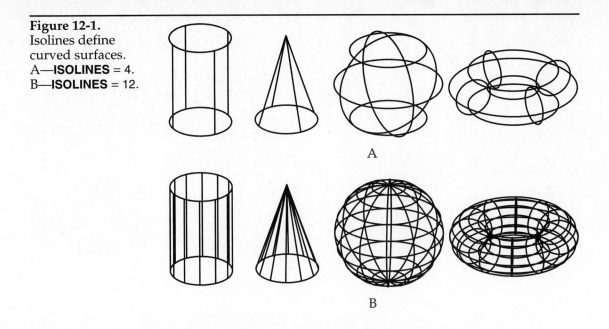

Figure 12-1.
Isolines define
curved surfaces.
A—**ISOLINES** = 4.
B—**ISOLINES** = 12.

A

B

Creating a display silhouette with DISPSILH

Solids can appear in two forms when the **HIDE** command is used. The default form shows the model as if it is composed of many individual faces. These faces are defined by tessellation lines. The number of tessellation lines is controlled by the **ISOLINES** variable for wireframes and by the **FACETRES** variable in all other displays. The model can also appear smooth, with no tessellation lines on the surface. This is controlled by the **DISPSILH** (display silhouette) system variable. Figure 12-2 shows solids with **DISPSILH** set to 1 after using **HIDE**.

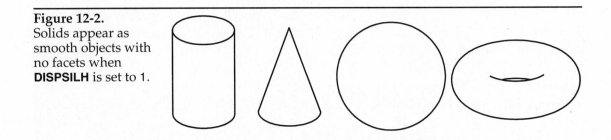

Figure 12-2.
Solids appear as
smooth objects with
no facets when
DISPSILH is set to 1.

Controlling surface smoothness with FACETRES

The smoothness of shaded or rendered images is controlled by the **FACETRES** system variable. This variable determines the number of polygon faces that are applied to the solid model. The default value is .5. Values can range from 0.01 to 10.0. The illustrations in Figure 12-3 show the effect of two different **FACETRES** settings.

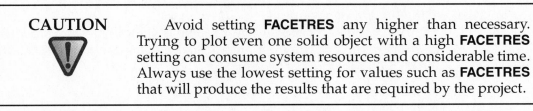

CAUTION

Avoid setting **FACETRES** any higher than necessary. Trying to plot even one solid object with a high **FACETRES** setting can consume system resources and considerable time. Always use the lowest setting for values such as **FACETRES** that will produce the results that are required by the project.

Figure 12-3.
The images in the top row have hidden lines removed, while the bottom row is rendered.
A—The **FACETRES** setting of 0.5 produces these images.
B—The **FACETRES** setting of 5.0 produces smoother surfaces.

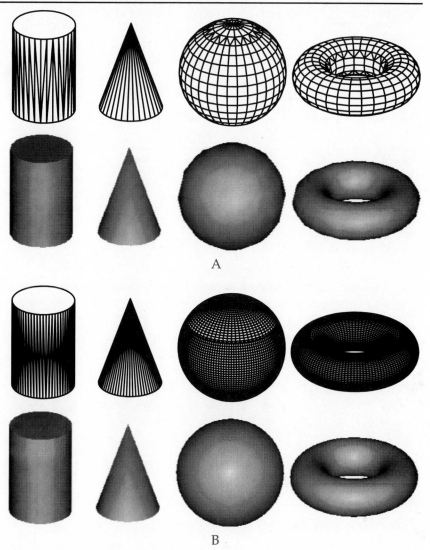

A

B

EXERCISE 12-1

❏ Begin a new drawing named EX12-1.
❏ Construct the object shown below using the dimensions given.
❏ Change **ISOLINES** to 6, 8, and 12, and observe the results.
❏ Use the **HIDE** command.
❏ Change **DISPSILH** to 1 and use **HIDE**. Observe the difference.
❏ Set **FACETRES** to .1, .5, 1, and 2 and use **HIDE** after each setting. Observe the results.
❏ Save the drawing as EX12-1. This drawing is used in the remainder of the chapter exercises.

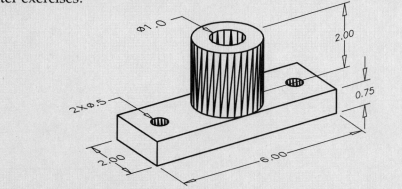

You can "cut" through a 3D solid model to view its internal features and profiles. The **SECTION** command allows you to create a 2D region of the model that is cut. The **SLICE** command allows you to create a 3D cutaway view of the model. These commands can be selected from the **Solids** cascading menu in the **Draw** pull-down menu. See Figure 12-4.

Figure 12-4.
The **SECTION** and
SLICE commands
can be executed
from the **Solids**
cascading menu in
the **Draw** pull-down
menu. The
commands are
shown here
highlighted.

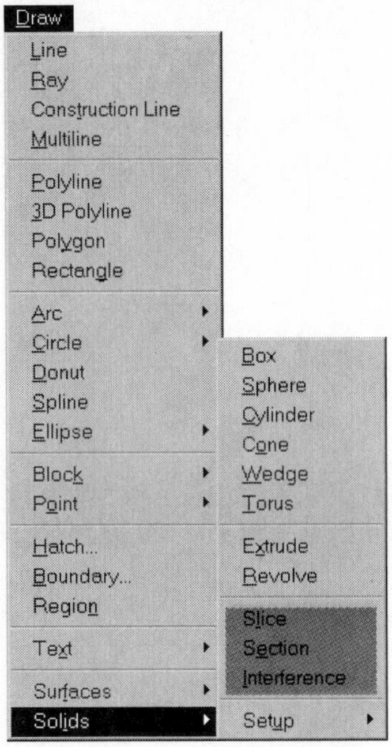

Draw
Line
Ray
Construction Line
Multiline
Polyline
3D Polyline
Polygon
Rectangle
Arc ▶
Circle ▶
Donut
Spline
Ellipse ▶
Block ▶
Point ▶
Hatch...
Boundary...
Region
Text ▶
Surfaces ▶
Solids ▶

Box
Sphere
Cylinder
Cone
Wedge
Torus
Extrude
Revolve
Slice
Section
Interference
Setup ▶

Creating a 3D solid model section

SECTION
SEC

Draw
↳ **Solids**
↳ **Section**

Solids
toolbar

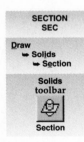

Section

The **SECTION** command places a cutting plane line through your model in the selected location. The default option of **SECTION** is to select three points to define the cutting plane. To access the command, pick **Section** from the **Solids** cascading menu of the **Draw** pull-down menu, pick the **Section** button in the **Solids** toolbar, or type SEC or SECTION at the Command: prompt. The following example selects two quadrant points and one center point on the object in Figure 12-5 to define the cutting plane.

Command: **SEC** *or* **SECTION**↵
Select objects: *(pick the solid to be sectioned)*
Select objects: ↵
Section plane by Object/Zaxis/View/XY/YZ/ZX/⟨3points⟩: *(pick the quadrant at point 1)*
2nd point on plane: *(pick the center at point 2)*
3rd point on plane: *(pick the quadrant at point 3)*
Command:

The section created is a 2D region. It has no section lines and is created on the current layer. See Figure 12-5B. If you wish to use the new region as the basis for a 2D, hatched section view of the model, do the following:

1. Move or copy the region to a new location. See Figure 12-6A.
2. Explode the region. This creates individual regions if there are two or more separate areas in the section.
3. Explode each separate region again. This breaks the region into objects. These individual objects can be used by AutoCAD to create a boundary for hatching purposes.

Figure 12-5.
A—Three points are picked to define a cutting plane. B—The section is drawn as a region without section lines.

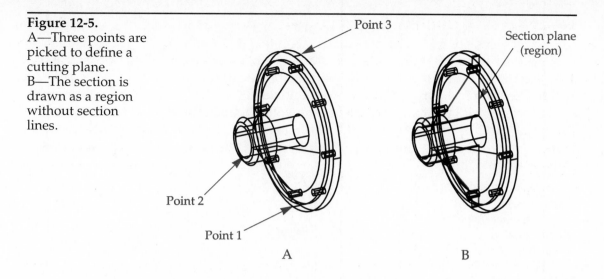

Point 3

Point 2

Point 1

Section plane (region)

A   B

4. Use **BHATCH** to draw section lines inside the areas. See Figure 12-6B. Be sure that the UCS is set to the plane of the area to be hatched. If not, a boundary definition error will appear when an object is selected.
5. Draw any connecting lines required to complete the section view. See Figure 12-6C.
Additional options of the **SECTION** command enable you to specify sectioning planes in a variety of ways. These are explained below.

*   **Object.** The section plane is aligned with a selected object, such as circle, arc, ellipse, 2D spline, or 2D polyline.
*   **Zaxis.** Select a point on the new section plane, then pick a point on the positive Z axis of that plane.
*   **View.** Select a point on the new section plane and AutoCAD aligns the section perpendicular to the viewpoint in the current viewport.
*   **XY.** The new section plane is aligned with the XY plane of the current UCS. The point selected specifies the location of the plane.
*   **YZ.** The new section plane is aligned with the YZ plane of the current UCS. The point selected specifies the location of the plane.
*   **ZX.** The new section plane is aligned with the ZX plane of the current UCS. The point selected specifies the location of the plane.

Figure 12-6.
Using a region as a section view. A—First move the region. B—Add section lines. C—Add any other lines needed to complete the section view.

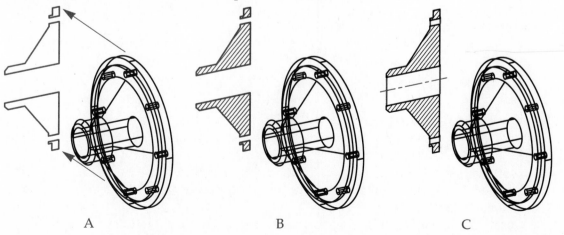

A   B   C

SLICE
SL

Draw
→ Solids
→ Slice

Solids
toolbar

Slice

Slicing a solid model

A true 3D sectioned model is created with the **SLICE** command. You can create a new solid by discarding one side of the cut, or both parts of the sliced object can be retained. **SLICE** does not draw section lines or create regions.

To slice an object, select **Slice** from the **Solids** cascading menu in the **Draw** pull-down menu, pick the **Slice** button from the **Solids** toolbar, or type SL or SLICE at the Command: prompt. The options of the **SLICE** command are the same as those of **SECTION**. In the following example, the **YZ** option of **SLICE** is used to define the cutting plane. Refer to Figure 12-7.

    Command: **SL** or **SLICE**↵
    Select objects: *(pick the solid)*
    Select objects: ↵
    Slicing plane by Object/Zaxis/View/XY/YZ/ZX/⟨3points⟩: **YZ**↵
    Point on YZ plane ⟨0,0,0⟩: ↵
    Both sides/⟨Point on desired side of the plane⟩: *(pick point 1 to keep the far side of the object)*

Both sides of the slice can be kept if desired. To do so, select the **Both sides** option at the following prompt:

    Both sides/⟨Point on desired side of the plane⟩: **B**↵

The slice plane appears the same as the section plane shown in Figure 12-7B, but the solid is now two separate objects. Test this by picking one side to display grips. Either side can be moved, copied, or rotated. See Figure 12-8.

Figure 12-7.
A—Specify the cutting plane and pick the side of the object to keep. B—The completed slice. C—The sliced object after **HIDE**.

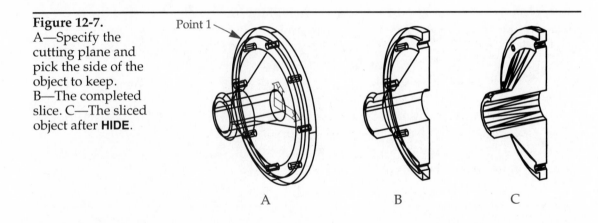

Point 1

A   B   C

Figure 12-8.
A—The slice plane appears as a section when both sides are kept. B—Each part of the sliced object can be moved, copied, or rotated.

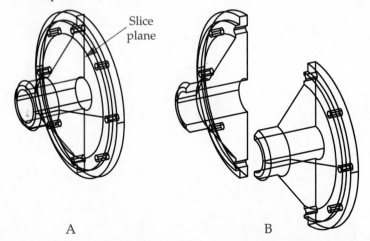

Slice
plane

A   B

Creating special sections with SLICE

You are not limited to a single slice through an object. For example, you can create a half section of the object in Figure 12-9 by using the **SLICE** command a second time to cut away the top half of the object nearest to you. The example shown in Figure 12-9A shows the use of the **3points** option of **SLICE** to remove one quarter of the original object. The results are shown in Figure 12-9B and Figure 12-9C.

Figure 12-9.
A—A cutting plane is selected to remove one quarter of the original object. B—The cutaway view in wireframe. C—A rendered view of the cutaway.

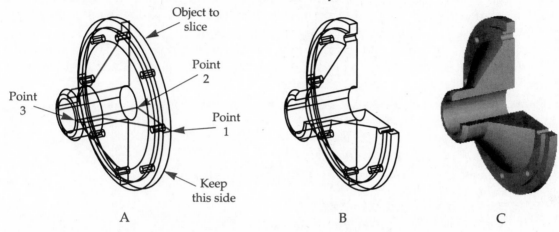

A   B   C

EXERCISE 12-2

❏ Open drawing EX12-1 if it is not on your screen.
❏ Create a full section that cuts through the centers of all three holes.
❏ Move the section region outside the object. Add section lines and connect the section areas with lines to complete the view.
❏ The completed section should look like A shown below.
❏ Create a slice through the object on the same plane as the previous section.
❏ Retain both sides of the slice and move both sides apart.
❏ Slice through the large hole on the near side and remove one half of the side.
❏ The completed objects should look like B shown below.
❏ Save the drawing as EX12-2.

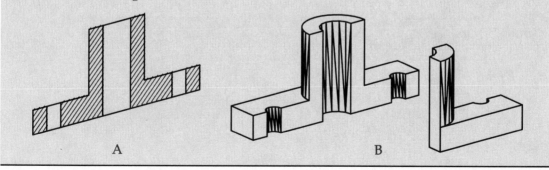

A   B

Creating and Using Multiview Layouts

Once a solid model has been constructed, it is easy to create a multiview layout using the **SOLVIEW** command. This command allows you to create a paper space layout containing orthographic, section, and auxiliary views. The **SOLDRAW** command can then be used to complete profile and section views. **SOLDRAW** must be used after **SOLVIEW**. The **SOLPROF** command can be used to create a profile of the solid in the current view.

Creating views with SOLVIEW

To use the **SOLVIEW** command, first restore the WCS. This will help avoid any confusion. Then, display a plan view. See Figure 12-10. It helps to have additional User Coordinate Systems created prior to using **SOLVIEW**. This allows you to construct orthographic views based on a specific named UCS.

Next, create an initial view from which other views can project. This is normally the top or front. In the following example, the top view is constructed first. The top view is created by using the plan view of a UCS named Left.

To initiate the **SOLVIEW** command, select **View** from the **Setup** cascading menu after selecting **Solids** from the **Draw** pull-down menu, pick the **Setup View** button from the **Solids** toolbar, or type SOLVIEW at the Command: prompt as follows:

```
Command: SOLVIEW↵
Entering Paper space. Use MVIEW to insert Model space viewports.
Regenerating paperspace.
Ucs/Ortho/Auxiliary/Section/〈eXit〉: U↵
Named/World/?/〈current〉: N↵
Name of UCS to restore: LEFT↵
Enter view scale〈1.0000〉: .5↵
View center: (pick the center of the view)
View center: ↵
Clip first corner: (pick the first corner of a paper space viewport outside the object)
Clip other corner: (pick the opposite corner of the viewport)
View name: TOP↵
Ucs/Ortho/Auxiliary/Section/〈eXit〉:
```

Figure 12-10.
Before using
SOLVIEW, display
the plan view of
the WCS.

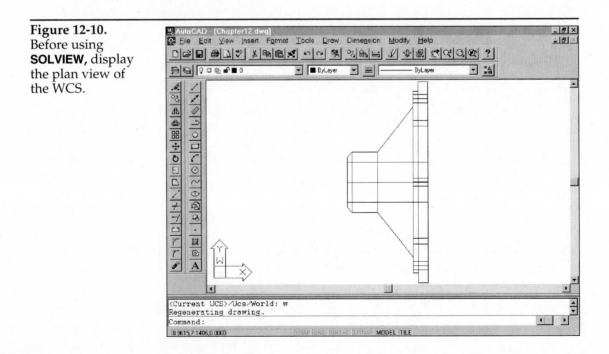

AutoCAD and its Applications—Advanced

You must provide a name for the view in order to continue using **SOLVIEW**. The view shown in Figure 12-11 is displayed.

The **SOLVIEW** command remains active until you use the **eXit** option or press the [Esc] key. If you exit **SOLVIEW** at this time, you can still return to the drawing and create additional orthographic viewports. Continue and create a section view to the right of the top view as follows:

Ucs/Ortho/Auxiliary/Section/⟨eXit⟩: **S**↵
Cutting Plane's 1st point: *(pick the quadrant of point 1 in Figure 12-12)*
Cutting Plane's 2nd point: *(pick the quadrant of point 2)*
Side to view from: *(pick point 3)*
Enter view scale⟨0.5000⟩: ↵
View center: *(pick the center of the new section view)*
View center: ↵
Clip first corner: *(pick one corner of the viewport)*
Clip other corner: *(pick the opposite corner of the viewport)*
View name: **SECTION**↵
Ucs/Ortho/Auxiliary/Section/⟨eXit⟩: ↵

Figure 12-11.
The initial view named TOP is created with the **Ucs** option of **SOLVIEW**.

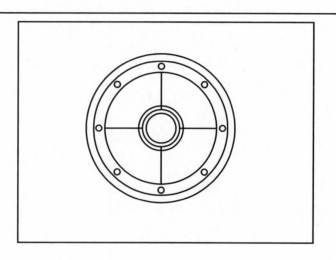

Notice in Figure 12-12 that the new view is shown as a wireframe and not as a section. This is normal. **SOLVIEW** is used to create the views. The **SOLDRAW** command draws the section lines. **SOLDRAW** is discussed later in this chapter.

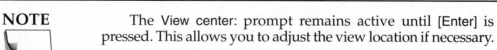

NOTE   The View center: prompt remains active until [Enter] is pressed. This allows you to adjust the view location if necessary.

A standard orthographic view can be created using the **Ortho** option of **SOLVIEW**. This is illustrated in the following example:

Ucs/Ortho/Auxiliary/Section/⟨eXit⟩: **O**↵
Pick side of viewport to project: *(pick the bottom edge of the left viewport)*
View center: *(pick the center of the new view)*
View center: ↵
Clip first corner: *(pick one corner of the viewport)*
Clip other corner: *(pick the opposite corner of the viewport)*
View name: **FRONT**↵

The new orthographic view is shown in Figure 12-13.

Figure 12-12.
The section view created with **SOLVIEW** (shown on the right in both A and B) does not show section lines.

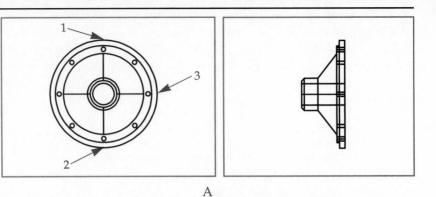

A

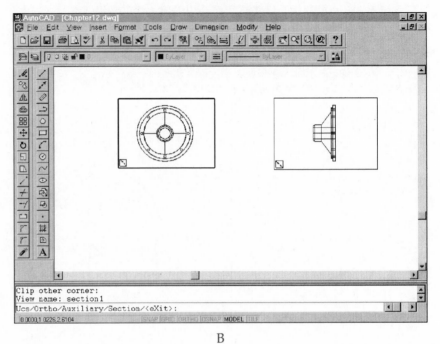

B

Figure 12-13.
An orthographic front view is created with the **Ortho** option of **SOLVIEW**. This is the view shown at the lower left.

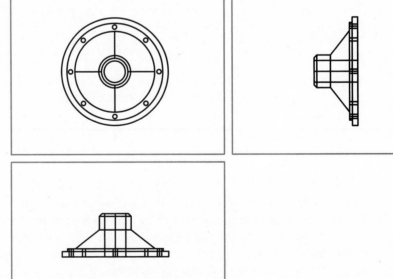

AutoCAD and its Applications—Advanced

The **SOLVIEW** command creates new layers that are used by **SOLDRAW** when profiles and sections are created. The layers are used for the placement of visible, hidden, dimension, and section lines. Each layer is named as the name of the view with a three letter tag. The layers are:

Layer name	Object
view name-vis	Visible lines
view name-hid	Hidden lines
view name-dim	Dimension lines
view name-hat	Hatch patterns (sections)

The use of these layers is discussed in the next section.

EXERCISE 12-3

❑ Open drawing EX12-1 if it is not on your screen.
❑ Return the display to a plan view of the WCS.
❑ Use **SOLVIEW** to create a top view of the solid. Locate the view near the top of the screen. Name the view TOP.
❑ Use **SOLVIEW** to create a front section view of the solid located below the top view. Name the view SECTION.
❑ The drawing should look similar to the one shown below.
❑ Save the drawing as EX12-3.

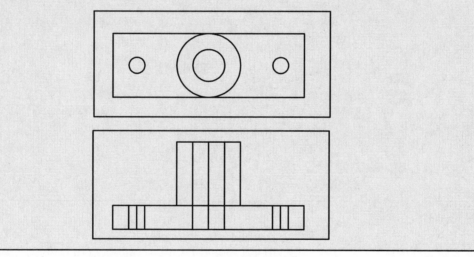

Creating finished views with **SOLDRAW**

SOLVIEW saves information specific to each viewport when a new view is created. This information is used by **SOLDRAW** to construct a finished profile or section view. **SOLDRAW** first deletes any information currently on the *view name*-vis, *view name*-hid, and *view name*-hat layers for the selected view. Visible, hidden, and section lines are automatically placed on the appropriate layer. Therefore, you should avoid placing objects on any layer other than the *view name*-dim layer.

The **SOLDRAW** command automatically creates a profile or section in the selected viewport. If you select a viewport that was created using the **Section** option of **SOLVIEW**, the **SOLDRAW** command uses the current values of the **HPNAME**, **HPSCALE**, and **HPANG** system variables to construct the section. These three variables control the angle, boundary, and name of the hatch pattern.

If a view is selected that was not created as a section in **SOLVIEW**, the **SOLDRAW** command constructs a profile view. All new visible and hidden lines are placed on the *view name*-vis or *view name*-hid layer. All existing objects on those layers are deleted.

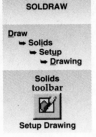

SOLDRAW

Draw
➥ Solids
➥ Setup
➥ Drawing

Solids
toolbar

Setup Drawing

To initiate the **SOLVIEW** command, select **Drawing** from the **Setup** cascading menu after selecting **Solids** from the **Draw** pull-down menu, pick the **Setup Drawing** button from the **Solids** toolbar, or type SOLDRAW at the Command: prompt as follows:

    Command: **SOLDRAW**↵
    Select viewports to draw: (*pick the three viewport outlines*)
    Select objects: 1 found
    Select objects: ↵
    One solid selected.

After the profile construction is completed, lines that should be a hidden linetype are still visible (solid). This is because the linetype set for the *view name*-hid layer is Continuous. Change the linetype to Hidden and the drawing should appear as shown in Figure 12-14.

Figure 12-14.
The new front profile view shows hidden lines after the linetype is set to dashed for the Front-hid layer.

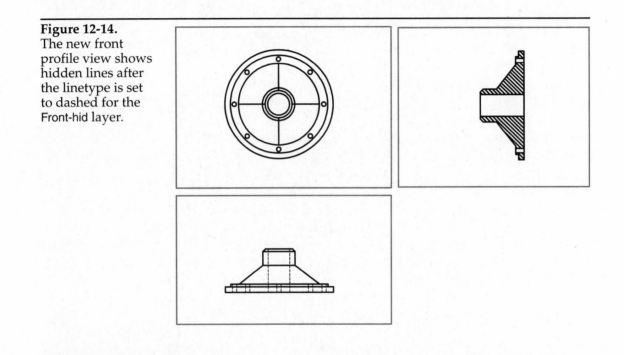

PROFESSIONAL TIP   If you wish to dimension views created with **SOLVIEW** and **SOLDRAW**, use the view-specific dim layers. These layers are created for that purpose and are only visible in one view. **SOLDRAW** does not delete information on the dim layers when it constructs a view.

Adding a 3D viewport to the drawing layout

If you want to add a viewport that contains a 3D view of the solid, use the **MVIEW** command. Create a single viewport by picking the corners. The object will appear in the viewport. Next, use **VPOINT** to achieve the desired 3D view. Pan and zoom as necessary. If you want hidden lines removed on the 3D view when the drawing is plotted, use the **MVIEW Hideplot** option and select the 3D viewport. See Figure 12-15. Remember the following points when working with **SOLVIEW** and **SOLDRAW**:

- Use **SOLVIEW** first then **SOLDRAW**.
- Do not draw on the *view name*-hid and *view name*-vis layers.
- Place dimensions for each view on the *view name*-dim layer for that specific view.

Figure 12-15.
Create a 3D viewport with **MVIEW** and hide the lines with the **MVIEW Hideplot** option. This view is shown at the lower right.

- After using **SOLVIEW**, use **SOLDRAW** on all viewports in order to create hidden lines or section views.
- Change the linetype on the *view name*-hid layer to Dashed or Hidden.
- Create 3D viewports with the **MVIEW** command. Remove hidden lines when plotting with the **MVIEW Hideplot** option.
- Plot the drawing in paper space at the scale of 1:1.

EXERCISE 12-4

❏ Open drawing EX12-3 if it is not on your screen. If you have not completed any of the exercises in this chapter, complete EX12-1 now and then complete EX12-3.

❏ Use **SOLDRAW** to create profile and section views of the two views on your screen. Adjust layer linetypes so hidden lines show properly.

❏ Add a 3D view to the right of the first two. The drawing should look similar to the one shown below.

❏ Save the drawing as EX12-4.

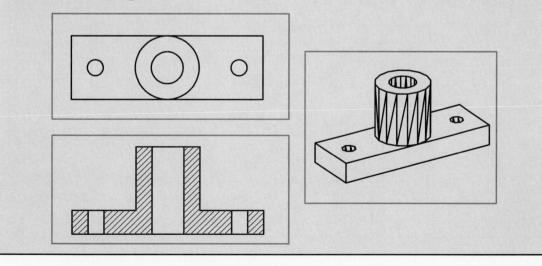

Creating a profile with SOLPROF

The **SOLPROF** command creates a profile view from a 3D solid model. This is similar to the **Profile** option of the **SOLVIEW** command. **SOLPROF** is limited to creating a profile view of the solid for the current 3D view only.

SOLPROF creates a block of all lines forming the profile of the object. It also creates a block of the hidden lines of the object. The original 3D object is retained. Each of these blocks is placed on a new layer with the name of Ph-*view handle* and Pv-*view handle*. A *view handle* is a name composed of numbers and letters that is automatically given to a viewport by AutoCAD. For example, if the view handle for the current viewport is 2C9, the **SOLPROF** command creates the layers Ph-2c9 and Pv-2c9. You must be in model space to use **SOLPROF**.

To initiate the **SOLVIEW** command, select **Profile** from the **Setup** cascading menu after selecting **Solids** from the **Draw** pull-down menu, pick the **Setup Profile** button from the **Solids** toolbar, or type SOLPROF at the Command: prompt as follows:

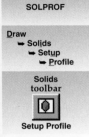
Command: **SOLPROF**↵
Select objects: 1 found
Select objects: ↵
Display hidden profile lines on separate layer? ⟨Y⟩: ↵
Project profile lines onto a plane? ⟨Y⟩: ↵

If you answer yes to this prompt, the 3D profile lines are projected to a 2D plane and converted to 2D objects. This produces a cleaner profile.

Delete tangential edges? ⟨Y⟩: ↵

Answering yes to this prompt produces a proper 2D view by eliminating lines that would normally appear at tangent points of arcs and lines.

One solid selected:
Command:

The original object and the profile created with **SOLPROF** are shown in Figure 12-16.

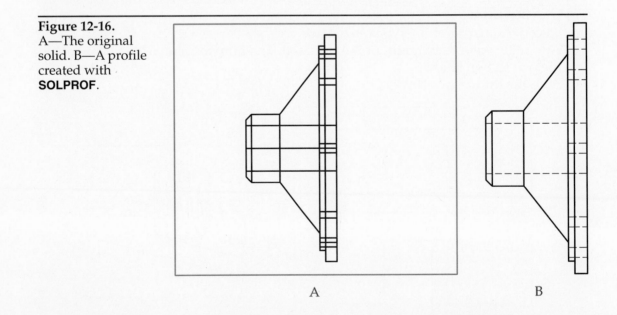

Figure 12-16.
A—The original solid. B—A profile created with **SOLPROF**.

A   B

NOTE	When plotting views created with **SOLPROF**, hidden lines may not be displayed unless you freeze the layer that contains the original 3D object.

Solid Model Analysis

The **MASSPROP** command allows you to analyze a solid model for its physical properties. There is only one material in Release 14—mild steel.

The data obtained from **MASSPROP** can be retained for reference by saving it to a file. The default file name is the drawing name. The file is an ASCII text file with an .mpr extension (mass properties). The analysis can be used for third party applications to produce finite element analysis, material lists, or other testing studies.

Select the **MASSPROP** command by selecting **Inquiry** in the **Tools** pull-down menu and then picking **Mass Properties**, Figure 12-17. You can also pick the **Mass Properties** button in the **Inquiry** flyout of the **Standard** toolbar (or in the **Inquiry** toolbar), or type MASSPROP at the Command: prompt:

MASSPROP

Tools
➡ Inquiry
➡ Mass
   Properties

Inquiry
toolbar

Mass Properties

> Command: **MASSPROP**↵
> Select objects: *(pick the solid model)*
> Select objects: ↵

AutoCAD analyzes the model and displays the results on the text screen. See Figure 12-18. The following properties are listed:

- **Mass.** A measure of the inertia of a solid. In other words, the more mass an object has, the more inertia it has. Note: Mass is *not* a unit of measurement of inertia.
- **Volume.** The amount of 3D space the solid occupies.
- **Bounding box.** A 3D box that fully encloses the solid.
- **Centroid.** A point in 3D space that represents the geometric center of the mass.
- **Moments of inertia.** A solid's resistance when rotating about a given axis.
- **Products of inertia.** A solid's resistance when rotating about two axes at a time.
- **Radii of gyration.** Similar to moments of inertia. Specified as a radius about an axis.
- **Principal moments and X-Y-Z directions about a centroid.** The axes about which the moments of inertia are the highest and lowest.

Figure 12-17.
The **MASSPROP** command is found in the **Inquiry** cascading menu of the **Tools** pull-down menu.

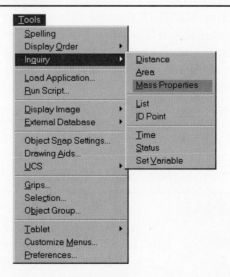

Figure 12-18.
The **MASSPROP** command displays a list of solid properties in the text screen. Each of these properties are explained in the text.

```
■ AutoCAD Text Window                                    _ □ ✕
 Edit
 Select objects:

 ----------------      SOLIDS      ----------------

 Mass:                     11.5476
 Volume:                   11.5476
 Bounding box:       X: 4.3750   --  6.3750
                     Y: 2.7500   --  7.7500
                     Z: -2.5000  --  2.5000
 Centroid:           X: 5.9227
                     Y: 5.2500
                     Z: 0.0000
 Moments of inertia: X: 344.0157
                     Y: 419.8898
                     Z: 738.1816
 Products of inertia: XY: 359.0635
                      YZ: 0.0000
                      ZX: 0.0000
 Radii of gyration:  X: 5.4581
                     Y: 6.0301
                     Z: 7.9953
 Press ENTER to continue:
 Principal moments and X-Y-Z directions about centroid:
                     I: 25.7338 along [1.0000 0.0000 0.0000]
                     J: 14.8193 along [0.0000 1.0000 0.0000]
                     K: 14.8292 along [0.0000 0.0000 1.0000]

 Write to a file ? <N>:                            ◀ █    ▶
```

PROFESSIONAL TIP

Advanced applications of solid model design and analysis are possible with Autodesk's Designer and Mechanical Desktop software. These products allow you to create parametric designs and assign a wide variety of materials to the solid model.

Solid Model File Exchange

AutoCAD drawing files can be converted to files that can be used for testing and analysis with the **ACISOUT** command or **Export Data** dialog box. This creates a file with an .sat extension. These files can be imported into AutoCAD with the **ACISIN** command or by using the **Select ACIS File** dialog box.

Solids can also be exported for use with stereo lithography software. These files have an .stl extension. Use the **STLOUT** command or the **Export Data** dialog box to create .stl files.

Release 14 and Release 13 solids use the ACIS modeling language. Release 12 uses the AME modeling language. However, solids created in Release 12 can be converted to Release 14 ACIS models with the **AMECONVERT** command.

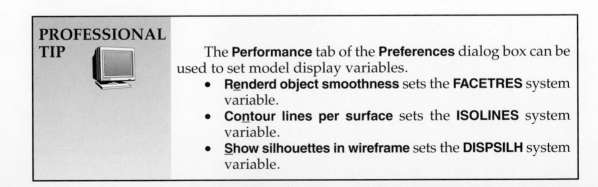

PROFESSIONAL TIP

The **Performance** tab of the **Preferences** dialog box can be used to set model display variables.
- **Re̲nderd object smoothness** sets the **FACETRES** system variable.
- **Co̲ntour lines per surface** sets the **ISOLINES** system variable.
- **Show silhouettes in wireframe** sets the **DISPSILH** system variable.

Importing and exporting solid model files

A solid model is frequently used with analysis and testing software or in the manufacturing of a part. The **ACISOUT** command allows you to create this type of file. You can type ACISOUT at the Command: prompt. This displays the **Create ACIS File** dialog box. See Figure 12-19A.

You can also use the **Export Data** dialog box by picking **Export...** from the **File** pulldown menu or typing EXP or EXPORT at the Command: prompt. Pick the **ACIS (.sat)** selection in the **Save as type:** list box in the **Export Data** dialog box. See Figure 12-19B.

An .sat file can be imported into AutoCAD and automatically converted into a drawing file by selecting **ACIS Solid...** from the **Insert** pull-down menu or entering ACISIN at the Command: prompt. This displays the **Select ACIS File** dialog box. See Figure 12-20A.

You can also import a file using the **IMPORT** command. Type IMP or IMPORT at the Command: prompt to display the **Import File** dialog box. Pick the **ACIS (.sat)** selection in the **Files of type:** list box, Figure 12-20B.

Figure 12-19.
A—The **Create ACIS File** dialog box.
B—Pick **ACIS (.sat)** in the **Export Data** dialog box to create a solid model export file.

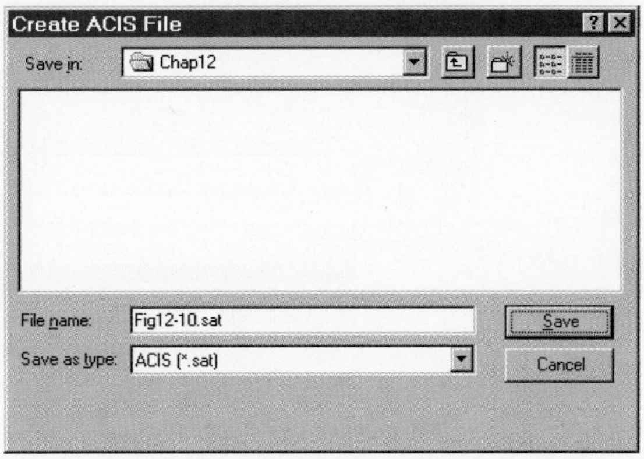

A

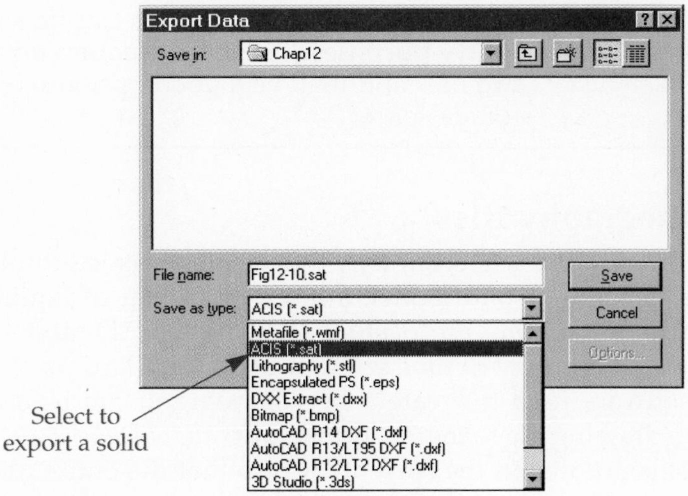

Select to export a solid

B

Figure 12-20.
A—The **Select ACIS File** dialog box.
B— Pick **ACIS (.sat)** in the **Import File** dialog box to import a solid model file.

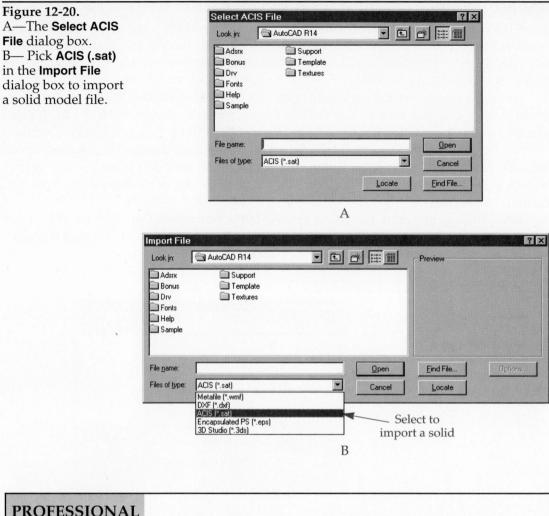

A

B

Select to
import a solid

PROFESSIONAL TIP

Solid model drawing files can be saved as .sat files for archive purposes. These files require far less disk space than .dwg files and may be a good option when you have limited storage space.

Stereolithography files

Stereolithography is a technology that creates plastic prototype 3D models using a computer-generated solid model, a laser, and a vat of liquid polymer. This technology is also called *rapid prototyping*. A prototype 3D model can be designed and formed in a short amount of time without using standard manufacturing processes.

Most software used to create a stereolithograph can read an .stl file. AutoCAD can export a drawing file to the .stl format, but *cannot* import an .stl file. Also, the solid model must be located in the current UCS so that the entire object has positive XYZ coordinates.

Use the **Export Data** dialog box to export an .stl file, or type STLOUT at the Command: prompt as follows:

Command: **STLOUT**↵
Select a single solid for STL output:
Select objects:

You can only select a single object. If you select more than one object, AutoCAD prompts you with the following:

Only one solid per file is permitted.

Select one object and press [Enter]. You are then asked if you want to create a binary .stl file. If you answer no to the prompt, an ASCII file is created. Keep in mind that a binary .stl file may be as much as five times smaller than the same file in ASCII format. After you choose the type of file, the **Create STL File** dialog box is displayed. Type the file name in the **File name:** edit box and pick **OK** or press [Enter].

Converting Release 12 AME solids

The **AMECONVERT** command allows you to convert AutoCAD Release 12 AME solids into Release 14 ACIS solids. The solids must be either AME Release 2 or 2.1 regions or solids. First load the Release 12 drawing into AutoCAD. Then type AMECONVERT at the Command: prompt. Select all solids to be converted. Then, press [Enter] to convert the solids.

EXERCISE 12-5

❑ Open drawing EX12-4 if it is not on your screen.
❑ Perform a mass properties analysis of the solid.
   ❑ What is the mass? _____
   ❑ What is the volume? _____
   ❑ What is the bounding box?
   ❑ X: _____
   ❑ Y: _____
   ❑ Z: _____
   ❑ What is the centroid?
   ❑ X: _____
   ❑ Y: _____
   ❑ Z: _____
❑ Export an .sat file and name it EX12-5.
❑ Begin a new drawing. Import the .sat file named EX12-5.
❑ Export an .stl file and name it EX12-5.
❑ Do not save the drawing.

Chapter Test

Write your answers in the spaces provided.

1. What is the function of the **ISOLINES** system variable? _____

_____

_____

2. What variable controls the display of a solid primitive silhouette? _____

3. What is the function of the **FACETRES** system variable? _____

_____

_____

4. What command creates a 2D region that represents a cutting plane through the solid? _____

_____

5. What command can display the true 3D shape of internal features and object profiles? _____

_____

6. Which command should be used first, **SOLDRAW** or **SOLVIEW**? _____

7. What command allows you to create a multiview layout from a 3D solid model?

_____

8. Which option of the command in Question 7 is used to create an orthographic view? _____

_____

9. Name the layer(s) that the command in Question 7 automatically creates. _____

_____

10. Which layer(s) in Question 9 should you avoid drawing on? _____

_____

11. What command can automatically complete a section view using the current settings of **HPNAME**, **HPSCALE**, and **HPANG**? _____

12. When plotting, how are hidden lines removed in a viewport that contains a 3D view? _____

_____

_____

13. Which command creates a profile view from a 3D model? _____

14. What is the function of the **MASSPROP** command? _____

_____

_____

15. What is the extension of the ASCII file that can be created by **MASSPROP**? _____

16. What is a centroid? _____

_____

_____

17. What commands export and import solid models? _____

_____

18. What kind of file has an .stl extension? _____

_____

19. What command creates the file in Question 18? _____

20. How can AutoCAD Release 12 solids be converted into AutoCAD Release 14 solids? _____

_____

_____

Drawing Problems

1. Open one of your solid model problems from a previous chapter and do the following:
   A. Set the **DISPSILH** variable to 1 and use **HIDE**.
   B. Set the **FACETRES** variable to .5 and produce a shaded model. Set **FACETRES** to 1 and shade the model again.
   C. Change the **SHADEDGE** and **SHADEDIF** variables, set **FACETRES** to 2 and shade the model.
   D. Create a rendering of the model.
   E. Save the drawing as P12-1.

2. Open one of your solid model problems from a previous chapter and do the following:
   A. Construct a section through the model. Cut through as many features as possible.
   B. Move the new section region to a space outside the 3D solid.
   C. Explode the resulting regions as needed and place section lines in the appropriate areas. Add lines to complete the section.
   D. Cut a slice through the original solid in the same location as the previous section.
   E. Retain the piece of the solid that is the same side as the section.
   F. Remove the other side of the slice.
   G. Save the drawing as P12-2.

3. Open one of your solid model problems from a previous chapter and do the following:
   A. Create a paper space multiview layout of the model. One of the views should be a section view. Create a minimum of three 2D views.
   B. Use **SOLVIEW** and **SOLDRAW** to create the views. Be sure that section lines and hidden lines are displayed properly.
   C. Create a fourth viewport that contains a 3D view of the solid. Label the view PICTORIAL VIEW.
   D. Plot the drawing so the 3D view is displayed with hidden lines removed.
   E. Save the drawing as P12-3.

4. Open one of your solid model problems from a previous chapter and do the following:
   A. Display the model in a plan view.
   B. Use **SOLPROF** to create a profile view. Wblock the profile view to a file named P12-2PLN.
   C. Display the original model in a 3D view.
   D. Use **SECTION** to construct a front-view section of the model. Delete the original 3D solid.
   E. Display the section as a plan view.
   F. Insert the wblock P12-2PLN above the section view. Adjust the views so that they align properly.
   G. Save the drawing as P12-4.

5. Choose five solid model problems from previous chapters and copy them to a new directory on the hard drive. Then, do the following:

A. Open the first drawing, then export it as an .sat file to the new directory.

B. Do the same for the remaining four files.

C. Compare the sizes of the .sat files with the .dwg files. Compare the combined sizes of both types of files.

D. Begin a new drawing and import one of the previous .sat files.

Using Raster and Vector Graphics Files

Learning Objectives

After completing this chapter, you will be able to:
- ○ Import and export raster files using AutoCAD.
- ○ Set image commands to manipulate inserted raster files.
- ○ Import and export vector files using AutoCAD.
- ○ Import and export PostScript files using AutoCAD.

This chapter introduces using AutoCAD to work with raster and vector graphics files. This includes importing and exporting raster files into and out of AutoCAD. Several different types of vector files can also be imported and exported. PostScript fonts and creating PostScript files for printing are also covered in this chapter.

The Windows Clipboard can be an important part of creating presentation graphics. In addition, object linking and embedding (OLE) can be used to incorporate AutoCAD graphics into electronic presentations. Both of these topics are covered thoroughly in Chapter 24.

Working with Raster Files

AutoCAD | User's | 15
Guide

AutoCAD drawing files are composed of vectors. A *vector* is defined by XYZ coordinates. *Pixels* (picture elements) are the "dots" or "bits" that make up your display screen. There is no relationship between the physical pixels in your monitor and a vector object. Pixels simply show the object at the current zoom percent.

Many illustrations created with drawing, painting, and presentation software are saved as raster files. A *raster file* defines objects by the location and color of the screen pixels. Raster files are usually called *bitmaps*. There are several types of raster files used for presentation graphics and desktop publishing. The most common types are covered in the next section.

Raster file types

You can work with raster files using the **Image** dialog box. Some of the most common raster files used in industry today are the following:
- **.GIF (Graphics Interchange Format).** A file format developed by CompuServe to exchange graphic images over an on-line computer service.
- **.PCX (Personal Computer Exchange).** A file format developed by Z-Soft Corporation.
- **.TIF (Tagged Image File Format).** A file format developed by Aldus Corporation and Microsoft Corporation.

- **.BMP (Bitmap).** A file format developed by Microsoft Corporation.
- **.PCT (Picture).** A proprietary graphics file format owned by Apple that uses Apple's *QuickDraw* language.
- **.JPG (JPEG or Joint Photographic Experts Group).** Creates a compressed graphics image file of approximately 1/20th the original size.
- **.FLC or .FLI (Flick).** Developed by Autodesk for Animator software movies.

Other file types can also be imported into AutoCAD. If you have a raster image that cannot be imported directly, you will need to first import the file into a paint or draw program. Then, export the image in one of the usable formats.

The Windows Clipboard can also be used to import file types not listed here into AutoCAD. This feature is discussed in Chapter 24.

Inserting raster images

IMAGE
IM

Insert
→ Raster
   Image...

Reference
toolbar

Image

Raster images inserted into AutoCAD drawings using the **IMAGE** command are treated much like externally referenced drawings. They are not added to the database, but are attached and referenced by a path name to the raster file's location. Therefore, any changes to the image content cannot be done in AutoCAD, but must be made with the original file using the appropriate software. Settings and commands in AutoCAD can control the portion of the image shown and its appearance.

Images can be inserted, removed, and modified using commands found in the **Reference** toolbar, Figure 13-1. These functions are discussed in detail in this chapter.

To activate the **IMAGE** command, select **Raster Image...** in the **Insert** pull-down menu, pick the **Image** button in the **Reference** toolbar, or enter IM or IMAGE at the Command: prompt. This displays the **Image** dialog box, Figure 13-2. This dialog box lists the images attached to a drawing. From this dialog box, you can insert a new image, delete an image from the drawing, and view information about the image.

Figure 13-1.
The **Reference** toolbar contains buttons for the **Image** family of commands.

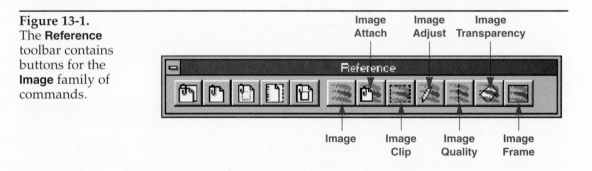

Figure 13-2.
Raster images can be inserted or deleted from the **Image** dialog box.

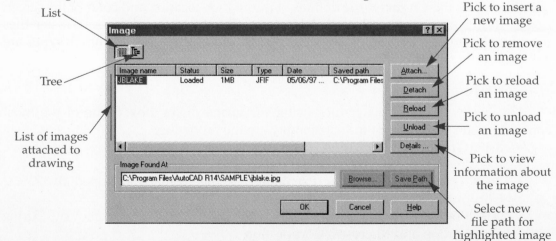

A raster image is not actually inserted into a drawing. The image details are not stored in the drawing file. Instead, the directory path to the location of the image file is added to the drawing file. Then, whenever the drawing is opened, it locates the image file and reloads it into the drawing.

The **IMAGEATTACH** command is used to attach an image file to a drawing. To access this command, pick the **Attach...** button in the **Image** dialog box, pick the **Image Attach** button in the **References** toolbar, or type IAT or IMAGEATTACH at the Command: prompt. The **Attach Image File** dialog box is displayed, Figure 13-3. Pick the **Files of type** drop-down list to display the raster file types that can be used in AutoCAD. If a folder contains a wide variety of raster files, you can quickly narrow your search by picking one file type in this list. Select the raster file name and pick **Open**. This displays the **Attach Image** dialog box, Figure 13-4.

The image name and current path are displayed here. You can preset image parameters, or choose to specify them on-screen. The **Include path** box is checked by default. When this item is checked, it ensures that the path to the image is saved with the drawing file. If this box is not checked, AutoCAD searches through the Support Files Search Path as defined in the **Files** tab of the **Preferences** dialog box.

IMAGEATTACH
IAT

Reference
toolbar

Image Attach

Figure 13-3.
Select the image file to be attached to the drawing in the **Attach Image File** dialog box. Pick the **Files of type** drop-down list to display the raster file types that can be used.

Figure 13-4.
The image name and current path are displayed in the **Attach Image** dialog box. In addition you can preset image parameters, or choose to specify them on-screen.

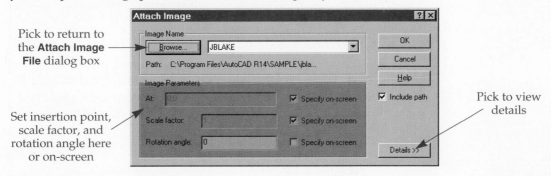

Pick to return to the **Attach Image File** dialog box

Set insertion point, scale factor, and rotation angle here or on-screen

Pick to view details

PROFESSIONAL TIP

If you are working on a project that requires the use of xrefs and attached images, it is good practice to establish a project files search path. A *project files search path* is a project name and folder in which AutoCAD can automatically search for files that are attached to a drawing. This process can be set up quickly and applied to any drawing.

1. Pick **Preferences...** in the **Tools** pull-down menu.
2. Pick the **Files** tab in the **Preferences** dialog box.
3. Pick the Project Files Search Path file cabinet icon, then pick the **Add** button. This creates a new name called Project1. See Figure A. You can retain this name or enter a new one at the keyboard. This is the name of the project, and not the location of project files. The name you enter here should also be entered at the Command: prompt using the **PROJECTNAME** system variable.
4. Next pick the **Add** button and enter the path location of your project image files. If you don't remember the exact path, pick the **Browse** button. This displays the **Browse for Folder** dialog box, from which you can select the proper folder.
5. The project name and new path name are now displayed under the Project Files Search Path file icon. See Figure B.
6. Pick **OK** to close the dialog box.

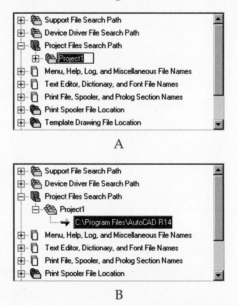

A

B

You can create as many project files search path locations as needed. When AutoCAD must find an attached image, it will search through the project paths you have indicated. You can narrow the search so that files are found quicker by using the **PROJECTNAME** system variable.

Command: **PROJECTNAME**↵
New value for PROJECTNAME, or . for none <"">:
  (Enter a project name)

The value entered for the **PROJECTNAME** variable is saved with the drawing file only. The default is a period (.) for "none."

You can view image resolution information in the **Attach Image** dialog box by picking the **Details >>** button. See Figure 13-5. The default value for all images is unit-less, unless the image contains resolution information that allows you to set the units.

The image appears as a frame attached to the crosshairs and you are prompted for an insertion point.

Insertion point ⟨0,0⟩: *(pick a point)*
Base image size: Width: 1.00, Height: *varies* ⟨Unitless⟩
Scale factor ⟨1⟩: *(pick a second point or enter a scale factor)*

When the second point is picked or a scale value is entered, the image is drawn. See Figure 13-6.

Figure 13-5.
The **Attach Image** dialog box expands to include the **Image Information** area when the **Details** button is picked.

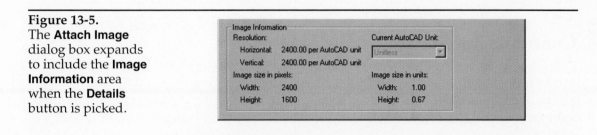

Figure 13-6.
The jblake.jpg raster image attached to an AutoCAD drawing. This image is contained in the AutoCAD R14\Sample folder.

Managing attached images

The **Image** dialog box is used to control the raster images that are inserted in the drawing. The file list box displays the image name, whether it is loaded or unloaded, the file size, type, date it was last saved, and the file path. Four options are available to help you manage the images.

- **Attach.** Enables you to search for and attach an image file.
- **Detach.** Removes or detaches the selected image file from the current drawing.
- **Reload.** Reloads the selected image file. The Status column will indicate Reload if this option is selected. If you pick **OK** and return to this dialog box later, the Status column will indicate Loaded.
- **Unload.** Unloads the selected image. The Status column will indicated Unload if this option is selected. If you pick **OK** and return to this dialog box later, the

Status column will indicate Unloaded. If an image has been unloaded, only its frame is displayed in AutoCAD. Simply select the file and pick the **Reload** button to redisplay the image. An unloaded image is still attached to the current drawing, but it is not displayed.

PROFESSIONAL TIP

It is good practice to unload attached image files if they are not needed during the current working session. Although inserted images are still attached, they are removed from the display and the drawing is regenerated faster.

Controlling image file displays

Once an image has been inserted and attached to the current drawing, its display can be adjusted to meet the needs of the project. The commands used to adjust images can be accessed from the **Reference** toolbar, or by picking the command from the **Image** submenu of the **Object** cascading menu of the **Modify** pull-down menu, Figure 13-7.

Clipping an image

The **IMAGECLIP** command enables you to select a portion of the image for display. The image can be clipped using a rectangular or polygonal clipping frame. Use the command as follows:

Command: **ICL** *or* **IMAGECLIP**↵
Select image to clip: *(pick the image frame)*
ON/OFF/Delete/⟨New boundary⟩: ↵
Polygonal/⟨Rectangular⟩: **R**↵
First point: *(pick the first corner)*
Select second corner: *(pick the second corner)*

IMAGECLIP
ICL

Modify
↳ Object
  ↳ Image Clip

Reference
toolbar

Image Clip

Figure 13-7.
Commands used to
control image files
are found in the
Image cascading
menu.

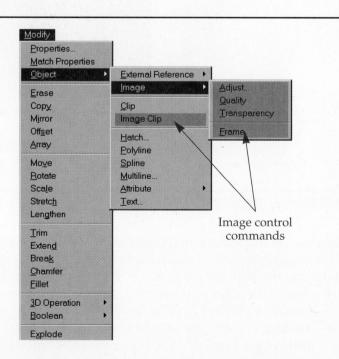

Image control
commands

AutoCAD and its Applications—Advanced

The **Polygonal** option allows you to construct a clipping frame composed of three or more points as follows:

Polygonal/⟨Rectangular⟩: **P**↵
First point: *(pick first point)*
Undo/⟨Next point⟩: *(pick second point)*
Undo/⟨Next point⟩: *(pick third point)*
Close/Undo/⟨Next point⟩: *(pick additional points as needed)*
Close/Undo/⟨Next point⟩: ↵

Figure 13-8 shows the results of using the **Rectangular** and **Polygonal** options of the **IMAGECLIP** command on the r300-20.jpg raster image. This file is included in the AutoCAD R14\Sample folder.

Three additional options of **IMAGECLIP** allow you to work with the display of the clipped image.

- **ON.** Turns the clipped image on to display the previous clipped area if it has been turned off.
- **OFF.** Turns off the clipped image to display the entire original image and frame.
- **Delete.** Deletes the clipping frame and displays the original image.

Figure 13-8.
A—A rectangular image clip. B—A polygonal image clip.

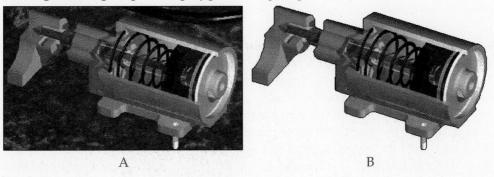

A   B

> **NOTE**
>
> You can pick an unclipped image frame to display the grips for editing. If one grip is stretched it affects the entire image by enlarging or reducing it proportionally. On the other hand, if you select a clipped image for grip editing, stretching the image frame does not change the size or shape of the image, but alters the size of the frame and retains the size of the image.

Adjusting an image

The **IMAGEADJUST** command provides controls over the brightness, contrast, and fade of the image. These adjustments are made in the **Image Adjust** dialog box, Figure 13-9. Access the dialog box by picking the **Image Adjust** button in the **Reference** toolbar, selecting **Adjust...** from the **Image** cascading menu, or typing IAD or IMAGEADJUST at the Command: prompt. Values can be entered numerically or by using the slider bars. The following settings can be adjusted:

- **Brightness.** Controls pixel whiteness and indirectly affects the contrast. Values range from 0 to 100, with 50 as the default value. Higher values increase the brightness.
- **Contrast.** Controls the contrast of the image, or how close each pixel is moved toward its primary or secondary color. Values range from 0 to 100, with 50 as the default value. Higher values increase the contrast.

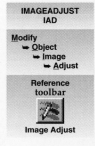

IMAGEADJUST
IAD

Modify
➥ Object
➥ Image
➥ Adjust

Reference
toolbar

Image Adjust

Figure 13-9.
Brightness, contrast, and fade values can be entered numerically or by using the slider bars in the **Image Adjust** dialog box.

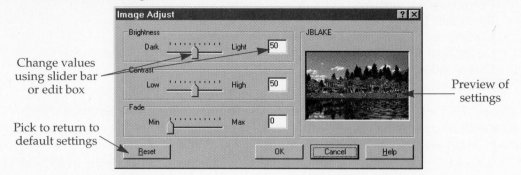

Change values
using slider bar
or edit box

Pick to return to
default settings

Preview of
settings

- **Fade.** Controls the fading of the image, or how close the image is to the background color. Values range from 0 to 100, with 0 as the default value. Higher values increase the fading.

The preview tile provides a small view of all changes to the image. Pick the **Reset** button to return all values to their defaults.

Other image controls

The **IMAGEQUALITY** command provides only two options, **High** and **Draft**. The high quality setting produces the best image display, but requires longer to generate. If you are working with several images in a drawing, it is best to set the **Draft** option. The image that is displayed is lower quality but requires less time to display.

Change the **IMAGEQUALITY** setting by picking the **Image Quality** button from the **Reference** toolbar, selecting **Quality** from the **Image** cascading menu, or typing IMAGEQUALITY at the Command: prompt.

Some raster image files have transparent background pixels. The **TRANSPARENCY** command controls the display of these pixels. If **TRANSPARENCY** is on, the drawing will show through the image background. Images are inserted with this feature turned off.

The **TRANSPARENCY** setting can be changed by picking the **Image Transparency** button from the **Reference** toolbar, selecting **Transparency** from the **Image** cascading menu, or typing TRANSPARENCY at the Command: prompt.

The **IMAGEFRAME** command controls the appearance of frames around all images in the current drawing. There are two settings: on and off. When **IMAGEFRAME** is on, a frame appears around the image.

The **IMAGEFRAME** setting can be changed by picking the **Image Frame** button from the **Reference** toolbar, selecting **Frame** from the **Image** cascading menu, or typing IMAGEFRAME at the Command: prompt.

IMAGEQUALITY

Modify
➥ Object
  ➥ Image
    ➥ Quality

Reference
toolbar

Image Quality

TRANSPARENCY

Modify
➥ Object
  ➥ Image
    ➥ Transparency

Reference
toolbar

Image Transparency

IMAGEFRAME

Modify
➥ Object
  ➥ Image
    ➥ Frame

Reference
toolbar

Image Frame

> **NOTE**
>
> Several system variables that controlled the appearance of imported raster files have been discontinued in Release 14. They are **RIASPECT**, **RIBACKG**, **RIEDGE**, **RIGAMUT**, **RIGREY**, and **RITHRESH**.

Exporting raster files

You can save or export raster files in four formats: .tga, .tif, .gif, and .bmp. The **SAVEIMG** command is used to save .tga, .tif, and .gif files. To access the command, pick **Save...** from the **Display Image...** cascading menu in the **Tools** pull-down menu or type SAVEIMG at the Command: prompt. This displays the **Save Image** dialog box. Use the dialog box to save the image. This process is discussed in detail in Chapter 14. Saving a .bmp file is discussed in the next section.

Bitmap files

A raster image is often called a bitmap. A bitmap is simply a record of colored pixels, rather than geometric objects. When you draw a line, the pixels between the endpoints of the line are filled in. However, the pixels are not associated with one another and do not form a single object. A bitmap file is often used by paint-style programs, such as Windows Paintbrush.

To create a bitmap image file, select **Export...** from the **File** menu or type EXP or EXPORT at the Command: prompt. Then, select .bmp in the **Save as type:** drop-down list of the **Export Data** dialog box, Figure 13-10A. You can also type BMPOUT at the Command: prompt to display the **Create BMP File** dialog box. In this case, the file type is automatically selected. See Figure 13-10B.

After entering a file name, you must select the objects you want in the bitmap. The image file is a rectangular area that represents the current viewing area in AutoCAD. However, only selected objects are placed in the bitmap. Unselected objects are not placed in the bitmap file.

The current screen resolution affects the appearance of the image in the bitmap. The bitmap background size is the size of the AutoCAD graphics screen when the bitmap is created, and the background color is always white.

Figure 13-10.
Use one of these dialog boxes to export a bitmap. A—The **Export Data** dialog box.
B—The **Create BMP File** dialog box.

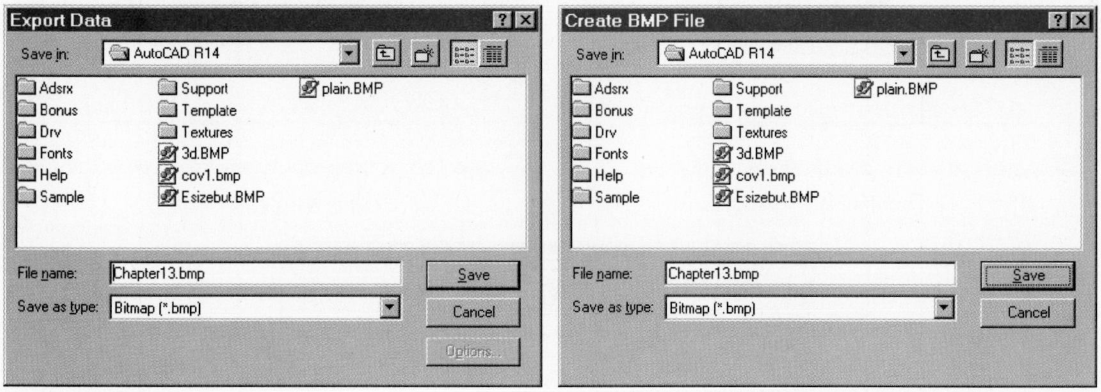 Export Data	Create BMP File
Save in: AutoCAD R14	Save in: AutoCAD R14
Adsrx Support plain.BMP	Adsrx Support plain.BMP
Bonus Template	Bonus Template
Drv Textures	Drv Textures
Fonts 3d.BMP	Fonts 3d.BMP
Help cov1.bmp	Help cov1.bmp
Sample Esizebut.BMP	Sample Esizebut.BMP
File name: Chapter13.bmp Save	File name: Chapter13.bmp Save
Save as type: Bitmap (*.bmp) Cancel	Save as type: Bitmap (*.bmp) Cancel
Options...	
A	B

NOTE

The **BMPOUT** command creates a *compressed* .bmp file by default. This type of file uses less disk space, but some applications may not be able to read this file.

Uses of raster files in AutoCAD

One use of raster images is sketching or tracing. For example, you may need a line drawing of an image that is only available as a .gif file. After importing the raster image, use the appropriate commands to sketch or trace the image. After the object is sketched, the original raster image can be deleted or frozen, leaving the tracing. You can then add other elements to the tracing to create a full drawing. See Figure 13-11.

Raster files can be combined with AutoCAD drawing and modeling features in many ways to complete or complement the design. For example, company marks or logos can be easily added to title blocks, style sheets, and company drawing standards. Drawings and designs that require designs, labels, and a variety of text fonts can be created using raster files and the wide variety of TrueType fonts available with Release 14.

You can also add features to raster files. For example, you can import a raster file, dimension or annotate it, and even add special shapes to it. Then, export it as the same type of file with a command such as **SAVEIMG**. Now you can use the revised file in the original software in which it was created. As with any creative process, let your imagination and the job requirements determine how you use this capability of AutoCAD. Refer to Chapter 14 for a discussion on the **SAVEIMG** command.

Figure 13-11.
Using a raster image as a model for a drawing. A—Import the raster image.
B—Use AutoCAD commands to trace the image. Then either delete the image or freeze its layer. C—The completed drawing.

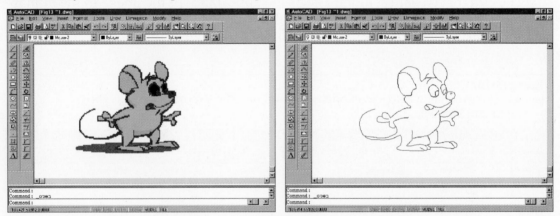

A—Raster image

B—Image tracing

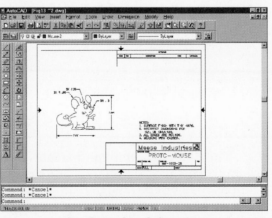

C—Completed drawing

AutoCAD and its Applications—Advanced

❏ Start a new drawing named EX13-1.
❏ Find a raster file with a .gif, .pcx, or .tif extension. It can be a sample file from other software or a file downloaded from the Internet or a computer on-line service such as CompuServe or America Online.
❏ Use the proper command to import the image into your drawing.
❏ Resize the image using grips, then clip a portion of the image using rectangular and polygon clipping frames.
❏ Adjust the brightness, contrast, and fade of the image.
❏ Make two new layers. Name one Image and the other Lines.
❏ Make the Lines layer current. Use commands such as **SKETCH**, **PLINE**, and **SPLINE** to trace a portion of the image.
❏ Make the Image layer current, freeze the Lines layer, then erase all of the entities on the Image layer.
❏ Thaw the Lines layer and save the drawing as EX13-1.

Working with Vector Files

A vector file contains objects defined by XYZ coordinates. AutoCAD allows you to work with several different vector files using the **Export Data** and **Import File** dialog boxes. The most common is the AutoCAD drawing file (.dwg). Other vector file types are .dxf, .3ds, .wmf, and .sat.

The .dxf file is an ASCII version of the drawing data. The .3ds file exports AutoCAD objects to the native format of Autodesk's 3D Studio. Both .dxf and .3ds files are discussed in Chapter 15 of *AutoCAD and its Applications—Basics, Release 14*.

The .sat file format is used with solid models and statistical analysis. Refer to Chapter 12 of this text for a discussion on .sat files.

The .wmf file format is a Windows metafile. This file format is often used to exchange data with desktop publishing programs. The next section covers using Windows metafiles with AutoCAD.

Creating vector files using AutoCAD

The Windows metafile format works best for importing files into object-based drawing programs. An object-based program creates objects such as lines, arcs, and circles in the same way as AutoCAD. This means that a line is drawn as a single object, rather than a collection of colored pixels on the screen. The .wmf file format is an object-based format.

To save a .wmf file, select **Export...** from the **File** pull-down menu or type EXP or EXPORT at the Command: prompt. This displays the **Export Data** dialog box. Select .wmf in the **Save as type:** drop-down list. You can also type WMFOUT at the Command: prompt. This displays the **Create WMF File** dialog box. In this dialog box, the .wmf file type is automatically selected.

After specifying the file name and folder location in either dialog box, you must select the objects to place in the file. Press [Enter] when all of the objects are selected and the .wmf file is saved.

Only the portions of selected objects visible on-screen are written into the file. If part of a selected object goes off the screen, only the visible part is written to the file. For example, if a selected circle is partially off the screen, it appears as an arc in the .wmf file. This is because a Windows metafile is a vector format translated from a raster image.

AutoCAD
User's
Guide | Appendix **C**

Also, the current view resolution affects the appearance of a Windows metafile. For example, when **VIEWRES** is set low, circles in your AutoCAD drawing may look like polygons. When saved to a Windows metafile, the objects are polygons rather than circles.

To import a Windows metafile, select **Windows Metafile...** from the **Insert** pull-down menu or type IMP or IMPORT at the Command: prompt. This opens the **Import File** dialog box. Select .wmf in the file type list and then select a file. You can also type WMFIN at the Command: prompt. This displays the **Import WMF** dialog box. Both of these dialog boxes have a preview window where you can see the image before you import it. See Figure 13-12.

A Windows metafile is imported as a block made up of all the objects in the file. You can explode an imported Windows metafile if you need to edit the objects within it. If an object isn't filled, it is created as a polyline when brought into AutoCAD. This includes arcs and circles. Objects composed of several closed polylines to represent fill are created from solid fill objects, as if created using the **SOLID** command with **Fill** off.

There are two settings used to control the appearance of Windows metafiles imported into AutoCAD. Type WMFOPTS at the Command: prompt. The **WMF Import Options** dialog box is displayed, Figure 13-13. The dialog box contains the following two check boxes:

- **Wire Frame (No Fills).** When checked, filled areas are imported only as outlines. Otherwise, filled areas are imported as filled objects.
- **Wide Lines.** When this option is checked, the relative line widths of lines and borders from the .wmf file are maintained. Otherwise, they are imported using a zero width.

Figure 13-12.
The **Import File** and **Import WMF** dialog boxes display the highlighted file in the preview windows.

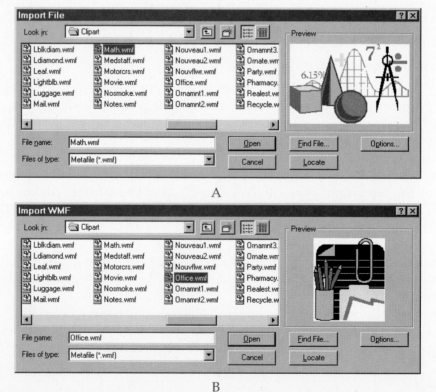

A

B

AutoCAD and its Applications—Advanced

Figure 13-13.
The **WMF Import Options** dialog box.

PostScript is a copyrighted page description language developed by Adobe Systems. PostScript files are widely used in desktop publishing. AutoCAD can import and export PostScript files. This allows you to work with raster or vector files to create presentation-quality graphics and then save the graphics in a format that most desktop publishing software can read.

Working with Postscript

The **PSIN** and **PSOUT** commands are used to import and export PostScript files. The **IMPORT** and **EXPORT** commands can also be used. The **PSDRAG** command controls the visibility of the imported image as it is being inserted. The quality, or resolution, of the displayed image is controlled with the **PSQUALITY** command. The pattern that fills the graphic is set with the **PSFILL** command.

Adding fill patterns to an object

Using the **PSFILL** command, you can add PostScript fill patterns to a closed polyline. The types of fill patterns available are shown in Figure 13-14. To access the

Figure 13-14.
The fill patterns available with the **PSFILL** command.

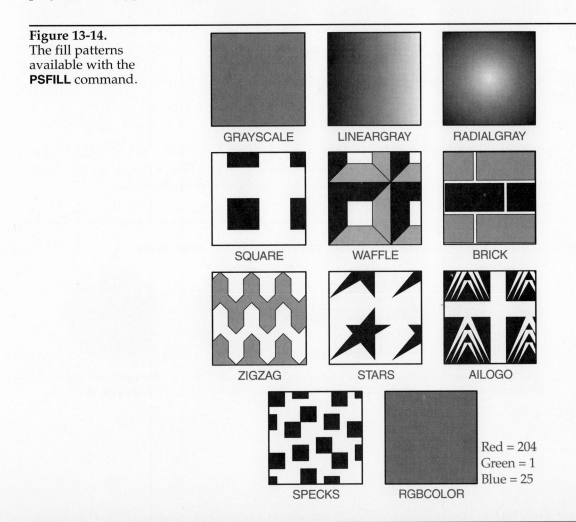

command, type PSFILL at the Command: prompt. Type the full name of the pattern you wish to use. Enter a question mark if you wish to see a list of available pattern names.

Each pattern prompts for different values. For example, you can enter a value from 0 to 100 when using the Grayscale pattern. In this case, the value is a percentage of black. To fill an area with a grayscale value of 15 (15% black), enter the following:

Command: **PSFILL**↵
Select polyline: *(pick the polyline to be filled)*
PostScript fill pattern (. = none) ⟨.⟩/?: **GRAYSCALE**↵ *(type ? to see the available fill patterns)*
Grayscale ⟨50⟩: **15**↵

Notice that no change appears on the screen. However, the pattern is included in the file when you use the **PSOUT** command.

The Radialgray fill pattern displays a highlight in the center of the selected polyline, and darkens toward the outer edges. You can control the brightness of the highlight (ForegroundGray), and the darkness of the edges (BackgroundGray).

Command: **PSFILL**↵
Select polyline: *(pick the polyline to be filled)*
PostScript fill pattern (. = none) ⟨.⟩/?: **RADIALGRAY**↵
Levels ⟨256⟩: ↵
ForegroundGray ⟨0⟩: ↵
BackgroundGray ⟨100⟩: ↵

The appearance of several Radialgray settings are shown in Figure 13-15.

When the **PSOUT** command is used, all **PSFILL** patterns are automatically surrounded by a polyline. This polyline shows on the final print. If you do not want a polyline to surround the fill, place an asterisk (*) in front of the pattern name like this:

PostScript fill pattern (. = none) ⟨.⟩/?: ***GRAYSCALE**↵

You can remove a fill pattern from a polyline by entering a period at the PostScript fill pattern: prompt.

PostScript fill pattern (. = none) ⟨.⟩/?: **.**↵

Custom fill patterns can be added to the acad.psf file. This is an ASCII text file and can be edited with any text editor. However, the proper PostScript language must be used. See the *AutoCAD Customization Guide* for the correct procedures.

Figure 13-15.
Changing the value of the Radialgray **PSFILL** pattern creates different effects.

| **Foreground** = 0 | **Foreground** = 10 | **Foreground** = 30 | **Foreground** = 100 |
| **Background** = 100 | **Background** = 90 | **Background** = 70 | **Background** = 0 |

❏ Begin a new drawing named EX13-2.
❏ Draw four rectangles, each measuring 1 × 2 units.
❏ Use the following **PSFILL** patterns to fill the rectangles.
   ❏ Lineargray (2 cycles)
   ❏ Radialgray
   ❏ Waffle
   ❏ Stars (BackgroundGray = 20, ForegroundGray = 85)
❏ Save the drawing as EX13-2.

Exporting a PostScript image

Any drawing created in AutoCAD can be converted to a PostScript file using the **EXPORT** or **PSOUT** commands. A PostScript file is usually created if PostScript fonts or images are added to the drawing, or if the **PSFILL** command is used to add patterns. Remember, an .eps file can only be printed by a PostScript printer.

If you use the **PSOUT** command, the **Create PostScript File** dialog box is displayed. Enter a name and pick the **OK** button. If you entered EXPORT, the **Export Data** dialog box appears. Pick .eps in the file type list, enter a name, and pick **OK**.

NOTE
If you use the **EXPORT** command to export a PostScript file, all prompts are automatically answered with the defaults. You are not given the opportunity to change any of the settings.

A screen preview image can be included with the file. A preview is used by many desktop publishing programs. It allows an artist to see the image. To specify a preview image, select the **Options** button from the export dialog box. The **Export Options** dialog box appears with the **PostScript Out** tab. See Figure 13-16.

To create a preview image, select the **EPSI** or **TIFF** radio button in the **Preview** area and then select an image size from the **Pixels** area. The default size of 128 × 128 pixels is small, so it does not slow down the software when the image is imported. Enter appropriate values in the **What to plot**, **Size Units**, **Scale**, and **Paper Size** areas. Pick the **OK** button and the PostScript file is created.

Figure 13-16.
The **Export Options** dialog box is used to select settings when creating a PostScript file.

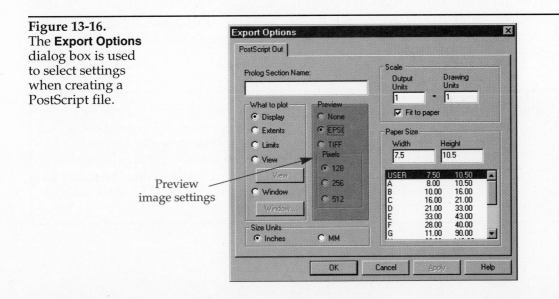

Preview image settings

Printing PostScript files

After the file has been created, it can be printed by a PostScript printer at the DOS prompt. The DOS prompt can be accessed by selecting Programs from the Windows Start menu and then picking MS-DOS Command Prompt. Then, type the following:

C:*path to file* ⟩ **PRINT** *filename*.**EPS**↵

NOTE

You cannot use the Windows "drag and drop" capability to print PostScript files. If you try to drag and drop a file to the printer icon, you are prompted that there is no association with this file. If you pick <u>V</u>iew then <u>O</u>ptions... in My Computer, your .eps file must be associated with AutoCAD. Then, when you drag and drop the .eps file to the printer icon, the drawing file that you select is printed, not your .eps file.

Importing a PostScript image

You can use the **IMPORT** or **PSIN** commands to import a PostScript file into AutoCAD. If you use the **IMPORT** command, you must specify .eps in the file type list of the **Import File** dialog box. If you use the **PSIN** command, .eps is automatically selected in the **Select PostScript File** dialog box. Select the file and pick the **OK** button. It may take a few moments to load the file, depending on its size. Then, the following prompts appear:

Insertion point⟨0,0,0⟩: ↵
Scale factor: (*drag the image to fit and pick*)

If **PSDRAG** is set to 0, only the outline of the box that represents the image is displayed until you set the scale factor. If you wish to see the image as you drag it, set **PSDRAG** to 1.

Now you can place additional entities or text on the drawing. You can then save it again as a PostScript file with the **PSOUT** command or save it as a .dwg drawing file.

PostScript file quality

The **PSIN** command renders an image according to the value of the **PSQUALITY** system variable. If **PSQUALITY** is set to 0, only a box representing the image is displayed with the file name inside. The default value is 75. This displays the image with 75 pixels per AutoCAD drawing unit. Higher quality values mean longer rendering time. A negative value, such as –75, renders at the same resolution but does not fill PostScript outlines.

PROFESSIONAL TIP

When you use **PSIN** to import an image into AutoCAD, a file named acadps.arx is used to interpret the PostScript file into a *Ghostscript* format so the entities are compatible with AutoCAD. You can then save the drawing, edit it later, or give the drawing to someone else to work with. The acadps.arx file is no longer needed.

Chapter Test

Write your answers in the spaces provided.

1. Name four common formats of raster images that can be imported into AutoCAD. _____

   _____

   _____

2. Name the raster file that is the CompuServe image format. _____

   _____

3. What command allows you to attach a raster file to the current AutoCAD drawing? _____

4. What is the display status of an inserted image that has been unloaded? _____

   _____

5. What two shapes can be used to clip a raster image? _____

   _____

6. What is the function of the **IMAGEADJUST** command? _____

   _____

   _____

7. Name two commands that allow you to export bitmap files. _____

   _____

8. Give the name and file type of the vector file that can be exchanged between object-based programs. _____

   _____

9. Name the two commands that allow you to import and export the file type in Question 7. _____

   _____

10. Name the two commands that enable you to import and export PostScript files in AutoCAD. _____

    _____

11. When using the **PSFILL** command, what is the numerical value range of grays that are available? _____

12. What is the three-letter extension given to PostScript files when they are exported? _____

Drawing Problems

1. Locate some sample raster files with the .gif, .pcx, or .tif file extensions. These files are often included as samples with software. They can also be downloaded from the Internet, or from computer on-line services such as CompuServe and America Online. With the permission of your instructor or supervisor, create a subfolder on your hard disk drive and copy the raster files there.

2. Choose one of your smaller raster files and import it into AutoCAD.

   A. Insert the image so that it fills the entire screen.

   B. Undo and insert the image again using a scale factor that fills half the screen with the image.

   C. Stretch the original object using grips, then experiment with different clipping boundaries. Stretch the image after it has been clipped and observe the result.

   D. Create a layer named Raster. Create a second layer named Object. Give each layer the color of your choice. Set the current layer to Raster.

   E. Import the same image next to the previous one at the same scale factor.

   F. Set the current layer to Object and use any AutoCAD drawing commands to trace the outline of the second raster image.

   G. Turn off the Object layer and erase the raster image. Turn the Object layer on.

   H. Save the drawing as P13-2.

3. For this problem, you will import several raster files into AutoCAD. Then, you will trace the object in each file and save it as a block or wblock to be used on other drawings.

   A. Find as many raster files as you can that contain simple objects, shapes, or figures that you might use in other drawings. Save these to diskettes or a hard drive directory.

   B. Create a template drawing containing Object and Raster layers.

   C. Import each raster file into AutoCAD using the appropriate command. Set the Object layer and trace the shape or objects using AutoCAD drawing commands.

   D. Delete the raster information, keeping only the traced lines of the object.

   E. Save the object as a block or wblock using an appropriate file-naming system.

   F. After all blocks have been created, insert each one into a single drawing and label each with its name. Include a path if necessary.

   G. Save the drawing as P13-3.

   H. Print or plot the final drawing.

4. In this problem, you will create either a style sheet to be used for drawing standards or a presentation sheet for a detail, assembly, or pictorial drawing.

   A. Begin a new drawing and name it P13-4. The drawing should be set up to A-size dimensions and the orientation should be portrait. (A portrait orientation has the long side orientated vertically.)

   B. Create at least two new text styles using TrueType fonts.

   C. Draw one or more closed shapes, such as rectangles. Use the **PSFILL** command to place a pattern of your choice inside the shapes.

   D. Use the various text styles to place title and related text on your drawing. See the example below. Add other graphics or text as desired.

   E. Save the drawing as P13-4. Then, use the **PSOUT** command to save the file as P13-4.EPS.

   F. Plot the drawing on a plotter or laser printer. If you have a PostScript printer, generate a printed copy of the .eps file.

5. Begin a new drawing named P13-5 using P13-4 as the prototype.

   A. Insert the blocks you created in Problem 3 into your style sheet. Arrange them in any order you wish.

   B. Add any notes you need to identify this drawing as a sheet of library shapes. Be sure each shape is identified with its file name and location (path).

   C. Save the drawing with the current name (P13-5). Then, use the **PSOUT** command to create an .eps file using the same name.

   D. Print or plot the drawing.

   E. If you have a PostScript printer, create a PostScript print of the file.

6. Add a raster image to one of your title block template drawings as a design element or a company logo. Import an existing raster image or create your own using a program such as Windows Paint.

Rendering with AutoCAD

Learning Objectives

After completing this chapter, you will be able to:
- ○ Create shaded and rendered drawings.
- ○ Place light sources.
- ○ Apply surface textures and materials to models.
- ○ Map materials onto AutoCAD objects.
- ○ Create a background for a model.
- ○ Use fog to create the appearance of depth and distance.
- ○ Locate and manipulate landscaping objects.
- ○ Save views, scenes, and image files.
- ○ Render and save bitmaps using Windows Clipboard.

Three-dimensional computer models can provide more information than a set of two-dimensional blueprints. The computer allows you to visualize the model from all sides, including the inside. Surface textures can be added to the model. Rendering "colors" the model with the assigned surface. The model can also be placed in a scene with lights, shading, textured materials, background, and landscaping objects. Views and scenes can then be saved, rendered, and placed in documents.

You can render a model with either the **SHADE** command or the **RENDER** command. The **SHADE** command, which is covered in Chapter 9, provides limited control over the type of display and lighting. The **RENDER** command gives you complete control over the lighting and surfaces of your model.

> **NOTE** You have almost unlimited options and variations when rendering 3D models. Components such as color, light, shadow, sunshine, time of year, location on earth, material, texture, reflections, roughness, viewpoint, and scene (and combinations of all of these) lead to a wide variety of renderings. The purpose of this chapter is to introduce you to the features found in AutoCAD's renderer. This chapter does not cover all the possibilities and details surrounding use of the renderer. Use the online help files in AutoCAD for additional information. If you want additional instruction in rendering and animation, sign up for a course at an Autodesk Training Center in your area.

Lighting

AutoCAD uses four types of lighting: ambient, distant, point, and spot. See Figure 14-1. It is important to understand how each type applies light to a model.

Ambient light is like natural light. It is the same intensity everywhere. All faces of the object receive the same amount of light. Ambient light cannot create highlights. You can change the intensity of ambient light or turn it off, but ambient light cannot be concentrated in one area.

A *distant light* is a directed light source with parallel light rays. This acts much like the sun, striking all objects in your model on the same side and with the same intensity. The direction and intensity of a distant light can be changed.

A *point light* is like a lightbulb, shining out in all directions. A point light can create highlights. The intensity of a point light "falls off," or weakens, over distance. Other programs, such as 3D Studio, call these lights *omni lights*.

A *spotlight* is like a distant light, but it projects in a cone shape. A spotlight is placed closer than a distant light to the object.

Figure 14-1.
AutoCAD uses ambient, spot, point, and distant light. Ambient light is an overall light and does not have an icon representation. You can see here how the other three lights strike objects.

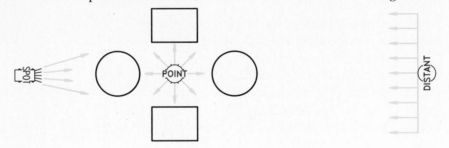

Properties of lights

There are several properties that affect how a light illuminates an object. These include the angle of incidence, reflectivity of the object's surface, and the distance that the light is from the object.

Angle of incidence

AutoCAD renders the faces of a model based on the angle that light rays strike the faces. This angle is called the *angle of incidence*. See Figure 14-2. A face that is perpendicular to light rays receives the most light. As the angle of incidence decreases, the amount of light striking the face decreases.

Reflectivity

The angle at which light rays are reflected off a surface is called the *angle of reflection*. The angle of reflection is always equal to the angle of incidence.

The "brightness" of light reflected from an object is actually the number of light rays that reach your eyes. A surface that reflects a bright light, such as a mirror, is reflecting most of the light rays that strike it.

The amount of reflection you see is called the *highlight*. The highlight is determined by the angle of the viewpoint relative to the angle of incidence. Refer to Figure 14-2.

The surface of the object affects how light is reflected. A smooth surface has a high *specular factor*. The specular factor indicates the number of light rays that have the same angle of reflection. Surfaces that are not smooth have a low specular factor. These surfaces are called *matte*. Matte surfaces *diffuse*, or "spread out," the light as it strikes the surface. This means that few of the light rays have the same angle of reflection. Figure 14-3 illustrates the difference between matte and high specular finishes.

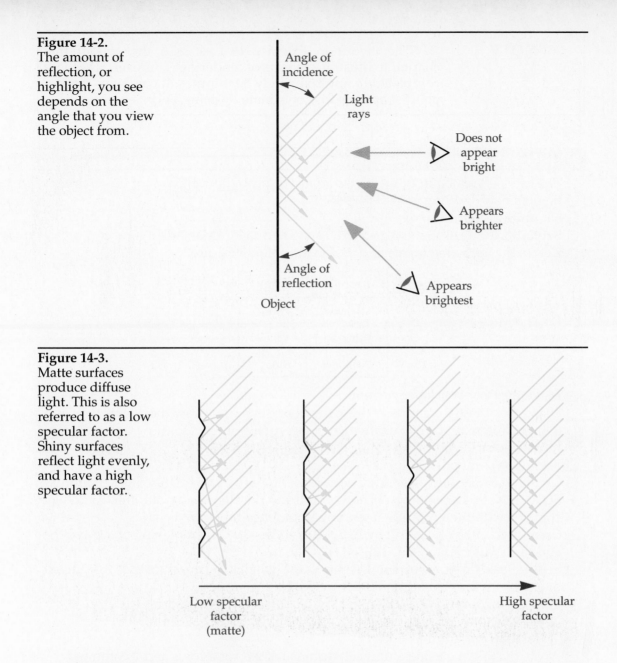

Figure 14-2.
The amount of reflection, or highlight, you see depends on the angle that you view the object from.

Angle of incidence

Light rays

Does not appear bright

Appears brighter

Angle of reflection

Object

Appears brightest

Figure 14-3.
Matte surfaces produce diffuse light. This is also referred to as a low specular factor. Shiny surfaces reflect light evenly, and have a high specular factor.

Low specular factor (matte)

High specular factor

Surfaces can also vary in *roughness*. Roughness is a measure of the polish on a surface. This also affects how diffused the reflected light is.

Distance

The farther an object is from a point light or spotlight, the less light that reaches it. The intensity of light decreases over distance. This decrease is called *falloff* or *attenuation*. Attenuation only applies to point lights and spotlights. The following attenuation settings are available:

- **None.** Applies the same light intensity regardless of distance. In other words, no falloff is calculated.
- **Inverse Linear.** The illumination of an object decreases in inverse proportion to the distance. For example, if an object is 2 units from the light, it receives 1/2 of the full light. If the object is 4 units away, it receives 1/4 of the full light.
- **Inverse Square.** The illumination of an object decreases in inverse proportion to the square of the distance. For example, if an object is 2 units from the light, it receives $(1/2)^2$, or 1/4, of the full light. If the object is 4 units away, it receives $(1/4)^2$, or 1/16, of the full light. As you can see, falloff is greater with the **Inverse Square** option than with the **Inverse Linear** option.

NOTE	The layout in Exercise 14-1 is used throughout this chapter to illustrate aspects of rendering. This exercise can be completed in approximately 30 minutes. It combines the use of 3D shapes, User Coordinate Systems, and viewports.

EXERCISE 14-1

❏ The models created in this exercise are used throughout the rest of this chapter.
❏ Begin a new drawing named 3DSHAPES.
❏ Set units to architectural.
❏ Set limits to 24′,18′. Set the grid to 6″ and snap to 2″. Zoom all.
❏ Create the following layers and assign the colors indicated:

Layer	Color
Floor-wall	Cyan
Table	Red
Pyramid	Yellow
Cone	Green
Torus	Blue

❏ Make the Floor-Wall layer current.
❏ Using the **3DFACE** command, draw the floor 8′ square. Draw the wall 8′ long and 6′ high. You may have to change your viewpoint or UCS to draw the wall. This forms the background.
❏ Set a viewpoint of –2.5,–3,1.5.
❏ Create a UCS at the lower-front corner of the floor. Save this UCS orientation as FLOOR. Note: Depending on how you drew the floor and wall, this UCS may coincide with the WCS. If it does, you do not need to save the UCS.
❏ Create a 1″ cube on layer 0 by using **Box** in the **3D Objects** dialog box. Save the cube as a wblock named CUBE.
❏ Set the Table layer as current. Use the CUBE wblock to construct the table. Insert one cube for the first leg and enter the following values:
  ❏ Insertion point: X = 2′10″, Y = 2′
  ❏ Scale factors: X = 4, Y = 4, Z = 16
  ❏ Rotation angle = 0°
❏ Array the first leg using a unit cell distance of 24″ for 2 rows and 2 columns.
❏ Use the CUBE wblock again for the tabletop as follows:
  ❏ Insertion point: X = 2′10″, Y = 2′, Z = 16″
  ❏ Scale factors: X = 28, Y = 28, Z = 2
  ❏ Rotation angle = 0°
❏ Establish a new UCS at the top-front of the tabletop.
❏ Change the current layer to Pyramid. Select **Pyramid** from the **3D Objects** dialog box. Locate the first base point of the pyramid at X = 12, Y = 10. Locate the second base point as @0,–8. Locate the third point as @8,0. Locate the fourth point as @0,8. Locate the apex point at 16,6,12. Use the **ROTATE** command or grips to rotate the pyramid 45°. Use the second point of the pyramid (closest to the UCS origin) as the rotation base point.
❏ Set the Cone layer as current and draw a cone at X = 8, Y = 20 with an 8″ diameter base, 0″ diameter top, and a 12″ height. Leave the number of segments at 16.
❏ Set the current layer to Torus. Set **ISOLINES** = 12. Draw a solid torus located at X = 14, Y = 14, Z = 22. The torus diameter is 18″ and the tube diameter is 5″.
❏ The drawing should look like the one shown on the following page.
❏ Restore the UCS orientation named FLOOR.

❏ Save the drawing as 3DSHAPES and remain in the drawing editor. These objects are used throughout this chapter.

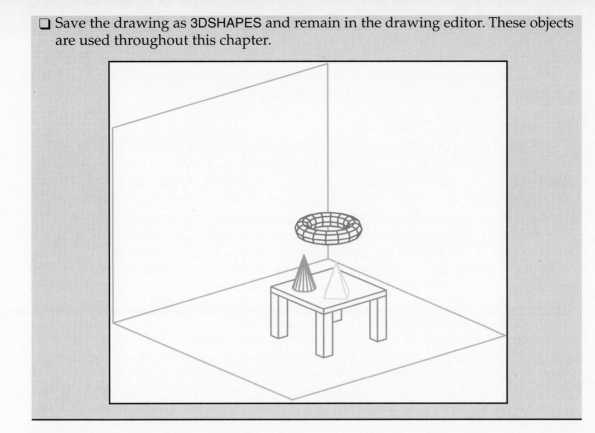

Preparing for rendering

If you are creating a drawing or model that will be rendered, you must plan to provide enough space around the model to place lights. Creating three viewports using the **VPORTS** command can help. The large view can be used to see a 3D view of the model. The two small viewports can be used for a plan view and a different 3D view. The lights can be placed in the plan view.

An example of this type of layout is shown in Figure 14-4. To create this layout, first use the default settings of the **VPORTS** command to create three viewports. Then, divide each of the two left viewports using the **2** option of the **VPORTS** command. This

Figure 14-4.
The final arrangement of viewports for the tutorial in the text.

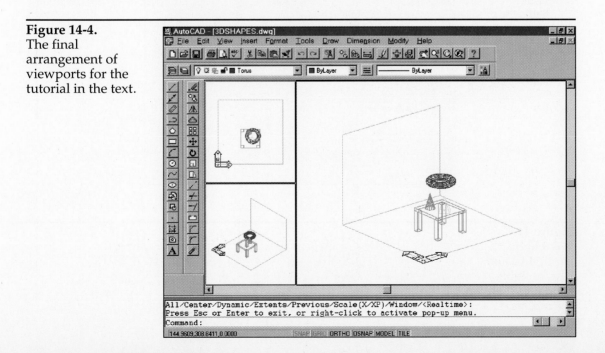

creates four small viewports on the left side. Now, use the **Join** option of **VPORTS** to join the two small viewports oriented vertically in the middle of the screen. Next, join the large viewport with the tall thin one in the middle. The final step is to display a plan view in the upper-left viewport and a Southeast isometric view in the lower-left viewport. This gives you the arrangement shown in Figure 14-4.

Using the Lights dialog box

After the objects in your model are constructed, placing lights is the first step in creating a scene for rendering. Consider the properties for each type of light when choosing the lights for the model. Place as many lights as you want. When you create a scene, pick only the lights needed for that scene. You can select a different combination of lights for each scene. A *scene* is like a photograph of your model.

Lights are placed using the **LIGHT** command. Access this command by picking the **Lights** button in the **Render** toolbar, selecting **Lights...** from the **Render...** cascading menu in the **View** pull-down menu, or typing LIGHT at the Command: prompt. The **Lights** dialog box is then displayed, Figure 14-5. Each light (other than ambient) must be named. The name can be up to eight characters long. Uppercase and lowercase letters can be used, and all light names must be different.

When placing lights in a drawing, use XYZ coordinates or filters to specify a 3D location. Once a light is placed, an icon representing the light appears in the drawing editor. The icons representing point, distant, and spotlights are shown in Figure 14-6.

Ambient light is also set in the **Lights** dialog box. Use the slider bar or type a value in the text box in the **Ambient Light** area to adjust the intensity. You can also change the ambient light color by adjusting the appropriate slider bars. Adjusting light color is discussed later in the chapter.

After lights are created, you can fine-tune them by changing their intensity, location, and color. Lights can also be turned off or deleted if needed. Once a light is selected from the list in the **Lights** dialog box, pick the **Modify...** button to adjust intensity, position, color, and falloff.

LIGHT

View
➡ Render
➡ Lights...

Render
toolbar

Lights

Figure 14-5.
The **Lights** dialog box.

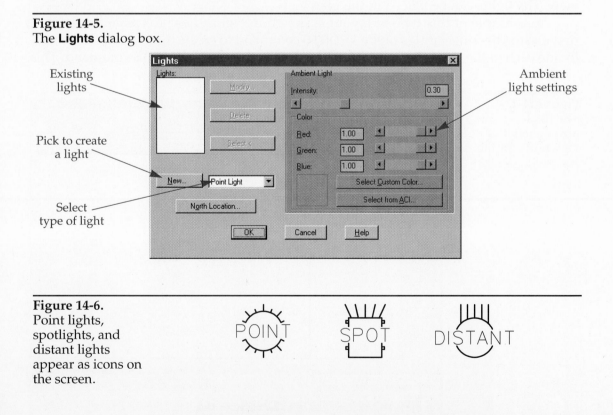

Figure 14-6.
Point lights, spotlights, and distant lights appear as icons on the screen.

AutoCAD and its Applications—Advanced

Placing point lights in the model

A point light radiates light rays outward from a central point, much like a light-bulb. Other programs, such as 3D Studio, call point lights *omni lights*. A point light requires a location and a name. Remember, a name can have up to eight characters.

To place a point light in the 3DSHAPES drawing created in Exercise 14-1, first select **Point Light** in the drop-down list at the left of the **Lights** dialog box. Then, pick the **New...** button. This displays the **New Point Light** dialog box shown in Figure 14-7A. Enter the name, such as P-1, in the **Light Name:** text box and pick **OK**. The **Lights** dialog box returns and P-1 is displayed and highlighted in the **Lights:** list box.

Now, pick **Modify...** and the **Modify Point Light** dialog box shown in Figure 14-7B is displayed. Pick the **Modify** button in the **Position** area and you are returned to the graphics window. The prompt on the command line requests a light location. You can pick the location, use filters, or enter coordinates at the keyboard as follows:

> Enter light location ⟨*current*⟩: **4',3'2",8'**↵

The dialog box then reappears. Pick **OK** in the **Modify Point Light** and **Lights** dialog boxes to complete the command and return to the graphics window. Now, zoom all in the right viewport.

Figure 14-7.
Specifying a point light. These two dialog boxes are identical except for the title bar. A—The **New Point Light** dialog box. B—The **Modify Point Light** dialog box.

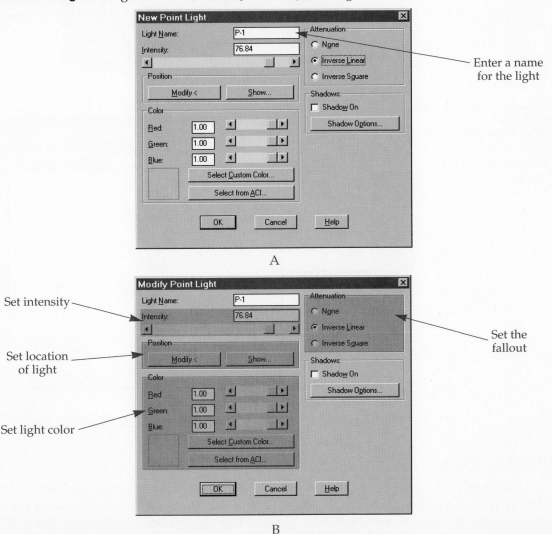

A

B

Setting the icon scale

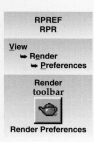

RPREF
RPR

View
➥ Render
➥ Preferences

Render
toolbar

Render Preferences

After you place the point light, you should see the light icon directly above the torus. However, it is too small to be seen clearly. You can change the scale of icons in the **Rendering Preferences** dialog box, Figure 14-8. To access this dialog box, pick the **Preferences** button in the **Render** toolbar, select **Preferences...** from the **Render** cascading menu in the **View** pull-down menu, or type RPR or RPREF at the Command: prompt. Pick the **Light Icon Scale:** text box and enter 24. Pick **OK** to return to your model, Figure 14-9. The icon is now large enough to be seen clearly. The light name P-1 appears in the icon.

Figure 14-8.
The icon scale is set in the **Rendering Preferences** dialog box.

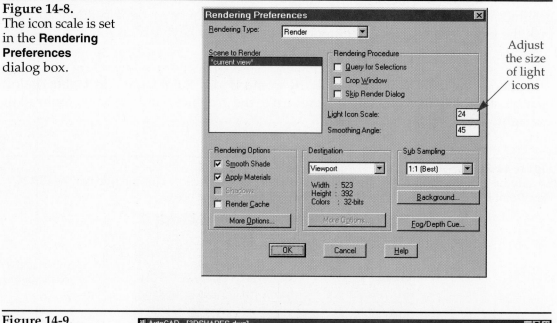

Figure 14-9.
After increasing the icon scale, the light icons are larger and can be clearly seen on the screen.

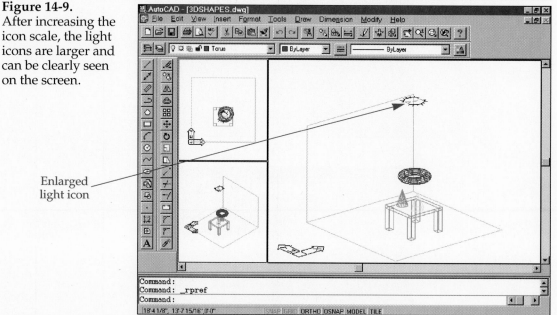

Placing distant lights in the model

The sun's rays are approximately parallel when they reach earth, and strike all objects with the same intensity. The distant light functions as the sun's rays in your models. An accurate representation of the sun's angle can be achieved by using the sun angle calculator.

Distant lights are placed in the same way as point lights. However, a target location is needed as well as a light location. To place a distant light, first open the **Lights** dialog box. Then, pick **Distant Light** from the lights drop-down list. Pick the **New...** button to display the **New Distant Light** dialog box, Figure 14-10. Notice that this dialog box is different than the **New Point Light** dialog.

Enter a name, such as D-1, in the **Light Name:** text box. The location of the distant light can be entered as XYZ values in the **Light Source Vector** text boxes. Remember, these coordinates are relative to the origin of the current UCS. In addition, you can graphically select the location of the light using the **Azimuth:** and **Altitude:** image tiles. The *azimuth* is the angle *in* the XY plane. This can also be equated with the angular direction of the sun from the North Pole. The *altitude* is the angle *from* the XY plane. This measurement represents the angle of the sun above the horizon. The location can also be set by picking the **Modify** button and entering coordinates at the Command: prompt as follows:

```
Enter light direction TO ⟨current⟩: (pick P1 in Figure 14-11)
Enter light direction FROM ⟨current⟩: 6',-4',30↵
```

Figure 14-10.
The **New Distant Light** dialog box.

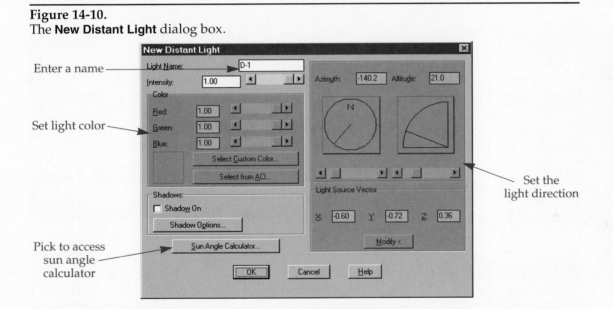

Figure 14-11.
The pick points for setting a distant light in the tutorial.

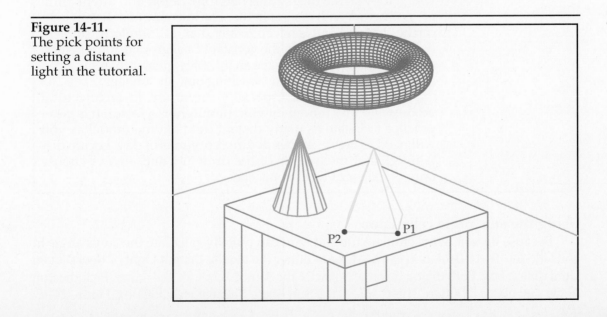

Pick **OK** to return to the **Lights** dialog box. Pick **OK** in that dialog box to return to the graphics window. The distant light is placed in the drawing.

You may not see the light in the 3D view. However, it will show in the plan view and possibly in your other view. Place one more distant light in your model using the following information:

Name	Light direction to	Light direction from
D-2	Point P2 in Figure 14-11	–2′,0,30

Your model should look like Figure 14-12 after you place the second distant light.

Figure 14-12.
The tutorial model with distant lights placed.

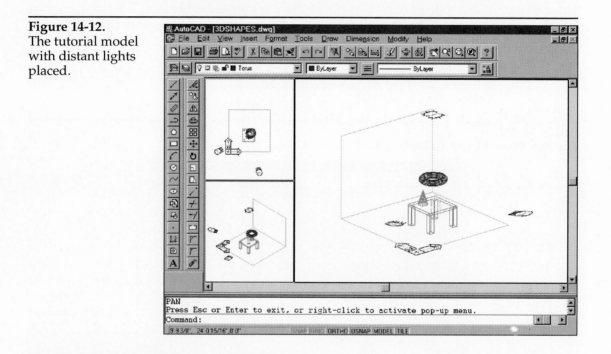

PROFESSIONAL TIP
The intensity of the sun's rays do not diminish from one point on earth to another. They are weakened by the angle at which they strike the earth. Therefore, falloff and attenuation are not factors with distant lights. The intensity of a distant light can be changed, but is never greater than 1.0. Similarly, ambient light—which represents the constant background illumination of all objects—can never have an intensity greater than 1.0. Keep ambient light low to avoid "washing out" the image.

Distant lights are especially important in architectural models and any model in which sunlight is a factor. It is good practice to locate as many distant lights in the model as you will need to create scenes at different times of day. Locate distant lights at the extents of the drawing, and always choose only one distant light per scene.

Using the sun angle calculator

Because distant lights emulate the sun, you can quickly calculate the sun's angle in your model. This calculation can be done in either the **Modify Distant Light** or **New Distant Light** dialog box. Both dialog boxes are exactly the same except for the name. Pick the **Sun Angle Calculator...** button. This displays the **Sun Angle Calculator** dialog box, Figure 14-13.

AutoCAD and its Applications—Advanced

Figure 14-13.
Distant lights can be placed using the sun angle calculator.

Set date and time

Set time zone

Hemispheres

Graphic representation of settings

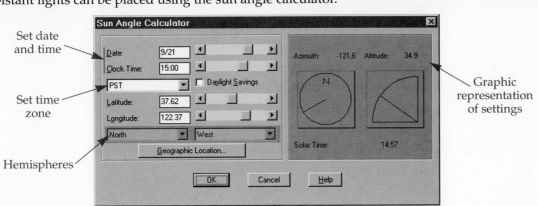

The left side of the dialog box contains all the values that adjust the sun's angle. The image tiles on the right side graphically reflect all of the values on the left as they are changed.

- **Date.** Enter the day of year in the text box, or move the slider bar to set the date. One pick on the slider bar arrow changes the date by one day, and one pick in the space to the left or right of the slider bar changes the date by one month. Pick and hold the slider bar and move it left and right. As you do, watch the azimuth and altitude image tiles automatically adjust.

- **Clock Time.** This is a 24-hour clock. One pick on the slider bar arrow changes the time by ten minutes, and one pick in the space to the left or right of the slider bar changes the time by one hour. As you move the slider bar, the azimuth and altitude image tiles automatically adjust. Do not forget to select your time zone from the drop-down list, and pick the **Daylight Savings** check box if it applies.

- **Latitude.** This is the angular location of the sun from the equator to the north or south. This is an angular measurement from the center of the earth, with the equator being 0° and the north and south poles 90°. This measurement represents the seasonal and daily movements of the sun, and most directly affects the altitude.

- **Longitude.** This represents the east/west location of the sun as the earth rotates. It most directly affects the angle of the sun above the horizon (altitude). This angle determines shadow length.

- **Hemispheres.** Below the **Longitude** text box are two drop-down lists that enable you to select either the north or south hemisphere, and either the east or west hemisphere. North America is located in the northern and western hemispheres.

If you are unsure of the exact latitude and longitude location of your model, you can select your location by picking the **Geographic Location...** button. This displays the **Geographic Location** dialog box, Figure 14-14. Use the following steps to select your location:

1. Pick the continent in the drop-down list above the map.
2. Pick the city in the **City:** list on the left of the dialog box. The location and its latitude and longitude are displayed in the lower left of the dialog box.

   If you do not know the nearest city to your location, do the following:

1. Complete step 1 above.
2. Be sure a check mark appears in the **Nearest Big City** check box.
3. Pick your location on the map. The nearest big city is located by the blue crosshairs, and its name is highlighted in the **City:** list.

Figure 14-14.
Selecting the geographic location of your model automatically sets the latitude and longitude.

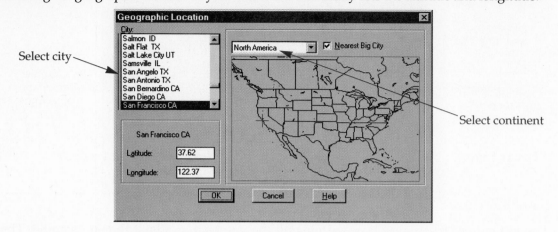

Select city →

Select continent

The lower-left area of this dialog box displays the latitude and longitude of your selected city. You can change the latitude and longitude values, but the changes are not graphically updated on the map. If you pick the **OK** button, your changes are displayed in the **Sun Angle Calculator** dialog box.

In order for shadows to be displayed accurately in the model, the north direction must be set properly. By default, AutoCAD locates north in the positive Y direction of the World Coordinate System. To change the north direction in your model, pick the **North Location...** button in the **Lights** dialog box. This displays the **North Location** dialog box shown in Figure 14-15.

A new north direction can be assigned by entering an angle in the **Angle:** text box or moving the slider bar. The north line changes in the image tile as the slider bar moves. If you want north to be the X direction in the WCS, enter 90 in the **Angle:** text box. You can also orient north along the Y axis of any named UCS. Just pick the UCS name from the **Use UCS:** list. Before selecting a UCS, be sure that the **X/Y Plane** angle is 0.

Figure 14-15.
The **North Location** dialog box.

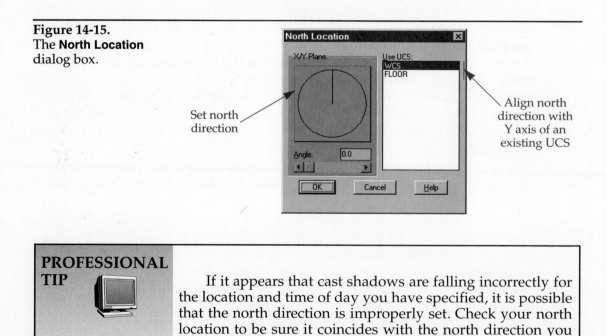

Set north direction

Align north direction with Y axis of an existing UCS

PROFESSIONAL TIP   If it appears that cast shadows are falling incorrectly for the location and time of day you have specified, it is possible that the north direction is improperly set. Check your north location to be sure it coincides with the north direction you have established for your model.

Placing spotlights in the model

A spotlight produces a cone of light. The *hotspot* is the central portion of the cone, where the light is brightest. The *falloff* is the outer portion of the cone, where the light begins to blend to shadow.

Spotlights are located in the same way as distant lights. First, pick **Spotlight** in the **Lights** drop-down list of the **Lights** dialog box, then pick the **New...** button. This displays the **New Spotlight** dialog box, Figure 14-16. Name the spotlight S-1.

The angle of the hotspot and the angle of the fallout can be set in the **Hotspot** and **Fallout** edit boxes. If you want the hotspot to illuminate a cone of 30° and the falloff angle to be 45°, enter 30 and 45 in the appropriate text boxes. Figure 14-17 illustrates the two cones of light and the values entered in the **New Spotlight** dialog box.

Figure 14-16.
The **New Spotlight** dialog box.

Figure 14-17.
The hotspot of a spotlight is the area that receives the most light. The falloff receives light, but less than the hotspot.

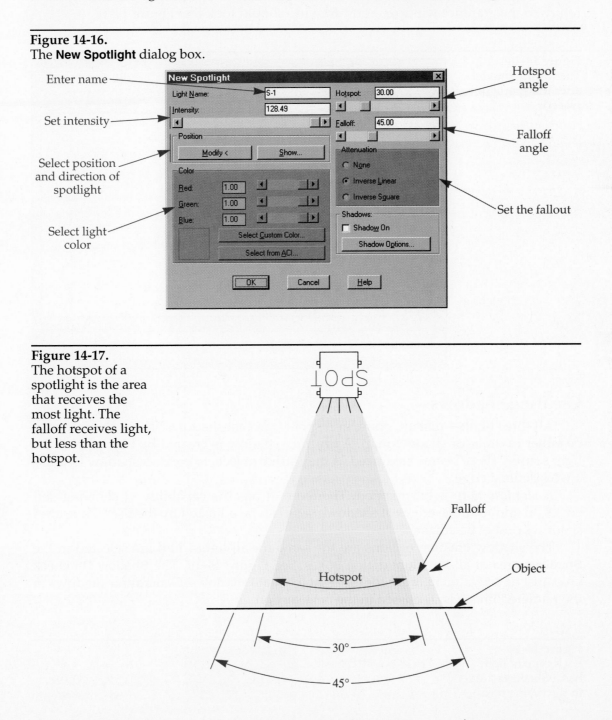

NOTE
The hotspot value must be less than or equal to the falloff value.

Pick the **Modify** button to locate the light on the graphics screen. Enter the location at the Command: prompt as follows:

Enter light target ⟨*current*⟩: *(pick the apex of the pyramid)*
Enter light location ⟨*current*⟩: **@24,-36,48**↵

The dialog box returns. Pick **OK** in both dialog boxes to complete the command and return to the graphics window. Your drawing should look like Figure 14-18.

Figure 14-18.
The tutorial model after the spotlight is placed.

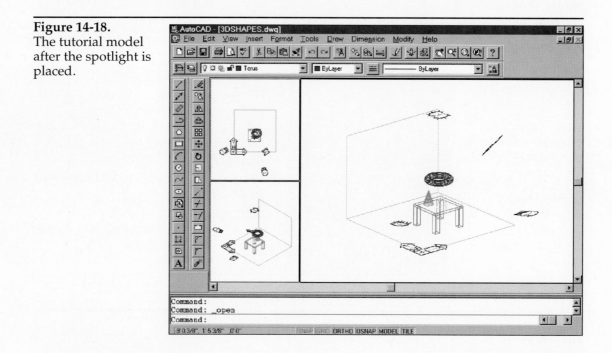

Creating shadows

All three lights—distant, point, and spot—can cast shadows. These shadows can be either raytrace or shadow map. A *raytrace* shadow is created by beams from the light source. These beams are traced as they strike objects to create a shadow that has a well-defined edge.

A *shadow map* is bit mapped. Therefore, it has the capability of showing soft edges. In addition, the edges of shadow maps can be adjusted by the user. Raytraced shadows cannot be adjusted.

The shadow creation options are the same for all lights, and are selected in the **Shadows** area of all the **Light** dialog boxes. See Figure 14-19. The **Shadow On** check box must be activated in order for the light to create shadows. Generating shadows in the rendered image is discussed in the next section.

Figure 14-19.
Each type of light has a **Shadows** area in the dialog box.

Pick to activate shadows

Pick to select type of shadows

If casting shadows is an important aspect of the model, be sure that shadows are turned on for each of the lights in the model. Create a variety of scenes and carefully place a distant light in each representing the time of year and day.

If you wish to experiment with different lighting effects in your scenes, it may also be helpful to create a full set of lights for each scene. This is especially true if you will be using several scenes for rendering purposes. Remember, you can place an unlimited number of lights in the model and then create as many scenes as you need, using any of the lights. Scenes are discussed later in the chapter.

Rendering the Model

You can render your model anytime. If there are no lights in your model, AutoCAD places one behind your viewpoint. If you have placed lights in your model but have not yet constructed a "scene," AutoCAD uses all of the lights and renders the current view in the active viewport.

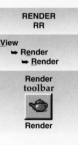

To render your model, pick the **Render** button from the **Render** toolbar, select **Render** from the **Render** cascading menu in the **View** pull-down menu, or type RR or RENDER at the Command: prompt. All three methods open the **Render** dialog box. Pick the **Render** button in this dialog box. AutoCAD then displays the rendering of your model in the active viewport. See Figure 14-20.

AutoCAD produces three different types of renderings: the default render, photo real, and photo raytrace. These types of rendering are shown in the **Rendering Type:** drop-down list at the top of the **Render** dialog box, Figure 14-21.

Figure 14-20.
The tutorial model rendered after the lights are placed.

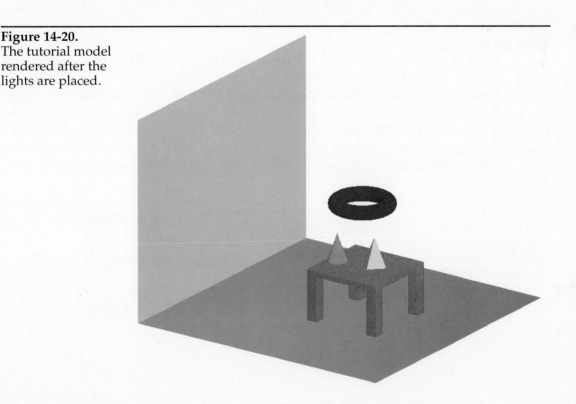

Figure 14-21.
Three types of renderings are available in the **Render** dialog box.

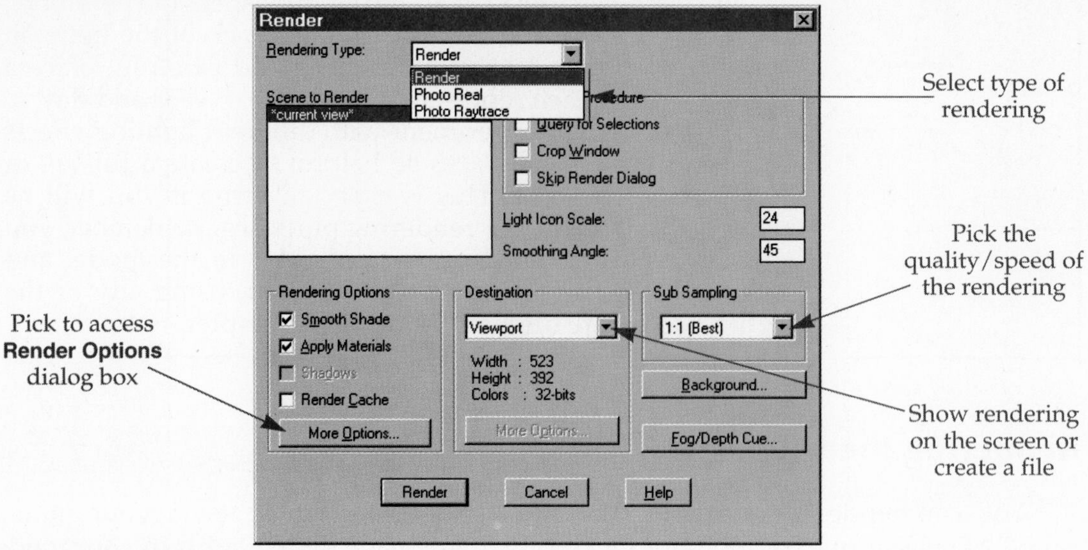

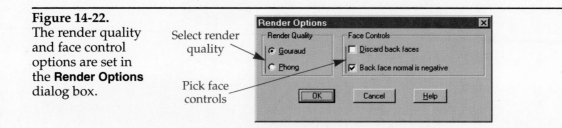

Select type of rendering

Pick the quality/speed of the rendering

Pick to access **Render Options** dialog box

Show rendering on the screen or create a file

Standard rendering

This default type of rendering does not support shadows. Notice that the **Shadows** check box in the **Rendering Options** area is disabled. Picking the **More Options...** button displays the **Render Options** dialog box, Figure 14-22. In this dialog box, you can choose the render quality and the 3D face controls.

The type of render quality determines the points where light intensity is calculated. The two options are the following:

- **Gouraud.** Light intensity is calculated at each vertex. The intensity of the space between vertices is estimated. This is the lesser realistic of the two options.
- **Phong.** Light intensity is calculated at each pixel. This creates realistic lighting.

The **Face Controls** area contains two items that determine whether or not hidden faces are calculated:

- **Discard back faces.** AutoCAD does not calculate hidden faces when rendering. This setting can speed the rendering process.
- **Back face normal is negative.** A *normal vector* is perpendicular to a face. A front face has a normal vector that points outward toward the viewer and is positive. A back face normal vector points away from the viewer and is negative. This setting determines which faces on the model are back faces. When **Discard back faces** is turned on, faces with negative normals are not calculated.

Figure 14-22.
The render quality and face control options are set in the **Render Options** dialog box.

Select render quality

Pick face controls

Photo real rendering

This type of rendering produces a more realistic image than the default render method. When **Photo Real** is selected, the **Shadows** check box is enabled. You can refine the rendered image by selecting the **More Options...** button. This displays the **Photo Real Render Options** dialog box. See Figure 14-23.

In addition to the face controls discussed previously, you can adjust the anti-aliasing, depth map shadow controls, and texture map sampling.

Figure 14-23.
This dialog box is used to select settings for a photo real rendering.

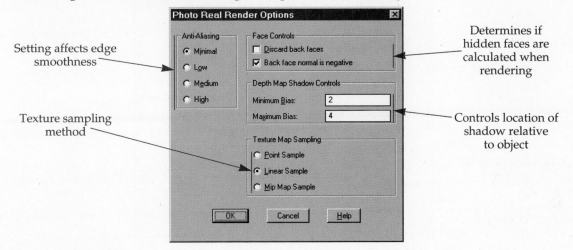

Setting affects edge smoothness

Texture sampling method

Determines if hidden faces are calculated when rendering

Controls location of shadow relative to object

Anti-aliasing

Aliasing is the jagged edges, or "jaggies," that appear on many computer text and graphic images. *Anti-aliasing* refers to methods used to smooth these jagged edges. A variety of colors and shades per pixel can produce a smoother edge. AutoCAD provides four different settings for this option. Each successive option requires a longer time to render the image.

- **Minimal.** The default method uses only horizontal anti-aliasing. This option requires the least amount of time to render.
- **Low.** Uses horizontal anti-aliasing and four shading samples per pixel.
- **Medium.** Uses horizontal anti-aliasing and nine shading samples per pixel.
- **High.** Uses horizontal anti-aliasing and sixteen shading samples per pixel.

Depth map shadow controls

These settings control the location of the shadow in relation to the object casting the shadow. This helps prevent detached and misplaced shadows. The following settings are available:

- **Minimum Bias.** The default setting is 2 and maximum is 20.
- **Maximum Bias.** The default setting is 4 and maximum is 20.

Texture map sampling

When a bitmap texture is projected onto an object that is smaller than the texture map, a sampling method must be used in order to "map" the texture to the object.

- **Point Sample.** The nearest pixel in the bitmap is selected for each sample.
- **Linear Sample.** Four pixels nearest the sample point in the bitmap are averaged for each sample. This is the default setting.
- **Mip Map Sample.** Each sample is averaged using the *mip* method, which is a pyramidal average taken from a square sample area.

Photo raytrace rendering

Photo raytrace rendering provides more options for controlling the appearance of the scene. These options provide further control of the anti-aliasing process and control of the depth of rays used in raytracing. Selecting the **More Options...** button in the **Render** dialog when **Photo Raytrace** is selected displays the **Photo Raytrace Render Options** dialog box. See Figure 14-24.

Figure 14-24.
The **Photo Raytrace Render Options** dialog box is used to control photo raytrace renderings.

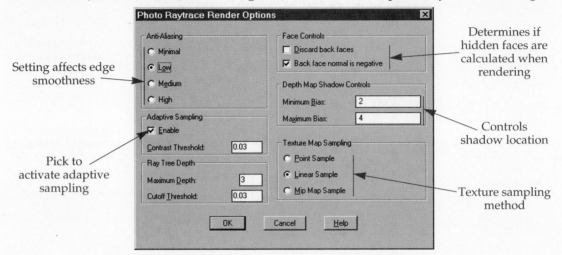

Setting affects edge smoothness

Pick to activate adaptive sampling

Determines if hidden faces are calculated when rendering

Controls shadow location

Texture sampling method

Adaptive sampling

When a contrast threshold is set, AutoCAD determines how many samples it needs to process to produce the level of anti-aliasing resolution specified. The following items are located in the **Adaptive Sampling** area of the dialog box:

- **Enable.** When this box is checked, adaptive sampling is enabled.
- **Contrast Threshold.** Values between 0.0 and 1.0 are valid in the text box. A low value means that a greater number of samples will be taken to achieve the selected level of anti-aliasing. The greater the number of samples, the longer the rendering time.

Ray tree depth

The **Ray Tree Depth** area contains two ray tree settings. These settings control the depth of the ray tree used to track rays. In other words, how far the ray bounces (reflects).

- **Maximum Depth.** Values between 3 and 10 are suggested, with 3 being the default.
- **Cutoff Threshold.** This value controls the additional percentage that the last pixel in the ray must contribute before the ray is cut off. A value of .05 means that at least 5% must be contributed to the final pixel value. If the 5% is reached, the ray continues. If the 5% is not contributed, the ray is stopped.

Rendering destination

The rendering can be displayed in a viewport, in the **Render** window, or it can be sent to a file. These options are found in the drop-down list in the **Desti<u>n</u>ation** area of the **Render** dialog box. See Figure 14-25. Rendering to a **Render** window is discussed in detail later in the chapter.

If you choose the **File** option, the **More Options...** button is enabled. Pick this button if you wish to select the file type and adjust the file's options. The **File Output Configuration** dialog box is displayed. See Figure 14-26.

The selected file type determines which options in the four areas are selectable. The available file types are .bmp, .pcx, PostScript, .tga, and .tif. Pick each one of these file types and notice the different options that are available. The following four areas are found in the dialog box:

- **<u>F</u>ile Type.** Select the type of output file desired, then pick the file resolution in the next drop-down list. Note that the X and Y values of resolution and the aspect ratio can only be set if **User Defined** is picked in the resolution drop-down list.
- **Colors.** The options available in this area depend on the file type. The widest variety of color options is available with the .tga file type.
- **TGA Options.** These are active for the .tga file type. You can select a compressed file, images that are scanned from the bottom left, or select an interlaced or noninterlaced file. **None** is the default and produces a *noninterlaced* image, which is scanned one horizontal line at a time from top to bottom. A noninterlaced monitor produces images that are easier to view because they have little or no flicker. Pick **2 to 1** or **4 to 1** to create an interlaced file. These images are for use on an *interlaced* monitor, which scans every other line and then returns to scan the remaining lines of the image. It requires more time to produce the same image and can therefore produce flicker.

Figure 14-25.
The **Destination** area of the **Render** dialog box.

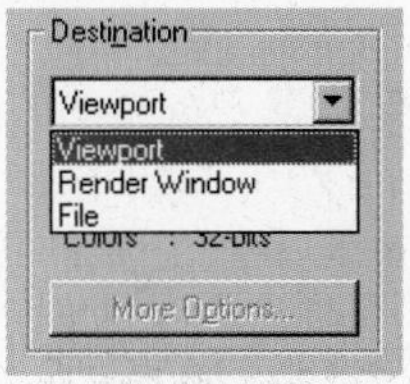

Figure 14-26.
When rendering to a file, parameters can be set in the **File Output Configuration** dialog box.

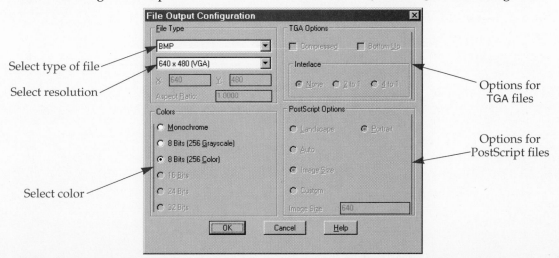

- **PostScript Options.** These are available only when the PostScript file type is selected. You can choose landscape or portrait format, and you can select the method of image sizing. **Auto** instructs AutoCAD to automatically scale the image, whereas **Image Size** uses the exact image size. When **Custom** is selected, you can enter the size in the **Image Size** text box.

Preview renderings

The **Sub Sampling** area of the **Render** dialog box allows you to specify the amount of time and level of quality you want for your renderings. See Figure 14-27. These settings sample a fraction of the pixels in your model. The **1:1** setting produces the best quality image while the **8:1** setting provides the lowest quality, but the quickest rendering. Regardless of the value you select, other effects you have selected, such as shadows and materials, are still used. Figure 14-28 shows the difference among various sub sampling settings.

Figure 14-27.
The **Sub Sampling** setting affects the quality and speed of the rendering.

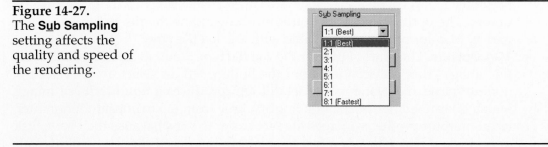

Figure 14-28.
A drawing rendered at various sub sampling settings. A—**1:1 (Best)**. B—**4:1**. C—**8:1 (Fastest)**.

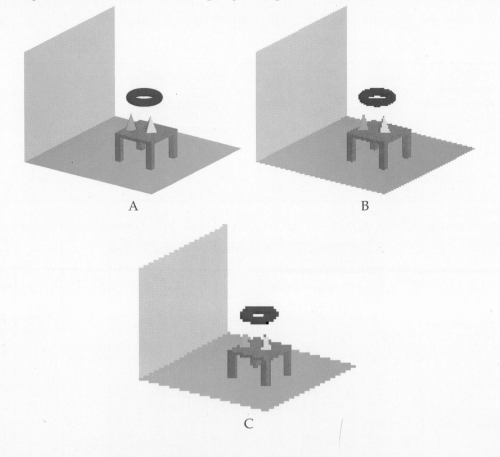

Rendering procedures

By default, the entire active viewport is rendered. However, there are times when you may want to render only some of the objects, or a portion of the viewport. When performing a series of renderings, you may wish to have the rendering performed immediately, without the appearance of the **Render** dialog box.

The options listed in the **Rendering Procedure** area of the **Render** dialog box can be used in these situations. See Figure 14-29. The options are described as follows:

- **Query for Selections.** This allows you to select specific objects to be rendered.
- **Crop Window.** Check this option in order to window a specific area of the model for rendering.
- **Skip Render Dialog.** Eliminates the display of the **Render** dialog box in all successive uses of the **Render** command. This is a good option if render settings are used for a series of renderings. You can use the **Rendering Preferences** dialog box to change this setting so that the dialog box appears. To access the **Rendering Preferences** dialog box, pick the **Render Preferences** button in the **Render** toolbar, select **Preferences...** from the **Render** cascading menu in the **View** pull-down menu, or type RPR or RPREF at the Command: prompt.

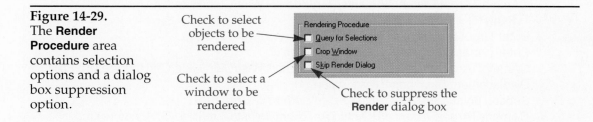

Figure 14-29.
The **Render Procedure** area contains selection options and a dialog box suppression option.

Check to select objects to be rendered

Check to select a window to be rendered

Check to suppress the **Render** dialog box

Additional rendering options

The **Rendering Options** area of the **Render** dialog box provides options that give you a wide range of control over how the model is rendered. These options not only control the appearance of the rendering, but also the speed in which it is produced. See Figure 14-30.

- **Smooth Shade.** AutoCAD blends colors between two or more surfaces to produce a smoother surface. This option requires a longer rendering time. The **Smoothing Angle** (located just below **Light Icon Scale**) determines at what angle an edge is defined. Angles less than the default of 45° are smoothed. Angles greater than 45° are not smoothed.
- **Apply Materials.** If materials have been assigned to objects in the model, AutoCAD renders them if this box is checked. This option requires a longer rendering time that will vary depending on the number and complexity of the textures and materials.
- **Shadows.** Check this box if you want the renderer to generate cast shadows. Remember, only those lights whose shadows have been turned on will cast shadows. Check the lights using the **Modify Light** dialog box if you are unsure.

Figure 14-30.
The **Rendering Options** area of the **Render** dialog box.

Rendering Options
- ☑ Smooth Shade
- ☑ Apply Materials
- ☐ Shadows
- ☐ Render Cache

More Options...

- **Render Cache.** All of the rendering settings and values are saved to a *cache file* on the hard disk. If you do not change any of the settings in the **Render** dialog box, AutoCAD can use the cache file for additional renderings. This can save considerable time because *tessellation lines*, which define 3D surfaces and solids, do not need to be recalculated.

Creating Views and Scenes

A *scene* is like a photograph. It is made up of a view and one or more lights. You can have as many scenes in a model as you want. The current view in the active viewport is used as the "camera" for the scene. You can use the **VIEW**, **VPOINT**, or **DVIEW** commands to set the viewpoints you want, then use the **VIEW** command to create named views. For the tutorial model, create the following views using the **DVIEW** command. Be sure the large viewport is active and the current UCS is FLOOR (or the WCS, depending on how you constructed the floor and walls).

> Command: **DVIEW**↵
> Select objects: *(window the entire model)*
> Select objects: ↵
> CAmera/TArget/Distance/POints/PAn/Zoom/TWist/CLip/Hide/Off/Undo/⟨eXit⟩:
>   **POINTS**↵
> Enter target point ⟨*current*⟩: *(pick P2 in Figure 14-11)*
> Enter camera point ⟨*current*⟩: **@-8'6",-6',4'**↵
> CAmera/TArget/Distance/POints/PAn/Zoom/TWist/CLip/Hide/Off/Undo/⟨eXit⟩: **PAN**↵
> Displacement base point: *(pick a point)*
> Second point: *(pick a second point to center the drawing)*
> CAmera/TArget/Distance/POints/PAn/Zoom/TWist/CLip/Hide/Off/Undo/⟨eXit⟩: ↵

The view should look like the one shown in Figure 14-31.

Figure 14-31.
The view created
and saved as VIEW1.

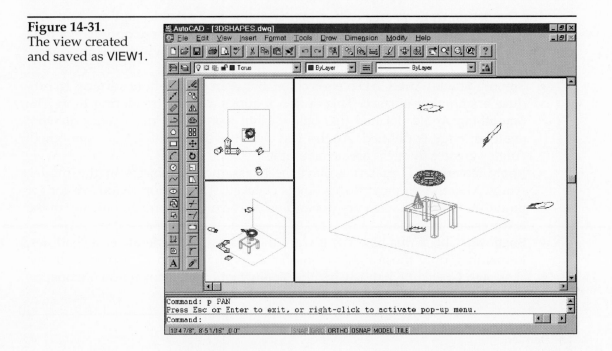

Now you can use the **VIEW** or **DDVIEW** command to save the current display as a new view named VIEW1. Next, set up a second viewpoint with the **DVIEW** command as follows:

    Command: **DVIEW**↵
    Select objects: **P**↵
    Select objects: ↵
    CAmera/TArget/Distance/POints/PAn/Zoom/TWist/CLip/Hide/Off/Undo/⟨eXit⟩:
        POINTS↵
    Enter target point ⟨*current*⟩: *(pick top of cone)*
    Enter camera point ⟨*current*⟩: **@-2',-8'6",5'**↵

Now, turn perspective on by setting a distance.

    CAmera/TArget/Distance/POints/PAn/Zoom/TWist/CLip/Hide/Off/Undo/⟨eXit⟩: **D**↵
    New camera/target distance ⟨*current*⟩: **14'**↵
    CAmera/TArget/Distance/POints/PAn/Zoom/TWist/CLip/Hide/Off/Undo/⟨eXit⟩: ↵

Your display should look like Figure 14-32. Create another view of the current display and name it VIEW2.

Now that you have two views, make a couple of scenes by picking the **Scenes** button from the **Render** toolbar, selecting **Scene...** from the **Render** cascading menu in the **View** pull-down menu, or typing SCENE at the Command: prompt. This displays the **Scenes** dialog box. See Figure 14-33. Pick **New...** to display the **New Scene** dialog box, Figure 14-34. This dialog box lists all views and lights in the drawing.

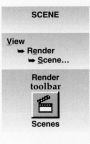

Figure 14-32.
The view created
and saved as VIEW2.

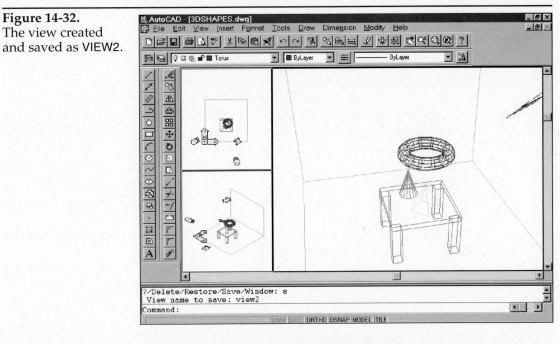

Figure 14-33.
The **Scenes** dialog
box.

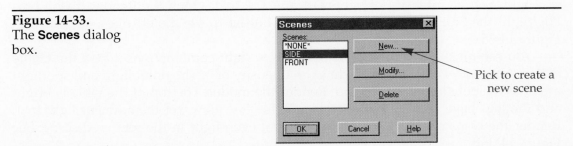

Pick to create a new scene

Figure 14-34.
The **New Scene**
dialog box.

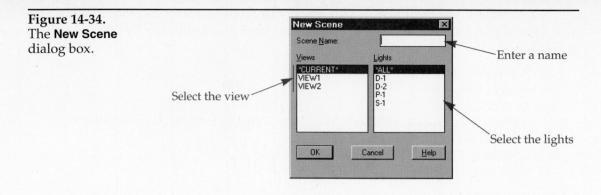

Enter FRONT in the **Scene Name:** text box. Now you need to assign a view and lights to the new scene. Pick VIEW1, then hold the [Ctrl] key and pick lights D-1 and P-1. Pick the **OK** button to save the scene. Pick **New...** again and make another scene named SIDE. Use VIEW2 and lights D-2 and S-1. The **Scenes** dialog box now lists the two scenes, as shown in Figure 14-33. Pick **OK**.

Render the scene with the **RENDER** command. In the **Render** dialog box, select a scene from the list at the left and pick the **Render** button. The **RENDER** command renders the view used to define the selected scene. Therefore, the rendering may not be the same view currently displayed in the active viewport.

Create a third scene named SIDE2. Use the **DVIEW** command to establish a new view named VIEW3 using the same target as VIEW1. Make the camera location X = –5′, Y = –8′6″, and Z = 12′. Set the distance in **DVIEW** to 11′6″. Use VIEW3 and lights S-1, P-1, and D-1 for scene SIDE2.

Changing light intensities

The full intensity of point lights and spotlights should strike the first object in the model. Full intensity of any light is a value of one. Remember that spotlight falloff (attenuation) is calculated using either the **Inverse Linear** or **Inverse Square** setting.

In the 3dshapes.dwg model you have been working with, the top of the torus is approximately 55″ from the point light. The spotlight is approximately 43″ from the torus. Use the following calculations for each spotlight setting:

- **Inverse Linear.** If the point light is 55 units above the highest object (torus), that object receives 1/55 of the light. Set intensity to 55 so the light intensity striking the torus has a value of 1. Since the spotlight is 43″ from the nearest object, set its light intensity to 43.
- **Inverse Square.** Set light intensity to 55^2, or 3025, for the point light. Set the intensity to 43^2, or 1849, for the spotlight.

To change the light intensity for your model, open the **Lights** dialog box. First, set the **Ambient Light Intensity** to 0. With ambient light at 0, you can see the effects of changing other lights. Highlight P-1 in the **Lights:** list box, and then pick the **Modify...** button. Enter 55 in the **Intensity:** text box and pick **OK**. Modify S-1 and set the intensity to 43. Be sure the **Inverse Linear** radio button is active for the point light and the spotlight. Set the intensity of lights D-1 and D-2 to 1. Open the **Render** dialog box. Highlight the SIDE2 scene. Pick the **Render** button to see the changes, as shown in Figure 14-35.

You can quickly see the effects of different light combinations. Open the **Lights** dialog box and set each distant light to an intensity of 0. The point light and spotlight are now the only lights that are on. Render the model. The top of the table is bright and the legs have no highlight. See Figure 14-36A. Now, set the ambient light to 1. Render the scene again. Notice the additional even light in the rendered scene. See Figure 14-36B.

AutoCAD and its Applications—Advanced

Figure 14-35.
The SIDE2 scene rendered.

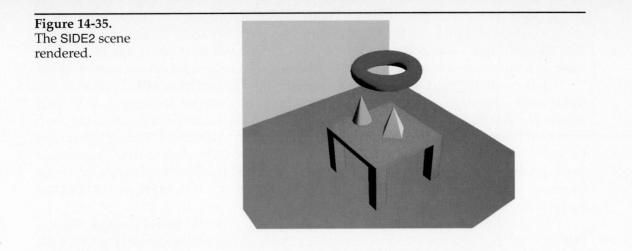

Figure 14-36.
A—The SIDE2 scene rendered with just the point light and spotlight. B—The SIDE2 scene rendered with the point, ambient, and spotlight.

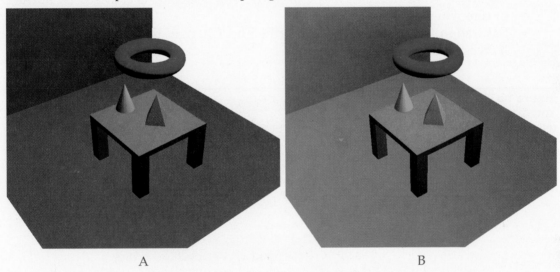

A   B

Try turning the point light off, and turn on only one of the distant lights at a time. First, set the intensity of light D-2 to .8, then render the model. The left sides of the objects are illuminated. Now turn off D-2 and give light D-1 an intensity of 1. Render the model. The front of the objects and the back wall are illuminated. The floor is dark because it is parallel to the light rays. Try additional combinations on your own.

> **NOTE**
>
> If you render a scene and the image appears black, you may have selected a scene in which all the lights have been turned off. Unless you want to save power, check the lights in the scene to be sure they have been given an intensity greater than zero.

Changing light color

The color of a light can be adjusted if you want the objects in the model to appear tinted differently than they appear in white light. The amount of red, green, or blue (RGB) can be adjusted to produce any color from white to black. White is the presence of all colors. This is a setting of 1.0 for red, green, and blue. Black is the absence of all colors. This is a setting of 0.0 for red, green, and blue.

To set a color for a light, open the **Lights** dialog box. Then, highlight the light you want to adjust and pick the **Modify...** button. In the **Modify Light** dialog box, the **Color** area allows you to adjust the amount of red, green, and blue using the RGB slider bars. In addition, you can select a standard AutoCAD color or choose a custom color.

If you want to select a predefined color, pick the **Select from ACI...** button in the **Color** area. This displays the **Select Color** dialog box shown in Figure 14-37. *ACI* stands for AutoCAD Color Index. These are the predefined colors that come with AutoCAD. You can choose one of the standard colors (numbers 1 through 9), one of six gray shades (numbers 250 to 255), or select from the full-color palette. The number of colors displayed in the full-color palette is controlled by your display device. Color numbers 10 through 249 are shown here. Note that the **BYLAYER** and **BYBLOCK** options do not apply to lights.

The third way to adjust the color of a light is to pick the **Select Custom Color...** button. This displays the Windows standard **Color** dialog box shown in Figure 14-38. HLS and RGB color values appear in this dialog box. HLS stands for hue, lightness (luminescence), and saturation.

- **Hue.** A single color in a range of colors.
- **Lightness (luminescence).** The brightness of the color is changed by adding or removing white.
- **Saturation.** The content of black in the hue. Changes the purity of the hue by increasing or decreasing the gray.

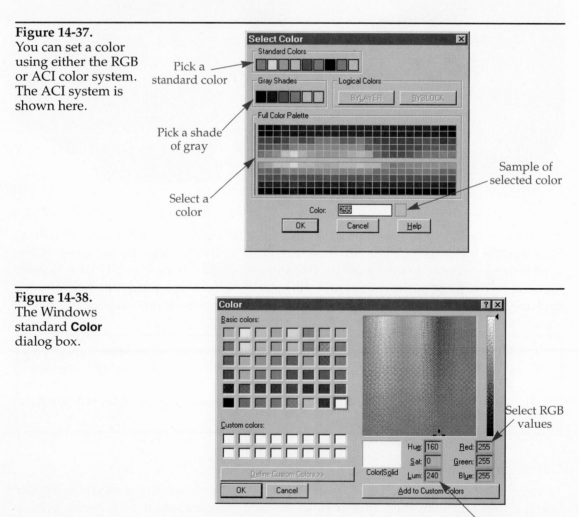

Figure 14-37.
You can set a color using either the RGB or ACI color system. The ACI system is shown here.

Pick a standard color

Pick a shade of gray

Select a color

Sample of selected color

Figure 14-38.
The Windows standard **Color** dialog box.

Select RGB values

Select HLS values

You can create a custom color using several methods.

1. Pick one of the basic colors. It is displayed in the **Color|S_olid** image tile.
2. Enter new values in the **Hu_e:**, **S_at:**, and **L_um:** boxes, or
3. Enter new values in the **Red:**, **G_reen:**, and **Bl_ue:** boxes, or
4. Pick a location in the large color palette image tile, then adjust the slider arrow along the tall thin color sample to the extreme right of the dialog. This is a visual method to change the numerical values of the color.

When you have created a color that you want to keep, pick the **A_dd to Custom Colors** button. This places the new color in the **_Custom Colors:** palette.

PROFESSIONAL TIP

The best way to see how colored lights affect your model is to experiment. Remember, you can render individual objects in the model. This allows you to see how light intensity and color change each object.

Creating Surface Finishes with Materials

AutoCAD User's Guide **14**

A *finish* in AutoCAD can be a shiny surface, dull surface, or any gradation between. You can create a variety of finishes by specifying how a surface reflects light. When you create a finish, it can be assigned to an entity color that you created or to a specific AutoCAD Color Index (ACI) number. If you assign a finish to an ACI, all objects in your model with that color number are given the finish.

To create a new finish, first pick the **Materials** button in the **Render** toolbar, select **Materials...** from the **Render** cascading menu in the **_View** pull-down menu, or type RMAT at the Command: prompt. This displays the **Materials** dialog box, Figure 14-39A. The **New** drop-down list provides four material types: **Standard**, **Marble**, **Granite**, and **Wood**. Select **Standard**, then pick the **New...** button to display the **New Standard Material** dialog box, Figure 14-39B.

RMAT

_View
➡ **Render**
   ➡ **Materials...**

Render toolbar

Materials

Material attributes are set in the **Attributes** area of the **New Standard Material** dialog box. The following seven radio buttons are available:

- **_Color/Pattern.** This refers to the reflected color of the object and the bitmap used as a pattern. Use the **_Value** and **Color** adjustment controls to change the color. If the **By ACI** box has been checked, the color controls are not available. A bitmap can also be specified as a pattern and can be blended with the color. Load any bitmap file for this purpose. For example, in Figure 14-40 the checker.tga bitmap file has been attached to the floor. Adjust bitmap blend to show more or less of the material color through the bitmap.
- **Ambient.** This is the color of the ambient light reflected from the object.
- **R_eflection.** This is the color of the highlight. The highlight is the shiniest spot on the object. This is also called the *specular* reflection or highlight. A bitmap can be selected as a reflection map. Be sure that the reflection value is high and the roughness value is low. The strength of the reflection bitmap that appears in the object is based on value set for **Bitmap Blen_d**.
- **R_oughness.** This controls the size of the specular reflection. A larger highlight is created when the roughness value is higher.
- **_Transparency.** Controls how transparent the object is. Set this value to 1.0 if you want the object to appear completely transparent. Transparency falls off toward the edges of closed objects when photo real and photo raytrace renderings are used. A bitmap for transparency is called an *opacity map*. The color white is opaque, while black is completely transparent. Colors between

Figure 14-39.
A—The **Materials** dialog box. Pick the **New...** button to display the **New Standard Material** dialog box. B—The **New Standard Material** dialog box.

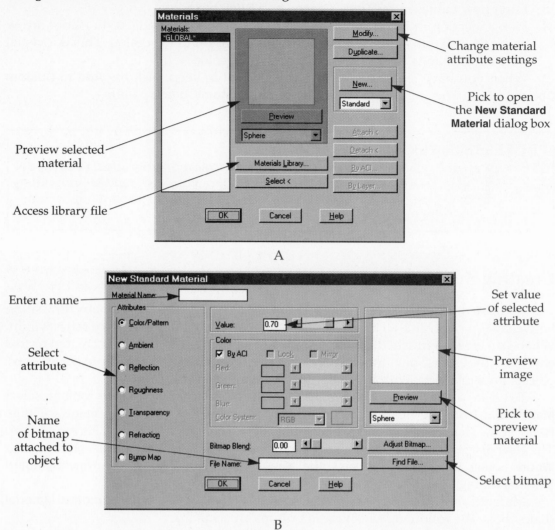

Change material attribute settings

Pick to open the **New Standard Material** dialog box

Preview selected material

Access library file

A

Enter a name

Select attribute

Name of bitmap attached to object

Set value of selected attribute

Preview image

Pick to preview material

Select bitmap

B

Figure 14-40.
A bitmap can be attached to an object or surface.

black and white have varying degrees of opacity or transparency depending on their equivalent grayscale value.

An opacity map can be placed over other materials or textures to create different effects. For example, for the **Color/Pattern** option you can use a checkered pattern for a texture map floor covering. Then select the same pattern for the **Transparency** option, but adjust the bitmap so the pattern scale is larger, and adjust the bitmap blend to a value less than 1.0. When rendered, this produces the checkered floor pattern with the appearance of a larger checkered pattern superimposed over the top, producing different shades of gray. See Figure 14-41.

- **Refraction.** Use the **Value** control to specify how refractive the material is. Active for photo raytrace rendering only.
- **Bump Map.** Any bitmap image can be used as a texture or background to give the appearance of a "bumpy" or embossed surface. Even though the geometry of the bitmap image may not be 3D, the bump map option can give the effect of raised areas. Using this option increases the rendering time. For example, you can specify the brown brick as the **Color/Pattern** bitmap and set the bitmap scale at 4.0. Then select the brown brick as the **Bump Map** bitmap using the same scale. Using a bump map gives a 3D appearance to the original pattern. See Figure 14-42. You can increase or decrease this effect by adjusting the bitmap blend value. A lower blend value may produce a more pleasing effect.

Figure 14-41.
An opacity map is a bitmap used for transparency.

Figure 14-42.
Selecting a bitmap with the **Bump Map** attribute creates the appearance of raised areas. A—The brnbricb.tga bitmap used on the floor. B—An additional **Bump Map** has been added.

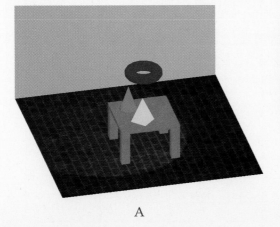

A   B

By default, the **By ACI** check box is active for color. The main color is determined by the color of the object you assign the material to. Pick both the **Ambient** and **Reflection** radio buttons. Notice that the **Lock** check box is active. This means that the attribute's color is locked to the main color. You can change these colors by picking the check box to remove the lock. This activates the **By ACI** check box. Pick to remove the check and the color slider bars and the **Color System** selections are activated.

There is also a **Value:** area in the **New Standard Material** dialog box. This represents the level, or intensity, of the attribute's color. Notice that the default **Value** setting for **Color** is 0.70. When combined with a 0.30 value for **Reflection**, a matte finish is produced. A polished finish is created with a 0.30 setting for **Color** and a 0.70 setting for **Reflection**. The greater the **Ambient** value, the more pale the object appears. The default setting of 0.10 is best here, combined with a setting of 0.30 in the **Lights** dialog box. To have the brightest reflection, keep the **Color** value low and the **Reflection** value at least 0.70.

The **Value** area is also used with **Roughness**. The smaller the value, the smaller the area of highlight. A small specular highlight makes the surface appear shiny. Set a high value for **Roughness** and a low value for **Reflection** if you want the surface to appear rough or dull.

Preview the results of your settings by picking the **Preview** button. AutoCAD renders a sample sphere with the material created by the settings. See Figure 14-43. After you preview, you can make any changes necessary and preview again.

For the tutorial, enter TORUS in the **Material Name** text box. The maximum length of a material name is 16 characters. Set the **Color** value to 0.70, **Ambient** to 0.10, **Reflection** to 0.30, and **Roughness** to 1.00. Pick **OK** to exit the **New Standard Materials** dialog box and return to the **Materials** dialog box. Now you must assign the new material to an object. Pick the **Attach** button and the following prompt appears:

```
Select objects to attach "TORUS" to: (pick the torus)
Select objects: ↵
```

The dialog box returns. Pick **OK** to exit. As new materials are created they are listed on the left side of the **Materials** dialog box.

To best see how the light and material changes affect the model, create a close-up view of a single object. Zoom-in close to the torus and create a new view named TORUS. Now create a new scene named TORUS. Use the TORUS view and lights S-1 and D-2. Render the scene and notice the wide area of the reflection. See Figure 14-44A. Now, edit the material TORUS. Change the roughness to 0.10, color to 0.30, and reflection to 0.70. Render the model again. Notice that the area of reflection is much smaller. There is also less diffused light, indicating a smoother surface. See Figure 14-44B.

Figure 14-43.
A preview of the TORUS material.

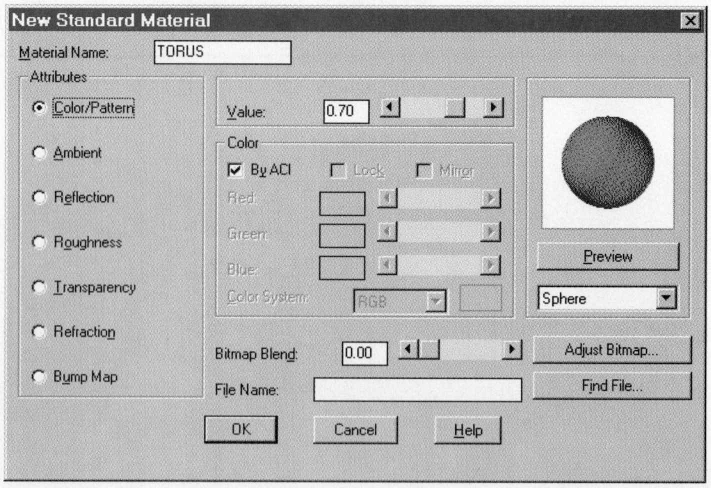

AutoCAD and its Applications—Advanced

Figure 14-44.
Adjusting material attributes affects the rendering. A—The TORUS material with high roughness and color values and low reflection value. B—The TORUS material with low values for roughness and color and a high reflection value.

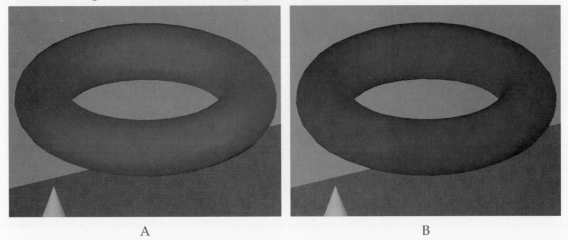

A   B

Other features of the **Materials** dialog box

There are several other features of the **Materials** dialog box. These help you work with materials and are explained below.

- **Preview.** Picking this button displays a sphere or cube with the attributes of the selected material in the image tile. This works the same as the preview function of the **New Material** dialog box.
- **Materials Library... button.** Displays the **Materials Library** dialog box. This is discussed later in the chapter.
- **Select.** Returns to the graphics screen and allows you to apply materials to selected objects.
- **Modify... button.** Displays the **Modify Material** dialog box. This is the same as the **New Materials** dialog box and allows you to adjust material attributes.
- **Duplicate... button.** Displays the **New Material** dialog box. The current material is duplicated and can be edited to create a new material.
- **New... button.** Displays the **New Material** dialog box.
- **Attach.** Displays the graphics screen so the current material can be attached to selected objects.
- **Detach.** Displays the graphics screen so the current material can be detached from selected objects.
- **By ACI... button.** Displays the **Attach by AutoCAD Color Index** dialog box. See Figure 14-45A. The current material is attached to all objects in the drawing with the color that you pick from the **Select ACI:** list.
- **By Layer... button.** Displays the **Attach by Layer** dialog box. See Figure 14-45B. The current material is attached to all objects in the drawing on the selected layer.

Figure 14-45.
Materials can be attached to colors and layers. A—The **Attach by AutoCAD Color Index** dialog
box. B—The **Attach by Layer** dialog box.

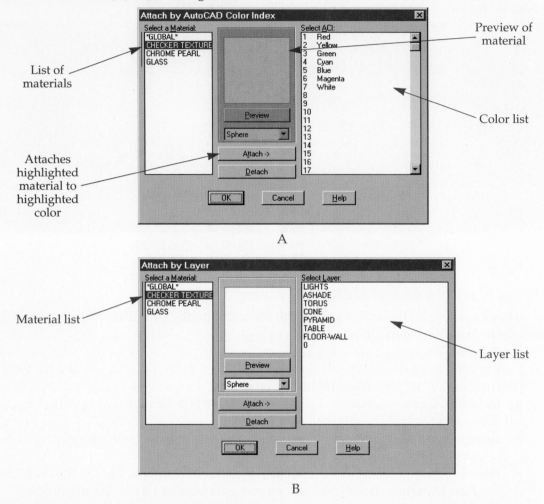

List of
materials

Attaches
highlighted
material to
highlighted
color

Preview of
material

Color list

A

Material list

Layer list

B

EXERCISE 14-2

❑ Open the 3DSHAPES drawing if it is not on your screen.
❑ Zoom-in on the cone and pyramid. Create a new view named EX14-2.
❑ Create a new scene and name it EX14-2. Use light D-1 and P-1.
❑ Create a new material for the cone. Give it a dull surface by adjusting the material attributes. Name the material EX14-2.
❑ Render the new scene.
❑ Modify the material to create a shiny surface with a highlight.
❑ Render the scene.
❑ Save the drawing as EX14-2.

Granite, marble, and wood

In addition to the **Standard** material, you can also select from the **Granite**, **Marble**, and **Wood** options from the **New...** drop-down list in the **Materials** dialog box, Figure 14-46. These options are selected when you create a new material. Pick **Granite**, then pick the **New...** button. The **New Granite Material** dialog box is displayed. This is basically the same as the **New Standard Material** dialog box, except some of the attributes are different. Figure 14-47 shows the different attributes for granite, marble, and wood.

Figure 14-46.
The **New...** drop-down list in the **Materials** dialog box.

Figure 14-47.
The various materials have different attributes available.

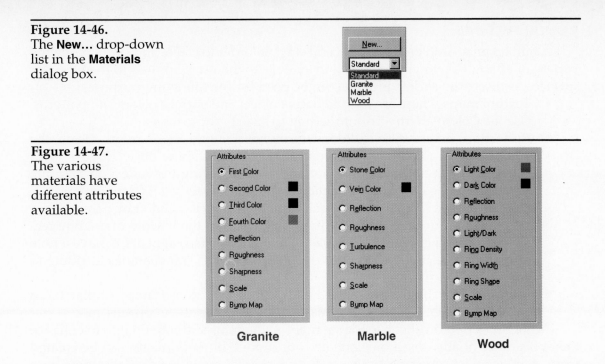

Granite can have up to four colors. If you want only one or two colors, set the colors you do not need to a value of zero. **Sharpness** determines how blurred or distinct the different granite colors are. A value of 1.0 produces distinct colors and a value of 0 creates blurred colors.

Marble allows you to choose stone color and the color of the veins that run through the stone. Colors can be set using only the RGB or HLS color systems. **Turbulence** refers to how much vein color is present and the amount of swirling the veins display. A higher turbulence value increases swirling and vein color.

The **New Wood Material** dialog box provides several attributes that enable you to refine the appearance of the wood color and grain.

- **Light Color.** Controls the color value of light wood.
- **Dark Color.** Controls the color value of dark wood. Only RGB and HLS color systems control the light and dark attributes.
- **Light/Dark.** This controls the ratio of light to dark rings in the wood, with a value of 1.0 being light and a value of 0 being dark.
- **Ring Density.** A scale value that sets the number of rings in the wood. Fine, tight rings are achieved with a large value.
- **Ring Width.** This controls the variation in the width of the rings. A variety of ring widths is produced with a value of 1.0, and consistent ring width is achieved with a value of 0.
- **Ring Shape.** Irregular-shaped rings are produced with a value of 1.0, while concentric circular rings result from a value of 0.

PROFESSIONAL TIP

Be creative when testing new materials and try out a variety of attribute settings. You can quickly view the result of new attributes, colors, and values by picking the **Preview** button.

Using bitmaps

A bitmap image can be used in several ways in order to create and simulate a wide variety of effects. A bitmap is *mapped* to an object when it is applied to the object or surface. As discussed earlier, bitmaps can be used for the following purposes:

- **Texture maps.** These are used to define object and surface colors and patterns. Use the **Color/Pattern** attribute setting to specify these maps.
- **Reflection maps.** Also called *environment maps*, these maps create the appearance of a scene reflected on the surface of a shiny object. Figure 14-48 shows one object rendered before and after applying the reflection map file named sunset.tga. Use the **Reflection** attribute to specify a reflection map.
- **Opacity maps.** These maps specify areas of opacity and transparency. For example, if your bitmap image is a black circle in the middle of a white rectangle and you apply it as an opacity map, the surface appears to have a hole in it where the circle maps onto the object. Use the **Transparency** attribute to specify an opacity map.
- **Bump maps.** These can create the appearance of raised areas similar to an embossed effect. Use the **Bump Map** attribute to specify an opacity map.

AutoCAD's photorealistic renderer enables you to use bitmap images to enhance the appearance of any object or plane in your model. Bitmap images can be created from an image on a computer screen, a photograph taken with a digital camera, or a paper photo translated by a photo processing service.

Figure 14-48.
A reflection map creates the appearance of a scene reflected on a shiny surface.
A—Without reflection map. B—With reflection map.

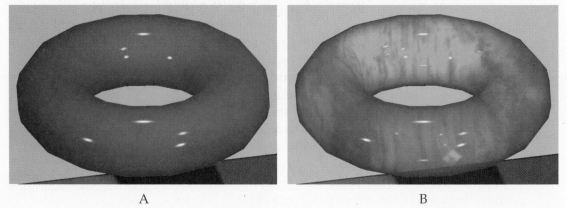

A   B

> **NOTE** Materials, textures, and patterns specified by bitmaps will only display when the photo real or photo raytrace rendering option is used.

If you plan to work with 3D models and apply photorealistic textures and patterns, you should begin collecting a variety of bitmap images to use with those models. For example, architects and interior designers use a variety of carpeting textures, wallpaper designs, flooring tiles, vinyls, and window covering samples. These images can all be easily created using one of the wide variety of digital cameras on the market.

Adjusting material bitmaps

All of the material dialog boxes provide the same type of options. For example, each allows you to select and adjust colors, attributes, and their values. In addition, each dialog allows you to select bitmap textures, and provides a means to adjust and scale the bitmap texture on the object. You can select from a wide range of bitmap textures supplied with AutoCAD by picking the **Find File...** button to access the Textures subfolder in the AutoCAD R14 folder. After you have loaded a bitmap file, you can adjust it to fit the object you are applying it to.

Pick the **Adjust Bitmap** button to display the **Adjust Material Bitmap Placement** dialog box. See Figure 14-49. The **Offset** option controls the location of the bitmap on the object(s) and the **Scale** option controls the size of the bitmap. You can see the results of your adjustments easier by selecting the **Cube** option for the **Preview** image. Offset and scale values are shown as **U** and **V**, with **U** representing a horizontal adjustment and **V** representing the vertical value.

As an example, enter .2 in the **Offset U** text box and press [Enter]. Notice that the red box remains in place and the box with the magenta bottom and right sides moved to the right in the **Scale** image tile. Now enter .2 in the **Offset V** text box. You have just moved the bitmap texture's origin on the object. **Offset U** and **V** values can also be changed by moving the bottom and right slider bars, respectively. Now pick the **CROP** radio button in the **Tiling** area. To see how this would appear when the object is rendered, pick the **Preview** button. When **CROP** is selected, all areas outside the bitmap are rendered in the material colors. This is also called a *decal map*. See Figure 14-50. If you want the entire object covered with the bitmap after the origin has been adjusted, pick the **TILE** radio button.

The bitmap image can be increased or decreased in size by using the **Scale U** and **V** text boxes, or by adjusting the upper and left slider bars, respectively. A scale value less than 1.0 increases the bitmap size in relation to the object, and a value greater than 1.0 decreases the bitmap size. If you want the **U** and **V** values of the bitmap scale to remain proportional to each other, pick the **Maintain Aspect Ratio** check box. Then, when you change one scale value, the other automatically changes. Test the scale values of .5 and 2.0, and do a preview of each to see how the bitmap is affected on both a box and sphere. Figure 14-51 shows how a scale value of 2 appears with tiling set to crop.

> **NOTE**
>
> The values of **U** and **V** are used as horizontal and vertical adjustment values for bitmap offsets. They are referred to as *mapping axes*, and are separate from the XY coordinate axes.

Figure 14-49.
The **Adjust Material Bitmap Placement** dialog box.

Figure 14-50.
A decal map is created by cropping the bitmap. In this example, the bitmap is offset.
A—The dialog box settings. B—The rendered image.

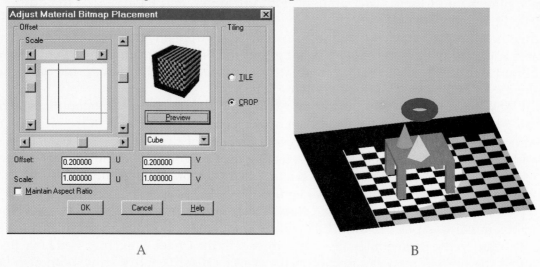

A

B

Figure 14-51.
A scale value greater than one reduces the size of the bitmap. A—The dialog box settings.
B—The rendered image.

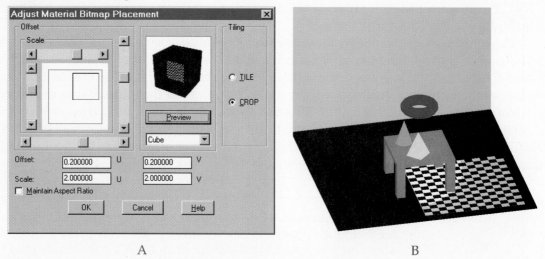

A

B

EXERCISE 14-3

❑ Open Exercise 14-1 if it is not on your screen.
❑ Display one of the 3D views previously created. If a 3D view does not exist, establish a 3D viewpoint.
❑ Create a new wood material and assign attributes of your choosing. Preview each of the changes you make to the new wood material.
❑ Save the material with the name of TABLEWOOD.
❑ Attach the wood material to the table in the drawing.
❑ Render the drawing using the **Photo Real** option and the scene of your choice.
❑ Save the drawing as EX14-03.

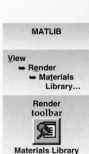
The standard materials library is an ASCII file named render.mli. This file contains a list of materials that are displayed in the **Library List:** area of the **Materials Library** dialog box. This dialog box can be used to import and export materials, and to perform housekeeping functions on the current materials list and the library list. By default, the render.mli library file is located in the \AutoCAD R14\Support folder.

The **Materials Library** dialog box is accessed by picking the **Materials Library** button in the **Render** toolbar, selecting **Materials Library...** from the **Render** cascading menu in the **View** pull-down menu, or typing MATLIB at the Command: prompt. In addition, you can also pick the **Materials Library...** button in the **Materials** dialog box.

MATLIB

View
➡ Render
➡ Materials
Library...

Render toolbar

Materials Library

PROFESSIONAL TIP

You can import an AutoVision or 3D Studio material library file (.mli) using the **Open...** button in the **Materials Library** dialog box. However, AutoCAD only displays the color, ambient, reflection, and roughness parameters of AutoVision materials. The transparency or texture mapping is *not* displayed.

Editing the materials list and materials library

The **Materials List:** area is on the left side of the **Materials Library** dialog box. This list displays all the materials defined in the current drawing. See Figure 14-52. The **Library List:** on the right side of the dialog displays all of the materials in the current library file. The name of the current library file appears above the list.

You can use a material from the default render.mli library by highlighting the material name in the material library list and picking the **Import** button. This copies the material from the library list to the materials list, making it available in the current drawing.

You may want to use a different library file than the default render.mli. For example, you may create several different libraries for different projects or customers. Also, if you are using the modeling capabilities of AutoCAD in conjunction with the rendering and animation capabilities of 3D Studio, you may want to have a common library used by both programs. A different library file can be used by picking the **Open...** button, which displays the **Library File** dialog box. Change to the folder where

Figure 14-52.
The **Materials Library** dialog box.

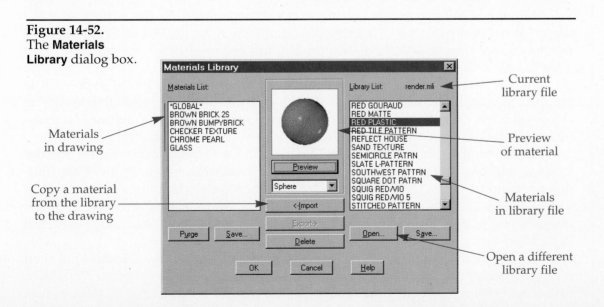

Current library file

Materials in drawing

Copy a material from the library to the drawing

Preview of material

Materials in library file

Open a different library file

the library file is located. Then, highlight the file name and pick **OK**. The materials in that library file are now displayed in the **Library List**.

If you want to use a material that you have created in the current drawing for other applications, you need to export it to the library file. Highlight the material in the **Materials List:** and pick the **Export** button. The material name appears in the **Library List**. Next, pick the **Save...** button to open the **Library File** dialog box and save the file.

If you make changes to the library list in the **Materials Library** dialog box and pick **OK** without saving, the **Library Modification** dialog box appears. See Figure 14-53. This gives you the chance to save the changes, discard the changes, or cancel and return to the **Materials Library** dialog box. Pick the appropriate button and continue.

To delete a material, highlight the name and pick the **Delete** button. You can delete materials from the current drawing by picking a name from the **Materials List**. You can also delete a material from the current library file by picking the name from the **Library List**. You cannot delete materials that are attached to objects.

The **Purge** button deletes all unused materials from the current drawing. This is similar to typing PURGE at the Command: prompt to delete all unused layers, blocks, and linetypes. The current material library file is unaffected by the **Purge** button.

Figure 14-53.
If you make changes to a library file and try to exit without saving, this dialog box appears.

Library Modification	✕
The current materials library has been changed.	
Save Changes...	Discard Changes	Cancel Command

Mapping Textures to Objects

There are three basic components to creating an object that possesses realistic qualities.
1. **Material.** Attach a material from the materials library to the object. The material is enhanced by giving it attributes such as colors, lighting, roughness, and reflectivity.
2. **Texture/Pattern.** The material can be given textures and patterns by attaching additional bitmaps to the object.
3. **Mapping.** Placing the bitmap patterns and textures on the object so that it appears realistic when it is rendered.

Mapping is the process of placing a 2D bitmap image on the surface of a 3D object. Whenever you select a bitmap and attach it to an object, it is attached (mapped) in a default direction. Mapping is not required if 3D objects have been assigned materials and texture maps already.

It is always best to preview the material or do a quick rendering to see if it is mapped to your liking. If not, change the offset, scale, and tiling first. If sides of the object are not rendered properly, you can use mapping to adjust the texture. Use mapping to rotate the currently assigned texture or to move it to a different plane.

The **Mapping** dialog box is accessed by picking the **Mapping** button in the **Render** toolbar, selecting **Mapping...** from the **Render...** cascading menu in the **View** pull-down menu, or typing SETUV at the Command: prompt. Mapping applies to individual objects, so you are first presented with a Select objects: prompt. Pick the object(s) you wish to map and press [Enter]. The **Mapping** dialog box is displayed. See Figure 14-54.

Pick the method of projection—**Planar**, **Cylindrical**, **Spherical**, or **Solid**—and then pick the **Preview** button to see the results. If the mapping appears correct, pick **OK** to exit. If an existing object in your model has the mapping variables you wish to use,

SETUV

View
➥ Render
  ➥ Mapping...

Render
toolbar

Mapping

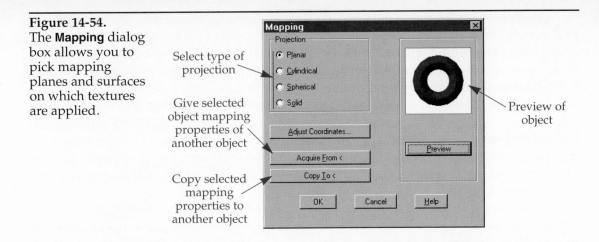

Figure 14-54.
The **Mapping** dialog box allows you to pick mapping planes and surfaces on which textures are applied.

Select type of projection

Give selected object mapping properties of another object

Copy selected mapping properties to another object

Preview of object

pick the **Acquire From** button, then pick the object in the model. If you want to give another object the mapping properties of the currently selected object, pick the **Copy To** button, and pick the object to be mapped.

The **Adjust Coordinates...** button accesses the **Adjust Coordinates** dialog box. This dialog box varies slightly for each type of projection. The **Adjust Planar Coordinates** dialog box is shown in Figure 14-55. The offset adjustments here (XY) are similar to the offset adjustments made when adjusting bitmaps earlier in the chapter.

The **Parallel Plane** area provides three planes to which the bitmap can be mapped. In addition, you can pick any plane using the **Pick Points** button. Picking this button displays the model and you are prompted to pick three corners of the new plane. Use object snap for accuracy.

Place the lower left corner of the mapping plane: *(pick lower-left corner)*
Place the lower right corner of the mapping plane: *(pick lower-right corner)*
Place the upper left corner of the mapping plane: *(pick upper-left corner)*

The dialog box returns and the **Picked Plane** radio button is selected.

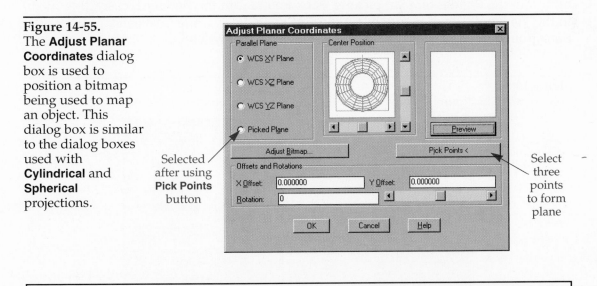

Figure 14-55.
The **Adjust Planar Coordinates** dialog box is used to position a bitmap being used to map an object. This dialog box is similar to the dialog boxes used with **Cylindrical** and **Spherical** projections.

Selected after using **Pick Points** button

Select three points to form plane

NOTE

If the points you pick are the same as one of the WCS axes, AutoCAD saves this as the WCS axis. The next time the **Adjust Coordinates** dialog box appears, the button indicates the WCS plane, rather than the **Picked Plane**.

The **Center Position** area indicates the orientation of the object on the current parallel plane. This appears as red lines. The current projection square for the mapped image shows as a blue square with a small tick mark on the top of the square. The projection square represents the extents of the object's parallel projection. Use the scroll bars to change the position of the projection axis.

The **Adjust Bitmap...** button displays the **Adjust Object Bitmap Placement** dialog box. This is the same dialog discussed previously, but it contains a **DEFAULT** radio button in the **Tiling** area. This allows you to accept the default appearance of the bitmap.

The **Offsets and Rotations** area in the **Adjust Coordinates** dialog box enables you to offset or rotate the map. These are XY offsets because it adjusts the map plane and not the bitmap image.

If **Cylindrical** projection is selected, the **Adjust Coordinates...** button displays the **Adjust Cylindrical Coordinates** dialog box. This provides the same options as the planar dialog, except the cylindrical shape is displayed in the **Central Axis Position** area and the **Pick Points** button is used to set the **Picked Axis** projection.

If **Spherical** projection is selected, the **Adjust Coordinates...** button displays the **Adjust Spherical Coordinates** dialog box. The spherical shape is displayed in the **Polar Axis Position** area, and the red mesh of the object is shown perpendicular to the current axis. A green radius line indicates the wrap line, and the blue circle is the projection axis.

If for any reason you need to detach a map from an object, you must do so at the Command: prompt as follows:

> Command: **(C:SETUV "D" (SSGET))**⏎
> Select objects: *(pick the object)*
> Select objects: ⏎

Creating Backgrounds for Models

The background for your scene can be a solid color, a gradient of colors, a bitmap file, or the current AutoCAD drawing. Establish a background by picking the **Background** button in the **Render** toolbar, picking **Background...** in the **Render...** cascading menu in the **View** pull-down menu, or typing BACKGROUND at the Command: prompt. The **Background** dialog box is displayed, as shown in Figure 14-56.

Figure 14-56.
Four types of backgrounds can be created using the **Background** dialog box.

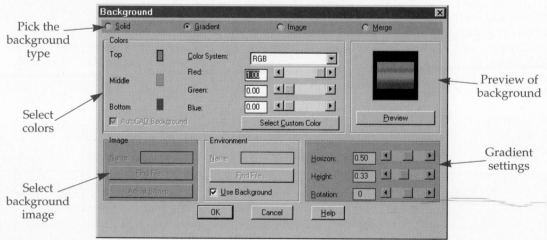

AutoCAD and its Applications—Advanced

Solid backgrounds

Four radio buttons at the top of the dialog indicate the background options. The default is the solid AutoCAD background. When the **AutoCA<u>D</u> Background** check box is inactive, you can select either the RGB or HLS color system. Either enter numeric values or use the slider bars to set the **Top** color swatch. Pick the **<u>P</u>review** button to see a larger color sample. A color can also be selected from the **Color** dialog box by picking the **Select <u>C</u>ustom Color...** button.

Gradient backgrounds

A **<u>G</u>radient** background can be composed of two or three colors. These are shown in the **Colors** area of the dialog box as **Top**, **Middle**, and **Bottom**. Pick each color swatch in order to set its value. When **<u>G</u>radient** is picked, the three values in the lower-right corner are activated.

- **Horizon.** This is a percentage value that determines the center of the gradient.
- **H<u>e</u>ight.** The starting location of the second color in a three-color gradient is determined by this percentage. A two-color gradient composed of the top and bottom colors results if this value is 0.
- **Rotation.** The angle at which the gradient background is rotated.

Image backgrounds

Any bitmap image can be used as a background. This can be used to produce realistic or imaginative settings for your models. Pick the **Im<u>a</u>ge** radio button. This activates the **Image** and **Environment** areas. Use the **<u>F</u>ind File...** button to locate the bitmap, and use the **Adjust <u>B</u>itmap...** button to alter the offset and scale. Figure 14-57 shows the result of using an image for the background.

An *environment* is an image that is mapped on a sphere that surrounds the scene. This "environment-in-a-sphere" is used by the photo raytrace renderer to project additional images onto objects that have reflective surfaces. The **<u>U</u>se Background** check box must be inactive in order to use an environment. Environment files can be .bmp, .gif, .jpg, .pcx, .tga, and .tif.

The **<u>M</u>erge** option uses the current AutoCAD image as the background.

Figure 14-57.
An image can be used as the background for a model.

LSNEW

View
→ Render
→ Landscape
New

Render
toolbar

Landscape New

Landscaping the Model

You can landscape your model with bushes, trees, road signs, and people. Pick the **Landscape New** button in the **Render** toolbar, select **Landscape New...** from the **Render** cascading menu in the **View** pull-down menu, or type LSNEW at the Command: prompt. This displays the **Landscape New** dialog box, Figure 14-58.

The library list on the left side contains the contents of the render.lli file. This is a landscape library file that you can add to. The contents of this file are .tga images. Select the file you want and pick the **Preview** button to view it. Adjust the height by entering a value in the **Height:** text box, or use the slider bar.

The **Geometry** area allows you to specify the number of faces on the landscape object and how the view is aligned. Pick **Single Face** to display the object as a single plane. If the **View Aligned** box is checked, the object's face is placed perpendicular to the line of sight of the camera. A single-face object renders faster than a two-face object. The **Crossing Faces** option creates objects with two faces that intersect at a 90° angle. This object creates more realistic images and raytraced shadows. The faces are oriented at a 45° angle to the camera if they are view-aligned. Pick the **Position** button and locate the object in your model using standard AutoCAD methods.

A single-face, view-aligned object is identified by a single triangle with the name of the object at the bottom. This object cannot be rotated. A single-face fixed object (not view-aligned) is displayed as a rectangle, and its name may be forward or backward to the camera. This object can be rotated. The objects are drawn to the specified height. A crossing-face object is drawn as two intersecting triangles. If they are view-aligned, they cannot be rotated. Figure 14-59 shows the difference between the object symbols and the rendered versions.

Figure 14-58.
Landscape objects can be placed and sized using the **Landscape New** dialog box.

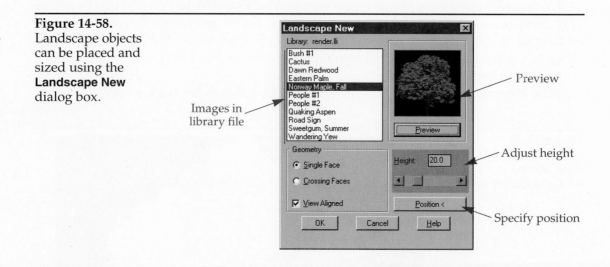

Figure 14-59.
A—Single-face and crossing-face object symbols are shown after placement in the model.
B—The same two objects after rendering.

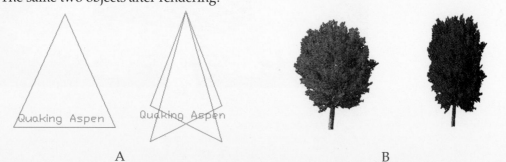

A   B

Editing landscape objects

The triangular shapes of landscape objects can be edited using standard AutoCAD methods. The objects have grips at the apex, base, and corners of the triangle. The objects can be moved using the grip at the middle of the base. The size and height of the object is changed using the top and lower corner grips. The size always remains proportional.

The geometry, position, and height of individual landscape objects can also be edited. Pick the **Landscape Edit** button in the **Render** toolbar, select **Landscape Edit...** from the **Render** cascading menu in the **View** pull-down menu, or type LSEDIT at the Command: prompt. You are prompted to select a landscape object. After the object is selected, the **Landscape Edit** dialog box is displayed.

The **Landscape Edit** dialog box is the same as the **Landscape New** dialog box, except landscape objects are not selectable. If you need to locate a different object in place of the one selected, just erase it and create a new one. Using this dialog box, you can convert between single-face and double-face objects. Enter a new value to change the height, and pick the **Position** button to relocate the object.

Remember these points when editing landscape objects.

✓ View-aligned objects cannot be rotated.

✓ Fixed objects (not view-aligned), can be rotated.

✓ The position, height, and width of objects can be quickly changed with grips.

LSEDIT

View
➡ Render
➡ Landscape Edit

Render toolbar

Landscape Edit

Editing the landscape library

The landscape library files, and the individual bitmap files contained in them, can be edited. Pick the **Landscape Library** button in the **Render** toolbar, select **Landscape Library...** from the **Render** cascading menu in the **View** pull-down menu, or type LSLIB at the Command: prompt. This displays the **Landscape Library** dialog box, Figure 14-60. This dialog box contains the following buttons:

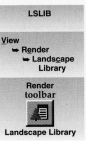

LSLIB

View
➡ Render
➡ Landscape Library

Render toolbar

Landscape Library

- **Modify.** Highlight the landscape object that you want to edit, then pick this button. The **Landscape Library Edit** dialog box appears, Figure 14-61. The current name of the object is given, as are the two files associated with it. Each object has an image file and an opacity map file, which is used to portray the see-through parts of the image. You can change the name of this item and replace the current image and opacity files with different ones. You can also change the default geometry that is displayed in the **Landscape New** dialog box.

- **New.** Displays the **Landscape Library New** dialog box, which is exactly the same as the **Landscape Library Edit** dialog box. Here you provide the name of a new landscape object, select the files that define it, and specify the default geometry settings.

- **Delete.** Removes the highlighted object.

- **Open.** Displays the **Open Landscape Library** dialog box in order to open a landscape library file (.lli).

- **Save.** Displays the **Save Landscape Library** dialog box to save the revised landscape library file.

Figure 14-60.
The landscape library files, and the individual bitmap files contained in them, can be edited using the **Landscape Library** dialog box.

```
Landscape Library                    ☒
Library: render.lli
┌─────────────────────┐   ┌─────────┐
│ Bush #1             │   │ Modify... │
│ Cactus              │   └─────────┘
│ Dawn Redwood        │   ┌─────────┐
│ Eastern Palm        │   │  New...  │
│ Norway Maple, Fall  │   └─────────┘
│ People #1           │   ┌─────────┐
│ People #2           │   │ Delete  │
│ Quaking Aspen       │   └─────────┘
│ Road Sign           │   ┌─────────┐
│ Sweetgum, Summer    │   │  Open...  │
│ Wandering Yew       │   └─────────┘
└─────────────────────┘   ┌─────────┐
                          │  Save...  │
                          └─────────┘
┌────┐  ┌────────┐  ┌──────┐
│ OK │  │ Cancel │  │ Help │
└────┘  └────────┘  └──────┘
```

Figure 14-61.
Individual landscape objects can be edited using the **Landscape Library Edit** dialog box.

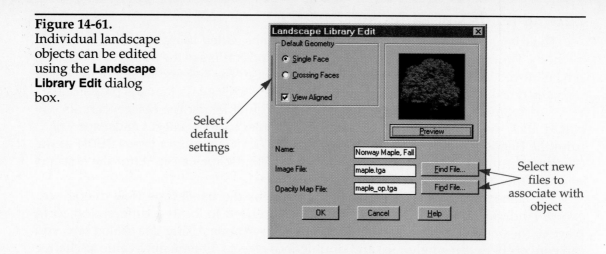

Select default settings

Select new files to associate with object

Fogging up the Model

Fog is actually a method of using colors to visually portray the distance between the camera and objects in the model. To activate fog, pick the **Fog** button in the **Render** toolbar, select **Fog...** from **Render** cascading menu in the **View** pull-down menu, or type FOG at the Command: prompt. This displays the **Fog/Depth Cue** dialog box. See Figure 14-62.

Turn on fog by picking the **Enable Fog** check box. Picking the **Fog Background** check box applies fog to the background in the model. Fog is composed of three components: color, distance, and percentage.

- **Color.** The color controls are the same as previously discussed. First, select **RGB** or **HLS** from the **Color System** drop-down list. Then enter numerical values for each color, or use the slider bars. You can also select a custom color from the Windows standard **Color** dialog box, or select an ACI color.
- **Distance.** The **Near Distance** value is a percentage of the distance from the camera to the rear of the model, or its back "clipping plane." The camera has a value of 0 and the back of the model is 1.0, or 100%. Enter values in the text boxes or use the slider bars.
- **Fog percentage.** These values are the percentages of fog at the near distance and far distance. A value of 0 is no fog, and a value of 1.0 is 100% fog. The **Near Fog Percentage** value takes effect at the **Near Distance** value and increases to the **Far Fog Percentage** value at the back of the model.

Figure 14-62.
The **Fog/Depth Cue** dialog box is used to visually portray the distance between the camera and objects in the model.

Check to enable options

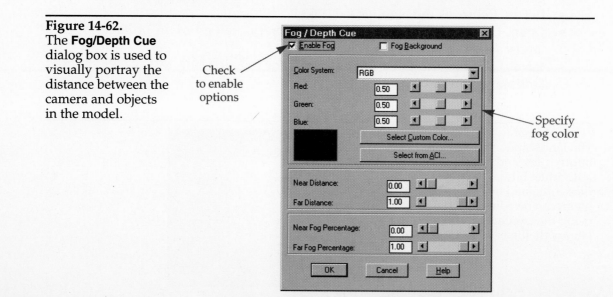

Specify fog color

FOG

View
→ Render
→ Fog...

Render toolbar

Fog

Specifying Rendering Preferences

The **Rendering Preferences** dialog box is exactly the same as the **Render** dialog box. See Figure 14-63. To access this dialog box, pick the **Render Preferences** button in the **Render** toolbar, select **Preferences...** in the **Render** cascading menu in the **View** pull-down menu, or type RPR or RPREF at the Command: prompt. You can use this dialog box to establish the rendering options, and then pick the **Skip Render Dialog** check box. Then when you use the **RENDER** command, the model is immediately rendered.

All of the options in the **Rendering Preferences** dialog box have been discussed previously, but note the two buttons at the lower right: **Background** and **Fog/Depth Cue**. These buttons open the background and fog dialog boxes discussed previously.

You might note that in the **Scene to Render** list is the entry *current view*. Pick this if you would rather render the current view instead of one of the named views in a scene.

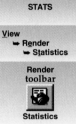

RPREF
RPR

View
➡ Render
➡ Preferences

Render
toolbar

Render Preferences

Rendering statistics

The **STATS** command provides information about the last rendering performed. Pick the **Statistics** button from the **Render** toolbar, pick **Statistics...** from the **Render** cascading menu in the **View** pull-down menu, or type STATS at the Command: prompt. The **Statistics** dialog box displays information that cannot be altered, but can be saved to a file. See Figure 14-64.

STATS

View
➡ Render
➡ Statistics

Render
toolbar

Statistics

Figure 14-63.
The **Rendering Preferences** dialog box is used to establish all the rendering options.

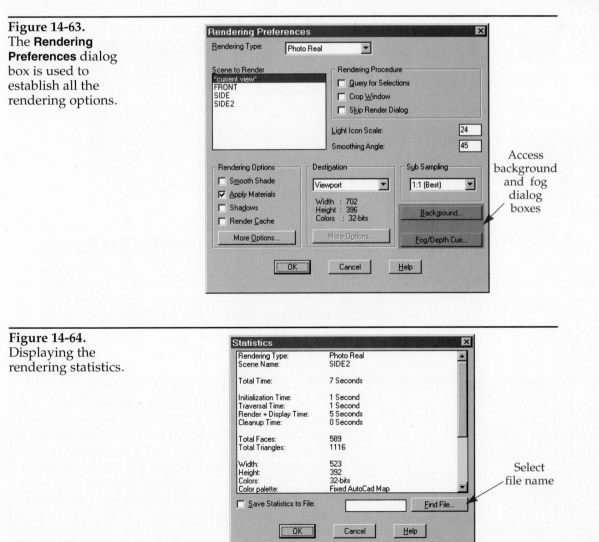

Access background and fog dialog boxes

Figure 14-64.
Displaying the rendering statistics.

Select file name

Saving Image Files with SAVEIMG

SAVEIMG

Tools
➥ Display Image
  ➥ Save...

You can save a rendered image to a file in a variety of raster file formats. These images can then be used with other software, such as a desktop publishing program. As previously discussed in the *Rendering destination* section, the model can be rendered directly to a file.

Images can be saved by picking **Save...** from the **Display Image** cascading menu in the **Tools** pull-down menu or by typing SAVEIMG at the Command: prompt. This displays the **Save Image** dialog box. See Figure 14-65.

You must render the scene *before* using the **SAVEIMG** command. Also, there are only three file types available in this dialog box. The .tga and .tif formats can be saved as compressed files. Pick the **Options...** button to open the **TGA Options** or **TIFF Options** dialog box. See Figure 14-66. The compressed form for .tga files is **RLE** (run length encoded). A .tif file can be compressed as **PACK** for Macintosh. Pick **OK** to close the dialog box and the **Image File** dialog box appears. Enter a file name and pick **OK** to save the image.

Using the **Save Image** dialog box, you can crop the image by specifying the XY pixel values. The **Offset X:** and **Y:** text boxes define the lower-left corner of the image. The **Size X:** and **Y:** text boxes define the upper-right corner of the image. You can also use the pointing device and pick the two corners in the **Portion** area of the dialog box to define the image area. Pick the **Reset** button to return the image to its default size.

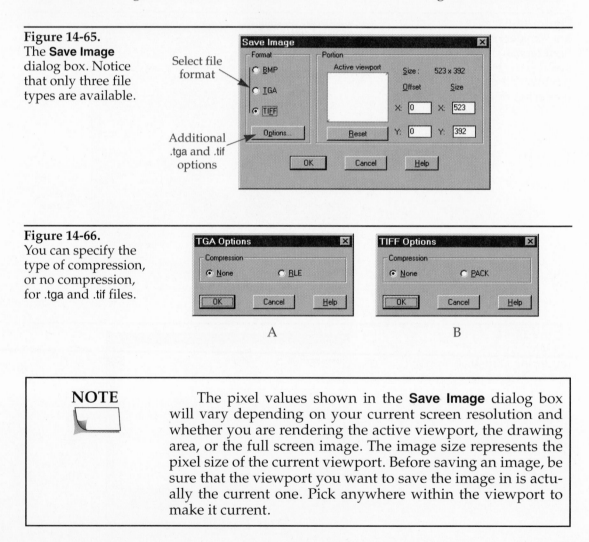

Figure 14-65.
The **Save Image** dialog box. Notice that only three file types are available.

Select file format

Additional .tga and .tif options

Figure 14-66.
You can specify the type of compression, or no compression, for .tga and .tif files.

A   B

NOTE

The pixel values shown in the **Save Image** dialog box will vary depending on your current screen resolution and whether you are rendering the active viewport, the drawing area, or the full screen image. The image size represents the pixel size of the current viewport. Before saving an image, be sure that the viewport you want to save the image in is actually the current one. Pick anywhere within the viewport to make it current.

Replaying image files

Images saved as .tga, .tif, and .bmp files can be displayed in AutoCAD with the **REPLAY** command. Access the command by selecting **Display Image** and then **View...** from the **Tools** pull-down menu or by typing REPLAY at the Command: prompt. This displays the **Replay** dialog box. Select the folder and file you want to display and pick the **Open** button. The **Image Specifications** dialog box then appears. This dialog box allows you to specify the exact portion of the image you want to display. See Figure 14-67.

The image tile on the left side of the dialog box is titled **IMAGE**. The size of the image is given in pixels just above the image tile. You can pick two points inside this tile to crop the image for display. When you do this, notice that the offset location of the image in the **SCREEN** image tile changes. You can also change the image size by entering the cropped size of the image in the **Image Offset** and **Image Size** text boxes. The image offset defines the lower-left corner of the image. The image size defines the upper-right corner of the image.

In addition to cropping the size of the image, you can determine where it will be displayed on the screen. Do this visually by picking a point in the **SCREEN** image tile. This point becomes the center of the image on your screen. You can also specify the location by entering **Screen Offset** values in the boxes below the tile. Notice that the **Screen Size** values cannot be changed. The **Reset** button returns the image and screen values to their defaults. Pick **OK** when you are ready to display the image.

REPLAY

Tools
→ Display Image
  → View...

Figure 14-67.
The **Image Specifications** dialog box.

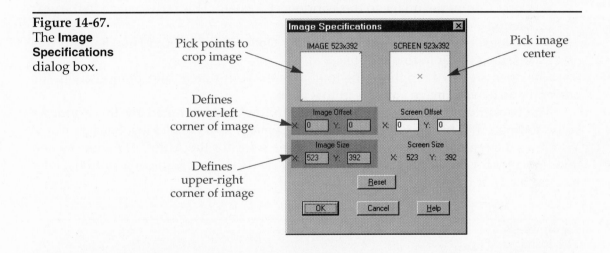

Pick points to crop image

Pick image center

Defines lower-left corner of image

Defines upper-right corner of image

❏ Load EX14-1 into AutoCAD if it is not on your screen.
❏ Save an image of the entire model in a raster file format. Save it as EX14-4.
❏ Replay the image to occupy the entire screen.
❏ Replay the image again, but display only the center of the image. Locate it in the upper-right portion of the screen.

Advanced Rendering

Some of the advanced capabilities of AutoCAD Render include rendering to a separate window, copying the rendered image to the Windows Clipboard, and advanced printing options. This section discusses each of these capabilities.

The Render window

Rendering to a window is activated by picking **Render Window** in the **Destination** area of the **Render** dialog box. Subsequent renderings are generated in the **Render** window. An image rendered to the **Render** window can be saved as a bitmap (.bmp) or printed. The **Render** window can also be used to open and display a bitmap image.

The **Render** window is made up of several elements, Figure 14-68. These elements include a menu bar, toolbar, and status area. The menu bar contains the **File**, **Edit**, and **Window** pull-down menus. The toolbar contains five buttons that are shortcuts to the commands in the **File** and **Edit** pull-down menus, Figure 14-69. The following commands are available:

- **Open.** Opens a bitmap (.bmp) image selected from the **Open** dialog box. If the **Preview** check box is checked, the selected image is previewed before it is displayed in the **Render** window.
- **Save.** Saves a rendered image to a file using the **Save BMP** dialog box.
- **Print.** Prints the bitmap.
- **Copy.** Copies the image to the Windows Clipboard. This is discussed in the next section.
- **Options.** Displays the **Windows Render Options** dialog box. This dialog box is discussed later in this chapter.

The open area to the right of the toolbar is the status area. Information about the currently displayed image appears in this area.

The background color for the **Render** window is determined by the Windows color settings. To change the color, use the Control Panel by picking **Settings** in the Windows Start menu. You may want to use one color for the AutoCAD window and another color for the **Render** window. To learn more about screen color options, refer to Chapter 17 of this text.

Figure 14-68.
The 3dshapes drawing rendered to the **Render** window.

Menu bar

Status area

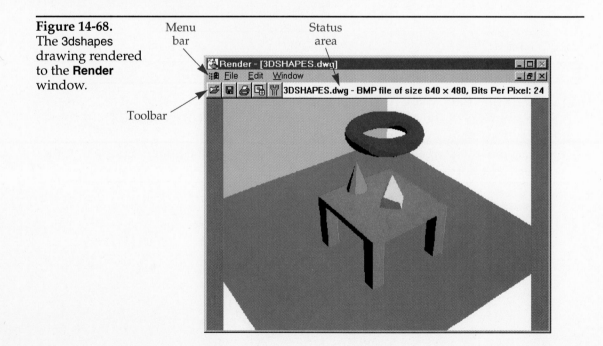

Toolbar

Figure 14-69.
The buttons
available in the
Render window
toolbar.

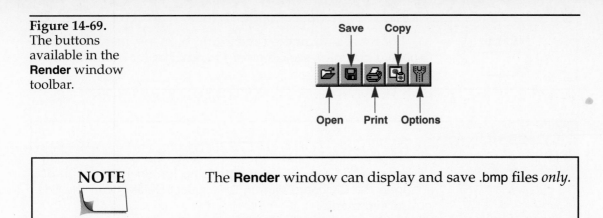

Save   Copy

Open   Print   Options

NOTE

The **Render** window can display and save .bmp files *only.*

Copying a rendered image to the Clipboard

Once an image has been rendered, it can be copied to the Windows Clipboard. Think of the Clipboard as a temporary storage area for text and graphic information. Once an image is copied into the Clipboard, it can be "pasted" into another Windows application, such as a desktop publishing program. Information copied to the Clipboard stays there until something else is copied to the Clipboard, information is deleted from the Clipboard, or you quit Windows.

To copy a rendered image to the Clipboard, pick the **Copy** button, select **Copy** from the **Edit** pull-down menu, or use the [Ctrl]+[C] key combination. For example, suppose you want to include your 3dshapes drawing as a rendered image in a memo or letter. First, render the drawing to the **Render** window. Next, copy the image to the Clipboard. Once information is on the Clipboard, start a Windows-compatible word processing program. Finally, paste the contents of the Clipboard into the document. See Figure 14-70.

The Clipboard Viewer is used to view the contents of the Clipboard. To open this application, select Clipboard Viewer from the Accessories submenu in the Programs menu in the Windows Start menu. The Local ClipBook is displayed first. To view the Clipboard, select 1 Clipboard from the Window pull-down menu.

Figure 14-70.
Once a rendered
image is copied to
the Clipboard, it can
be pasted into a
word processing
document.

MEMO

To:	Otto Desque
From:	Ima Drafter II
Date:	Thursday, March 14
Subject:	AutoCAD Render

Dear Otto,

Guess what I discovered? I can render an image to a window! Not only that, I can then copy it to the Windows Clipboard. Once it's on the clipboard I can paste it into any document I wish. For example, look how nicely I managed to paste it into this memo. This has the potential to make me more productive, and also more valuable to the design team.

This is probably grounds for a promotion, wouldn't you think? I anxiously await your reply.

NOTE For more information regarding bitmaps, metafiles, and Clipboard graphics, see Chapter 13 and Chapter 24 of this text.

PROFESSIONAL TIP To conserve system memory, clear the contents of the Clipboard when the copied image is no longer needed. To do so, open the Clipboard Viewer, then select <u>D</u>elete from the <u>E</u>dit pull-down menu.

EXERCISE 14-5

❑ Load EX14-4 if it is not already on your screen.
❑ Render a bitmap image to the **Render** window.
❑ Save the bitmap image with the name EX14-5.BMP. Then, copy the image to the Windows Clipboard.
❑ Return to the Accessories menu and activate the Clipboard Viewer. If necessary, use the horizontal and vertical scroll bars to display different portions of your copied bitmap rendering.
❑ If you have a Windows-compatible word processing program, begin a new file and paste the contents of the Clipboard into your document.
❑ When you are finished, clear the contents of the Clipboard and exit the Clipboard Viewer. Do not close the **Render** window or exit AutoCAD.

Render window display options

The **Render** window has options that let you arrange the open display windows. These options are located in the **Window** pull-down menu, Figure 14-71. These options are explained below:

- **Tile.** This menu item arranges the open display windows so they are adjacent to each other. Figure 14-72 shows four tiled bitmap images. Only one window can be active. In Figure 14-72, the Prairie Wind.bmp window is active, as indicated by the highlighted title bar.
- **Cascade.** This menu item arranges the open display windows so they overlap one another, Figure 14-73. As with a tiled display, only one of the open windows can be active at a time.
- **Arrange Icons.** Automatically aligns minimized display windows along the bottom of the **Render** window.
- **Reuse Window.** By default, **Render** opens a new rendering window whenever a new rendering is produced. The **Reuse Window** selection clears any existing image from the active **Render** window and uses the same window for the new rendered image.

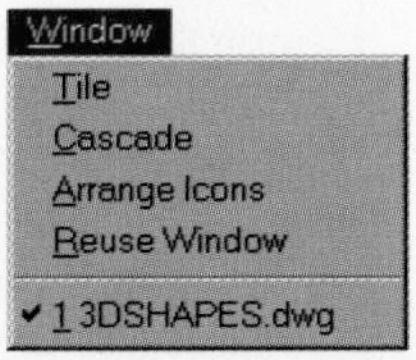

Figure 14-71.
The **Window** pull-down menu of the **Render** window.

Window
<u>T</u>ile
<u>C</u>ascade
<u>A</u>rrange Icons
<u>R</u>euse Window
✓ <u>1</u> 3DSHAPES.dwg

Figure 14-72.
Four images tiled in
the **Render** window.
The active image is
the one with the
highlighted title bar.

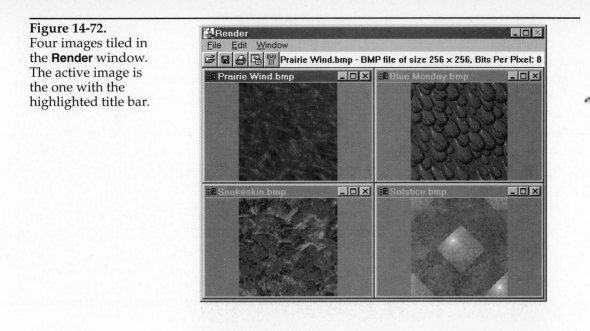

Figure 14-73.
The four images
from Figure 14-72
cascaded.

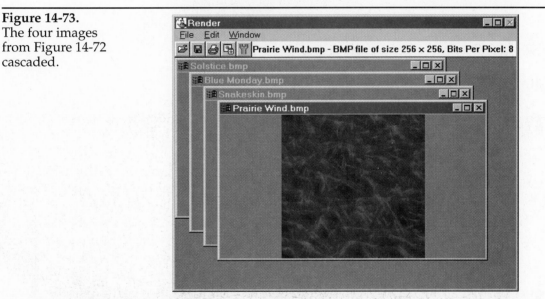

EXERCISE 14-6

❑ Activate the **Render** window and open four bitmap files of your choice from the
Windows folder.

❑ Produce a tiled display similar to that shown in Figure 14-72.

❑ Produce a cascaded display similar to that shown in Figure 14-73.

❑ Minimize each of the display windows to an icon using one of the methods
described in this chapter.

❑ Align the icons at the bottom of the render window with the **Arrange Icons**
option.

❑ Turn on **Reuse Window** and open EX14-5.BMP from the previous exercise.

❑ Maximize each of the icons at the bottom of the render window. Close each open
display window and then close the **Render** window.

The **Windows Render Options** dialog box

You can choose pixel and color resolutions for rendered bitmap images in the **Windows Render Options** dialog box, Figure 14-74. To access this dialog box, pick the **Options** button on the **Render** window toolbar or select **Options...** from the **Render** window **File** pull-down menu. Any changes made in this dialog box do not take effect until you render again.

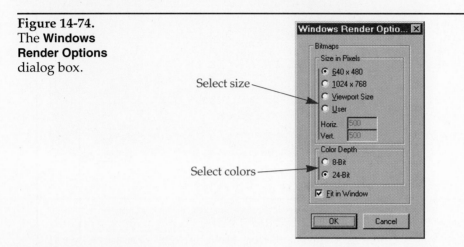

Figure 14-74.
The **Windows Render Options** dialog box.

Select size

Select colors

Bitmap rendering options

You can specify the screen resolution for your rendered image using one of the four radio buttons located in the **Size in Pixels** area of the **Windows Render Options** dialog box. These four radio buttons are explained below:

- **640 × 480.** This is the resolution of a standard VGA display system.
- **1024 × 768.** This is the resolution of many 17" and larger video displays.
- **Viewport Size.** This button sets the size of the bitmap to the size of the **Render** window. The larger the window, the larger the displayed image.
- **User.** This button lets you manually set the horizontal and vertical size of the bitmap. The default values are 500 pixels on both the horizontal and vertical axes. You can set a maximum size of 4096 × 4096 pixels.

Also, notice the **Fit in Window** check box at the bottom of the dialog box. This option is on by default and permits you to scale your bitmap according to the size of the display window. Therefore, the **Fit in Window** option overrides the **Size in Pixels** settings described above. As an example, suppose you have rendered an image at a given resolution and then substantially reduce the size of the **Render** window. It is likely that only a portion of your rendered image is displayed in the reduced window. To display the entire rendered image again while maintaining the correct aspect ratio, return to the **Windows Render Options** dialog box and pick the **Fit in Window** check box. The image is then automatically rescaled to fit inside the smaller window.

In addition to the pixel size options, you can render either an 8-bit or 24-bit image. Select one of the radio buttons in the **Color Depth** area of the **Windows Render Options** dialog box. Even when working on a system set up for 8-bit color display (256 colors), you can still render and save a 24-bit (16.7 million colors) image. When the image is displayed on a system set up for 24-bit color, the image displays in true color.

Printing a rendered image

You can print a rendered bitmap from the **Render** window. Select **Print...** from the **File** pull-down menu or pick the **Print** button on the toolbar. The **Print** dialog box shown in Figure 14-75 appears. The rendered image is displayed in a border that represents the paper size and orientation (portrait or landscape) currently set in the

Figure 14-75.
This **Print** dialog box appears when printing from the **Render** window.

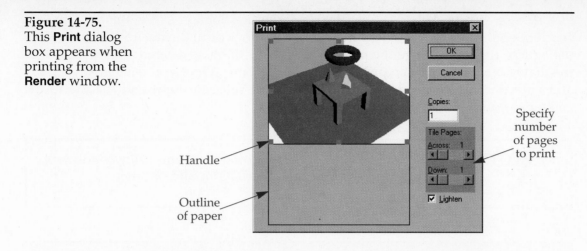

Handle

Outline of paper

Specify number of pages to print

Windows Print Manager (Windows NT), or System Printer (Windows 95). The current system printer is used, regardless of the current printer/plotter in AutoCAD.

In Figure 14-75, the rendered 3dshapes drawing from Exercise 14-1 appears in the dialog box. Notice that the image is located near the top of the outline. The outline represents the paper. Where the image appears in the outline is where it will print on the paper. You can change the position of the printed image by picking anywhere on the image, holding the pick button down, and dragging the image to a new location.

You can also change the size of the printed image. Notice the solid-filled squares around the boundary of the image. These squares are called *handles* and are used to change the size of the image both horizontally and vertically. Handles function much like a hot grip. When you move your cursor over a handle, it changes to a double-headed arrow. Simply hold down the pick button and drag the image to the desired size. If you pick a corner handle, the image is rescaled with the correct aspect ratio.

Once the image is scaled and located as needed, you can set the number of printed copies using the **Copies:** text box. You can also lighten the printed image with the **Lighten** check box. With this box checked, the entire image is printed lighter. Darker colors are lightened more than lighter colors. When you are ready to print, pick the **OK** button.

PROFESSIONAL TIP If you are using a laser or inkjet printer, the **Lighten** feature should be used whenever possible to save toner or ink.

Printing across multiple pages

You can print an image that is larger than the paper using the tiling feature of the **Render** window's **Print** dialog box. *Tiling* is printing an image on more than one sheet of paper. The sheets are then placed together to form the completed image.

The **Tile Pages: Across:** and **Down:** slider bars indicate the number of pages the image will print on. The maximum number of pages that can be tiled depends on the printer you are using. The image can be moved or resized across the tiled pages using the handles.

Printing a rendered image as a PostScript file

You can print a rendered image as a PostScript file. To do so, first double-click the Printers icon in the Windows Control Panel. Set up a new printer and select a PostScript printer. You can select a printer that is not connected to the computer since you are printing to file. In the **Add Printer** wizard, select FILE: as the port.

Next, switch to AutoCAD, set the rendering destination as the **Render** window, and render the image. Then, from the **Render** window, print the image. When the **Print** dialog box appears, change the position, size, and tiling as desired. Pick **OK** to close the dialog box. You are then prompted for a file name. Once you have given a name and path, the file is saved in PostScript format. You can then send the file to the printer as you would any other PostScript file.

NOTE   Refer to the documentation that came with Windows for complete printer setup instructions and options.

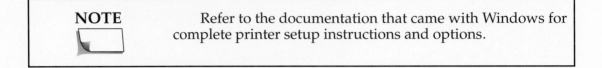

EXERCISE 14-7

❑ If you are connected to a printer, open EX14-1 if it is not currently displayed on your screen.
❑ Set the rendering preferences to render to a window. Without changing any of the printing parameters, print the rendered image.
❑ Turn off **Lighten** in the **Print** dialog box. Print the rendered image again. Compare the two printed images. Which do you prefer?
❑ Return to the **Print** dialog box. Set the slider bars to tile 3 pages across and 3 pages down. Print the multiple page image.

Chapter Test

Write your answers in the spaces provided.

1. Define the following rendering terms:
   Ambient light _____
   Distant light_____
   Point light _____
   Spotlight _____
   Roughness_____
   Diffused light _____

2. When using the **RENDER** command, what is a scene made up of? _____
   _____

3. Which dialog box allows you to specify the shininess and roughness of a surface?
   _____
   _____
   _____

4. What is the relationship between the numerical value of roughness and the size of the highlight on a shiny surface?_____
   _____
   _____
   _____

5. What is the meaning of *altitude* and *azimuth* in the sun angle calculator? _____

_____

_____

_____

6. How must the values of **Hotspot** and **Falloff** relate to each other? _____

_____

_____

_____

7. What types of renderings can produce cast shadows? _____

_____

_____

8. What is *anti-aliasing*? _____

_____

_____

9. Where do you set the option to send the rendering to a file? _____

_____

10. What command allows you to crop an image by pixels and save it as a file? What types of files can be saved? _____

_____

_____

11. What effect does selecting **Smooth Shading** have on the computer model after it has been rendered? _____

_____

_____

12. What are the advantages of rendering to a bitmap? _____

_____

_____

_____

13. To produce a bitmap rendering, how should you configure the **Rendering Preferences** dialog box? _____

_____

_____

14. When working with materials, which attributes allow the use of a bitmap? _____

_____

_____

15. What is the function of a bump map? _____

_____

_____

16. List the steps involved in loading a material, customizing the material, and applying it to a defined surface._____

_____

_____

_____

_____

17. What is the difference between point lights and distant lights when they are applied to a drawing? _____

_____

_____

18. What is *attenuation*? Which lights have this attribute? _____

_____

19. What is *mapping*? _____

_____

_____

20. How do you remove mapping from an object?_____

_____

_____

21. Name the different types of backgrounds that can be applied to a model. _____

_____

_____

22. Name two ways in which landscape objects can be displayed. _____

_____

_____

23. What aspects of a landscape object can be edited? _____

_____

_____

24. What is the function of fog? _____

_____

_____

25. How do you prevent the display of the **Render** dialog box when the **RENDER** command is used? _____

_____

26. What determines the background color of the **Render** window? _____

_____

_____

27. What is the purpose of the Windows Clipboard? What kind of files can be saved using the Clipboard? _____

_____

_____

28. When rendering bitmap images, the **Fit in Window** check box takes precedence over other screen resolution options. (True/False) _____

29. How can you resize the image area in the **Print** dialog box without losing the correct aspect ratio? _____

    _____

30. When printing across multiple pages, what determines the maximum number of pages that can be tiled? _____

    _____

Drawing Problems

1. In this problem, you will draw some basic 3D shapes, place lights in the drawing, and then render it.

    A. Begin a new drawing and name it P14-1.

    B. Draw the following 3D shapes using the layer names and colors as indicated.

Shape	Layer Name	Color
Box	Box	Red
Pyramid	Pyramid	Yellow
Wedge	Wedge	Green
Cone	Cone	Cyan
Dome	Dome	Blue
Dish	Dish	Magenta
Sphere	Sphere	White

    C. Draw the shapes in a circular layout, as shown below. Each shape should be one unit in size.

    D. Place a point light in the center of the objects, 3 units above them.

    E. Place two distant lights as shown in the drawing, having target points in the center of the objects. Light D-1 should be located at $Z = 3$ and light D-2 should be located at $Z = 2$.

    F. Place two spotlights as shown in the figure. Light S-1 has a target of the cone apex and light S-2 has a target of the pyramid apex. Light S-1 should be located at $Z = 2.5$ and light S-2 should be located at $Z = 2$.

    G. Render the drawing.

    H. Save the image as a bitmap file named P14-1.

    I. Save the drawing as P14-1.

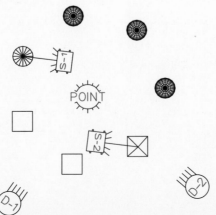

2. Open drawing P14-1. Generate the following scenes and renderings using the light values given. Adjust the values of the spotlights based on their distance from the objects. See the illustration below for proper view orientations.

View name	Scene name	Ambient	Point	D-1	D-2
VIEW1	ONE	.7	2	1	0
VIEW2	TWO	.3	2	0	1
VIEW3	THREE	0	5	1	0

A. Create a material for the sphere with a color of 0.3, reflection of 0.7, and roughness of 0.1. Name it SPHERE1.

B. Create a second material for the sphere named SPHERE2 with a color of 0.7, reflection of 0.3, and roughness of 1.0.

C. Create a third material for the sphere named SPHERE3 with a roughness of 0.7, color of 0.5, and a reflection of 0.5.

D. Set finish SPHERE1 as current and render scene ONE.

E. Set finish SPHERE2 as current and render scene ONE.

F. Set finish SPHERE3 as current and render scene ONE.

G. Save the drawing as P14-2. Create a bitmap and save it as P14-2.

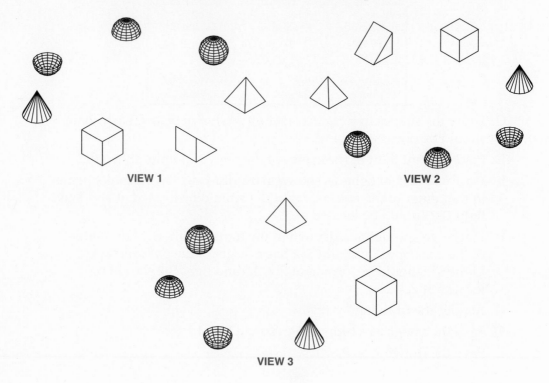

VIEW 1

VIEW 2

VIEW 3

3. This problem enables you to attach materials and textures to some of the objects in your drawing.

   A. Open the drawing P14-2.

   B. Attach materials to the following objects as indicated.

Object	Material
Box	Wood
Pyramid	Marble
Dome	Granite

   C. Give the wood a dark color with narrow rings of a concentric shape. The marble should have a lot of vein color and swirling. The granite should have a highly polished look. Choose your own colors for the marble and granite.

   D. Create a rendering of these three objects only using each of the rendering types.

   E. Create a rendering of all objects using shadows. Create a bitmap and save it as P14-3.

4. This problem will add additional light to a drawing. You will then use the Windows Clipboard and place the drawing in a written document.

   A. Open the drawing P14-1.

   B. Place a new point light directly over the cone and a new distant light to one side and slightly below the "ground." Render the drawing.

   C. Send the drawing to the Windows Clipboard.

   D. Minimize AutoCAD.

   E. Open the Windows Clipboard Viewer to verify the image is there.

   F. Minimize the Windows Clipboard Viewer.

   G. Open your Windows-compatible word processor.

   H. Type the following sentence: This is an example of what AutoCAD can do for documents.

   I. Using the Edit menu of your word processor, paste the rendered drawing into the document. Save the file as P14-4.

5. Open a 3D drawing from a previous chapter. Do the following:

   A. Place two point lights around the model.

   B. Place two distant lights around the model.

   C. Place two spotlights around the model.

   D. Create a solid background for the model using a color that complements the model.

   E. Add three appropriate landscape objects in or around the model. Edit them as needed.

   F. Create three scenes of the model. Choose two different lights for each scene.

   G. Set the ambient light to a value of your choice.

   H. Render each scene once. Change the light attributes to create highlights. Render each scene again.

   I. Render one scene as a .tga file, one as a .tif file, and one as a .gif file.

   J. Replay each image.

   K. Save the drawing as P14-5.

6. Open problem P14-5. Do the following:
    A. Configure AutoCAD to render to a window.
    B. Render each one of the three scenes.
    C. Display the rendered images in a tiled format in the **Render** window.
    D. Display the rendered images in a cascade format in the **Render** window.
    E. Minimize each of the image tiles.
    F. Open a .bmp file from the Windows folder.
    G. Print one of the images centered on a page. Reduce the image size and move it to the upper-right corner. Print it again.
    H. Copy one of the images to the Windows Clipboard.
    I. Paste the Clipboard image into a word processor document.
    J. Print the document.
    K. Save the document as P14-6.

AutoCAD and the Internet

Learning Objectives

After completing this chapter, you will be able to:
- ○ Explain what the Internet is and its basic operation.
- ○ Identify the various components of the Internet.
- ○ Launch a Web browser and access Web sites from AutoCAD.
- ○ Create drawing web format (.dwf) files.
- ○ View a .dwf file using a Web browser.
- ○ Create a simple Web (.html) document containing a .dwf file.
- ○ Attach URLs to an AutoCAD drawing.
- ○ Open and insert drawings from the Web.
- ○ Save drawings to the Web.
- ○ Download the WHIP plug-in.

The Internet started in 1969 as a network consisting of four computers. It now includes literally millions of computers worldwide, connected to one another through the use of telecommunication lines. The Internet is a powerful and versatile communications medium. One of the widest uses of the Internet is for sending and receiving electronic mail. Electronic mail, or *e-mail*, is used to create, send, and receive text messages and other files by telecommunication.

Another widely known application of the Internet is the World Wide Web (WWW). The *World Wide Web*, often called "the Web", uses HyperText Markup Language (HTML) files to provide an intuitive way to access Internet information. The term *hypertext* refers to text that is linked to other information. This information is displayed when the hypertext is picked. These links can be attached to text or images in a document, and are often referred to as *hyperlinks*.

A type of software known as a *Web browser* views the HTML files, providing a graphical user interface for sending and receiving information—much in the same way that Windows provides a graphical user interface to your operating system. Using a Web browser allows even inexperienced computer users to navigate the Internet easily.

AutoCAD Release 14 now incorporates a set of tools called the Internet Utilities to allow you to communicate AutoCAD drawing information using the Web. A drawing can be saved in a format that can be viewed using a Web browser and placed on a Web site. A *Web site* is a collection of HTML documents (which can include text, graphics, and sound files) that others can view on the Internet using a Web browser. Only a Web browser is required, so you can now share drawing information with systems that do not have AutoCAD installed.

Incorporating Internet technologies with the AutoCAD drafting software opens up whole new worlds of possibilities. With geographic and software restrictions removed, you can now communicate your designs to anyone, anywhere in the world.

This communications capability lends itself to creating effective virtual workgroups. A *virtual workgroup* is a group of individuals separated by geographical distances who collaborate on a project through the use of telecommunication technologies, such as e-mail and the World Wide Web. This chapter covers the Internet applications available to AutoCAD Release 14 users.

Getting Connected to the Internet

The Internet uses publicly accessible telecommunications lines to send information between computers. Many large organizations, schools, and governmental agencies are connected using the "T-carrier" digital transmission system, providing extremely fast file transmission speeds. Other Internet users use modems and standard telephone lines to connect to the Internet. A *modem* is a device that **mo**dulates (converts) digital computer information into sounds that can be sent through the telephone service to another computer modem, where they are **dem**odulated, or converted back to computer data.

If your computer system is part of a network, you may already have access to the Internet. To find out, and to learn to access it, ask your network administrator or instructor for assistance. For users who are not connected to a network, a modem and access to a telephone line is one possible solution.

PROFESSIONAL TIP

When selecting a modem, the general guideline is: *faster is better*. Modems slower than 28.8 Kbps (kilobits per second) may take a long time to transmit or receive large files. A 56 Kbps modem is often a better choice when connecting to a standard telephone line.

In many areas, *integrated services digital network* (*ISDN*) lines are available. ISDN lines offer speeds up to 128 Kbps, but require an ISDN adapter instead of a modem. Two levels of service are currently available: the Basic Rate Interface (BRI) for small businesses and individuals, and the Primary Rate Interface (PRI) for larger users. For frequent or heavy Internet use, the initial cost and monthly charge for an ISDN line can be easily recovered in reduced wait times when accessing Web resources or transmitting and receiving files.

The next thing you will need is an *Internet Service Provider* (*ISP*). One good place to look for an ISP is in the telephone book, or you can ask a friend or coworker with Internet access. Online service providers such as CompuServe® and America Online® (AOL) also provide Internet access. The ISP normally provides the software you need to access the Internet, and will often assist you in any minor system configurations needed to get you connected. An ISP typically provides you with e-mail access and your own e-mail address.

The Internet Explorer Web browser is included with the Windows95 and the Windows NT 4.0 operating systems. Both powerful and versatile, Netscape Navigator software is a popular Web browser. Netscape software can be purchased at a local software store, or if you want to try before you buy, you can download an evaluation version. Regardless of which browser you use, it should be the latest version available. Your Web browser should be "Java enabled".

Launching a Web browser

Selecting the **Launch Browser** button in the **Standard** toolbar automatically launches your default Web browser. The **BROWSER** command can also be entered at the Command: prompt. When you pick the toolbar button, the **BROWSER** command uses the current default Uniform Resource Locator. The *Uniform Resource Locator* (*URL*) refers to the location, or address, of a Web file on the Internet. When entered at the keyboard, the **BROWSER** command allows you to enter a specific URL:

BROWSER

Standard
toolbar

Launch Browser

> Command: **BROWSER.⏎**
> Location 〈http://www.autodesk.com/acaduser〉:

The initial default URL takes you to the Autodesk Web site, and specifically to the AutoCAD home page. Here you can find information about AutoCAD and AutoCAD related topics. Figure 15-1 shows the AutoCAD home page as it appears in the Internet Explorer Web browser.

Figure 15-1.
The AutoCAD home page is the initial default URL for the **BROWSER** command. (Autodesk, Inc.)

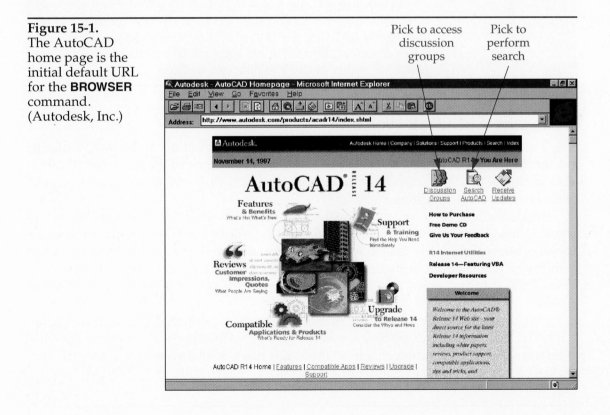

Pick to access discussion groups

Pick to perform search

The default URL is stored in the **INETLOCATION** system variable. You can change this value at the Command: prompt as follows:

Command: **INETLOCATION.⏎**
New value for INETLOCATION ⟨"http://www.autodesk.com/acaduser"⟩:
    HTTP://WWW.CADNET1.COM.⏎
Command:

The default URL should be the location you most frequently access when you start your browser. This may be your own Web site, a client's Web site, or any other site that you frequently access.

As mentioned earlier, the **BROWSER** command launches the default Web browser indicated in your system registry. If you have not installed another Web browser, Microsoft's Internet Explorer is probably your default browser. If Netscape is installed, the option to specify Netscape as your default browser is offered during the installation and configuration process.

PROFESSIONAL TIP

When using both AutoCAD and your Web browser, you can easily move between the two applications by using your task bar or by using the [Alt]+[Tab] keystroke. To see both windows at once, right-click on the task bar and select Cascade Windows or one of the Tile Windows options.

Using the Autodesk Web site

The Autodesk Web site offers a great deal of information and many valuable resources to AutoCAD users of every experience level. Some of the information available includes product support information, reviews, tips and tricks, white papers, and compatible applications.

To most effectively use any Web site, look for a search option. Using a search tool reduces the amount of time required to find the information or document you are looking for. Selecting the Search AutoCAD option on the AutoCAD home page takes you to the page shown in Figure 15-2. Use the toggles to narrow down your search area. Then specify a word or word combination in the edit box and pick the **Submit** button.

The pages that match your area of interest are then displayed, as shown in Figure 15-3. The total number of matches is shown, along with titles of matching pages and brief summary information. Each of the page titles is presented as a link, so that picking a title takes you to that page.

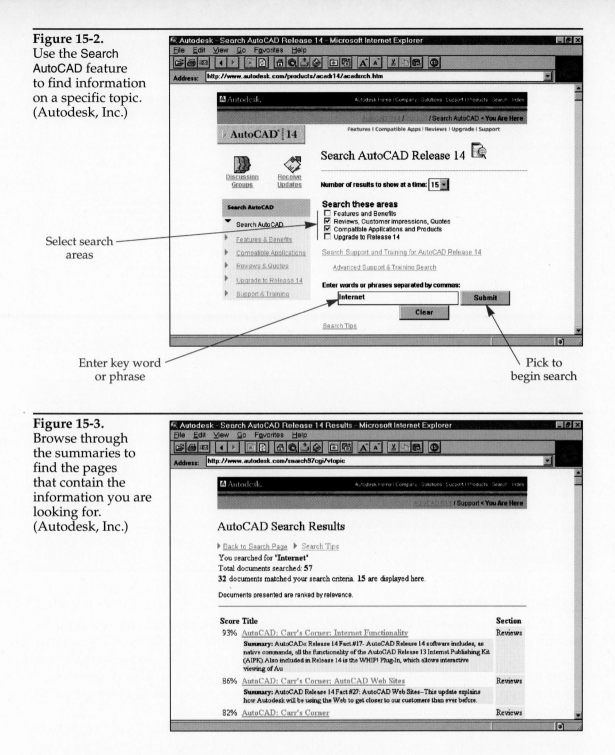

Figure 15-2.
Use the Search AutoCAD feature to find information on a specific topic. (Autodesk, Inc.)

Select search areas

Enter key word or phrase

Pick to begin search

Figure 15-3.
Browse through the summaries to find the pages that contain the information you are looking for. (Autodesk, Inc.)

Another very useful aspect of the Autodesk Web site is the discussion group access. A *discussion group* is an area where you can post messages for others to read. Participants in the discussion groups include many Autodesk staff members and other AutoCAD users (from novice to expert). The discussion groups are divided by area of interest, and include general topics, Internet use, connecting to databases, customization, and more. The main discussion group list is shown in Figure 15-4.

If you have questions regarding an AutoCAD topic, you can get them answered in the discussion group. Likewise, you may be able to answer a question for another user on a topic you understand well.

Netscape Navigator has a built-in discussion group viewer. Picking one of the discussion group links starts the viewer automatically. If you are unable to view the discussion groups, ask your system administrator or instructor for assistance.

Figure 15-4.
The discussion groups represent a valuable resource, enabling you to get specific questions answered by other professionals. (Autodesk, Inc.)

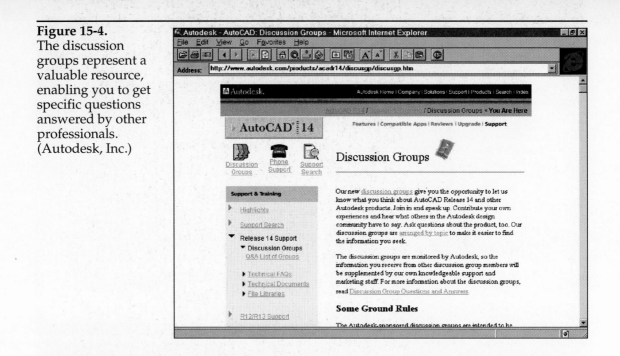

EXERCISE 15-1

❑ Ask your system administrator or instructor for guidance on accessing the Internet. Also, verify that you have a Web browser program available.

❑ In AutoCAD, check the value of the **INETLOCATION** system variable. Set it to http://www.autodesk.com/acaduser if it is currently set to a different value.

❑ In AutoCAD, pick the **Launch Browser** button.

❑ Once you have reached the Autodesk Web site, select the search tool.

❑ From the search window, initiate two or three searches to get a feel for how to find things. After each search is complete, select the browser's Back button to return to the search page.

Creating a Web site

With the variety of powerful Web document creation tools available, creating the documents that constitute a simple Web site is not too difficult. Many new word processing applications, such as Microsoft Word 7, now offer the option to save your document as a Web document. Using this option, you can build a Web page using a familiar tool, and then save the results as an HTML file. In addition, there are many web design companies that can design your site for you.

In order to publish your documents on the World Wide Web, you must have some space available on a Web server. A *Web server* is a computer connected to the Web that transmits files requested by Web browsers. Most ISPs provide a small amount of space on their Web server for clients. You can use this space if it is sufficient, or you may need to contact an Internet host to review your options. An *Internet host* is an organization that provides space on its Web server for a fee.

Many companies obtain a domain name. A *domain name* is a unique identifier for a Web site. For example, the domain name for the main Autodesk Web site is www.Autodesk.com. Domain names must be registered with an organization known as InterNIC, which charges a one-time fee for this registration. Domain names fall within a specific top-level domain, depending on the purpose of the site. Sites that end in .com are commercial sites, .gov indicates a government site, .edu is used for educational organizations, .org is for nonprofit organizations, and .mil is for military sites. An Internet host can assist you in getting your domain name registered.

AutoCAD and its Applications—Advanced

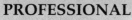

PROFESSIONAL TIP If you are designing your own Web site, you can benefit from the many web design resources available on the World Wide Web. Use your browser's search tool and search the web for a phrase such as HTML Resources. You will find that there are many Web sites dedicated to providing assistance to those learning to create web documents.

EXERCISE 15-2

❑ Use your browser's Internet search tool to look for sites that provide HTML Resources.

The Internet Utilities

Using Web technologies in conjunction with AutoCAD Release 14 provides powerful tools and new options for real-time data communications with clients, vendors, and colleagues. It is now possible to get drawings from, or save them to, a Web site using the Internet Utilities. With Autodesk's *WHIP!*™ plug-in for Netscape or Internet Explorer, drawing files can be viewed and printed within the Web browser.

Creating drawing web format (.dwf) files

AutoCAD Release 14 incorporates a new file type for saving AutoCAD drawings—the .dwf, or *drawing web format*, file. A .dwf file is a highly compressed 2D vector file that can be viewed using a Web browser equipped with Autodesk's WHIP plug-in. A *plug-in* is an external application used as part of your browser program. Getting and setting up the WHIP plug-in are covered later in this section.

Using the **DWFOUT** command in AutoCAD creates .dwf files, or you can use the **EXPORT** command and specify the .dwf format. Using the **DWFOUT** command displays the dialog box shown in Figure 15-5.

The **DWFOUT** command creates a .dwf file using all of the drawing data currently being displayed. Any geometry that is beyond the visible screen area is not included in the .dwf file. Before creating the file, you can set up the available options by picking the **Options...** button. This displays the **DWF Export Options** dialog box, as shown in Figure 15-6.

Figure 15-5.
The **Create DWF File** dialog box is used to create .dwf files.

Pick to set file options

Figure 15-6.
The **DWF Export Options** dialog box allows you to set up the parameters used to create the .dwf file.

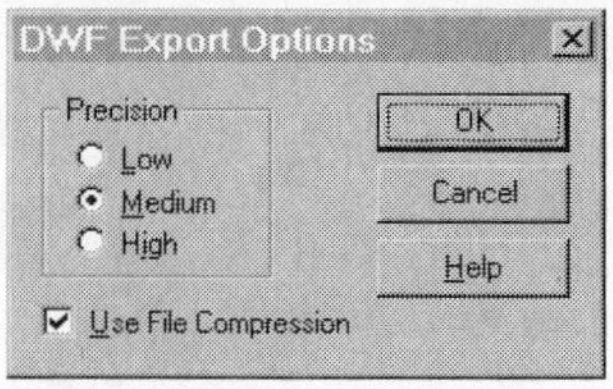

DWF Export Options

Precision
○ Low
● Medium
○ High

☑ Use File Compression

OK
Cancel
Help

The items in the **DWF Export Options** dialog box are primarily associated with controlling the size of the .dwf file. Restrictions in data transmission speed make it desirable to keep file sizes as small as possible. The precision setting controls the number of decimal places used in the .dwf file. **Low** indicates 16 bits, **Medium** is 20 bits, and **High** is 32 bits. The level of precision affects the accuracy of the resulting .dwf file. For smaller drawings with little detail, there is not much difference between these settings. However, with larger drawings that have small details, a higher precision level is best.

Keep in mind that the greater the precision level, the larger the resulting .dwf file. Typically, a low-precision .dwf file can be as small as 1/8 the size of the original .dwg file. Generally speaking, the low-precision setting produces a file that is 40% smaller than medium precision. Medium precision is 30% smaller than high precision. The **Use File Compression** option produces a file size 25% or less of the same file generated without using compression.

The **DWFOUT** command cannot be used in paper space. If multiple viewports exist in model space, the .dwf drawing is created using only the contents of the currently active viewport.

NOTE

The contents of a .dwf file are affected by commands that control the display of geometry on screen, such as **VIEWRES**, **FACETRES**, **DISPSILH**, and **HIDE**. Also, .dwf files are generated using the current AutoCAD graphics screen background color. Rendered objects are not supported, and shaded objects in a .dwf file produce unexpected results.

PROFESSIONAL TIP

TrueType fonts in a drawing file cause the corresponding .dwf file to be very large because the text using these fonts must be tessellated. To help keep .dwf file size as small as possible, use .shx fonts in these drawings.

Loading the **Internet Utilities** menu

The Internet Utilities can be accessed by typing commands at the Command: prompt or picking buttons from the **Internet Utilities** toolbar, Figure 15-7. The **Internet Utilities** toolbar menu is defined in a file named inet.mnu, located in the Support folder under your AutoCAD program directory. If this menu file has been loaded, you can access it through the **Toolbars** dialog box by picking **Toolbars...** from the **View** pulldown menu. From the **Menu Group:** drop-down list, select the menu group named inet. The toolbar name appears in the **Toolbars:** list. Pick the toggle to make the toolbar visible.

If the INET group is not found in the drop-down list, you must first load the menu using the **MENULOAD** command. To use this command, pick **Customize Menus...** from the **Tools** pull-down menu or type MENULOAD at the Command: prompt. In the **Menu**

Figure 15-7.
The **Internet Utilities**
toolbar.

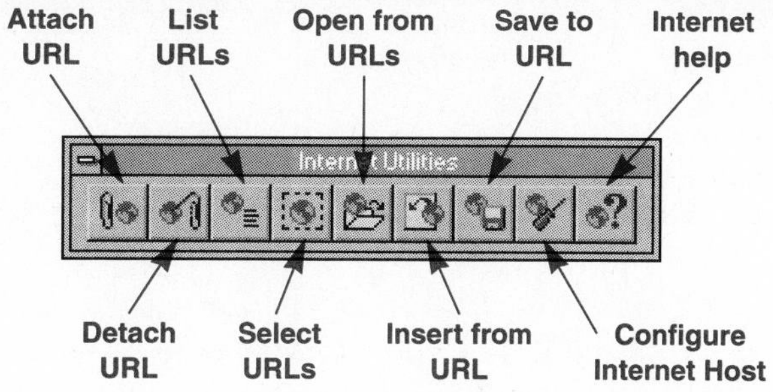

Attach   List   Open from   Save to   Internet
URL   URLs   URLs   URL   help

Detach   Select   Insert from   Configure
URL   URLs   URL   Internet Host

Customization dialog box, pick the **Browse...** button to locate the INET menu in the Support folder then pick **Open**. When you return to the **Menu Customization** dialog box, pick the **Load** button. Now the INET menu group will be visible in the **Toolbars** dialog box and you can display it as described above.

EXERCISE 15-3

❑ Use the **MENULOAD** command to display the **Menu Customization** dialog box.
❑ Select the **Browse...** option, locate the inet.mnu file in the Support folder and double-click on it.
❑ When you return to the **Menu Customization** dialog box, pick **Load**.
❑ If the **Internet Utilities** toolbar is not visible, use the **Toolbars** dialog box to display it.

Using the Attach URL option

A URL, or Uniform Resource Locator, is the address of a document file on the World Wide Web. AutoCAD allows you to attach URL links to areas and objects within a .dwf file. When viewing the resulting .dwf file using the WHIP plug-in, these links can be picked to display other files. The new file can be another Web document or even another .dwf file.

For example, an assembly drawing can be created with each part within the assembly having a link to its detail drawing. Individual parts can be linked directly to a Web page that displays text information such as part numbers, supplier name, and prices.

To attach a URL in a drawing, pick the **Attach URL** button or type ATTACHURL at the Command: prompt. Two options are available: **Area** and **Objects**. The default option, **Objects**, allows you to attach a URL to one or more selected objects. In the resulting .dwf file, picking any of these objects activates the link and displays the new URL. Using the **Objects** option produces the standard Select objects: prompt, and objects can be selected using any available selection method.

```
Command: ATTACHURL↵
URL by (Area/⟨Objects⟩): ↵
Select objects: (select any number of objects)
Select objects: ↵
Enter URL: HTTP://WWW.CADNET1.COM/R14VWG.HTML↵
Command:
```

As indicated previously, the URL can be the address of any web document. This includes text documents, images, sound files, or even another .dwf drawing file. The URL is attached to the object using an area described as the bounding box. A *bounding box* is a nonrotated rectangular area that encompasses an object. As an example, the bounding box for an angled line is shown in Figure 15-8. In the .dwf file, picking anywhere within the bounding box activates the indicated link. This can cause problems if the bounding boxes for objects with differing URLs overlap.

ATTACHURL

Internet Utilities
toolbar

Attach URL

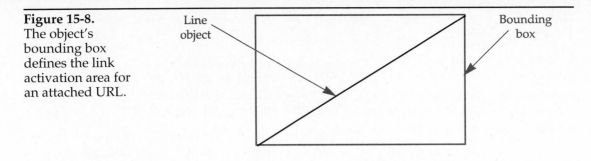

Figure 15-8.
The object's bounding box defines the link activation area for an attached URL.

Line object

Bounding box

The **ATTACHURL** command allows you to attach a URL to a rectangular area of the drawing. The following sequence is used to attach a URL to an area of a drawing:

Command: **ATTACHURL**↵
URL by (Area/⟨Objects⟩): **A**↵
First corner: *(Pick first corner)*
Other corner: *(Pick other corner)*
Enter URL: **HTTP://WWW.CADNET1.COM/R14VWG.HTML**↵
Command:

A red rectangle appears in your drawing to show the defined area. The rectangle is on a new layer named Urllayer. Objects on the Urllayer will show up on your hard copy if the layer is visible when you plot, so you must freeze it or turn it off to suppress the items. However, if Urllayer is not visible when you use **DWFOUT**, then the URLs attached to areas of your drawing are not saved in the .dwf file. Using **ATTACHURL** on an object or area that already has a URL attached updates the URL to the new entry.

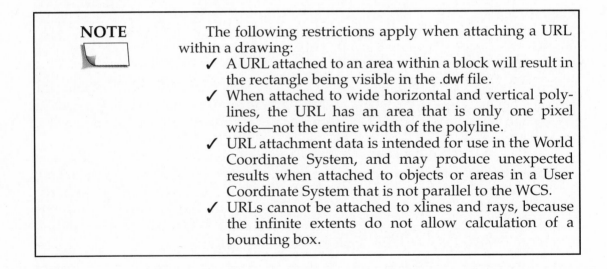

NOTE

The following restrictions apply when attaching a URL within a drawing:
- ✓ A URL attached to an area within a block will result in the rectangle being visible in the .dwf file.
- ✓ When attached to wide horizontal and vertical polylines, the URL has an area that is only one pixel wide—not the entire width of the polyline.
- ✓ URL attachment data is intended for use in the World Coordinate System, and may produce unexpected results when attached to objects or areas in a User Coordinate System that is not parallel to the WCS.
- ✓ URLs cannot be attached to xlines and rays, because the infinite extents do not allow calculation of a bounding box.

AutoCAD and its Applications—Advanced

Detaching a URL

DETACHURL

Internet Utilities
toolbar

Detach URL

The **DETACHURL** command is used to remove a URL attachment from an object or an area in the drawing. Either select the **Detach URL** button from the **Internet Utilities** toolbar or type DETACHURL at the Command: prompt to activate this command. At the Select objects: prompt, you can select objects that have URLs attached, or you can select the rectangles created by the **Area** option of the **ATTACHURL** command. In the following sequence, a selection window is used to pick both an object and an area:

> Command: **DETACHURL**↵
> Select objects: *(pick the first corner of an implied window)*
> Other corner: *(pick the other corner)*
> 7 found
> 5 were filtered out.
> Select objects: ↵
> DetachURL, deleting the Area

All objects that do not have associated URLs are automatically filtered out of the selection set. When an area is removed, a message indicates that the area was deleted. Erasing an area also removes the associated URL link.

PROFESSIONAL TIP
After adding, changing, or deleting URL information, you must update the .dwf file using **DWFOUT** for the changes to take effect.

Listing URLs in a drawing

LISTURL

Internet Utilities
toolbar

List URLs

To determine the URL associated with an object, pick the **List URLs** button from the **Internet Utilities** toolbar or type LISTURL at the Command: prompt. Any number of objects can be selected at the prompt. However, no indication is given with the listing as to which object the specified URL is associated with. The following sequence lists the URLs for three objects selected with an implied window:

> Command: **LISTURL**↵
> Select objects: *(pick the first corner of an implied window)*
> Other corner: *(pick the other corner)*
> 6 found
> 3 were filtered out.
> Select objects: ↵
>   URL for selected object is: http://www.cadnet1.com/index.htm
>   URL for selected object is: http://www.cadnet1.com/index.htm
>   URL for selected object is: http://www.cadnet1.com/index.htm
> Command:

Objects with no URL attachments are automatically filtered out of the selection, and the URLs for the remaining objects are listed.

Identifying objects with URLs

SELECTURAL

Internet Utilities
toolbar

Select URLs

To quickly determine which objects in your drawings have attached URLs, pick the **Select URLs** button from the **Internet Utilities** toolbar or type SELECTURL at the Command: prompt. All objects and areas with attached URLs in the current viewport are selected.

The **SELECTURL** command offers a convenient method to edit all URLs in your drawing simultaneously. For example, to remove all URLs from a drawing, use **SELECTURL** followed by **DETACHURL**. Similarly, all URLs can be changed or listed. Remember that only the objects or areas visible in the active viewport are selected.

❑ Start a new drawing session in AutoCAD. Set your limits to 0,0 and 12,9, then perform a **ZOOM All**. Using the circle command, create a circle at 6,4.5 with a diameter of 3 units.

❑ Use the **ATTACHURL** command to attach a URL to the circle object. Specify a URL of CIRCLE.HTML.

❑ Use the **SELECTURL** command to display linked objects.

❑ View the URL for the selected circle by picking **LISTURL**.

❑ Remove the URL from the circle using **DETACHURL**.

❑ Use the **ATTACHURL** option to attach a new URL to the circle object. Specify a URL of CIRCLE1.HTML.

❑ Using the **DWFOUT** command, export the drawing as EX15-4.DWF and place it in its own directory folder. Save the drawing as EX15-4.DWG.

Configuring the Internet host

An *Internet host* is any computer that has two-way access to other computers on the Internet. While you are connected to the Internet, your computer becomes an Internet host. The **INETCFG** command is used to configure your system to be able to communicate with a remote system that is also connected to the Internet.

INETCFG

Internet Utilities toolbar

Configure Internet Host

To access the **INETCFG** command, pick the **Configure Internet Host** button from the **Internet Utilities** toolbar or type **INETCFG** at the Command: prompt. The **INETCFG** command displays the **Internet Configuration** dialog box, as shown in Figure 15-9.

The login protocols include **FTP Login** and **HTTP Secure Access**. *Login* is the process used to connect to the remote system and gain authorization for file access. *Protocol* is the set of rules and methods of communication between computers.

Figure 15-9.
Use the **Internet Configuration** dialog box to set up your communications with the remote system.

Enter user name and password for accessing secured areas

Type of connection

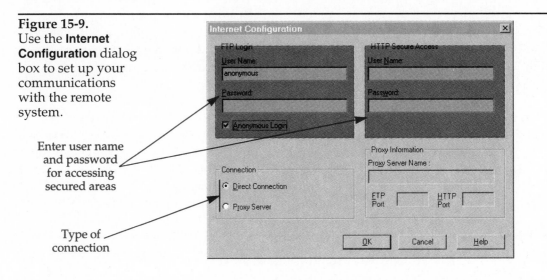

FTP login

Transmission Control Protocol/Internet Protocol (*TCP/IP*) is the backbone of all Internet communication. *File Transfer Protocol* (*FTP*) is one of the protocols that is part of TCP/IP. Using FTP, you can send and receive files between your system and your Web server. Additionally, FTP allows you to copy, move, rename, and delete files and folders found on the Web server.

Areas on a Web server that are not secure may allow an *anonymous login*. Picking the **Anonymous Login** toggle in the **Internet Configuration** dialog box sets the user name to Anonymous and uses no password. Accessing a secure area requires entry of the appropriate user name and password. Enter your user name in the **User Name:**

text box and your password in the **Password:** box. Note that your password is not saved across AutoCAD sessions. This prevents unauthorized access to your FTP site. In a subsequent AutoCAD session, if you have not previously entered the password before attempting to access a secure FTP site, the password entry is requested.

HTTP secure access

HyperText Transfer Protocol (*HTTP*) is the basis for World Wide Web documents. Web sites, or even individual Web documents, can also implement security measures to prevent unauthorized access to sensitive files. If the user name and password are not entered in the **Internet Configuration** dialog box, you will need to enter them in the **User Authentication** dialog box for each login attempt for secure HTTP access. However, if you regularly access a specific site and want the login to occur automatically, the user name and password can be specified in the **Internet Configuration** dialog box. Similar to the FTP login parameters, the password is not remembered between AutoCAD sessions.

Connection

If you connect to the Internet through a modem and an ISP, you need to select the **Direct Connection** option. Selecting **Direct Connection** disables the **Proxy Information** settings area, because a direct connection does not use a proxy server. Generally speaking, a *gateway* is a network computer that acts as an entrance to another network. A *proxy server* is a computer that acts as a gateway between the company's internal intranet and the Internet. An *intranet* is a network of computers within a company or enterprise.

A proxy server allows implementation of a firewall. *Firewalls* provide access to the Internet for those operating within the network, or from behind the firewall. However, the firewall restricts outside access to files or systems within the intranet. If you have questions regarding whether you need to access a proxy server, ask your instructor or system administrator.

Proxy information

If you are using a proxy server, the **Proxy Information** area needs to be completed. Your instructor or network system administrator should be able to provide you with the proxy server name and port numbers.

> **NOTE** The user name and password fields provided in the **User Authentication** dialog box are only for file access on remote servers. Secure access through a proxy server (firewall) is not supported.

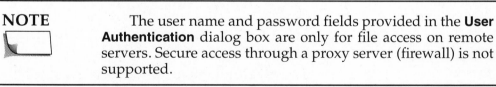

EXERCISE 15-5

- ❏ Ask your system administrator or instructor for assistance as needed for each of the items in this exercise.
- ❏ Use the **INETCFG** command to display the **Internet Configuration** dialog box.
- ❏ Enter the appropriate FTP login information required for your FTP site, or check **Anonymous Login** if allowed by your Internet server.
- ❏ Enter the appropriate HTTP login information required to log into your Web site.
- ❏ If the sites you are logging into are part of your company's official Web site, you should set up a separate folder to work in where your activities cannot cause problems with any existing files.
- ❏ If your Internet access is through a proxy server, complete the **Proxy Information** section.

Opening a drawing from the Web

If you know the URL of a drawing file on the Web, you can use the **OPENURL** command to open the file locally. AutoCAD then copies the drawing to a temporary file on your hard disk and loads it into the drawing editor. Using the **QSAVE** command saves any changes to the drawing in the local version of the file.

OPENURL

Internet Utilities toolbar

Open from URL

The **OPENURL** command can be accessed by selecting the **Open from URL** button from the **Internet Utilities** toolbar, or by typing OPENURL at the Command: prompt. The **OPENURL** command displays the **Open DWG from URL** dialog box, shown in Figure 15-10.

When specifying the URL of the file in the **Open DWG from URL:** text box, it is important to enter the URL accurately using acceptable syntax. Acceptable syntax examples are shown here:

> http://*servername/pathname/filename*.dwg
> ftp://*servername/pathname/filename*.dwg
> file:///*drive:/pathname/filename*.dwg
> file:///*drive:/pathname/filename*.dwg
> file://*localPC\pathname\filename*.dwg
> file:////*localPC/pathname/filename*.dwg
> file://localhost/*drive:/pathname/filename*.dwg
> file://localhost/*drive:/pathname/filename*.dwg

In order to open a drawing from a URL, you must have permission to access the requested file. This typically involves entering a user name and password when logging onto the remote server. Select the **Options...** button in the **Open DWG from URL** dialog box to display the **Internet Configuration** dialog box. Once you specify a suitable URL and pick **Open**, the computer attempts to complete the requested file transfer. The **Remote Transfer in Progress** dialog box shows the status of the transfer.

Figure 15-10.
The **Open DWG from URL** dialog box allows drawings to be opened from a file on the World Wide Web.

PROFESSIONAL TIP

When copying files from the Internet to your local system, the drawings are placed in your temporary file directory, typically C:\Temp. These files are not automatically removed, so it is important to periodically check the temporary directory and remove unneeded files.

AutoCAD does not check to confirm that an Internet connection exists when you attempt a transfer. If you are not connected to the Internet when attempting to connect to a URL, the **Transfer Status** dialog box will display 0 bytes and 0% complete until you pick **Cancel**, or the time out occurs. The term *time out* refers to a process being canceled because no progress is detected after a given amount of time.

Inserting a drawing from a URL

It is possible to insert a drawing from the Web into the current drawing. This is similar to opening a drawing from the Web. The drawing is inserted using the **INSERTURL** command.

The **INSERTURL** command is accessed by picking the **Insert from URL** button from the **Internet Utilities** toolbar or by typing INSERTURL at the Command: prompt. The **Insert DWG from URL** dialog box is identical to the **Open DWG from URL** dialog box. After the drawing is downloaded, AutoCAD initiates the **INSERT** command to bring in the new drawing. As with other applications of the **INSERT** command, an insertion point, scale factor, and rotation angle must be specified. The drawing then becomes a locally defined block.

Saving a drawing to the Web

The **SAVEURL** command is accessed by picking the **Save to URL** button from the **Internet Utilities** toolbar or by typing SAVEURL at the Command: prompt. This command displays the **Save DWG to URL** dialog box and allows you to save drawings directly to a Web site. Again, the **Remote Transfer in Progress** dialog box indicates the status of the transfer. The URL for saving a drawing must be specified as an FTP address using the following syntax:

ftp://*servername/pathname/filename*.dwg

PROFESSIONAL TIP

If you try to open, insert, or save a drawing on your Internet server and AutoCAD reports that it is unable to connect, you may have forgotten to reset your user name and password in the **Internet Configuration** dialog box. The password data is not saved between AutoCAD sessions. To correct this, pick the **Options...** button in the URL entry dialog box.

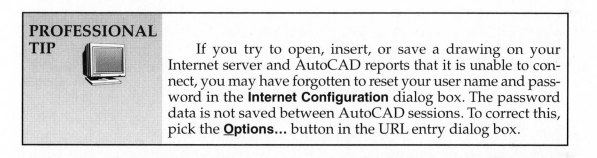

EXERCISE 15-6

❑ Open the drawing EX15-4 in AutoCAD.
❑ Use the **SAVEURL** command to save the file to an appropriate location on your Internet server.
❑ Start a new drawing session. Now use **OPENURL** to open the drawing that you just saved to a URL.
❑ Start a new drawing session again. This time, use **INSERTURL** to insert the drawing into the current drawing. Save this drawing as EX15-6.

Getting the WHIP Plug-In

In order to continue in this chapter, you will need the capability to view .dwf files. To view .dwf files, you will need the WHIP plug-in. The WHIP plug-in is freely available on the Autodesk Web site. Release 1 of WHIP is not fully functional with AutoCAD R14, so you must install Release 2 or later. To download the WHIP plug-in, log onto this URL:

http://www.autodesk.com/prodsol/ddraft/products/whip/reg2.htm

Follow the links to the latest version of WHIP that is compatible with AutoCAD Release 14. You may be required to electronically "sign" a license agreement, Figure 15-11. Then you can freely download the required files. Be certain to review the system requirements and installation instructions.

Figure 15-11.
Before downloading
the WHIP plug-in,
you must complete
a product
registration form.
(Autodesk, Inc.)

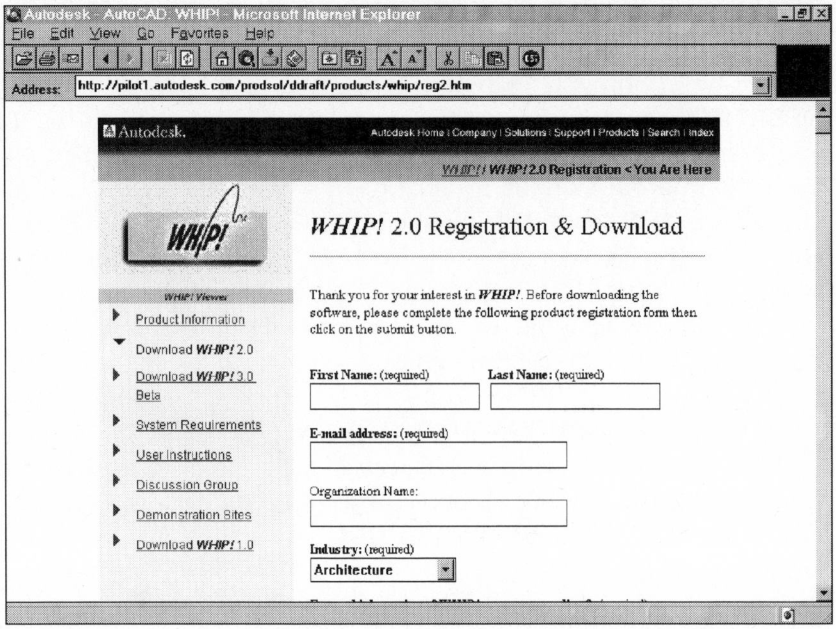

You will be asked to specify the location where the downloaded file should be placed. The WHIP 2 plug-in is about 3.5 Mb in size and can take an hour or more to download using a 28.8 Kbps modem. If you are connected to the Internet with a "T-carrier" or ISDN line, the download can be completed in a matter of minutes.

The name of the file being downloaded is displayed in the dialog box showing the download progress. When the download is complete, exit from your browser and execute the downloaded file. You can use Explorer to find the file and double-click on it, or you can select Run... from the Start menu and Browse... to find the file.

The plug-in is activated after the installation procedure is complete. The next time you open a Web document that contains a .dwf file, the WHIP plug-in is automatically started for viewing the file.

Publishing a .dwf file on the Web

Primary benefits of .dwf files include greatly reduced file size and extended viewing capabilities. The reduced file size provides for much faster file transfer. The viewing capabilities are extended because the drawing can be viewed or printed from computers that do not have access to AutoCAD. Using a Web browser with the WHIP plug-in, anyone can view these drawings. There is currently no way to edit this file type—so you can keep your data secure.

In order to make a .dwf file easily accessible on the Web, it is best to place it within an HTML document. It is not within the scope of this text to detail the use of HTML, nor to cover the use of HTML editors. In this example, minimal HTML coding is included and a simple text editor is used to create the HTML document.

The following HTML code creates a very simple HTML document, showing only a title and a text heading. To follow along with this example, create a text file using this code and save it as SAMPLE1.HTML.

```
<html>
<head>
   <title>Title: A Simple HTML Document Example</title>
</head>
<body bgcolor="ffffff">
<h2>This page demonstrates the use of a .dwf file</h2>
</body>
</html>
```

AutoCAD and its Applications—Advanced

Viewed in Internet Explorer, this HTML code produces the results shown in Figure 15-12.

Also in this example, a file named example1.dwf has been created, and exists in the same folder as the HTML document. To incorporate the .dwf file into the document, add the following new code (the existing code is shown in red):

```
<html>
<head>
   <title>Title: A Simple HTML Document Example</title>
</head>
<body bgcolor="ffffff">
<h2>This page demonstrates the use of a .dwf file</h2>
<OBJECT width=420
   height=315
   classid="clsid:B2BE75F3-9197-11CF-ABF4-08000996E931"
   codebase="ftp://ftp.autodesk.com/pub/autocad/plugin/whip.cab#version=2,0,0,0"
>
<PARAM name="Filename"
   value="EXAMPLE1.dwf"
>
<EMBED SRC="EXAMPLE1.dwf"
   PLUGINSPAGE="http://www.autodesk.com/products/autocad/whip/whip.htm"
   WIDTH=420
   HEIGHT=315
   name="EXAMPLE1"
>
</OBJECT>
</body>
</html>
```

Figure 15-12.
A simple HTML document viewed in the Internet Explorer.

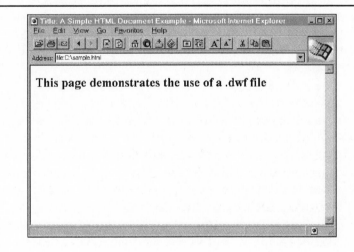

When viewed using Netscape Navigator, this HTML code appears as shown in Figure 15-13. To reproduce these results using your own .dwf file, follow these steps:
1. Create your drawing and export the .dwf file.
2. Create an HTML document using the sample code shown above in a normal text file (save it using the .html file extension), substituting the name of your .dwf file for each occurrence of **EXAMPLE1**.
3. For increased functionality, place a copy of the original drawing file in the same location as the .dwf and .html files.

Figure 15-13.
The .dwf file is now displayed in the Netscape Navigator.

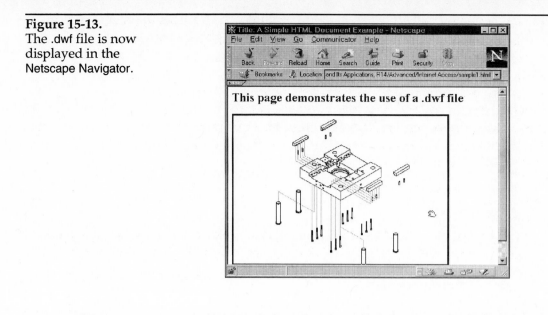

This page demonstrates the use of a .dwf file

NOTE   Unless your Web site is secure, all information posted there will be fully accessible to anyone with a Web browser. Do not post any confidential or sensitive information until appropriate security measures are in place.

Using the WHIP plug-in

When viewing a .dwf drawing file using the WHIP plug-in from your browser, you have several options for changing the display. To display the WHIP menu, right-click while the cursor is within the display area of the .dwf drawing. The WHIP menu is shown in Figure 15-14. The following options are available:

- **Pan.** Just like AutoCAD's realtime pan feature, allows you to slide into a new position.
- **Zoom.** Works like AutoCAD's realtime zoom.
- **Zoom Window.** Zooms to display the contents of a user-defined rectangle.
- **Named Views.** Displays the **Named View** dialog box, where any defined view can be restored.
- **Full View.** Fills the browser window with the .dwf drawing file.
- **Highlight URLs.** All URL links in the .dwf drawing are displayed.
- **Print.** Sends the current view of the drawing to the system printer.
- **Save As.** Allows the .dwf file to be saved locally. The current view can also be saved as a .bmp file. If a .dwg file exists in the same location as the .dwf file and you have appropriate permissions, you can save as a .dwg file.

Figure 15-14.
The **WHIP** menu is displayed by right-clicking in a .dwf drawing display area.

✔ Pan
Zoom
Zoom to Rectangle
Fit to Window
Named Views...
Full View

Highlight URLs
Print...
Save As...

About WHIP!...

Back
Forward

- **About Whip!.** Provides a dialog box that identifies the version of WHIP you are using. Also provides the URL for the Autodesk Web site, as well as information about the .dwf file you are viewing.
- **Back.** Works like the Back button in your browser.
- **Forward.** Works like the Forward button in your browser.

While viewing a .dwf file, the cursor changes to the familiar hand with an extended index finger when it is over a link. These links may display other drawings or Web documents, show animations, play sounds, or provide downloadable files. The possibilities are almost endless.

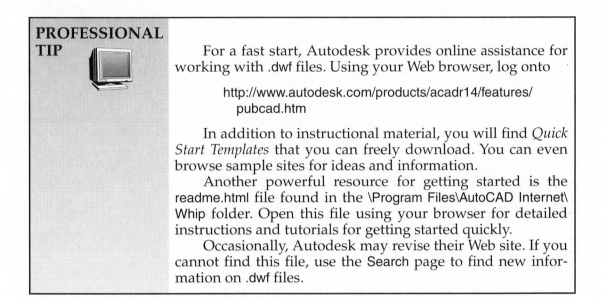

PROFESSIONAL TIP

For a fast start, Autodesk provides online assistance for working with .dwf files. Using your Web browser, log onto

http://www.autodesk.com/products/acadr14/features/ pubcad.htm

In addition to instructional material, you will find *Quick Start Templates* that you can freely download. You can even browse sample sites for ideas and information.

Another powerful resource for getting started is the readme.html file found in the \Program Files\AutoCAD Internet\ Whip folder. Open this file using your browser for detailed instructions and tutorials for getting started quickly.

Occasionally, Autodesk may revise their Web site. If you cannot find this file, use the Search page to find new information on .dwf files.

EXERCISE 15-7

❑ Open Notepad or a similar text editor. Create a document using the following HTML code:

```
<html>
<head>
   <title>Exercise 15-4</title>
</head>
<body>
<h2>This circle has a diameter of 3.0 units.</h2>
</body>
</html>
```

❑ Save the text file in the same folder where the ex15-4.dwf file was saved. Name the text file CIRCLE1.HTML.
❑ Open your browser, then open Windows Explorer. Using Windows Explorer, find ex15-4.dwf, then drag and drop it into your browser window. It should appear in the browser window as a drawing.
❑ Remember that in Exercise 15-4, you attached the URL CIRCLE1.HTML to the circle. Point at the circle and you will see by the change in your cursor that the circle contains a hyperlink. Pick the circle to activate the link.
❑ Now the CIRCLE1.HTML file is displayed in the browser window. You can use your browser's Back button to return to the .dwf file.
❑ Consider the possible applications of linking Web documents to objects in a drawing to provide more detailed information to those viewing the drawings.

INETHELP

Internet Utilities
toolbar

Internet Help

Internet utilities help

The **Internet Help** button in the **Internet Utilities** toolbar accesses the **AutoCAD Internet Utilities** help window. This window can also be accessed by typing INETHELP at the Command: prompt. This is a very useful resource, especially as you first begin exploring the Internet capabilities of AutoCAD.

Virtual Workgroups and Shared Designs on the Web

Not long ago, the only feasible way to share a drawing with someone who did not have AutoCAD software was to plot a hard copy and send the drawing. But now, because the person viewing your drawings doesn't need access to AutoCAD, you can share your designs with almost anyone. You can allow existing and potential customers to view your drawings and designs while visiting your Web site. Anyone with a WHIP-enabled browser and the required permission can view your .dwf drawings.

Using overnight delivery could mean two or three days wait time on getting customer feedback on proposed design changes. Using Web technologies, you can make the drawings available anywhere in the world within minutes, and receive the revised drawings or even an approval on the same day.

Another natural development from these technologies is the advent of effective virtual workgroups. Imagine having a collaborative design team where the members are hundreds of miles away from each other, yet are able to view the same drawing at the same time while having a virtual meeting via conference call (or even using video-conferencing capabilities).

Chapter Test

Write your answers in the spaces provided.

1. What are the two most widely used applications of the Internet? _____
_____
_____

2. What is the name of the software used to view documents on the World Wide Web? _____
_____

3. What is the minimum recommended modem speed for Internet work? _____
_____

4. What does *ISP* stand for? _____
_____

5. What AutoCAD command can be used to launch your default Web browser software? _____

6. What does the **INETLOCATION** system variable control? _____
_____

7. A computer that transmits files requested by Web browsers is called a _____
_____

8. Define the term *Internet host*. _____
_____
_____

9. What does *HTML* stand for? _____

10. What is the file extension of a compact, 2D version of a drawing created for viewing by a Web browser? _____

11. In order to view the files described in Question 10, your browser must be equipped with: _____
_____

12. The **DWFOUT** command creates a file using what portion of a drawing? _____
_____

13. What is the name and location of the menu that contains the Internet Utilities? _____

14. What command is used to access the menu file referenced in Question 13? _____
_____

15. What does URL stand for and to what does it refer? _____
_____
_____

16. What simple security measure is used in the Internet configuration to help prevent unauthorized access to your Internet files? _____
_____
_____

17. What version of the WHIP plug-in must be used with AutoCAD Release 14? ____

_____

18. What is a *virtual workgroup*? _____

_____

_____

Problems

1. Open an existing drawing. Use the **ATTACHURL** option and attach two URLs to components or areas in the drawing. Select components or areas that you can generate a few lines of text information about. Specify the new URLs to be P15-1A.HTML and P15-1B.HTML. Save the drawing as a .dwf file named P15-1.

2. Create two .html documents using Notepad (or another text editor) as follows, and place them in the same directory as P15-1.DWF:

        <html>
        <head>
           <title>Chapter 15 DWF Links Problem</title>
        </head>
        <body>
        <h2>
        (Write one or two lines of information about the component or area in this section of the document.)
        </h2>
        </body>
        </html>

3. Use your text editor to create an .html document named P15.HTML using guidelines and examples in this chapter, and embed the .dwf file in the .html document. Save the document as P15.HTML. Use your Web browser to open P15.html. Pick the links and ensure that all links work properly.

Introduction to the AutoCAD SQL Environment (ASE)

When creating an AutoCAD drawing, you are actually creating a very powerful graphical database. This database can be linked to other database software applications to use the data from the drawing in a variety of ways. The *AutoCAD SQL Extension* (*ASE*) provides a means to freely exchange and update information between AutoCAD drawings and other database applications. *Structured Query Language* (also called *SQL* or *Sequel*) is the language used to manage and exchange data between database applications. This chapter introduces you to the use of ASE for maximizing the functionality of your AutoCAD drawings.

What Is a Database?

A database is a collection of information with contents that can be easily accessed, managed, and updated. The information stored in many databases represents large collections of data records or files such as inventories, employee records, and customer files. Modern databases are most often stored in computer files. There are many different software programs, called *database management systems* (*DBMS*), used to create, edit, and manage these databases. Most DBMS applications provide capabilities such as quick retrieval of files, report generation, and even the capability to freely exchange information with other software programs.

Two popular DBMS applications include Borland's dBase and Microsoft Access. AutoCAD is another very powerful database management system. With many DBMS programs, records are created and managed by entering text information in specific locations. These locations are called fields. The interface for these applications is often a set of rows and columns, where each row is a record and each column within a record represents a specific field. The term *field* refers to a data position within a record designed to hold a specific type of data. For example, the table in Figure 16-1 represents a portion of an employee record database. Each row represents a single record, and each column represents a field within the record.

An AutoCAD drawing file is also a database. It stores a collection of graphical information that makes up the drawing. In the AutoCAD database, each record contains the information needed to define a single object, such as a line, arc, circle, or block. For example, a line object is defined by starting and ending points, as well as other pertinent data such as color, layer, and linetype.

Instead of using a table with rows and columns, the interface for creating and editing an AutoCAD database is the drawing editor. Using ASE, an AutoCAD database can be linked to an outside database. This establishes an information pool that can be edited and updated by either AutoCAD or the external database application.

Linked database applications

There are many applications for linking drawings to outside databases. One very common application in industry is in the area of facilities management. *Facilities management* involves the management of buildings, furnishings, equipment, and resources.

An effective facilities management system maintains a record of all physical assets of a company. This record helps the company use existing resources effectively by reducing the number of unnecessary purchases. The records of personnel, physical assets, budgets, and company growth plans can be combined and used to control spending and ensure that the needs of the company are met.

Most companies maintain floor plans in CAD, and also maintain conventional database records of equipment and furnishings. Changes in these assets need to be entered into two different systems. When the conventional data is linked directly to the graphic data using ASE, changes in one database are automatically applied to the other. Therefore, changes to the database are reflected in the drawing, and the database records are updated if the drawing is edited.

The real power of ASE is the capability it gives a designer or planner to organize spatial information sources by linking AutoCAD data directly to related textual data. This streamlines the process of generating reports and plans regarding space inventory, furniture and equipment inventories, and asset deployment. Equipment and furniture can be tracked when it is moved from one location to another. Any physical asset can be instantly located whenever it is needed.

Database File Structure

The terminology used to describe the components in a database file can be confusing at first. Also, the appearance of database information used by ASE may not appear in an AutoCAD dialog box as you expected. This can be confusing as well. Therefore, read this section carefully. When you understand the nature of a database table, working with ASE becomes much easier.

Sample database layouts

In the simplest form, a database is a list of items. This list usually appears in a table. A *table* is data arranged in rows and columns. A *row* is a horizontal group of entries. A *column* is a vertical group of entries. A table based on the employee.dbf file is shown in Figure 16-1. This file is one of three sample database files included with AutoCAD, and can be used to help you gain an understanding of ASE. In this example, the row across the top of the table contains the name of each column, such as LAST_NAME, FIRST_NAME, and TITLE. The column name indicates the name of the field for the information found in that column.

Figure 16-1.
Many databases can be represented as tables, where each row is a record, and each column is a field.

Employee.dbf						
EMP_ID	LAST_NAME	FIRST_NAME	DEPT	TITLE	ROOM	EXT
1000	Meredith	Dave	Sales	V.P.	101	8600
1001	Williams	Janice	Sales	Western Region Mgr.	102	8601
1003	Smith	Jill	Sales	Central Region Mgr.	104	8603
1004	Nelson	Kirk	Sales	Canadian Sales Mgr.	109	8640
1005	Clark	Karl	Sales	Educational Sales Mgr.	106	8605

Database file components

Notice in Figure 16-2 that an entry in a row of the employee table begins with the EMP_ID number. Six additional items complete the row. A row is also called a *record*. Each column represents a specific element, or field, within the record. For example, LAST_NAME, FIRST_NAME, and DEPT columns define fields within each record. See Figure 16-3.

A database table usually has a key. A *key* is a column in the table used to identify different rows in the table. The key is used as a search option. For example, the key

Figure 16-2.
A row is an element or entry in a table.

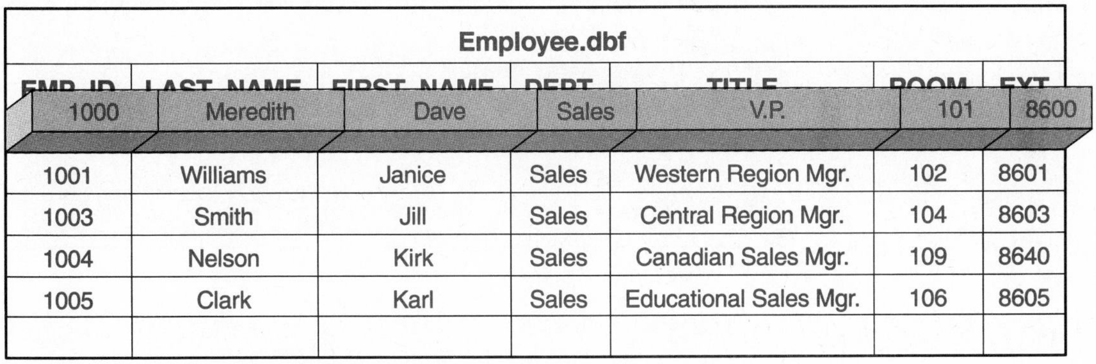

Employee.dbf						
EMP_ID	LAST_NAME	FIRST_NAME	DEPT	TITLE	ROOM	EXT
1000	Meredith	Dave	Sales	V.P.	101	8600
1001	Williams	Janice	Sales	Western Region Mgr.	102	8601
1003	Smith	Jill	Sales	Central Region Mgr.	104	8603
1004	Nelson	Kirk	Sales	Canadian Sales Mgr.	109	8640
1005	Clark	Karl	Sales	Educational Sales Mgr.	106	8605

Figure 16-3.
A column contains an element of the row.

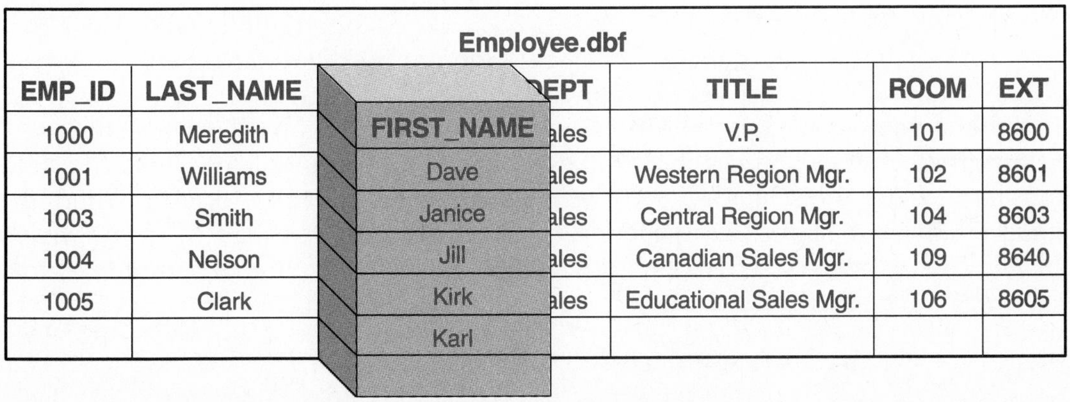

Employee.dbf						
EMP_ID	LAST_NAME	FIRST_NAME	DEPT	TITLE	ROOM	EXT
1000	Meredith		Sales	V.P.	101	8600
1001	Williams	Dave	Sales	Western Region Mgr.	102	8601
1003	Smith	Janice	Sales	Central Region Mgr.	104	8603
1004	Nelson	Jill	Sales	Canadian Sales Mgr.	109	8640
1005	Clark	Kirk	Sales	Educational Sales Mgr.	106	8605
		Karl				

for a sales projection table may be the MONTH column. The key can then be used to identify all of the sales projections for a certain month, such as February (the FEBRUARY row).

If more than one row can have the same value for each column, two or more columns can be specified as keys. This is called a *compound key*. A compound key allows a search to be more selective.

Database rows displayed in ASE

When working with ASE, you are most often using the information contained in a row. You can view the information, edit it, and link it to a graphic entity in your drawing. However, when you see a row displayed in a dialog box in AutoCAD, it does not appear horizontally. It is displayed vertically in what looks like a column. See Figure 16-4. This is an example of the **Rows** dialog box you will be working with later.

Look at the capitalized items on the left side of the list box. They may seem like different rows in a table. However, they are actually column names. The values after the I symbol are the entries in that column. Compare the information in Figure 16-4 with that in Figure 16-2.

Figure 16-4.
Row elements are listed vertically in the **Rows** dialog box.

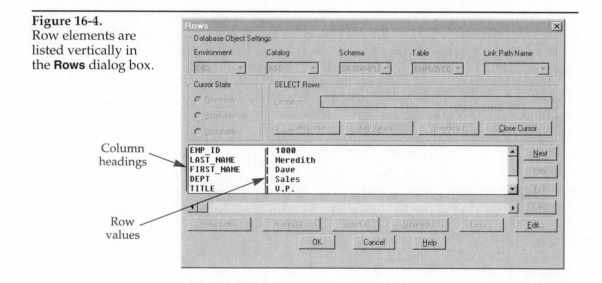

Getting Started with ASE

Now that you are familiar with the meaning and structure of databases and their files, you can develop an understanding of how the various components of databases and AutoCAD fit together. Figure 16-5 illustrates the relationship of the DBMS, database files, and tables.

AutoCAD Release 14 uses SQL2. *SQL2* is a set of international standards that make up for some of the deficiencies in the original SQL standard. SQL uses databases and tables. SQL2 uses environments, catalogs, and schema. The *environment* refers to the database management system, the databases it can access, and the users and programs that can access the databases. The SQL2 *catalog* is the directory path name that locates the schemas, and a *schema* is the subdirectory location where the database tables are stored. Each catalog must have a schema called the *information schema*. This schema describes the other schemas in the catalog and the tables that each schema contains.

Figure 16-5.
The relationship of
the DBMS, database
files, and tables.

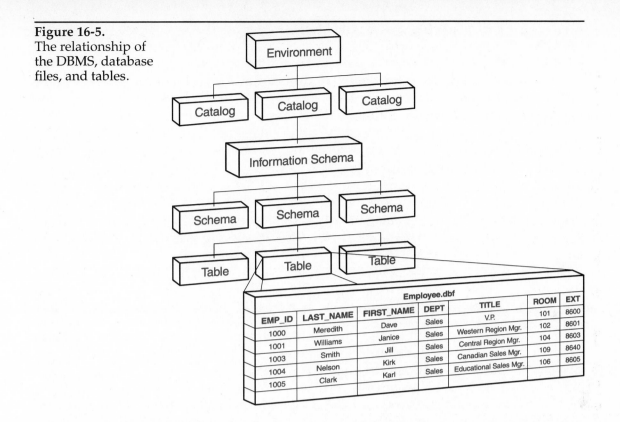

		Employee.dbf					
EMP_ID	LAST_NAME	FIRST_NAME	DEPT	TITLE		ROOM	EXT
1000	Meredith	Dave	Sales	V.P.		101	8600
1001	Williams	Janice	Sales	Western Region Mgr.		102	8601
1003	Smith	Jill	Sales	Central Region Mgr.		104	8603
1004	Nelson	Kirk	Sales	Canadian Sales Mgr.		109	8640
1005	Clark	Karl	Sales	Educational Sales Mgr.		106	8605

Making backup copies of the database tutorial files

Always make backup copies of database files before using them with ASE. The ASE commands can alter the content of the database files. Before you begin working through this tutorial, make copies of the following files:

    C:\Program Files\AutoCAD R14\Sample\asesmp.dwg
    C:\Program Files\AutoCAD R14\Sample\Dbf\computer.dbf
    C:\Program Files\AutoCAD R14\Sample\Dbf\employee.dbf
    C:\Program Files\AutoCAD R14\Sample\Dbf\inventry.dbf

These locations are based on AutoCAD being installed on the C: drive using the Release 14 defaults. When you want to restore the original files, simply copy them back to the original locations.

The **External Database Configuration** utility

Before you can get started using a database application with AutoCAD, it is necessary to specify which databases you are using and enter the locations of the database tables. As discussed earlier, the database connection requires you to specify an environment, a catalog, and a schema. If you selected a full installation when installing AutoCAD (or a custom installation with External Databases selected), AutoCAD is automatically configured for connecting to the dBASE III DBMS and the included sample .dbf files. No further setup is required unless you wish to connect to a different database management system. The examples in this chapter use the sample dBASE III files.

To run the **External Database Configuration** utility, select the Start button on your task bar, pick Programs, and select the External Database Configuration option from the AutoCAD R14 group. This displays the **External Database Configuration** dialog box. This dialog box is used to configure AutoCAD to work with your DBMS. Always check with your system administrator or instructor prior to adding, removing, or changing database configurations.

Creating the Database Environment

To begin working through the examples in this chapter, the programs that run ASE must be loaded. The following procedure loads ASE, directing AutoCAD to the database information.

The administration procedure must be completed each time you work with ASE. This procedure creates links between the proper database files, catalogs, schema, and tables. Once ASE is loaded into your drawing, you can work with any of the sample databases that come with AutoCAD.

> **NOTE**
>
> Dialog boxes are used extensively in the examples in this chapter. Be sure the **CMDDIA** system variable is on (1) as you begin to explore ASE and databases.

ASEADMIN
AAD

Tools
➥ External Database
➥ Administration...

External Database
toolbar

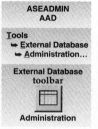

Administration

The **Administration** dialog box is used to set up links between databases and to edit database fields. Access this dialog box by picking the **Administration** button from the **External Database** toolbar, selecting **Administration...** from the **External Database** cascading menu in the **Tools** pull-down menu, or typing AAD or ASEADMIN at the Command: prompt. The **Administration** dialog box is shown in Figure 16-6.

A list of defined environments is displayed. Highlight DB3 (which stands for dBASE III) in the **Database Objects:** list and pick the **Connect...** button. The **Connect to Environment** dialog box is displayed, Figure 16-7. If your environment requires a user name and password information, enter them. If it does not, select the **OK** button.

Figure 16-6.
The ASE environment is set in the **Administration** dialog box.

Environment list

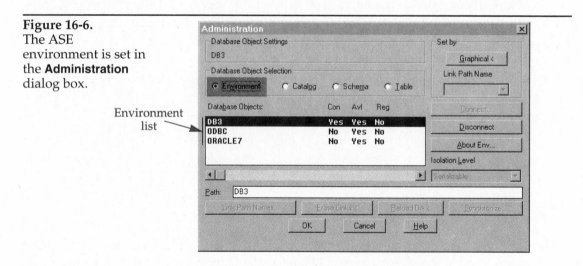

Figure 16-7.
If a user name and password are needed, enter them in the **Connect to Environment** dialog box. If security is not a concern, pick the **OK** button without entering any information.

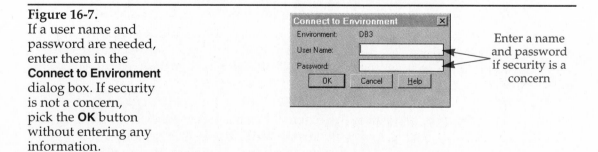

Enter a name and password if security is a concern

Next, select the **Catalog** radio button in the **Administration** dialog box. This displays a list of available catalogs in the environment. Highlight ASE. See Figure 16-8.

Pick the **Schema** radio button next. This is the database table held in the designated location. Highlight DB3SAMPLE. See Figure 16-9.

Pick the **Table** radio button. This displays the database information, organized in rows and columns. Highlight EMPLOYEE. You have loaded ASE and now have access to the EMPLOYEE database table. See Figure 16-10.

Figure 16-8.
The **Catalog** radio button displays available catalogs.

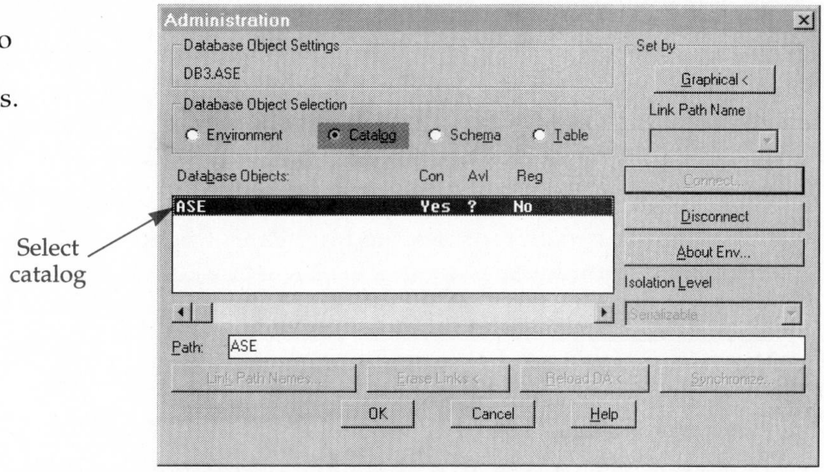

Figure 16-9.
Picking the **Schema** radio button lists the DB3SAMPLE schema.

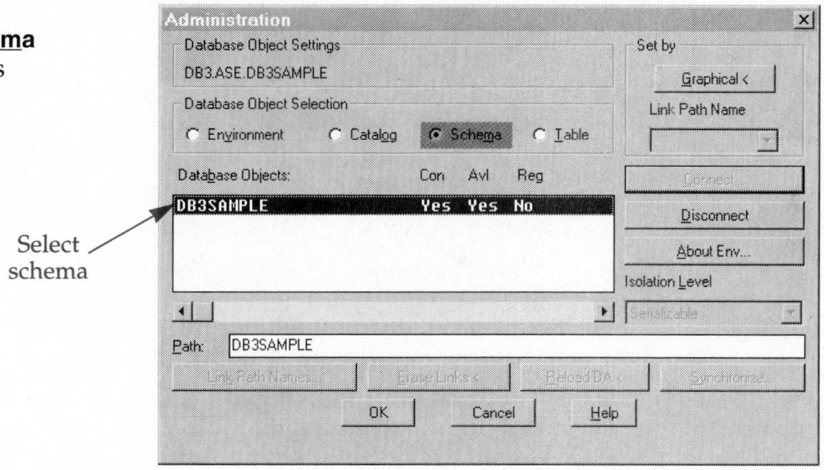

Figure 16-10.
The completed **Administration** dialog box.

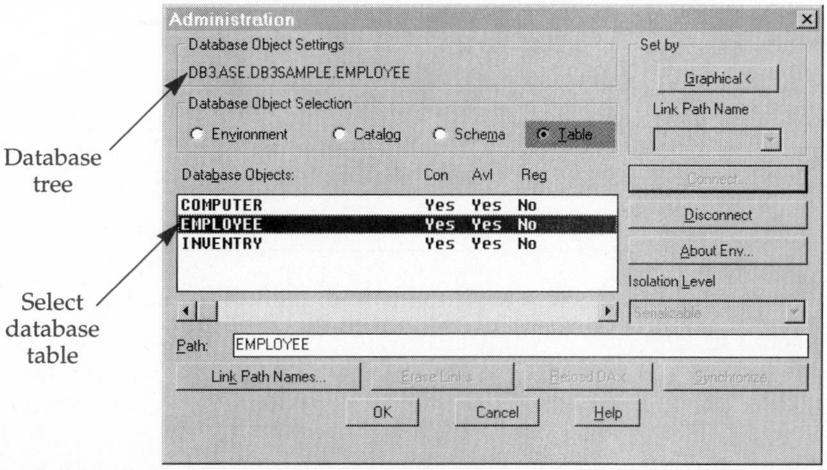

Linking a drawing to a database

After loading ASE and connecting database objects, you are able to link drawings to the database. When you highlight a table in the **Administration** dialog box, the **Link Path Names...** button is enabled. Picking this button displays the **Link Path Names** dialog box, as shown in Figure 16-11. This dialog box provides an area for key column selection.

A *key* specifies a column or set of columns whose values will be used to identify a specified row in the table. To set a column as a key, highlight the column and then pick the **On** button. More than one column can be selected as a key. Set the LAST_NAME and DEPT columns as keys.

Once the key items are selected, enter a new path name in the **New:** text box, then pick **New**. When you exit the dialog box, the new path name will be registered and you return to the **Administration** dialog box. Set a new path as EMPLOYEE_INFO.

There are three columns in the **Database Objects:** list of the **Administration** dialog box: **Con**, **Avl**, and **Reg**. **Con** indicates if a database object is *connected* to the DBMS loaded into memory. **Avl** indicates that an environment listed in the asi.ini file has been connected and is *available* for use. **Reg** indicates that key columns have been *registered* in an associated table.

Figure 16-11.
Key columns are selected in the **Link Path Names** dialog box.

Multiple columns can be selected as keys

Activates column as a key

Enter new path

Activates new path

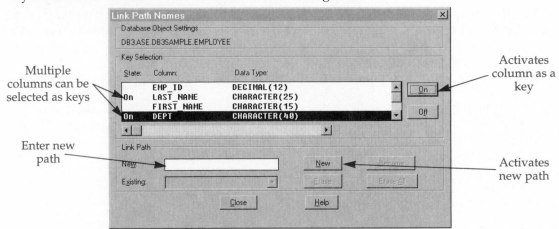

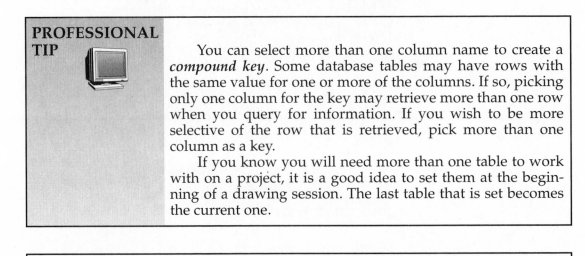

PROFESSIONAL TIP

You can select more than one column name to create a *compound key*. Some database tables may have rows with the same value for one or more of the columns. If so, picking only one column for the key may retrieve more than one row when you query for information. If you wish to be more selective of the row that is retrieved, pick more than one column as a key.

If you know you will need more than one table to work with on a project, it is a good idea to set them at the beginning of a drawing session. The last table that is set becomes the current one.

NOTE

When a drawing is saved and AutoCAD is closed, you must reload ASE every time you open the drawing. The catalogs, schemas, and tables are saved to the database, but AutoCAD loses the database link.

❏ In the **Administration** dialog box, select the INVENTRY table.
❏ Use the INV_ID column as the key.
❏ Select the COMPUTER table.
❏ Use the COMP_CFG column as the key.
❏ Do *not* save the drawing.

Using SQL

The purpose of the following example and the exercises in this chapter is to illustrate the use of ASE to link graphic entities in an AutoCAD drawing with rows in a database table. The first part of this exercise steps through information that is already in the database. You will then add new information to the database file (table).

Open the drawing named asesmp.dwg located in the C:\Program Files\AutoCAD R14\Sample folder. After the drawing is loaded, you need to initialize ASE, using the steps explained previously. Set the current table to EMPLOYEE. You are now ready to edit the EMPLOYEE section of this table.

The SQL editor executes SQL statements from the user interface, from files, or from a list of previously executed commands saved in memory. To access the **SQL Editor** dialog box, pick the **SQL Editor** button from the **External Database** toolbar, select **SQL Editor...** from the **External Database** cascading menu in the **Tools** pull-down menu, or enter ASQ or ASESQLED at the Command: prompt. The **SQL Editor** dialog box appears, as shown in Figure 16-12.

Enter the following in the **SQL Statement:** text box:

    select * from employee where room = '104'

Pick the **Execute** button or press [Enter].

The database is queried directly. The results are displayed in the **SQL Cursor** dialog box, as shown in Figure 16-13. This is an example of how you can use an SQL query to select information. Pick **Close** to remove the dialog.

ASESQLED
ASQ

Tools
→ External Database
→ SQL Editor...

External Database toolbar

SQL Editor

Figure 16-12.
Queries of the database can be made in the **SQL Editor** dialog box.

Query — select * from employee where room = '104'

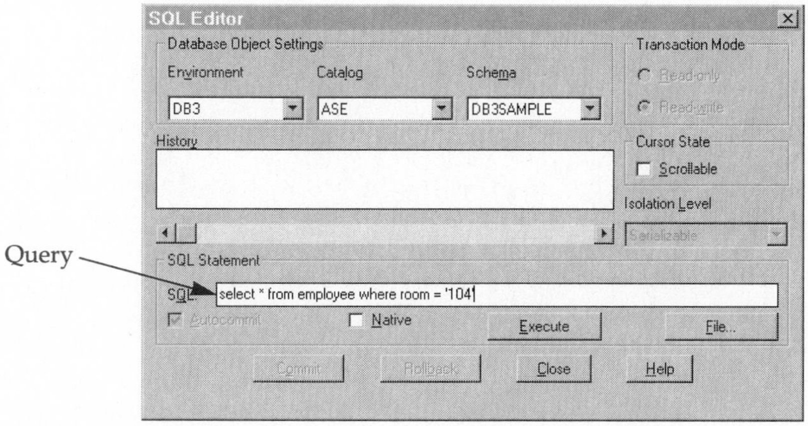

Figure 16-13.
The query result is displayed in the **SQL Cursor** dialog box.

Query

Response

SQL Cursor

SELECT Statement:

select * from employee where room = "104"

EMP ID		1003
LAST_NAME		Smith
FIRST_NAME		Jill
DEPT		Sales
TITLE		Central Region Mgr.
ROOM		104

Next
Prior
First
Last

Name: EMP_ID

Value: 1003

Update   Delete   Close   Help

Working with Rows

Most of your work in ASE will be either viewing, editing, displaying, or linking rows to a drawing entity. Remember that a row is an entry in a database file (schema) that contains several attributes. The following discussion shows you how to use rows in a variety of ways.

Understanding the Rows dialog box

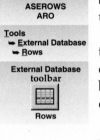

ASEROWS
ARO

Tools
➥ External Database
➥ Rows

External Database
toolbar

Rows

The last table to be set remains the current one, and will be displayed when the **Rows** dialog box is opened. Before setting a row, be sure the correct table is current using the **Administration** dialog box.

To access the **Rows** dialog box, pick the **Rows** button from the **External Database** toolbar, select **Rows...** from the **External Database** cascading menu in the **Tools** pull-down menu, or type ARO or ASEROWS at the Command: prompt. The **Rows** dialog box is displayed, as shown in Figure 16-14. Notice the three areas at the top of the dialog box.

Figure 16-14.
Rows from any table can be displayed in the **Rows** dialog box.

Rows

Database Object Settings

| Environment | Catalog | Schema | Table | Link Path Name |
| DB3 | ASE | DB3SAMPLE | EMPLOYEE | |

Cursor State
◉ Read-only
○ Scrollable
○ Updatable

SELECT Rows

Condition:

Select to display current row

Open Cursor   Key Values...   Graphical <   Close Cursor

Enter an SQL query

Next
Prior
First
Last

Make Link   Make DA   Select   Unselect   Links   Edit...

OK   Cancel   Help

- **Database Object Settings.** Displays the current database settings. Each setting can be changed by picking the drop-down list.
- **Cursor State.** The *cursor* is the current row that is displayed. Using the three radio buttons in this area, you can control how you work with the information in the current row.
- **SELECT Rows.** Using this area you can select a row using one of several methods.

The items displayed in the **Database Object Settings** area indicate the settings previously created in the **Administration** dialog box. Notice that the list box in the center of the dialog box is blank. Row data in the current table can be displayed in this list area.

Displaying row data

The current row can be displayed by pressing [Enter] or by picking the **Open Cursor** button. This displays the columns for the first row in the EMPLOYEE table, as shown in Figure 16-15. Also notice that the row is displayed in a column fashion. The column headings are displayed on the left side of the list. You can use the scroll bar to see the remaining columns in the table. When you are finished viewing the data, pick the **Close Cursor** button.

A second method for displaying row data is to write an SQL query in the **Condition:** text box. This statement must begin with a column name, then an equal sign (=), and end with the search string in single quotes. For example, if you wanted to display employees with the last name of Williams, enter the following in the **Condition:** text box, and press [Enter]:

    LAST_NAME = 'Williams'

The first row that matches your query is displayed in the list box, and all of the **SELECT Rows** options are disabled except for the **Close Cursor** button. See Figure 16-16. If more than one row matches your query, pick the **Next** button to view it. When you are finished viewing the data, pick the **Close Cursor** button. This returns to the default state of the dialog box.

A third method for searching for row data is to enter key values. Pick the **Key Values...** button to display the **Select Row by Key Values** dialog box. This displays the key columns that you initially selected in the **Administration** dialog box.

Figure 16-15.
Picking the **Open Cursor** button displays the first row of the current table.

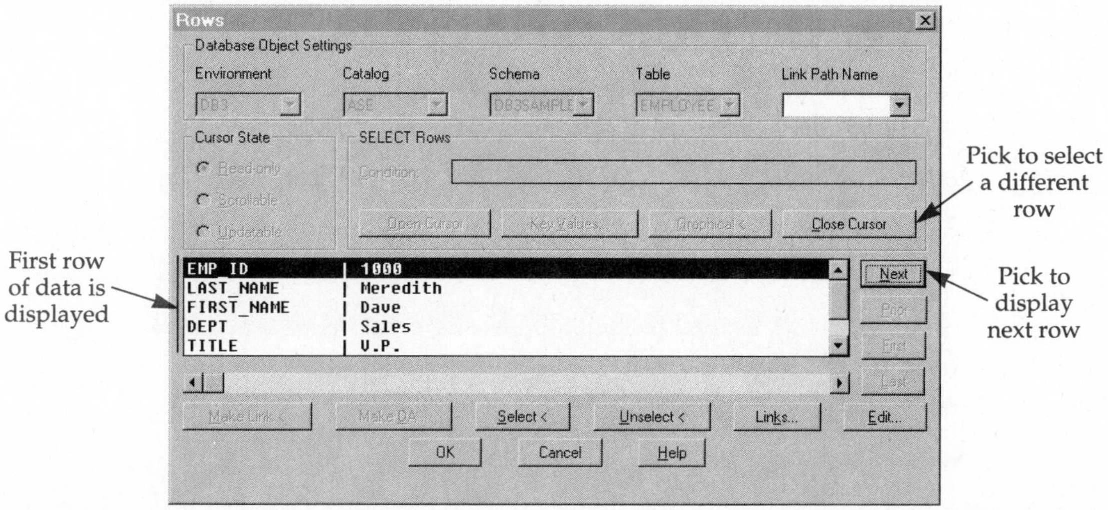

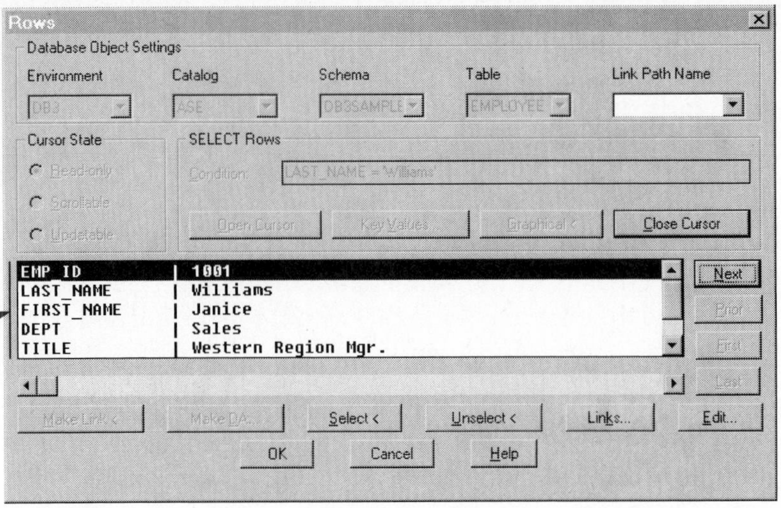

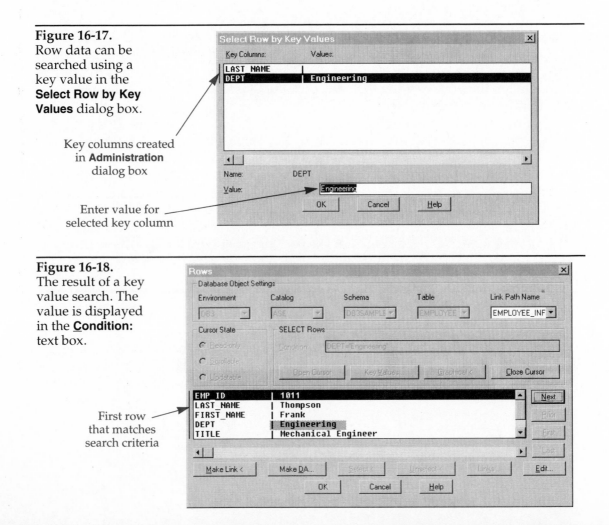

Figure 16-16.
Row data can be displayed as a result of a query in the **Condition:** text box of the **Rows** dialog box.

Row matching search criteria

Begin the search by highlighting the key value in the list box that you wish to use. In this example, the DEPT key is selected. This is displayed in the **Name:** field below. Now enter the selection criteria in the **Value:** text box and press [Enter]. This value is then displayed in the list box under the **Values:** heading. See Figure 16-17. Pick **OK** to begin the search.

The first row that meets the search criteria is displayed in the **Rows** dialog box. Notice in Figure 16-18 that the search value you used is now listed in the **Condition:** text box.

Figure 16-17.
Row data can be searched using a key value in the **Select Row by Key Values** dialog box.

Key columns created in **Administration** dialog box

Enter value for selected key column

Figure 16-18.
The result of a key value search. The value is displayed in the **Condition:** text box.

First row that matches search criteria

The fourth method for displaying row data is to select an object in the AutoCAD drawing by picking the **Graphical** button. If this button is disabled, pick the **Close Cursor** button to remove the current row display and activate the row selection options.

Picking the **Graphical** button returns the graphic screen and issues the Select object: prompt. Pick office number 109. The **Links** dialog box is displayed with the key value of the row that is linked to your selection, as shown in Figure 16-19. In this case, the link is to employee number 1009. Pick **OK** to return to the **Rows** dialog box, which now contains the row data for employee number 1009.

When row data is displayed, you can view the next row by picking the **Next** button. The remaining three scrolling buttons are disabled if the **Scrollable** radio button in the **Cursor State** area is not selected. You can activate the scrolling buttons by first picking **Close Cursor**, and then picking the **Scrollable** radio button. Now pick **Open Cursor**. Notice that the **Prior**, **First**, and **Last** buttons can now be used. These enable you to move through the rows quickly.

Figure 16-19.
The **Links** dialog box displays row data linked to a selected object.

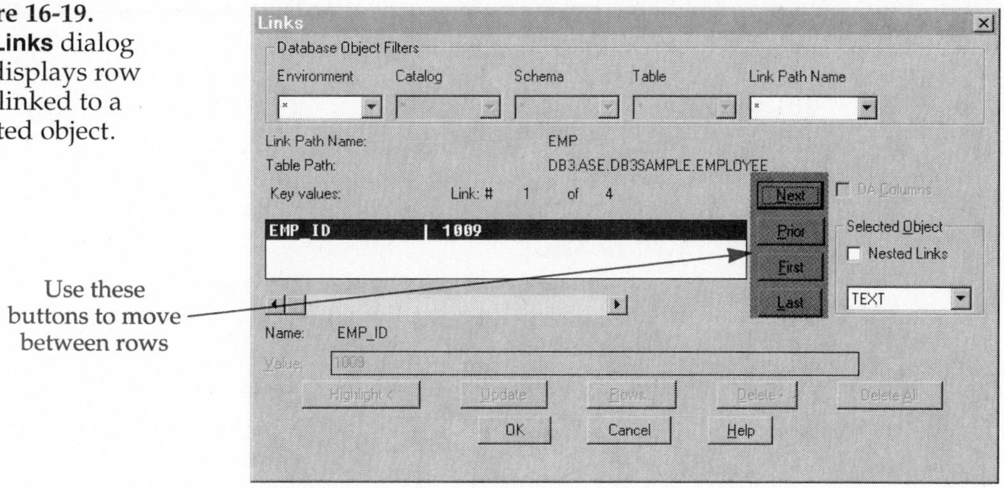

Use these buttons to move between rows

Editing a row

You can edit the row in the database table. In the **Rows** dialog box, select the **Close Cursor** button. This temporarily clears the window, but allows you to change the **Cursor State**. Choose the **Updatable** radio button. If you do not pick the **Updatable** radio button you will not be able to edit the row data. Remove any information listed in the **Condition:** text box, and pick the **Open Cursor** button. Use the **Next** button to find the employee 1007. Select the **Edit...** button to display the **Edit Row** dialog box. See Figure 16-20.

In the **Edit Row** dialog box, scroll to find the room number and pick it. The column name appears in the **Name:** field below the list box. The **Value:** of the current room appears, which in this case is 109. Change the room number to 121 and press [Enter]. The **Update** button becomes active. Select it and the Row is updated message is displayed in the lower-left corner. See Figure 16-21. Pick **Close** to save the change. Check the **Rows** dialog box to be sure that the room number has changed to 121.

Figure 16-20.
The **Edit Row** dialog box.

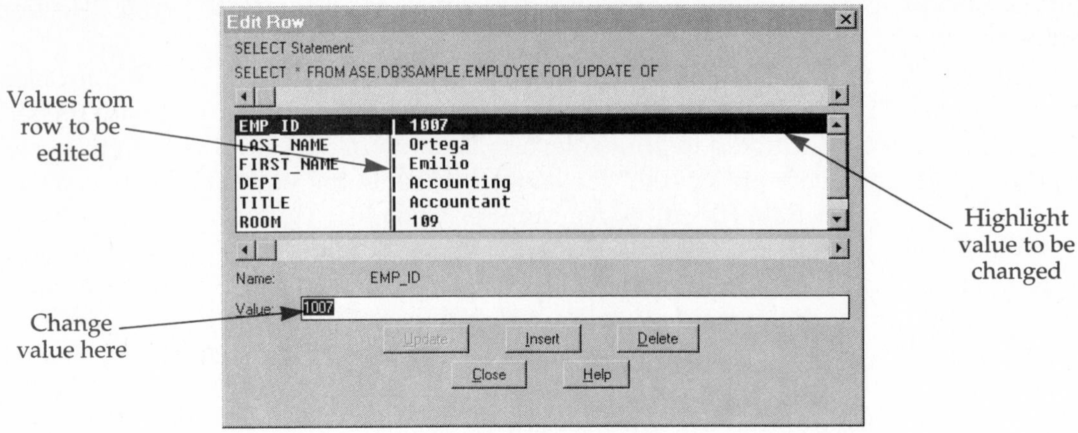

Values from
row to be
edited

Highlight
value to be
changed

Change
value here

Figure 16-21.
The updated row is displayed in the **Edit Row** dialog box.

New room
number

Message verifies
that row has
changed

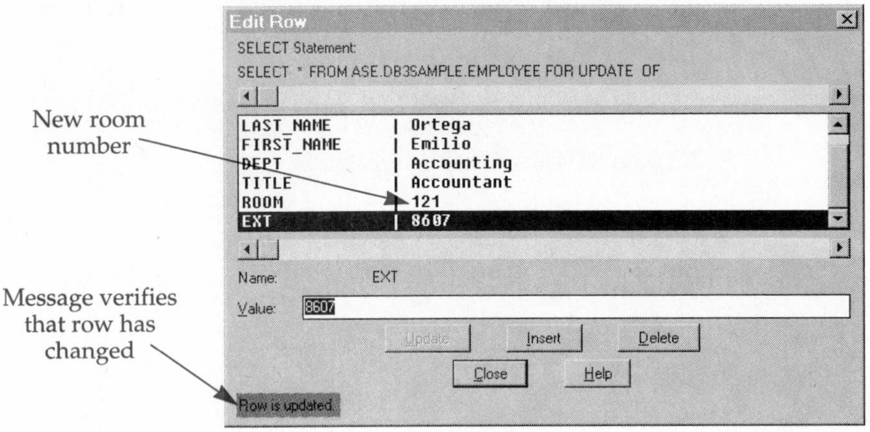

Adding a row

You can also add a row using the **Rows** dialog box. To insert a new employee you must close the cursor, select the **Updatable** radio button, and then pick the **Edit...** button. The **Edit Row** dialog box appears. The row data is blank. See Figure 16-22.

The column that is highlighted in the list box is displayed in the **Name:** field below. You can type a new value for this column in the **Value:** text box, then press [Enter]. This new value is entered in the list box and the LAST_NAME column is highlighted. The **Value:** text box becomes current, so type the last name and press [Enter]. Continue in this manner until all values for the new row have been entered. Type the following to create a new row:

```
EMP_ID        |2000
LAST_NAME     |Wilbourn
FIRST_NAME    |Rachel
DEPT          |CAD
TITLE         |Engineer
ROOM          |108
EXT           |0002
```

Pick the **Insert** button to insert the new row. AutoCAD displays the Row is inserted message. See Figure 16-23.

AutoCAD and its Applications—Advanced

Figure 16-22.
A row can be added in the blank **Edit Row** dialog box.

Input values for new row

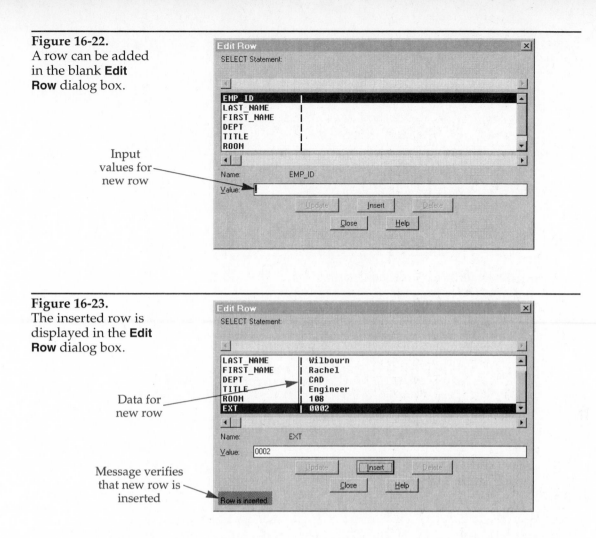

Figure 16-23.
The inserted row is displayed in the **Edit Row** dialog box.

Data for new row

Message verifies that new row is inserted

Close this dialog box and pick **OK** to exit the **Rows** dialog box. Use the **SQL Editor** to see if the employee has been added to the database. Open the **SQL Editor** dialog box and type the following in the **SQL:** text box:

select * from EMPLOYEE where emp_id = 2000

Pick the **Execute** button to begin the search. The **SQL Cursor** dialog box displays the results. See Figure 16-24. Close the dialog box to return to the **SQL Editor** dialog box.

Figure 16-24.
A search query issued in the **SQL Editor** dialog box is displayed in the **SQL Cursor** dialog box.

Query

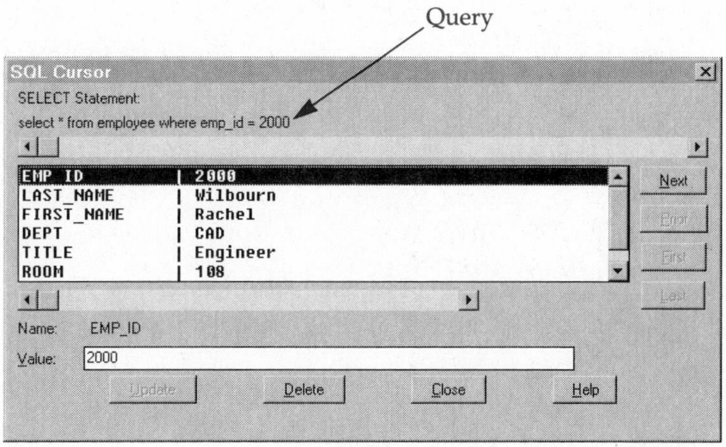

❑ Open the asesmp.dwg.
❑ Open the **Administration** dialog box.
❑ Add a new row to the EMPLOYEE table. Use the following information:

Column	Value
EMP_ID	1038
LAST_NAME	Desque
FIRST_NAME	Otto
DEPT	Publications
TITLE	Graphics Specialist
ROOM	122
EXT	8627

❑ View the current row to check your work.
❑ Set the INVENTRY table as current and add a new row with the following values:

Column	Value
INV_ID	2158
TYPE	Hardware
DESCRIPT	Personal inventory
MFR	HARDWIRE HARDWARE
MODEL	cpu7
COMP_CFG	7
PRICE	4900.00
ROOM	122
EMP_ID	1038

❑ View the current row to check your work.
❑ Save the drawing as EX16-2.

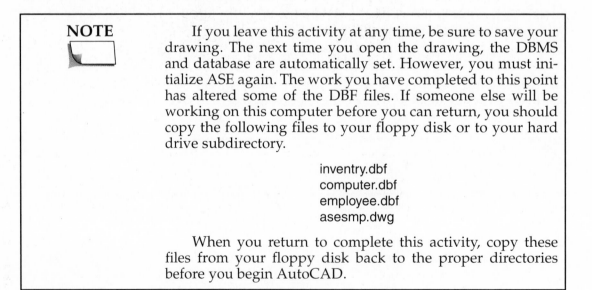

NOTE

If you leave this activity at any time, be sure to save your drawing. The next time you open the drawing, the DBMS and database are automatically set. However, you must initialize ASE again. The work you have completed to this point has altered some of the DBF files. If someone else will be working on this computer before you can return, you should copy the following files to your floppy disk or to your hard drive subdirectory.

inventry.dbf
computer.dbf
employee.dbf
asesmp.dwg

When you return to complete this activity, copy these files from your floppy disk back to the proper directories before you begin AutoCAD.

Working with Selection Sets

Simple selection sets can be created using the **Rows** dialog box. These selection sets can be used for finding and viewing objects linked to the current row data. The selected objects can be used in editing operations.

The **ASESELECT** command allows you to create two selection sets based on textual and graphical data. These two selection sets can be combined or subtracted from each other to create a more defined set.

Using the Rows dialog box to create a selection set

In order to create a selection set in the **Rows** dialog box, row data must be shown in the list box. Display a row using any one of the methods described previously. Be sure that the current **Link Path Name** is EMP. Next pick the **Select** button. The dialog box is dismissed and all AutoCAD objects linked to the current row are highlighted. Press [Enter] and the highlighted objects are added to the selection set. See Figure 16-25. In the example used in Figure 16-25, office number 101 was highlighted because it is the only AutoCAD object linked to the current row.

Figure 16-25.
The **Rows** dialog box can be used to create a selection set.

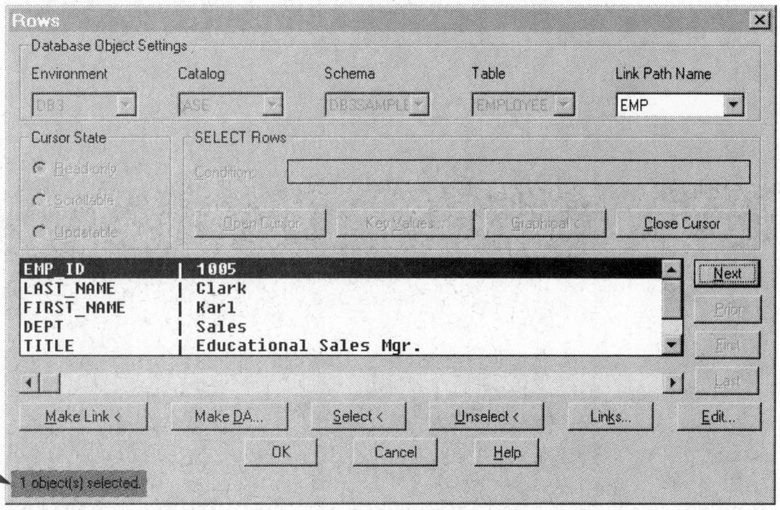

Message displays the number of objects

Using the Select Objects dialog box to create a selection set

The **ASESELECT** command is used to access the **Select Objects** dialog box. This dialog box can be used to create two different selection sets, A and B. Set A is composed of textual data specified in the **Select Objects** dialog box. Set B is composed of AutoCAD objects that are linked to selection set A.

Access the **Select Objects** dialog box by picking the **Select Objects** button in the **External Database** toolbar, selecting **Select Objects** from the **External Database** cascading menu in the **Tools** pull-down menu, or typing ASE or ASESELECT at the Command: prompt. See Figure 16-26.

To create a selection set you must set the **Database Object Filters** to the proper environment. These are the same settings used in the **Administration** dialog box to begin a session. The settings for the INVENTRY table look like those in Figure 16-27.

A selection set can now be created in two different ways. Objects can be selected from the graphics screen using the **Graphical** button, or a condition statement can be used to specify the contents of the set. First type a statement in the **Condition:** text box that describes the object you wish to select, then press [Enter]:

    descript = '36x12 file cabinet'

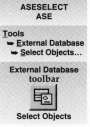

ASESELECT
ASE

Tools
➥ External Database
➥ Select Objects...

External Database
toolbar

Select Objects

Figure 16-26.
The **Select Objects**
dialog box is used
to create combined
selection sets.

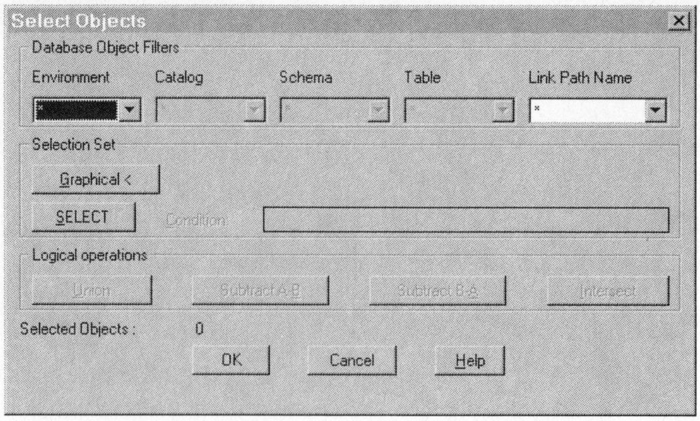

Figure 16-27.
The **Database Object Filters** are used to create a selection set.

Pick to select
objects in
drawing

These values
must be set
to the proper
environment

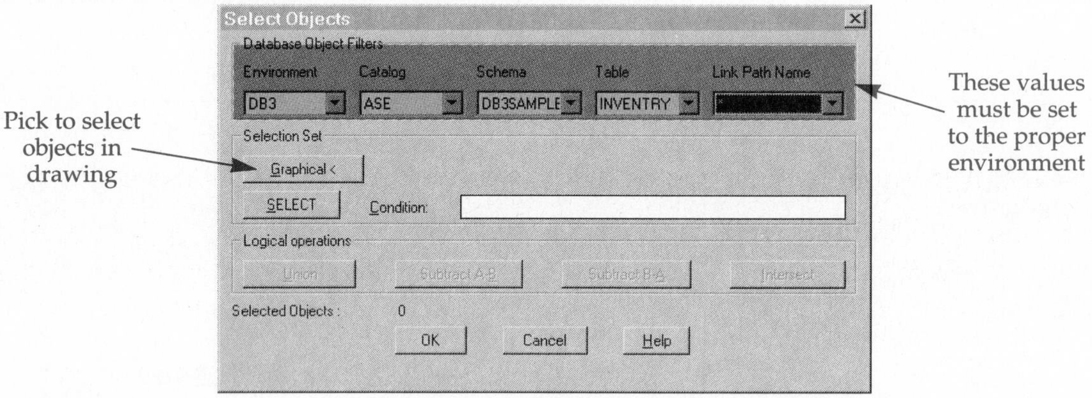

This creates set A, the textual description. Now pick the **Intersect** button to create a selection set that combines set A and set B. Next pick the **Graphical** button. AutoCAD dismisses the dialog box for you to select the objects to be included in this selection set. Make a window selection around all of the rooms along the top of the drawing, then press [Enter]. This creates selection set B.

Even though AutoCAD reports that you selected about 300 objects, when the dialog box returns, a message indicates that five objects were selected. That is because you specified that the selection set was to be an *intersection* of sets A and B. Therefore, AutoCAD applied the conditional specification of a 36×12 file cabinet to only those rooms you selected and found five objects. See Figure 16-28.

Figure 16-28.
An intersect selection set combines textual and graphical information.

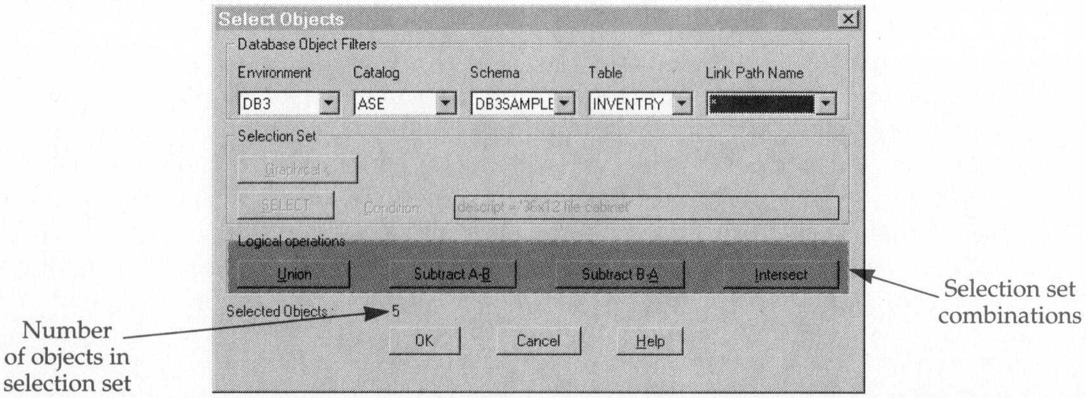

Number
of objects in
selection set

Selection set
combinations

A new selection set can be created in four different ways using a union, intersection, subtraction of set A from set B, or subtraction of set B from set A. These functions are displayed as buttons in the **Logical operations** area of the **Select Objects** dialog box.

- **Union.** Combines all criteria and objects in sets A and B to create a selection set.
- **Intersect.** Creates a selection set of only those objects defined by both set A and set B.
- **Subtract A-B.** Set B is subtracted from set A to create the new selection set.
- **Subtract B-A.** Set A is subtracted from set B to create the new selection set.

The new selection set can be displayed quickly by using the **SELECT** button or any edit command and the **Previous** option.

Linking the Database to the Drawing

In ASE, a *link* is a connection between a graphic object in the AutoCAD drawing and a row from a table within a database. You can select an object in the drawing, such as a computer, and have immediate access to all of the information stored in the database about that computer. Using ASE and the **ASELINKS** command, you can create, delete, view, and edit links.

Viewing an existing link

To initiate the **ASELINKS** command, pick the **Links** button from the **External Database** toolbar, select **Links...** from the **External Database** cascading menu in the **Tools** pull-down menu, or type ALI or ASELINKS at the Command: prompt. The Select object: prompt appears. Zoom in to room 109 at the upper-right corner of the drawing, then pick the number 109. The **Links** dialog box is then displayed, as shown in Figure 16-29.

The list box displays the key values of the first row that is linked to the selected object. The **Link:** field just above the list box indicates how many links exist to the selected object. In this case there are four links. You can scroll through the links by using one of the scroll buttons to the right of the list box.

To view more than just the key values of the current link, pick the **Rows...** button. This displays the **Rows** dialog box and all of the data on the current row.

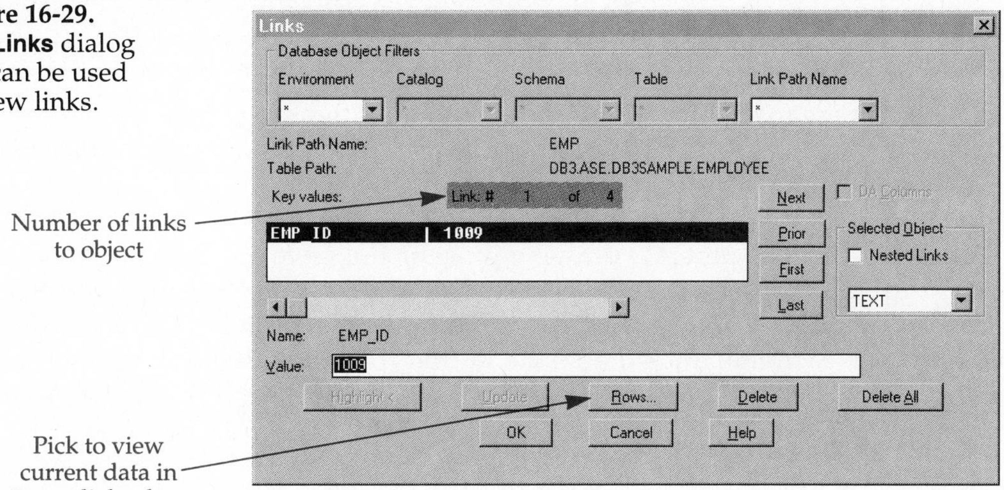

ASELINKS
ALI

Tools
➥ External Database
➥ Links...

External Database
toolbar

Links

Figure 16-29.
The **Links** dialog box can be used to view links.

Number of links to object

Pick to view current data in **Rows** dialog box

Creating a link

A link can be created between a row in a table and an AutoCAD object. An AutoCAD object can have links to more than one row in a table, and also to more than one table or database.

Links are made using the **Rows** dialog box. First, be sure you have set up the proper environment with a path link and key values. Then pick the **Make Link** button in the **Rows** dialog box. Select the objects in the AutoCAD drawing that you want to link to the current row, then press [Enter]. A message in the lower-left of the dialog box indicates that the link has been made. See Figure 16-30.

You can check to see if the link was successful by using the process described in the previous section.

Figure 16-30.
A new link is created in the **Rows** dialog box.

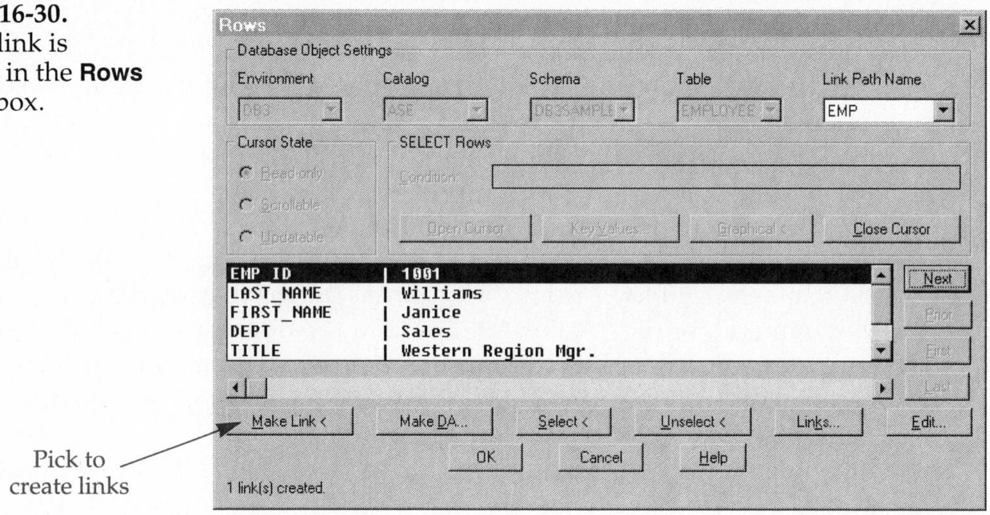

Pick to create links

Editing an existing link

Links between AutoCAD objects and database rows may need to be changed. This process is as easy as creating a link. First use the **ASELINKS** command and select the object whose link must be edited. The **Links** dialog box is displayed. Check to see if there are multiple links. If so, scroll to the link you wish to edit and pick the **Rows...** button. This displays the **Rows** dialog box.

Use one of the row selection methods previously described to make the new row current. This row will become the new link after you pick **OK** to exit the dialog box.

Deleting an existing link

If an object in an AutoCAD drawing must be linked to a row, it might be necessary first to delete any existing links. Use the **ASELINKS** command and select the desired object(s). The **Links** dialog box displays all current links. Use the scroll buttons to display each link. Pick the **Delete** button to remove the link to the row currently displayed. Pick the **Delete All** button to remove all links. A message in the lower-left indicates that the link is deleted. Pick **OK** when you are done.

❏ Open asesmp.dwg if it is not already loaded.
❏ Use **ASEADMIN** to establish the environment and set the INVENTRY table current.
❏ View the links to the computer in the upper-right corner of room 105. Fill in the following data regarding the computer.

EMP_ID	1004
PRICE	1300
INV_ID	126
MODEL	CPU1

❏ Janice Williams and Jill Smith have exchanged rooms. They took their computers with them, but all other furniture remained. Edit all of the links associated with these two employees.
❏ Dave Meredith retired and was replaced by Rosalyn Cramer. She took his office. Delete and edit all necessary links.
❏ Save your drawing as EX16-3.

Displayable Attributes

A *displayable attribute* is similar to a block attribute, except it gets its text information from the database table. The text is an AutoCAD block and is composed of values from a row that you select. For example, you can select any of the column values of a row in the EMPLOYEE table to be displayed in that employee's office. The text will reflect the attribute values in the linked row. You can store the text information in the drawing near the entity it describes.

In the **Rows** dialog box, pick the **Updatable** radio button then pick the **Graphical** button. This temporarily closes the dialog box to allow you to pick entities. Pick the room number 106. The dialog box is redisplayed with the linked row information in the list box. See Figure 16-31.

Choose the **Make DA...** button. The **Make Displayable Attribute** dialog box appears with the table columns listed on the left. Select the first column you wish displayed then pick the **Add** button. This displays the table column in the **DA Columns:** list. Repeat this process for each column that you want to be a displayable attribute. The **Add All** button makes all columns displayable attributes. The **Remove All** button removes all of the entries from the **DA Columns:** list. If you wish to remove a single item from the **DA Columns:** list, highlight it and pick the **Remove** button.

Figure 16-31.
The **Rows** dialog box is used to select an object for attaching a displayable attribute.

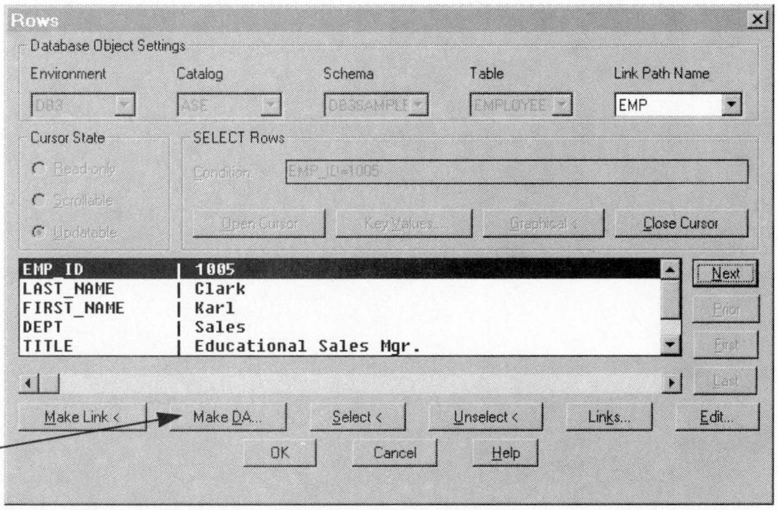

Pick to display attributes

The displayable attribute text can also be formatted. If you have predefined text styles, choose one from the **Text Style:** drop-down list. For this example, choose the **Justification** drop-down list and center the text. Change the text height to 15. See Figure 16-32. Pick **OK**. AutoCAD prompts you to select your center point for the text. Once you do, the **Rows** dialog box reappears with the text information in the box. Pick **OK** and the attributes are displayed at the selected point, Figure 16-33.

Figure 16-32.
Displayable attributes are created in the **Make Displayable Attribute** dialog box.

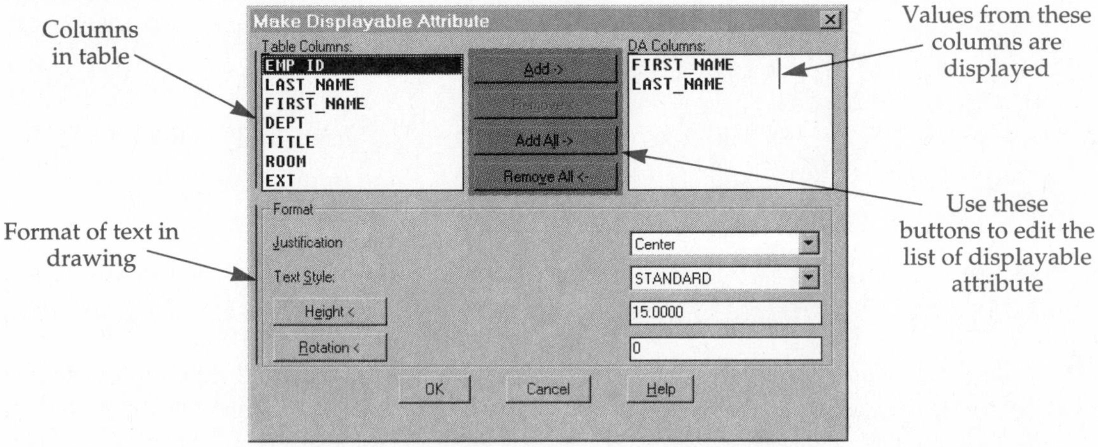

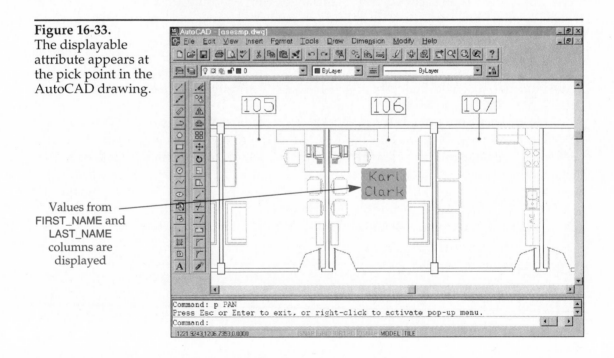

Figure 16-33.
The displayable attribute appears at the pick point in the AutoCAD drawing.

Values from FIRST_NAME and LAST_NAME columns are displayed

AutoCAD and its Applications—Advanced

Resolving Data and Drawing Conflicts

Errors and conflicts can creep into your drawing and database files due to several factors. Persons working on the drawing can erase or alter drawing entities, and other people using the database files can delete or alter keys or rows to linked entities. In order for the drawing and database to maintain their integrity, you can use the **ASEADMIN** command with the **Synchronize** option. This option reports invalid links within the database objects, links the existing information to a record that has been altered or deleted, and links information to entities that have been altered or deleted.

In the **Administration** dialog box, select the EMPLOYEE table. Be sure that you have a selected catalog and schema. Pick the **Synchronize...** button. The **Synchronize Links** dialog box appears and defines any errors in the link. If there are errors, pick the **Synchronize** button in this dialog box. AutoCAD repairs the link error and returns the table blank. Pick **Close** in this dialog box, then **OK** in the **Administration** dialog box, and the errors are repaired.

NOTE This chapter is intended to be an introduction to the capabilities of ASE. It is suggested that you go through the documentation in Chapter 17 of the *AutoCAD Users Guide*, Accessing External Databases. Begin to create your own small database and create a drawing that relates to it. This project should be a subject that is useful for you, and one that you can update and maintain easily. You will begin to see the value of working with a text and graphic relational database.

Chapter Test

Write your answers in the space provided.

1. What is a database? _____

    _____

    _____

2. What is a DBMS? _____

    _____

    _____

3. A common three-letter extension of a database file is _____.

4. What is a field? _____

    _____

    _____

    _____

    _____

5. What does SQL stand for?_____

    _____

    _____

6. The letters ASE stand for _____.

7. What is a database table? _____

---

8. What are the two principal components of a table? _____

9. The horizontal component of a table is also known as a(n) _____.

10. The vertical component of a table is also known as a(n) _____.

11. What does the environment comprise? _____

_____

_____

12. What is a catalog? _____

_____

_____

_____

_____

_____

_____

_____

13. What is a schema? _____

_____

_____

_____

_____

_____

_____

_____

_____

14. What command must be used before ASE can function? _____

15. What command is used to add and edit rows? _____

16. What does the **ASESELECT** command do? _____

_____

_____

_____

17. Define "link". _____

_____

_____

18. How can you display a link you just created? _____

_____

_____

_____

_____

19. How do you find link errors from the entities to the database? _____

_____

_____

_____

_____

_____

20. What is the command name for the **SQL Editor**?_____

Drawing Problems

1. Make a copy of the asesmp drawing and name it P16-1. Open P16-1 and set the DBMS and database used earlier in this chapter.

A. Add the following rows to each table shown below. Use **ASESQLED** to find a vacant room for the new employee, and enter that number in the proper column. For any column left blank in the lists below, find the next available number in the existing tables and use that value.

EMPLOYEE.DBF
EMP_ID—_____
LAST_NAME—Robinson
FIRST_NAME—Lonnie
DEPT—Human Resources
TITLE—Counselor
ROOM—_____
EXT—_____

INVENTRY.DBF
INV_ID—_____
TYPE—Laser printer
DESCRIPT—Personal inventory
MFR—Quasar Lasers
MODEL—QLP-600
COMP_CFG—0
PRICE—1245.00

B. View the new rows to check for errors.

C. Link the new employee and the new laser printer to the room number you selected in the drawing. Save the drawing as P16-1.

2. Open drawing P16-1 and edit the following existing rows of the tables given.

A. EMPLOYEE table: Change EMP_ID 1006's last name to Wilson-Jenkins, and change her TITLE to International Sales Mgr.

B. INVENTRY table: Change the price of INV_ID 141 to 5300.00, and change the MFR to Tradewinds Computers.

C. COMPUTER table: Change COMP_CFG 5's RAM to 64MB, and the GRAPHICS to Metheus.

D. View each table after completion to check for errors.

3. If you have database software, create a database for each computer in your lab named COMPUTER.DBF. Columns in the table should be:
   - COMP_ID
   - CPU
   - HDRIVE
   - INPUT
   - MFR
   - RAM
   - FDRIVE
   - GRAPHICS

   A. Before constructing the database file, make a list of each computer and record the components of each according to the requirements of the database table. Then enter all of the data at one time at the computer.

   B. Generate a printed copy when you have completed the database.

4. Construct a drawing of your computer lab. Create blocks for each workstation.

   A. Set the proper database and table in order to work with the computers in your drawing.

   B. Link each one of the computers in the drawing with the appropriate row in your database table created in Problem 3.

   C. View the links you created to check for accuracy. Edit any links that are not correct.

   D. Create displayable attributes for each workstation. The attributes should use the COMP_ID and MFR columns.

   E. Place a label in the title block, or as a general note, referring to the database name that is linked to this drawing.

   F. Save the drawing as P16-4 and print or plot a copy of the drawing.

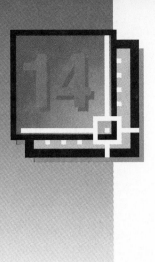

Chapter 17

Customizing the AutoCAD Environment

Learning Objectives

After completing this chapter, you will be able to:
- ○ Assign colors and fonts to the text and graphics windows.
- ○ Set environment variables.
- ○ Resize and reposition the text and graphics windows.
- ○ Modify program item properties.
- ○ Set up AutoCAD for multiple configurations.

AutoCAD provides a variety of options to customize the user interface and working environment. These options permit users to configure the software to suit personal preferences. These options include defining colors for the individual window elements, assigning preferred fonts to both the graphics and text windows, and customizing toolbars and buttons.

Setting Preferences

The options for customizing the AutoCAD user interface and working environment are found in the **Preferences** dialog box, Figure 17-1. This dialog box is accessed by selecting **Preferences...** from the **Tools** pull-down menu, or by typing PR or PREFERENCES at the Command: prompt.

PREFERENCES
PR

Tools
➥ Preferences...

Changes are not made until either the **Apply** or the **OK** button is picked. If you pick the **Cancel** button, all changes are discarded. Each time you change the preferences settings, the system registry is updated and the changes are used in subsequent drawing sessions.

Customizing the AutoCAD graphics window

Numerous options are available to customize the graphics window to your personal liking. Refer to the **Preferences** dialog box in Figure 17-1. Select the **Display** tab to view the display control options area, shown in Figure 17-2. An "X" in any of the check boxes in the **Drawing window parameters** area enables the specified option. By default, the scroll bars are turned on, the screen menus are turned off, and the AutoCAD window is maximized upon startup.

Figure 17-1.
The **Preferences**
dialog box is used
to customize the
AutoCAD working
environment.

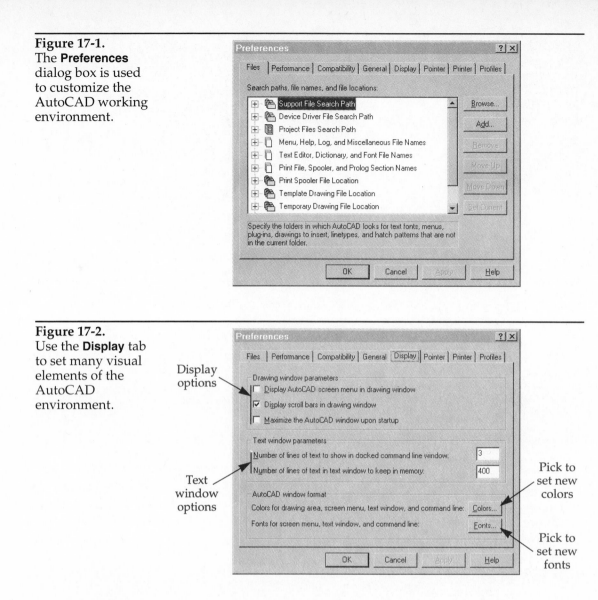

Figure 17-2.
Use the **Display** tab
to set many visual
elements of the
AutoCAD
environment.

Display options

Text window options

Pick to set new colors

Pick to set new fonts

Changing colors

By customizing colors, you can add your personal touch and make AutoCAD stand out among other active Windows applications. AutoCAD Release 14 provides this capability with the **AutoCAD Window Colors** dialog box, shown in Figure 17-3. This dialog box is accessed by picking the **Colors...** button in the **AutoCAD window format** area near the bottom of the **Display** tab in the **Preferences** dialog box.

The **Window Element:** drop-down list allows you to select elements of the graphics and text windows. These elements include the graphics area, the screen menu and command area, text window background, text in the graphics window or text window, and the full-screen crosshairs. To customize colors, do the following:

1. Pick the **Color...** button in the **Preferences** dialog box. The **AutoCAD Window Colors** dialog box appears.
2. If you have a monochrome display monitor, the **Monochrome Vectors** box is checked. If you have a grayscale display monitor and are experiencing problems displaying elements of AutoCAD, try checking this box.
3. Pick an area in the graphics or text window samples at the left of the dialog box, or select the element to change from the **Window Element:** drop-down list. The elements that can be selected are shown in Figure 17-4.

Figure 17-3.
Change AutoCAD color settings using the **AutoCAD Window Colors** dialog box.

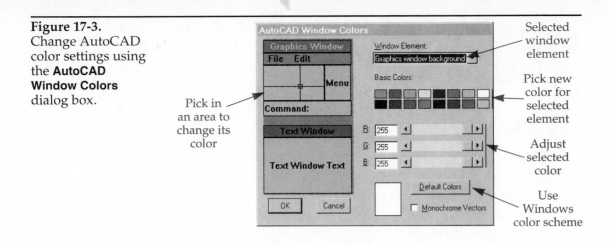

Pick in an area to change its color

Selected window element

Pick new color for selected element

Adjust selected color

Use Windows color scheme

Figure 17-4.
The colors of six elements can be adjusted in the **AutoCAD Window Colors** dialog box.

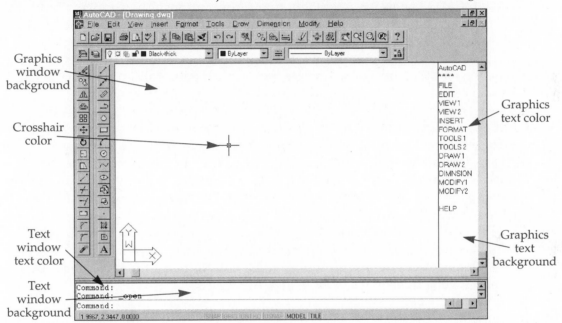

Graphics window background

Crosshair color

Text window text color

Text window background

Graphics text color

Graphics text background

4. Pick the color you want from the available colors displayed in the **Basic Colors:** section. The color you select is immediately reflected in the sample area at the left of the dialog box, and in the color swatch at the bottom.

5. You can modify the selected color by using the horizontal slider controls labeled **R:**, **G:**, and **B:** to change the red, green, and blue (respectively) components of the color. You can also type a number between 0 and 255 in the text boxes.

6. You can customize the AutoCAD windows to match the system colors defined in the Windows Control Panel. To do so, pick the **Default Colors** button.

7. Once you have made your color selections, pick the **OK** button and then pick **Apply** in the **Preferences** dialog box to implement your color changes. Or, if you are finished making changes in the **Preferences** dialog box, simply pick **OK**. The graphics window regenerates and displays the color changes you made. If you modified the colors for the text window as well, you should see the difference in the floating command window.

Changing fonts

You can also change the font used in the toolbar, command area, screen menu, and text window. The font you select has no effect on the text in your drawings, nor is the font used in the AutoCAD dialog boxes. To change the font used in the graphics and text windows, do the following:

1. Pick the **Fonts...** button on the **Display** panel of the **Preferences** dialog box. The **Graphics Window Font** dialog box appears, Figure 17-5.
2. The **AutoCAD Window** area contains two radio buttons. The **Graphics** button is selected by default, indicating that changes you make will modify the graphics window font. Pick the **Text** radio button to modify the text window font.
3. The default font used by AutoCAD for the graphics window is MS Sans Serif. The font style for MS Sans Serif is Regular (not bold or italic), and it defaults to a size of 10 points. You can retain this font and just change the style and size.
4. To select a different font, select the new font from the **Font:** list. This list displays each of the fonts installed in the \Windows\System folder. If you have any third-party fonts, such as TrueType or Adobe Type Manager, they also appear in this list. The **Sample Graphics Window Font** box at the bottom of the dialog box displays a sample of the selected font. If you are selecting a font for use in the text window, the title of the dialog box changes to **Text Window Font** and this box is labeled **Sample Text Window Font**.
5. Once you have selected the desired fonts, font styles, and sizes for the graphics and text windows, pick the **OK** button to assign the new fonts.
6. The **Preferences** dialog box is redisplayed. Pick **OK** to exit the **Preferences** dialog box and save your changes to the AutoCAD registry.

As with color modifications, changes made in font selection force a regeneration of the AutoCAD graphics window. When the regeneration is complete, the new font is displayed. Figure 17-6 illustrates font changes.

Figure 17-5.
Use the **Graphics Window Font** dialog box to change the fonts in the text and graphics windows.

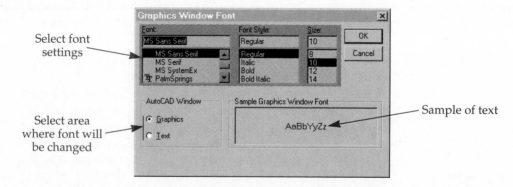

Select font settings

Select area where font will be changed

Sample of text

Figure 17-6.
The fonts used in the graphics and text windows can be changed to suit your preference. Times New Roman font is used in the graphics window and Monotext font is used in the text window.

12 point Times New Roman Bold Italic font

14 point Monotext font

NOTE

If you are using the screen menu, you may note that some fonts do not display properly because the menu area is not wide enough and the menu selections are truncated. This does not affect the usability of the menu, but menu names that are not fully displayed may result in incorrect selections.

PROFESSIONAL TIP

The **UNDO** command does not affect changes made to your system using the **Preferences** dialog box. If you have made changes that you do not want to save, pick **Cancel** to dismiss the **Preferences** dialog box. Picking **Cancel** does not dismiss changes that have been applied using the **Apply** button.

EXERCISE 17-1

❑ Start AutoCAD.
❑ Use the **Preferences** dialog box to change the color elements and fonts of both the graphics and text windows to your personal liking.
❑ Once you are satisfied with your modifications, pick **OK** to save your changes.

Text window parameters

In addition to changing the colors and fonts used in the AutoCAD text window, there are other setting options available. The following two additional options are available in the **Text window parameters** area of the **Display** tab.

- **Number of lines of text to show in docked command line window.** This controls the number of lines that are visible on the floating command window when it is docked. The default is 3 lines, but this value can be set higher so that more of your commands are visible. Increasing the number of lines displayed here will affect the size of your drawing area. Also, you can dynamically change the size of the floating command window (whether floating or docked) using the *resizing* cursor. Figure 17-7 shows the resizing cursor. Changing the size of the command window in this manner will automatically update the value in the edit box.

- **Number of lines of text in text window to keep in memory.** AutoCAD generates a listing of command area prompts and messages in a separate text window. You can scroll through the window to see previous command input and information returned by AutoCAD. The text box allows you to set the number of lines of text stored in the text window (from 25 to 2048 lines). The default is 400 lines.

Figure 17-7.
The cursor appears like this when resizing the command window.

Pointer

AutoCAD allows you to specify what pointing device you want to use for working within AutoCAD. The default is the current system pointing device, usually your mouse. If you have a digitizer tablet, you may need to change the pointer setting. To specify which pointer AutoCAD will use, select the **Pointer** tab from the **Preferences** dialog box, Figure 17-8. The available drivers are shown in the list. To select a different one, highlight it and pick the **Set Current** button.

You must configure your tablet using the **TABLET** command before it can be used. Refer to the *AutoCAD Installation Guide* for more information about digitizer configuration options. For detailed instructions on using your tablet as a digitizing device, see Chapter 21 of this text or Chapter 29 of *AutoCAD and its Applications—Basics, Release 14*.

The size of the cursor can be adjusted in the **Cursor size** area of the **Pointer** tab. The cursor size is set as a percentage of the screen size, and the default is 5%. This refers to the size of your desktop area, not the size of the AutoCAD window. To change the value, either type in the new value or use the up and down arrows to adjust the value. A larger cursor can be a useful visual aid, but may be distracting.

Figure 17-8.
Select the pointing device from the **Pointer** tab of the **Preferences** dialog box.

Pointing device drivers

Pick to select highlighted pointing device

Adjust cursor size

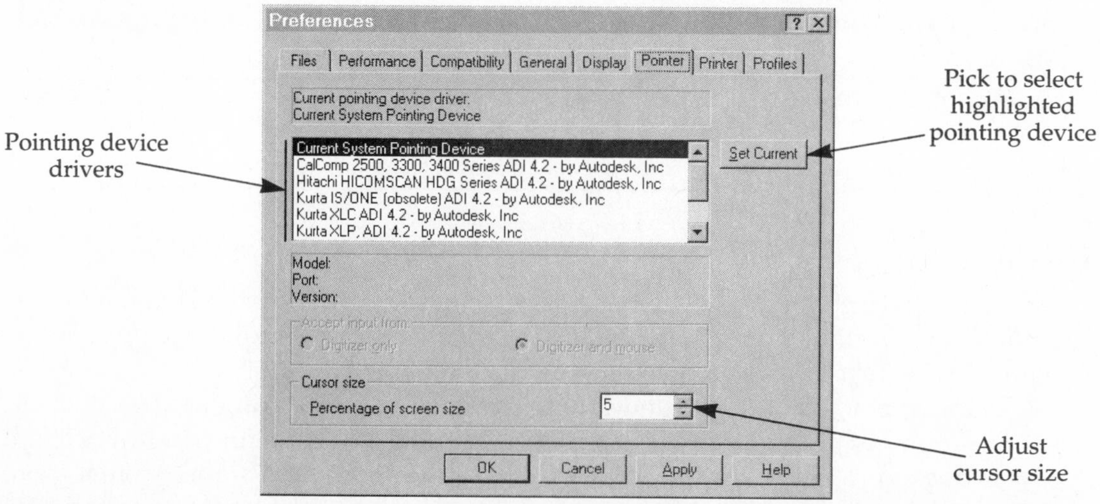

Safety precautions

When working in AutoCAD, there is always a risk of data loss. This data loss can occur due to a sudden power outage or an unforeseen system error. AutoCAD provides several safety precautions to help you minimize data loss when these types of events occur. These settings are found in the **Drawing session safety precautions** area in the **General** tab of the **Preferences** dialog box, see Figure 17-9A.

When the **Automatic save** check box is enabled, AutoCAD automatically creates backup files at a specified interval. The **Minutes between saves:** edit box sets this interval (the edit box contains the value of the **SAVETIME** system variable). Removing the check sets **SAVETIME** to 0.

The automatic save feature does not overwrite the source drawing file with its incremental saves. Rather, AutoCAD creates a drawing to save temporary files. This name is specified in the **Files** tab in the **Preferences** dialog box, Figure 17-9B. The default name for this file is auto.sv$.

This auto.sv$ file can be renamed with a .dwg file extension to make it usable by AutoCAD. Having an extra backup copy of a drawing file can be extremely valuable when a power outage or system error results in a corrupt drawing file.

The interval setting you should use is based on working conditions and file size. It is possible to adversely affect your productivity by setting your **SAVETIME** value too small. For example, in larger drawings (1 Megabyte and above), a **SAVE** command can take a significant amount of time. If a save takes two minutes and your auto save

Figure 17-9.
AutoCAD can create backup files automatically to help prevent data loss.
A—The **General** tab of the **Preferences** dialog box.
B—The location of the automatically saved filed is stored in the **Files** tab.

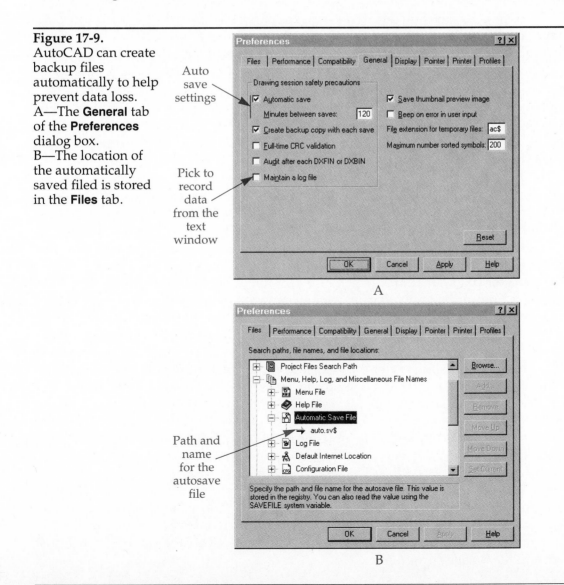

A

B

is set to save every five minutes, then you would spend more than fifteen minutes of every hour waiting on AutoCAD to finish saving the file.

Ideally, it is best to set your **SAVETIME** variable to the greatest amount of time you can afford to repeat. While it may be acceptable to redo the last fifteen minutes or less of work, it is unlikely that you would feel the same about having to redo the last hour.

PROFESSIONAL TIP
Setting and resetting the **SAVETIME** variable according to any given situation is often the best approach. The factors that should influence the current setting include not only file size, but also the working conditions. If your computer system is experiencing frequent lock-ups or crashes, your automatic saves should occur often. Weather can also be a factor. Wind or electrical storms should be an immediate cue to reduce the value of the **SAVETIME** variable.

The automatic save feature saves the current drawing in a specified file. Unfortunately, when you open a new drawing, this drawing may then overwrite the automatic save file from the previous drawing. Therefore, the automatic save feature is only a temporary safety precaution. AutoCAD can also create a backup of the current drawing file that uses the same name as the drawing with a .bak file extension instead of .dwg. Because this file uses the same name as the drawing, it is not overwritten when other drawings are opened or saved.

When a check mark is placed in the check box labeled **Create backup copy with each save**, the backup file feature is enabled. When you save a drawing, the previously existing version of it is renamed from a .dwg file to a .bak file and the current drawing data is written to the .dwg file. The first time you save a drawing, no backup file is created. If there is no check in this toggle box, the file is not backed up when you save. Unless you prefer to take unnecessary risks, it is usually best to leave this feature enabled.

Full-time CRC validation is a feature that you can use when drawing files are being corrupted and you suspect that a hardware or software problem may exist. CRC stands for *cyclic redundancy check*, which verifies that the number of data bits sent was the same as the number received. When using full-time CRC validation, the CRC check is done every time data is read into the drawing. This ensures that all of the data was received correctly.

Audit after DXFIN or DXBIN, when enabled, forces an audit after importing a .dwf or .dxb file. The audit simply verifies that all drawing data is valid. If you are experiencing problems with importing these file types, you should enable this feature.

When the **Maintain a log file** check box is activated, AutoCAD creates a file named acad.log. The name and location of the log file can be specified using the **Log File** option found in the listing under the **Files** tab of the **Preferences** dialog box (shown in Figure 17-9B). When activated, all prompts, messages, and responses that appear in the text window are saved to this file. Exiting AutoCAD or turning off this check box disables the log file feature.

The log file status can also be set using the **LOGFILEON** and **LOGFILEOFF** commands. Each individual session of AutoCAD contained in a single log file is separated by a line of dashes with a date and time stamp.

The log file can serve a variety of purposes. The source of drawing errors can be determined by reviewing the commands that produced the incorrect results. Additionally, log files can be reviewed by a CAD manager to determine the need for training and customization of the system. Figure 17-10 shows an example of a log file opened in the Notepad program.

Figure 17-10.
The acad.log file viewed using Notepad.

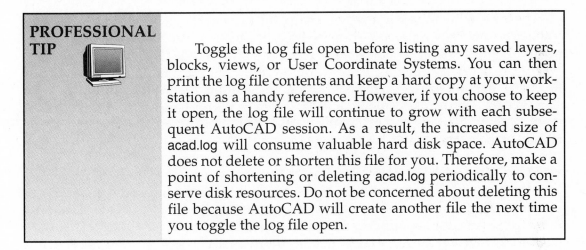

```
acad log - Notepad                                                   _ |□| x|
File   Edit   Search   Help
[ AutoCAD - Tue Sep 30 14:39:24 1997   ]-------------------------------

Command:
Command: rec RECTANGLE
Chamfer/Elevation/Fillet/Thickness/Width/<First corner>: 2,2

Other corner: 8,8

Command: z ZOOM
All/Center/Dynamic/Extents/Previous/Scale(X/XP)/Window/<Realtime>: .5x

Command: dim

Dim: *Cancel*

Command: dl
Unknown command "DL".   Press F1 for help.

Command: dimlinear

First extension line origin or press ENTER to select: _int of
Second extension line origin: _int of
Dimension line location (Mtext/Text/Angle/Horizontal/Vertical/Rotated):
```

PROFESSIONAL TIP

Toggle the log file open before listing any saved layers, blocks, views, or User Coordinate Systems. You can then print the log file contents and keep a hard copy at your workstation as a handy reference. However, if you choose to keep it open, the log file will continue to grow with each subsequent AutoCAD session. As a result, the increased size of acad.log will consume valuable hard disk space. AutoCAD does not delete or shorten this file for you. Therefore, make a point of shortening or deleting acad.log periodically to conserve disk resources. Do not be concerned about deleting this file because AutoCAD will create another file the next time you toggle the log file open.

The **Save thumbnail preview image** check box allows control over the preview image generated when a drawing is saved. This preview image is displayed in the **Preview** area of the **Select File** dialog box when opening a drawing. By leaving this box unchecked, no preview is generated. Checking the option specifies that a preview is saved within the drawing file.

Keystrokes

AutoCAD supports the common keystroke combinations recognized by many other Windows applications. For example, pressing [Ctrl]+[S] activates the **QSAVE** command to save your file. The [Ctrl]+[P] keystroke prints (plots) your file, [Ctrl]+[O] opens a drawing, and [Ctrl]+[N] starts a new drawing. In all releases previous to Release 13, the [Ctrl]+[C] key combination is used as a **CANCEL**. However, to conform with Windows standards, this combination now starts the '**COPYCLIP** command, and the [Esc] key now cancels.

For an experienced user of AutoCAD upgrading to Release 14, it may be a significant hurdle to "unlearn" several years of canceling with a [Ctrl]+[C]. For these users, AutoCAD provides a way to switch the new keystroke model with the old keystroke standards. Picking **AutoCAD classic** in the **Priority for accelerator keys** area on the **Compatibility** tab of the **Preferences** dialog box enables the old-style keystroke model. Picking **Windows standards** enables the new keystrokes. See Figure 17-11.

Figure 17-11.
Select the set of
keyboard shortcuts
you wish to use.

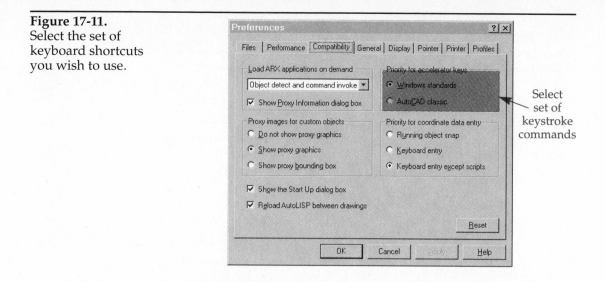

Setting AutoCAD Environment Variables

There are numerous settings that control the manner in which AutoCAD behaves in the Windows environment. These settings are made through the use of environment variables. These variables are used to specify such items as which folders to search for driver and menu files, and the location of your temporary and support files. The default settings created during installation are usually adequate, but changing the settings sometimes results in better performance. While several different options exist for setting many of the environment variables, the simplest method is to use the **Preferences** dialog box.

Specifying support file directories

The **Files** tab of the **Preferences** dialog box is used to specify the path AutoCAD searches to find support files and driver files. It also specifies the placement of temporary page (swap) files. Support files include text fonts, menus, AutoLISP files, ADS files, blocks to insert, linetypes, and hatch patterns.

The folder names shown under the Support File Search Path heading in the **Search paths, files names, and file locations:** list are automatically created by the AutoCAD installation procedure. See Figure 17-12. The Support, Fonts, and Help folders are created in a standard installation. The Bonus\Cadtools folder is only created if a full installation is performed. You can add the path of any new folders you create that contain support files.

Figure 17-12.
Folder paths can be
changed in the **Files**
tab of the **Preferences**
dialog box.

AutoCAD and its Applications—Advanced

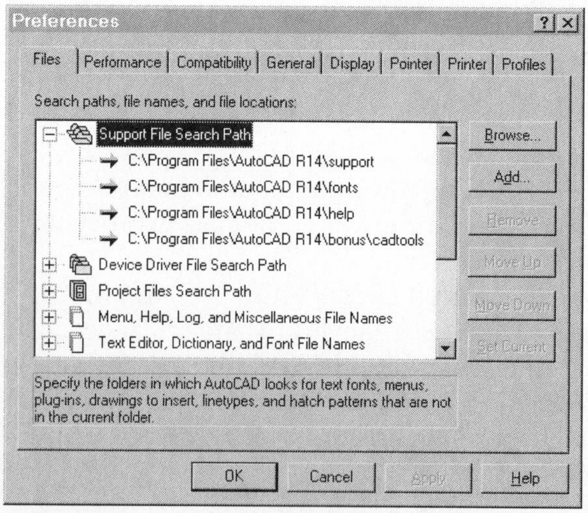

As an example, suppose you store all of the blocks you typically use in a separate folder named \Blocks on the C: drive. Unless this folder name is placed in the support files search path, AutoCAD will not be able to find your blocks when you attempt to insert them (unless you specify the entire folder path location).

You can add this folder to the existing search path in two ways. The first method is to highlight the **Support File Search Path** heading and pick the **Add...** button. This places a new, empty, listing under the heading. You can now type C:\BLOCKS to complete the entry. Alternatively, instead of typing the path name, you can pick the **Browse...** button to display the **Browse for Folder** dialog box. You can then use this dialog box to select to the desired folder. The new setting takes effect as soon as you pick **Apply** or the **OK** button and close the **Preferences** dialog box.

NOTE The terms *directory*, *subdirectory*, and *folder* are used interchangeably.

Specifying the help file

The AutoCAD help file is named acad.hlp. During installation, this file is placed in the AutoCAD R14\Help subfolder. You can use the Help file heading under the Menu, Help, Log, and Miscellaneous File Names entry to specify a different path and file name for the help file. This is particularly handy if you want to locate the help file on a network drive, or if you are using a custom help file.

AutoCAD is able to use any Windows format or platform-independent help file, so custom help files can be generated as needed. This can be a formidable undertaking, and is usually done by third-party developers to supplement their software add-ons. If you are using a third-party application with AutoCAD, you may have an alternate help file.

Other environment settings

Another setting that can be specified from the **Files** panel is the location of ADI (Autodesk Device Interface) driver files. The *Autodesk Device Interface* is a specification that allows dealers, manufacturers, and users to develop device drivers for peripherals that work with AutoCAD and other Autodesk products.

By default, the drivers supplied with AutoCAD are placed in the \AutoCAD R14\Drv folder. If you purchase a third-party driver to use with AutoCAD, be sure to load the driver into this folder. If the third-party driver must reside in a different folder, you should specify that folder using the Device Driver Search Path heading under the **Search paths, file names, and file locations** listing. Otherwise, the search for the correct driver is widespread and likely to take longer.

Some other file locations listed in the **Files** tab include the following:

- **Project Files Search Path.** Sets the value for the **PROJECTNAME** system variable and specifies of project path names.
- **Menu, Help, Log, and Miscellaneous File Names.** Specifies which files are used for the menu, help file, automatic save file, log file, default Internet location, configuration file, and license server.
- **Text Editor, Dictionary, and Font File Names.** Specifies which files are used for the text editor application, main and custom dictionaries, alternate font files, and the font mapping file.
- **Print File, Spooler, and Prolog Section Name.** Sets the file names for the print file, the print spool executable file, and the Postscript prolog section name.
- **Print Spooler File Location.** Sets the location of the print spooler file.
- **Template Drawing File Location.** Specifies the default location for template files.

- **Temporary Drawing File Location.** Sets the directory location where AutoCAD stores temporary drawing files.
- **Temporary External Reference File Location.** Indicates where temporary external reference files are placed.
- **Texture Maps Search Path.** Tells AutoCAD where to look for texture map files for rendering.

There are many other settings available in the **Preferences** dialog box that do not fall directly into any of the previous discussion areas. Some affect the performance of AutoCAD, others affect the functionality of the program. The following is a synopsis of these additional settings. Some of these variables are discussed in other chapters.

Performance tab

- **Rendered object smoothness** controls the smoothness, or number of facets, on curved surfaces of rendered objects. This sets the **FACETRES** system variable.
- **Contour lines per surface** specifies the number of contour lines used to represent curved surfaces on 3D models. This sets the **ISOLINES** system variable.
- **Show silhouettes in wireframe** specifies whether silhouette curves of body objects are displayed as wireframes. This sets the **DISPSILH** system variable.
- **Show text boundary frame only** sets the **QTEXTMODE** system variable, specifying whether text objects are displayed as rectangles.
- **Show raster image content** controls whether raster images are displayed during real-time display changes, and while dragging the images. This sets the **RTDISPLAY** system variable.
- **External reference file demand load** sets the **XLOADCTL** variable, which specifies the method of demand loading for xrefs.
- **Display object being dragged** options specify the way that dragged objects are displayed. This sets the **DRAGMODE** system variable..
- **Arc and circle smoothness** controls the smoothness of circles, arcs, and ellipses. Also controlled by **VIEWRES**.
- **Segments per polyline curve** sets **SPLINESEGS**, which controls how many line segments are used to represent polyline curves.
- **Incremental Save %** specifies how much wasted space is tolerated within a drawing file. When the value is reached, a full save is done instead of an incremental save. This sets the **ISAVEPERCENT** system variable.
- **Maximum active viewports** indicates the maximum number of viewports that can be active at one time. This sets the **MAXACTVP** system variable.

Compatibility tab

- **Load ARX applications on demand** specifies if and when AutoCAD loads third party applications associated with objects in the drawing.
- **Proxy images for custom objects** controls how objects created by a third party application are displayed.
- **Show the start up dialog box** indicates whether the **Start Up** dialog box is displayed when beginning an AutoCAD session.
- **Reload AutoLISP between drawings** turns the persistent AutoLISP feature on or off.
- **Priority for coordinate data entry** controls whether coordinates entered at the keyboard or by script files respect running object snap modes.

General tab

- **Beep on error in user input** specifies whether AutoCAD alerts you of incorrect user input with an audible beep.
- **File extension for temporary files** sets the file extension used for temporary AutoCAD files.
- **Maximum number sorted symbols** controls the **MAXSORT** variable, which specifies the maximum number of objects to sort.

Saving Your Configuration Profiles

The AutoCAD environment settings can be saved as a user profile. A *profile* is a set of custom preferences. In cases where multiple users are using the same workstation at different times, each user can save an individual profile and then reload it at every session. Various profiles may also be useful to a single user with different preferences for different projects.

If no one has previously created a custom profile, the only profile listed will be <<Unnamed Profile>>. Unless you have defined a custom profile and set it to be current, AutoCAD saves all of your preference changes to <<Unnamed Profile>>.

Pick the **Profiles** tab of the **Preferences** dialog box to define or load a profile. The available and current profiles are displayed as shown in Figure 17-13. Select the profile that most closely matches your preferences, or <<Unnamed Profile>> if none already exist. You can create your own profile from the selected profile by picking the **Copy...** button. The **Copy Profile** dialog box, shown in Figure 17-14, is used to name and create a description for a new profile.

Figure 17-13. Collections of settings can be saved in the **Profiles** tab of the **Preferences** dialog box.

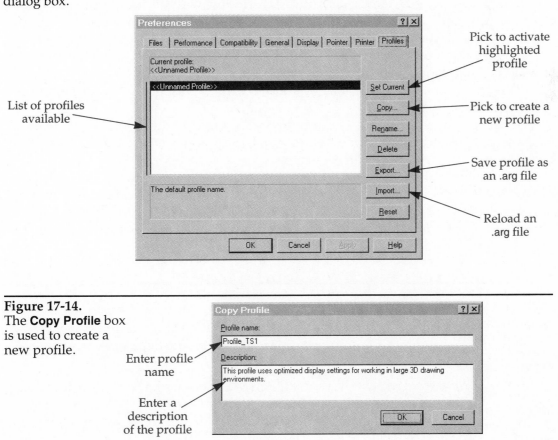

Figure 17-14.
The **Copy Profile** box is used to create a new profile.

Enter profile name

Enter a description of the profile

Next, set the new profile name to be the current profile by highlighting it and picking the **Set Current** button. Now, all changes that you make to your preferences are saved in this profile. At any point, you can make a different profile active by highlighting it and picking the **Set Current** button.

It is possible for another user to unknowingly change your preferences if the current profile is not changed before editing preferences. To ensure maximum safety of a profile, you can save the profile data to a file on disk. Pick the **Export...** button to display the **Export Profile** dialog box. The default file extension is .arg, and you can specify any valid file name. To access the saved settings at a later time, pick the **Import...** button to display the **Import Profile** dialog box. Now you can select any saved profile to import.

Positioning the AutoCAD Graphics and Text Windows

Perhaps the greatest advantage offered by the Microsoft Windows environment is the ability to have several applications displayed in separate windows simultaneously. It is then a simple matter to pick anywhere within an open window to activate the application within it. Naturally, the number and size of the displayed windows is a function of the current screen resolution and monitor size.

When AutoCAD is installed, the graphics window fills the entire display screen. The text window is only displayed when you press the [F2] function key. When you want to return to the graphics window, you simply pick once more anywhere within its displayed border or press [F2] again.

By default, AutoCAD is maximized on startup. This means that it fills the entire screen. When a window is maximized, the upper-right corner of the window displays three buttons, as shown in Figure 17-15A.

The **Minimize** button closes the AutoCAD window without ending your AutoCAD session. AutoCAD is then displayed as a button on your Windows task bar. Picking the application button on the task bar restores the window to its previous state.

The **Restore** button changes the AutoCAD window to a *floating* window. When a window is floating, it can be freely adjusted and repositioned.

The third button is the **Close Window** button. Picking this button closes the window and exits AutoCAD.

A floating window displays the buttons shown in Figure 17-15B. The **Minimize** and **Close Window** buttons work the same as before, and the **Maximize** button can be used to cause the window to fill the screen.

You can reposition a floating AutoCAD window by picking within the title bar at the top of the window. Hold the pointing device button down, drag the window to the desired location, and release the pointing device button. When floating, the windows will remain at the defined locations for all subsequent AutoCAD sessions until you relocate them and save the new position settings.

Figure 17-15.
The buttons in the upper-right corner of a window are used to change window display.
A—These buttons are found in a maximized window.
B—These buttons are found in a floating window.

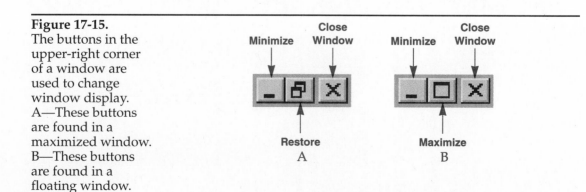

Sizing the AutoCAD Graphics and Text Windows

Apart from repositioning the graphics and text windows on your display, you may also find it useful to size the windows to different values. Sizing a window can be accomplished as easily as moving its location.

To stretch (or shrink) a window along its vertical axis, simply pick and hold at the top or bottom border of the window. The pointing device then assumes the shape of a double arrow, Figure 17-16A. Drag the border to the desired size and release the pointing device button. For example, to stretch (or shrink) a window along its horizontal axis, pick and hold at the left or right border of the window. Then, drag the border to the desired size and release the pointing device button.

To stretch (or shrink) a window along both axes simultaneously, pick and hold one of the four corners of the window. The pointing device assumes the shape of a double arrow at an angle, Figure 17-16B. Drag the corner to the desired position and release the pointing device button.

To help select the window border, you may find it useful to increase the width of the window border. To do so, pick Settings and then Control Panel from the Start menu, Figure 17-17. When the Control Panel window appears, double-click the Display icon, Figure 17-18.

Figure 17-16.
To change the size of a window, position the cursor on the edge of the window. The cursor changes to a resizing cursor and you can drag the edge. A—Stretching the window vertically. B—This cursor appears at edge corners. Both edges are stretched at the same time.

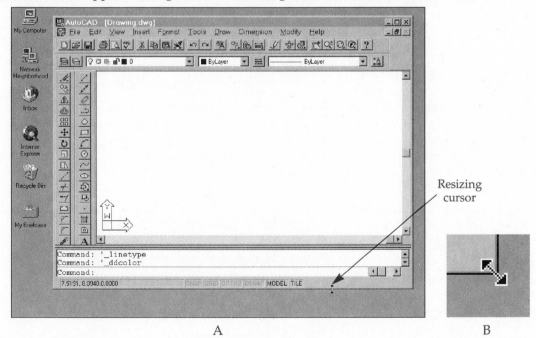

Resizing cursor

A   B

Figure 17-17.
Pick Control Panel from the Settings menu to access the Control Panel window.

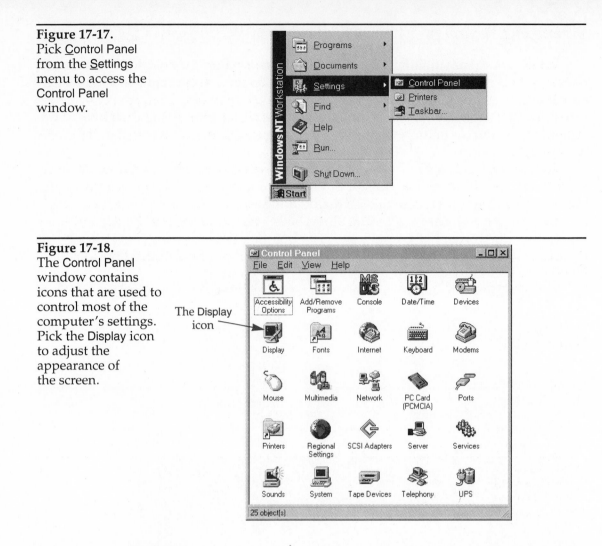

Figure 17-18.
The Control Panel window contains icons that are used to control most of the computer's settings. Pick the Display icon to adjust the appearance of the screen.

The Display icon

Pick the Appearance tab in the Display Properties dialog box. Then pick the active window border to make it the current option (or you can select Active Window Border from the Item: drop-down list). The Size option is used to adjust the width of the border, Figure 17-19. The border width is measured in pixels, and the default is 1 pixel.

Figure 17-19.
The width of window borders can be adjusted using the Appearance tab in the Display Properties dialog box.

Select item to adjust

Adjust window border size

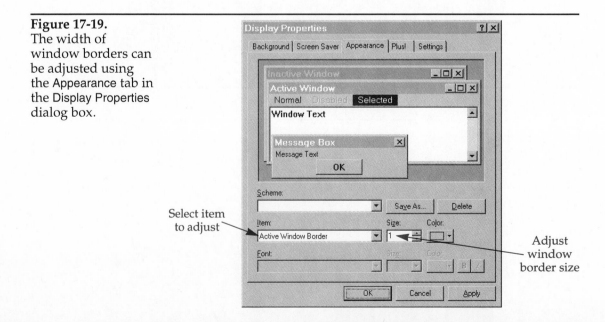

Changing Program Properties

When AutoCAD is first installed on your computer, the installation program setup.exe automatically creates the AutoCAD group and several program items, then places a shortcut on your desktop. If desired, you can then modify the program properties. These properties include such things as the file attributes, the directory where AutoCAD is started, and even choosing a new icon that AutoCAD uses to represent the application shortcut.

To modify the AutoCAD program properties, first right-click the AutoCAD icon on the desktop. Next, select Properties from the pop-up cursor menu, Figure 17-20. You can also single-click the AutoCAD icon and then use the [Alt]+[Enter] key combination. Either action displays the AutoCAD R14 Properties dialog box, Figure 17-21.

Figure 17-20.
This pop-up cursor menu appears when you right-click on an icon in the Windows desktop.

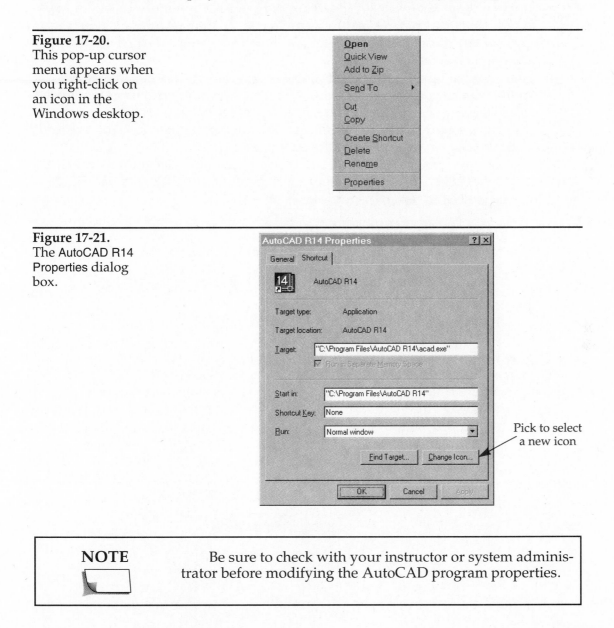

Figure 17-21.
The AutoCAD R14 Properties dialog box.

| NOTE | Be sure to check with your instructor or system administrator before modifying the AutoCAD program properties. |

There are two tabs, General and Shortcut. The following items can be specified in this dialog box:

- **Attributes.** These radio buttons on the General tab can be used to quickly and easily set the attributes for the file containing the shortcut information.
- **Target.** This text box contains the name of the executable program and its path. If the drive or folder that contains the AutoCAD executables has changed, this line can be edited so that it still links to the correct file. If you are not sure of the exact path name, you can pick the **Find Target** button to locate it.
- **Start in.** This text box specifies the name of the folder where the AutoCAD program files are located. The folder specified in this text box becomes the current directory when AutoCAD is running. Any newly created files are placed here.
- **Shortcut Key.** Microsoft Windows provides a special feature called an *application shortcut key*. This feature permits you to launch AutoCAD with a user-defined key combination. Assigning a shortcut key for AutoCAD is described later in this section.
- **Run.** This listing offers options to run the program in a normal, maximized, or minimized window. It is not recommended to run the program minimized, otherwise AutoCAD appears only as a button on the task bar when you run it. You can easily restore or maximize it, but when it does not automatically appear on screen, it may be confusing to newer users.

When you are finished making your changes, pick the OK button to exit the AutoCAD R14 Properties dialog box. Since any changes you make take effect immediately, there is no need to restart Windows.

Changing the AutoCAD icon

The AutoCAD R14 Properties dialog box provides the option to change the program icon used by AutoCAD. To change the icon, do the following:

1. Pick the Change Icon... button in the Shortcut tab of the AutoCAD R14 Properties dialog box.
2. The Change Icon dialog box is then displayed, Figure 17-22.
3. Observe that there are many icons from which to choose, but none of these icons represent the AutoCAD application. To display icons for AutoCAD, use the Browse... button to find the file named acad.exe in the AutoCAD R14 folder. Pick the Open button to display the AutoCAD icons, as shown in Figure 17-23. Six icons are shown—the standard icon, a drawing icon, two that closely resemble the AutoCAD text window, one for the aerial view window, and the standard icon for an AutoLISP file.

Figure 17-22.
A new icon can be selected in the Change Icon dialog box.

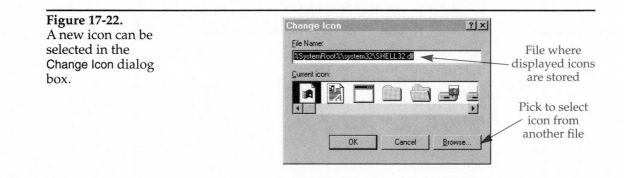

File where displayed icons are stored

Pick to select icon from another file

Figure 17-23.
Icons available in
the acad.exe file.

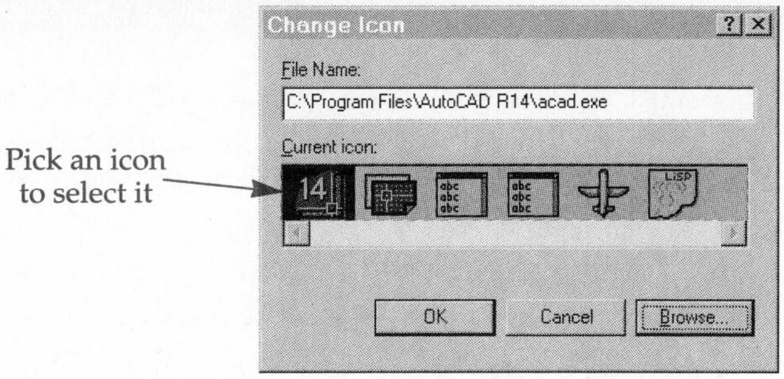

Pick an icon
to select it

4. Select the icon you wish to use and pick the OK button to exit the Change Icon dialog box.
5. Your icon selection is now displayed in the AutoCAD R14 Properties dialog box.

Defining a shortcut key

Microsoft Windows provides the option of assigning a shortcut key that starts a new application running no matter where you are in Windows. You can use any letter, number, or special character for a shortcut key. Whichever key you choose, Windows automatically adds a [Ctrl]+[Alt] in front of it. To assign a shortcut key for launching AutoCAD, do the following:

1. Return to the desktop and open the AutoCAD R14 Properties dialog box.
2. Pick within the Shortcut Key: text box. The flashing vertical cursor appears at the end of the word None.
3. Now, press [A] (or whichever key you prefer).
4. The character string Ctrl + Alt + A appears in the text box, Figure 17-24.
5. Pick OK to exit the AutoCAD R14 Properties dialog box.

Your new shortcut key is immediately active. Now, no matter which Windows-based application is running, you can start AutoCAD with the keyboard combination [Ctrl]+[Alt]+[A]. Refer to the Microsoft Windows *User's Guide* for more information regarding shortcut keys.

Figure 17-24.
Setting the
[Alt]+[Ctrl]+[A] key
combination to
automatically start
AutoCAD.

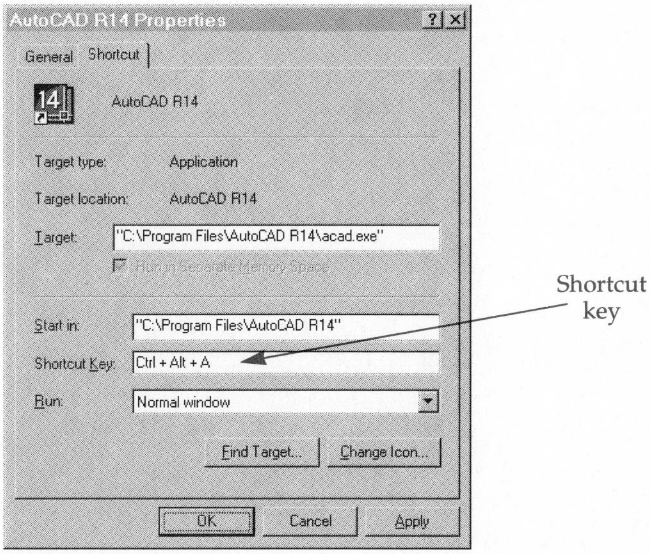

Shortcut
key

Creating Alternate AutoCAD Configurations

The information you specify for AutoCAD regarding the pointing and printing devices is recorded in a configuration file. Your pointing and printing devices are specified in the **Preferences** dialog box, but the information is stored in the current configuration file.

The default configuration file is acad14.cfg. By default, this file is located in the folder that contains the AutoCAD program files. Each time you specify a new pointing or printing device, the existing acad14.cfg file is overwritten with the new information.

Under most circumstances, a single configuration file is all that is necessary. Some users, however, may require multiple configurations. As an example, if you use a mouse most of the time but sometimes need a digitizer tablet for your AutoCAD work, you may find it convenient to set up AutoCAD to use multiple configurations. This can save you the time required to reconfigure AutoCAD each time you need to switch your pointing devices.

To save multiple configurations, you must specify a new location for AutoCAD to store the acad14.cfg so that it does not overwrite the previous version. This way you actually have more than one configuration file, with each file located in a specific folder.

As you set up your system for multiple AutoCAD configurations, the first step is to create an alternate folder where the new configuration file will be placed. Do this using Windows Explorer, or any regular file dialog box. It is recommended that these folders be placed under the AutoCAD R14 directory so they are easy to locate. For this example, create a directory named AutoCAD R14\Altcfg. Now, find the acad14.cfg file in the AutoCAD R14 directory and copy it to your new directory.

Press the [Ctrl] key and pick the AutoCAD icon and drag it to copy the desktop shortcut. This creates a new icon for the starting of the new configuration. Open the AutoCAD R14 Properties dialog box and go to the Shortcut tab. In the <u>T</u>arget: edit box, place a /c after the existing target, followed by the directory path location for the alternate configuration. For example, in Figure 17-25, the configuration directory is entered as:

> "C:\Program Files\AutoCAD R14\acad.exe" **/c "C:\Program Files\AutoCAD R14\altcfg"**

Figure 17-25.
If multiple configurations are used, the location of the alternate configuration file must be specified in the **Target** edit box.

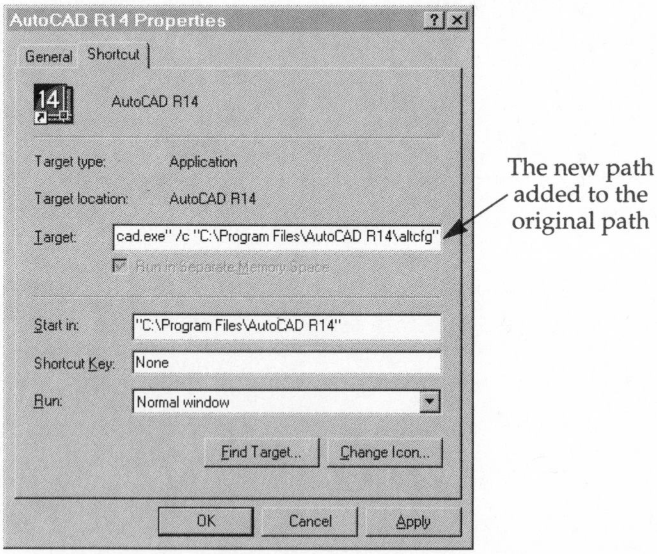

The new path added to the original path

The new path must be placed in quotation marks due to the space in the path name. The /c is not in quotation marks. Command line switches are separated by spaces, and the space is interpreted as the end of the path name.

It is also recommended that you change the title of the shortcut icon on the desktop to match the configuration. For example, one shortcut icon could be called AutoCAD R14 – Mouse and the other could be called AutoCAD R14 – Digitizer. Do this by picking the text below the icon once, pausing for a moment, then picking again. Now you can enter the new text.

When you start AutoCAD using the new icon, the alternate configuration file directory is used. This means that any configuration changes you make are stored in the new configuration file and do not affect other configurations.

NOTE

You can set up unique shortcut keys for each AutoCAD shortcut icon on your desktop. To summarize the procedure:

1. Create a folder for AutoCAD's alternate configuration files.
2. Copy the acad14.cfg file into the alternate configuration folder.
3. Hold down the [Ctrl] key and drag the AutoCAD icon to copy it.
4. Pick the new AutoCAD icon to highlight it.
5. Press [Alt]+[Enter] to access the AutoCAD R14 Properties dialog box.
6. Add the /c switch and new path to the target just after acad.exe. For example:

"C:\Program Files\AutoCAD R14\acad.exe" **/c**
"C:\Program Files\AutoCAD R14\altcfg"

7. Pick OK to exit the AutoCAD R14 Properties dialog box.
8. Change the title of the desktop icon.

Chapter Test

Write your answers in the spaces provided.

1. List two methods used to access the **Preferences** dialog box. _____

   _____

   _____

2. How do you access the **AutoCAD Window Colors** dialog box? _____

   _____

   _____

3. What are the advantages of toggling the log file open? The disadvantages? _____

   _____

   _____

   _____

   _____

   _____

---

4. Name the two commands that toggle the log file on and off. _____
_____

5. AutoCAD resides in the C:\Program Files\AutoCAD R14\ folder on your workstation. You have created two folders under \AutoCAD R14 named Projects and Symbols. You want to store your drawings in the Projects folder and your blocks in the Symbols folder. What should you enter in the Support File Search Path area so these directories are added to the search path? _____
_____
_____

6. What is a *profile*? _____
_____
_____

7. How and why are profiles used? _____
_____
_____
_____
_____

8. How do you increase the width of a window border? _____
_____
_____
_____

9. Which file must be copied to a separate folder before creating an alternate AutoCAD configuration? _____

Problems

1. Create an alternate configuration for AutoCAD dedicated to 3D modeling and rendering using the methods described in this chapter. Use the following instructions:
   A. Assign a different program icon to the 3D configuration.
   B. Name the program icon AutoCAD 3D.
   C. Define a shortcut key for the configuration.
   D. Add a directory to the support path that contains 3D shapes.

2. Create another alternate configuration for AutoCAD dedicated to dimensioning. Use the following instructions to complete this problem:
   A. Assign a different program icon to the dimensioning configuration.
   B. Name the program icon AutoCAD Dimensioning.
   C. Define a shortcut key for the configuration.
   D. Add a directory to the support path that contains 3D shapes.

Chapter 18

Customizing Toolbars

Learning Objectives

After completing this chapter, you will be able to:
- Position and resize toolbars.
- Display and hide toolbars.
- Modify existing toolbars.
- Create new toolbars.
- Create new toolbar tools.
- Construct new button images.
- Create and modify flyout menus.
- Describe the purpose and function of the AutoCAD menu files.

One of the easiest ways of altering the AutoCAD environment is to customize the toolbars. This requires no programming and little use of text editors. Existing toolbars can be modified quickly by removing and adding buttons, or changing toolbar shape. New tools can also be created and assigned to an existing toolbar. The most powerful aspect of customizing toolbars is the ability to quickly create entirely new functions and buttons to help you in your work.

Working with Toolbars

Toolbars provide access to most AutoCAD commands with one or two quick "picks." This graphical interface provides much flexibility. Toolbars can be quickly and easily resized, repositioned, hidden from view, or made visible.

Positioning and sizing toolbars

A *docked toolbar* is positioned so that it appears as if it is part of the AutoCAD window. By default, the **Standard** and **Object Properties** toolbars are docked at the top of the screen and the **Draw** and **Modify** toolbars are docked at the left side of the screen. When a visible toolbar is not docked, it is a floating toolbar. A *floating toolbar* appears as a small window with a title bar. When a toolbar is floating, it can be adjusted and repositioned like any other window.

A docked toolbar can be *floated* by pointing to any area on the toolbar that is not a button, and then pressing and holding the pick button. Now, move your cursor and you drag an outline of the toolbar. When you release the pick button, the toolbar appears in the new location.

To reposition a floating toolbar, place the cursor on the title bar, press and hold the pick button, and move the toolbar to the new location. The outline of the toolbar is visible while you are moving it, Figure 18-1A. Release the pick button when the toolbar is where you want it.

Unlike windows, toolbars can only be resized in one direction at a time. Moving the cursor to a vertical border changes the cursor to a horizontal resizing cursor. Again, press and hold the pick button and an outline is displayed. Move the cursor to resize the toolbar. Release the pick button to create the new size. Figure 18-1B and Figure 18-1C show the **Draw** toolbar being resized.

To dock a toolbar, reposition it at any edge of the AutoCAD window. A toolbar can be docked on the right, left, top, or bottom of the window. Figure 18-2 shows the **Draw** toolbar docked on the left side of the screen and the **Modify** toolbar in the process of being docked on the right side. Note that the outline of the toolbar changes shape and is displayed with a thinner line when it is in position to be docked. Releasing the pick button completes the docking operation.

If you need to place a floating toolbar near the edge of the AutoCAD window but you do not want it to dock, simply hold the [Ctrl] key down while you reposition the toolbar. This information appears on the status line as you move a toolbar, as shown in Figure 18-2. To float a docked toolbar, place your cursor anywhere on the toolbar that is not a button, then press and hold the pick button. Now, move the toolbar away from the edge and it floats. This technique can also be used to adjust the position of a docked toolbar.

Figure 18-1.
A—Repositioning a floating toolbar.
B—Resizing a floating toolbar horizontally.
C—Resizing a toolbar vertically.

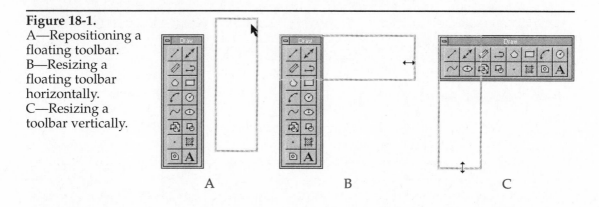

A   B   C

Figure 18-2.
Toolbars can be docked on the edge of the AutoCAD window. Press the [Ctrl] key while moving the toolbar to prevent docking.

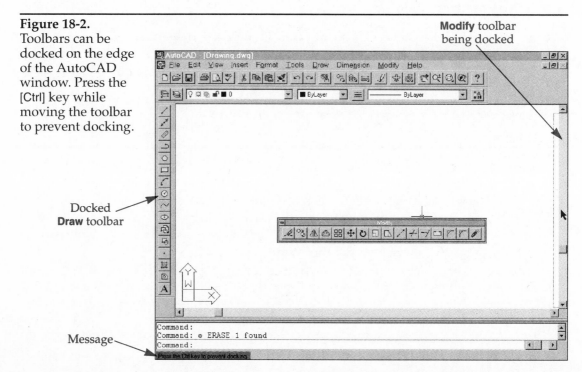

Modify toolbar being docked

Docked **Draw** toolbar

Message

       AutoCAD and its Applications—Advanced

Controlling toolbar visibility

You can adjust the AutoCAD screen so that only the toolbars you need are visible. This helps conserve drawing window space. If too many toolbars are visible at one time, the drawing window can become small and crowded. When your drawing area is small, too much of your time is spent making display changes so you can clearly see parts of the drawing. Figure 18-3 shows an example of a small and crowded drawing window.

Also, look closely at the **Dimension** toolbar docked on the left side of the window. It is partially hidden from view. The combined length of the **Dimension** and **Insert** toolbars is longer than the available space. Remember this when arranging your toolbars. You must have access to all of the buttons.

Toolbars can be turned on and off using the **TOOLBAR** command. Access this command by selecting **Toolbars...** from the **View** pull-down menu or typing TO or TOOLBAR at the Command: prompt. This command displays the **Toolbars** dialog box, Figure 18-4. Right-clicking on a toolbar button will also access the **Toolbars** dialog box. There are several options available in this dialog box for controlling the visibility and appearance of toolbars.

TOOLBAR
TO

View
➡ Toolbars...

Figure 18-3.
Too many toolbars visible at once can cut down on the useful drawing area.

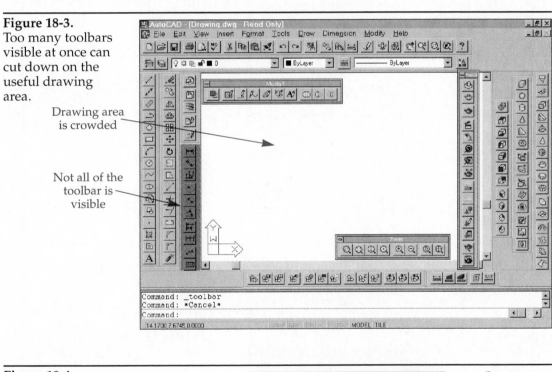

Drawing area is crowded

Not all of the toolbar is visible

Figure 18-4.
The **Toolbars** dialog box is used to turn toolbars on and off, create new toolbars, and customize existing toolbars.

An "X" means the toolbar is visible

Toolbars in this menu are listed

Display options

Create a new toolbar

Delete highlighted toolbar

Add buttons to or subtract buttons from a toolbar

Pick to change properties

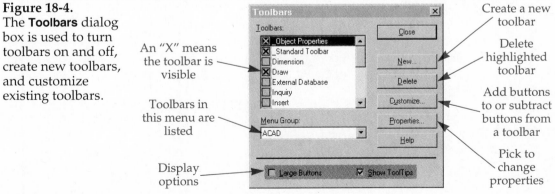

If there are toolbars defined in more than one menu, select the appropriate menu from the **Menu Group** drop-down list. If you loaded partial menus in addition to your primary menu, you must make the menu group name current to access the toolbars defined in that menu.

The **Toolbars:** list shows all of the toolbars defined in the selected menu group. To make a toolbar visible, place a check in the check box next to the toolbar name by picking the box. To hide a toolbar, remove the check. The results are immediate. When you are finished, pick the **Close** button.

Another way to hide a floating toolbar is to pick on the menu control button, Figure 18-5. If you wish to hide a docked toolbar, you can first move it away from the edge to make it a floating toolbar. Then, pick the menu control button. However, if you hide a docked toolbar in this manner, it will appear in the floating position when you make it visible again. When the **Toolbars** dialog box is used to hide a docked toolbar, it remains in its docked position.

The **Toolbars** dialog box displays two check boxes at the bottom. They are toggles for the button features they represent:

- **Large Buttons.** Checking this box increases the size of your toolbar buttons from 16×16 to 32×32 pixels. At very high screen resolutions, such as 1280×1024, the smaller 16×16 buttons can be difficult to see. Setting the buttons to the larger size is easier on the eyes. At lower screen resolutions, the large buttons take up too much of the available space in the AutoCAD window.
- **Show ToolTips.** This allows you to turn off the ToolTips feature, which displays the name of the button that you are pointing to. Unless you are very familiar with the button interface, it is usually best to leave ToolTips on.

Figure 18-5.
Pick the menu control button and the toolbar is hidden.

Menu control button

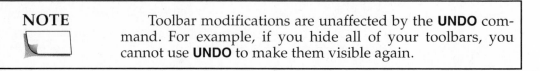

NOTE

Toolbar modifications are unaffected by the **UNDO** command. For example, if you hide all of your toolbars, you cannot use **UNDO** to make them visible again.

Working with toolbars at the command line

Use the **-TOOLBAR** command to work with toolbars at the command line. When using this method, you are prompted for the toolbar name. The toolbar name consists of the menu group and toolbar name, separated by a period. For example, the toolbar name for the **Draw** toolbar defined in the acad.mnu menu is ACAD.DRAW. After specifying the toolbar name (or selecting ALL for all toolbars), you can select an option from the following prompt:

```
Command: -TOOLBAR↵
Toolbar name (or ALL): ACAD.DRAW↵
Show/Hide/Left/Right/Top/Bottom/Float:
```

The options are used to hide, show, or specify a location for the toolbar. The following options are available:

- **Show.** This option makes the toolbar visible. Selecting this option is identical to activating the check box next to the toolbar name in the **Toolbars** dialog box.
- **Hide.** This option causes the toolbar to disappear. Selecting this option is identical to disabling the check box next to the toolbar name in the **Toolbars** dialog box.
- **Left.** Places the toolbar relative to a docked position at the left side of the window.
- **Right.** Places the toolbar relative to a docked position at the right side of the window.
- **Top.** Places the toolbar relative to a docked position at the top of the window.
- **Bottom.** Places the specified toolbar relative to a docked position at the bottom of the window.
- **Float.** Places the toolbar as a floating toolbar.

The **Left/Right/Top/Bottom/Float** options show a toolbar (if it is not already visible) and place it in the specified position in the AutoCAD window. To dock the **Modify** toolbar on the left side of the AutoCAD window, use the following command sequence:

```
Command: -TOOLBAR↵
Toolbar name (or ALL): ACAD.MODIFY↵
Show/Hide/Left/Right/Top/Bottom/Float: ⟨Show⟩: LEFT↵
Position ⟨0,0⟩: ↵
```

The Position ⟨0,0⟩: prompt is asking for a pixel value. *Pixel* stands for picture elements and refers to the smallest unit of display on your monitor. For example, an 800×600 resolution screen has 800 pixels horizontally and 600 vertically. When docked, a horizontal toolbar is approximately 32 pixels high and a vertical toolbar is about 34 pixels wide.

Pixels used as screen coordinates are specified using the upper-left portion of the screen as 0,0. In the case of docked toolbars, the upper-left area of the docking area is considered 0,0. The previous example places the **Modify** toolbar in the upper-left corner of the toolbar docking area at the left side of the screen. Placing another toolbar in the same location (0,0) pushes the existing toolbar down on a vertical (**Left/Right**) configuration, or to the right on a horizontal (**Top/Bottom**) configuration.

The last option of the **TOOLBAR** command is the **Float** option. This places the toolbar in a floating position specified in pixels at the Position ⟨0,0⟩: prompt. The anchor point of a floating toolbar is the upper-left corner. If you place the toolbar at 400,300, the upper-left corner of the toolbar is at this coordinate location. You are then asked to establish the shape of the new toolbar by specifying the number of rows of buttons for the toolbar. For example, this sequence places the **Draw** toolbar as shown in Figure 18-6:

```
Command: -TOOLBAR↵
Toolbar name (or ALL): ACAD.DRAW↵
Show/Hide/Left/Right/Top/Bottom/Float: ⟨Show⟩: FLOAT↵
Position ⟨0,0⟩: 400,300↵
Rows ⟨1⟩: 2↵
```

While using the **-TOOLBAR** command is very accurate for placement, it is also time-consuming. Using the cursor is much quicker, though not as accurate. When using floating toolbars, it is also possible to overlap the toolbars to save screen space. To bring a toolbar to the front, simply pick on it. Be sure to leave part of each toolbar showing.

Another capability of the **-TOOLBAR** command is to show or hide all toolbars at once. When prompted for the toolbar name, enter ALL. The only two options that appear are **Show** and **Hide**. If you use the **Hide** option, no toolbars are displayed. Then, you can use the **Toolbars** dialog box menu to select the toolbars you need.

Figure 18-6.
Locating a floating toolbar at a 400,300 position using the **-TOOLBAR** command.

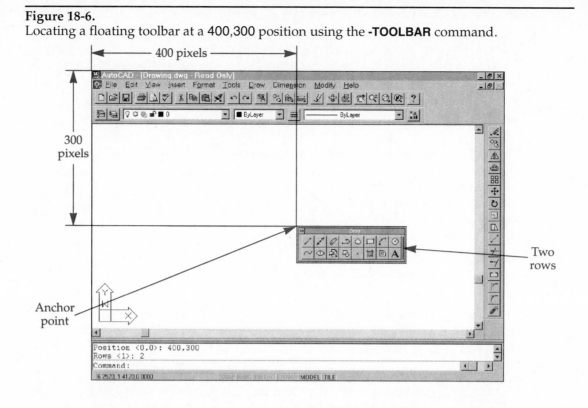

NOTE	The command line version of the **-TOOLBAR** command is most useful when creating menu macros, script files, or AutoLISP functions designed to perform automated toolbar setups.

EXERCISE 18-1

❑ Open AutoCAD and maximize it so that it occupies the entire screen.
❑ Use the appropriate method to display the **Draw**, **Modify**, and **Dimension** toolbars.
❑ Position the three toolbars in a floating configuration. Move them to several different floating positions around the screen.
❑ Move the **Draw** and **Modify** toolbars to a docked position at the top of the screen.
❑ Move the **Dimension** toolbar to a docked position at the right side of the screen.
❑ Position all three toolbars in a docked position at the right side of the screen.
❑ Position each of the toolbars in two additional docked positions on the screen.
❑ Return the screen to the original configuration.

Customizing Toolbars

In addition to positioning and sizing toolbars, you can also customize the toolbar interface. You can add new buttons or place existing buttons in new locations for quick access. Infrequently used tools can be deleted or moved to an "out-of-the-way" location. Entirely new toolbars can be created and filled with redefined buttons, or custom button definitions can be created. Toolbars are customized using the **Toolbars** dialog box.

Adding, deleting, moving, and copying tools

The **Toolbars** dialog box allows you to manipulate toolbars and toolbar buttons. One common modification to the toolbars is to place an existing tool in a new location. For example, if your current project requires you to modify the properties of existing hatch patterns, you may wish to have access to the **Edit Hatch** tool. One approach would be to make the **Modify II** toolbar visible, but if you do not want an extra toolbar on your screen, you can simply move or copy the **Edit Hatch** button to a currently visible toolbar.

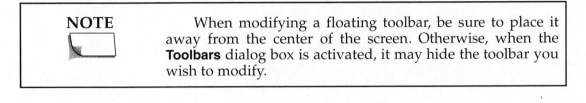

NOTE When modifying a floating toolbar, be sure to place it away from the center of the screen. Otherwise, when the **Toolbars** dialog box is activated, it may hide the toolbar you wish to modify.

The following sequence adds the **Edit Hatch** tool to the **Modify** toolbar. First, start the **TOOLBAR** command, or right-click on any visible toolbar button. The **Toolbars** dialog box is displayed. To begin customizing your toolbar, pick the **Customize...** button. This displays the **Customize Toolbars** dialog box, Figure 18-7A. The **Customize Toolbars** dialog provides access to all of AutoCAD's predefined toolbar buttons.

The **Categories:** drop-down list contains general command classifications. Some of these correspond to toolbar names. Use this list to select the **Modify** category, where the **Edit Hatch** button is located. The **Customize Toolbars** dialog box changes, as shown in Figure 18-7B.

The buttons displayed in the dialog box can be added to an existing toolbar. Point to the button, then press and hold the pick button. Drag the button to the toolbar and release the pick button. Figure 18-8 shows the **Edit Hatch** button being dragged from the **Customize Toolbars** dialog box to the **Modify** toolbar.

Figure 18-7.
The **Customize Toolbars** dialog box.
A—First select the proper category for the command.
B—Pick a displayed button to view its description.

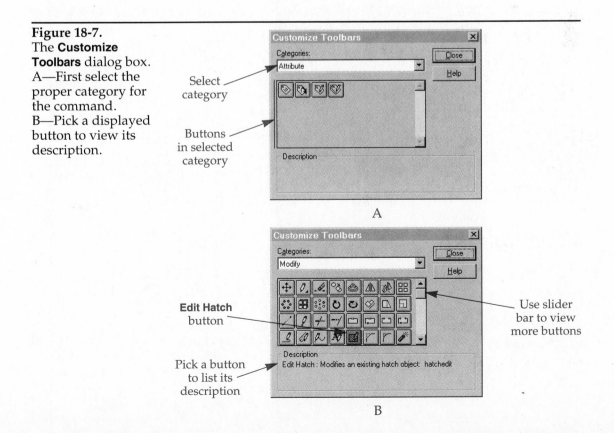

Select category

Buttons in selected category

A

Edit Hatch button

Use slider bar to view more buttons

Pick a button to list its description

B

Figure 18-8.
Adding the **Edit Hatch** button to the **Modify** toolbar. A—Dragging the button from the **Customize Toolbars** dialog box. B—Positioning the button in the toolbar. C—The toolbar with the added button.

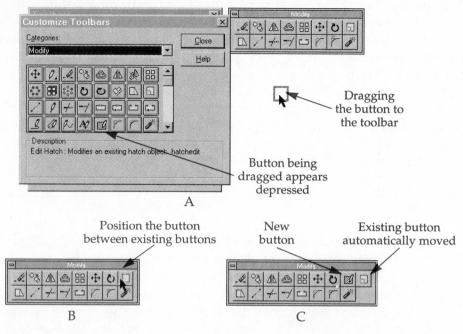

A

Dragging the button to the toolbar

Button being dragged appears depressed

Position the button between existing buttons

New button

Existing button automatically moved

B   C

Position the button in the toolbar where you would like it to be located. If you position it between two other buttons, it is placed between them. The existing buttons are adjusted to accommodate the new button.

You can continue to customize toolbars while the **Customize Toolbars** dialog box is open. To remove an existing button from a toolbar, first point to the button. Then, press and hold the pick button on your pointing device. Now drag the toolbar button out to a clear area of the graphics screen and release the pick button. The toolbar button disappears and is removed from the toolbar.

Moving a button to a new location is accomplished the same way. Simply drag it to the new location. This includes repositioning a button on the same toolbar, or moving it to a new toolbar. By pressing and holding the [Ctrl] key while you move a button, a small plus sign is added to the outline being dragged, Figure 18-9. This indicates that the button is being *copied* to the new location rather than being *moved*. A copied button appears in both the new and old locations.

Figure 18-9.
When dragging a button and pressing the [Ctrl] key, the plus sign indicates that the toolbar button is being copied.

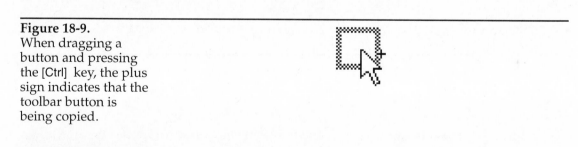

PROFESSIONAL TIP

You will notice that many buttons are displayed in the **Customize Toolbars** dialog box. Some of them may be familiar and some may not. Unfortunately, ToolTips are not available for the buttons displayed in this dialog. If you are unsure of what a specific button is, pick it and read the description.

Toolbar properties

The basic properties of a toolbar include the toolbar name, help string, and its current visibility status. Each of these properties can be adjusted by picking the **Properties...** button in the **Toolbars** dialog box. This displays the **Toolbar Properties** dialog box for the currently selected toolbar. See Figure 18-10.

The **Toolbar Properties** dialog box lists the name, help string, and alias for the toolbar. The toolbar name appears in the list in the **Toolbars** dialog box and in the title bar of a floating toolbar. The help string appears at the left of the status bar when the cursor is over the toolbar. To change the name of a toolbar or the associated help string, enter the new text in the appropriate edit box. The **Apply** button is grayed-out unless a change has been made. However, changes are not applied until the **Apply** button is picked. To close the dialog box without saving changes, pick the menu control button or press [Esc].

Figure 18-10.
The **Toolbar Properties** dialog box.

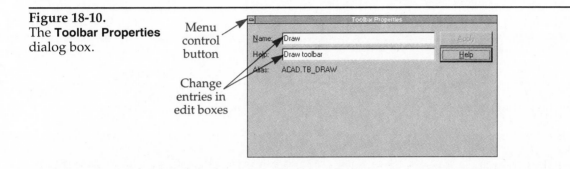

Menu control button

Change entries in edit boxes

EXERCISE 18-2

❏ Begin AutoCAD. Display the **Draw** and **Modify** toolbars as floating toolbars.
❏ If you have not added the **Edit Hatch** button to the **Modify** toolbar, do so now.
❏ Copy the **Donut** button to the **Draw** toolbar, and place it adjacent to the **Circle** button.
❏ Copy the **3D Polyline** button to the **Draw** toolbar, and place it adjacent to the **Polyline** button.
❏ Move the **Mirror** button to a new position in the **Modify** toolbar.
❏ Remove the **Donut**, **Edit Hatch**, and **3D Polyline** buttons from the **Draw** and **Modify** toolbars.
❏ Modify the title of the **Draw** toolbar to read **Draw/Construct**.
❏ Modify the help string of the **Draw** toolbar to read Displays the Draw/Construct toolbar.
❏ Change the title and help string of the **Draw** toolbar to the original wording and apply the changes.

Creating new toolbars

To create a new toolbar, pick the **New...** button in the **Toolbars** dialog box. The **New Toolbar** dialog box is displayed. See Figure 18-11A. Enter a name for the toolbar. This name will appear in the list in the **Toolbars** dialog box and in the title bar of the toolbar when it is floating. Select the menu group in which to store the toolbar. Pick the **OK** button and the new toolbar appears on-screen, Figure 18-11B.

The toolbar can now be customized just as any other toolbar. Add predefined buttons by picking the **Customize...** button in the **Toolbars** dialog box and dragging buttons into the new toolbar.

Figure 18-11.
A—Creating a toolbar named **Custom Tools** in the **New Toolbar** dialog box. B—The newly created toolbar.

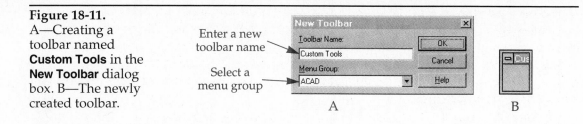

Enter a new toolbar name

Select a menu group

A

B

Creating new buttons

New buttons can be created and added to toolbars. To create a new button, pick the **Customize...** button from the **Toolbars** dialog box. Using the **Categories:** drop-down list, pick the **Custom** category. This category displays a standard button and a flyout button, Figure 18-12. Notice that both of these buttons are blank.

To begin creating your own custom button, drag a blank button to the new toolbar. Now, point to it and right-click your mouse (or pick using the return button of a digitizer). The **Button Properties** dialog box is displayed. See Figure 18-13. This dialog box allows you to define a new button.

Figure 18-12.
The blank buttons available in the **Customize Toolbars** dialog box. The first step in creating a customized button is to drag the blank button to a toolbar.

Drag a blank button to a toolbar

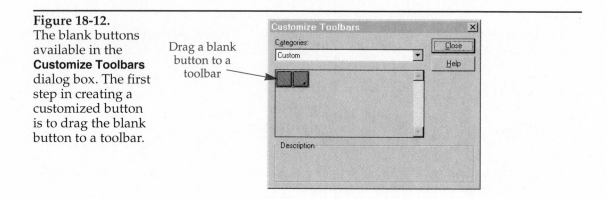

Figure 18-13.
Right-click on a blank button in a toolbar to access the **Button Properties** dialog box.

Enter a button name

Enter a help string

Define the commands performed by the button

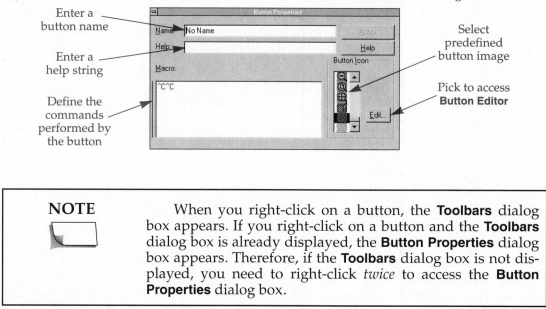

Select predefined button image

Pick to access **Button Editor**

NOTE

When you right-click on a button, the **Toolbars** dialog box appears. If you right-click on a button and the **Toolbars** dialog box is already displayed, the **Button Properties** dialog box appears. Therefore, if the **Toolbars** dialog box is not displayed, you need to right-click *twice* to access the **Button Properties** dialog box.

AutoCAD and its Applications—Advanced

When the **Button Properties** dialog box is open, No Name appears by default in the **Name:** text box. The characters ^C^C appear the **Macro:** field. These represent two cancel commands. No graphic appears initially. You can fill in all of the fields as desired. For the purpose of this example, a macro will be created that draws an E-size rectangular border (44" × 34") using a wide polyline, sets the drawing limits, and finishes with **Zoom Extents**.

First, enter a name in the **Name:** field. All buttons must have a name, or AutoCAD will not accept the button definition. For this example, assign the name **E-Size Setup**. This will appear as the ToolTip after you finish defining the button.

The next field is the **Help:** field. This is where you specify the help string that appears on the status line when you point to the button with the cursor. All help strings should provide a clear description of what the associated button actually does. While help strings should be clear, they should also be brief. Set this help string to read Draws an E-Size sheet, sets and displays the limits.

Now it is time to define the macro to be performed when the button is picked. Move your cursor to the **Macro:** field. Whenever a command is not required to operate transparently, it is best to begin the macro with two cancel keystrokes (^C^C) to cancel any current command and return to the Command: prompt. Two cancels are required to be sure you begin at the Command: prompt. If you are using a command at the Dim: prompt and issue one cancel by pressing the [Esc] key, you are returned to the Dim: prompt. Pressing the [Esc] key a second time cancels the Dim: prompt and returns you to the Command: prompt.

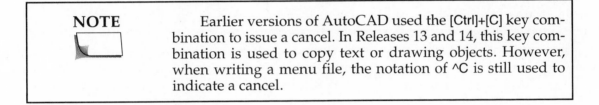

NOTE Earlier versions of AutoCAD used the [Ctrl]+[C] key combination to issue a cancel. In Releases 13 and 14, this key combination is used to copy text or drawing objects. However, when writing a menu file, the notation of ^C is still used to indicate a cancel.

The macro information must match the requirements of the activated commands perfectly. For example, if the **LINE** command is issued, the subsequent prompt expects a coordinate point to be entered. Any other data is inappropriate and will cause an error in your macro.

It is best to walk through each step in the desired macro manually, writing down each step and the data required by each prompt. The following sequence walks through the creation of the polyline border. The polyline is set at .015 line width and is a rectangle from 0,0 to 44,34.

```
Command: PLINE↵
From point: 0,0↵
Current line-width is 0.0000
Arc/Close/Halfwidth/Length/Undo/Width/⟨Endpoint of line⟩: W↵
Starting width ⟨0.0000⟩: .015↵
Ending width ⟨0.0150⟩: .015↵
Arc/Close/Halfwidth/Length/Undo/Width/⟨Endpoint of line⟩: 44,0↵
Arc/Close/Halfwidth/Length/Undo/Width/⟨Endpoint of line⟩: 44,34↵
Arc/Close/Halfwidth/Length/Undo/Width/⟨Endpoint of line⟩: 0,34↵
Arc/Close/Halfwidth/Length/Undo/Width/⟨Endpoint of line⟩: C↵
Command:
```

Creating the menu macro involves duplicating the above keystrokes, with a couple of differences. Some symbols are used in menu macros to represent keystrokes. For example, the ^C is not entered by pressing the [Ctrl]+[C] button combination. Instead, the [Shift]+[6] key combination is used to access the *caret* symbol, which is used to represent the [Ctrl] key in combination with the subsequent character (a 'C' in this case).

Another keystroke represented by a symbol is the [Enter] or return key. An [Enter] is shown as a semicolon (;). A space can also be used to designate [Enter]. However, the semicolon is more commonly used because it is very easy to count to make sure that the correct number are supplied. Spaces are not so easy to count.

Keeping these guidelines in mind, the following entry draws the required polyline:

^C^CPLINE;0,0;W;.015;.015;44,0;44,34;0,34;C;

Compare this with the previous command line entry example to identify each part of the menu macro. The next step is to set the limits and zoom to display the entire border. To do this at the command line would require the following entries:

Command: **LIMITS**↵
Reset Model space limits:
ON/OFF/⟨Lower left corner⟩ ⟨0.0000,0.0000⟩: **0,0**↵
Upper right corner ⟨12.0000,9.0000⟩: **44,34**↵
Command: **ZOOM**↵
All/Center/Dynamic/Extents/Left/Previous/ Scale(X/XP)/Window/⟨Realtime⟩: **E**↵
Regenerating drawing.

Continue to develop this macro by entering the following sequence immediately after the previous one (shown in italics):

*^C^CPLINE;0,0;W;.015;.015;44,0;44,34;0,34;C;*LIMITS;0,0;44,34;ZOOM;E

Note that an automatic carriage return is issued at the end of the macro, so it is not necessary to enter a semicolon at the end. Having completed the fields of the dialog, the **Button Properties** dialog box now appears as shown in Figure 18-14.

Next, you should create a graphic image for the button. A button can be selected from the scrolling graphic list in the **Button Icon** area of the **Button Properties** dialog box. However, having duplicate images can be a source of confusion. It is best to either modify an existing image or create a brand new one using the **Button Editor**.

Figure 18-14.
The properties for the **E-Size Setup** button.

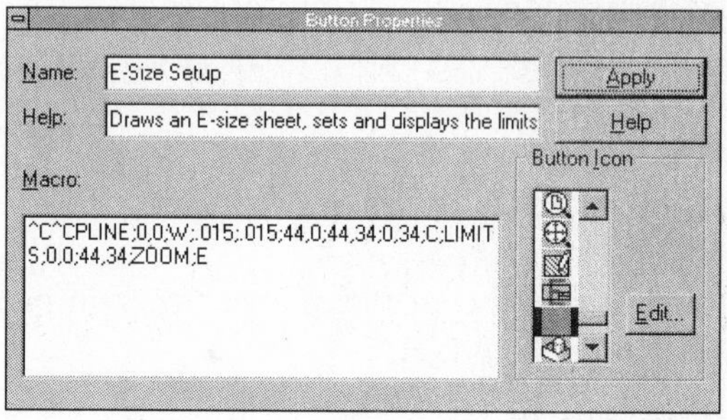

Creating button images

It is important to consider the needs of the persons who will be using your custom menu system when you design buttons. All of the standard buttons in AutoCAD show a graphic that implies something about the command that the button executes. Buttons you create will be most effective if they use this principle as well.

Simple abstract designs may be recognizable to you because you created them and you know what they do. When someone else uses this menu system, they may not recognize the purpose of the button.

Rather than edit an existing button in this example, an entirely new button will be created. Highlight one of the blank button icons in the **Button Icon** list of the **Button Properties** dialog box. Next, pick the **Edit...** button. The **Button Editor** dialog box is displayed, Figure 18-15.

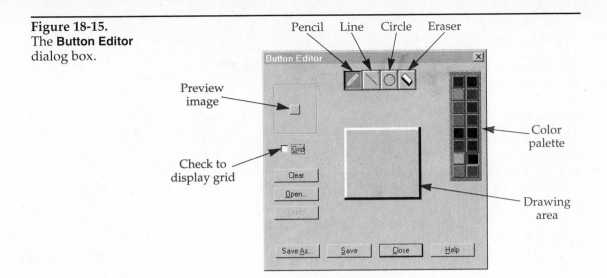

Figure 18-15.
The **Button Editor**
dialog box.

Pencil   Line   Circle   Eraser

Preview
image

Check to
display grid

Color
palette

Drawing
area

The **Button Editor** dialog box has basic pixel painting tools and several features to simplify the editing process. The four tools are shown as buttons at the top of the dialog box. The pencil paints individual pixels in the current color. The line tool allows you to draw a line between two points. The circle tool allows you to draw center/radius style ellipses and circles. The erase tool clears the color from individual pixels. The current color is selected from the color palette on the right side of the dialog box. Anything you draw will appear in this color.

Drawing a graphic is usually much easier with the grid turned on. The grid provides outlines for each pixel in the graphic. Each square is representative of one pixel. Picking the **Grid** check box toggles the state of the grid.

The area just above the **Grid** toggle is the button preview area. The preview displays the appearance of the button in its actual size while you draw the image.

When the toolbar buttons are set in their default size, the button editor provides a drawing area 16 pixels high by 16 pixels wide. If **Large Buttons** is turned on in the **Toolbars** dialog box, then this will be a 32×32 pixel image.

Buttons require two separate images, one at 16×16 and one at 32×32. If you only create a 16×16 pixel image, your custom buttons will be blank when you switch to large buttons because they have no image defined at that size. You must create a second 32×32 pixel image for the large button.

Other tools available in the **Button Editor** include the following:
- **Clear.** If you want to erase everything and start over, pick the **Clear** button to clear the drawing area.
- **Open….** Use this button to open existing bitmap files (.bmp).
- **Undo.** You can undo the last operation by picking this button. An operation that has been undone cannot be redone. Only the last operation can be undone.
- **Save As….** Saves a file using the **Save As** dialog box. Use this when you have opened a file and want to save it as well as keep the original on file.
- **Save.** Saves the current bitmap file. If the current image has not yet been saved, then the **Save As** dialog is displayed.
- **Close.** Ends the **Button Editor** session. A message is displayed if you have unsaved changes.
- **Help.** Provides context-sensitive help.

Figure 18-16A shows a 16×16 pixel image created for the **E-Size Setup** button with the **Grid** turned on. After saving your button image, pick the **Close** button to return to the **Button Properties** dialog box. Your newly created image appears above the **Edit…** button, as shown in Figure 18-16B. Pick the **Apply** button to apply the changes. Your button will display the new image, Figure 18-16C.

Figure 18-16.
Creating a new
button image.
A—A 16×16 pixel
image for the **E-Size
Setup** button.
B—The **Button
Properties** dialog
box displays the
new image.
C—The **E-Size Setup**
button after
applying the new
image.

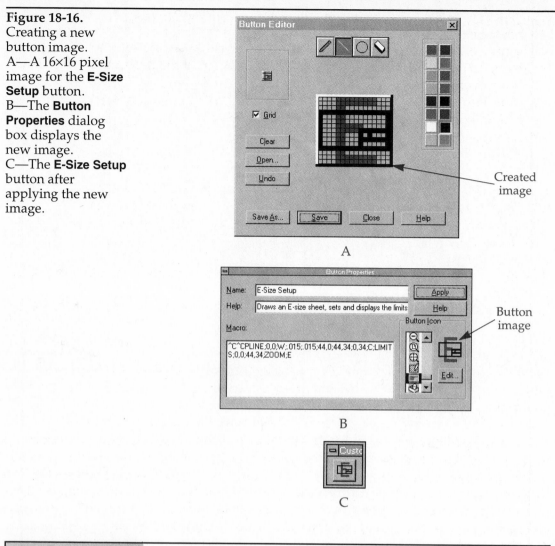

Created
image

A

Button
image

B

C

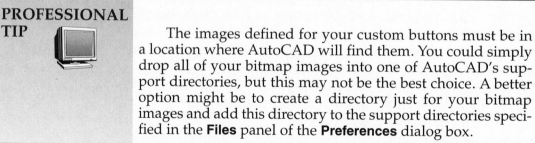

PROFESSIONAL TIP

The images defined for your custom buttons must be in a location where AutoCAD will find them. You could simply drop all of your bitmap images into one of AutoCAD's support directories, but this may not be the best choice. A better option might be to create a directory just for your bitmap images and add this directory to the support directories specified in the **Files** panel of the **Preferences** dialog box.

When you have completed your button and applied the changes, pick the menu control button in the upper left of the **Button Properties** dialog box to close it. Pick the **Close** button in the **Customize Toolbars** dialog box, then pick **Close** in the **Toolbars** dialog box.

The menu file is then recompiled, adding your new changes. More discussion of menu files is found at the end of this chapter and in Chapter 19.

❑ Begin AutoCAD. Use the **TOOLBAR** command to display the **Toolbars** dialog box.
❑ If you have not created the **Custom Tools** toolbar and the **E-Size Setup** button as shown in the previous discussion, do so now.
❑ Copy the **Paper Space** button from the **Standard** category into the **Custom Tools** toolbar, and place it to the left of the **E-Size Setup** button.
❑ Create a new macro that does the following:
  ❑ Executes the **MVIEW** command.
  ❑ Selects the **4** option of **MVIEW** to construct four viewports.
  ❑ Uses the **Fit** option to fit the four viewports in the current display.
❑ Test these commands at the keyboard before entering the code as a macro.
❑ Name the button **4 PS Viewports**, and enter the following as the help string: Fits 4 paper space viewports into the current drawing.
❑ Create a button icon of your own design.
❑ Place the new button to the right of the **E-Size Setup** button in the **Custom Tools** toolbar.
❑ Close each dialog box in proper order to save the new macro and toolbar configuration.
❑ The arrangement of the three icons allows you to first enter paper space, then create an E-size layout, then divide it into four paper space viewports.

Working with Flyouts

A flyout is a single button that can display all the buttons from an associated toolbar. A pick on a flyout button activates the command assigned to the currently visible toolbar button. When you point to a flyout and hold the pick button, the buttons from the associated toolbar are displayed. Move the cursor to the desired button and release the pick button. This activates the associated command or macro, and leaves this button's image displayed as the image for the flyout.

In order to create a new flyout button, you should create the associated toolbar first. You can then associate the toolbar with the flyout using the **Flyout Properties** dialog box.

Creating a toolbar with frequently used buttons can help you to save time and increase productivity. However, each new toolbar that is displayed takes up some of the available screen area. If too many toolbars are displayed at once, this can become a problem, especially with low-resolution screens.

You can conserve on-screen space using flyouts. Follow through this discussion to create a customized toolbar flyout for working with 3D projects.

First, enter the **TOOLBAR** command to display the **Toolbars** dialog box. Now, select the **New...** button and name the new toolbar **3D Tools**. The toolbar appears on the screen, ready to be customized. Pick the **Customize...** button, then pick the **Categories** drop-down list in the **Customize Toolbar** dialog box. Use the predefined buttons found in the **Surfaces, Render,** and **Standard** categories, and set up your new toolbar as shown in Figure 18-17.

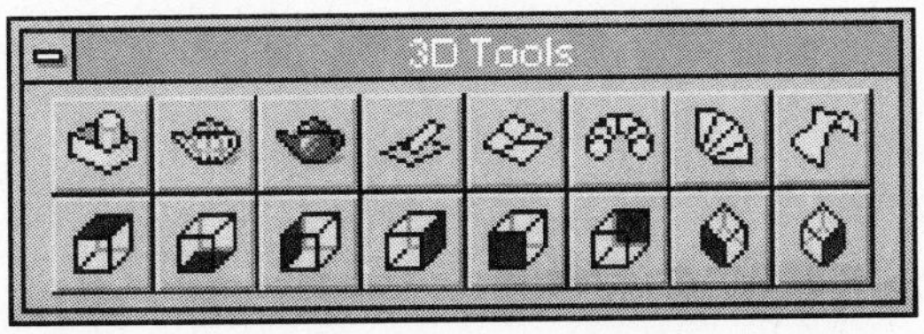

Figure 18-17.
The customized **3D Tools** toolbar is created using a combination of buttons in existing toolbars.

After you have set up your **3D Tools** toolbar, use the drop-down list to access the **Custom** category. Drag and drop a blank flyout button to your **Modify** toolbar. Right-click on this button to activate the **Flyout Properties** dialog box. Complete the fields for the dialog box as shown in Figure 18-18, and highlight the ACAD.3D Tools line in the **Associated Toolbar:** field.

Picking the **Apply** button activates the changes, and the upper-left button in the **3D Tools** toolbar becomes the current image in the flyout on the **Modify** toolbar. Close the **Flyout Properties** dialog box by picking the menu control button. Pick the **Close** button in the **Customize Toolbars** dialog box. Next, pick the **Close** button in the **Toolbars** dialog box and the menu is recompiled. Now when you pick the flyout, your custom **3D Tools** toolbar is displayed, as shown in Figure 18-19.

When you point at the flyout button, the name and help string you supplied in the **Flyout Properties** dialog box are not used. This is because the flyout button is defined as having no icon (or image) of its own. It assumes the identity of the most recently used button in its associated toolbar.

By picking the check box for **Show This Button's Icon** in the **Flyout Properties** dialog box, we can define a flyout that has its own identity and properties. If this box is checked, you need to define an icon image using the **Button Editor**.

After this is done, the assigned properties are displayed when the flyout is pointed to, as shown in Figure 18-20. The ToolTip now displays the button's name, and the help string also displays the information associated with this flyout.

While both methods of creating a flyout are acceptable, it is most effective to allow the flyout to be "transparent"—or assume the identity of the most recently picked button. Commands are often used several times consecutively in a standard editing session. For example, rarely will you need to draw only a single line. Normally, several lines must be drawn in sequence. This is generally true of many different AutoCAD commands. Therefore, having the last button picked as the default makes it more convenient to select it again. This can increase your efficiency by requiring fewer picks for the same amount of work.

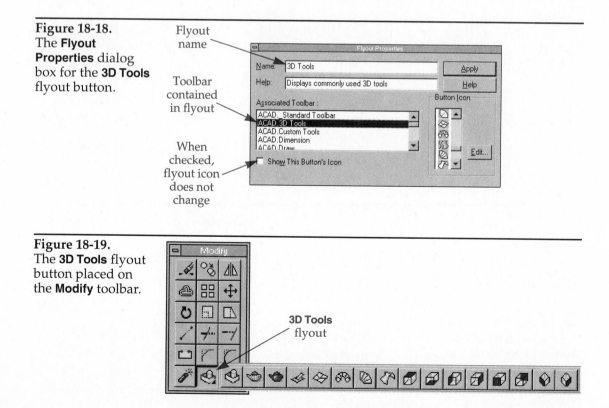

Figure 18-18.
The **Flyout Properties** dialog box for the **3D Tools** flyout button.

Flyout name

Toolbar contained in flyout

When checked, flyout icon does not change

Figure 18-19.
The **3D Tools** flyout button placed on the **Modify** toolbar.

3D Tools flyout

AutoCAD and its Applications—Advanced

Figure 18-20.
The new flyout displays its own ToolTip and help string.

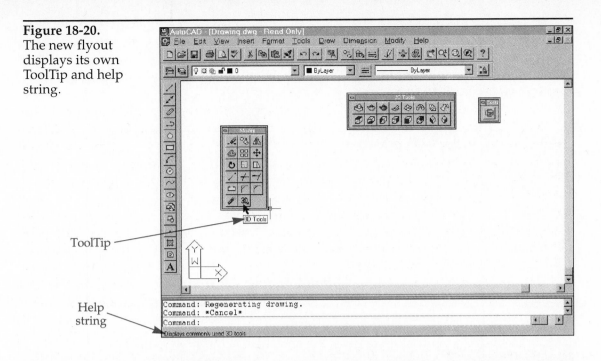

ToolTip

Help string

Toolbars and Menu Files

As toolbars are adjusted and customized, the changes are stored in files. AutoCAD maintains a record of these changes in one of several files associated with the menu system. Each of these files has the same file name, but different file extensions. The standard menu provided with the AutoCAD software is named ACAD, and the files associated with this menu are located in the \AutoCAD R14\Support folder.

It is important to understand the handling of menu files, otherwise it is very easy for your toolbar customization work to simply disappear. The menu files associated with the ACAD menu are as follows:

- **ACAD.MNU.** This is the fully documented *template* file. This provides the initial menu setup. If this menu is edited and then loaded using the **MENU** command, it creates a new menu *source* file.
- **ACAD.MNS.** This is the menu *source* file. Most documentation is stripped from the file to reduce its size. All code changes to the toolbar menu are recorded into this file. (Position data is recorded in the acad.ini file.) This is the file that is used in the creation of a *compiled* menu file.
- **ACAD.MNC.** This is a *compiled* menu file. AutoCAD creates this optimized file to handle the menus in your drawing sessions.
- **ACAD.MNR.** This is the menu *resource* file. It stores all of the bitmap images associated with the menu for quick access.

As noted, the .mns file is the location for code changes to the toolbars. However, when an .mnu file is loaded, it overwrites the current .mns file—losing all of your changes to the toolbars. A warning to this effect is displayed whenever you attempt to load an .mnu file. In order to make your changes permanent, you should open both files with an ASCII text editor and cut and paste the new or changed data from the .mns to the .mnu file. That way, when the .mnu file is loaded, it keeps these changes and writes them again to the new .mns file.

Editing a menu file is done using any ASCII text editor. You will find that the menu files are too large for Notepad, but can be opened with WordPad. If you are using WordPad, be sure that you specify the Text Document file type when saving. If you do not, WordPad will save the menu file as a Word document and will incorporate printer and text formatting codes that AutoCAD will not recognize.

Once you have opened the file, use a text search option to find the text ***TOOLBARS—this begins the toolbar data section. You can then find the listings in each file for changed toolbars and update the .mnu using the code in the .mns file. New toolbars can be copied and pasted into the .mnu file. More information on editing menu files is found in Chapter 19.

PROFESSIONAL TIP

There are other approaches to making your menu changes permanent. You can rename or delete the .mnu file, since it is not necessary to AutoCAD. You can also copy the .mns file directly over the .mnu file.

These approaches are used by AutoCAD professionals, but there is a drawback for those who are just learning to work with menus. The .mnu file is well-documented and can be a valuable tool for learning your way around the menu file. It may be best to keep this file on hand while you are learning to work with menus.

If you wish to keep the .mnu file available, you should make a copy of the .mns file each time you modify the toolbar menus. Keep this file in an alternate directory as a backup in case you accidentally overwrite the original .mns file.

Chapter Test

Write your answers in the spaces provided.

1. What four toolbars are shown by default when AutoCAD is loaded? _____
   _____

2. Describe the flexibility inherent in a floating toolbar. _____
   _____
   _____

3. How is resizing toolbars different than resizing other windows? _____
   _____
   _____
   _____

4. How do you prevent a floating toolbar from being docked when repositioning it?
   _____
   _____
   _____

5. Which command provides the means to show, hide, or position toolbars? _____
   _____

6. When using the command in Question 5, what name would you enter to display the **Modify** toolbar? _____

7. What option of the command in Question 5 would you use to remove a toolbar from the display? _____

8. In which dialog box can you find all predefined buttons divided by category?
_____

9. How do you copy an existing button from a toolbar category to another toolbar?
_____

10. How do you remove an existing button from a toolbar? _____
_____
_____
_____

11. How can you copy an existing button to a new location? _____
_____
_____

12. How do you access the **New Toolbar** dialog box in order to create a new toolbar?
_____

13. Once the new empty toolbar is displayed on the screen, how do you place the first blank button inside it? _____
_____
_____

14. When the new toolbar is displayed on the screen with a blank button inside it, how do you access the **Button Properties** dialog box in order to create a custom macro?
_____
_____

15. How do you create a ToolTip for a new button? _____
_____
_____

16. How do you create a help string for a new button? _____
_____
_____

17. How should you develop and test a new macro before creating it in a new button?
_____
_____
_____

18. Name two ways to specify an [Enter] or RETURN in a macro, and indicate which of the two is the safest. _____
_____
_____

19. What type of file (file extension) is a button graphic saved as? _____
_____

20. Name the four tools that are provided in the **Button Editor** dialog box. _____
_____
_____

21. What is the default size (in pixels) of the button editor drawing area? _____
_____

22. If **Large Buttons** is turned on in the **Toolbars** dialog box, what is the size (in pixels) of the button editor drawing area? _____
_____

23. What is the most efficient location for saving button icon graphic files? _____
_____
_____

24. How do you insert a flyout button into a toolbar? _____
_____
_____

25. How do you access the **Flyout Properties** dialog box in order to supply a ToolTip and help string to a new flyout button? _____
_____
_____

26. Why is it more effective to allow a flyout button to assume the identity of the most recently picked button? _____
_____
_____

27. What is the name and extension of the AutoCAD menu file in which all code changes to the toolbar are recorded? _____

28. Which AutoCAD menu file is fully documented and is used to create a new menu source file? _____

Drawing Problems

Before customizing or creating any menus, check with your instructor or supervisor for specific instructions or guidelines.

1. Create a new toolbar using the following information:
    A. Name the toolbar **Draw/Modify**.
    B. Copy at least three, but no more than six, commonly used draw buttons into the new toolbar.
    C. Copy at least three, but no more than six, commonly used edit buttons into the new toolbar.
    D. Use only existing buttons, do not create new ones.
    E. Remove the default **Draw** and **Modify** toolbars from the display.
    F. Dock the new **Draw/Modify** toolbar to the upper-left side of the screen.

2. Create a new toolbar using the following information:

A. Name the toolbar **My 3D Tools**.

B. Copy the following existing buttons from the **Surfaces** toolbar into the new toolbar:

Dish	**Box**	**Wedge**
Torus	**Pyramid**	**Cone**
Sphere	**Dome**	

C. Copy the following existing buttons from the **View** toolbar into the new toolbar:

Top View	**Bottom View**	**Left View**
Right View	**Front View**	**Back View**

D. Copy the following existing buttons from the **UCS** toolbar into the new toolbar:

Save UCS	**Named UCS**	**World UCS**
Origin UCS	**3 Point UCS**	**Previous UCS**

E. Use only existing buttons, do not create new ones.

F. Size the new toolbar to display two rows or columns and dock it in a location of your choice.

3. Create a new toolbar using the following information:

A. Name the toolbar **Paper Space Viewports**.

B. The toolbar should contain eight buttons that use the **MVIEW** command to create paper space viewports as follows:

- 1 viewport—allow user to pick location
- 2 viewports (horizontal)—allow user to pick location
- 3 viewports allow user to pick orientation and location
- 4 viewports allow user to pick location
- 1 viewport—fit
- 2 viewports—vertical
- 3 viewports—right
- 4 viewports—fit

C. The toolbar should contain two additional buttons that do the following:

- Switch to floating model space (**TILEMODE** variable should remain 0)
- Switch to paper space from floating model space

D. Construct new button icon graphics for the ten buttons. Save the images in a new directory that has been specified in the AutoCAD support environment.

E. Dock the toolbar on the right side of the screen.

4. Create a new toolbar that contains eight new buttons for the insertion of a paper space border and title block drawings.

   A. All buttons should use the **MVSETUP** command to either create or insert the drawings. The eight buttons should do the following:

      - Insert an A-size mechanical title block
      - Insert a B-size mechanical title block
      - Insert a C-size mechanical title block
      - Insert a D-size mechanical title block
      - Insert an A-size architectural title block
      - Insert a B-size architectural title block
      - Insert a C-size architectural title block
      - Insert a D-size architectural title block

   B. Create your own architectural title blocks and borders, or modify the mechanical versions to suit your needs. Be sure that new title blocks are added to the list that is available in the **MVSETUP** command.

   C. Construct your own button icon images for each of the eight new buttons. Save the images in a new directory that has been specified in the AutoCAD support environment.

   D. Dock the toolbar on the left side of the screen.

5. Customize the **Open** button on the **Standard** toolbar to display a flyout menu of the eight title blocks you created in Problem 4. Use the following information for this problem:

   A. Use the **OPEN** command for each of the buttons.

   B. The **OPEN** command should always be the default button of the flyout menu and should not be replaced by the most recently used button.

   C. Construct your own button icon images for each of the eight new buttons, or use the same images created in Problem 4. Save the images in a new directory that has been specified in the AutoCAD support environment.

Chapter 19

Customizing Screen and Button Menus

In Chapter 17, you learned how to customize the AutoCAD working environment to suit your preferences. AutoCAD menus can also be customized to suit specific needs. Users can add special commands to the standard menus or create their own menu system from scratch. As with customized toolbar and toolbar buttons, existing commands can be used in a macro. A *macro* is a function that combines the capabilities of multiple commands and options.

All of the aspects of the menu system can be changed. This includes the cursor button functions, standard screen menus, pull-down menus, and image file menus. Study this chapter carefully to create your own menus.

AutoCAD's Menu Structure

Before constructing your own menus, look at AutoCAD's standard menu structure to get a feel for the layout. This will give you a better understanding of the tools and techniques you can use to build custom menus. The basic components of a menu are the main sections, submenus, item titles, and command codes.

For Chapter 19–Chapter 22, it is assumed that you are familiar with a programmer's text editor or a word processor program. You must be familiar with the commands or keys in your text editor that allow you to scroll or page through a file.

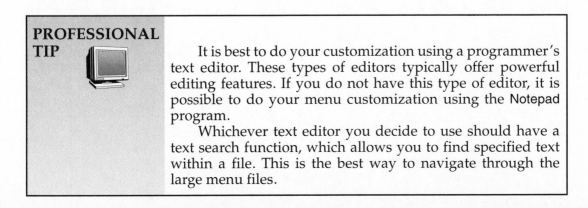

PROFESSIONAL TIP

It is best to do your customization using a programmer's text editor. These types of editors typically offer powerful editing features. If you do not have this type of editor, it is possible to do your menu customization using the Notepad program.

Whichever text editor you decide to use should have a text search function, which allows you to find specified text within a file. This is the best way to navigate through the large menu files.

AutoCAD's menu files

Several files are used to produce AutoCAD's menu system. As noted in Chapter 18, the file names may vary, but the file extensions are the same. AutoCAD comes with one primary menu file. This file is named ACAD. Figure 19-1 shows the AutoCAD screen with this menu loaded.

Figure 19-1.
The AutoCAD screen with the ACAD menu loaded.

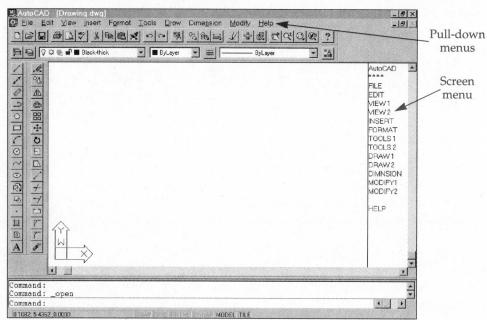

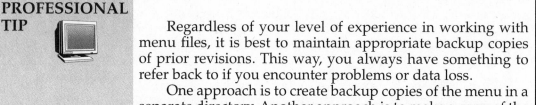

Regardless of your level of experience in working with menu files, it is best to maintain appropriate backup copies of prior revisions. This way, you always have something to refer back to if you encounter problems or data loss.

One approach is to create backup copies of the menu in a separate directory. Another approach is to make a copy of the current menu with a different name for your customization work. For example, make a copy of the acad.mns file named work.mns and do your customization in the new file to protect the original menu. Also, this would give you something to refer back to if you have difficulties getting the new menu to function.

PROFESSIONAL TIP

The ACAD menu files are discussed in this chapter. The primary files are acad.mnu, acad.mns, acad.mnl, acad.mnc, and acad.mnr. The acad.mnl is a menu LISP file that holds the AutoLISP program code. This defines any AutoLISP functions used in the menu. The acad.mnc and acad.mnr files are automatically created and updated by AutoCAD whenever an edited .mnu or .mns is loaded and compiled. More information on menu files is provided later in this chapter.

The menu files that you can directly edit include both the .mnu and the .mns files. As mentioned in Chapter 18, the .mnu file is more completely documented and is, therefore, a bit easier to navigate through and understand. All work in this chapter requires the .mnu file to be edited.

Loading an edited .mnu file overwrites the existing .mns file of the same name. Since all of your interactive toolbar modifications are written to the .mns file, they would be overwritten and lost.

Rather than edit the current menu structure, a copy of the .mnu file should be created. This way, any changes you make to the menu will not affect your standard menu. Additionally, since the menu you will be editing will have a different name, previous toolbar changes will not be lost as you work in this chapter.

To give you a clear idea of how the two menus differ, look at the excerpts of menu code in Figure 19-2. Note that the acad.mnu file has documentation that explains the purpose of the code.

Figure 19-2.
The acad.mnu file contains helpful documentation not found in the acad.mns file.

ACAD.MNU	ACAD.MNS

//
//   Default AutoCAD NAMESPACE declaration:
//
***MENUGROUP=ACAD
 	
//
//   Begin AutoCAD Digitizer Button Menus
//
***BUTTONS1
// Simple + button
// if a grip is hot bring up the Grips Cursor Menu
   (POP 17), else send a carriage return
$M=$(if,$(eq,$(substr,$(getvar,cmdnames),1,5),GR
   IP_),$P0=ACAD.GRIPS $P0=*);
$P0=SNAP $p0=*
^C^C
^B
^O
^G
^D
^E
^T
	//
	// AutoCAD menu file - C:\Program
	   Files\AutoCAD R14\support\acad.mnc
	//
	
	***MENUGROUP=ACAD
	
	***BUTTONS1
	$M=$(if,$(eq,$(substr,$(getvar,cmdnames),1,5),GR
	   IP_),$P0=ACAD.GRIPS $P0=*);
	$P0=SNAP $p0=*
	^C^C
	^B
	^O
	^G
	^D
	^E
	^T

Menu section labels

Open the acad.mnu file found in the \AutoCAD R14\Support folder using your text editing program. Use your keyboard cursor keys and the [Page Up]/[Page Down] keys to page through the file.

As you look through the menu file, notice the menu section headings. Major menu headings are identified by three asterisks (***) in front of the name. Submenus are listed with two asterisks (**) in front of the name. The following are the major menu headings:

```
***MENUGROUP
***BUTTONS1
***BUTTONS2
***BUTTONS3
***BUTTONS4
***AUX1
***AUX2
***AUX3
***AUX4
***POP0 through POP10
***POP17
***TOOLBARS
***IMAGE
***SCREEN
***TABLET1
***TABLET2
***TABLET3
***TABLET4
***HELPSTRINGS
***ACCELERATORS
```

In this chapter, you will be working with button and screen menus. Pull-down menus and image tiles are discussed in Chapter 20, and tablet menus are discussed in Chapter 21. The AUX1 and AUX2 menus are used for a system mouse that comes with operating systems such as Windows/NT, Macintosh, or SPARCstation.

Menu layout

Before beginning any editing of the acad.mnu file, take a few minutes to peruse it. Load the acad.mnu file into your text editor and locate the line containing ***BUTTONS1. The following portion of the menu should be displayed:

```
***BUTTONS1
// Simple + button
// if a grip is hot bring up the Grips Cursor Menu (POP 17), else send a carriage
    return
$M=$(if,$(eq,$(substr,$(getvar,cmdnames),1,5),GRIP_),$P0=ACAD.GRIPS $P0=*);
$P0=SNAP $p0=*
^C^C
^B
^O
^G
^D
^E
^T

***BUTTONS2
// Shift + button
$P0=SNAP $p0=*

***BUTTONS3
// Control + button

***BUTTONS4
// Control + shift + button
```

This is the first part of the acad.mnu file. The entire file has well over 10,000 lines. The first line, ***BUTTONS1, is the beginning of the button menu. The items that follow are specific assignments to the buttons on your pointing device.

Scroll down until you see the ***POP1 heading. This is the first pull-down menu, which appears at the left end of the menu bar near the top of the AutoCAD graphics window. Notice that the first word on each line is preceded with the characters "ID_". This is known as a *tag*, and allows AutoCAD to associate other lines in the menu with these tags. Tags are covered later in this chapter. The next item is the label, enclosed in brackets ([ ]). Any word or character string appearing inside these brackets is displayed in the pull-down menu or on the menu bar.

Also note that one of the characters within the brackets is preceded by an ampersand (&). The character preceded by an ampersand in a pull-down menu title defines the keyboard shortcut key used to enable that menu. Thus, since the title of the **File** pull-down menu is defined as [&File], it can be accessed by pressing [Alt]+[F].

Once a pull-down menu is displayed, a menu item within it may be selected using a single mnemonic character key. The mnemonic keys defined for the **New...** and **Open...** commands in the **File** pull-down menu appear in acad.mnu as &New and &Open. Therefore, these menu items are enabled with the [N] and [O] keys, respectively. Do not confuse mnemonic keys with *accelerator keys*, which are the windows keystrokes such as [Ctrl]+[N] and [Ctrl]+[O].

Menu item titles

Learn to use the "search" function of your text editor. This function is extremely useful in moving around a file. Use the search function, or the [Page Down] key to find the **09_DRAW1 menu. Remember, the two asterisks represent a subheading under a major section. The **09_DRAW1 menu is the first page of the **DRAW1** screen menu. In Figure 19-3, the **DRAW1** screen menu as seen in AutoCAD is shown on the left, and the same page is shown on the right as it appears in the acad.mnu file.

Figure 19-3.
On the left is the **DRAW1** screen menu as it appears on-screen. On the right is the related command lines from the acad.mnu file.

AutoCAD Screen Menu (DRAW1)	ACAD.MNU Menu Code
* * * *	**09_DRAW1 3
Line	[Line]^C^C_line
Ray	[Ray]^C^C_ray
Xline	[Xline]^C^C_xline
Mline	[Mline]^C^C_mline
Pline	[Pline]^C^C_pline
3Dpoly	[3Dpoly]^C^C_3dpoly
Polygon	[Polygon]^C^C_polygon
Rectang	[Rectang]^C^C_rectang
Arc	[Arc]^C^C_arc
Circle	[Circle]^C^C_circle
Donut	[Donut]^C^C_donut
Spline	[Spline]^C^C_spline
Ellipse	[Ellipse]^C^C_ellipse

Notice that the command name in the menu is the same as its file listing inside the brackets ([]). A screen menu name can be up to eight characters long. You can have longer names and descriptions inside the brackets. However, only the first eight characters are displayed.

The characters to the right of the closing bracket are the command codes. Figure 19-4 shows the difference between title information and command code. Any text after the eighth character is comments.

Figure 19-4.
A—Information that can be included inside the title brackets. B—Information outside the brackets is processed by AutoCAD.

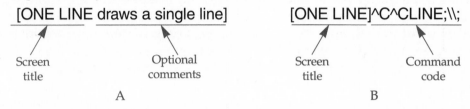

Menu command codes and syntax

When paging through the menu file, you probably noticed several characters and symbols that did not make much sense, such as $S=ACAD.01_FILE and \. These are menu codes, and have explicit functions in the menu. You will be using these codes to create menus.

The characters listed here can be used for button and screen menus. Special characters used in pull-down menus are described later. The following is a list of characters and their functions:

Character	Function
***	Major menu sections—Must be placed directly in front of the name of the section, for example: ***SCREEN.
**	Submenu section—Appears in front of the submenu name. The **DRAW1** screen menu shown in the previous section has the name **09_DRAW1.
[ ]	The name of a menu item is enclosed in brackets. Only the first eight characters inside the brackets are displayed on the side screen menu in AutoCAD.
$S=	This indicates that another screen menu is to be displayed and enables AutoCAD to move between submenus. Other similar codes are $B (BUTTONS), $T (TABLET), $I (IMAGE), $P (PULL-DOWN or POP), and $A (AUXILIARY).
^C^C	This cancels any current command. If you are in a transparent or DIM: command, two ^Cs are needed to get you out. Placing this in front of your commands ensures that you begin the new command cleanly by canceling any command you are in.
;	The semicolon represents pressing [Enter].
\	The backslash represents a pause for user input, where information must be typed at the keyboard or entered with the pointing device.
+	The plus symbol is placed at the end of a long menu line and tells AutoCAD that there is more of this sequence on the next line.
=*	The current cursor, pull-down, or image tile menu is displayed.
(space)	A blank space between items is the same as pressing [Enter] or the space bar.
*^C^C	Creates a repeating command.
si	Specifies immediate action on a single selected item. Placed at the end of the macro; for example: Erase;si

Button menus control the functions of the pointing device buttons. If you use a stylus or a mouse with only one or two buttons, you will not be using button menus. If you have a pointing device with two or more buttons, you can alter the functions of the buttons to suit your needs. This can add to your drawing productivity and speed the access of commonly used commands.

The BUTTONS*n* (where *n* represents a number from one to four) menu sections are applied to pointing devices such as a digitizer puck. The AUX*n* menus are used for a system mouse, such as the mouse you use in Windows 95 or Windows NT. A simple mouse does not provide as much room for customization as a digitizer puck. The pick button on a mouse cannot be changed by editing the menu file. Therefore, a two button mouse has a single button that can be customized, and a three button mouse has two customizable buttons. Still, by using the [Shift]+, [Ctrl]+, and [Ctrl]+[Shift]+ combinations described in this section, added functionality is possible even for a mouse.

Standard button menu layout

The main button menu is BUTTONS1. It is arranged for a device with nine programmable buttons. A list of this button menu and its functions is shown in Figure 19-5.

Figure 19-5.
On the left is the ***BUTTONS1 menu and on the right is the meaning of the command lines.

Menu File Listing	Button Number and Function
***BUTTONS1	Menu Name
$M=$(if,$(eq,$(substr,$(getvar,cmdnames),1,5),	#1 Return, or display Grips menu
GRIP_),$P0=ACAD.GRIPS $P0=*);	#2 Displays cursor object snap menu
$P0=SNAP $p0=*	#3 Cancel
^C^C	#4 Snap on/off toggle
^B	#5 Ortho on/off toggle
^O	#6 Grid on/off toggle
^G	#7 Coordinate on/off toggle
^D	#8 Isoplane crosshair toggle
^E	#9 Tablet on/off toggle
^T	#0 Pick button—nonprogrammable

Additional button menus

You can have instant access to the four button menus, BUTTONS1 through BUTTONS4. Each of these menus can be accessed with a keyboard and puck button combination:

Action	Button Menu
puck button only	BUTTONS1
[Shift]+puck button	BUTTONS2
[Ctrl]+puck button	BUTTONS3
[Ctrl]+[Shift]+puck button	BUTTONS4

Each of these button menus can contain any commands you need. For example, you can place a variety of display commands in the BUTTONS2 menu. To access these commands, simply hold down the [Shift] key on the keyboard and press the appropriate puck button.

Copying the ACAD.MNU file

Before you edit the acad.mnu file, check with your instructor or supervisor to find out what procedures should be used. As discussed previously, you should first copy the acad.mnu file to your own folder or floppy disk. Then experiment and make changes to your copy. This protects the original program. It also prevents undue frustration for students or employees who find that the revised menu does not function properly.

To avoid confusing acad.mnu with your menu, name the new copy mymenu.mnu. You can also use your first name, such as nancy.mnu. This distinguishes it from all others.

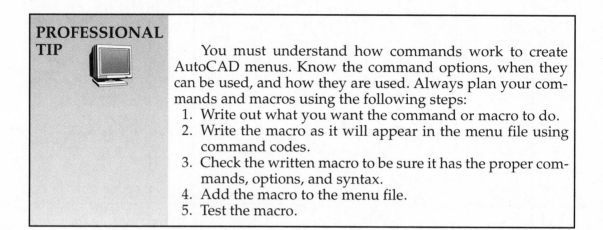

PROFESSIONAL TIP

You must understand how commands work to create AutoCAD menus. Know the command options, when they can be used, and how they are used. Always plan your commands and macros using the following steps:
1. Write out what you want the command or macro to do.
2. Write the macro as it will appear in the menu file using command codes.
3. Check the written macro to be sure it has the proper commands, options, and syntax.
4. Add the macro to the menu file.
5. Test the macro.

Replacing button menu items

The process of replacing button menu items is the same as editing a line in a text file. An example is replacing the existing button commands shown in Figure 19-6 with the new commands given. Place a double cancel before each command. This cancels the current command when the button is picked.

When you have finished editing, the new button menu should look like this:

```
***BUTTONS1
$M=$(if,$(eq,$(substr,$(getvar,cmdnames),1,5),GRIP_),$P0=ACAD.GRIPS $P0=*);
$P0=SNAP $p0=*
^C^C
^B
^C^CLINE
^C^CERASE
^C^CCIRCLE
^C^CARC
^T
```

Before testing the new menu, you must load it into memory with the **MENU** command, otherwise AutoCAD will work with the old copy. The **MENU** command displays the **Select Menu File** dialog box, Figure 19-7. Select the **Files of type:** drop-down list. Note that you can specify either .mns/.mnc files or .mnu files.

Figure 19-6.
Existing button commands can be easily replaced with new commands.

Button	Existing Command	New Command
#5	Ortho	LINE
#6	Grid	ERASE
#7	Coords	CIRCLE
#8	Isoplane	ARC

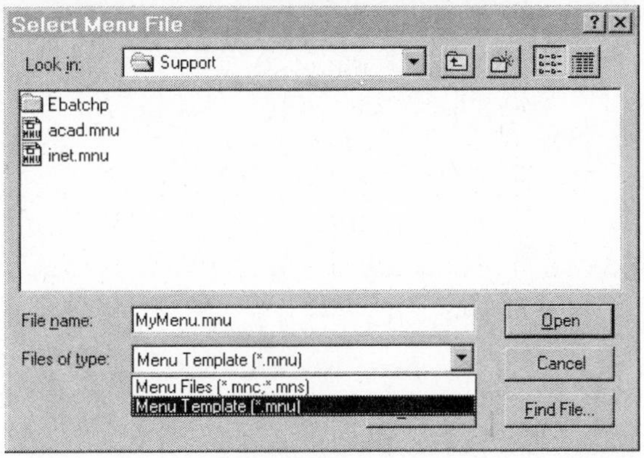

Figure 19-7.
The **Select Menu File**
dialog box is used
to load the new
menu file into
memory.

Select the .mnu option and find your menu file using the directory windows. Then, pick your menu from the file list and select the **OK** button. A warning dialog is displayed:

Loading of a template menu file [MNU file] overwrites and redefines the menu source file [MNS file], which results in the loss of any toolbar customization changes that have been made.

Continue loading menu file?

In this case, you want to load the .mnu file, so pick the **OK** button. There is a slight delay as AutoCAD compiles the .mnu file into an .mnc file. The .mnc file is written in a format that makes it usable by AutoCAD. You cannot directly edit the .mnc file.

If the system variable **FILEDIA** is turned off, load your menu file from the command line:

Command: **MENU**⏎
Menu file name or . for none ⟨C:\AutoCAD R14\Support\Acad⟩ **MYMENU**⏎
Compiling menu C:\AutoCAD R14\Support\Mymenu.mnu…

Providing for user input

An important aspect of menu customization is having a good grasp of AutoCAD's commands and options. Most commands require some form of user input—picking a location on the screen or entering values at the keyboard.

The final action of any input is using a button on the pointing device or pressing [Enter] on the keyboard. The symbol that is used to indicate a pause for user input is the backslash (\). A second important aspect of menu customization is inserting returns, or specifying when the [Enter] key is pressed. This is handled with the semicolon (;).

When a command is listed in a menu file, AutoCAD automatically inserts a space after it, which is interpreted as a return. The following command executes the **LINE** command and prompts for the From point:

LINE

If the command is followed by a semicolon, backslash, or plus sign, AutoCAD does not insert a space. Therefore, there is no automatic return. If you want to allow for user input, and then provide a return, you should end the line with a semicolon:

LINE;\\;

This executes the **LINE** command, waits for the user to pick the start and end points of a line, and then terminates the command.

The button menus perform additional functions with the user input symbols. If a backslash is provided after the command, the coordinates of the crosshairs on the screen are recorded when the pick button is pressed. Therefore, the following button command accepts the location of the crosshairs as the From point: for the **LINE** command when the button is pressed, and the prompt that is displayed is the To point: prompt:

LINE;\

This instant input can be used for other applications. For example, object snaps can be set up to be transparently executed using a button menu.

Adding new button menus

You are not limited to the four button menus. You can create as many as needed. However, one of the buttons should be used to switch menus. Here are a few things to keep in mind when creating new button menus:

- There is no screen display of button names. Use brackets in your menu file to contain button labels or numbers. AutoCAD does not act on anything inside brackets. For example:

  ```
  ***BUTTONSn
  [5]^C^CLINE
  [6]^C^CERASE
  [7]^C^CCIRCLE
  [8]^C^CARC
  ```

- The letter B is used to call button menu names. The code $B= is used to call other button submenus, just as $S= is used to call other screen submenus. For example, you could specify button 9 in the ***BUTTONS1 menu to call submenu **B1 as follows:

  ```
  [9]$B=B1
  ```

  When button 9 is pressed, submenu **B1 is activated and the buttons change to reflect the new menu.

- A button menu selection can also call a screen menu in the same manner. For example, button 9 could call the **OSNAP** screen menu in addition to changing the button submenu to B1. The entry in the menu file would look like this:

  ```
  [9]$B=B1 $S=OSNAP
  ```

  You will alter the **OSNAP** screen menu for using buttons in one of the chapter problems.

- A button menu selection can display a pull-down menu as follows:

  ```
  $P10=*
  ```

  The P10 calls for pull-down menu 10 (the **Help** pull-down menu), and the =* displays it on screen.

- In the file, a space is not required after a button submenu to separate it from its submenus.

The following example shows revisions to the ***BUTTONS1 menu. It includes a selection for button 9 that switches to the B1 button menu and also displays the **OSNAP** screen menu. The B1 menu provides eight object snap options, and button 9 returns to the BUTTONS1 menu and displays the **S** screen menu.

```
***BUTTONS1
[1] $M=$(if,$(eq,$(substr,$(getvar,cmdnames),1,5),GRIP_),$P0=ACAD.GRIPS
    $P0=*);
[2]$P0=SNAP $p0=*
[3]^C^C
[4]^B
[5]^C^CLINE
[6]^C^CERASE
[7]^C^CCIRCLE
[8]^C^CARC
[9]$B=B1 $S=OSNAPB
**B1
[1]ENDpoint
[2]INTersect
[3]MIDpoint
[4]PERpendicular
[5]CENter
[6]TANgent
[7]QUAdrant
[8]NEArest
[9]$B=BUTTONS1 $S=S
```

PROFESSIONAL TIP

When using button submenus, it is a common technique to combine menu calls with the macro in order to automatically reset the previous button menu. For example:

```
**B1
[1]$B=BUTTONS1 ENDpoint
```

EXERCISE 19-1

❑ Copy the acad.mnu file into your folder or onto a floppy disk. Change the name of the file to mymenu.mnu or use your name.
❑ Create a button submenu named **B2.
❑ Include three drawing commands and three editing commands in the submenu.

Creating Standard Screen Menus

AutoCAD Custom Guide 4

Once enabled, standard screen menus are located along the right side of the screen. They are created with the same techniques used for button menus. Screen menus are more versatile than button menus because you can see the command titles.

The positions of commands within the screen menu are referred to as *screenboxes*. The number of boxes available depends on the current size of the AutoCAD program window. You can find out how many boxes are available using the **SCREENBOXES** system variable as follows:

Command: **SCREENBOXES**↵
SCREENBOXES = 27(read only)

Most people rarely use all of the commands found in AutoCAD's screen menus. In time, you will find which commands you use most often, and those you seldom use. Begin to develop an idea of what the menu structure should look like. Then start constructing custom menus, even though you may not completely know what to include. Menus are easy to change, and can be revised as many times as needed.

NOTE   If screen menus are not enabled, the **SCREENBOXES** system variable returns a value of 0.

PROFESSIONAL TIP   Develop a plan for your menus, but build them over time. Create one command or macro and then test it. It is much easier to create one macro and test it than to create an entire untested menu. Building menus a small portion at a time is also more efficient. It can be done as you work or study, or when you have a spare minute.

Screen menu items

A screen menu item is composed of the command name and the command code. The command name is enclosed in brackets. The code is a combination of commands, options, and characters that instruct AutoCAD to perform a function or series of functions. Take a closer look at the example in Figure 19-8. It is the same one that was introduced in Figure 19-4. The following parts are included in the macro:

- Brackets ([ ]) enclose the screen title. The first eight characters inside the brackets are displayed on the screen.
- The command name ONE LINE is displayed on the screen. Try to give descriptive names to your commands so they indicate what the command does.
- The double cancel (^C^C) cancels out any command that is active when you pick the menu item.
- AutoCAD commands determine what function the macro performs (**LINE**).
- A return (;) represents pressing the [Enter] key after typing LINE at the keyboard.
- The two backslashes (\\) pause for user input to the From point: and To point: prompts. Remember, each backslash indicates a value entered at the keyboard or a selection made with the pointing device.
- A final return (;) represents pressing the [Enter] key to end the **LINE** command.

As you can see, you need to know the commands, prompts, options, and entries required to perform AutoCAD functions before you can modify screen menus. Look at the next menu item and try to determine what it is doing.

[Erase 1]^C^CERASE;\;

The title should give you a clue. It erases a single object. The **ERASE** command is followed by a return, which is followed by a single backslash. This allows one pick on the screen. The second return completes the command. Here is another one.

[Extend 1]^C^CEXTEND;\;\;

This macro issues the **EXTEND** command, then allows for one user input to pick a boundary edge. Then a return is entered and one additional user input is allowed for the object to extend. After one object is picked, the last return completes the command automatically.

Look at one more menu item that combines two commands. What function do you think this macro performs?

    [Line T]^C^CLINE;\\;;MID;\\;

Notice that the first half of the item is exactly the same as the macro shown in Figure 19-8. It draws a single line. The return just before MID selects the **LINE** command again. MID specifies an object snap mode for the From point: prompt. At the first backslash, pick the line on which the midpoint is needed. The second backslash is the To point: prompt. The final return ends the command.

Figure 19-8.
The components of
a screen menu item.

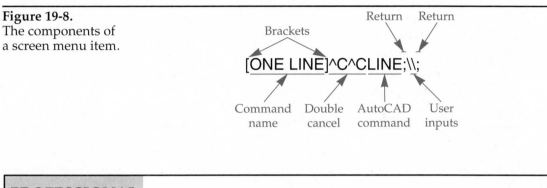

PROFESSIONAL TIP
When writing menu commands and macros, write them as if you are entering the commands and options at the keyboard. Use the semicolon (;) for the [Enter] key. Use first letters where appropriate for command options.

Constructing menu commands

When you think of a useful command or function to include in a menu, the first step is to write it out in longhand. This gives you a clear picture of the scope of the command. The second step is to list the keyboard steps required to execute the new function. Third, write out the menu item as it will appear in the menu file. The following examples each use this three-step process:

Example 1
1. Make a menu pick called ERASE L to erase the last object drawn.
2. **ERASE**↵
   LAST↵
   ↵
3. [ERASE L]^C^CERASE;L;;

Example 2
1. Make a menu pick called ERASE 1 that erases one entity and returns to the Command: prompt.
2. **ERASE**↵
   (select entity)↵
3. [ERASE 1]^C^CERASE;\;

Example 3
1. Make a menu pick called ZOOM D that enters the **ZOOM Dynamic** display without the user having to pick the **Dynamic** option.
2. **ZOOM**↵
   DYNAMIC↵
3. [ZOOM D]^C^CZOOM;D

Example 4

1. Make a menu pick called ZOOM P that zooms to the previous display.
2. **ZOOM⏎**
   PREVIOUS⏎
3. [ZOOM P]^C^CZOOM;P

Example 5

1. Make a menu pick that draws as many circles as needed.
2. **MULTIPLE CIRCLE⏎**
3. [M CIRCLE]^C^CMULTIPLE CIRCLE or *^C^CCIRCLE

These examples should give you the feel for the process used when creating menu items. The command items can now be written to a menu file and tested. Before doing this, though, take a look at two more examples that are a little more involved.

Example 6

1. Create a new menu pick called 25FILLET that can set a .25 fillet radius on a polyline without restarting the **FILLET** command.
2. **FILLET⏎**
   RADIUS⏎
   .25⏎
   FILLET⏎
   POLYLINE⏎
   (select 2D polyline)
3. [25FILLET]^C^CFILLET;R;.25;;P;\

Example 7

1. Create a new menu pick called DWG AIDS that sets the grid to .5, sets the snap grid to .25, and turns **Ortho** on.
2. **GRID⏎**
   .5⏎
   SNAP⏎
   .25⏎
   ORTHO⏎
   ON⏎
3. [DWG AIDS]^C^CGRID;.5;SNAP;.25;ORTHO;ON

Adding macros to the menu file

The next step is to add the new macros to the menu file and then test them. Create a new submenu after the **S menu. Load your copy of the acad.mnu file into your text editor and search to find the following:

    ***SCREEN
    **S

Listed below **S is AutoCAD's familiar root menu. Find the last sequential command in that menu, which is [LAST]. If you are editing the acad.mnu file, then just below the [LAST] option is the **SNAP_TO menu. It is preceded by 3 lines of comments. Move your cursor to the beginning of the first comment line and press the [Enter] key twice, then press the up arrow key once. Your cursor will now be on a blank line that is separated from the subsequent menu by an additional blank line.

This can be done between the end of any screen submenu and the start of the next. Remember that the first screen menu listed in the ***SCREEN section is displayed when you enter the drawing editor. (If you insert your submenu in front of the **S menu, yours will be the first displayed when AutoCAD enters the drawing editor.)

Name this first submenu TEST. Type the entries in your text editor exactly as they are shown below. Be sure to press [Enter] at the end of each line. Your first entries in this menu should look like the following:

```
**TEST 3 (the "3" begins the menu on the third line from the top of the screen)
[ TEST]
[ MENU]
[Erase L]^C^CERASE;L;;
[Erase 1]^C^CERASE;\;
[Zoom W]^C^CZOOM;W
[Zoom P]^C^CZOOM;P
[M Circle]^C^CMULTIPLE CIRCLE
[25Fillet]^C^CFILLET;R;.25;;P;\
[Dwg Aids]^C^CGRID;.5;SNAP;.25;ORTHO;ON
```

Long menu items

If a menu item occupies more than one line, instruct AutoCAD that there is more to the item. Type a plus symbol (+) at the end of the line. Do not put spaces in before or after the mark. Use the long-line technique to create a command that does the following:

- **ZOOM All**.
- Set **LIMITS** to 0,0 and 20,12.
- Set **SNAP** to 0.25.
- Set **GRID** to 0.50.
- Draw a **PLINE** border from 0.5,0.5. The border should be 17″ × 11″.
- Set **MIRRTEXT** to zero.
- Set the **APERTURE** to 3.
- Set **ORTHO** to on.
- Turn the **GRID** on.
- Set **UNITS** to three decimal places.
- **ZOOM Extents**.

The item name and code for this macro is written as follows:

```
[B-11x17]^C^CZOOM;A;LIMITS;;20,12;SNAP;.25;GRID;.5;PLINE;0.5,0.5;+
17.5,.5;17.5,11.5;0.5,11.5;C;MIRRTEXT;0;APERTURE;3;ORTHO;+
ON;GRID;ON;ZOOM;E
```

Place your menu in the root menu

You have created your first screen menu, but how do you access it from the root menu of AutoCAD? There is nothing in the root menu that calls the **TEST** menu. You need to add that item to the root menu now.

Look again at the **S menu and notice that only 18 lines are occupied with commands inside brackets. You can insert your menu name on the line after [HELP], or any other blank line in this area. Insert the following item:

```
[TEST] $S=ACAD.TEST
```

Do not press [Enter] at the end of the line or you will insert an additional line in the menu. This could push the last menu item off the screen if the AutoCAD window displays only 26 lines in the menu area.

The menu stack

The item you entered above calls your submenu TEST. A screen menu call is different from other menu calls because the previous menu is not removed prior to displaying the subsequent menu. Instead, the new menu is overlaid on the existing menu, with the first item being placed on the specified line. This creates a menu stack.

For example, the **TEST menu has a 3 following the menu name. This indicates that the first two lines are to remain unchanged and the menu data placement begins on line 3 of the screen menu display area. The new items are then used to replace existing screen menu selections.

In the **TEST menu, ten items are defined with the menu beginning on the third line. The previous menu, **S, has many additional lines. Since the **TEST menu only redefines lines 3 through 12, lines 13 and on remain unchanged. To clear these lines out when the submenu is displayed, place an appropriate number of blank lines after the code for the submenu. Figure 19-9A shows the **S menu with the addition of the TEST menu call, and Figure 19-9B shows the screen menu after calling the **TEST menu.

The standard approach is to begin submenus on the third line of the menu display area. This results in the first two lines of the **S menu being preserved regardless of which submenu is currently displayed. This is important because of the functions performed by these two items. The top of the **S menu looks like this:

        AutoCAD
          * * * *

Picking the word **AutoCAD** displays the **S menu (the root menu), and picking the four asterisks displays an object snap menu. This way, no matter where you are in the menu system, it takes only one pick to get to these frequently needed items.

Figure 19-9.
A—The screen menu with the **TEST** menu call added below **HELP**.
B—Calling the **TEST submenu results in this display.

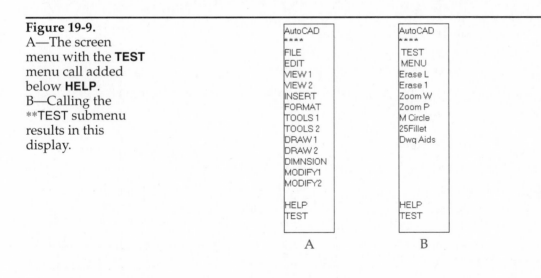

A   B

PROFESSIONAL TIP

When creating screen menus, always use the standard convention for menu label appearances. On the AutoCAD screen menu, the label for an item that calls another menu is shown with all UPPERCASE characters. Items that start a command are shown in Title Case, with the first character of each word in uppercase.

Using variables and control characters

AutoCAD system variables and control characters can be used in screen menus. They can be included to increase the speed and usefulness of your menu commands. Become familiar with these variables so you can make use of them in your menus:

- **^B. Snap** on/off toggle
- **^C. Cancel**
- **^D. Coords** on/off toggle
- **^E. Isoplane** on/off toggle
- **^G. Grid** on/off toggle
- **^H.** Issues a backspace
- **^M.** Issues a ↵
- **^O. Ortho** on/off toggle
- **^P. MENUECHO** Variable on/off toggle
- **^T. Tablet** on/off toggle
- **^V.** Switches current viewport

EXERCISE 19-2

❑ Use the three-step process to write the menu items given below.
❑ Use the spaces provided to write the macros.
  ❑ [GRID]—Turn the snap and grid on or off. _____
  ❑ [TEXT-S.1]—Set the snap at .1 and select the **TEXT** command._____
  ❑ [MIRROR]—Turn the **MIRRTEXT** variable off and select the **Window** option of the **MIRROR** command. Do not delete the old object. This command should return the user to Command: prompt. _____
  ❑ [BREAK @]—Break a single line into two parts._____
  ❑ [CHMFER.5]—Set a chamfer distance of .5 and allow two lines to be picked.
  _____

Chapter Test

Write your answers in the spaces provided.

1. The name and extension of the file that contains all of the fully documented menus for AutoCAD is_____.

2. List the names of the major sections in AutoCAD's default menu. _____
_____
_____

3. All interactive toolbar modifications are written to which file? _____
_____

4. Why should you edit a copy of the acad.mnu file when customizing menus? ____
_____
_____
_____

5. How many different button menus can you have?_____
_____

6. What kind of symbol is used to indicate a screen submenu? _____

7. Describe the function of each of the following screen menu commands:

    A. [Trim 1]^C^CTRIM;\;\;_____

    _____

    _____

    B. [Copy W]^C^CCOPY;W;\\ _____

    _____

    _____

    C. [Change 1]^C^CCHANGE;\; _____

    _____

    _____

8. Give the function of the following menu command codes:

    Brackets ([]) _____

    Semicolon (;) _____

    Backslash (\)_____

    _____

    _____

    Plus sign (+)_____

    Single (si) _____

9. How many button menus can be accessed with combinations of key and button
    picks? _____

    _____

10. How would the following button menu command function? _____
    Erase;_____

11. What system variable lists the number of screen menu items?_____

    _____

12. List the three steps you should use when creating a new menu command._____

    A. _____

    B. _____

    C. _____

13. Suppose you add a new menu to the acad.mnu file. How does the new menu get
    displayed on the screen?_____

    _____

    _____

14. Define a menu stack. _____

    _____

15. Define the use of the following control characters.

    ^B—_____

    ^G— _____

    ^O— _____

    ^V—_____

Drawing Problems

1. Begin an entirely new AutoCAD menu composed of a general button section and an **OSNAP** button menu and screen menu. Name the menu P19-1.MNU. Plan your menu items before you begin. The main button menu (***BUTTONS1) should have the following items:

Button Number	Function
1	Select text and allow user to reword.
2	Cancel last and activate the **LINE** command.
3	Cancel last and activate the **CIRCLE** command.
4	**ZOOM Dynamic**.
5	Leave blank.
6	Erase one object and end the **ERASE** command.
7	Cancel last and **ZOOM Window**.
8	[Enter].
9	Cancel last and **ZOOM Previous**.

The **BUTTONS2 menu is an object snap interrupt menu. All object snap items should activate the **OSNAP** mode and select a point when the button is pressed. The **BUTTONS2 menu should contain the following items:

Button Number	Function
1	**Endpoint**
2	**Intersection**
3	**Perpendicular**
4	**Midpoint**
5	**Center**
6	**Tangent**
7	**Quadrant**
8	Return to main button and screen menus.
9	**Node**

Write the menus in small segments and be sure to test all items. Generate a printed copy of the menu file.

2. Add the menu given below to the P19-1.MNU file you created in Problem 1. The section name should be ***SCREEN. The main menu name should be **S. Plan all of your menu items before entering them in the text editor. The following items should be included.

Position	Menu Items
1	Menu title [HOME]
2	Cancel and **ARC**.
3	Cancel and **POLYGON**.
4	Cancel and **PLINE**.
5	Cancel and **LIST**.
6	Cancel and **DIST**.
7	Cancel and **SCALE**.
8	Cancel and **OFFSET**.
9	Cancel and **ROTATE**.
10	Cancel and **STRETCH**.
11	Blank.
12	Cancel and **ZOOM**.
13	Blank.
14	Rotate crosshairs axis to user-specified angle. Allow user to set base point and leave **SNAP** on.
15	Reset crosshairs axis to zero and turn **SNAP** off.
16	Allow user to pick multiple objects and change all to a new layer.
17	Select text string and allow user to input new height.

Test all menu items to ensure that they are working properly before going to the next problem. Generate a printed copy of the menu file.

3. Add the following screen menu to your P19-1.MNU file. This is an editing menu and should be named **EDIT. At position 18 in your main screen menu (see Problem 2), add an item that calls the **EDIT** menu. Place the following items in the **EDIT** menu:

Position	Menu Items	Function
1	[Erase-F]	Erase with **FENCE** option.
2	[Copy-WP]	Copy with **Window Polygon** option.
3	[Move-W]	Move with **Window** option.
4	[Break-F]	Activate **BREAK**, allow user to select object, then pick first and second points without entering F.
5	[Change-1]	Activate **CHANGE**, select object, and stop for user input.
6	[Reword-M]	Allow user to reword one to four lines of text without restarting command.
7	[0-Fillet]	Select two lines and clean up corners with zero radius fillet. Allow selection of five clean-ups without restarting the command.
8	[0-Break]	Select line or arc and split into two parts.
9	[0-Corner]	Select two intersecting lines at the intersection. Clean up corner using two picks.

Generate a printed copy of the menu file.

4. Add an item to the main button menu at button 5 that calls the **BUTTONS2 menu and a new screen menu called **OSNAP. The line should read:

[5]$B=BUTTONS2 $S=OSNAP

The new **OSNAP screen menu should contain the following items:

Position	Menu Item	Function
1	[BUTTONS]	Label
2	[1=Endpt]	Show button assignment and activate normal **OSNAP** if picked from the screen.
3	[2=Inter]	Show button assignment and activate normal **OSNAP** if picked from the screen.
4	[3=Perp]	Show button assignment and activate normal **OSNAP** if picked from the screen.
5	[4=Middle]	Show button assignment and activate normal **OSNAP** if picked from the screen.
6	[5=Center]	Show button assignment and activate normal **OSNAP** if picked from the screen.
7	[6=Tangent]	Show button assignment and activate normal **OSNAP** if picked from the screen.
8	[7=Quad]	Show button assignment and activate normal **OSNAP** if picked from the screen.
9	[8=HOME]	Page back to main button and screen.
10	[9=Node]	Show button assignment and activate normal **OSNAP** if picked from the screen.
11	[Nearest]	Activate **Nearest OSNAP** from screen.
12	[Insert]	Activate **Insert OSNAP** from screen.

Generate a printed copy of the menu file.

5. Alter the **OSNAPB menu in your copy of acad.mnu to function with a button menu in the same manner as given in Problem 4. If you have not added a **BUTTONS2 menu to your acad.mnu file (explained earlier in this chapter), do so for this problem.

Customizing Pull-Down Menus and Image Tiles

Learning Objectives

After completing this chapter, you will be able to:
- ○ Create single- or multiple-page pull-down menus.
- ○ Understand the structure of pull-down menus.
- ○ Create user-defined accelerator keys.
- ○ Describe the purpose and function of image tile menus.
- ○ Describe the purpose and the function of a slide library.
- ○ Create slides for image tile menus.
- ○ Create a slide library for an image tile menu.
- ○ Create an image tile menu file listing.

Pull-Down Menus and Accelerator Keys

AutoCAD Custom Guide **4**

The names of the standard pull-down menus appear in the menu bar at the top of the AutoCAD graphics window. They are selected by placing the cursor arrow over the menu item and picking to select it.

Pull-down menus are referred to as "POP" menus in the menu file, and are listed as POP0, POP1, etc. POP0 is the object snap cursor menu, which provides quick access to frequently used items. The object snap cursor menu is enabled by simultaneously pressing the [Shift] key and clicking the [Enter] button on your mouse or digitizer tablet puck. By default, this cursor menu displays each of the object snap modes. The **Grips** cursor menu is also defined in the menu file, under POP17. It displays the **Grips** options. Other cursor menus, such as the **Zoom** cursor menu, are handled by AutoCAD and are not part of the menu file.

Once you understand how pull-down menus are designed, you can customize existing menus and create your own. Some basic information about pull-down menus follows:
- You can have from 1 to 16 pull-down menus.
- The name of the pull-down menu, or "header," can be up to 14 characters long. On low resolution displays, headers should average less than five characters if all 16 pull-down menus are used. This will allow all of the titles to fit on the screen.
- Menu item labels can be any length. The menu is as wide as its longest label.
- Each menu can have multiple cascading submenus.
- A pull-down menu can have up to 999 items (including cascading submenus).
- A cursor menu can have up to 499 items (including cascading submenus).

- If a pull-down menu title duplicates the title of a standard Windows pull-down menu (such as File, Edit, or Help), that section of the menu is ignored and does not appear in the menu bar.

Pull-down menu structure and codes

Many of the same codes used for writing screen menus are used for pull-down menus. The primary difference is the sequence of characters, or *syntax*, used for cascading submenus. This different syntax allows for the definition of accelerator and mnemonic shortcut keys used in the pull-down menus.

This is best seen by loading your copy of the acad.mnu file into your text editor. Look for the ***POP3 heading. This is the **View** pull-down menu. The first part of this menu is shown in Figure 20-1.

Compare the appearance of the menu file syntax and the pull-down menu. A few new menu syntax characters are found in this menu. These characters are explained below. They provide a separator line, indicate where cascading submenus begin and end, and define accelerator and mnemonic shortcut keys.

Character	Function
[--]	Two hyphens are used to insert a separator line across the pull-down menu. The line is automatically drawn the width of the menu.
->	Indicates this item has a cascading submenu.
<-	Indicates this is the last item in the cascade.
<-<-	Indicates this item is the last item in the submenu and the last item of the previous menu (parent menu).
&c	The ampersand specifies the mnemonic key in a pull-down or cursor menu label. The "c" shown here represents any character.

Figure 20-1.
The first part of the ***POP3 **View** pull-down menu. Note the placement of the ampersand character (&) to define accelerator and mnemonic shortcut keys.

```
***POP3
**VIEW
ID_MnView        [&View]
ID_Redrawall     [&Redraw]'_redrawall
ID_Regen         [Re&gen]^C^C_regen
ID_Regenall      [Regen &All]^C^C_regenall
                 [--]
ID_MnZoom        [->&Zoom]
ID_ZoomRealt         [&Realtime]'_zoom ;
                     [--]
ID_ZoomPrevi         [&Previous]'_zoom _p
ID_ZoomWindo         [&Window]'_zoom _w
ID_ZoomDynam         [&Dynamic]'_zoom _d
ID_ZoomScale         [&Scale]'_zoom _s
ID_ZoomCente         [&Center]'_zoom _c
                     [--]
ID_ZoomIn            [&In]'_zoom 2x
ID_ZoomOut           [&Out]'_zoom .5x
                     [--]
ID_ZoomAll           [&All]'_zoom _all
ID_ZoomExten         [<-&Extents]'_zoom _e
ID_MnPan         [->&Pan]
```

Menu entry   Resulting pull-down menu

Marking menu items

Menu items can be marked with a check mark (✓) or other character of your choosing. You can also have items "grayed-out." The following characters are used for these purposes:

Character	Function
[~]	The tilde grays out any characters that follow.
!.	The combination of an exclamation point and a period places a check mark (✓) before the menu item.

When these marking characters are used in a menu, they mark an item permanently. This may be desirable for the separator line and for graying out specific items, but a check mark is often related to an item that is toggled on or off. Look at the following example menu file and its pull-down menu in Figure 20-2.

Figure 20-2.
An example of
check mark and
grayed-out
character definition
in a pull-down
menu.

```
***POP11
**TEST
[T&est]
[!.Checkmark]
[--]
[~Grayed out text]
[--]
[~!.Grayed out checkmark]
```

Menu entry   Resulting pull-down menu

Creating "smart" pull-down menu items

A check mark is often placed by any item to indicate that it has been selected, or that it is on. You can add this capability to your pull-down menus by using a new string expression language called DIESEL. A *string* is simply a group of characters that can be input from the keyboard or from the value of a system variable. DIESEL (Direct Interpretively Evaluated String Expression Language) uses a string for its input and provides a string for output. In other words, you give DIESEL a value, and it gives something back to you.

Using the check mark is an excellent example of how DIESEL can be used in menu items. For example, you may want to put the **ORTHO** command in a pull-down menu and indicate when it is on with a check mark. Use the following line in your menu:

    [$(if,$(getvar,orthomode),!.)&Ortho]^O

The first $ signals the pull-down menu to evaluate a DIESEL macro. This macro gets the value (getvar) of the **ORTHOMODE** system variable, and places the check mark by the item if the value is 1 (on). Notice that the AutoCAD command being executed is **ORTHO** (^O).

Figure 20-3 shows how two DIESEL additions to the previous **Test** menu look in the menu file and the pull-down menu. The pull-down menu shows that **ORTHO** is on.

The use of DIESEL expressions in your menus can enhance their power and make them more "intelligent." See Chapter 5 of the AutoCAD *Customization Guide* for a complete discussion of the DIESEL language.

Figure 20-3.
An example of DIESEL macros added to a pull-down menu. Note that **Ortho** is toggled on.

```
***POP11
**TEST
[T&est]
[$(if,$(getvar,orthomode),!.)&Ortho]^O
[$(if,$(getvar,snapmode),!.)&Snap]^B
[!.Checkmark]
[--]
[~Grayed out text]
[--]
[~!.Grayed out checkmark]
```

Menu entry   Resulting pull-down menu

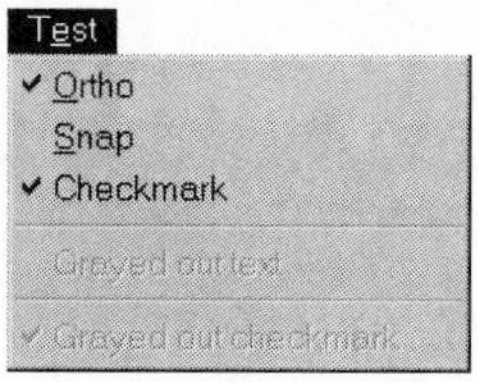

Referencing other pull-down menus

A pick on one menu can activate, or "reference" another pull-down menu. A menu pick can also gray out or place a marking character by another pull-down menu item. The following character codes are used for these purposes:

Character	Function
$p*n*=	Makes another pull-down menu current, where "*n*" is the number of the menu. Alternately, any specified alias for the menu can be referenced. The alias is defined by the **alias* label after the menu section name.
$p*n*=*	Displays the currently active pull-down menu.
$p*n*.1=	References a specific item number on another pull-down menu.

When referencing other pull-down menus, you can combine the marking symbols to add "gray out" or place check marks. Study the following menu item examples. The first example activates POP11 and displays it.

    $p11=*

The next menu item places a check mark on item 4 of POP11.

    $p11.4=!.

Now, study these menu item examples. The first entry grays out item 3 of POP6.

    $p6.3=~

The following menu item places a check mark by item 2 of POP8 and grays it out.

    $p8.2=!.~

The next menu item removes all marks and "gray outs" from item 2 of POP8.

    $p8.2=

The following examples show how these techniques can be combined in a macro.

    [Insert desk]^C^Cinsert;desk;\\\\$p2=*
    [Setup .5]^C^Cgrid;.5;snap;.25;$p2.1=!. $p2.2=!.~
    [Defaults]^C^Cgrid;off;snap;off;$p2.1= $p2.2=

Figure 20-4 shows an example using these techniques, and the appearance of the pull-down menu it defines.

Figure 20-4.
A sample of linking
pull-down menu
items.

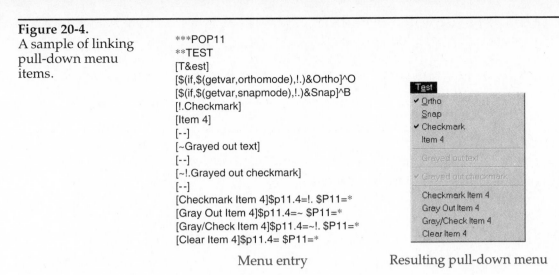

```
***POP11
**TEST
[T&est]
[$(if,$(getvar,orthomode),!.)&Ortho]^O
[$(if,$(getvar,snapmode),!.)&Snap]^B
[!.Checkmark]
[Item 4]
[--]
[~Grayed out text]
[--]
[~!.Grayed out checkmark]
[--]
[Checkmark Item 4]$p11.4=!. $P11=*
[Gray Out Item 4]$p11.4=~ $P11=*
[Gray/Check Item 4]$p11.4=~!. $P11=*
[Clear Item 4]$p11.4= $P11=*
```

Menu entry   Resulting pull-down menu

NOTE   Menu item numbering begins with the first line of the pull-down menu below the title and continues to the bottom of the file. AutoCAD numbers items consecutively through all submenus, without considering submenu levels.

Creating a new pull-down menu

When adding a new pull-down menu, first scroll through the acad.mnu file until you find the ***POP17 pull-down menu. If you want to add any additional pull-down menus, they should be inserted before the ***POP17 section. Your new pull-down menus will be located in the menu bar after the **Help** menu. Be sure to leave an empty line between pull-down menus.

Test each item of a new menu to make sure it works properly. Remember, when you return to the drawing editor, you must use the **MENU** command to reload the revised menu. If you neglect to do this, you will be working with the old version of the menu.

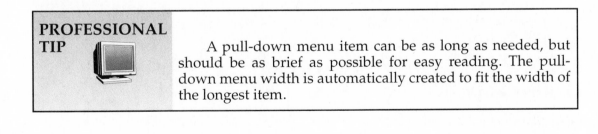

PROFESSIONAL TIP   A pull-down menu item can be as long as needed, but should be as brief as possible for easy reading. The pull-down menu width is automatically created to fit the width of the longest item.

Sample menu items

The following examples show how AutoCAD commands and options can be used to create pull-down or screen menu items. They are listed using a three-step process:

- Step 1 is a verbal description of the macro.
- Step 2 lists the keyboard strokes required for the macro.
- Step 3 gives the actual macro as it appears in the menu file.

Example 1

1. This **HEXAGON** command will start the **POLYGON** command and request a six-sided polygon inscribed in a circle.
2. **POLYGON**⏎

   6⏎

   (select center)⏎

   I⏎
3. [Hexagon]*^C^Cpolygon;6;\I

As mentioned earlier, you can indicate a return in a command or macro by using either a space or a semicolon. Notice the following two commands. Both commands perform the same function.

        [Hexagon]*^C^Cpolygon 6 \I
        [Hexagon]*^C^Cpolygon;6;\I

The first example uses spaces and the second example uses semicolons to represent pressing the [Enter] key. The technique you use is a matter of personal preference, but it is recommended to use semicolons.

PROFESSIONAL TIP 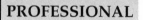 It is generally preferred to use a semicolon for a return to clearly indicate that a return has been inserted. Spaces can be difficult to count, and when using spaces, an extra space can slip into a menu item and go unnoticed until the item is tested.

Example 2

1. This **DOT** command should draw a solid dot, .1 inch in diameter. Use the **DONUT** command. The inside diameter is 0 (zero) and the outside diameter is .1.
2. **DONUT**⏎

   0⏎

   .1⏎
3. [&Dot]^C^Cdonut;0;.1

Example 3

1. This **X-POINT** command sets **PDMODE** = 3 and draws an X at the pick point. The command should be repeated.
2. **PDMODE**⏎

   3⏎

   POINT⏎

   (Pick the point)
3. [&X-Point]*^C^Cpdmode;3;point

Example 4

1. This command, named **Notation**, could be used by a drawing checker or instructor. It allows them to circle features on a drawing and then add a leader and text. It first sets the color to red, then draws a circle, snaps a leader to the nearest point that is picked on the circle, and prompts for the text. User input for text is provided, then a cancel returns the Command: prompt and the color is set to white.

2. **COLOR.⏎**
   RED⏎
   CIRCLE⏎
   (Pick center point)
   (Pick radius)
   DIM⏎
   LEADER⏎
   NEA⏎
   (Pick a point on the circle)
   (Pick end of leader)⏎
   (Press [Enter] for automatic shoulder)
   (Enter text)⏎
   (Press [Esc] to cancel)
   COLOR⏎
   WHITE⏎

3. [&Notation]^C^Ccolor;red;circle;\\dim;leader;nea;\\;\^Ccolor;white

Example 5

1. A repeating command named **Multisquare**, which draws one inch squares oriented at a 0° horizontal angle.

2. **RECTANG⏎**
   (Pick lower left corner)
   @1,1⏎

3. [&Multisquare]*^C^Crectang;\@1,1

EXERCISE 20-1

❑ Use your text editor and create a new file named EX20-1.MNU. Put the following three commands in a new ***POP11 menu titled **Custom**.
  ❑ [Copy M]—Make multiple copies. Allow two picks.
  ❑ [Rotate45]—Rotate an object 45° counterclockwise. Should be an automatic command.
  ❑ [Fillet .5]—A repeating command that applies a .5 fillet.
❑ All commands should display their mnemonic keys.
❑ Use the spaces below to write out the commands before you enter them in the computer.

  [Copy M]— _____

  [Rotate45]— _____

  [Fillet .5]—_____

Creating help strings for pull-down menus

Help strings are the brief descriptions on the status line describing the menu item currently highlighted. These can provide helpful information to those who are using your menu. It becomes very important to create appropriate help strings when you are adding new items to the menu, since these items may be unfamiliar to even experienced AutoCAD users. To get an idea of the ideal content of a help string for your menu item, carefully review some of AutoCAD's existing help strings. Help string definitions are placed in the ***HELPSTRINGS section in your menu file, but references to a help string can be placed throughout your menu file. For example, if a 0.5" wide polyline option is added to a pull-down menu, the menu code might look like this:

    [0.5 Polyline]^C^Cpline;\w;0.5;0.5;

To create a help string for this selection, open your menu file and find the ***HELPSTRINGS section. The beginning of the ***HELPSTRINGS section looks like this:

```
***HELPSTRINGS
ID_3darray      [Creates a three-dimensional array:  3darray]
ID_3dface       [Creates a three-dimensional face:  3dface]
ID_3dmesh       [Creates a free-form polygon mesh:  3dmesh]
ID_3dpoly       [Creates a polyline of straight line segments in three-dimensional
                space:  3dpoly]
ID_3dsin        [Imports a 3D Studio file:  3dsin]
ID_3dsurface    [Creates three-dimensional surface objects using a dialog box]
ID_About        [Displays information about AutoCAD:  about]
ID_Acisin       [Imports an ACIS file:  acisin]
ID_Ai_box       [Creates a three-dimensional box polygon mesh:  ai_box]
ID_Ai_cone      [Creates a cone-shaped polygon mesh:  ai_cone]
```

The format for an entry in the ***HELPSTRINGS section is as follows:

    ID_*tagname* [*Help message...*]

The ID_*tagname* should be unique. Duplicate tags can cause unexpected results. Do a text search using your text editor's "find" function to see if the tag name you select is already in use. The help message should be short enough to fit along the bottom of the screen, and as clearly worded as possible. A search of the acad.mnu file reveals that the ID tag name selected for the wide polyline (ID_Wpline) is not already in use. To prepare the help string for use, find the ***HELPSTRINGS section of your menu file and enter the following line:

    ID_Wpline [Draws a 0.5" wide polyline.]

Now that the help string definition has been created, any menu item referencing the ID_Wpline tag will display this help string. To place a reference to this help string, you need to precede the menu item label with the ID tag name as follows:

    ID_Wpline [0.5 Polyline]^C^Cpline;\w;0.5;0.5;

When the **0.5 Polyline** menu item is highlighted, the help string "Draws a 0.5" wide polyline" is displayed on the status line.

PROFESSIONAL TIP    A new help string can be placed anywhere within the help string section. Since this section is rather extensive, it can be helpful to place all of your custom help string definitions together at the bottom. This makes them easy to locate when you need to edit them.

❏ Use your text editor and open the menu file EX20-1.MNU from Exercise 20-1. You can also make a copy of the acad.mnu file and name it TEST.MNU. Using this file, do the following:

❏ Create a ***HELPSTRINGS section in your menu file if one does not exist.

❏ Create a help string for each of the three new commands you developed in Exercise 20-1.

❏ Test each command to be sure each help string is displayed properly.

❏ Use the spaces below to write the notation for each help string before you insert it into your menu.

[Copy M]— _____

[Rotate45]— _____

[Fillet .5]— _____

Creating and using accelerator keys

AutoCAD Release 14 supports user-defined accelerator keys. The accelerator keys are the keystrokes available when you specify **Windows standards** in the **Priority for accelerator keys** area of the **Compatibility** tab of the **Preferences** dialog box. These include [Ctrl]+[C] as **COPYCLIP**, [Ctrl]+[V] as **PASTECLIP**, [Ctrl]+[S] as **QSAVE**, and [Ctrl]+[P] as **PRINT**. If you select **AutoCAD Classic** keystrokes, the accelerator keys cannot be used.

The accelerator key definitions are contained in the ***ACCELERATORS section of your menu file:

```
***ACCELERATORS
[CONTROL+"K"]$M=$(if,$(and,$(getvar,pickadd),1),'_pickadd 0,'_pickadd 1)
[CONTROL+"L"]^O
[CONTROL+"R"]^V
ID_Copyclip     [CONTROL+"C"]
ID_New          [CONTROL+"N"]
ID_Open         [CONTROL+"O"]
ID_Print        [CONTROL+"P"]
ID_Save         [CONTROL+"S"]
ID_Pasteclip    [CONTROL+"V"]
ID_Cutclip      [CONTROL+"X"]
ID_Redo         [CONTROL+"Y"]
ID_U            [CONTROL+"Z"]
```

There are two different ways to specify an accelerator key. The second entry defines the [Ctrl]+[L] keystroke as an **Ortho** mode toggle. This method allows you to specify the keystroke as a label, followed by any menu code required. For example, to define a [Ctrl]+[I] keystroke to start the **DDINSERT** command, enter the following line into your ***ACCELERATORS section:

```
[CONTROL+"I"]^C^CDDINSERT
```

It is also possible to create macros associated with accelerator keys. Simply enter the menu code just as you would for any other menu area. For example, to create a [Ctrl]+[A] accelerator key that automatically sets up A-size drawing limits and draws a 0.15 wide polyline border, enter the following in the ***ACCELERATORS section:

```
[CONTROL+"A"]^C^CLIMITS;;11,8.5;PLINEWID;0.15;RECTANG;0.5,0.5;10.5,8;ZOOM;A
```

The second accelerator key definition references an ID_*tagname* for a menu pick as the source code, followed by the keystroke definition. Any item on a pull-down menu that displays a help string can be used in this manner. For example, under the **Tile_d Viewports** cascading menu in the **View** pull-down menu, the **4 Viewports** selection displays a help string when highlighted. Searching through the menu for this item reveals the following code for this menu pick:

        ID_Vports 4 [&4 Viewports]^C^C_vports 4

The ID_Vports 4 tag can be referenced in the ***ACCELERATORS section to execute the menu code listed for this item as follows:

        ID_Vports 4 [CONTROL+"4"]

Pressing [Ctrl]+[4] now activates the **4 Viewports** menu selection. Basically, it is the same as entering the following under ***ACCELERATORS:

        [CONTROL+"4"]^C^C_vports 4

Either way works equally well, but it is unnecessary to duplicate existing menu code if you reference the ID tag.

PROFESSIONAL TIP  Accelerators have some specific limitations. For example, an accelerator cannot pause for user input or use repeating commands.

EXERCISE 20-3

❏ Use your text editor and open the menu file you used in Exercise 20-2. Do the following:
  ❏ Create an ***ACCELERATORS section in your menu file if one does not exist.
  ❏ Create an accelerator key for each of the three new commands you developed in Exercise 20-1.
  ❏ Test each command to be sure that each accelerator functions properly.
  ❏ Use the spaces below to write the notation for each accelerator before you insert it into your menu.

      [Copy M]— _____

      [Rotate45]— _____

      [Fillet .5]— _____

Some notes about pull-down menus

Here are a few more things to keep in mind when developing pull-down menus:
- If the first line of a pull-down menu (the title line) is blank, that menu is not displayed in the menu bar, and all menus to the right are moved left to take its place.
- Pull-down menus are disabled during the following commands:
  ✓ **DTEXT**, after the rotation angle is entered.
  ✓ **SKETCH**, after the record increment is set.
- Pull-down menus that are longer than the screen display are truncated to fit on the screen.
- The cursor menu is named POP0. It can contain items that reference other pull-down and screen menus.

Menu Groups and Partial Menus

In addition to the **MENU** command, two other menu file handling commands are provided. The **MENU** command initially loads a base menu in its default condition, and provides no menu display options. However, it is possible to load multiple menus at one time and use only the desired elements of each, or modify the way a base menu is displayed by using the **MENULOAD** command.

The purpose of the **MENULOAD** command is to allow loading of partial menus. This allows you to add to your base menu (e.g. ACAD or MYMENU) additional options from a different menu. This allows you to customize your menu so that you have access to desired features from two or more different menu files.

AutoCAD menu files are assigned menu group names. For example, in the beginning of the acad.mnu file, you will find the line:

***MENUGROUP=ACAD

This assigns the group name ACAD to this menu. However, if you open the sample menu file AC_BONUS.MNU, which is found in the \AutoCAD R14\Bonus\Cadtools folder, you will find the specification:

***MENUGROUP= AC_BONUS

This identifies items in this menu as being in the AC_BONUS menu group. This allows you to identify items from different menus easily. For example, when working with screen menus, your calls to submenus were preceded by ACAD. This identified the group containing the desired menu. In Chapter 19, your call to the TEST screen submenu appeared as:

$S=ACAD.TEST

If the AC_BONUS menu was loaded and also had a screen submenu named TEST, your menu call would specify from which group to obtain the definition for the TEST menu.

If you have not changed the group name and you try to load your MYMENU menu with **MENULOAD** while the ACAD menu is already loaded, you will get an error message. This is because these two menus both use the same group name. You can force AutoCAD to replace existing group definitions with newly loaded menu data.

The **MENULOAD** command can be accessed by picking **Customize Menus...** from the **Tools** pull-down menu, or it can be typed directly at the Command: prompt. Entering the **MENULOAD** command displays the **Menu Customization** dialog box, as shown in Figure 20-5. There are several options available:

* **Menu Groups.** This list shows the currently loaded menu groups. Items on this list can be highlighted in preparation for other actions.

MENULOAD

Tools
➡ Customize
Menus...

Figure 20-5.
The **Menu Groups**
tab of the **Menu Customization**
dialog box.

After a menu
group is loaded,
its group name
appears here

Specify menu
file to be added

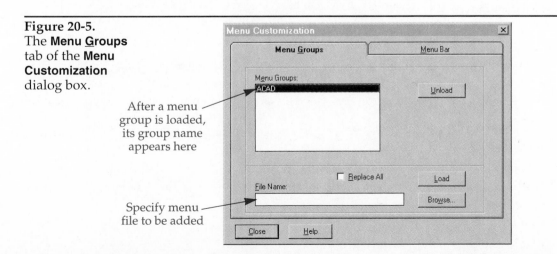

- **File Name.** This edit box shows the name of the currently selected menu file.
- **Replace All.** A check in this check box forces newly loaded group names to replace existing duplicate file names.
- **Unload.** This button unloads the definition for the menu group highlighted in the **Menu Groups** list box.
- **Load.** This button loads the menu file specified in the **File Name:** edit box and places its associated group name in the **Menu Groups** list box.
- **Browse....** This is often the easiest way to specify a new menu file name for loading. It displays the **Select Menu File** dialog box and allows you to select a menu file. This is often easier than typing the entire path and file name.

To practice loading an additional menu, use the **Select Menu File** dialog box to find the ac_bonus.mnu file. Remember that you must first specify *.mnu in the **Files of type:** drop-down list.

After selecting the ac_bonus.mnu file, you are returned to the **Menu Customization** dialog box. The ac_bonus.mnu file and path name appear in the **File Name:** edit box. Pick the **Load** button to load the menu definition and the new group name will be displayed in the **Menu Groups:** list box.

Now that you have loaded an additional menu definition, you can specify which menus to display. First, pick the **Menu Bar** tab, Figure 20-6. The features of this tab are as follows:

- **Menu Group.** This drop-down list provides access to the currently loaded menu group names. The currently selected menu group name is displayed here.
- **Menus.** All of the available pull-down menu names defined in this group are displayed here.
- **Menu Bar.** This list shows the pull-down menus that are currently available on the menu bar. The top item of the list takes a position at the far left of the menu bar, and each subsequent menu title is displayed to the right of the previous one.
- **Insert.** Picking this button inserts the currently highlighted menu in the **Menus:** list into the highlighted position in the **Menu Bar:** list.
- **Remove.** Removes the currently highlighted menu title from the **Menu Bar:** list.
- **Remove All.** Removes all menu titles from the **Menu Bar:** list.

The AC_BONUS menu group displays only one menu name, because that is all that is contained in the menu file. Other menu files may display one or more menu names. By selecting the desired group name and adjusting the various individual menu titles, you can completely customize the menu bar to have only the pull-down menus that are necessary for your current project.

Figure 20-6. The **Menu Bar** tab of the **Menu Customization** dialog box.

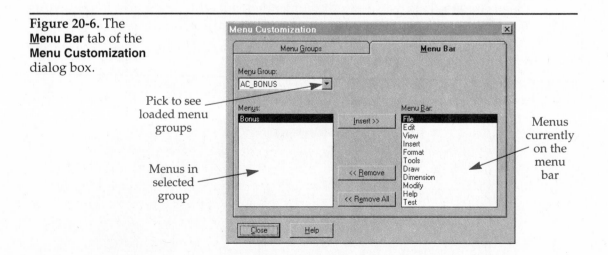

Pick to see loaded menu groups

Menus in selected group

Menus currently on the menu bar

Image Tile Menus

Image tile menus contain graphic symbols displayed in dialog boxes. They appear in certain dialog boxes, such as the **3D Objects** dialog box, Figure 20-7. This dialog box is accessed by selecting **3D Surfaces...** from **Surfaces** cascading menu in the **Draw** pull-down menu.

The dialog box shown contains several small boxes. Each box contains a small image. These displays are AutoCAD slides.

The slides are saved in a file created with the SLIDELIB program. This DOS-based program creates a file with an .slb extension. The slides can be used in an image tile menu by entering the required data in the menu file. Chapter 28 of *AutoCAD and its Applications—Basics, Release 14* explains the use of the SLIDELIB program.

Figure 20-7.
The **3D Objects** dialog box has an image tile menu.

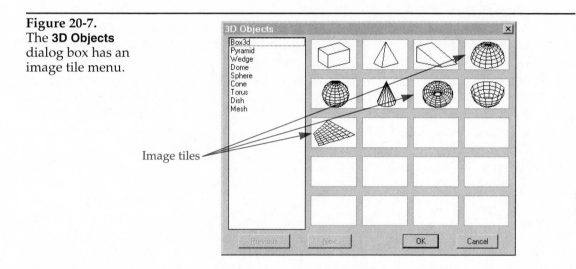

Image tiles

Image tile menu creation

The addition of image tile menus can enhance the operation of AutoCAD. However, you must create images using certain guidelines:

- ✓ Keep images simple. This saves display time and storage space. The image can be a simplified version of the actual symbol.
- ✓ When making slides, fill the screen with the image to be sure the image tile is filled. Center long items on the screen using **PAN**. This centers them in the image tile.
- ✓ Use image tile menus for symbols only. Do not clutter your program with image tile menus of text information. This slows the system down.
- ✓ AutoCAD does not display solid filled areas in image tiles. If you use fills, such as arrowheads, use the shade command prior to making the slide image file.
- ✓ A maximum of 20 slides can be displayed in one image tile menu. The names of the images are automatically displayed in a list box to the left of the image tiles. Image names (up to 17 characters) are displayed in the list box.

✓ If you have more than 20 slides in an image tile menu, AutoCAD creates additional "pages," each containing a **Next** and a **Previous** button for changing pages. The **OK** and **Cancel** buttons are automatically provided in the image tile menu.

✓ If an item label in an image tile menu has a space before the first character, no image is displayed for that label, but the label name is shown. This can be used to execute other commands or call other image tile menus.

Making symbols and slides for the image tile menu

Image tile menus can be used for a variety of purposes, but they are most commonly used to display images of blocks. Regardless of the types of symbols used, follow these steps when making image tile menus:

1. Draw the symbol or block.
2. Center the drawing on the display screen. When the drawing appears in the image tile menu, it is displayed in a box with a 1.5:1 ratio of width to height. With your drawing on the screen, set **TILEMODE** = 0, and create a 3 × 2 viewport. Now, **ZOOM Extents** and then switch back to model space. The drawing is now at the correct ratio.
3. Make a slide of the symbol using the **MSLIDE** command.
4. Write the SLIDELIB file.
5. Write the image tile menu file and test it.

Draw the three shapes shown in Figure 20-8. They represent a table, desk, and chair. Draw them any size you wish. Save each as a wblock, and name them TABLE, DESK, and CHAIR. Do not include text or attributes.

Use the **MSLIDE** command to make a slide of each one of the blocks, centering the slide as previously discussed. Give the slides the same name as the block. This completes the second step. Now you will use the SLIDELIB program to make the slide file.

Figure 20-8.
These objects are saved as blocks and used in a new image tile menu.

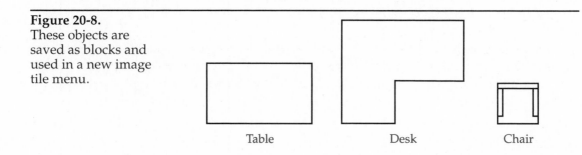

Table   Desk   Chair

Using the **SLIDELIB** program for an image tile menu

The SLIDELIB program operates in DOS and allows you to create a list of slide (.sld extension) files. This list of slides can then be used for slide shows and image tile menus.

To use the SLIDELIB program, you must launch the MS-DOS Prompt from your Windows task bar. You can also use the **SHELL** command from within AutoCAD. Either method opens an MS DOS window.

The creation of a slide file called FURNITUR begins as follows:

```
Command: SHELL↵
OS Command: ↵
```

You will now see the following on your screen:

```
Microsoft(R) Windows NT(TM)
(C) Copyright 1985-1996 Microsoft Corp.
C:\Program Files\AutoCAD R14⟩ SUPPORT\SLIDELIB FURNITUR↵
SLIDELIB 1.2 (3/8/89)
(C) Copyright 1987-1989,1994,1995 Autodesk, Inc.
    All Rights Reserved
TABLE↵
CHAIR↵
DESK↵
  ↵
  ↵
```

The second [Enter] on a blank line after the last slide name exits the SLIDELIB program. Check to see that the slide library file was created by listing all files with a .slb extension. It should be listed as furnitur.slb.

```
C:\Program Files\AutoCAD R14⟩ DIR *.SLB↵
```

Type EXIT to return to the AutoCAD graphics window.

```
C:\Program Files\AutoCAD R14⟩ EXIT↵
```

A second method of creating a slide library involves using an existing list of slides in a text file. This method is useful if you add slide names to a text file (.txt) as the slides are made. The method is discussed in Chapter 28 of *AutoCAD and its Applications—Basics, Release 14*.

Creating an image tile menu file listing

Load your copy of the acad.mnu into the text editor and page through the file until you find the ***image section. You can insert your new image tile menu between any of the existing ones. Be sure to leave a space between the previous and next menus.

Now begin a menu called furniture below the last image tile heading, **image_vporti. The first item in the menu is used as the title. If you neglect to put a title here, the first line of the menu will be used as the title. Your new menu should look like the following:

```
**image_furniture
[Select Furniture]
[furnitur(Table)]^C^Cinsert;table
[furnitur(Desk)]^C^Cinsert;desk
[furnitur(Chair)]^C^Cinsert;chair
[ Plants]$I=plants $I=*
```

Notice the space in the last entry, [Plants], after the left bracket. This produces a label without an image tile. This label is used to execute other commands, or as in this case, display other image tile menus.

These are called *branching* image tile menus. In this example, the Plants menu may show images of several types of plants. You can have as many branching image tile menus as needed.

The new image tile menu is still not usable because there is no selection that calls this menu to the screen. The **Draw** pull-down menu is a good place to put the call for this menu. Insert the following line in the pull-down menu:

```
[Furniture]$I=image_furniture $I=*
```

The first part of this entry, $I=furniture, calls the new furniture menu. The second part, $I=*, displays the menu and makes the items selectable.

Save the file and use the **MENU** command to reload the menu. Test all the items in the menu and correct any problems. The new image tile menu should look like the one in Figure 20-9.

Figure 20-9.
The customized image tile menu uses previously created objects.

A block can be selected with the label or the image tile

A label with no image is used to initiate a command or access another menu

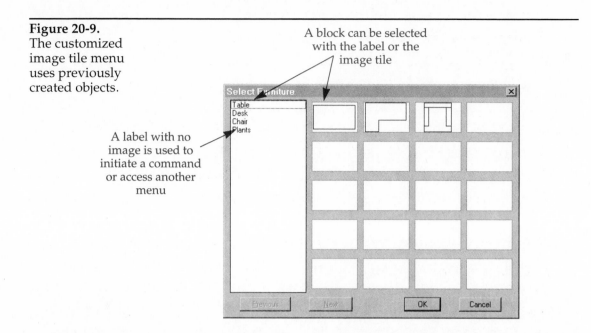

EXERCISE 20-4

❏ Using your text editor, create an image tile menu named **EX20-4** using three blocks that you have on file.
❏ Plan this menu so that you can add to it in the future.
❏ Remember to include an entry in the **Draw** pull-down menu that calls the new icon menu.

PROFESSIONAL TIP   Your primary goal in developing menus is to eliminate extra steps required to perform a function. The end result is that you can execute a thought or idea with one pick, rather than labor through a series of commands and options.

Chapter Test

Write your answers in the spaces provided.

1. How many items can a pull-down menu contain? _____

2. Define the following pull-down menu characters.

   A. -> _____

   B. <- _____

   C. <-<- _____

   D. &_____

3. Provide the character(s) required to perform the following functions:

   A. Insert a separator line across the pull-down menu. _____

   B. "Gray out" characters. _____

   C. Place a check mark before the menu item. _____

   D. Specify a mnemonic key shortcut. _____

4. What is a macro? _____

   _____

   _____

5. What code is used to make pull-down menus display and be selectable? _____

6. Describe the uses of the following menu codes:

   A. [*] _____

   B. [--] _____

   C. [~] _____

7. Name two ways to represent a return in a menu item. _____

   _____

8. How many pull-down menus can be displayed on one screen?_____

9. If sixteen pull-down menus are used, what should be the average length of the pull-down menu headings? _____

10. How wide is a pull-down menu? _____

11. What is the function of the following DIESEL expression?

    [$(if,$(getvar,snapmode),!.)Snap]^B_____

    _____

    _____

12. What is the function of the following menu item characters?

    $p3=* _____

    $p4.1=~ _____

    $p6.7=!. _____

13. What is the maximum number of pull-down menus? _____

14. Interpret the following menu item:

    ^C^Crectang;\@1,1 _____

    _____

15. Why is it a good idea to make a copy of the acad.mnu file before you begin experimenting or customizing?_____

    _____

16. In the acad.mnu file, how is a menu group name specified in an item that calls a specific menu?_____

17. Write the proper notation for the ***HELPSTRINGS section as it appears in the acad.mnu file. _____

    _____

18. You wish to create a new macro that executes the **PURGE** command, and uses the **Blocks** option. Write the macro as it would appear in the menu file, and the correct notation in the ***HELPSTRINGS section of the acad.mnu file.

    Menu file _____

    Help string_____

19. What is the key combination called that allows you to press the [Ctrl] key and one additional key to execute a command? _____

20. Write the proper notation to define the type of key mentioned in Question 19 using the [M] key to execute the **MVIEW** command. _____

    _____

21. What is the purpose of the **MENULOAD** command? _____

    _____

    _____

22. In the acad.mnu file, how is a menu group name specified in an item that calls a specific menu? _____

    _____

    _____

23. Which command is used to create the slide file that is used for an image tile menu?

    _____

    _____

24. What is the first line of an image tile menu called? _____

25. List the steps required to create an image tile menu.

    1. _____
    2. _____
    3. _____
    4. _____
    5. _____

26. Write the correct syntax for executing the SLIDELIB program at the DOS prompt. The syntax should include a slide library name of CIVIL. _____

    _____

27. Describe the function of the following entry in an image tile menu file.

    [Fittings]$I=fittings $I=*_____

28. How would the title of an image tile menu named FITTINGS appear in the file listing? _____

    _____

Drawing Problems

1. Create a dimensioning pull-down menu. Place as many dimensioning commands as you need in the menu. Use cascading submenus if necessary. One or more of the submenus should be dimensioning variables. Include mnemonic keys.

2. Create a pull-down menu for 3D objects. Add it to your copy of acad.mnu. Include mnemonic keys. The contents of the menu should include the following items:

   - 3D solid objects
   - 3D surface objects
   - **ELEV** command
   - **3DFACE** command
   - **VPOINT** command
   - **VPORTS** command
   - **DVIEW** command
   - **HIDE** command
   - Filters

3. Create a new pull-down menu named **Special**. The menu should include the following drawing and editing commands:

   - **LINE**
   - **ARC**
   - **CIRCLE**
   - **POLYLINE**
   - **POLYGON**
   - **RECTANGLE**
   - **DTEXT**
   - **ERASE**
   - **MOVE**
   - **COPY**
   - **STRETCH**
   - **TRIM**
   - **EXTEND**
   - **CHAMFER**
   - **FILLET**

   Use cascading submenus if necessary. Include a separator line between the drawing and editing commands, and specify appropriate mnemonic shortcut keys.

4. Create a single pull-down menu that is used to insert a variety of blocks or symbols. These symbols can be for any drawing discipline that you use. Use cascading menus and mnemonic keys if necessary. This menu should have a special group name that will enable it to be loaded with the **MENULOAD** command. This menu can be added to the existing pull-downs in the ACAD menu, or it can replace one of them.

5. Create a single pull-down menu that is used to insert a variety of blocks, or drawing files of symbols. These symbols can be for any drawing discipline that you use. Use cascading menus and mnemonic keys if necessary. This menu should have a special group name that will enable it to be loaded with the **MENULOAD** command. This menu can be added to the ACAD menu.

6. Choose one of the previous five problems and create help strings for each of the new menu items. Use existing defined help strings whenever possible. When you define new help strings, always do a search of the menu file to see if the string is being used.

7. Refer to Problem 3. Create an accelerator key for each of the drawing and editing commands in that problem. Search the menu file to see if any of the commands are currently tagged with an accelerator key to avoid duplication.

---

8. Construct an image tile menu of a symbol library that you use in a specific discipline of drafting or design. This menu can be selected from the **Draw** pull-down menu, or from a new pull-down menu of your own creation. Use as many image tiles as needed. You can call additional image tile menus from the initial one. The following are examples of disciplines that could be used:

- Mechanical
- Architectural
- Civil
- Structural
- Piping
- HVAC

- Electrical
- Electronics
- PC board layout
- Geometric tolerancing
- 3D construction

9. Modify the existing **3D Objects** dialog box and image tile menu to include additional 3D objects of your own creation. You can insert an additional nine images to the existing dialog box. Create additional menus, or "pages," if needed.

10. Create a new image tile menu and dialog box that illustrates a variety of hatch patterns. When an image is selected, it should set a specific hatch pattern, then execute the **HATCH** command so that the user can set the scale and angle for the hatch pattern. Be sure to include the proper name of the hatch pattern in your menu file so that the user does not have to enter it when the **HATCH** command is executed.

11. Create a new image tile menu that provides images of a variety of dimensioning styles. When a specific image is picked, it should automatically set the appropriate dimension variables in order to achieve the appearance of the dimension in the selected image. Test each of these selections carefully before incorporating them into the file. This may be an excellent menu for using branching image tile dialog boxes in order to display variations in different dimension styles.

AutoCAD and its Applications—Advanced

Customizing *21*
Tablet Menus

Learning Objectives

After completing this chapter, you will be able to:
- ○ Configure and use the AutoCAD tablet menu template.
- ○ Customize the AutoCAD tablet menu.
- ○ Create a new tablet menu.

If you have a digitizer, the AutoCAD standard tablet menu is an alternative to keyboard entry or picking screen commands. The tablet menu template is a thick piece of plastic that measures 11″ × 12″. Printed on it are many of the commands available in AutoCAD. Some commands are accompanied by small symbols, or icons, which indicate the function of the command. The menu is helpful because it provides a clear display of various AutoCAD commands.

Like the screen menus, the tablet menu can be customized. Notice the empty spaces at the top of the tablet. This space is available for adding commands and symbols. You can have several overlays for this area.

Most people discover that many of the commands in the AutoCAD tablet are not used for specific types of drawings, so they construct their own tablet menus. This is similar to creating screen menus.

Using the AutoCAD Tablet Menu

To use a tablet menu, the digitizer must be configured for your specific hardware configuration and the type of menu you will be using. When you initially configure AutoCAD to recognize a digitizer, the entire surface of the tablet represents the screen pointing area. The **TABLET** command allows you to configure the digitizer to recognize the tablet menu overlay. This includes informing AutoCAD of the exact layout of the menu areas and the size and position of the screen pointing area. Depending on the type of pointing device you are using with Microsoft Windows, there are additional aspects of tablet configuration to be considered.

Using the digitizer tablet for all Windows applications

If you are using your digitizer as the sole pointing device for all Windows applications, you will require a driver called WINTAB. The WINTAB driver configures a digitizer to act as a mouse for Windows-based applications, but permits you to use the tablet screen pointing area and menus when running AutoCAD. This is called *absolute mode*.

You must install the WINTAB driver as your system pointing device in Windows before starting AutoCAD. WINTAB drivers are supplied by the digitizer tablet manufacturers, not by Autodesk. If you have access to CompuServe®, you can easily download the current WINTAB driver for your particular digitizer tablet.

Tablet menu layout

The AutoCAD tablet menu presents commands in related groups. See Figure 21-1. Notice the headings below each menu area. Find the **TEMPLATE** command in the **TOOL** section of the menu template. This command is used to calibrate, configure, and toggle your tablet.

Figure 21-1.
The AutoCAD tablet menu template. The area name is listed below the items in the area. The large area across the top of the template is the **User** area. (Autodesk, Inc.)

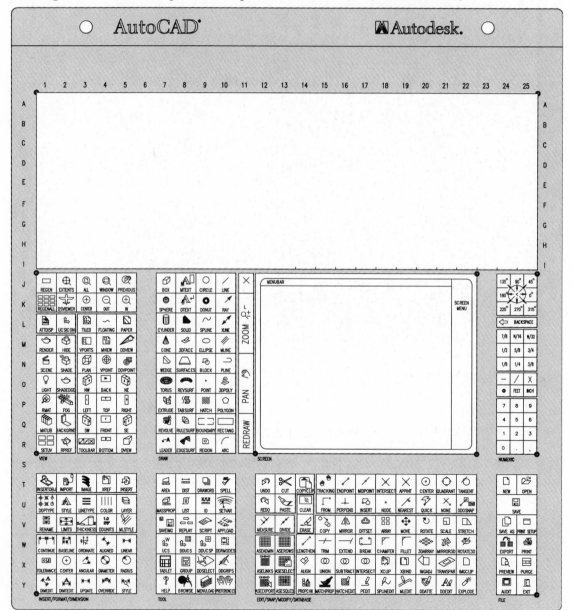

Many third-party applications supply their own customized menu files. An example of one such application is illustrated in Figure 21-2. The custom tablet menu shown is from Design Pacifica's ANSI Mechanical™, a widely used advanced mechanical and design annotation application for AutoCAD.

This program uses the available menu space for its specialized functions. This unused portion is called Menu Area 1. As you develop your own customized tablet menu, make a point of taking advantage of this unused space. Suggestions and instructions for customizing Menu Area 1 appear later in this chapter.

Figure 21-2.
Third-party applications, such as ANSI Mechanical™, often include their own specialized tablet menu templates. (Design Pacifica)

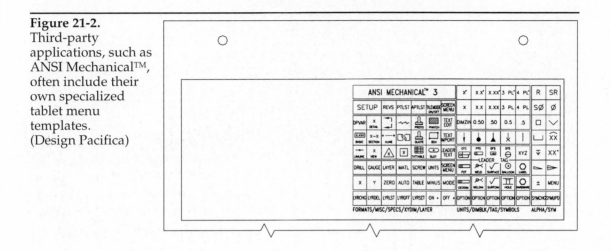

Configuring the tablet menu

The **TABLET** command is used to tell AutoCAD the layout of the tablet menu. It prompts for three corners of each menu area and the number of columns and rows in each area. The screen pointing area is defined by picking two opposite corners. Three corners of each menu area are marked with small doughnuts. As you read the following example, look at Figure 21-3. It illustrates the configuration of the standard AutoCAD tablet menu and shows the doughnuts marking menu area corners.

> Command: **TABLET**↵
> Option (ON/OFF/CAL/CFG): **CFG**↵
> Enter number of tablet menus desired (0-4): **4**↵

If tablet menus are currently in use and the same number is specified for menu areas, AutoCAD prompts as follows:

> Do you want to realign the tablet menu areas?⟨N⟩: **Y**↵

Next, you are prompted to select the points that define each menu area with the digitizer pointing device.

> Digitize upper-left corner of menu area 1: *(pick the doughnut at the upper-left corner)*
> Digitize lower-left corner of menu area 1: *(pick the point)*
> Digitize lower-right corner of menu area 1: *(pick the point)*
> Enter the number of columns for menu area 1: (*n-nnnn*) ⟨25⟩: ↵
> Enter the number of rows for menu area 1: (*n-nnnn*) ⟨9⟩: ↵

Figure 21-3.
Small doughnuts mark the corners of the menu areas on the AutoCAD template.
(Autodesk, Inc.)

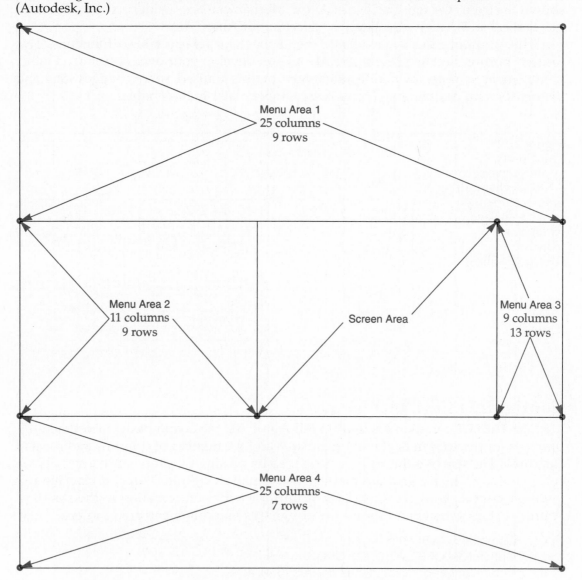

You have now given AutoCAD the location of Menu Area 1 and specified the number of boxes that are available. The command continues with Menu Area 2:

> Digitize upper-left corner of menu area 2: *(pick the point)*
> Digitize lower-left corner of menu area 2: *(pick the point)*
> Digitize lower-right corner of menu area 2: *(pick the point)*
> Enter the number of columns for menu area 2: (*n-nnnn*) ⟨11⟩: ↵
> Enter the number of rows for menu area 2: (*n-nnnn*) ⟨9⟩: ↵
> Digitize upper-left corner of menu area 3: *(pick the point)*
> Digitize lower-left corner of menu area 3: *(pick the point)*
> Digitize lower-right corner of menu area 3: *(pick the point)*
> Enter the number of columns for menu area 3: (*n-nnnn*) ⟨9⟩: ↵
> Enter the number of rows for menu area 3: (*n-nnnn*) ⟨13⟩: ↵
> Digitize upper-left corner of menu area 4: *(pick the point)*
> Digitize lower-left corner of menu area 4: *(pick the point)*
> Digitize lower-right corner of menu area 4: *(pick the point)*
> Enter the number of columns for menu area 4: (*n-nnnn*) ⟨25⟩: ↵
> Enter the number of rows for menu area 4: (*n-nnnn*) ⟨7⟩: ↵

Next, you must locate opposite corners of the screen pointing area. The screen pointing area is an area of the tablet that translates the digitizer motion into cursor movement on your screen. This mimics mouse movement. The screen pointing area maps to the computer display *absolutely*. This means that when you are pointing within the screen pointing area, the digitizer can be used to access windows, menus, and other applications outside of AutoCAD's drawing window area.

You can configure two different screen pointing areas, one fixed and one floating. The *fixed* screen pointing area is the entire tablet by default. You can reconfigure the area of the tablet that is used as the fixed screen pointing area to match the size of drawings you will be digitizing:

> Do you want to specify the Fixed Screen Pointing Area? ⟨N⟩: **Y**↵
> Digitize lower-left corner of Fixed Screen pointing area: *(pick the point)*
> Digitize upper-right corner of Fixed Screen pointing area: *(pick the point)*
> Do you want to specify the Floating Screen pointing area? ⟨N⟩: **Y**↵
> Do you want the Floating Screen Pointing Area to be the same size as the Fixed
>   Screen Pointing Area? ⟨Y⟩: *(enter Y or N; if you enter Y, digitize the lower-left and*
>   *upper-right corners of the floating screen pointing area when prompted.)*
> The F12 Key will toggle the Floating Screen Pointing Area ON and OFF.
> Would you like to specify a button to toggle the Floating Screen Area? ⟨N⟩: *(enter Y or N)*

If you choose to use a digitizer puck button as the toggle, the following prompt is issued:

> Press any non-pick button that you wish to designate as the toggle for the Floating
>   Screen Area.

Press the button of your choice. Do not press the pick button.

The tablet configuration is saved in the acad14.cfg file, which is in your AutoCAD R14 folder. The system reads this file when loading AutoCAD to determine what kind of equipment you are using. It also determines which menu is current. Use this same process when configuring the tablet for your custom menus.

Configuring the AutoCAD template menu can be done more simply by selecting the **Reconfig** option from the **TABLET** screen menu. First enable the screen menu in the **Display** tab of the **Preferences** dialog box. Then pick **TOOLS2** from the AutoCAD root menu. Next, pick **Tablet** and then select **Reconfig**. The **TABLET** screen menu options are shown in Figure 21-4.

Figure 21-4.
Select **Reconfig** from the **TABLET** screen menu to configure the tablet menu.

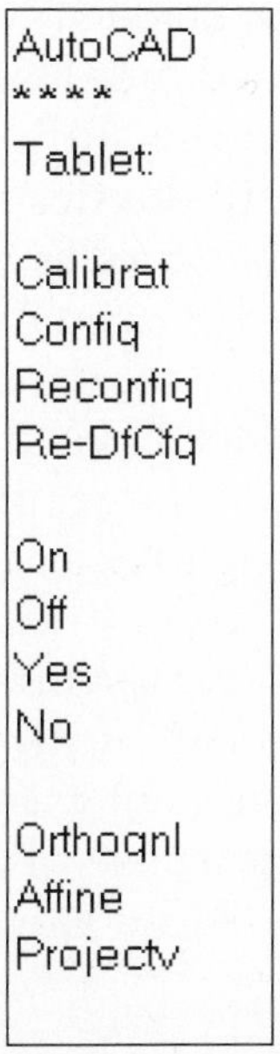

```
AutoCAD
* * * *
Tablet:

Calibrat
Config
Reconfig
Re-DfCfg

On
Off
Yes
No

Orthognl
Affine
Projectv
```

When the **Reconfig** option is selected, the configuration prompts appear as shown earlier. However, you do not need to enter the number of columns and rows. The **Reconfig** option assumes you are realigning the AutoCAD template. Therefore, it only requires the locations of the menu area and the screen pointing area. Use this screen menu option when you wish to return to the standard AutoCAD template after using a custom menu.

Customizing the AutoCAD Tablet Menu

The empty upper portion of the AutoCAD tablet menu can be used to add custom commands. This is Menu Area 1. It contains 225 boxes that can be programmed for additional commands, macros, scripts, and blocks. It is a good place to locate often used symbols and shapes.

An overlay containing block names and drawings can be plotted and slipped under the plastic template. Several overlays can be added for different disciplines, and can be structured to operate in different ways.

Plan the overlay

Before adding items to the AutoCAD template, take time to think about what the overlay should include. Ask yourself the following questions:
- ✓ For what kinds of drawings will the overlay be used?
- ✓ What kind of symbols should be placed in an overlay?
- ✓ What additional commands or macros should be in the overlay?
- ✓ Should the symbols be stored as blocks or drawings?
- ✓ Which symbols and blocks are used most often?
- ✓ If the symbols are blocks, should they be stored in a prototype drawing?

After answering these questions, you will be able to lay out a quality overlay. The next step is to draw the overlay.

Draw the overlay

Part of your plan should be drawing or sketching the menu area. The quickest way to make an accurate drawing is to plot Menu Area 1 from the tablet14.dwg drawing. This drawing is located in the AutoCAD R14\Sample folder. The following steps should be used to create the drawing of Menu Area 1:
1. Open the drawing file named tablet14.dwg.
2. **ZOOM Window** around Menu Area 1. See Figure 21-5.
3. Freeze all layers except Borders.
4. Make a new layer named Area1, and give it the color cyan.
5. Use **PLINE** to trace over the outline of Menu Area 1.
6. Draw a vertical line between tick marks on the right or left side and array it in 24 columns. Use object snap modes to set the correct spacing.
7. Draw a horizontal line between tick marks at the top or bottom and array 8 rows. Use object snap modes to set the correct spacing.
8. Erase the remaining black lines in the menu. See Figure 21-6.
9. Plot the menu on B-size or larger paper. A plot using a 1.5 = 1 or 2 = 1 scale provides a larger drawing, which is easier to work with for initial menu design purposes.
10. Erase all unnecessary layers.
11. Save the drawing as TABAREA1 (tablet area one) for future use.

Make several copies of your drawing. Pencil in the command and symbol names. Try more than one arrangement based on some of the considerations mentioned above. Keep in mind the purpose of the overlay you are making. Symbols that are used frequently should be placed along the outer edges for quick selection.

Figure 21-5.
Menu Area 1 is located at the top of the AutoCAD template. It contains a grid of 225 boxes inside the menu area border.

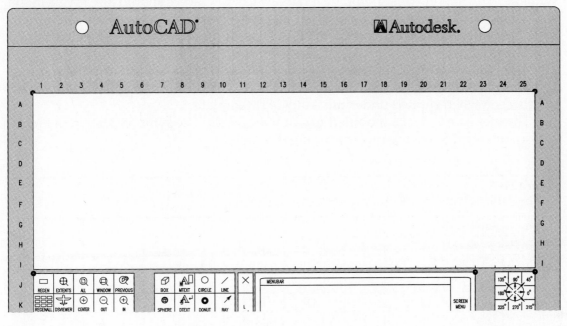

Figure 21-6.
A—The tablet14 drawing in its unedited form.
B—Menu Area 1 after drawing vertical lines.
C—Completed Menu Area 1.

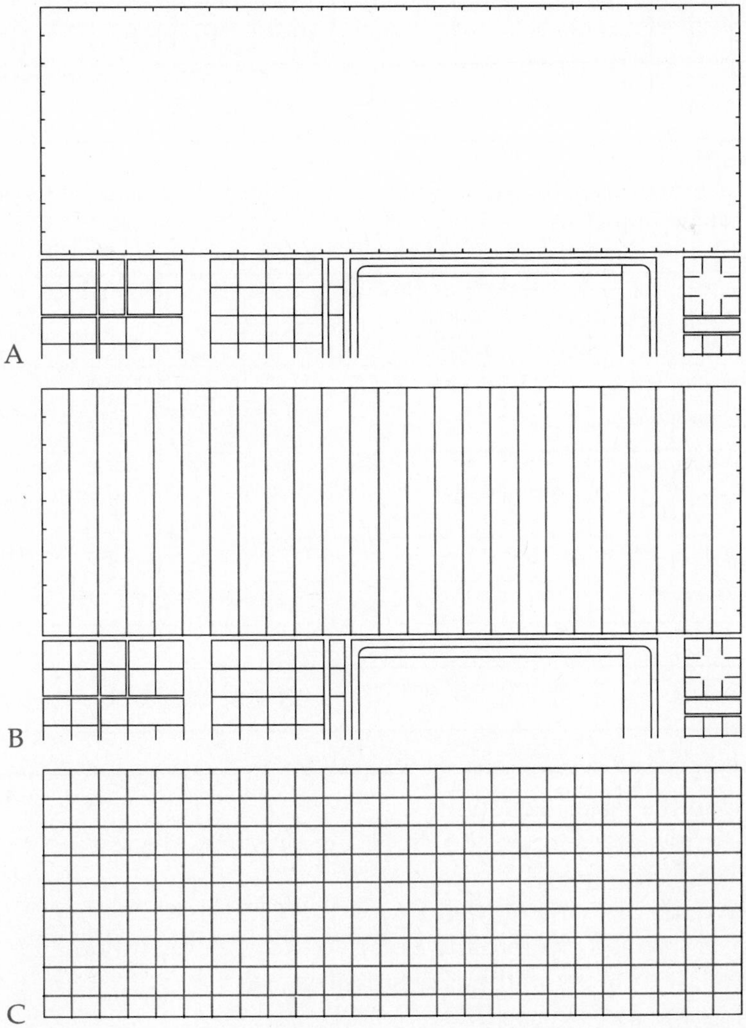

Complete the menu drawing

The next step in creating your customized AutoCAD template is to draw the symbols in the menu. This should be relatively easy. Symbols should already be in the form of blocks. They can now be inserted into the boxes of the menu. You will need to scale the symbols down to make them fit. The menu should now resemble that shown in Figure 21-7.

After drawing the menu, plot it at full scale (1 = 1). Use vellum or polyester film and wet ink. Use black rather than colored ink. This produces a good-quality plot, clearly seen when slipped under the AutoCAD template.

The menu area can be modified to suit your needs. The symbols shown in Figure 21-8 are used for isometric process piping drawings.

Figure 21-7.
Symbols (blocks) are inserted into the boxes of the menu.

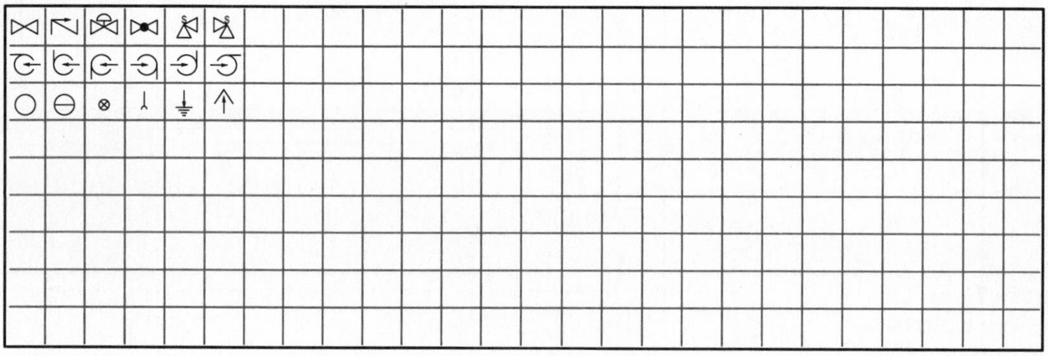

Figure 21-8.
This custom overlay for Menu Area 1 is used for isometric process piping drawings. (Willamette Industries, Inc.)

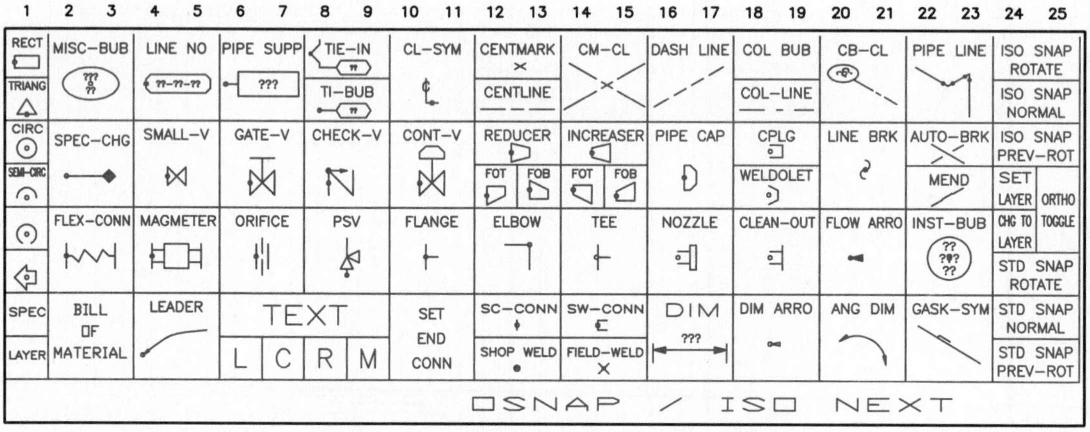

❑ Open the tablet14 drawing.
❑ Edit the drawing as shown in the previous discussion to create a tablet Menu Area 1 with boxes.
❑ Save the drawing of Menu Area 1 as EX21-1.
❑ Insert two blocks into the first two boxes of the menu area.
❑ Scale the blocks so they fit in the boxes.
❑ Save the drawing as EX21-1.

Write the menu file

The final step in customizing the AutoCAD template is to write the code in the ***TABLET1 section of the menu file. Load the acad.mnu file into your text editor and find the section label ***TABLET1. It should look like the following:

```
***TABLET1
**TABLET1STD
[A-1]\
[A-2]\
[A-3]\
[A-4]\
[A-5]\
```

Look at the tablet menu template in Figure 21-5 and notice the row and column numbers and letters along the top and sides of the tablet. These correspond to the numbers in brackets in the acad.mnu file under the ***TABLET headings. Each row contains 25 boxes numbered from left to right. There are 225 boxes in all. Therefore, box number 70 would also be C-20.

Notice in Figure 21-7 that the symbols placed in the menu occupy the first six boxes of each row. The first box of each row is labeled [A-1], [B-1], and [C-1], respectively.

The code can be entered in two ways. It can replace the box numbers listed in the menu file, or it can be entered after the box numbers. The latter method is recommended because it provides you with reference numbers for the tablet box. There are no screen labels for tablet menus. Thus, anything inside brackets is not displayed, nor is it read by AutoCAD. The notations inside the brackets can be left as helpful reminders.

Before making changes to the menu, make a copy of the acad.mnu file. Then load your copy of acad.mnu into the text editor. The following example shows the menu entries for the customized template shown in Figure 21-7.

```
**TABLET1STD
[A-1]^C^Cinsert;gatevalve
[A-2]^C^Cinsert;checkvalve
[A-3]^C^Cinsert;controlvalve
[A-4]^C^Cinsert;globevalve
[A-5]^C^Cinsert;safetyvalv-r
[A-6]^C^Cinsert;safetyvalv-l

[B-1]^C^Cinsert;pumpr-top
[B-2]^C^Cinsert;pumpr-up
[B-3]^C^Cinsert;pumpr-dn
[B-4]^C^Cinsert;pumpl-dn
[B-5]^C^Cinsert;pumpl-up
[B-6]^C^Cinsert;pumpl-top

[C-1]^C^Cinsert;instr-loc
[C-2]^C^Cinsert;instr-pan
[C-3]^C^Cinsert;trans
[C-4]^C^Cinsert;instr-con
[C-5]^C^Cinsert;drain
[C-6]^C^Cinsert;vent
```

After you edit or create a new menu in this manner, save the menu file and then exit the text editor. Use the **MENU** command to load your copy of the acad.mnu file. Be sure to enter the proper path to the file. If you will be editing your menu often, consider making a menu pick on the screen that automatically loads the menu file:

```
[LOADMENU]^C^Cmenu;folder path/menu name
```

Alternate ways to use the menu

The method just discussed uses blocks that have been saved in a prototype drawing. In order to use the blocks, the prototype must first be inserted into the current drawing. Or, the new drawing can be started based on a template containing the blocks.

For example, suppose the piping flow diagram symbols are saved in a template drawing called pipeflow.dwt. You can use the symbols if you specify **Use a Template** in the **Create New Drawing** dialog box, and select the pipeflow template. All the blocks in the pipeflow template can then be picked from your new tablet menu.

Another method uses the blocks located in another drawing. You can insert one drawing into another using the **INSERT** command. You may consider putting an insertion command on your tablet menu. Only the named items, such as blocks, views, and layers are inserted.

```
Command: INSERT↵
Block name (or ?): PIPEFLOW↵
Insertion point:(press [Esc] to cancel)
```

Remember to cancel the **INSERT** command at the Insertion point: prompt. Wait for all of the named items to be inserted into the drawing. You can insert prototype drawings (.dwg files), but you cannot insert template drawings (.dwt files).

The **Insert Prototype Drawing** pick in your tablet menu file can be written as follows:

```
^C^CINSERT;PIPEFLOW;^C
```

A third way to use the menu is to use drawing files instead of blocks. This method does not require using symbol drawings. The drawing files can be on the hard disk or floppy disks. Remember that symbols stored as drawing files require more disk storage space. Disk access time also is often slower.

PROFESSIONAL TIP

Evaluate your present use of blocks and drawing files when making or modifying tablet menus. Take into account your current method of symbol creation, storage, and usage when developing tablet menus for symbols. If symbol drawings (prototypes) are working best for your application, develop your tablet menu around these. If individual drawing files are used, the menus should access these.

Designing a New Tablet Menu

A tablet menu is somewhat inefficient because it requires you to move your eyes away from the screen to find a tablet command. However, there are advantages of tablet menus over screen menus.

- Screen menus must be "paged" or "cascaded" when looking for a command. Flipping through pages of screen menus and submenus slows down the drawing process.
- A tablet menu provides immediate access to most commands. If necessary, it can be paged for additional commands and symbols.
- Available tablet commands can be chosen with only one pick of the input device.
- Graphic symbols on the template make it easy to identify commands.
- Numerous commands can be printed on a tablet menu. This enables users to select commands that they might seldom select if using just screen menus.

Any technique that increases your efficiency and productivity should be investigated and incorporated as part of your operating procedures. You will find that making custom tablet menus is one such procedure. They can be used alone or together with screen menus. A tablet menu pick can display a specialized screen menu or load new tablet menus. After gaining experience and confidence in your menu-creating abilities, you will become aware of the value of tablet menus.

Plan your new tablet menu

Planning a custom AutoCAD menu was discussed earlier in the text. Planning is also needed when developing new tablet menus. The creation of a tablet menu should not be the first thing you do when customizing AutoCAD. There are several important preliminary steps that should be taken before designing a menu:

✓ List the commands that you use most often.
✓ Develop macros that automate your CAD work as much as possible.
✓ List the different types of symbol overlays you may need.
✓ List each group of symbols used in order of most often used to least often used.

PROFESSIONAL TIP

When designing macros, think of the commands and functions you use most often. Automate these first. Keep in mind that your goal is to create a drawing or design. This requires knowledge of the specific discipline. You want to spend more time using your knowledge and skills rather than picking the proper succession of AutoCAD commands and options. Therefore, for each function that you automate, reduce the number of picks required to complete the function. In doing so, your time spent at the computer will be more productive.

After listing the items just mentioned, begin the process of creating commands, macros, and menus.

1. Develop and test individual macros in a screen menu or tablet menu.
2. Determine major groups of commands and macros based on their frequency of use.
3. Design the tablet menu layout. Draw it larger than actual size, using a pencil. This gives you room for lettering and sketches. You can have up to four menu areas and a screen pointing area. Some common layouts are shown in Figure 21-9.
4. Draw the basic menu layout with AutoCAD. This should be a preliminary test menu. Do not add text or graphics yet. Pencil in commands on a plotted copy of the menu.

Figure 21-9.
Some common tablet menu layouts.

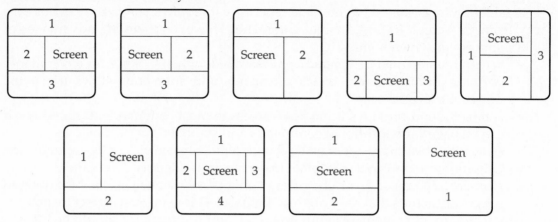

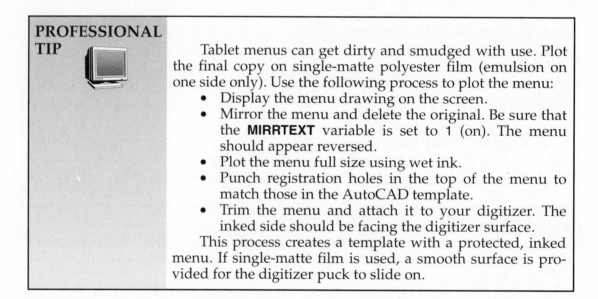

5. Write the code for the menu and test each function for convenience.
6. Add text and graphics to the menu, then plot it. Revise the menu as needed to make it more efficient.

PROFESSIONAL TIP

Tablet menus can get dirty and smudged with use. Plot the final copy on single-matte polyester film (emulsion on one side only). Use the following process to plot the menu:
- Display the menu drawing on the screen.
- Mirror the menu and delete the original. Be sure that the **MIRRTEXT** variable is set to 1 (on). The menu should appear reversed.
- Plot the menu full size using wet ink.
- Punch registration holes in the top of the menu to match those in the AutoCAD template.
- Trim the menu and attach it to your digitizer. The inked side should be facing the digitizer surface.

This process creates a template with a protected, inked menu. If single-matte film is used, a smooth surface is provided for the digitizer puck to slide on.

Creating a menu definition file

The process of developing your own menu is similar to customizing the AutoCAD template. Of course, it takes longer because you are creating the entire menu. But do not let this bother you. Autodesk has developed a menu definition and compiling process that can speed up the menu creation process.

A menu definition file is a preliminary menu file in which macros can be created to represent frequently used functions. In addition, a command located in several boxes of the menu can be defined once using a multiple line definition. The menu definition file is created with an .mnd file extension. If you are developing a menu named TEST, name the file test.mnd.

The definition file must be compiled before it can be used by AutoCAD. This is done with the mc.exe program. The relationship between the mc.exe, .mnd, .mnu, .mns, and .mnc files is shown in Figure 21-10. The .mnd file is written first. Then the mc.exe program, run from DOS, compiles the .mnd file into an .mnu file. AutoCAD then reads the .mnu file and further compiles it into an .mnc file. This is the version used for drawing.

Figure 21-10.
The .mnd file must
be compiled twice
before it can be used
by AutoCAD for
drawing purposes.

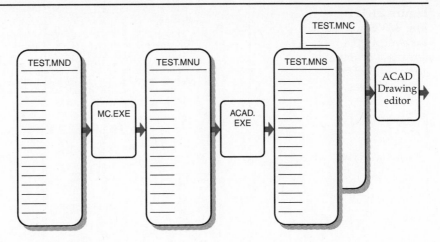

Creating menu definition file macros

A menu definition file is a preliminary file that can be constructed with the aid of macros. For example, suppose several commands in your menu use ^C^C. You can define that function at the beginning of the menu as any word or character. The menu definition macro must be listed at the beginning of the file, before the first menu section. If you assign the letter C to the double cancel, it would be written as:

{C}= ^C^C

Put this in the menu file immediately after the section heading. Anything inside the braces represents the macro given after the equals sign. Place a {C} in your menu where you need a ^C^C in the compiled .mnu file.

Defining multiple lines

The menu definition file also allows you to specify multiple lines (template boxes) that have the same command. For example, suppose menu boxes 5, 6, 30, and 31 should have the **'REDRAW** command. This can be written as:

⟨5,6,30,31⟩'REDRAW

This is interpreted by the mc.exe program to mean that menu boxes 5, 6, 30, and 31 are assigned the **'REDRAW** command. Multiple definitions such as this must be entered immediately below the menu heading.

```
***TABLET1
⟨5, 6,30,31⟩'REDRAW
```

The ability to specify multiple line definitions is especially useful for tablet menus. There may be several boxes on the template that represent the same thing. Look at the **FILE** area of the AutoCAD template and notice the **SAVE** box, Figure 21-11. AutoCAD does not see the **SAVE** area as one large box because tablet Menu Area 4 is divided into 175 equally sized boxes. The **SAVE** command on the template is located across two boxes. Therefore, two lines in the menu file must have the **SAVE** command.

Load acad.mnu into your text editor and page to the ***TABLET4 section. You should notice several lines on which there is just a backslash (\). These specify the blank, gray space above tablet Menu Area 4. Now scroll down until you find two lines that read '_qsave. These are boxes 49 and 50. These two boxes would be defined at the beginning of the .mnd file as:

```
***TABLET4
⟨49,50⟩'SAVE
```

Figure 21-11.
The **SAVE** box on the AutoCAD template is actually composed of two smaller boxes.

A sample tablet menu

An example of a custom menu is shown in Figure 21-12. It is similar to the AutoCAD template, but contains fewer boxes. The template shows a grid of numbers along the top and letters down the left side. These locations are used at the beginning of each line of code in the menu file for reference:

```
***TABLET1STD
[A-1]
[A-2]
[A-3]
```

Figure 21-12.
A sample custom menu layout.

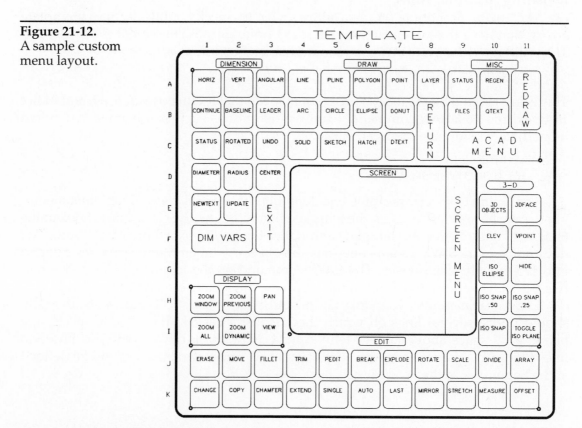

AutoCAD and its Applications—Advanced

Anything inside brackets in a tablet menu section is not displayed, and does not affect the menu code. It is only a helpful reference. The same notation is used in the acad.mnu file. It indicates the tablet section and box number within that section.

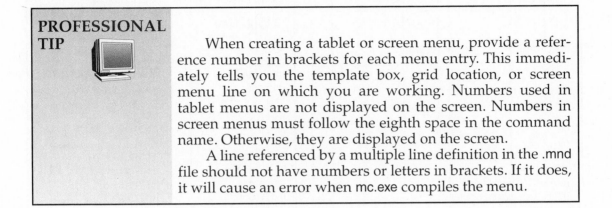

PROFESSIONAL TIP

When creating a tablet or screen menu, provide a reference number in brackets for each menu entry. This immediately tells you the template box, grid location, or screen menu line on which you are working. Numbers used in tablet menus are not displayed on the screen. Numbers in screen menus must follow the eighth space in the command name. Otherwise, they are displayed on the screen.

A line referenced by a multiple line definition in the .mnd file should not have numbers or letters in brackets. If it does, it will cause an error when mc.exe compiles the menu.

In Figure 21-12, notice that often used commands, such as **RETURN**, **REDRAW**, **ACADMENU** (loads the AutoCAD menu), **DIM VARS**, and **EXIT** (from the dimension menu), are placed inside large boxes. This allows you to pick them quickly.

The code for this menu can be written as an .mnu or .mnd file. Remember, the menu definition (.mnd) file involves less typing if you use its macro functions. Both versions are given here for comparison. As you look through the code in Figure 21-13, compare the entries to the appropriate template boxes in Figure 21-12. Also, note the codes located at the beginning of the menu and the box numbers left blank in the .mnd file. A blank line indicates that the function of the box was defined in one of the multiple line codes at the beginning of the tablet section. The grid locations of each menu item are indicated in brackets for quick identification. The button menu is for a 12 button cursor.

If you plan to try this menu, enter the code with your text editor. Assign the name MENU1.MND. After creating the menu definition file, you must compile it with the mc.exe program. The program is found in the AutoCAD R14\Support folder. Both the mc.exe file and your .mnd file should be in the same directory, or you must provide a path for MC to find your definition file.

The MC program runs from the DOS prompt. If you are in Windows, select Programs and then MS-DOS Command Prompt from the Start menu. Be sure that the AutoCAD R14\Support folder is current.

The mc.exe program can now be run to compile the menu1.mnd file and create a file named menu1.mnu. In the following example, the MC program is run after entering the **SHELL** command and changing to the AutoCAD R14\Support folder in the MS DOS Window.

```
Command: SHELL↵
OS Command:↵
C:\Program Files\AutoCAD R14〉 CD SUPPORT↵
C:\Program Files\AutoCAD R14\Support〉 MC MENU1↵
AutoCAD Menu Compiler 2.71  (08/09/94)
Copyright (c) 1985-91 Throoput, Ltd.
C:\Program Files\AutoCAD R14\Support〉
```

Check to see that the .mnu file has been created by getting a directory listing of all files with .mnu extensions:

```
C:\Program Files\AutoCAD R14\Support〉 DIR *.MNU↵
C:\Program Files\AutoCAD R14\Support〉 CD...↵
C:\Program Files\AutoCAD R14〉 EXIT↵
```

Figure 21-13.
The menu code for the template shown in Figure 21-12. Either an .mnd or .mnu file can be used to define the menu.

MENU1.MND	MENU1.MNU	MENU1.MND	MENU1.MNU
***BUTTONS	***BUTTONS	[D-3]{D};center	[D-3]^C^Cdim;center
;	;	[E-1]{D};newtext	[E-1]^C^Cdim;newtext
'REDRAW	'REDRAW	[E-2]{D};update	[E-2]^C^Cdim;update
^C	^C	[E-3]exit	[E-3]exit
^B	^B	[F-1]{DV}	[F-1]^C^Cdim $s=var1
^O	^O	[F-2]{DV}	[F-2]^C^Cdim $s=var1
^G	^G	[F-3]exit	[F-3]exit
^D	^D	[G-1]	[G-1]
^E	^E	[G-2]	[G-2]
^T	^T	[G-3]	[G-3]
{D}=^C^Cdim		[H-1]'zoom;w	[H-1]'zoom;w
{C}=^C^C		[H-2]'zoom;p	[H-2]'zoom;p
{MA}=^C^Cmenu;acad		[H-3]'pan	[H-3]'pan
{DV}=^C^Cdim $s=var1		[I-1]'zoom;a	[I-1]'zoom;a
		[I-2]'zoom;d	[I-2]'zoom;d
***TABLET1	***TABLET1	[I-3]{C}view	[I-3]^C^Cview
⟨11,22⟩redraw			
⟨19,30⟩"		***TABLET3	***TABLET3
[A-1]{D};horiz	[A–1]^C^Cdim;horiz	[D-10]	[D-10]
[A-2]{D};vert	[A-2]^C^Cdim;vert	[D-11]	[D-11]
[A-3]{D};angular	[A-3]^C^Cdim;angular	[E-10]$i=3dobjects $I=*	[E-10] $i=3dobjects $I=*
[A-4]{C}line	[A-4]^C^Cline	[E-11]{C}3dface	[E-11]^C^C3dface
[A-5]{C}pline	[A-5]^C^Cpline	[F-10]{C}elev	[F-10]^C^Celev
[A-6]{C}polygon	[A-6]^C^Cpolygon	[F-11]{C}vpoint;;	[F-11]^C^Cvpoint;;
[A-7]{C}point	[A-7]^C^Cpoint	[G-10]{C}ellipse;i	[G-10]^C^Cellipse;i
[A-8]{C}layer	[A-8]^C^Clayer	[G-11]{C}hide	[G-11]^C^Chide
[A-9]{C}status	[A-9]^C^Cstatus	[H-10]{C}snap;s;i;.5	[H-10]^C^Csnap;s;i;.5
[A-10]{C}regen	[A-10]^C^Cregen	[H-11]{C}snap;s;i;.25	[H-11]^C^Csnap;s;i;.25
	[A-11]'redraw	[I-10]{C}snap;s;s;;	[I-10]^C^Csnap;s;s;;
[B-1]{D};continue	[B-1]^C^Cdim;continue	[I-11]{C}^E	[I-11]^E
[B-2]{D};baseline	[B-2]^C^Cdim;baseline		
[B-3]{D};leader	[B-3]^C^Cdim;leader	***TABLET4	***TABLET4
[B-4]{C}arc	[B-4]^C^Carc	[J-1]{C}erase	[J-1]^C^Cerase
[B-5]{C}circle	[B-5]^C^Ccircle	[J-2]{C}move	[J-2]^C^Cmove
[B-6]{C}ellipse	[B-6]^C^Cellipse	[J-3]{C}fillet	[J-3]^C^Cfillet
[B-7]{C}donut	[B-7]^C^Cdonut	[J-4]{C}trim	[J-4]^C^Ctrim
	[B-8]^C^C;	[J-5]{C}pedit	[J-5]^C^Cpedit
[B-9]{C}files	[B-9]^C^Cfiles	[J-6]{C}break	[J-6]^C^Cbreak
[B-10]{C}qtext	[B-10]^C^Cqtext	[J-7]{C}explode	[J-7]^C^Cexplode
	[B-11]'redraw	[J-8]{C}rotate	[J-8]^C^Crotate
[C-1]{D};status	[C-1]^C^Cdim;status	[J-9]{C}scale	[J-9]^C^Cscale
[C-2]{D};rotated	[C-2]^C^Cdim;rotated	[J-10]{C}divide	[J-10]^C^Cdivide
[C-3]{D};undo	[C-3]^C^Cdim;undo	[J-11]{C}array	[J-11]^C^Carray
[C-4]{C}solid	[C-4]^C^Csolid	[K-1]{C}change	[K-1]^C^Cchange
[C-5]{C}sketch	[C-5]^C^Csketch	[K-2]{C}copy	[K-2]^C^Ccopy
[C-6]{C}hatch	[C-6]^C^Chatch	[K-3]{C}chamfer	[K-3]^C^Cchamfer
[C-7]{C}dtext	[C-7]^C^Cdtext	[K-4]{C}extend	[K-4]^C^Cextend
	[C-8]^C^C;	[K-5]single	[K-5]single
[C-9]{MA}	[C-9]^C^Cmenu;acad	[K-6]auto	[K-6]auto
[C-10]{MA}	[C-10]^C^Cmenu;acad	[K-7] last	[K-7]last
[C-11]{MA}	[C-11]^C^Cmenu;acad	[K-8]{C}mirror	[K-8]^C^Cmirror
		[K-9]{C}stretch	[K-9]^C^Cstretch
***TABLET2	***TABLET2	[K-10]{C}measure	[K-10]^C^Cmeasure
[D-1]{D};diameter	[D-1]^C^Cdim;diameter	[K-11]{C}offset	[K-11]^C^Coffset
[D-2]{D};radius	[D-2]^C^Cdim;radius		

The new menu cannot be used until it is loaded into AutoCAD using the **MENU** command. In the following example, the system variable **FILEDIA** is set to 0:

Command: **MENU**↵
Menu file name or . for none ⟨*current*⟩: **SUPPORT\MENU1**↵

The compiled version of the menu file has an .mnc extension. AutoCAD looks for the latest version of the compiled menu file when you begin a new drawing. If there is no such file, AutoCAD compiles the menu file again.

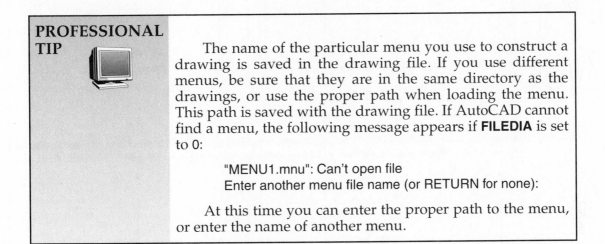

PROFESSIONAL TIP

The name of the particular menu you use to construct a drawing is saved in the drawing file. If you use different menus, be sure that they are in the same directory as the drawings, or use the proper path when loading the menu. This path is saved with the drawing file. If AutoCAD cannot find a menu, the following message appears if **FILEDIA** is set to 0:

"MENU1.mnu": Can't open file
Enter another menu file name (or RETURN for none):

At this time you can enter the proper path to the menu, or enter the name of another menu.

After loading your new menu, select the **TABLET** command and configure the new template. If you select the **TABLET** command from the screen menu, do not pick the **Reconfig** option. This starts the configuration routine for the ACAD tablet menu. Instead, use the **Config** option.

The configure routine prompts for the number of tablet menus. The MENU1 template requires four. You are then asked if you want to realign tablet menu areas. Answer Y (Yes). Now digitize the upper-left, lower-left, and lower-right corners of each of the four tablet menu areas. When prompted, provide the number of columns and rows in each area. The corners of MENU1 are shown in Figure 21-14. The columns and rows in each area are given in the following chart:

Menu Area	Columns	Rows
1	11	3
2	3	6
3	2	6
4	11	2

The final prompt in the configure process asks you to specify the lower-left and upper-right corners of the screen pointing area. These are also shown in Figure 21-14.

Test all of the menu items to be sure they function properly. Correct any mistakes you find. You may encounter one shortcoming if you select the **ACAD MENU** item in Menu Area 1. The AutoCAD menu will be loaded, but how do you get back to the MENU1 template? There must be a call, or item in the AutoCAD menu, that loads the MENU1 template. Load the acad.mnu file into your text editor and add the following line to the **S menu, or to a pull-down menu:

[MENU1]^C^Cmenu;menu1

If you insert this entry between two existing items, do not press [Enter]. Otherwise you will insert a blank line into the menu.

Figure 21-14.
Digitize the corners of the MENU1 tablet menu areas indicated here. Also, pick the lower-left and upper-right corners of the screen pointing area to properly configure the template.

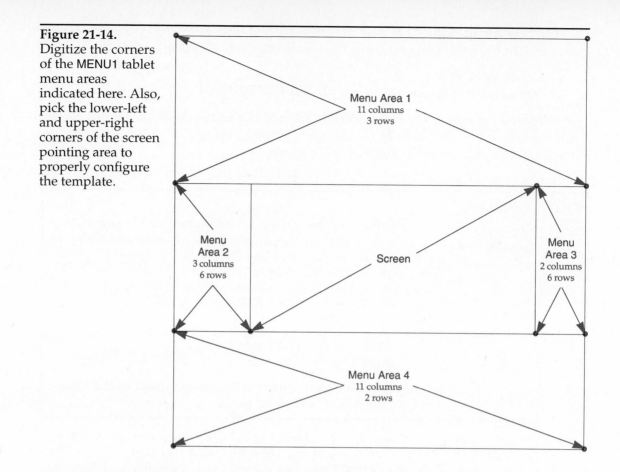

Automating the menu editing process

Modifying screen or tablet menus requires loading the text editor on a regular basis. This can become tedious. The process can be automated if you place a macro in a menu that loads the text editor and .mnu file. If you are using the Notepad editor, add the following item to your menu:

[EDITMENU]^C^CNOTEPAD;menu1.mnu;

When picked, this item cancels the current command and executes the **NOTEPAD** command (your text editor). The file name of the menu is entered automatically.

If you use a text editor other than Notepad, just substitute its name in place of edit. For example, suppose an application named TextPad is used. The following entry is placed in the screen menu section:

[EDITMENU]^C^CTEXTPAD;menu1.mnu;

The **TEXTPAD** command will not work when entered at the Command: prompt unless you have altered the acad.pgp file as discussed in Chapter 28 of *AutoCAD and its Applications—Basics, Release 14*. In order for the menu item above to work properly, you must first add a line to the acad.pgp file to make **TEXTPAD** a valid command in AutoCAD. Edit your acad.pgp file by adding the following line:

Textpad, Start C:\Program Files\TextPad\txtpad32, 0,*File to edit:,

Be sure the information in the second entry, "C:\Program Files\TextPad\txtpad32," is the proper name of your text editor's executable file (txtpad32.exe).

Tablet Menu Tips

Tablet menus can be as simple or as complex as you want, and can contain just about any function you need. As you experiment with helpful commands and options, think of the problems you face when drawing. Design AutoCAD macros to solve problems and eliminate tedious tasks. Add them to your menu. Keep in mind the following guidelines:

✓ Use tablet menu picks to call button, screen, and image tile menus.

✓ Use tablet menu picks to call other tablet menus.

✓ Use a tablet menu pick that inserts a group of blocks from a prototype drawing into the current drawing. If the prototype drawing name is elec001, the menu items should look like this:

    ^C^Cinsert;elec001;^C

This inserts only the blocks and not the rest of the drawing information.

✓ Use tablet menu picks to display help screens and frequently used slides.

✓ Plot menu templates on heavy polyester film for durability.

✓ Be sure your template does not extend beyond the active area of your digitizer.

✓ When customizing tablet Menu Area 1 of the AutoCAD template, change the number of boxes to any number you need. Draw a new overlay containing the revised boxes. When configuring the AutoCAD tablet menu, be sure to specify **Config** and not **Reconfig**. Enter the revised number of columns and rows.

✓ Any portion of the AutoCAD template can be changed to suit your needs. Just alter the portion of the acad.mnu file that you wish to change.

✓ When customizing the acad.mnu file, always work with a copy, not the original file.

✓ If you work at a computer that other people use, return the tablet and menu configuration to the way it was before you changed it.

✓ Build your menu in small pieces as you work.

Chapter Test

Write your answers in the spaces provided.

1. How many menu areas are on the AutoCAD template? _____

2. Provide the command and option responses that allow you to initially set up the AutoCAD template.

   Command: _____

   Option (ON/OFF/CAL/CFG): _____

3. Fill in the number of columns and rows found in each of the following tablet menu areas of the AutoCAD template.

Menu Area	Columns	Rows
1	_____	_____
2	_____	_____
3	_____	_____
4	_____	_____

4. When you select the **TABLET** command from the screen menu, which option allows you to set up the AutoCAD template without entering the number of rows and columns? _____

   _____

   _____

   _____

5. How many boxes are in the user portion of the AutoCAD template? _____

6. Identify the first step to customize the AutoCAD template. _____

   _____

   _____

   _____

7. Describe how the tablet Menu Area 1 boxes are numbered in the acad.mnu file.

   _____

   _____

   _____

   _____

   _____

8. Explain why it is a good idea to leave the box numbers in the menu file. _____

   _____

   _____

   _____

   _____

   _____

9. List two advantages of using tablet menus instead of screen menus. _____

_____

_____

_____

_____

10. Which commands should you automate first when designing a screen or tablet menu?_____

_____

_____

11. Define a menu definition file._____

_____

_____

_____

_____

_____

_____

_____

12. The extension of the menu file AutoCAD uses for drawing purposes is_____.

13. How would a custom macro that represents **REDRAW** be shown in an .mnd file?

_____

_____

_____

14. Suppose boxes 25, 50, 75, and 100 are to be used for the **REDRAW** command. How would they be listed in the .mnd file as a multiple line function?_____

_____

15. Give the advantage of creating an .mnd file instead of an .mnu file. _____

_____

_____

_____

_____

_____

_____

16. Explain the purpose of the mc.exe program. _____

_____

_____

_____

17. How do you combine different menus to form a larger menu? _____

_____

_____

_____

_____

18. Why is it a good idea to combine screen menus with a tablet menu? _____

_____

_____

_____

_____

Drawing Problems

1. Add ten new commands or macros to the user area of the AutoCAD template. Follow these guidelines:

   A. Place the commands along the bottom line (I) of the template. They should occupy boxes I-1 through I-10.

   B. Plot a copy of the Menu Area 1 grid and sketch the commands in the boxes.

   C. Sketch graphic symbols to represent the commands.

   D. Draw the command text and graphics in a copy of the Menu Area 1 grid.

   E. Plot a final copy of the overlay on vellum or polyester film.

   F. Make a copy of the acad.mnu file and write the code for the new commands.

2. Create a menu overlay for the user area of the AutoCAD template containing graphic symbols for one of the following drafting disciplines:
   - Architectural
   - Structural
   - HVAC
   - Mechanical
   - Industrial Piping
   - Electrical
   - Electronics

   A. Use existing blocks or symbols that you have on file, or create new ones.

   B. Provide a tablet pick that allows you to insert all symbols into a drawing without inserting the additional prototype drawing data.

   C. Provide a tablet pick that calls the AutoCAD menu.

3. Redesign the user area of the AutoCAD template so that it contains a complete selection of dimensioning commands, options, and variables. Follow these guidelines:

   A. Use the standard 225 boxes or change the numbers of boxes to suit your personal requirements.

   B. Provide access to dimensioning dialog boxes.

   C. Design a special section for dimensioning variables. Draw a small graphic symbol for each variable in the menu box.

   D. Plot a menu overlay on vellum or polyester film that can be slipped under the AutoCAD template.

4. Design a new tablet menu that occupies only the lower half of your digitizer. Follow these guidelines:

   A. The menu should contain a screen pointing area and two menu areas.

   B. Design the menu so it can work with the AutoCAD screen menus.

   C. Provide an area of symbols (blocks) and an area for special commands that you have created.

   D. Make a drawing of the new tablet overlay and plot it on vellum or polyester film. Plot the overlay as a mirror image of the original as discussed earlier in this chapter.

5. Design a new tablet menu that occupies the entire active area of your digitizer. Follow these guidelines:

   A. Provide four menu areas and a screen pointing area.

   B. Provide access to the AutoCAD menu.

   C. Include custom commands you have created, plus an area for symbols. Allow the user to change the symbols section of the menu to a different set of drawing symbols.

   D. Draw an overlay for the new tablet menu. Draw two separate, smaller overlays for the two sets of drawing symbols.

   E. Draw graphic symbols to represent commands and place them in the menu overlay.

   F. Insert scaled-down copies of blocks into the symbol overlays of the menu.

   G. Plot test copies of the template and two symbol overlays and use them for several days.

   H. Plot a final copy of the template on vellum or polyester film using the mirror image technique discussed in this chapter.

6. Design a custom tablet overlay for a specific drafting field, such as electronics, piping, or mapping. Follow these guidelines:

   A. Create as many menu areas as you need, between one and four.

   B. Provide space for a complete selection of symbols. These should reflect the type of drawing for which you will be designing the template.

   C. Place only those commands on the template that you will use often for this type of drawing.

   D. Place commands used less frequently in special screen menus. These should be accessed from the template.

   E. Provide the ability to load a variety of prototype drawings from the template.

   F. Create menu selections that allow you to do the following:
      - Edit a file using your text editor or word processor.
      - Edit the menu template file that you design for this problem.
      - Exit to DOS.
      - List all drawing files in your active subdirectories in an MS DOS window.

   G. Plot the template overlay on vellum or film using the mirroring technique.

Learning Objectives

After completing this chapter, you will be able to:
- ○ Locate, load, and run existing AutoLISP programs.
- ○ Use basic AutoLISP commands.
- ○ Write screen and tablet menu macros using AutoLISP.
- ○ Write basic AutoLISP programs.

AutoLISP is a derivative, or dialect, of the LISP programming language. *LISP* (List Processing) is a high-level computer programming language used in artificial intelligence (AI) systems. In this reference, the term *high-level* does not mean *complex*, rather it means *powerful*. As a matter of fact, many AutoCAD users refer to AutoLISP as the "non-programmer's language" because it is easy to understand.

The AutoLISP dialect is specially designed by Autodesk to work with AutoCAD. It has special graphic features designed to work in the drawing editor. It is a flexible language that allows the programmer to create custom commands and functions that can greatly increase productivity and drawing efficiency.

AutoLISP can be used in several ways. It is a built-in feature of AutoCAD and is therefore available at the Command: prompt. When AutoLISP commands and functions are issued inside parentheses, the AutoLISP interpreter automatically evaluates the entry and carries out the specified tasks. AutoLISP functions can be incorporated into the AutoCAD menu as toolbar buttons, screen menu items, and tablet menu picks. AutoLISP command and function definitions can be saved in an AutoLISP program file and then loaded into AutoCAD when needed. Items that are used frequently can be placed in the acad.lsp file, which is automatically loaded when AutoCAD starts.

The benefits of using AutoLISP are endless. Third party applications (add-on software that enhances AutoCAD) use AutoLISP to perform specialized functions, such as creating special symbols.

A person with a basic understanding of AutoLISP can create new commands and functions to automate many routine tasks. Working through this chapter, you will be able to add greater capabilities to your screen, tablet, and toolbar menu macros. You can also enter simple AutoLISP expressions at the Command: prompt. More experienced programmers can create powerful programs that quickly complete very complex design requirements. Several powerful AutoLISP programs are found in the AutoCAD Release 14 Bonus Utilities. Other new functions include the following:
- Automatic line breaks when inserting schematic symbols.
- Automatic creation of shapes with associated text objects.
- Parametric design applications that create geometry based on numeric entry.

Knowing basic AutoLISP gives you a better understanding of how AutoCAD works. By learning just a few simple functions, you can create new commands that make a significant difference in your daily productivity levels. Read through this chapter slowly while you are at a computer. Type all of the examples and exercises as you read them. This is the best way to get a feel for AutoLISP. An excellent resource for learning to create useful AutoLISP applications is *AutoLISP Programming—Principles and Techniques*, published by Goodheart-Willcox.

AutoCAD Custom Guide 7

AutoLISP Basics

LISP stands for *list processing*, indicating that AutoLISP processes lists. In the LISP language, a list can be defined as any number of data items enclosed in parentheses. Each item in a list must be separated from other items by a space.

When any entry is made at the Command: prompt, it is first checked to see if the first character was a parenthesis. The opening parenthesis tells AutoCAD that an AutoLISP expression is being entered. AutoCAD then sends the expression to the AutoLISP Interpreter for evaluation. The initial input can be supplied as direct keyboard entry or even a menu macro.

When your entry starts with an open parenthesis, AutoCAD does not interpret the spacebar as an [Enter] keystroke, so you must press [Enter] when the expression is complete.

The format for an AutoLISP expression , called *syntax*, is as shown here:

    (FunctionName AnyRequiredData...)

The first item in the AutoLISP expression is a function name. Some functions require additional information. For example, the addition function requires numeric data:

    Command: (+ 2 4)↵
    6
    Command:

Any required data for a function is referred to as an ***argument***. Some functions use no arguments, others may require one or more arguments. When entering an AutoLISP expression, it is important to *close* it using a closing parenthesis prior to pressing [Enter]. When you press [Enter], the AutoLISP Interpreter checks to see that the number of opening and closing parenthesis match, and if they do not you are prompted as follows:

    Command: (+ 2 4↵
    1>

The 1> indicates that you are missing one closing parenthesis. In this example, all that is necessary is to enter the single missing parenthesis and the function is complete:

    1>)↵
    6
    Command:

When the AutoLISP Interpreter evaluates an AutoLISP expression, it *returns* a value. Expressions entered at the command line return their value to the command line. If a different prompt is active, the returned value is used as input for that prompt. For example, this next sequence uses the result of adding two numbers as the input at the Diameter/⟨Radius⟩: prompt. Checking **CIRCLERAD** verifies that the value returned by AutoLISP was in fact applied to the circle radius.

```
Command: C↵
3P/2P/TTR/⟨Center point⟩: (pick a point)
Diameter/⟨Radius⟩: (+ 14.25 3.0).↵
```

```
Command: CIRCLERAD.↵
New value for CIRCLERAD ⟨17.2500⟩: ↵
```

Basic AutoLISP functions

The best way to get started learning AutoLISP is to enter a few functions at the command line and see what they do. The following discussion includes basic AutoLISP functions that are part of the foundation for all AutoLISP programs. At first, these functions and expressions will be entered at the command line. Later in the chapter you will learn about creating and using AutoLISP program files. Practice using the functions as you read. Then, begin using them in menus and macros.

AutoLISP math functions

AutoLISP provides many different mathematical operators for performing calculations. All real number calculations in AutoLISP are accurate to 15 decimal places. AutoLISP distinguishes between real numbers and integers, handling each data type differently. Real numbers are numbers with a decimal point, such as 1.25, 7.0, and –0.438. Integers are whole numbers without a decimal point, such as 3, 91, and -115. If a mathematical expression has only integer arguments, the result is returned as an integer. If at least one real number is used, the result is returned as a real number. The following symbols are used for the four basic math functions:

Symbol	Function
+	Returns the sum of all the supplied number arguments.
-	Subtracts the sum of the second through the last number from the first number and returns the result.
*	Returns the product of all the supplied number arguments.
/	Divides the first number by the product of the second through the last numbers.

The following examples illustrate AutoLISP math expressions entered at the Command: prompt. As you practice entering these expressions, use the following procedure:
1. Start with an open parenthesis.
2. Separate each item in the expression with a space.
3. Close the expression with a closing parenthesis.

Using these guidelines, enter the following expressions at the Command: prompt. If you get lost at any time or do not return to the Command: prompt when expected, press the [Esc] key to cancel the AutoLISP entry.

```
Command: (+ 6 2).↵
8
Command: (+ 6.0 2).↵
8.0
Command: (- 15 9).↵
6
Command: (* 4 6).↵
24
Command: (/ 12 3).↵
4
Command: (/ 12 3.2).↵
3.75
Command: (/ 19 10).↵
1
```

An "incorrect" answer is returned in the last example. The result of dividing 19 by 10 should yield 1.9. When only integers are supplied as arguments, the result is returned as an integer. If it were rounded, it would round to 2. However, the result returned is simply the integer portion of the actual answer. The result is not rounded, it is truncated. To get the correct result in many division expressions, specify at least one of the arguments as a real number:

Command: (/ 19.0 10)↵
1.9

When entering real numbers between 1 and –1, you must include the leading zero or you will get an error message:

Command: (+ .5 16)↵
error: invalid dotted pair
Cancel
Command:

The correct entry follows:

Command: (+ 0.5 16)↵
16.5

❏ Solve the following equations by using AutoLISP functions at the Command: prompt. Write down the equation you used.

❏ 57 + 12 _____	❏ 8 × 4 _____
❏ 86.4 + 16 _____	❏ 16 × 5 × 35 _____
❏ 24 + 12 + 8 + 35 _____	❏ 7.3 × 22 _____
❏ 8 – 3 _____	❏ 45 / 9 _____
❏ 29 – 17 _____	❏ 60 / 2 / 2 _____
❏ 89.16 – 14.6 _____	❏ 76 / 27.3 _____

Nested expressions

The term *nested* refers to an AutoLISP expression that is used as part of another expression. For example, to add 15 to the product of 3.75 and 2.125, you can nest the multiplication expression in the addition expression:

Command: (+ 15 (* 3.75 2.125))↵
22.9688

Nested expressions are evaluated from the deepest nested level outwards. In the previous expression, the multiplication is evaluated first, and the result is applied to the addition expression. Here are some examples of nested expressions:

Command: (+ 24 (* 5 4))↵
44
Command: (* 12 (/ 60 20))↵
36
Command: (/ 39 (* 1.6 11))↵
2.21591

AutoLISP performs all mathematical calculations to 16 decimal places, but only displays six significant digits. For example, take a close look at this expression:

Command: **(+ 15 (* 3.75 2.125))**↵
22.9688

The actual result is 22.96875, but AutoLISP only displays six significant digits at the command line and rounds the number for display only. This is true for large and small numbers alike. The next example shows how AutoLISP uses exponential notation to display larger numbers using only 6 digits:

Command: **(* 1000 1575.25)**↵
1.57525e+006

The final example uses a numeric printing function set to show 8 decimal places in order to show that the number is not actually rounded, and that no precision is lost:

Command: **(RTOS (+ 15 (* 3.75 2.125)) 2 8)**↵
"22.96875000"

EXERCISE 22-2

❑ Use the proper AutoLISP format to solve the following problems. Write the AutoLISP notations and answers in the space provided.

❑ 56.3 + (12 / 3) _____

❑ 23 – (17.65 / 4)_____

❑ 14 ÷ (12 / 3.6)_____

❑ 47 / (31 – 16.4)_____

❑ 257 / (34 – 3.6)_____

❑ 123.65 + 84 – 43.8 _____

❑ 16 ÷ (46 – 23) _____

Variables

All programming languages make use of variables to temporarily store information. The variable name can be used in another expression anywhere in the program. When AutoLISP encounters a variable in an expression, it uses the value of the variable to evaluate the expression. A variable name cannot contain any of the following characters:

✓ Parenthesis (**( )**)
✓ Period (**.**)
✓ Apostrophe (**'**)
✓ Quotation marks (**""**)
✓ Semi-colon (**;**)

The **SETQ** function is used to set variable values. A **SETQ** expression requires a variable name and value as arguments. The following example shows an expression that creates a variable named A and assigns it a value of 5:

Command: **(SETQ A 5)**↵
5

If you try to use an illegal variable name, an error message is returned. The following example tries to create a variable named 2 and assign it a value of 7. Since 2 is not a valid variable name, an error message is returned:

```
Command: (SETQ 2 7).↵
error: bad argument type
(SETQ 2 7)
*Cancel*
```

Once a variable name has been assigned, it can be used in subsequent AutoLISP expressions or even accessed directly at the command line. To access a variable value at the command line, precede the variable name with an exclamation mark (!). For example:

```
Command: !A↵
5

Command: C↵
3P/2P/TTR/⟨Center point⟩: (pick a point)
Diameter/⟨Radius⟩: !A↵
Command: CIRCLERAD↵
New value for CIRCLERAD ⟨5.0000⟩: ↵
```

To use the value of a variable in any expression, simply include the variable in the appropriate location. The following sequence sets and uses a series of variables:

```
Command: (SETQ B (- A 1))↵
4
Command: (SETQ C (- A B))↵
1
Command: (SETQ D (* (+ A B) 2))↵
18
```

Look closely at the example illustrated in Figure 22-1. Find the three separate expressions inside parentheses. AutoLISP evaluates expression 3 first. The result is applied to expression 2, which is then evaluated. The result of expression 2 is applied to 1. The final evaluation determines the value of variable D.

Figure 22-1.
Each AutoLISP expression needs to be enclosed with parentheses. Expression 3 is evaluated first, then expression 2, and finally expression 1.

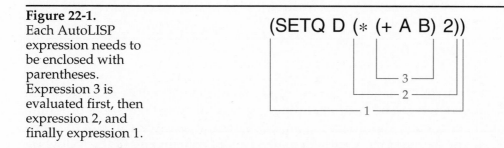

EXERCISE 22-3

❏ In the spaces provided, write the AutoLISP expressions in the proper format. After writing the expression, enter it into the computer to test your solution.

❏ Assign the value of 4 to the variable ONE. _____

❏ Assign the value of 3 + 2 to the variable TWO. _____

❏ Assign the value of ONE + TWO to the variable THREE. _____

❏ Assign the value of THREE + (TWO – ONE) to the variable FOUR. _____

AutoCAD and its Applications—Advanced

AutoLISP program files

Entering AutoLISP expressions at the command line is not a problem for expressions that are simple or unique. However, when developing more complex expressions or when the expressions you are using may be needed again, it is best to place the expressions in an AutoLISP program file. Even with AutoCAD's command line editing feature, AutoLISP code can be more effectively developed using a text editor.

A very common feature found in most AutoLISP files is a function definition. A *function definition* is a collection of AutoLISP code that performs any number of tasks. The function is assigned a name that is used to activate it. Some function definitions create new AutoCAD command names that can be typed at the command line.

Once written, an AutoLISP program file can be loaded and used whenever it is needed. AutoCAD automatically loads the acad.lsp file (if it is located in the support path). Any new AutoLISP commands or functions that you define in this file will be available in every drawing session.

An AutoLISP file must be a text file, so if you choose to use a word processing program (such as Microsoft Word or Word Perfect) to edit your AutoLISP files, you must be sure to save the files as text only. Word processing files use special printing codes that control the font appearances, and AutoLISP cannot understand these codes.

Defining new AutoCAD commands

In this section, you will use several of the built-in AutoLISP functions to create a brand new AutoCAD command. The **DEFUN** (Define Function) function is used to create new AutoCAD commands. The syntax for **DEFUN** is as follows:

```
(DEFUN FunctionName (ArgumentList)
   (Expression)...
)
```

The function name is any alphanumeric name, subject to the same conditions as any variable name assigned using the **SETQ** function. If you prefix the *FunctionName* with C:, the name can be entered at the Command: prompt.

You must include an argument list in every function definition, even if it is empty. The argument list is used to declare local variables, and in more advanced applications, to indicate what arguments are required by a function. For many applications, the argument list is simply left empty.

Any number of expressions can be included in a function definition. All of the expressions contained in the definition are evaluated when the function name is called.

A very powerful, yet simple, application for a function definition is to create a shortcut command similar to the command aliases contained in the acad.pgp file. However, a shortcut command defined using AutoLISP can specify command options and even multiple commands to use. Remember that the command aliases defined in the acad.pgp file can only start a single command, and they cannot specify any command options.

This first example shows the definition for a new function named **ZX** that performs a **ZOOM** command and the **Previous** option.

```
(DEFUN C:ZX ()
   (COMMAND "ZOOM" "PREVIOUS")
)
```

To see this function in action, enter the definition at the command line:

Command: **(DEFUN C:ZX () (COMMAND "ZOOM" "PREVIOUS"))**↵
C:ZX

Notice that the new function name is returned by the **DEFUN** expression. The C: prefix indicates that it is accessible at the Command: prompt as follows:

Command: **ZX**↵
Command: nil
Command:

When activated, defined functions return the value of the last thing evaluated in the expression. Since the **COMMAND** function always returns "nil", this is also returned when using the **ZX** function. The "nil" has no effect. You can suppress it if you do not want it to appear each time you use a defined function. To suppress the "nil", add a **PRINC** expression using no arguments to the end of the definition:

```
(DEFUN C:ZX ()
   (COMMAND "ZOOM" "PREVIOUS")
   (PRINC)
)
```

Typing a function definition at the Command: prompt is an inconvenient way to define custom functions. By storing these definitions in a text file, they can be loaded whenever needed.

PROFESSIONAL TIP

When defining new command names, keep in mind that most AutoCAD drafters are one-handed typists because the other hand uses the pointing device. For example, when deciding on the name for a function that does a **ZOOM Previous**, it may be easier for the keystroke combination ZX to be typed than ZP. The [Z] and [P] keys are in opposite diagonal corners of the keyboard.

Creating your first AutoLISP program file

As explained earlier, one of the most typical uses for an AutoLISP file is to hold function definitions. An AutoLISP program file can contain a single function or it can contain several.

Many AutoLISP files are created to perform a single specific task. For example, the ddinsert.lsp file creates and controls the **Insert** dialog box. Other AutoLISP files hold a large number of function definitions, all of which become available when the file is loaded. One common application for the acad.lsp file is to create a series of function definitions for shortcut commands used to speed up routine drafting tasks.

To create your first AutoLISP file, begin by opening Notepad, or another text editing application. In this first example, two function definitions are added to the file. The first is the **ZX** function from the previous example, and the second defines a command named **FC** (fillet corner) that sets the fillet radius to 0 and starts the fillet command.

```
(DEFUN C:ZX ()
  (COMMAND "ZOOM" "PREVIOUS")
  (PRINC)
)

(DEFUN C:FC ()
  (COMMAND "FILLET" "R" 0 "FILLET")
  (PRINC)
)
```

Adding appropriate documentation to your program files is recommended. When a semicolon (;) is encountered in a program file (except when part of a text string), any information to the right of the semicolon is ignored. This enables you to place comments and documentation in your AutoLISP files. The example below shows appropriate documentation for this file, called myfirst.lsp:

```
; MyFirst.lsp
; 3/27/98 by A. Novice

;C:ZX – Two key ZOOM Previous command
(DEFUN C:ZX ()
  (COMMAND "ZOOM" "PREVIOUS")
  (PRINC)
)

;C:FC – Fillet Corner, Sets fillet radius to 0 and starts Fillet command.
(DEFUN C:FC ()
  (COMMAND "FILLET" "R" 0 "FILLET")
  (PRINC)
)
```

After adding these functions into the new text file, save the file as myfirst.lsp in the Support folder.

APPLOAD
AP

Tools
↳ Load
   Application...

The **APPLOAD** command is used to load applications (such as AutoLISP files) into AutoCAD. To use this command, pick **Load Application...** from the **Tools** pull-down menu or enter AP or APPLOAD at the Command: prompt. The **Load AutoLISP, ADS, and ARX Files** dialog box appears, Figure 22-2.

Picking the **File...** button displays a file dialog box used to locate and select a file to place in the **Files to Load** list box. If the **Save List** toggle is checked, the files listed will be saved and displayed in subsequent **APPLOAD** sessions. This keeps you from having to use the file dialog box to locate frequently used files every time they are needed. The **Files to Load** list allows you to highlight any number of files, and picking the **Load** button loads all of the highlighted file names. Picking the **Remove** button removes the highlighted files from the listing, but does not affect the actual AutoLISP files.

Figure 22-2.
The **APPLOAD** command provides a dialog box for loading AutoLISP program files.

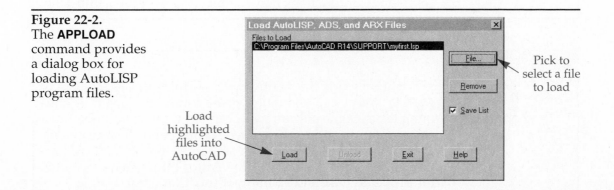

You can also load an AutoLISP file by highlighting the file in the Windows Explorer and dragging and dropping it into the AutoCAD graphics window. This method is extremely convenient if the Windows Explorer is active.

An AutoLISP file can be loaded using the **LOAD** function at the command line. The **LOAD** function requires an AutoLISP file name as its argument and requires that the file name be enclosed in quotation marks. To load the file myfirst.lsp using the **LOAD** function, the following sequence is used:

> Command: **(LOAD "MYFIRST").**↵
> C:FC
> Command:

When the file has an .lsp extension, it is not necessary to include the file extension in the **LOAD** expression. Therefore, you should use the standard .lsp file extension for all AutoLISP files you create. If you are loading an AutoLISP file that does not use an .lsp file extension, the actual extension must be included in the file name argument.

When an AutoLISP file is loaded and no errors are encountered, the result of evaluating the last expression in the file is returned to the screen. In the example above, the last expression in the file is the function definition for the **FC** function, so the function name is returned.

The **LOAD** function locates AutoLISP files located in the Support File Search Path. To load a file that exists elsewhere, the path name must also be specified. In the following example, the myfirst.lsp file is stored in the C:\My Documents\AutoLISP folder.

> Command: **(LOAD "C:/MY DOCUMENTS/AUTOLISP/MYFIRST").**↵
> C:FC

Notice that backslashes are not used in the path specification. In an AutoLISP text string, the backslash is used to specify special characters. For example, the string \n indicates a new line, or carriage return. When specifying directory path names, you can use either forward slashes or double-backslashes (\\). Therefore, in the example above, the file to load could also have been specified as C:\\My Documents\\AutoLISP\\MyFirst.

If you frequently load files that are in a folder not found on the Support File Search Path, it may be helpful to include the folder in the path. This is done using the **PREFERENCES** command. In the **Preferences** dialog box, pick the **Files** tab and select the Support File Search Path option.

As indicated previously, when you have defined one or more functions that you want to be available in all editing sessions, the definitions can be placed in the acad.lsp file.

NOTE  If the acad.lsp file already exists on your system, consult your system administrator or instructor prior to editing this file directly. The acad.lsp file is often used by third-party applications, and changing it or accidentally redefining existing commands or functions may render certain features unusable.

PROFESSIONAL TIP 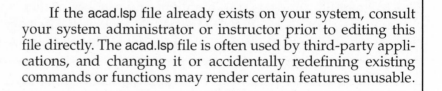 If you work frequently with AutoLISP files, you may wish to invest in a text editor geared more toward programming tasks. Some editors are equipped with useful tools such as bracket matching, which checks your parentheses to verify that none are missing. Some companies market editing programs designed specifically for AutoLISP, which can check for proper syntax and spelling of function names.

❑ Use the proper AutoLISP format to write the following expressions. Use the spaces provided to write the code. Test all of the exercise examples by entering them in the computer.

❑ Assign a point picked on the screen to the variable PNT1._____

❑ Assign a point picked on the screen to the variable PNT2._____

❑ Create the variable DIS and assign it the distance between PNT1 and PNT2.

_____

❑ Draw a line between PNT1 and PNT2.

_____

_____

_____

❑ Use the AutoLISP **DISTANCE** function to return the distance between PNT1 and PNT2._____

Getting text using AutoLISP

Variables can be given values other than numbers. You may need to assign a word or line of text to a variable. Use the **SETQ** command and enclose the word(s) in quotation marks as follows:

```
Command: (SETQ W "What Next?")↵
"What next?"
```

You can also assign a word or line of text to a variable with the **GETSTRING** function. This operates similar to the **GETPOINT** function, because it prompts the user to enter a value. Look at the following example:

```
Command: (SETQ E (GETSTRING))↵
```

Nothing is displayed on the command line because the optional prompt was not specified. AutoLISP is waiting for a "string" of characters. You can enter as many characters (numbers and letters) as needed. Once you press [Enter] or the space bar, the string is entered and displayed. To allow for spaces in the response, enter the letter T, without quotation marks, after the **GETSTRING** function as follows:

```
Command: (SETQ E (GETSTRING T))↵
HI THERE↵
"HI THERE"
Command:
```

Confirm the value of the variable as follows:

```
Command: !E↵
"HI THERE"
```

CAUTION The symbol T is a built-in AutoLISP constant. However, its value can be changed using the **SETQ** function. Be certain not to use the variable name T for any of your own variables, or other functions referencing this constant may not function properly.

The **PROMPT** function can be used to simply display a message. It has no value and is not assigned to a variable. AutoLISP indicates this by printing "nil" after the prompt.

> Command: **(PROMPT "Select an object:")**⏎
> Select an object: nil

You can use prompts in AutoLISP programs to provide information or prompt the user.

EXERCISE 22-6

❑ Use the proper AutoLISP format to write the following expressions. Use the spaces provided to write the code. Test all of the exercise examples by entering them in the computer.

❑ Assign the word Void to the variable VO. _____

❑ Assign the text Enter text height to the variable TE. _____

❑ Create the variable JP as a point that is picked on the screen. Issue the prompt Pick a point:. _____

❑ Create the variable KP as a point that is picked on the screen, and issue the prompt Pick a point:. _____

❑ Set the distance between points JP and KP to the variable LP. _____

❑ Issue a prompt that says This is only an exercise. _____

Basic AutoLISP review

Before applying these newly learned commands to an AutoLISP program, take a few minutes to review the following list. These commands are used in the next section.

- **(+, −, *, /).** Math functions—Must be the first part of an expression. Example: (+ 6 8).
- **(SETQ).** Set quote—This command allows a value to be assigned to a variable. Example: (SETQ CITY "San Francisco") sets the value San Francisco to the variable CITY.
- **(!).** Returns the value of a variable. Example: !CITY returns San Francisco.
- **(GETPOINT).** Get point—Gets a point entered at the keyboard or by the pointing device. Can be applied to a variable. Example: (SETQ A (GETPOINT)) assigns a point to the variable A.
- **(GETDIST).** Get distance—Gets a distance from two points entered at the keyboard or picked with the pointing device. Can be applied to a variable, and a prompt is allowed. Example: (SETQ D2 (GETDIST "Pick two points:")) gets a distance and assigns it to the variable D2.
- **(DISTANCE).** Distance—Returns a distance between two existing points. Example: (DISTANCE P1 P2) returns the distance between P1 and P2. Can also assign the distance to a variable. Example: (SETQ D (DISTANCE P1 P2)).
- **(GETSTRING).** Get string—Returns a word or group of characters. No spaces are allowed. Example: (GETSTRING) waits for a string of characters and displays the string when [Enter] or the space bar is pressed. Can be assigned to a variable. Spaces are allowed in the string if a T or number follows the **GETSTRING** function. Example: (SETQ TXT (GETSTRING T "Enter text:")) assigns the text entered to the variable TXT.
- **(PROMPT).** Prompt—Allows a message to be issued in a program. Example: (PROMPT "Select an entity:") prints the Select an entity: prompt.

EXERCISE 22-7

❏ Write an AutoLISP program that places NOTES: at a location that you pick on the screen. Name the file EX22-7.LSP.
❏ In the space below, write a description of the program in longhand. Then, write each line of code.
❏ Enter the program using your text editor and then test it in AutoCAD.
❏ The lines of your program should include the following:
  ❏ A remark line containing the author, date, and name of the file.
  ❏ The function defined is NOTES and has two local variables, P1 and T.
  ❏ Set the P1 variable. Provide a prompt for entering the text location at P1.
  ❏ Give the variable TXT the value NOTES:.
  ❏ Execute the **TEXT** command to do the following: Use P1 as the text location; enter text height of 0.25"; rotation angle of 0; and use the variable TXT as the text.

_____

_____

_____

_____

_____

_____

_____

_____

_____

_____

_____

_____

AutoLISP—Beyond the Basics

As you practice with AutoLISP, you will develop ideas for programs that require additional commands and functions. Some of these programs may require that the user pick two corners of a windowed selection set. Another program may use existing points to draw a shape. You may also need to locate a point using polar coordinate notation, or determine the angle of a line. All of these can be done with AutoLISP programs.

Getting additional input

The **GETREAL** function allows the user to enter a real number at the keyboard. Remember, as defined by AutoLISP, a real number is more precise than an integer because it has a decimal value.

The **GETREAL** function works with numbers as units. You cannot respond with a value of feet and inches. Once issued, the command waits for user input. If input is provided, a prompt is given and the real number is returned. **GETREAL** can be used to set the value of a variable as follows:

```
Command: (SETQ X (GETREAL "Enter number:").↵
Enter number: 34.↵
34.0
```

The **GETCORNER** command allows the user to pick the opposite corner of a rectangle. This is like placing a window around entities in a drawing. An existing point serves as the first corner. When positioning the opposite corner, a rubber band box appears on the crosshairs, similar to the window box. The command can also be used to set the value of a variable. The second corner can be picked with the pointing device or entered at the keyboard. An example use of **GETCORNER** follows:

```
Command: (SETQ PT1 (GETPOINT "\nPick a point:")).↵
Pick a point: (pick the point)
Command: (SETQ PT2 (GETCORNER PT1 "\nPick the second corner:")).↵
Pick the second corner: (pick the corner)
```

Notice that the value of PT1 is set first. Point PT1 becomes the base point for locating PT2. The two points (corners) located in this example can be used to construct an angled line, rectangle, or other shape. It can also be applied to other functions.

Using the values of system variables

AutoCAD's system variables can be accessed with the AutoLISP **GETVAR** and **SETVAR** functions. This can be useful if an application requires you to store the value of a system variable, change the variable for your program, and then reset it to its original value.

The **GETVAR** function is commonly used to see the value of a variable. Refer to the following example:

```
Command: (SETQ V1 (GETVAR "TEXTSIZE")).↵
current value of TEXTSIZE system variable
Command: (SETQ V2 (GETVAR "FILLETRAD")).↵
current value of FILLETRAD system variable
```

The **SETVAR** command is used to change a system variable. Assign the value to a variable as follows:

```
Command: (SETVAR "TEXTSIZE" 0.25).↵
0.25
Command: (SETVAR "FILLETRAD" 0.25).↵
0.25
```

Suppose you need to save a current system variable, reset the variable, and then reset the variable to its original value after the command is executed. The **GETVAR** command can be used to supply a value to a new variable, as shown in the previous "TEXTSIZE" example. When the program is complete, the **SETVAR** command is used to reset the text size to its original value as follows:

```
Command: (SETVAR "TEXTSIZE" V1).↵
0.125
```

This returns the value of TEXTSIZE to the variable V1, which is the default 0.125.

❏ In the spaces provided, write the following expressions in longhand using proper AutoLISP format. Enter the expressions into your computer to see if they work.

  ❏ Get the current aperture size and set it to the variable APER. _____

  ❏ Set the variable APER4 to the aperture size of four pixels._____

  ❏ Use the **LINE** command and an object snap setting to connect the line with other entities on the screen._____

  ❏ Reset the aperture to the original setting using AutoLISP commands and the variables previously set. _____

❏ Add the following capabilities to the EX22-7.LSP file that you created in the previous exercise:

  ❏ Create a variable V1 to hold the current text size. Insert this line after the "DEFUN" line. _____

  ❏ At the end of the program, reset the text size to its original size._____

Working with lists

A list is created when you pick a point on the screen in response to the **GETPOINT** command. The list is composed of three numbers—the X, Y, and Z coordinate values. You can tell it is a list because AutoLISP returns the numbers enclosed in parentheses. A number entered in response to the **GETREAL** command returns as a real number (it is not enclosed in parentheses). A single number is not a list. The following expression returns a list:

```
Command: (SETQ P1 (GETPOINT "Enter point:"))↵
Enter point: (pick a point)
(2.0 2.75 0.0)
```

The individual values in a list are called *elements*, and can be used in an AutoLISP program to create new points to draw shapes. The **CAR** function retrieves the first element of a list (the X coordinate in the above example). The variable P1 in the example above is composed of the list (2.0 2.75 0.0). Thus, **CAR** returns a value of 2.0. Enter the following:

```
Command: (CAR P1)↵
2.0
```

The second element of a list (the Y coordinate) is retrieved with the **CADR** function. Find the **CADR** of P1 by entering the following:

```
Command: (CADR P1)↵
2.75
```

You can create a new list of two coordinates by selecting values from existing points using the **CAR** and **CADR** functions. This is done with the **LIST** function. Values returned by the list function are placed inside parentheses. The coordinates of P1 can be combined with the coordinates of a second point P2 to form a third point P3. Study the following example, and the illustration in Figure 22-3.

```
Command: (SETQ P2 (GETCORNER P1 "Enter second point:"))↵
(6.0 4.5 0.0)
Command: (SETQ P3 (LIST (CAR P2) (CADR P1)))↵
(6.0 2.75)
```

Figure 22-3.
Point P3 has been
created using the
CAR of P2 and
CADR of P1.

+ P2
X = 6.0 (**CAR**)
Y = 4.5 (**CADR**)

+ P1
X = 2.0 (**CAR**)
Y = 2.75 (**CADR**)

+ P3
X = 6.0 (**CAR** P2)
Y = 2.75 (**CADR** P1)

In AutoLISP, a function is followed by an argument. An argument is data that a function operates on or with. An expression must be composed of only one function and any required arguments. Therefore, the functions **CAR** and **CADR** must be separated because they are two different expressions combined to make a list. The **CAR** value of P2 is to be the X value of P3, so it is given first. The **CADR** of P1 is placed second because it is to be the Y value of P3. Notice the number of closing parentheses at the end of the expression.

Now, with three points defined, there are many things you can do. For example, you can draw lines through the points to form a triangle, Figure 22-4. To do so, use the **COMMAND** function as follows:

Command: **(COMMAND "LINE" P1 P2 P3 "C").**↵

The **CAR** and **CADR** functions allow you to work with 2D coordinates. The **CADDR** function allows you to get the Z value of a 3D coordinate (the third element of a list). Enter the following at your keyboard:

Command: **(SETQ B (LIST 3 4 6)).**↵
(3 4 6)

You have created a list of three elements, or coordinate values. The third element is the Z coordinate. Retrieve that value with the **CADDR** function as follows:

Command: **(CADDR B).**↵
6

Since 6 is a single value as opposed to a list, it is not enclosed in parentheses. Now use **CAR** and **CADR** to find the other two elements of the list:

Command: **(CAR B).**↵
3
Command: **(CADR B).**↵
4

Figure 22-4.
Once the third
point P3 is created,
a triangle can be
drawn.

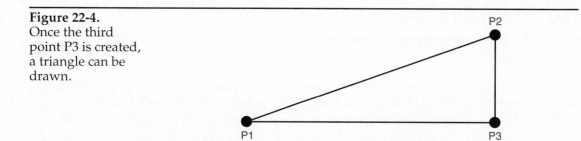

The following example shows a short AutoLISP file that uses these functions to place an X at the point midway between two selected points.

```
(DEFUN C:MDPNT (/ PT1 PT2 PT3)
  (SETQ PT1 (GETPOINT "\nEnter the first point:"))
  (SETQ PT2 (GETPOINT "\nEnter the second point:"))
  (SETQ PT3 (LIST (/ (+ (CAR PT1) (CAR PT2)) 2) (/ (+ (CADR PT1) (CADR PT2))
  2)))
  (SETVAR "PDMODE" 3)
  (COMMAND "POINT" PT3)
)
```

The **CDR** function allows you to retrieve the second and remaining elements of a list. Therefore, suppose the list (3 4 6) is assigned to variable B, as done earlier in this section. The **CDR** function returns the list (4 6). Try it:

```
Command: (CDR B).┘
(4 6)
```

This is now a separate list that can be manipulated with **CAR** and **CADR**, just like a 2D coordinate list. Study Figure 22-5 and the following examples:

```
Command: (CAR (CDR B)).┘
4
Command: (CADR (CDR B)).┘
6
```

The first example is asking for the first element (**CAR**) of the list (4 6). It originally was the last two elements (**CDR**) of the list for variable B. In the second example, the second element (**CADR**) of the list (4 6) is returned.

The four functions used to manipulate lists—**CAR**, **CADR**, **CADDR**, and **CDR**—may seem confusing at first. Practice using them and discover how they work. Practice with a list of numbers, coordinate values, or text strings. Remember, text strings must be enclosed in quotes. Try the following examples to see what happens. Enter the expressions at the Command: prompt exactly as shown and press [Enter] at the end of each line.

```
(SETQ NOTES (LIST "DO" "RE" "MI"))
(CAR NOTES)
(CADR notes)
(CADDR notes)
(CDR notes)
(SETQ last (cdr notes))
(CAR (CDR notes))
(CADR (CDR notes))
(CAR last)
(CADR last)
```

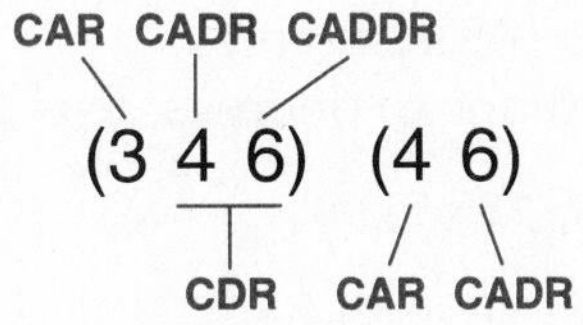

Figure 22-5.
The **CDR** function creates a list containing the second and remaining elements of a list.

Review of list-making functions
- **(CAR).** Returns the first element of a list.
- **(CADR).** Returns the second element of a list.
- **(CADDR).** Returns the third element of a list.
- **(CDR).** Returns the second and remaining elements of a list. Since the **CDR** function returns more than one element, the values it returns are always placed in a list.
- **(LIST).** Creates a list of all values entered after the function **LIST**.

EXERCISE 22-9

❑ Write an AutoLISP program that draws a right triangle. The 90° angle can be on either the left or right side.

❑ Write the program in proper AutoLISP format. Use your text editor and save it as EX22-9.LSP.

❑ Use the following items in writing the program:
  ❑ Define the function as "triangle."
  ❑ Set the variable P1 as the first point of the triangle. Use a prompt.
  ❑ Set the variable P2 as the endpoint of the hypotenuse (**GETCORNER**). Place the prompt on the next line.
  ❑ Set the variable P3 to the X coordinate of P2 and the Y coordinate of P1.
  ❑ Draw a line through all three points and close the triangle.

❑ Before saving the program, check for matching parentheses and quotes. Save the program and test it.

Polar Coordinates and Angles

The ability to work with angles is vital if you plan to do much AutoLISP programming. Four functions—**ANGLE**, **POLAR**, **GETANGLE**, and **GETORIENT**—allow you to use angles. AutoLISP works with these commands using the radian system of angle measurement. This system of measurement is explained in the next section.

Measuring an angle

The **ANGLE** function is used to calculate the angle between two given points. The value of the angle is given in radians. *Radian angle measurement* is a system where 180° equals "pi" (π). Pi is approximately equal to 3.14159.

AutoLISP functions use radians for angular measurement, but AutoCAD commands use degrees. Therefore, to use a radian angle in an AutoCAD command, it must first be converted to degrees. Conversely, a degree angle to be used by AutoLISP must be converted to radians. The following formulas are used for those conversions.

- To convert degrees to radians, use the formula

  (* pi (/ *AD* 180.0))

  where *AD* = angle in degrees.

- To convert radians to degrees, use the formula

  (/ (* *AR* 180.0) pi)

  where *AR* = angle in radians.

The following example illustrates how the angle between two points can be set to a variable, then converted to degrees.

```
Command: (SETQ P1 (GETPOINT "Enter first point:"))↵
Enter first point: 1.75,5.25↵
(1.75 5.25 0.0)
Command: (SETQ P2 (GETPOINT "Enter second point:"))↵
Enter second point: 6.75,7.25↵
(6.75 7.25 0.0)
Command: (SETQ A1 (ANGLE P1 P2))↵
0.380506
```

The angle A1 is measured in radians (0.380506). To convert this to degrees, use the following entry:

```
Command: (/ (* A1 180.0) pi)↵
21.8014
Command: !A1↵
0.380506
```

The value 21.8014 is the angle in degrees between P1 and P2. This conversion does not reset the variable to the degree value. Make the value permanent by assigning it to the variable using the following expression:

```
Command: (setq A1 (/ (* A1 180.0) pi))↵
21.8014
Command: !A1↵
21.8014
```

The variable A now has a value of 21.8014°.

The following list gives common angles measured in degrees, the AutoLISP expressions used to convert to radian values, and the values in radians.

Angle (degrees)	AutoLISP expression	Angle (radians)
0		0
30	(/ pi 6)	0.5236
45	(/ pi 4)	0.7854
60	(/ pi 3)	1.0472
90	(/ pi 2)	1.5708
135	(/ (* pi 3) 4)	2.3562
180	(+ pi)	3.1416
270	(+ pi (/ pi 2))	4.7124
360	(* pi 2)	6.2832

EXERCISE 22-10

❏ Using AutoLISP expressions, locate the endpoints of a line and store each endpoint as a variable.
❏ Use **ANGLE** to find the angle of the line.
❏ Use the proper formula to convert the radian value to degrees.
❏ Use the proper formula to convert the degree value back to radians.

Getting angular input

The **GETANGLE** function allows a user to input an angle value. This function is often used to set a variable that can be used by another function. The **GETANGLE** function automatically issues a Second point: prompt. The following example illustrates how you can set a variable to an angle input by the user:

> Command: **(SETQ A (GETANGLE "Pick first point:"))**↵
> Pick first point: *(pick first point)* Second point: *(pick point)*
> *angle (in radians)*

The angle value is given in radians. To convert this to degrees, use the formula presented in the previous section.

The **GETANGLE** function uses the current **ANGBASE** (angle 0 direction) and **ANGDIR** (clockwise or counterclockwise) system variables. Therefore, if you have angles set to be measured from north (**ANGBASE** = 90°), angles picked with **GETANGLE** will be measured from north. If the **ANGDIR** variable is set to measure angles clockwise, **GETANGLE** will accept input of clockwise values, but returns counterclockwise values. A companion function to **GETANGLE** is **GETORIENT**. It is used in exactly the same manner as **GETANGLE**, but always measures angles counterclockwise from east (0°), regardless of the current **ANGBASE** and **ANGDIR** settings.

EXERCISE 22-11

❏ Use **GETANGLE** to assign an angle to the variable ANG1.
    ❏ Convert the radian value to degrees using AutoLISP expressions.
    ❏ Convert the degree value back to radians using AutoLISP expressions.
❏ Use **GETORIENT** to find the angle in radians of any two points.
❏ Reset **ANGBASE** to 90.
    ❏ Use **GETORIENT** to find the angle of the two points.
    ❏ Use **GETANGLE** to find the angle of the two points.
❏ Compare the values. Explain the results. _____

_____

_____

Using polar coordinates

The **POLAR** function allows you to specify the angle and distance of a point relative to another point. Two variables must first be set for **POLAR** to work properly—the point that you are locating a new point from and the distance between the two points. For example, suppose you want to specify a point P1, then locate another point P2 at a specific distance and angle from P1. Enter the following expressions:

> Command: **(SETQ P1 (GETPOINT "Enter point:"))**↵
> Enter point: *(pick point or enter the coordinates at the keyboard)* **4.0,4.5.**↵
> Command: **(SETQ D (GETDIST P1 "Enter distance:"))**
> Enter distance: *(pick distance or enter at keyboard)* **3.0.**↵
> Command: **(SETQ A (* pi (/ 60 180.0)))**↵
> 1.0472

In this expression, the angle 60° is used. However, AutoLISP uses radians. Therefore, the 60° is converted to radians. The resulting angle of 1.0472 is saved as the variable A. A line can now be drawn from P1 at 60° using the **POLAR** command as follows:

> Command: **(SETQ P2 (POLAR P1 A D))**↵
> (5.5 7.09808)
> Command: **(COMMAND "LINE" P1 P2).**↵

❑ Write a program to draw a right triangle. If you need to, refer to EX22-9. However, use **POLAR** instead of **LIST** functions.

❑ Write the AutoLISP expressions for the program in the proper format. Save the file as EX22-12.LSP.

❑ Enter the program in your computer when you have finished writing it.

❑ Use the following items in the program:

    ❑ Define a function called POLARTRI.

    ❑ Set a variable P1 as the first corner of the triangle.

    ❑ Set a variable D as the length of one side.

    ❑ Set a variable P2 0° from P1 at a distance of D.

❑ Set a variable P3 90° from P2 at a distance of D.

❑ Use the **LINE** command to draw the triangle.

Locating AutoCAD's AutoLISP Files

One of the best ways to become familiar with AutoLISP is to enter expressions and programs on your computer. Look for programs in books or magazines that you read. Get a feel for how the functions and arguments go together and how they work in AutoCAD. Make a habit of reading through one of the AutoCAD journals. Experiment with AutoLISP routines printed in them. Also, refer to the *AutoCAD Customization Guide* for other samples.

A variety of AutoLISP programs are supplied with the AutoCAD Release 14 software. AutoLISP files typically use the file extension .lsp. There are three subfolders beneath your AutoCAD R14 program directory that contain various AutoLISP program files, shown in Figure 22-6.

The AutoLISP files found in the Support folder are standard files that support many of AutoCAD's built-in features. The Sample\Asilisp folder provide some examples of AutoLISP working with external database applications, and many very powerful AutoLISP programs are found in the Bonus\Cadtools folder. You can use the Windows Explorer to get a listing of the files in any of these directories. If you select Details from the View menu in Explorer, you can then sort the files by picking the Type button at the top of the Contents window. Sorting the files makes it easier to locate all of the AutoLISP files.

As stated earlier, the Support folder contains standard files that support built-in AutoCAD functions. When the command that starts the function is entered, the associated program file is automatically loaded, for example:

- **ddinsert.lsp.** This file supports the function of the **DDINSERT** command, providing the dialog based interface for inserting blocks and files.
- **3d.lsp.** This routine is activated when you select the **3D Surfaces...** option from the **Surfaces** cascading menu in the **Draw** pull-down menu. It activates the **3D Objects** dialog box.
- **3darray.lsp.** An arrangement of rows, columns, and levels of an object is possible with this routine. See Chapter 2 for a detailed explanation of using **3DARRAY**.

The files in the Sample\Asilisp folder provide examples for working with external database files using AutoLISP. Those found in the Cadtools folder are the files that make up the AutoCAD Bonus Utilities.

The easiest way to access the Bonus Utilities is by using the **MENULOAD** command to load the AC_BONUS menu file, which is also found in the Cadtools directory. **MENULOAD** is explained in Chapter 20. When the AC_BONUS menu has been loaded, you have access to toolbars and the **Bonus** pull-down menu for starting these functions.

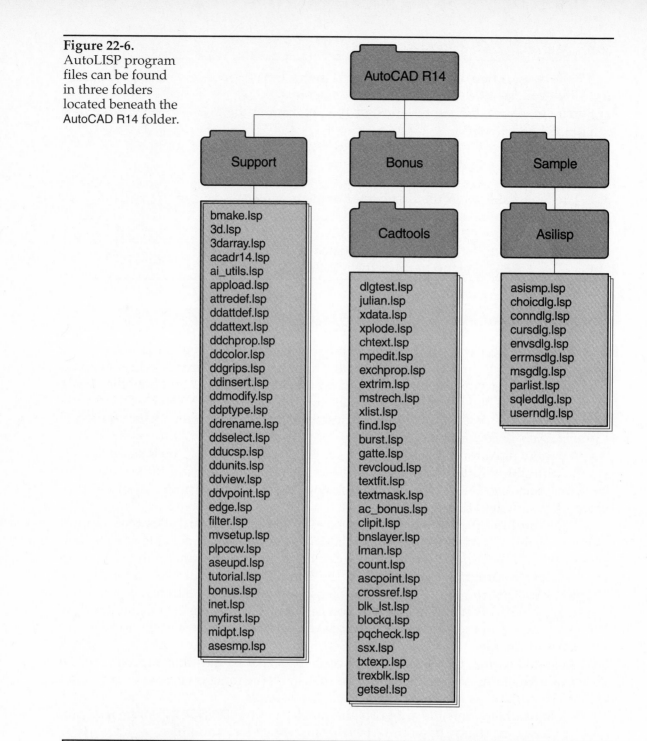

Figure 22-6.
AutoLISP program files can be found in three folders located beneath the AutoCAD R14 folder.

AutoCAD R14

Support

- bmake.lsp
- 3d.lsp
- 3darray.lsp
- acadr14.lsp
- ai_utils.lsp
- appload.lsp
- attredef.lsp
- ddattdef.lsp
- ddattext.lsp
- ddchprop.lsp
- ddcolor.lsp
- ddgrips.lsp
- ddinsert.lsp
- ddmodify.lsp
- ddptype.lsp
- ddrename.lsp
- ddselect.lsp
- dducsp.lsp
- ddunits.lsp
- ddview.lsp
- ddvpoint.lsp
- edge.lsp
- filter.lsp
- mvsetup.lsp
- plpccw.lsp
- aseupd.lsp
- tutorial.lsp
- bonus.lsp
- inet.lsp
- myfirst.lsp
- midpt.lsp
- asesmp.lsp

Bonus

Cadtools

- dlgtest.lsp
- julian.lsp
- xdata.lsp
- xplode.lsp
- chtext.lsp
- mpedit.lsp
- exchprop.lsp
- extrim.lsp
- mstrech.lsp
- xlist.lsp
- find.lsp
- burst.lsp
- gatte.lsp
- revcloud.lsp
- textfit.lsp
- textmask.lsp
- ac_bonus.lsp
- clipit.lsp
- bnslayer.lsp
- lman.lsp
- count.lsp
- ascpoint.lsp
- crossref.lsp
- blk_lst.lsp
- blockq.lsp
- pqcheck.lsp
- ssx.lsp
- txtexp.lsp
- trexblk.lsp
- getsel.lsp

Sample

Asilisp

- asismp.lsp
- choicdlg.lsp
- conndlg.lsp
- cursdlg.lsp
- envsdlg.lsp
- errmsdlg.lsp
- msgdlg.lsp
- parlist.lsp
- sqleddlg.lsp
- userndlg.lsp

PROFESSIONAL TIP

For easier access to any AutoLISP program file, add its folder in the Support File Search Path listing under the **Files** tab within the **Preferences** dialog box. Picking the **Browse...** button allows you to pick the folder rather than type the entire path. When using the Bonus Utilities, the Bonus\Cadtools folder should also be added in the support path listing if it is not already there.

Sample AutoLISP Programs

The following programs are provided for you to copy and add to your acad.lsp file or to your menus. Practice for a few minutes a couple of times a week. This will help you begin to better understand and use AutoLISP. Train yourself to learn a new function every week. Before long, you will be writing your own useful programs.

Erase the entire screen

This program sets two variables to the minimum and maximum screen limits. It then erases everything within those limits and redraws the screen. Name this program ZAP.LSP.

```
; ERASES ENTIRE LIMITS
(defun C:ZAP ( )
   (setq MIN (getvar "LIMMIN"))
   (setq MAX (getvar "LIMMAX"))
   (command "ERASE" "C" MIN MAX "")
   (command "REDRAW")
)
```

Set the current layer

Similar to the built-in **Make Object's Layer Current** tool, this program asks for the user to point to an object on the layer to be set current. The program finds the layer of the entity picked and sets the layer as current.

```
; Author : Rod Rawls
(defun C:LP (/ E)
   (while (not (setq E (entsel "\nSelect object on target layer...")))
        (alert "No object selected!")
   )
   (setq LN (cdr (assoc 8 (entget (car E)))))
   (command "LAYER" "S" LN "")
   (princ)
)
```

Clean overlapping corners

This program allows you to trim the overlapping ends of intersecting lines. You are requested to pick the two lines that intersect and overlap. The program does the rest. Name the program TRIMENDS.LSP.

```
; AUTHOR      : GEORGE HEAD
; PRINTED IN THE JANUARY, 1988 ISSUE OF "CADENCE" MAGAZINE
(defun C:CLEANC (/ O1 P1 P2)
   (setq O1 (getvar "OSMODE"))
   (setvar "OSMODE" 512)
   (command "FILLET" "R" 0)
   (setq P1 (GETPOINT "\nPick a line "))
   (setq P2 (GETPOINT "\nPick other line "))
   (command "FILLET" P1 P2)
   (setvar "OSMODE" O1)
)
```

Calculate the length of lines

This program calculates the length of all lines on a specified layer. It can be used for estimating and material takeoffs. This program works only with lines, not with polylines. Name the program LINEAR.LSP. After loading it into the AutoCAD drawing editor, respond to the first prompt by entering the name of the layer that contains the lines you wish to total. The answer is given in current drawing units.

```
; AUTHOR        : JOE PUCILOWSKI
; COMPANY       : JOSEPH & ASSOCIATES
; ADDRESS       : 7809A RIVER RESORT LANE, TAMPA, FL nnnnn
; PHONE         : (nnn) nnn-nnnn
; DATE          : 9/19/xx
; NOTE          : THIS PROGRAM FIGURES THE TOTAL NUMBER OF LINEAR
;                   UNITS (FEET, INCHES, ETC.) OF LINES ON A SPECIFIC LAYER.
; REVISED       : 10/8/xx BY ROD RAWLS
;
(defun C:LINEAR  ( )
  (setq  TOTAL    0
         E             (entnext)
         NUMLIN        0
         LAYPIK        (strcase
                          (getstring "\nAdd up lines on layer: ")
                        )
  )
  (if (tblsearch "LAYER" LAYPIK)
    (progn
      (while   E
        (setq ENTTYP (cdr (assoc 0 (setq EG (entget E)))))
              LAYNAM (cdr (assoc 8 EG))
        )
        (if
          (and
            (equal ENTTYP "LINE")
            (equal LAYNAM LAYPIK)
          )
          (progn
            (setq  LINLEN (distance (cdr (assoc 10 EG)) (cdr (assoc 11 EG)))
                   TOTAL (+ TOTAL LINLEN)
                   NUMLIN (+ 1 NUMLIN)
            )
          )
        )
        (setq  E (entnext E))
      )
      (princ
        (strcat "\nFound "
                (itoa NUMLIN)
                " lines on layer < "
                LAYPIK
                "> with a total of "
                (rtos TOTAL)
                " linear units."
        )
      )
    )
    (princ "\nLayer does not exist.")
  )
  (princ)
)
```

Easy grid rotation

This program, titled S.LSP, rotates the grid to the angle of any picked line. The second routine, SS.LSP, returns the grid to zero rotation.

```
; AUTHOR        : EBEN KUNZ
; COMPANY       : KUNZ ASSOCIATES ARCHITECTS
; Address       : 38 Greenwich Park, Boston, MA nnnnn
; Phone : (nnn) nnn-nnnn
;
(defun C:S (/ pt1 pt2)
   (setvar "orthomode" 0)
   (setq pt1 (osnap (getpoint "\nPick line to match new Grid angle: \n") "nea"))
   (setq pt2 (osnap pt1 "end"))
   (command "snap" "r" pt1 pt2)
   (setvar "snapmode" 0)
)
(defun C:SS ( )
   (prompt "\nReturn Grid to zero.")
   (command "snap" "r" "" 0.0)
   (setvar "snapmode" 0)
)
```

Move to current layer

This simple program quickly changes selected entities to the current layer.

```
; AUTHOR        : BILL FANE
; COMPANY       : WEISER, INC.
; Address       : 6700 Beresford St., Burnaby, B.C.
;
(DEFUN C:CL (/ THINGS)
   (SETQ THINGS (SSGET))
   (COMMAND "CHANGE" THINGS "" "P" "LA"
        (GETVAR "CLAYER") "" )
)
```

Change to selected layer

This routine allows you to move entities to a layer by picking an entity on the destination layer.

```
; AUTHOR        : SHELDON MCCARTHY
; COMPANY       : EPCM SERVICES LTD.
; Address       : 2404 Haines Road, Mississauga, Ontario
; Phone         : (nnn) nnn-nnnn
;
(DEFUN C:LA ( )
   (SETQ 1A (CDR (ASSOC 8 (ENTGET (CAR (ENTSEL "Entity on destination layer: "))))))
   (PROMPT "Select objects to change:")
   (SSGET)
   (COMMAND "CHANGE" "P" "" "P" "LA" 1A "")
)
```

Chapter Test

Write your answers in the spaces provided.

1. The extension used for AutoLISP files is _____.

2. Why is it a good idea to make a separate folder for LISP files? _____
   _____
   _____
   _____

3. A remark is indicated in an AutoLISP file with _____.

4. When in the drawing editor, how do you load an AutoLISP file named CHGTEXT.LSP?
   _____
   _____
   _____

5. Define an integer as related to AutoLISP._____
   _____
   _____

6. Define a real number as related to AutoLISP. _____
   _____
   _____

7. Write the following arithmetic expressions in the proper AutoLISP format.
   A. 23 + 54_____
   B. 12.45 + 6.28_____
   C. 56 – 34 _____
   D. 23.004 – 7.008 _____
   E. 16 × 4.6 _____
   F. 7.25 × 10.30_____
   G. 45 / 23_____
   H. 147 / 29.6 _____
   I. 53 + (12 × 3.8)_____
   J. 567 / (34 – 14) _____

8. Explain the purpose of the **SETQ** function. _____
   _____
   _____
   _____

9. Write the proper AutoLISP notation to assign the value of (67 – 34.5) to the variable
   NUM1._____

10. What does the **GETPOINT** function allow you to do? _____
    _____
    _____

11. Write the proper AutoLISP notation to assign the values of X = 3.5 and Y = 5.25 to
    the variable PT1._____

12. The AutoLISP function that allows you to find the distance between two points is

_____.

13. Explain the purpose of the **GETSTRING** function._____

_____

_____

14. Write the proper AutoLISP notation for assigning the string This is a test: to the variable TXT. _____

15. How do you allow spaces in a string of text when using the **GETSTRING** function?

_____

_____

16. Write the proper AutoLISP notation for using the **PLINE** command. _____

_____

17. How must an AutoCAD command be handled in an AutoLISP expression? ____

_____

_____

18. Define a function._____

_____

_____

19. Define an argument. _____

_____

_____

20. The AutoLISP function that describes the name of a function in a program is ___

_____.

21. Describe why indentation is used when writing AutoLISP programs._____

_____

_____

22. Explain the purpose of the **\n** function._____

_____

_____

23. The command that allows you to retrieve a decimal number is _____.

24. Which two commands allow you to work with system variables? _____

_____

25. Define the following AutoLISP functions:
    A. **CAR** _____
    B. **CADR**_____
    C. **CDR** _____
    D. **CADDR** _____
    E. **LIST**_____

26. Write the proper AutoLISP notation to return the last two numbers of the list (4 7 3).

_____

27. Write an expression to set a variable A to the result of Question 26. _____
_____

28. Write an expression to select the second element of the list returned in Question 27.
_____

29. Compare and contrast the **GETANGLE** and **GETORIENT** functions. _____
_____
_____

30. Write an expression to set the angle between points P3 and P4 to the variable A.
_____

31. What system of angle measurement does AutoLISP use? _____
_____

32. What is the value of 270° in the angular system AutoLISP uses? _____
_____

33. Explain the purpose of the **POLAR** function. _____
_____
_____
_____

Drawing Problems

1. Add the following capabilities to the right triangle function developed in Exercise 22-9.
   A. Use **GETDIST** instead of **GETCORNER**.
   B. Allow the angle of the hypotenuse to be picked.
   C. Allow the length of a side to be picked.

2. Create an AutoLISP program similar to that in Problem 1, but it should draw an equilateral triangle (equal angles and equal sides). Use the **POLAR** function.

3. Write a program to draw a rectangle. Use only the **GETPOINT** function to set opposite corners of the rectangle. Follow these guidelines:
   A. Set P1 as the first corner.
   B. Set P3 as the opposite corner.
   C. Set points P2 and P4 using the list functions of AutoLISP.
   D. Use the **LINE** command to draw the rectangle.

4. Revise the program in Problem 3 to draw a rectangle using the **GETCORNER** function to find the second corner.

5. Create an AutoLISP command to draw a square. Follow these guidelines:
   A. Set a variable for the length of one side.
   B. Set the variable P1 as the lower-left corner of the square.
   C. Use the **LINE** command to draw the square.

6. Revise the program in Problem 5 to draw a square using the **PLINE** command.

7. Use the program in Problem 6 to create a new command that draws a square and allows you to change the line thickness.

   A. Use either **PLINE** or **POLYGON** commands to draw the square.

   B. Set a variable to get the line thickness input by the user.

8. Add a **Fillet 0** command to your **Modify** pull-down menu. Use menu code and AutoLISP expressions to create the command. Follow these guidelines:

   A. Get the current fillet radius and assign it to an AutoLISP variable.

   B. Set the fillet radius to 0.

   C. Select two lines and enter a 0 fillet.

   D. Reset the fillet radius to the original value.

   E. Assign an appropriate mnemonic shortcut key to the new command.

9. Add a **DISTANCE** command to any pull-down menu. Use menu code and AutoLISP expressions to do the following:

   A. Get desired unit precision from user and store it as a variable.

   B. Store current unit precision as an AutoLISP variable.

   C. Set unit precision with a user variable.

   D. Reset unit precision to the original value.

   E. Assign an appropriate mnemonic shortcut key to the new command.

10. Write an AutoLISP program to draw parallel rectangles.

    A. Use the rectangle program in Problem 3, but replace **LINE** with the **PLINE** command.

    B. Get user offset distance for the inside rectangle.

    C. Use the **OFFSET** command to draw the parallel rectangle inside the original.

11. Write a program to draw a rectangle and place a circle having a user-specified diameter in the center of the rectangle.

    A. Incorporate the rectangle program in Problem 3.

    B. Use the **ANGLE, POLAR**, and **DISTANCE** functions to find the center point of the rectangle.

    C. Request the user to enter the diameter.

    D. Draw a circle at the center point of the rectangle.

12. Write a program to draw a leader with a diameter dimension having plus and minus tolerances.

    A. Prompt for and allow user to set **DIMTP** and **DIMTM** system variables.

    B. Activate the **DIM** command and turn **DIMTOL** on.

    C. Activate the **DIAMETER** command, select the circle, and cancel.

    D. Start the leader from the "last point" and allow two leader picks.

    E. End the leader and accept default dimension text.

    F. Turn tolerancing off and exit the **DIM** command.

---

13. Write a program to draw a leader with a bubble attached to the end.

A. Get the start point of the leader and set it to P1.

B. Get the endpoint of the leader and set it to P2.

C. Ask the user for text height and set it to a variable.

D. Ask for the text string (maximum of two characters) and set it to a variable.

E. Calculate the circle diameter 2.5 or 3 times the text height and set it to a variable.

F. Set the circle center point P3 to a value relative to P2 using **POLAR**.

G. Activate the **DIM** command and draw a leader from P1 to P2.

H. Erase the "last" portion of the leader.

I. Draw a circle at P3.

J. Draw text in the center of the circle using the appropriate option in the **TEXT** command.

14. Develop a program that writes a line of text and places a box around it.

A. Ask the user for the text height and set it to variable TXHT.

B. Ask for the lower-left corner to start box.

C. Ask the text string from the user.

D. Set string length to variable LG1. Use the **STRLEN** function.

```
(STRLEN) example:
    (setq TEXT (getstring T "Enter Text: "))
    (setq LG1 (strlen TEXT))
```

E. Set the X length to: (LG1 * TXHT).

F. Set the Y length to: (3 * TXHT).

G. Draw box to X and Y lengths.

H. Calculate center of the box, and set it to variable CENL1.

I. Draw the text string inside the box. Use the **M** justification option from point CENL1.

Introduction to Dialog Control Language (DCL)

Programmable dialog boxes can be used to completely customize the interface of your AutoLISP programs. This will allow your programs to work like many of AutoCAD's built-in functions. Using dialog boxes improves efficiency and reduces data entry errors.

Dialog boxes minimize the amount of typing required by the user. Rather than answering a series of text prompts at the command line, the user selects options from the dialog box. Dialog box fields can be filled in by the user in any order. While the dialog is still active, the user can revise values as necessary.

AutoLISP provides basic tools for controlling dialog boxes, but the dialog box itself must be defined using *Dialog Control Language*, (*DCL*). The definition is written to an ASCII file with a .dcl file extension.

DCL File Formats

A DCL file is formatted as an ASCII text file with a .dcl file extension. These files can have any valid file name, but a 1 to 8 character file name is recommended. Writing with DCL is easy—many of the components of a DCL file are normal English words.

The components of a dialog box—such as edit boxes, images, and drop-down lists—are referred to as *tiles*. Tiles are defined by specifying various *attribute* values. Each attribute controls a specific property of the tile being defined, such as size, location, and default values.

When writing a DCL file, you do not use parentheses (as with AutoLISP). When defining a dialog box or tile, all of the required attributes are placed within {braces}. Indentation helps to separate individual elements, making the file more readable. Comments are preceded by two forward slashes (//). Semicolons are used at the end of an attribute definition line.

To view an example of DCL code, open the acad.dcl and base.dcl files with your text editor. These two files are found in the \AutoCAD R14\Support folder. A portion of the acad.dcl file is shown in Figure 23-1.

Figure 23-1.
A portion of the
acad.dcl file.

```
acad_snap : dialog {                          Dialog definition
    label = "Drawing Aids";                   Label attribute
    : row {                                   adds a text string
      : column {
        : boxed_column {
          label = "Modes";
          : toggle {
            label = "&Ortho";
            key = "ortho";                    Key attribute
          }                                   identifies a text string
          : toggle {                          that associates the dialog
            label = "Solid &Fill";            tile with an AutoLISP
            key = "fill";                     function
          }
```

CAUTION The base.dcl file contains standard prototype definitions. The acad.dcl file contains definitions for all the dialog boxes used by AutoCAD. *Do not edit either one of these files!* Altering them can cause AutoCAD's built-in dialog boxes to crash.

DCL tiles

Your work in AutoCAD has provided you with a good background in how dialog boxes work. By now, you should be familiar with the use of buttons, edit boxes, radio buttons, and list boxes. This will be helpful as you design dialog interfaces for your AutoLISP programs.

DCL tiles are used individually or combined into structures called *clusters*. For example, a series of button tiles can be placed in a column tile to control the arrangement of the buttons in the dialog box. The primary tile is the dialog box itself.

This chapter is only an introduction to DCL, and will cover basic DCL file construction and a few common tile types. For a full discussion of DCL and dialog creation and management techniques, refer to *AutoLISP Programming: Principles and Techniques*, published by Goodheart-Willcox Co., Inc.

The best way to begin understanding the format of a DCL file is to study a simple dialog box definition. The following DCL code defines the dialog box shown in Figure 23-2.

Figure 23-2.
A sample custom
dialog box.

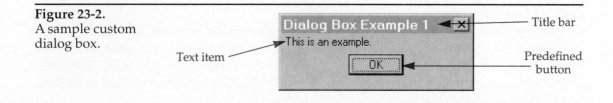

Title bar

Text item

Predefined button

```
main : dialog {
    label          = "Dialog Box Example 1";
    : text_part {
        value      = "This is an example.";
    }
    ok_only;
}
```

Now, let's take a closer look at the definition of this dialog box:

```
main : dialog {
    label          = "Dialog Box Example 1";
    : text_part {
        value      = "This is an example.";
    }
    ok_only;
}
```

The *dialog definition* is always the first tile definition. Everything within the braces defines the features of the dialog box. The word "main" indicates the name of the dialog box. This name is referenced by the controlling AutoLISP application. A colon (:) precedes all tile callouts. In the case of a dialog tile, the colon separates the name from the tile callout.

```
label    = "Dialog Box Example 1";
```

The *label* attribute of the dialog tile controls the text that appears in the title bar of the dialog box. The line is terminated with a semicolon. All attribute lines must be terminated with a semicolon.

```
: text_part {
    value          = "This is an example. ";
}
```

The *text_part* tile allows placement of text items in a dialog box. The *value* attribute is used to specify the text that will be displayed. Just as with the dialog tile, all of the attributes are defined between the braces.

```
ok_only;
```

This is a call to a *predefined tile* found in the base.dcl file. It is not preceded with a colon because it is not a specific definition. This line is terminated with a semicolon just like an attribute. No braces are required because this is not a tile definition, but a reference to a predefined tile.

There are many predefined tiles and subassemblies. A *subassembly* is a predefined tile cluster, such as OK_CANCEL and OK_CANCEL_HELP. The OK_ONLY tile shown here places an **OK** button at the bottom of the dialog box.

Once you have defined a dialog box, the definition must then be saved in a DCL file. For this example, the dialog definition above is saved in the file EXAMPLE1.DCL. This is treated as any other support file, and should be saved in the AutoCAD support path.

For reference, look at the **Insert** dialog box shown in Figure 23-3. Various tiles of this dialog box are identified with the corresponding portion of the ddinsert.dcl file.

Figure 23-3.
Some of the tile definitions and attributes associated with the **Insert** dialog box.

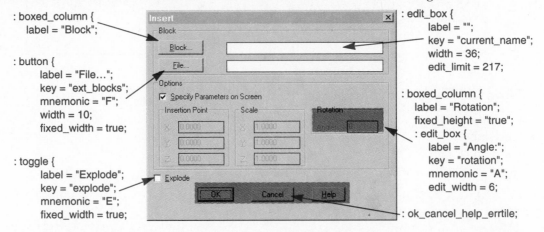

```
: boxed_column {
    label = "Block";


: button {
        label = "File...";
        key = "ext_blocks";
        mnemonic = "F";
        width = 10;
        fixed_width = true;


: toggle {
        label = "Explode";
        key = "explode";
        mnemonic = "E";
        fixed_width = true;
```

```
: edit_box {
        label = "";
        key = "current_name";
        width = 36;
        edit_limit = 217;


: boxed_column {
        label = "Rotation";
        fixed_height = "true";
    : edit_box {
            label = "Angle:";
            key = "rotation";
            mnemonic = "A";
            edit_width = 6;

: ok_cancel_help_errtile;
```

AutoLISP and DCL

A DCL file by itself is merely a definition of a dialog box, and cannot actually do anything without a controlling application. Both the AutoCAD Development System (ADS) and AutoLISP are frequently used to control dialog sessions. While the functions provided for handling dialog boxes differ in name and usage between ADS and AutoLISP, both applications have the same basic tool set. This section shows examples using the AutoLISP dialog handling functions.

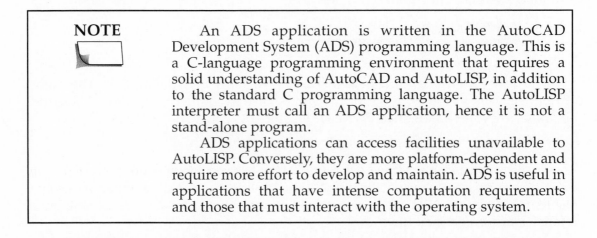

NOTE An ADS application is written in the AutoCAD Development System (ADS) programming language. This is a C-language programming environment that requires a solid understanding of AutoCAD and AutoLISP, in addition to the standard C programming language. The AutoLISP interpreter must call an ADS application, hence it is not a stand-alone program.

ADS applications can access facilities unavailable to AutoLISP. Conversely, they are more platform-dependent and require more effort to develop and maintain. ADS is useful in applications that have intense computation requirements and those that must interact with the operating system.

In order to display a dialog box, the controlling application must first load the dialog definition. The **LOAD_DIALOG** function loads the specified dialog definition file:

(load_dialog "*filename*.dcl")

The file name is enclosed in quotation marks. The **LOAD_DIALOG** expression returns a positive integer that identifies the loaded DCL file. If the attempted load was unsuccessful, a negative integer is returned.

Once the descriptions within a specific DCL file are no longer needed, they can be removed from memory by using the **UNLOAD_DIALOG** function:

(unload_dialog dcl_id)

> **CAUTION** Do not unload a dialog definition until your application is finished using the DCL file, otherwise your application may fail to function properly.

The next step is to activate a specific dialog box definition contained within the DCL file. The **NEW_DIALOG** function activates the dialog box specified, where *dlgname* is the name of the dialog box:

(new_dialog *dlgname* dcl_id)

This function is case-sensitive. The dialog definition used in the previous example was named main. Specifying Main or MAIN will not activate this dialog box, since the text string does not match exactly.

The dcl_id argument represents the integer value returned by **LOAD_DIALOG**. **NEW_DIALOG** also supports additional, optional arguments, which are not discussed here.

To actually begin accepting input from the user, the **START_DIALOG** function must be used:

(start_dialog)

This function has no arguments. It allows for input to be received from the dialog box initialized by the previous **NEW_DIALOG** expression.

With these basic AutoLISP functions, it is possible to display the dialog box shown in Figure 23-2. The controlling AutoLISP application named EXAMPLE1.LSP appears as follows:

```
(setq DCL_ID (load_dialog "EXAMPLE1.DCL"))
(if (not (new_dialog "main" DCL_ID))
   (exit)
)
(start_dialog)
```

Now, let's take a closer look at the controlling code for this dialog box:

(setq DCL_ID (load_dialog "EXAMPLE1.DCL"))

This expression loads the dialog definition found in example1.dcl and assigns the variable DCL_ID to the integer returned by **LOAD_DIALOG**.

(if (not (new_dialog "main" DCL_ID))
**   (exit)**
)

If **NEW_DIALOG** is unable to activate the specified dialog box for any reason, this function will exit the application. This is an important safety feature. In many cases, loading an incorrect or incomplete definition can cause your system to lock up, often requiring that the system be rebooted.

(start_dialog)

This expression starts the dialog session using the dialog box indicated by the previous **NEW_DIALOG** expression.

❑ Use the examples in the text to create EXAMPLE1.DCL and EXAMPLE1.LSP. Create each file in your text editor. You may wish to position a Notepad window alongside your AutoCAD window. In this manner, you can quickly jump from one application to another while writing and testing your dialog box. Load the AutoLISP program file in AutoCAD and run the dialog session.

Associating functions with tiles

Most tiles can be associated with actions. These actions vary from run-time error checking to performing tasks outside the dialog session. The **ACTION_TILE** function provides the basic means of associating tiles with actions:

(action_tile *"key" "action-expression"*)

The *key* references the attribute assigned in the DCL file. The *action-expression* is the AutoLISP expression performed when the action is called. Both the key and action-expression arguments are supplied as text strings.

In order to access a specific tile from AutoLISP, the key of the tile must be referenced. The key is specified as an attribute in the DCL file. Tiles that are static (unchanging) do not require keys. Any tile that must be referenced in any way—such as setting or retrieving a value, associating an action, or enabling/disabling the tile—requires a key.

This next example provides a button on the dialog box that updates the text_part value.

```
main : dialog {
    label           = "Dialog Box Example 2";
    : text_part {
        value       = "";
        key         = "time";
    }
    : button {
        key         = "update";
        label       = "Display Current Time";
        mnemonic = "C";
    }
    ok_only;
}
```

Save this file as EXAMPLE2.DCL. This DCL file is the same as example1.dcl, with the exception of the bold text. Note the addition of a key attribute to the text_part tile. This allows access by the AutoLISP application while the dialog session is running.

Another addition is the button tile. A key is provided in the button tile so an association can be created with an action-expression. The label attribute provides the text displayed on the button. The mnemonic attribute underlines the specified letter within the label to allow keyboard access.

The AutoLISP application used to manage this dialog session is shown below.

```
(setq DCL_ID (load_dialog "EXAMPLE2.DCL"))
(if      (not (new_dialog "main" DCL_ID))
         (exit)
)
(defun   UPDTILE ()
   (setq CDVAR (rtos (getvar "CDATE") 2 16)
         CDTXT (strcat "Current Time: "
                  (substr CDVAR 10 2)
                  ":"
                  (substr CDVAR 12 2)
                  ":"
                  (substr CDVAR 14 2)
               )
   )
   (set_tile "time" CDTXT)
)
(UPDTILE)
(action_tile "update" "(UPDTILE)")
(start_dialog)
```

Some AutoLISP functions that are not covered in this text are used in the above programming to retrieve and display the current date. The "update" button will display the current time when the button is picked. The dialog box displayed by this code is shown in Figure 23-4.

Commands that change the display or require user input (outside of the dialog interface) cannot be used while a dialog box is active. These AutoLISP functions are unavailable:

command	getangle	getpoint	grread	prompt
entdel	getcorner	getreal	grtext	redraw
entmake	getdist	getstring	grvecs	ssget (interactive)
entmod	getint	graphscr	menucmd	textpage
entsel	getkword	grclear	nentsel	textscr
entupd	getorient	grdraw	osnap	

When the desired action requires a large amount of AutoLISP code, it is best to define a function to perform the required tasks. This function is then called within the action-expression.

Figure 23-4.
The dialog box defined by example2.dcl and controlled by example2.lsp.

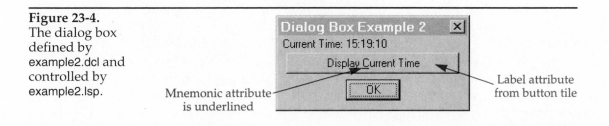

Mnemonic attribute is underlined

Label attribute from button tile

❏ Use the examples in the text to create EXAMPLE2.DCL and EXAMPLE2.LSP. Load the AutoLISP program file and run the dialog session. Note the action performed when the button is picked.

Working with DCL

There are many types of DCL tiles available. You can provide edit boxes for users to enter information directly, such as numeric or text information. You can create lists and drop-down lists to allow users to choose from preset selections. Buttons provide a simple means of initiating an action.

Images can be used to enhance dialog boxes. You can place company or personal logos on your dialog boxes. An interactive image, as shown in the **Viewpoint Presets** dialog box in Figure 23-5, can also be used. Tools such as text tiles, sliders, and clusters are used to control the layout of your tiles in a dialog box.

A wide variety of attributes are available for controlling the appearance and function of a dialog session. Additionally, several AutoLISP functions are provided to control your dialog session. You can disable or enable tiles, and change the active tile. It is even possible to change the value or state of a tile based on an entry in another tile.

The following section provides some applications that use various dialog boxes. Study these examples for additional insight into the creation of dialog sessions. Be sure to have an appropriate reference handy, such as the *AutoCAD Customization Guide*, to look up DCL and AutoLISP terms. You can adapt or modify these files to produce dialog sessions of your own.

Figure 23-5.
The **Viewpoint Presets** dialog box contains an interactive image.

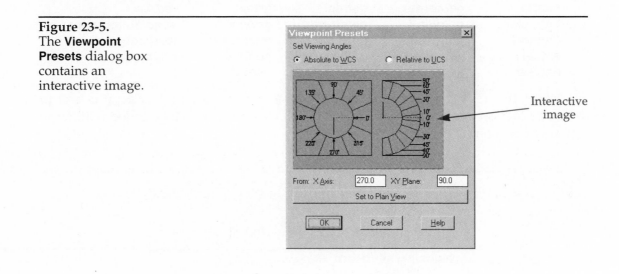

Interactive image

Dialog Example 3

Create the following two files as shown, then load the AutoLISP file. To initiate, type DRAW at the Command: prompt.

```
//EXAMPLE3.DCL
//Defines a dialog box that presents three drawing options to the user.
//
draw : dialog {
  label = "Select Drawing Option";
  :     text_part {
        label = "Select object type to draw: ";
  }
  : row {
    : button {
        key        = "line";
        label      = "Line";
        mnemonic   = "L";
        fixed_width = true;
    }
    : button {
        key        = "circle";
        label      = "Circle";
        mnemonic   = "C";
        fixed_width = true;
    }
    : button {
        key        = "arc";
        label      = "Arc";
        mnemonic   = "A";
        fixed_width = true;
    }
    : button {
        key        = "cancel";
        label      = "Cancel";
        is_cancel  = true;
        fixed_width = true;
    }
  }
}
```

```
;EXAMPLE3.LSP
;This file displays the dialog box defined in EXAMPLE3.DCL and begins the
; selected drawing command as specified by the user.
;
(defun C:DRAW (/ DCL_ID)
  (setq DCL_ID (load_dialog "EXAMPLE3.DCL"))
  (if    (not (new_dialog "draw" DCL_ID))
        (exit)
  )
  (action_tile "line" "(setq CMD $key) (done_dialog)")
  (action_tile "circle" "(setq CMD $key) (done_dialog)")
  (action_tile "arc" "(setq CMD $key) (done_dialog)")
  (action_tile "cancel" "(setq CMD nil) (done_dialog)")
  (start_dialog)
  (unload_dialog DCL_ID)
  (command CMD)
)
```

Dialog Example 4

This example allows you to select a new current layer from a drop-down list in a dialog box. To access the dialog box, type GOFOR at the Command: prompt.

```
//EXAMPLE4.DCL
// Presents a list of layers to the user.
fourth : dialog {
  label = "Select Layer";
  : popup_list {
    label        = "New Current Layer:";
    mnemonic     = "N";
    key          = "lyr_pop";
    allow_accept = true;
    width        = 32;
  }
  ok_cancel;
}
```

```
;;EXAMPLE4.LSP
;;
(defun  CHECKOUT ()
  (setq LD (tblsearch "LAYER" (nth (atoi (get_tile "lyr_pop")) LL))
        LN (cdr (assoc 2 LD))
        LS (cdr (assoc 70 LD))
  )
  (if    (and
            (/= 1 LS)
            (/= 65 LS)
         )
         (progn
           (setvar "CLAYER" (nth (atoi (get_tile "lyr_pop")) LL))
           (done_dialog)
         )
         (alert "Selected layer is frozen!")
  ) )
(defun C:GOFOR ()
  (setq DCL_ID (load_dialog "EXAMPLE4.DCL"))
  (if (not (new_dialog "fourth" DCL_ID)) (exit))
  (start_list "lyr_pop")
  (setq LL '()
        NL (tblnext "LAYER" T)
        IDX 0
  )
  (while   NL
           (if    (= (getvar "CLAYER") (cdr (assoc 2 NL)))
                  (setq CL IDX)
                  (setq IDX (1+ IDX))
           )
           (setq LL (append LL (list (cdr (assoc 2 NL)))))
                 NL (tblnext "LAYER")
  )        )
  (mapcar 'add_list LL)
  (end_list)
  (set_tile "lyr_pop" (itoa CL))
  (action_tile "lyr_pop" "(if (= $reason 4) (mode_tile \"accept\" 2))")
  (action_tile "accept" "(CHECKOUT)")
  (start_dialog)
  (unload_dialog DCL_ID)
  (princ)
)
```

Chapter Test

Write your answers in the spaces provided.

1. What are the three-letter extensions of the two types of files that must be created to construct a functioning dialog box? _____

2. When referring to a dialog box, what is a tile? _____
    _____
    _____
    _____

3. When defining a dialog or tile, inside of what are all of the required attributes for a tile definition placed? _____

4. What symbol indicates a comment inside a DCL file? _____

5. Write the appropriate notation for the first line of a DCL file that defines a dialog box named **Test**. _____

6. Write the appropriate notation in a DCL file that defines the text in the title bar of a dialog box named **Select Application**. _____
    _____

7. Write the notation for defining a cluster of four buttons labeled **OK**, **NEXT**, **CANCEL**, and **HELP**. _____
    _____

8. What type of file controls a DCL file? _____

9. Write the notation that would appear in the file in Question 8 that loads a dialog file named PICKFILE. _____
    _____

10. What is a *key* in a DCL file? _____
    _____
    _____

11. What is the function of a *mnemonic* attribute? _____
    _____
    _____

12. Write the proper DCL file notation for the first line that identifies a button. _____

Problems

1. Create a dialog box that contains the following items. Write the required DCL and AutoLISP files.

   A. Title bar—**Dialog Box Test**

   B. Label—**This is a test.**

   C. **OK** button

2. Create a dialog box that contains the following items. Write the required DCL and AutoLISP files.

   A. Title bar—**Date**

   B. Label—**Current date**

   C. Action button—**Display Current Date**

   D. **OK** button

3. Create a dialog box that performs the following tasks. Then, write the required DCL and AutoLISP files.

   A. Displays the current date.

   B. Displays the current time.

   C. Displays the current drawing name.

   D. Contains buttons to update current date and time.

   E. Contains an **OK** button.

Advanced AutoCAD Features and OLE

Advanced **Clipboard Support**

Copying, cutting, and pasting are the primary methods for relocating and duplicating data in Windows-based applications. With the help of the Windows Clipboard, AutoCAD Release 14 allows you to copy objects within a drawing, from one drawing to another, or from one application (software program) to another.

The Windows Clipboard is one of the applications that is included with Microsoft Windows. Anytime you cut or copy data in a Windows application, it is automatically stored in the Clipboard.

The Windows Clipboard provides a simple means of taking information from one application into another application, or from one drawing into another. Think of the Clipboard as a temporary storage area, or buffer, for text and graphic information. Once an image or text is copied to the Clipboard, it can be pasted as desired into any Windows program file, such as a word processor document, a spreadsheet, or even an AutoCAD drawing. Information copied to the Clipboard remains there until it is replaced by copying new information.

Copying, cutting, and pasting

The copy, cut, and paste features are typically found under the Edit pull-down menu of the Windows application you are using. Like most other Windows applications, AutoCAD has an **Edit** menu with these Clipboard-based options available. See Figure 24-1.

The primary function of each option is listed here. Detailed information on the use of these features is provided using several examples throughout this chapter.

- **Cut.** Removes the selected text or graphic objects and places them on the Clipboard. In AutoCAD, this starts the **CUTCLIP** command.
- **Copy.** Copies the selected text or graphic objects and places them on the Clipboard. In AutoCAD, this starts the **COPYCLIP** command.
- **Copy Link.** Copies all objects visible on the screen and places them on the Clipboard. In AutoCAD, this starts the **COPYLINK** command.

Figure 24-1.
The **Edit** pull-down menu in AutoCAD contains the Clipboard-based options.

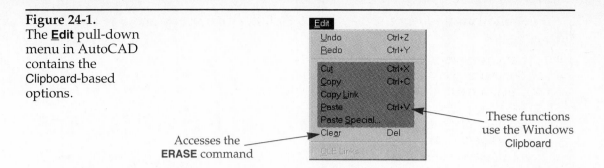

Accesses the **ERASE** command

These functions use the Windows Clipboard

- **Paste.** Pastes the contents of the Clipboard into the current drawing. In AutoCAD, this starts the **PASTECLIP** command. Note that pasted objects are not removed from the Clipboard. They can be pasted into multiple locations in your drawing.
- **Paste Special.** Opens the **Paste Special** dialog box where additional parameters can be set for the incoming data. In AutoCAD, this starts the **PASTESPEC** command.
- **Clear.** Starts the **ERASE** command. This option is included for Microsoft Office Compliance only, and is in no way different from the standard **ERASE** command in AutoCAD.

These Clipboard-based options can be used in many ways in AutoCAD. They can be used to copy information within a drawing session. Both drawing data and text data can be manipulated this way to help save time and maintain accuracy.

Copying, cutting, and pasting in an AutoCAD drawing session

Typically, when you need to copy or move drawing objects in AutoCAD, you use the **COPY** and **MOVE** commands. For most drawing requirements, these commands are easier to use than **COPYCLIP**, **CUTCLIP**, and **PASTECLIP**. When using these features, it is important to understand how each of the available commands works.

Both the **Cut** and the **Copy** options place drawing information on the Clipboard in the same manner. The difference is similar to the relationship between the **MOVE** and the **COPY** commands in AutoCAD. **Cut** works like **MOVE**—it removes the drawing information from its original location and places it on the Clipboard. **Copy**, however, places the same information on the Clipboard but leaves the original objects in place. Deciding which one to use depends on whether or not you require the original objects to remain in place.

The **Paste** option takes the information from the Clipboard and inserts it into the current drawing session. Note that the pasted objects come in as an *unnamed block*, a block that AutoCAD has named through an automated process. Unnamed blocks typically have names similar to A$C48534010. The pasted objects are assembled into a block, which you need to explode if you wish to edit the pasted objects.

The primary advantages of using the Clipboard for copying and moving objects in a drawing session are speed and convenience. By pressing the [Ctrl]+[C] keystroke or a menu pick, you enter the **COPYCLIP** command and can select objects to be copied. When using this command, there is no need to indicate a base point for the copy operation. To place the objects or copies in the desired location, press [Ctrl]+[V] or pick **Paste**. When the incoming data from the clipboard is AutoCAD geometry, the **PASTECLIP** command works just like the **INSERT** command, asking for an insertion point, scale factors, and rotation angles. In this situation, the insertion point is at the lower-left corner of the incoming block.

The following sequence shows the steps followed to copy and paste objects in a drawing:

Command: *(press [Ctrl]+[C])*
Command: '_copyclip
Select objects: *(select the desired objects)*
Select objects: ↵
Command: *(press [Ctrl]+[V])*
Command: '_pasteclip
Insertion point: *(select the insertion point)*
X scale factor ⟨1⟩ / Corner / XYZ: ↵
Y scale factor (default=X): ↵
Rotation angle ⟨0⟩: ↵
Command:

It is important to remember that the new object is actually a block and must be exploded before being edited. Also, this pasting example uses the default scale factors and rotation angles, but these values can be adjusted as required for any given situation. If the **COPYCLIP** command is used when objects are grip selected and Noun/Verb selection is enabled, the selected objects are copied directly to the Clipboard with no further prompts.

The Clipboard-based features can be very useful when editing dialog box text. Text objects in your drawing are treated like any other drawing object and become a block object when pasted. However, in an edit box within a dialog session, the text is copied, cut, and pasted as text only. This is true within any edit box in any dialog session, as well as the text-editing area of the **Multiline Text Editor** dialog box.

The following example shows the **Edit Attributes** dialog box while editing attributes in a drawing title block. In this example, the drawing was completed, checked, and approved on the same date. Observe how a quick copy and paste operation can be used to reduce typing requirements.

In Figure 24-2A, the text listed in the **Date drawn** edit box has been highlighted. The entire contents of an edit box can be highlighted by using the [Tab] key to set the keyboard focus, or you can double-click in the target edit box. After highlighting the text to be copied, press [Ctrl]+[C] to copy it to the clipboard. Now, move your cursor to the edit box that you are copying the text to, as shown in Figure 24-2B. Press [Ctrl]+[V] to paste the copied text to its destination.

Figure 24-2.
Copying and pasting in a dialog box. A—Within the edit box, highlight the text to be copied and then press [Ctrl]+[C]. B—Move the cursor to another edit box and press [Ctrl]+[V]. The copied text is inserted.

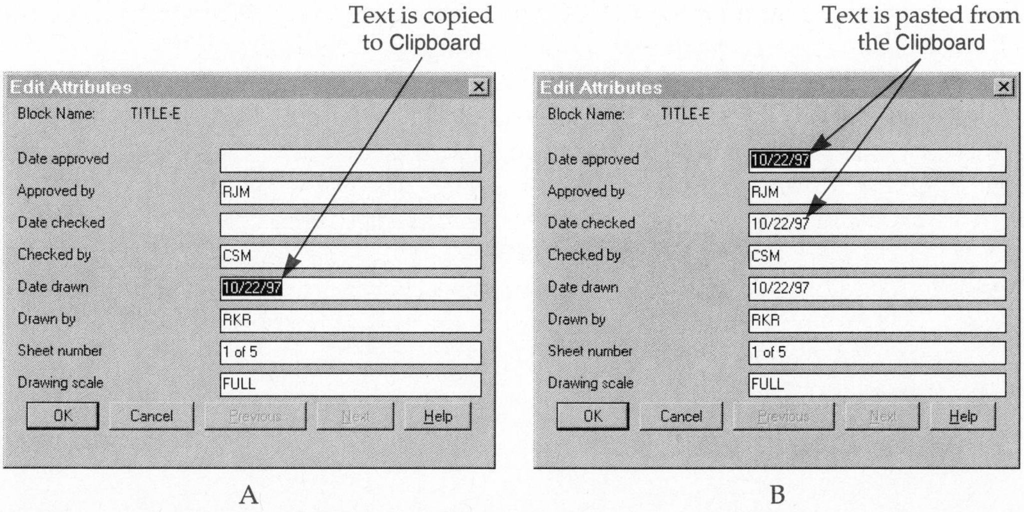

The previous example shows the entire contents of the edit box being copied, but it could just as well be only a portion of the contents. An example of this more specialized editing technique is demonstrated here using the **Multiline Text Editor** dialog box to copy part of one multiline text object into another. In this example, the customized portion of the text defined for a dimension object is cut and moved to another dimension.

Figure 24-3A shows the **Multiline Text Editor** dialog box after a dimension object has been selected for editing with the **DDEDIT** command. Highlighting the text is done by pointing to the start, pressing and holding the pick button, and then dragging the cursor to the end of the text and releasing the pick button.

In Figure 24-3B, a second dimension object is selected for editing with the **DDEDIT** command. In this illustration, the dimension text is the default value, as specified by the "⟨⟩" symbols.

Position the cursor where the Clipboard text is to be pasted. Next, press [Ctrl]+[V] to paste the Clipboard contents, Figure 24-3C.

Figure 24-3.
Copying and pasting text in the **Multiline Text Editor** dialog box. A—Highlight the text being copied and press [Ctrl]+[C]. B—Select a different dimension for editing and position the cursor where the new text is to be located. C—Press [Ctrl]+[V] to paste the text from the Clipboard.

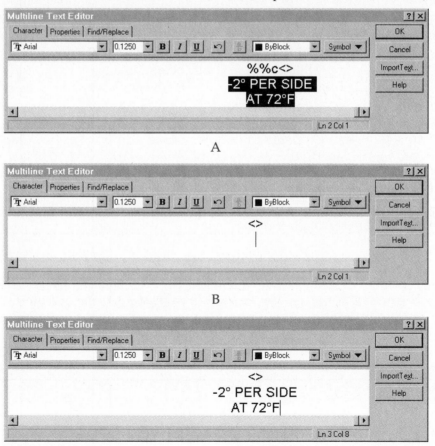

Copying information between drawings

The Windows 95 and Windows NT 4.0 operating systems allow multiple sessions of AutoCAD to be active at a time. This provides a powerful means for bringing partial drawing information from one drawing to another.

The following sequence shows an example of how to copy drawing information from one drawing to another using **COPYCLIP** and **PASTECLIP**. First, open both the drawing you wish to copy objects *from* and the drawing you wish to copy objects *to*. Because AutoCAD can only open one drawing per program window, you will need to open two different sessions of AutoCAD.

If no AutoCAD sessions are currently running, the easiest way is to simply double-click the AutoCAD icon on your desktop twice in a row. This will start two sessions of AutoCAD. If one session is already open, start another session by using the start menu, or you can minimize or move the current AutoCAD window so that you can access the AutoCAD icon on your desktop. An easy way to make both windows visible at once is to first close all windows except for the two AutoCAD graphics windows. Next, right-click on a blank area of the Windows task bar and select the Tile Windows <u>V</u>ertically option. Open the appropriate drawings and go to the AutoCAD window that contains the geometry you wish to copy. Now do the following:

```
Command: COPYCLIP↵
Select objects: (select the desired objects)
Select objects: ↵
Command:
```

Next, use either the [ALT]+[TAB] key combination, the task bar, or just pick the appropriate window to go to the drawing that you are copying the information *to*. Enter the **PASTECLIP** command:

```
Command: PASTECLIP↵
Insertion point: (select the insertion point)
X scale factor ⟨1⟩ / Corner / XYZ: ↵
Y scale factor (default=X): ↵
Rotation angle ⟨0⟩: ↵
Command:
```

NOTE

When picked from the toolbar, the <u>**Edit**</u> pull-down menu, or by using the available accelerator keys, the **COPYCLIP**, **CUTCLIP**, and **PASTECLIP** commands are entered using a leading apostrophe. This implies that the commands can be entered transparently, but these are not actually transparent commands. Attempting to enter one of these commands while another AutoCAD command is active has no effect, and issues a message that the command entry was ignored. The leading apostrophe has no adverse effects when entered at the Command: prompt.

PROFESSIONAL TIP

When pasted objects that include associative dimensions are exploded, the dimension objects are automatically updated to the current dimension variable settings. If you explode a pasted object containing associative dimensions, be sure to verify all included dimensions for correct formatting.

Pasting objects from other applications

When the contents of the Clipboard is text from a standard text editor (such as the Windows Notepad), pasting it into AutoCAD brings it in as a multiline text object. Normally, AutoCAD places the new object at the upper-left corner of the current drawing display area. However, if any objects are currently grip selected and Noun/Verb selection is enabled, AutoCAD replaces the grip-selected objects and places the text in the same location.

Other object types pasted from the Clipboard, such as Microsoft Word text, are brought in as OLE objects. OLE objects do not replace grip-selected AutoCAD objects. OLE objects are covered later in this chapter.

Using the **Clipboard Viewer**

Once a graphic image or an item of text is copied to the Clipboard, it remains there until something new is copied or until you exit Windows. The contents of the Clipboard can be available for use long after you have copied them. The application provided for you to work with the Clipboard contents is called the Clipboard Viewer.

The Clipboard Viewer allows you to examine the current contents of the Clipboard. Additionally, you can clear the Clipboard and save the contents to a file for later use. The program icon for the Clipboard Viewer is located in the **Accessories** group menu in the **Programs** menu, Figure 24-4.

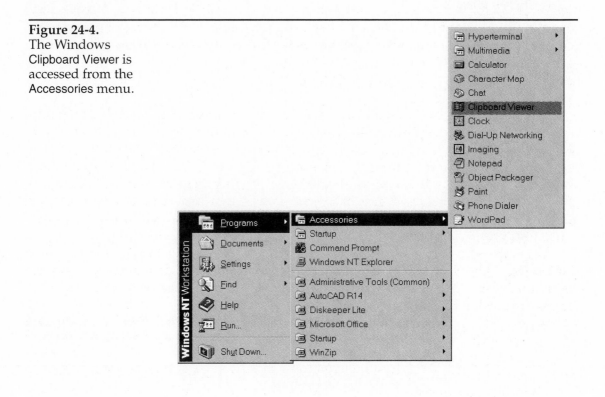

Figure 24-4.
The Windows Clipboard Viewer is accessed from the Accessories menu.

When the viewer is launched, it will display the currently stored data. If you cannot see all the image or text, use the scroll bars. In Figure 24-5, several AutoCAD objects have been copied and are displayed in the Clipboard Viewer window.

The contents of the Clipboard can also be saved to disk for later use. The Clipboard contents are saved as a .clp file, regardless of the type of information. This file can then be opened later using the Clipboard Viewer. To save a .clp file, select **Save As** from the **File** pull-down menu in the Clipboard Viewer. Specify the directory location and file name in the **Save As** dialog box. To open the saved file, select **Open** from the **File** menu and specify the file to open in the **Open** dialog box. When a .clp file is opened, the

Figure 24-5.
The Windows
Clipboard Viewer
displays the current
contents of the
Clipboard.

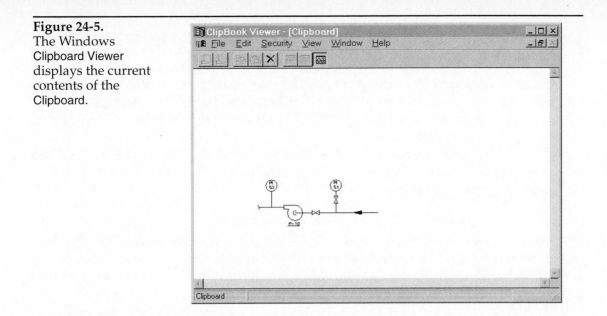

contents of the file are copied to the clipboard, and are then ready to be pasted into other applications.

If you have copied a very large image or many pages of text to the clipboard and no longer need the data, you can clear the contents of the Clipboard. This is useful when you are running low on memory and need to free up resources. To clear the contents of the Clipboard, select Delete from the Edit menu in the Clipboard Viewer.

Object Linking and Embedding (OLE)

Object Linking and Embedding, or *OLE*, is a feature of the Windows operating system that allows data from many different source applications to be combined into a single document. A technical document will often present data in several forms to ensure effective communications. For example, the technical documentation for a product might include formatted text from a word processor, technical drawings from AutoCAD, charts and graphs from a spreadsheet program, and even graphic images from a paint program. Understanding the use of OLE will help you to produce high quality documentation to communicate your ideas effectively.

As implied by the name, there are two distinct aspects to OLE: *linking* and *embedding*. Both linking and embedding allow you to insert data from one application into another, but they differ in the way they store the information. The following terms are used in the OLE process:

- **Object.** A piece of data created by a Windows application that supports OLE server functions. Such data could be text from a word processor, an AutoCAD drawing, or a graphic image.
- **OLE server.** A source application. For example, when using OLE to bring an AutoCAD drawing into your word processor, AutoCAD becomes the OLE server.
- **OLE client.** A destination application. AutoCAD is an OLE client when you use OLE to bring an object into AutoCAD from another application.

While working through these examples, you will be switching between applications in Windows. One convenient means of switching applications is using the [Alt]+[Tab] keystroke. Or, you may find it more convenient to have both windows visible at once on your desktop. Another option is to press [Ctrl]+[Esc] and select the application you need to be active.

Embedding objects in AutoCAD

The term *embedding* refers to storing a copy of an OLE object in a client document. Embedding differs from importing because an imported object maintains no association with its source application. An embedded object is edited using the source application, or server. For example, if a Corel Photo-Paint picture (.pcx) is embedded in an AutoCAD drawing, double-clicking on the picture starts the Corel Photo-Paint application and loads the selected picture. Using the **Image** command to bring a .pcx file into AutoCAD brings in the graphic image, but it has no association with the original application.

To embed an OLE object in an AutoCAD drawing, first copy it to the Clipboard from the source application. Return to AutoCAD and paste the Clipboard contents using **PASTECLIP**. When the contents of the Clipboard is not AutoCAD data and contains OLE information, it is embedded in the AutoCAD drawing.

One application for using embedded graphics is using a Paint picture in a title block for a logo design. In Figure 24-6, the Paint program has been used to design a logo graphic. Selecting the graphic image and pressing [Ctrl]+[C] copies the selected image to the Clipboard.

Once you have copied the image to the Clipboard, return to AutoCAD. Now press [Ctrl]+[V] to paste the Clipboard contents into the AutoCAD drawing. A pasted image appears in the upper-left corner of the graphics screen, Figure 24-7. Moving your cursor to point at the pasted image changes your cursor into a four-way arrow. Press and hold the pick button to move the image. Release the pick button when the image is in the desired location.

Figure 24-6.
A graphic image can be designed in the Paint program.

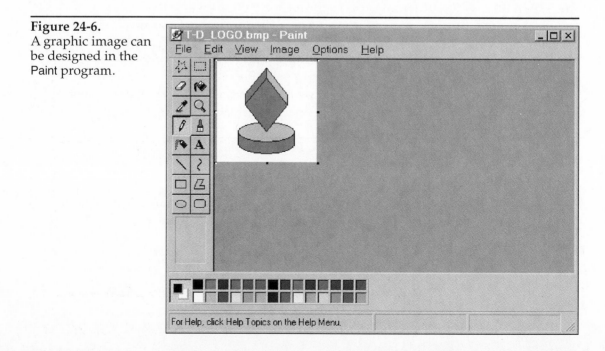

Figure 24-7.
The pasted image
appears in the
upper-left corner.

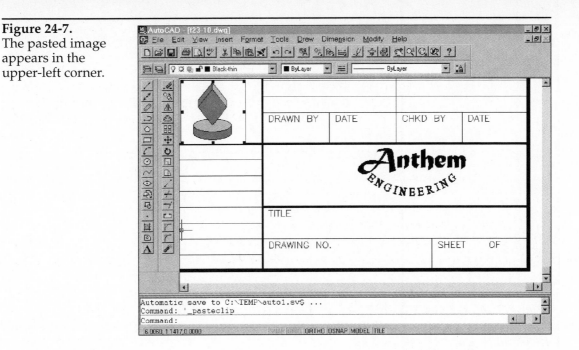

Once the image is positioned correctly, pick anywhere on the screen that is not on the image and the grips will disappear. Figure 24-8 shows the image in its final position within the title block.

Note that the filled squares surrounding the image can be used to adjust the size and proportions of the image. Pointing to the grips changes the cursor to the appropriate resizing cursor. Press and hold the pick button to move the grip. Release the pick button when you are finished adjusting the image. The illustration in Figure 24-9 shows the function of each of the grip points, as well as the appearance of the cursor when moving an image.

Because the image is embedded, it maintains an association with the original application. You can use the original application whenever you need to edit the image. The application can be initiated by double-clicking on the image. You can also use the **OLE Object Menu** to modify the object. This menu is displayed by right-clicking on the image. This displays the menu shown in Figure 24-10.

Figure 24-8.
The image moved to
the proper location.

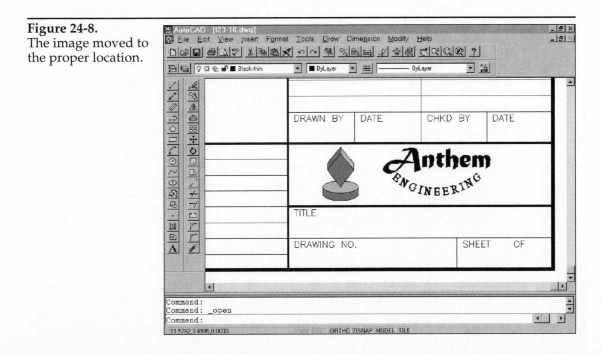

Figure 24-9.
The resize and
move cursor shapes
for pasted images.

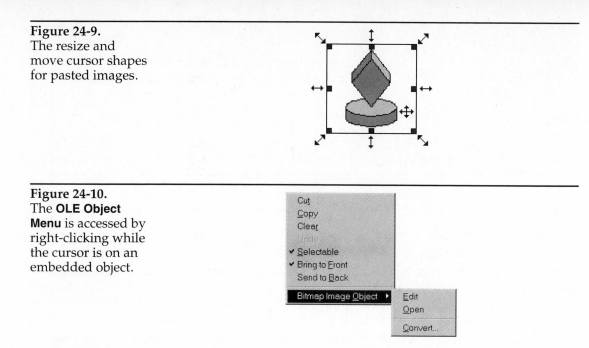

Figure 24-10.
The **OLE Object
Menu** is accessed by
right-clicking while
the cursor is on an
embedded object.

The bottom line on this menu indicates the type of object. In this case, it is a Bitmap Image Object. The menu items function as follows:

- **Cut.** Removes the OLE object and copies it to the Clipboard.
- **Copy.** Copies the object to the Clipboard.
- **Clear.** Removes the object from the drawing without copying it to the Clipboard.
- **Undo.** Reverses the last action performed with this menu. Similar to AutoCAD's **U** command, this can be used repeatedly. Note that this will not undo object updates done by the server application.
- **Selectable.** Controls whether the OLE object can be selected when using AutoCAD's editing commands. When a check mark appears by this option, the object can be selected by pointing at it and picking. Whether an item is selectable or not, right-clicking on it displays the **OLE Object Menu**.
- **Bring to Front.** Brings the item to the front, similar to the function of the **DRAWORDER** command.
- **Send to Back.** Sends the item to the back, similar to the function of the **DRAWORDER** command.
- **Object Type Cascade.** Displays options for editing, opening, and converting the object to other possible object types. For example, a Bitmap Image Object can be converted into a Picture Object. When converted to a Picture Object, the object has the same properties as an image attached using the **IMAGE** command. It loses its association with the Paint program.

It is possible to embed virtually any OLE object into an AutoCAD drawing. This includes word processing documents, charts, graphs, spreadsheets, audio clips, and video clips. Using these various OLE data types can transform a standard technical drawing into a complete multimedia presentation. As you use these techniques, try to use only objects that have significant communication value, rather than cluttering up a drawing with unnecessary "bells and whistles."

NOTE The **U** and **UNDO** commands in AutoCAD have no effect on any changes made to an OLE object. Additionally, the **REDO** command does not reverse an undo executed from the **OLE Object Menu**.

Embedding AutoCAD drawing objects in other documents

AutoCAD Release 14 provides both client and server OLE functions. This means that in addition to using embedded OLE objects, AutoCAD can provide objects for other applications. A common use for this feature is to combine technical drawings and illustrations with text in a technical document created with a word processing program.

If you already have a drawing created that you need to embed in another document, first open the drawing in AutoCAD. Press [Ctrl]+[C] or select **Copy** from the **Edit** pull-down menu and select the desired objects. This places the selected objects on the Clipboard. For this example, the entire AutoCAD drawing shown in Figure 24-11 is copied to the Clipboard.

In this example, the Windows WordPad program is used as the client application. In this next step, the destination document is opened in WordPad, Figure 24-12A. After opening the document, select the Edit menu and pick the Paste option to embed the AutoCAD drawing. Note that the embedded drawing will be placed at the current cursor location. You are not prompted for a location or a size. If you need to change either the location or the size, you can do so by clicking on the drawing or on the grips at the edges or corners and dragging the image. Figure 24-12B shows the document with the drawing embedded, resized, and moved to the center of the document.

Embedding an OLE object in an application also modifies the menu to display new options when the object is highlighted. The Edit menu in the WordPad program appears as shown in Figure 24-13 after highlighting the embedded drawing.

Once the drawing is embedded, it loses all connection with the original drawing file. This means that subsequent editing of this drawing will not affect the original

Figure 24-11.
To prepare to embed a drawing, copy it to the Clipboard using [Ctrl]+[C] or by picking **Copy** from the **Edit** pull-down menu.

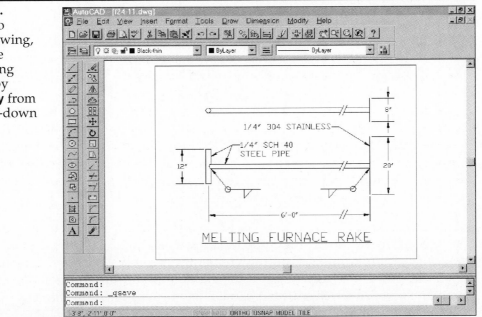

Figure 24-12.
Inserting an
AutoCAD drawing
object into a
WordPad document.
A—The original
document.
B—The document
after the drawing is
embedded.

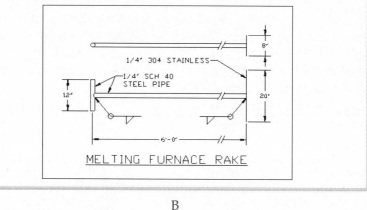

A

B

source file. In order to edit the embedded drawing, highlight the image and select Edit
Drawing Object from the Edit pull-down menu or simply double-click on the drawing.
When the AutoCAD window opens, examine the title bar and note the specified file
name. In Figure 24-14, the title bar shows the drawing name as Drawing in Document. If
you access the **SAVEAS** command, the current file name is set to something similar to

Figure 24-13.
New choices are
displayed on the
Edit menu when the
embedded drawing
is selected.

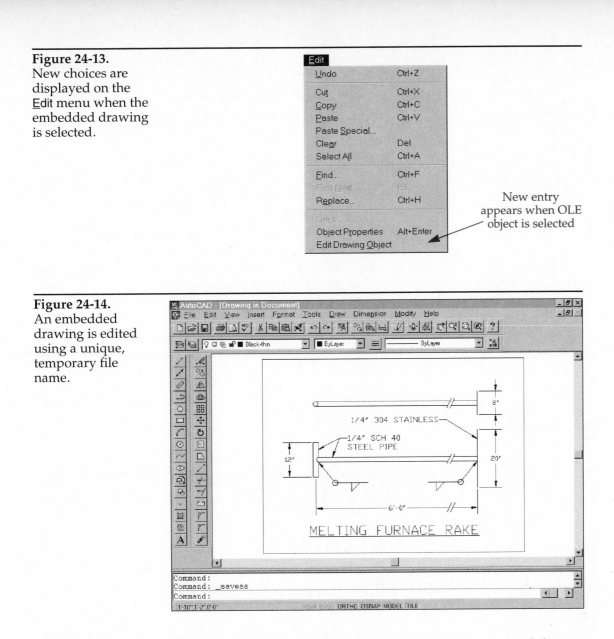

Figure 24-14.
An embedded
drawing is edited
using a unique,
temporary file
name.

A$C37DA7DFF.DWG. This is a temporary name assigned to the drawing while it is being edited, and may change from one editing session to another.

Updating refers to recording your changes to the embedded object within the client document. There are two ways to update the file when you have finished editing it. Picking the **File** pull-down menu displays a new option, such as **Update WordPad**. Selecting this option replaces the currently embedded drawing with the revised version. You also can simply exit AutoCAD. If changes have been made, the dialog box shown in Figure 24-15 will be displayed. Selecting the **Yes** button updates the client document.

Figure 24-15.
If there are unsaved
changes in your
drawing, this dialog
box is displayed.

Linking objects in AutoCAD

Linking is similar to embedding in that objects from one application are brought into another application. With linking, however, a direct link is maintained between the source data and the OLE object in the client application. Linked objects support *Dynamic Data Exchange (DDE)*. As the source data is modified, the link in the client application is updated.

To link an object within AutoCAD, first it must be copied to the clipboard. When bringing the object into AutoCAD, select the **Paste Special...** option from the **Edit** pull-down menu. Using this option activates the **Paste Special** dialog box, see Figure 24-16.

The source of the information currently on the Clipboard is displayed in the upper-left area of the dialog box. Two radio buttons allow you to specify whether or not to copy the information as a link. If **Paste** is active, the object will be embedded. If the **Paste Link** option is active, the object will be brought in as a link. If you are embedding the object, you may have several format options, depending on the type of data being pasted. These formats are shown in the **As:** list box. A linked object comes in as the file type that is associated with the server application.

Figure 24-16.
The **PASTESPEC** command opens the **Paste Special** dialog box. The Clipboard contains text from a Word document. A—The **Paste** option embeds the object, and several formats are available. B—The **Paste Link** option creates a link to the object, and only a single format can be used.

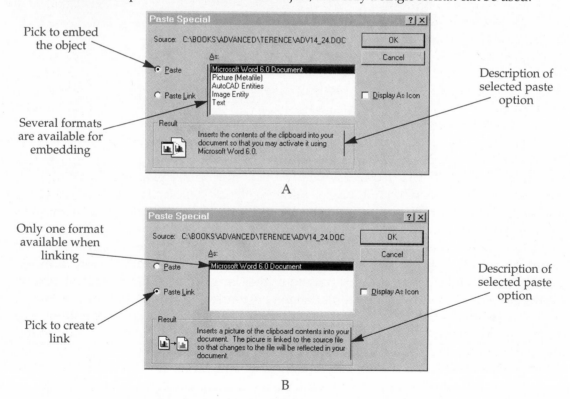

INSERTOBJ
IO

Insert
→ OLE Object...

Insert
toolbar

OLE Object

A linked object can also be inserted using the **INSERTOBJ** command. Select this command by picking the **OLE Object** button from the **Insert** toolbar, selecting **OLE Object...** from the **Insert** pull-down menu, or typing IO or INSERTOBJ at the Command: prompt. The following example uses this command.

First, create a simple image in Paint and save the image as a bitmap (.bmp) file. Then in AutoCAD, select **OLE Object...** from the **Insert** pull-down menu. The **Insert Object** dialog box appears, Figure 24-17A.

The **Create New** radio button is selected by default. The **Object Type:** list box shows the registered applications that support OLE functions. This list varies based on the software installed on your system. Read each selection carefully, because some programs can produce varied types of data. For example, if you have Microsoft Word installed, you may see options for producing a picture or a document. The option you select affects how the specified program is started, and the data type it will be sending back to AutoCAD.

To create a new object, highlight the desired program and pick the **OK** button. The appropriate application is called, and you can create the object. When you are finished creating the OLE object, select the Update option from your File menu or just exit the application. If you exit before you save, the application will ask you if you want to update the object before you exit.

If the object is already created and saved, select the **Create from File** radio button. The dialog box appears as shown in Figure 24-17B. Enter the path and file name in the **File:** edit box or pick the **Browse...** button to select the file from a selection dialog box. Activate the **Link** check box to create a link between the object file and the AutoCAD drawing. Pick the **OK** button, and a copy of the selected object appears in the upper-left corner of the graphics screen area. See Figure 24-18.

To edit the linked OLE object, double-click on it. This opens Paint, the server application. See Figure 24-19. Any changes you make to the image are updated in both the OLE object in the drawing and in the source file. The title bar of the Paint program shows that the object's original file is opened for editing.

All linked OLE objects behave in much the same manner as the previous example. In certain applications, the updates may be slower, but they are still automatic. To change the way a link is updated or to adjust current links in a drawing, select **OLE Links...** from the **Edit** menu. This opens the **Links** dialog box, as shown in Figure 24-20. If no links are present in the current drawing, this item is grayed-out in the pull-down menu.

The **Links:** list box displays all active links in the current drawing. The file name of the link and the update method are also shown. By default, a link is automatically updated. If you do not want the updates to be automatic, pick the **Manual** radio button. To force an update, select the **Update Now** button. The **Break Link** button removes link information from the OLE object and removes any association with the source file—effectively converting a linked object into an embedded object. Select the **Change Source...** button to change the source file with which the link is associated. Selecting **Open Source** opens the linked file using the originating application.

Figure 24-17.
The **Insert Object** dialog box can be used to link an object to an AutoCAD drawing.
A—To create a new object, select the type of object and pick **OK**. B—To create a link to the
object's file, pick the **Create from File** radio button, select the file name, and pick the
Link check box.

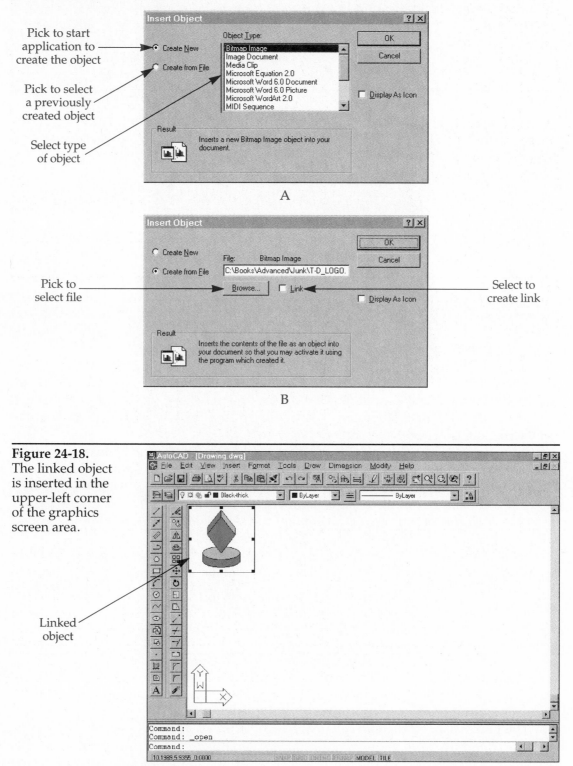

Pick to start
application to
create the object

Pick to select
a previously
created object

Select type
of object

A

Pick to
select file

Select to
create link

B

Figure 24-18.
The linked object
is inserted in the
upper-left corner
of the graphics
screen area.

Linked
object

Figure 24-19.
Double-clicking
on the linked object
starts the server
application
and opens the
source file.

Source
file

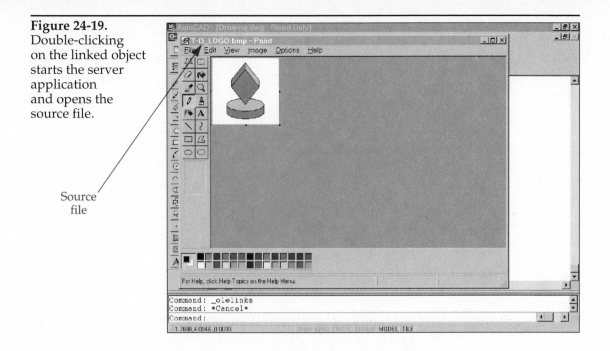

Figure 24-20.
The **Links** dialog box displays all active links.

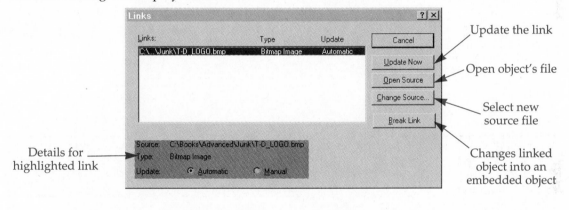

Update the link

Open object's file

Select new
source file

Changes linked
object into an
embedded object

Details for
highlighted link

NOTE   Some types of files (such as sound files, video clips, and animations) offer additional options within the AutoCAD drawing. For example, when you right-click on a linked or embedded video clip, the object type cascade shows a **Play** option. In the case of a video clip, the **Play** option is only enabled if an associated application for playing the clip is available.

Linking AutoCAD drawings in other applications

To embed an AutoCAD drawing in another application, the AutoCAD object is copied to the Clipboard using the **COPYCLIP** command and then pasted into the other application. To insert a linked AutoCAD object into another application, the **COPYLINK** command is used.

COPYLINK

Edit
➡ Copy Link

The **COPYLINK** command is accessed by selecting **Copy Link** from the **Edit** pull-down menu or entering COPYLINK at the Command: prompt. Using **COPYLINK** differs from **COPYCLIP** in that there is no selection process. All currently visible objects are automatically selected as they appear on screen. Also similar to **COPYCLIP**, the selected objects are displayed in a client application in the view that was active when the copy was made.

The Paste Special... selection found on the Edit menu of most Windows applications is used to paste a linked OLE object. The Paste Special dialog box displayed by picking this option may vary slightly from one application to the next, but several basic features are standard. See Figure 24-21. You can also select Object from the Insert pull-down menu in most applications. This is similar to using the **INSERTOBJ** command in AutoCAD.

Remember that the Paste Link option is only available if the source drawing has been saved to a file. Selecting AutoCAD Drawing Object as the data type maintains the pasted material as AutoCAD drawing data. Selecting Picture brings the information in as a .wmf file and Bitmap converts the incoming data to a .bmp file. Using bitmaps ensures that what you see on the screen is exactly what will print, but tends to make the client files very large and uses more memory. Your choice for the incoming data type has no effect on the original file, and the link is still maintained if the data type supports linking.

Figure 24-21.
The Paste Special dialog box is similar in most Windows applications.
A—Microsoft Word.
B—Windows WordPad.

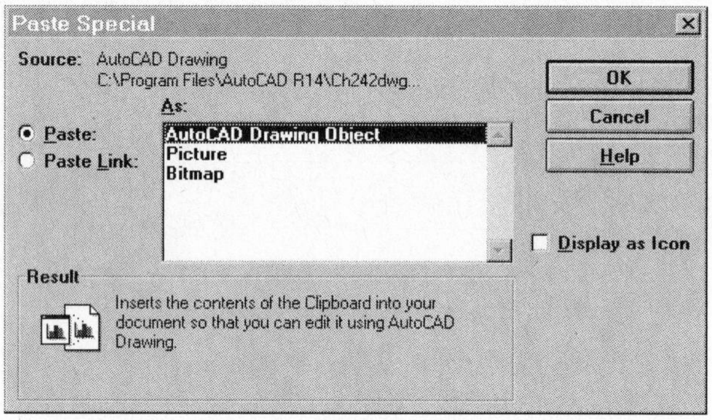

A

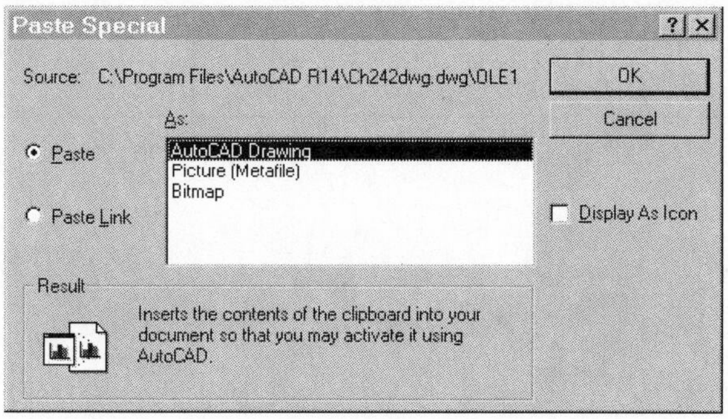

B

Chapter Test

Write your answers in the spaces provided.

1. What Windows application assists in copying objects from one software program to another? _____

    _____

    _____

2. How long does information copied to the application in Question 1 remain there?

    _____

    _____

    _____

3. What are the five commands in AutoCAD that allow you to work with the application in Question 1, and in which menu are they found? _____

    _____

    _____

    _____

4. What are the functions of the [Ctrl]+[C] and [Ctrl]+[V] keystrokes? _____

    _____

    _____

    _____

5. What two commands are used to copy drawing information from one AutoCAD drawing to another? _____

    _____

6. What type of file can be saved from the Clipboard Viewer? _____

    _____

7. What does OLE stand for? _____

    _____

8. Define the following terms:
    Object— _____

    _____

    OLE Server— _____

    _____

    OLE Client— _____

    _____

9. What does *embedding* mean? _____

    _____

    _____

    _____

10. How can you resize an object that has been pasted into another application? ___

    _____

    _____

    _____

11. How can you edit an object that has been embedded into an application? _____

_____

_____

_____

12. What does *linking* mean? _____

_____

_____

_____

13. How do you insert a new object that has not yet been created into an AutoCAD drawing? _____

_____

_____

_____

Drawing Problems

1. Begin a new drawing and name it P24-1, then do the following:
   A. Insert a title block.
   B. Open the Windows Paint program.
   C. Draw a company logo. Copy the design to the clipboard.
   D. Paste the design into the AutoCAD drawing.
   E. Position the design in the title block.
   F. Save the drawing.

2. Open one of your 3D drawings from a previous chapter, then do the following:
   A. Display the object in a hidden line removed format, or as a rendered image.
   B. Copy the object to the clipboard.
   C. Open a word processing program and paste the Clipboard contents to create an embedded object.
   D. Create a memo to a coworker or instructor in which you describe the process used to create the document.
   E. Save the document as P24-2 but do not close the application. Return to AutoCAD and close the drawing without saving.
   F. Return to the word processor and double-click on the pasted object.
   G. Edit the object in some way and save the drawing.
   H. Return to the document and save.

3. Open one of your 3D drawings from a previous chapter. Perform the same functions outlined in Problem 2, but this time create a link between the AutoCAD drawing and the word processing document. Edit the drawing in AutoCAD and observe the results in the document file. Save the document as P24-3 and close the word processor.

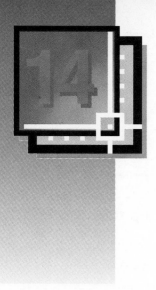

Solid Modeling Tutorial

Introduction

This tutorial is provided as a supplement to the solid modeling techniques presented in Chapter 10, Chapter 11, and Chapter 12. It is a step-by-step process intended as a guide. Directions are given for each step of the process, but exact details regarding which commands to use, where to find them, and exact coordinate locations are not always given. This allows you to use your knowledge of AutoCAD, to consult the online help files, and to refer to the text for answers. The model for this tutorial is the support base shown in Figure A-1.

Figure A-1.

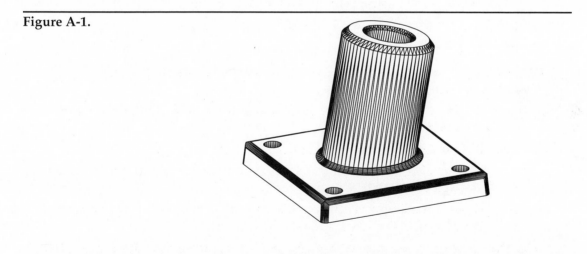

Constructing the Base of the Model

The base of the part is first drawn as a region. Then, the region is extruded into the finished height. Finally, holes are added to the base.
1. Draw an 8″ square and convert it to a region.
2. Draw a ∅.75″ solid cylinder, 1″ tall, with its center 1″ from each side of the region in the lower-left corner.
3. Create an array so that there is a cylinder in each corner of the region located the exact distance from the corners as the first. Your drawing should look like Figure A-2.
4. Extrude the base to a height of 1″ and give a taper angle of 5°.

5. Display the object in a 3D viewpoint. With hidden lines removed, your drawing should look like Figure A-3.
6. Subtract the four cylinders from the base.
7. Set the **FACETRES** value to 1.0 and remove the hidden lines. Your drawing should look like Figure A-4.

Figure A-2.

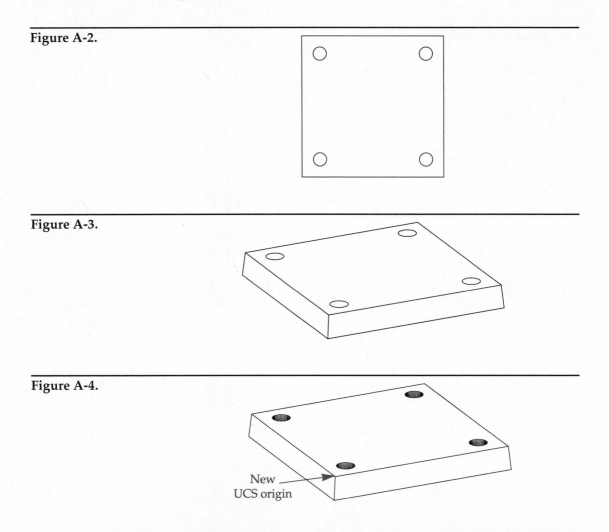

Figure A-3.

Figure A-4.

New ——
UCS origin

Constructing the Cylinder

First, the large cylinder is constructed. Then, holes are constructed inside the cylinder. Finally, the cylinder assembly is tilted on its axis.

1. Create a UCS on the top face of the base with the origin at the lower-left corner, as shown in Figure A-4. Display the UCS icon at the origin of the new UCS.
2. Draw a cylinder located at the exact center of the top of the base. Use a diameter of 4″ and a height of 6″.
3. Draw a ∅1.5″ cylinder 1.5″ high with its base centered on the bottom of the large cylinder.
4. Draw a ∅2″ cylinder 4.5″ high with its base centered on the top of the previous cylinder. See Figure A-5.
5. Move all three cylinders down into the base .5″.
6. Rotate all three cylinders 10° on the Y axis. See Figure A-6.
7. Union the two smaller cylinders.
8. Subtract the two small unioned cylinders from the large cylinder.
9. Union the base and large cylinder. Your drawing should look like Figure A-7.

Figure A-5.

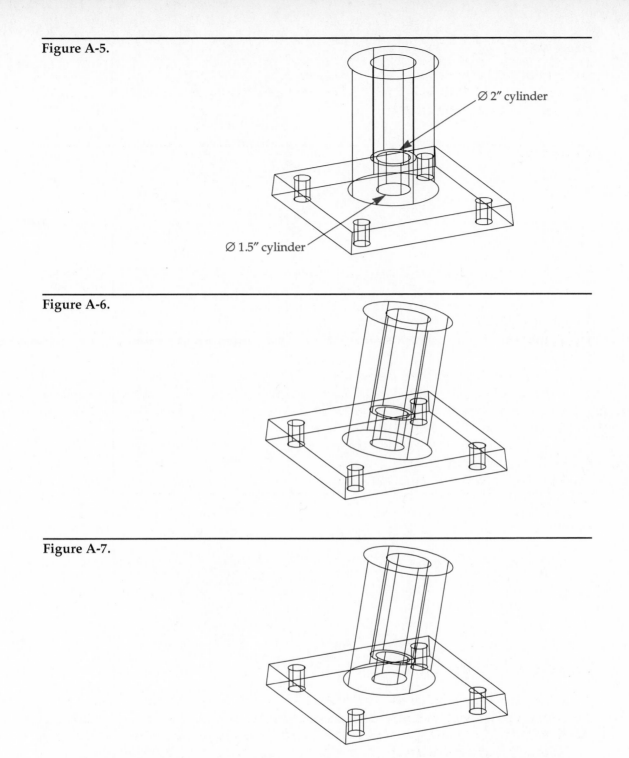

Ø 2" cylinder

Ø 1.5" cylinder

Figure A-6.

Figure A-7.

Adding Chamfers and Fillets

Fillets and chamfers are added to the union of the base and cylinder to complete the object.

1. Fillet the intersection of the cylinder and the base with a .25" radius.
2. Apply a .25", 45° angle chamfer to the top outside edge of the cylinder.
3. Apply a .15", 45° angle chamfer to the top inside edge of the hole in the cylinder. Your drawing should look like Figure A-8.

Figure A-8.

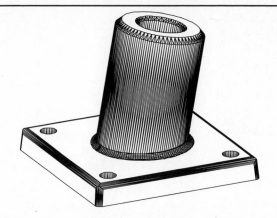

Creating Slices and Sections

To complete the model, you must create a section view. To do this, you must slice the finished object.

1. Rotate the current UCS 90° on the X axis. Move the origin to the center of the cylinders.
2. Create a slice through the center of the model on the current UCS. Select the back side of the object as the part to keep. The remaining part should look like Figure A-9.
3. Create a section through the center of the model on the current UCS. Use the **3point** option of the **SECTION** command.
4. Move the section above and to the left of the model. Add object and section lines, as shown in Figure A-10.
5. Save the drawing as TUTORIAL.

Figure A-9.

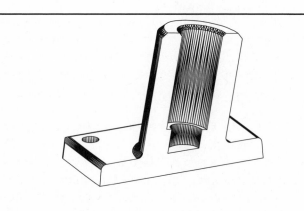

Figure A-10.

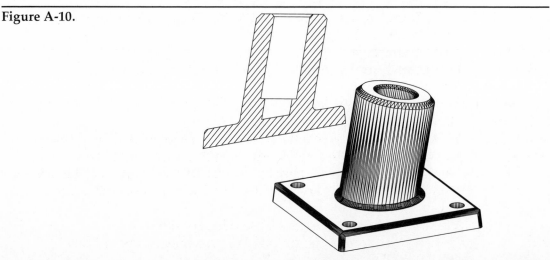

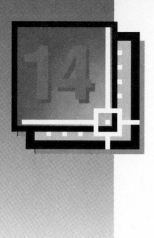

The following list gives common file extensions you may encounter when working with AutoCAD. A definition of each file type is also given.

File Extension	Description
3DS	This is a native 3D Studio file. They can be created with the **3DSOUT** command and imported with the **3DSIN** command.
AC$	A temporary work file.
ADS	An AutoCAD Development System application. Type (**XLOAD** *"filename"*) at the Command: prompt to load.
ADT	Audit report files created with the **AUDIT** command.
AHP	AutoCAD help files.
ARG	When you export a profile, you create a registry (.ARG) file. The documentation incorrectly lists this type of file as a .REG file.
ARX	An AutoCAD Runtime Extension application file. These applications run directly through AutoCAD and not through AutoLISP, like ADS applications. Type (**ARXLOAD** *"filename"*) at the Command: prompt to load.
BAK	Backup drawing files created by AutoCAD when the drawing is saved for the second time and anytime thereafter.
BAT	An MS-DOS batch file that executes a series of commands.
BK*n*	Emergency backup files numbered sequentially (BK1, BK2, BK3, etc.) when AutoCAD unexpectedly terminates. These files are numbered in this way to protect the original BAK file.
BMP	A Windows bitmap file. Use the **BMPOUT** command to export this file.
C	An ADS source code file.
CC	An ADS source code file.
CDF	An attribute extract file in the comma delimited format.
CFG	A configuration file.
CUS	A custom dictionary file.
DBF	Database file used with ASE.
DCC	An ASCII text file that contains color settings for all dialog box elements.
DCE	A dialog box error report file. AutoCAD creates the acad.dce text file if errors are found when trying to load a DCL file. It is placed in the current working directory and is deleted when another DCL file is read successfully.
DLL	A platform-specific, dynamic-linked library file.
DWF	Drawing Web format file for posting drawings on the Internet.

File Extension	Description
DWG	The native AutoCAD drawing file extension.
DWK	An AutoCAD drawing lock file.
DWL	A temporary lock file for an externally referenced drawing.
DXB	A drawing interchange file in binary format.
DXF	A drawing interchange file in ASCII format.
DXX	An attribute extract file in DXF format.
EPS	An encapsulated PostScript file.
ERR	An AutoCAD error file that contains diagnostic information. This type of file is created when AutoCAD "crashes."
EXE	An executable program file.
GIF	A graphics interchange format raster file. This type of file can be imported into AutoCAD using the **GIFIN** command.
H	An ADS include file.
HLP	A Windows help file.
HTM	HyperText Markup Language files for use with Internet applications.
INI	A program initialization file. This is where basic settings for the application are stored.
LIN	A linetype library file.
LOG	This file is a history of all commands and variables used in a drawing session.
LSP	An AutoLISP file.
MID	An identification information file.
MLI	A materials library file.
MLN	A multiline library file.
MNC	A compiled menu file.
MND	A menu description file created for use with the mc.exe program.
MNL	A menu AutoLISP file.
MNR	A menu resource file.
MNS	A menu source file.
MNU	A menu template file in ASCII format.
MSG	An AutoCAD message file that contains information displayed when AutoCAD is opened or when the **ABOUT** command is used.
OLD	The original version of a converted drawing file.
PAT	A hatch pattern library file.
PC2	Complete plot configuration file that stores all the information found in a PCP file plus device-specific information that would otherwise be defined in the acad.cfg file.
PCP	A plot configuration parameters file.
PCX	A bitmap raster image file. This file can be imported into AutoCAD with the **PCXIN** command.
PFA	A PostScript font file ASCII format.
PFB	A PostScript font file binary format.
PFM	A PostScript font metric file.
PLT	A plot output file. Also called a "plot file."
PS	A PostScript interpreter initialization file.
PSF	A PostScript font file.
RX	The acad.rx file contains a list of the ARX program files, which are loaded automatically when you start AutoCAD.
SAB	A binary file that stores solid model geometry.
SAT	An ASCII file that stores solid model geometry. Import and export this file type with the **ACISIN** and **ACISOUT** commands.
SCR	A command script file.

File
Extension	**Description**
SDF	An attribute extract file in the space delimited format.
SHP	This file extension is used for both AutoCAD shape and font source files.
SHX	A compiled AutoCAD shape and font file.
SLB	A slide library file.
SLD	A slide file.
STL	A stereolithography file.
SV$	An automatically saved drawing file.
TGA	A Truevision rendered replay file. Use the **REPLAY** command to display the image in AutoCAD.
TIF	A Tagged Image File format file. Use the **REPLAY** command to display the image in AutoCAD.
TTF	A TrueType font file.
TXT	An attribute extract or template file of SDF or CDF format.
UNT	A units conversion file.
WMF	A Windows Metafile format vector file. Use the **WMFIN** and **WMFOUT** commands to import and export this file type.
XLG	An external references log file.
XMX	An external message file.

A wireframe (top) may appear as nothing more than a mess of lines. However, when the **HIDE** command is used on the surface model, you can see that it is a '57 Chevy. (Autodesk)

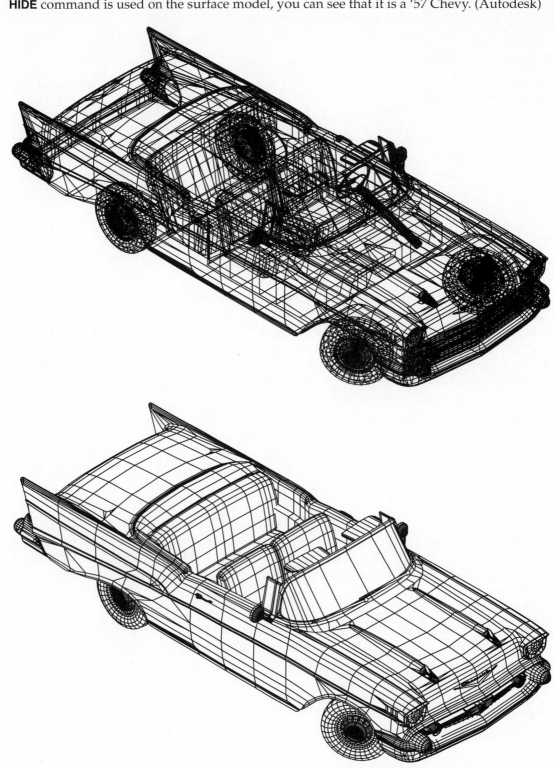

AutoCAD and its Applications—Advanced

Introduction

The following aliases for AutoCAD commands are found in the acad.pgp file. This file is located in the AutoCAD R14\Support folder. The examples given in this file are aliases for the most frequently used commands.

You can easily create your own aliases. The first part of the alias is the character(s) you type at the keyboard. The second part must begin with an asterisk followed by the name of the command the alias will execute. Do not put a space between the asterisk and the command.

Each alias you create requires a small amount of memory to function. Do not create a lot of aliases if your computer does not have sufficient memory resources. Always consult your instructor or supervisor before altering any file crucial to the operation of AutoCAD.

Aliases

The following aliases are included in the acad.pgp file. This file can be opened in any text editor or word processor that can read ASCII files. If you add your own aliases, it is a good idea to add them to the list alphabetically.

Command	Alias	Command	Alias	Command	Alias
3DARRAY	3A	ATTEDIT	-ATE	DDCOLOR	COL
3DFACE	3F	BHATCH	BH	DDEDIT	ED
3DPOLY	3P	BHATCH	H	DDGRIPS	GR
ALIGN	AL	BLOCK	-B	DDIM	D
APPLOAD	AP	BMAKE	B	DDINSERT	I
ARC	A	BOUNDARY	BO	DDMODIFY	MO
AREA	AA	-BOUNDARY	-BO	DDOSNAP	OS
ARRAY	AR	BREAK	BR	DDRENAME	REN
ASEADMIN	AAD	CHAMFER	CHA	DDRMODES	RM
ASEEXPORT	AEX	CHANGE	-CH	DDSELECT	SE
ASELINKS	ALI	CIRCLE	C	DDUCS	UC
ASEROWS	ARO	COPY	CO	DDUCSP	UCP
ASESELECT	ASE	DDATTDEF	AT	DDUNITS	UN
ASESQLED	ASQ	DDATTE	ATE	DDVIEW	V
ATTDEF	-AT	DDCHPROP	CH	DDVPOINT	VP

Command	Alias		Command	Alias		Command	Alias
DIMALIGNED	DAL		MEASURE	ME		TOLERANCE	TOL
DIMANGULAR	DAN		MIRROR	MI		TOOLBAR	TO
DIMBASELINE	DBA		MLINE	ML		TORUS	TOR
DIMCENTER	DCE		MOVE	M		TRIM	TR
DIMCONTINUE	DCO		MSPACE	MS		UNION	UNI
DIMDIAMETER	DDI		MTEXT	MT		UNITS	-UN
DIMEDIT	DED		MTEXT	T		VIEW	-V
DIMLINEAR	DLI		-MTEXT	-T		VPOINT	-VP
DIMORDINATE	DOR		MVIEW	MV		WBLOCK	W
DIMOVERRIDE	DOV		OFFSET	O		WEDGE	WE
DIMRADIUS	DRA		-OSNAP	-OS		XATTACH	XA
DIMSTYLE	DST		PAN	P		XBIND	XB
DIST	DI		-PAN	-P		-XBIND	-XB
DIVIDE	DIV		PASTESPEC	PA		XCLIP	XC
DONUT	DO		PEDIT	PE		XLINE	XL
DRAWORDER	DR		PLINE	PL		XREF	XR
DTEXT	DT		PLOT	PRINT		-XREF	-XR
DVIEW	DV		POINT	PO		ZOOM	Z
ELLIPSE	EL		POLYGON	POL			
ERASE	E		PREFERENCES	PR			
EXPLODE	X		PREVIEW	PRE			
EXPORT	EXP		PSPACE	PS			
EXTEND	EX		PURGE	PU			
EXTRUDE	EXT		QUIT	EXIT			
FILLET	F		RECTANGLE	REC			
FILTER	FI		REDRAW	R			
GROUP	-G		REDRAWALL	RA			
GROUP	G		REGEN	RE			
HATCH	-H		REGENALL	REA			
HATCHEDIT	HE		REGION	REG			
HIDE	HI		RENAME	-REN			
IMAGE	IM		RENDER	RR			
-IMAGE	-IM		REVOLVE	REV			
IMAGEADJUST	IAD		ROTATE	RO			
IMAGEATTACH	IAT		RPREF	RPR			
IMAGECLIP	ICL		SCALE	SC			
IMPORT	IMP		SCRIPT	SCR			
INSERT	-I		SECTION	SEC			
INSERTOBJ	IO		SETVAR	SET			
INTERFERE	INF		SHADE	SHA			
INTERSECT	IN		SLICE	SL			
LAYER	LA		SNAP	SN			
-LAYER	-LA		SOLID	SO			
LEADER	LE		SPELL	SP			
LENGTHEN	LEN		SPLINE	SPL			
LINE	L		SPLINEDIT	SPE			
LINETYPE	LT		STRETCH	S			
-LINETYPE	-LT		STYLE	ST			
LIST	LI		SUBTRACT	SU			
LIST	LS		TABLET	TA			
LTSCALE	LTS		THICKNESS	TH			
MATCHPROP	MA		TILEMODE	TI			

The following alternative aliases correspond to AutoCAD Release 13.

Command	Alias
DSVIEWER	AV
COPY	CP
DIMALIGNED	DIMALI
DIMANGULAR	DIMANG
DIMBASELINE	DIMBASE
DIMCONTINUE	DIMCONT
DIMDIAMETER	DIMDIA
DIMEDIT	DIMED
DIMTEDIT	DIMTED
DIMLINEAR	DIMLIN
DIMORDINATE	DIMORD
DIMRADIUS	DIMRAD
DIMSTYLE	DIMSTY
DIMOVERRIDE	DIMOVER
LEADER	LEAD
TILEMODE	TM

Command	Description
3D	This command allows you to create the following three-dimensional polygon mesh objects: box, cone, dish, dome, mesh, pyramid, torus, and wedge.
3DARRAY	This command allows you to create a three-dimensional polar or rectangular array.
3DFACE	This command creates a three-dimensional face. The face must have at least three and no more than four vertices.
3DMESH	This command creates a polygon mesh. You must give the coordinate location for each of the vertices in the mesh.
3DPOLY	This command creates a polyline in 3D space.
3DSIN	This command is used to import a 3D Studio into AutoCAD.
3DSOUT	This command is used to save an AutoCAD drawing in the native 3D Studio file format. Only 3D objects are saved. Any 2D objects are lost.
ACISIN	This command allows you to import an ACIS solid model (.sat) file into AutoCAD.
ACISOUT	This command allows you to save solid objects created in AutoCAD as an ACIS solid model file (.sat).
ALIGN	This command is used to move and rotate a selected object to align with other objects.
AMECONVERT	This command converts solid models created in AME to AutoCAD solids.
AREA	This command calculates the area and perimeter of selected objects or of defined areas.
ASEADMIN	This command is used to manage external database commands.
ASEEXPORT	This command exports link information for selected objects to an external database file.
ASELINKS	This command is used to manage links between objects and an external database.
ASEROWS	This command displays table data. You can edit data and create links and selection sets.
ASESELECT	This command creates a selection set from rows linked to text and graphic selection sets.
ASESQLED	This command executes Structured Query Language (SQL) statements.

Command	Description
ASEUNLOAD	This command removes an AutoCAD SQL Environment (ASE) application from system memory (RAM).
ATTACHURL	Enables you to attach a URL to areas or objects within a .dwf file.
BACKGROUND	Sets up the background for your scene.
BMPOUT	This command saves selected objects as a bitmap (.bmp) format file.
BOX	This command creates a three-dimensional solid box.
BROWSER	Launches the default Web browser defined in your system's registry.
CHAMFER	This command is used to bevel the edges of objects. A chamfer can be applied to a 2D or 3D object.
COMPILE	This command compiles shape and PostScript font files.
CONE	This command creates a three-dimensional solid cone.
COPYCLIP	This command copies selected objects to the Windows Clipboard.
COPYLINK	This command copies the current view to the Windows Clipboard for linking to Object Linking and Embedding (OLE) applications.
CUTCLIP	This command removes selected objects from the drawing and places them on the Windows Clipboard.
CYLINDER	This command creates a three-dimensional solid cylinder.
DDUCS	This command is used to manage defined User Coordinate Systems (UCS).
DDUCSP	This command allows you to select from several preset User Coordinate Systems.
DDVIEW	This command is used to create and restore saved views.
DDVPOINT	This command is used to set the viewing direction.
DETACHURL	Used to remove a URL attachment from an object or an area in a drawing.
DSVIEWER	This command allows you to change your view of the drawing using the **Aerial View** window. This command can only be used when your display is configured for a Windows accelerated display driver.
DVIEW	This command allows you to define a parallel projection or perspective view of selected objects.
DWFOUT	Exports a drawing Web format (.dwf) file.
EDGE	This command is used to make an edge of a 3D face visible or invisible.
EDGESURF	This command creates a three-dimensional polygon mesh using four objects to define the edges.
ELEV	This command is used to set the current elevation and thickness.
EXPORT	Saves objects to other file formats.
EXTRUDE	This command is used to create 3D solid primitives by extruding a 2D region.
FILLET	This command is used to place fillets and rounds on the edges of objects.
FOG	Provides visual cues for the apparent distance of objects.
GIFIN	This command is used to import a .gif image file into AutoCAD. A .gif file is a raster image file.
HIDE	This command is used to display 3D objects with hidden lines removed.

Command	Description
IMAGE	Inserts images in many formats into an AutoCAD drawing file.
IMAGEADJUST	Controls the brightness, contrast, and fade values of the selected image.
IMAGEATTACH	Attaches a new image object and definition.
IMAGECLIP	Creates new clipping boundaries for single image objects.
IMAGEFRAME	Controls whether the image frame is displayed on the screen or hidden from view.
IMAGEQUALITY	Controls the display quality of images.
IMPORT	This command is used to import several different types of files into AutoCAD.
INETCFG	Allows you to configure your system to be able to communicate with a remote system that is also connected to the Internet.
INSERTURL	Enables you to insert a drawing from the Web into the current drawing.
INTERFERE	This command is used to create a composite solid from the volume created by the interference of two or more solids.
INTERSECT	This command is used to create a composite solid or region from the intersection of two or more solids or regions.
LIGHT	This command is used to manage lights and lighting effects.
LISTURL	Any number of objects can be selected in the drawing in order to list the attached URLs.
LSEDIT	Lets you edit a landscape object.
LSLIB	Lets you maintain libraries of landscape objects.
LSNEW	Lets you add realistic landscape items, such as trees and bushes, to your drawings.
MASSPROP	This command calculates and displays the mass properties of regions or solids.
MATLIB	This command opens the **Materials Library** dialog box. This dialog box is used to import and export materials to and from a library of materials.
MENU	This command is used to load a menu file.
MENULOAD	This command is used to load partial menu files.
MENUUNLOAD	This command is used to unload partial menu files.
MIRROR3D	This command is used to construct a mirror image of selected objects in 3D space using a mirror plane.
MVIEW	This command is used to create floating viewports. It is also used to turn on existing floating viewports.
MVSETUP	Sets up the specifications of a drawing.
OLELINKS	This command is used to update, change, and cancel existing links.
OPENURL	Used to open the URL of a drawing file.
PASTECLIP	This command inserts the contents of the Windows Clipboard into the current drawing.
PASTESPEC	This command inserts the contents of the Windows Clipboard and allows you to control the format of what is being inserted.
PCXIN	This command is used to import a .pcx image file into AutoCAD. A .pcx file is a raster image file.
PFACE	This command allows you to create a three-dimensional polyface mesh. Each vertex must be individually specified.

Command	Description
PLAN	This command displays a plan view of the current User Coordinate System (UCS), a saved UCS, or the World Coordinate System (WCS).
PREFERENCES	Customizes the AutoCAD settings.
PSDRAG	Controls the appearance of a PostScript image as it is dragged into position with **PSIN**.
PSFILL	This command is used to fill a two-dimensional polyline outline with a PostScript pattern.
PSIN	This command is used to import an encapsulated PostScript file into AutoCAD.
PSOUT	This command saves the drawing as an encapsulated PostScript file. You must specify what portion of the drawing is to be saved.
PSPACE	This command switches from model space to paper space.
REGION	This command is used to create a region from selected objects.
REINIT	This command is used to reinitialize the I/O ports, digitizer, display, and program parameters file.
RENDER	This command opens the **Render** dialog box and also initializes the AutoCAD **Render** window. The **Render** dialog box is used to create a realistically shaded image of a three-dimensional object.
RENDERUNLOAD	This command closes the AutoCAD **Render** application. When you use this command, any rendered objects are returned to a wireframe.
RENDSCR	This command displays the last rendering created using the **RENDER** command. If **RENDERUNLOAD** has been used since the last rendering, this command has no effect.
REPLAY	This command is used to display a .gif, .tga, or .tif raster image.
REVOLVE	This command is used to create a 3D solid by revolving a closed two-dimensional object about an axis.
REVSURF	This command creates a 3D surface by rotating a 2D object about a selected axis.
RMAT	This command opens the **Materials** dialog box. This dialog box is used to manage materials used for rendering.
ROTATE3D	This command rotates selected objects about an axis in 3D space.
RPREF	Sets rendering preferences.
RULESURF	This command creates a 3D ruled surface between two path curves. The curves can be arcs, lines, or points.
SAVEIMG	This command saves a rendered image to a file in .gif, .tif, or .tga format.
SAVEURL	Allows you to save drawings directly to a Web site.
SCENE	This command is used to manage scenes.
SECTION	This command creates a region from the intersection of a plane and a solid. The region can then be used to create a section view.
SELECTURL	All objects and areas with attached URLs in the current viewport are selected for editing or listing.
SHADE	This command displays a shaded image of the drawing in the current viewport. This command is faster than the **RENDER** command, but the image quality is not as good.

Command	Description
SLICE	This command "cuts" a set of solids with a plane.
SPHERE	This command creates a three-dimensional solid sphere.
STATS	Displays rendering statistics.
SUBTRACT	This command creates a composite by subtracting the area or volume of one selection set from another selection set. This command can be used for 2D regions and 3D solids.
TABSURF	This command creates a 3D tabulated surface from a path curve and direction vector.
TIFFIN	This command is used to import a .tif file. A .tif file is a raster image file.
TORUS	This command creates a 3D solid that resembles a doughnut.
TRANSPARENCY	Controls whether background pixels in an image are transparent or opaque.
UCS	This command is used to create and manage User Coordinate Systems (UCS).
UCSICON	This command controls the visibility and placement of the UCS and WCS icons.
UNION	This command creates a composite by adding the area or volume of two selection sets. This command can be used with 2D regions or 3D solids.
VPOINT	This command is used to set the viewing direction. This command is commonly used to create a 3D display of the drawing.
VPORTS	This command is used to divide the graphics area into multiple viewports.
WMFIN	This command is used to import a Windows Metafile (.wmf).
WMFOPTS	This command sets the options for using the **WMFIN** command.
WMFOUT	This command saves selected objects as a Windows Metafile (.wmf).

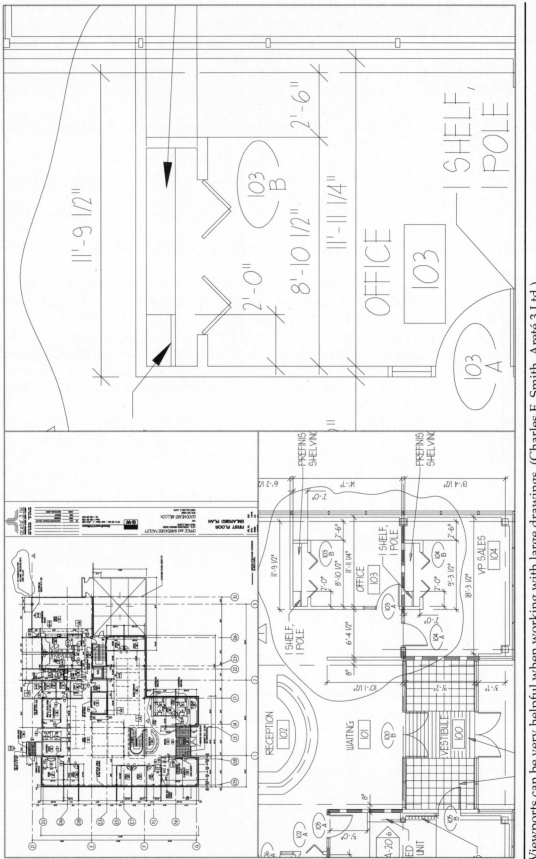

Viewports can be very helpful when working with large drawings. (Charles E. Smith, Areté 3 Ltd.)

Variable	Type	Saved In	Default Value	Description
CHAMFERA	Real	Drawing	0.0000	First chamfer distance.
CHAMFERB	Real	Drawing	0.0000	Second chamfer distance.
CHAMFERC	Real	Drawing	0.0000	Chamfer length.
CHAMFERD	Real	Drawing	0.0000	Chamfer angle.
CHAMMODE	Integer	Not saved	0	Sets the method for creating chamfers. 0 Two chamfer distances are used. 1 One chamfer length and an angle are used.
CVPORT	Integer	Drawing	2	Identification number of the current viewport. The identification number you specify must correspond to an active viewport. Also, the cursor must not be locked in that viewpoint. Tablet mode must be off.
DELOBJ	Integer	Drawing	1	Determines whether objects used to create other objects are deleted from the drawing database. 0 Delete objects. 1 Keep objects.
DISPSILH	Integer	Drawing	0	Display of silhouette curves of body objects in wireframe mode. 0 Off. 1 On.
EDGEMODE	Integer	Not saved	0	Cutting and boundary edges for the **TRIM** and **EXTEND** commands. 0 Uses only the selected edge. 1 Creates an imaginary extension from the selected object.
ELEVATION	Real	Drawing	0.0000	Stores the current 3D elevation relative to the current UCS for the current space.
FACETRES	Real	Drawing	0.5	Adjusts the smoothness of shaded and hidden line-removed objects. Value can range from 0.01 to 10.0.
FILLETRAD	Real	Drawing	0.0000	Fillet radius.
FRONTZ	Real	Drawing	(Read-only)	Stores the front clipping plane offset from the target plane for the current viewport.

Variable	Type	Saved In	Default Value	Description
INETLOCATION	String	Config		Holds the name of the default URL.
ISOLINES	Integer	Drawing	4	Specifies the number of isolines per surface. Values can range from 0 to 2047.
LENSLENGTH	Real	Drawing	(Read-only)	Stores the length of the lens (in millimeters) used in perspective viewing.
MAXACTVP	Integer	Not saved	16	Maximum number of viewports that regenerate at one time.
PFACEVMAX	Integer	Not saved	(Read-only)	Maximum number of vertices per face.
PROJMODE	Integer	Config	1	Projection mode for the **Trim** and **Extend** commands. 0　True 3D mode (no projection). 1　Project to the XY plane of the current UCS. 2　Project to the current view plane.
PROJECTNAME	String	Drawing	""	Stores the current project name.
PSPROLOG	String	Config	""	Assigns a name for a prologue section to be read from the acad.psf file when using **PSOUT**.
PSQUALITY	Integer	Drawing	75	Controls drawing of PostScript images. 0　Disables PostScript image generation. < 0　Sets the number of pixels per drawing unit for the PostScript image. > 0　Sets the number of pixels per drawing unit, shows PostScript paths as outlines and does not fill them.
RASTERPREVIEW	Integer	Drawing	0	Sets format of preview image. 0　BMP. 1　BMP and WMF. 2　WMF. 3　No preview image.
SHADEDGE	Integer	Drawing	3	Controls shading of edges in rendering. 0　Faces shaded, edges not highlighted. 1　Faces shaded, edges drawn in background color. 2　Faces not filled, edges in object color. 3　Faces in object color, edges in background color.
SHADEDIF	Integer	Drawing	70	Percent of diffuse reflective light relative to ambient light.
SPLFRAME	Integer	Drawing	0	Controls display of spline-fit polylines. 0　Does not display the control polygon. Displays the fit surface of a polygon mesh, but not the defining mesh. Does not display the invisible edges of 3D faces or polyface meshes. 1　Displays the control polygon. Only the defining mesh of a surface-fit polygon mesh is displayed (not the fit surface). Invisible edges of 3D faces and polyface meshes are displayed.
SPLINESEGS	Integer	Drawing	8	Number of line segments for each spline.

Variable	Type	Saved In	Default Value	Description
SPLINETYPE	Integer	Drawing	6	Type of spline curve to be generated by **PEDIT Spline**. 5 Quadratic B-spline. 6 Cubic B-spline.
SURFTAB1	Integer	Drawing	6	Number of tabulations generated for **RULESURF** and **TABSURF**. Mesh density in the *M* direction for **REVSURF** and **EDGESURF**.
SURFTAB2	Integer	Drawing	6	Mesh density in the *N* direction for **REVSURF** and **EDGESURF**.
SURFTYPE	Integer	Drawing	6	Controls the surface-fitting done by **PEDIT Smooth**. 5 Quadratic B-spline surface. 6 Cubic B-spline surface. 8 Bezier surface.
SURFU	Integer	Drawing	6	Surface density in the *M* direction.
SURFV	Integer	Drawing	6	Surface density in the *N* direction.
TARGET	3D point	Drawing	Read-only	Location of the target point for the current viewpoint in UCS coordinates.
THICKNESS	Real	Drawing	0.0000	Sets 3D thickness.
TILEMODE	Integer	Drawing	1	Controls access to paper space and the behavior of AutoCAD viewports. 0 Enables paper space and viewport objects (uses **MVIEW**). 1 Enables Release 10 Compatibility mode (uses **VPORTS**). Returns to Tiled Viewport mode. Paper space objects—including viewport objects—are not displayed, and the **MVIEW**, **MSPACE**, **PSPACE**, and **VPLAYER** commands are disabled.
TRIMMODE	Integer	Not saved	1	Controls edge trimming for chamfers and fillets. 0 Leaves edges intact. 1 Trims edges.
UCSFOLLOW	Integer	Drawing	0	Generates a plan view whenever you change from one UCS to another. Can be set separately for each viewport. The setting is maintained separately for both spaces, but it is always treated as if set to 0 while in paper space. 0 UCS does not affect the view. 1 Any UCS change causes a change to plan view of the new UCS in the current viewport.
UCSICON	Integer	Drawing	1	Displays the Coordinate System icon. 1 On. 2 Origin. The icon floats to the UCS origin, if possible.

Variable	Type	Saved In	Default Value	Description
UCSNAME	String	Drawing	(Read-only)	Stores the name of the current coordinate system. Returns a null string if the current UCS is unnamed.
UCSORG	3D point	Drawing	(Read-only)	Stores the origin point of the current coordinate system, in World coordinates.
UCSXDIR	3D point	Drawing	(Read-only)	Stores the X direction of the current UCS.
UCSYDIR	3D point	Drawing	(Read-only)	Stores the Y direction of the current UCS for the current space.
VIEWCTR	3D point	Drawing	(Read-only)	Stores the center of view in the current viewport, expressed in UCS coordinates.
VIEWDIR	3D vector	Drawing	(Read-only)	Stores the viewing direction in the current viewport expressed in UCS coordinates.
VIEWMODE	Integer	Drawing	(Read-only)	Controls viewing mode for the current viewport using bit-code. 0 Disabled. 1 Perspective view active. 2 Front clipping on. 4 Back clipping on. 8 UCS follow mode on. 16 Front clip not at eye.
VIEWSIZE	Real	Drawing	(Read-only)	Height of view in current viewport.
VIEWTWIST	Real	Drawing	(Read-only)	View twist angle for the current viewport.
VSMAX	3D point	Drawing	(Read-only)	Upper-right corner of the current viewport virtual screen, expressed in UCS coordinates.
VSMIN	3D point	Drawing	(Read-only)	Lower-left corner of the current viewport virtual screen, expressed in current UCS coordinates.
WORLDUCS	Integer	Not saved	(Read-only)	Relation between UCS and the World Coordinate System. 0 UCS and World Coordinate System are different. 1 UCS and World Coordinate System are the same.
WORLDVIEW	Integer	Drawing	1	Controls whether UCS changes to WCS during **DVIEW** or **VPOINT**. 0 Current UCS remains unchanged. 1 Current UCS is changed to the WCS.

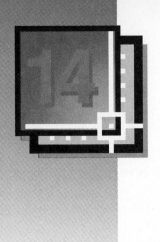

The following is a list of basic AutoLISP commands with a brief definition of each command. These commands are covered in Chapter 22 and Chapter 23 of this text. Detailed definitions of these and all other AutoLISP commands are found in the *AutoCAD Customization Guide*.

Command	Description
+ *(addition)*	Adds all the numbers.
– *(subtraction)*	Subtracts the second and following numbers from the first and returns the difference.
* *(multiplication)*	Multiplies all the numbers.
/ *(division)*	Divides the first number by the product of the remaining numbers and returns the quotient.
= *(equal to)*	Returns a total if all arguments are equal. Returns *nil* otherwise.
ANGLE	Returns the angle from the X axis of the current UCS to a line defined by two endpoints, as measured counterclockwise. The value is given in radians.
ARXLOAD	Loads an AutoCAD Runtime Extension application.
ARXUNLOAD	Unloads an AutoCAD Runtime Extension application.
CAR	Returns the first element of a list.
CADR	Returns the second element of a list.
CADDR	Returns the third element of a list.
CDR	Returns the second and remaining elements of a list. If the list contains more than two elements, the returned values are placed in a list.
DEFUN	Defines a function.
DISTANCE	Returns the distance between two points. The distance is measured in 3D space.
GETANGLE	Waits for a user-input angle and returns the angle in radians. The user can input the angle at the keyboard or use the pointing device to pick points on-screen.
GETCORNER	Waits for the user to input the second corner of a rectangle using the pointing device.
GETDIST	Waits for a userinput distance. The distance can be entered at the keyboard or using the pointing device to pick points on-screen.
GETORIENT	Waits for a user-input and returns the angle in radians. This is similar to the **GETANGLE** function, but the **ANGBASE** and **ANGDIR** system variables do not affect it.
GETPOINT	Waits for a user-input point and returns the point.

Command	Description
GETREAL	Waits for a user-input real number and returns the real number.
GETSTRING	Waits for a user-input string and returns the string.
GETVAR	Returns the value assigned to a specified AutoCAD system variable.
GRAPHSCR	If the text screen is currently displayed, switches to the AutoCAD graphics screen.
LOAD_DIALOG	Loads a Dialog Control Language file.
NEW_DIALOG	Opens a specified dialog box. This function can also specify a default action of the dialog box.
POLAR	Returns the coordinates of a 3D point a specified angle and distance from a specified point.
PRINC	Prints a specified expression on the command line. This function can also be used to write a specified expression to a file.
PROMPT	Displays a specified string on the command line.
START_DIALOG	Opens a specified dialog box and makes AutoCAD ready to accept user input.
STRLEN	Reports the number of characters in a string.
TERPRI	Prints a new line on the command line.
TEXTSCR	If the graphics screen is currently displayed, switches to the AutoCAD text screen.
UNLOAD_DIALOG	Unloads a Dialog Control Language file.
VMON	Provides virtual function paging. This function is no longer needed in Release 14, but is used for compatibility with previous releases.
XLOAD	Loads an AutoCAD Development System application.
XUNLOAD	Unloads an AutoCAD Development System application.

Index

Fog, 330
FOG command, 330
Fog/Depth Cue dialog box, 330
Fonts in AutoCAD display, 398–399
Frames for images, 274
FTP. *See* File Transfer Protocol

G

Gateway, 359
GETANGLE AutoLISP function, 524
GETCORNER AutoLISP function, 518
GETDIST AutoLISP function, 514, 516
GETORIENT AutoLISP function, 524
GETPOINT AutoLISP function, 513, 516
GETREAL AutoLISP function, 518
GETSTRING AutoLISP function, 515–516
GETVAR AutoLISP function, 518
GIF files, 267
Gouraud, 302
Gradient background, 327
Granite, 318–319
Graphics window, 395, 408–409
Grips, 145–146, 158–159
Grooves, 235

H

Help file, 405
Help strings, 466
Hidden line removal, 17, 182
HIDE command, 17, 182
    hiding text, 190
Highlight, 288
HLS color, 312
Holes, creating surfaces around, 112–113, 129–131
Hotspot, 299
HTML. *See* HyperText Markup Language
HTTP. *See* HyperText Transfer Protocol
Hue, 312
Hyperlinks, 347
Hypertext, 347
HyperText Markup Language (HTML), 347
    sample file, 362–363
HyperText Transfer Protocol (HTTP), 359

I

Icon, UCS. *See* UCS icon
Image background, 327
IMAGE command, 268
Image dialog box, 268
Image Specifications dialog box, 333
Image tile menu customization, 471–474
IMAGEADJUST command, 273–274
IMAGEATTACH command, 269, 271
IMAGECLIP command, 272–273
IMAGEFRAME command, 274
IMAGEQUALITY command, 274
Images,
    brightness, 273
    contrast, 273
    fade, 274
    frame, 274
    quality, 274
    replaying, 333
    transparency, 274
Importing,
    PostScript files, 282
    Windows metafile, 278
Incidence angle, 288
Inertia, 259
INETCFG command, 358
INETLOCATION system variable, 350
Information schema, 372
Insert Object dialog box, 562
Inserting,
    3D blocks, 116, 135
    blocks, 488
    drawings from the Web, 361
    raster images, 268–271
INSERTOBJ command, 561
INSERTURL command, 361
Integrated services digital network (ISDN), 348
INTERFERE command, 221–222
Interfering solids, 221–222
Internet, 347–352
    connections, 348
Internet Configuration dialog box, 358
Internet host, 352
    configuring, 358–359
Internet Service Provider (ISP), 348
Internet Utilities toolbar, 355
Internet Utilities, 353–361
    loading, 354
INTERSECT command, 220–221
Intersecting solids, 220
Intranet, 359

ISDN. *See* Integrated services digital network

ISOLINES system variable, 245
    spheres, 212–213
ISP. *See* Internet Service Provider

J

JPG files, 268

K

Key, 536, 540

L

Landscape Library dialog box, 329
Landscape objects, 328–329
    editing, 329
    library, 329
Layers, created by **SOLVIEW**, 255
Layout using paper space, 177–181
Leaders. *See* Dimensioning 3D objects
Lens, 175
Light,
    ambient, 183, 288
    diffuse, 183
LIGHT command, 292
Lighting, 288–300
    ambient, 183, 288
    intensity, 310–311
    properties, 288–289
    shadows, 300
Lights,
    color, 311–313
    distant, 288
    icon scale, 294
    intensity, 310–311
    point, 288
    shadows, 300
    spot, 288
Lights dialog box, 292
Linking, 560–564
    AutoCAD drawings to applications, 564
    drawings to databases, 376, 387–388
    objects in AutoCAD, 560–563
Links,
    creating, 388
    deleting, 389

editing, 388
    viewing, 387
Links dialog box, 381, 387, 563
LISP, 503. *See also* AutoLISP
LIST AutoLISP function, 519–520, 522
Listing URLs, 357
LISTURL command, 357
LOAD AutoLISP function, 512
Load AutoLISP, ADS, and ARX Files dialog box, 511
LOAD_DIALOG AutoLISP function, 538
Log files, 402
LOGFILEOFF command, 402
LOGFILEON command, 402
LSEDIT command, 329
LSNEW command, 328
Luminescence, 312

M

Macros,
    buttons, 427–428
    control characters, 455
Make Displayable Attribute dialog box, 390
Mapping, 320, 324
Mapping axes, 321
Mapping dialog box, 324–325
Mapping textures, 324–326
    cylindrical projection, 326
    planar projection, 324–325
    spherical projection, 326
Marble, 318–319
Mass, 259
Mass properties, 259–260
MASSPROP command, 259–260
Materials, 313–323
    applying, 307
    attaching, 317
    attributes, 313–316
    bit mapping, 320–322
    detaching, 317
    duplicating, 317
    granite, 318–319
    marble, 318–319
    New Standard Material dialog box, 314
    using materials library, 323–324
    wood, 318–319
Materials dialog box, 314, 317
Materials library, 323–324
Materials Library dialog box, 323

W

Web. *See* World Wide Web
Web browsers, 347–348
  launching, 349
Web servers, 352
Web sites, 347
  creating, 352
  See also Autodesk Web site
Wedge,
  solid, 216
  surface-modeled, 51–52

WEDGE command, 216
WHIP! plug-in, 361–365
  downloading, 361–362
  viewing options, 364–365
Windows Clipboard. *See* Clipboard
Windows metafile format, 277–278
WINTAB driver, 479–480
Wireframes, 24–26
WMF file, 277–278
Wood, 318–319
World Coordinate System, 69
World Wide Web (WWW), 347
  publishing drawings, 362–363